iOS 6 Programming Cookbook

Vandad Nahavandipoor

O'REILLY®

Beijing · Cambridge · Farnham · Köln · Sebastopol · Tokyo

iOS 6 Programming Cookbook

by Vandad Nahavandipoor

Copyright © 2013 Vandad Nahavandipoor. All rights reserved.
Printed in the United States of America.

Published by O'Reilly Media, Inc., 1005 Gravenstein Highway North, Sebastopol, CA 95472.

O'Reilly books may be purchased for educational, business, or sales promotional use. Online editions are also available for most titles (*http://my.safaribooksonline.com*). For more information, contact our corporate/institutional sales department: 800-998-9938 or *corporate@oreilly.com*.

Editors: Andy Oram and Rachel Roumeliotis		**Indexer:** Bob Pfahler	
Production Editor: Rachel Steely		**Cover Designer:** Karen Montgomery	
Copyeditor: Jasmine Kwityn		**Interior Designer:** David Futato	
Proofreader: Jason Schneiderman		**Illustrator:** Rebecca Demarest	

December 2012:   First Edition.

Revision History for the First Edition:

2012-11-19   First release

See *http://oreilly.com/catalog/errata.csp?isbn=9781449342753* for release details.

ISBN: 978-1-449-34275-3

[LSI]

1353339344

Table of Contents

Preface

The long-awaited iOS 6 SDK (Software Development Kit) is finally out, and we need to learn about all the great features that this release offers us. Apple did a great job adding new features to the SDK and, of course, to iOS itself. iOS 6 is much more stable than the previous versions of iOS, as you would expect. Things move very fast in Apple's world, and the iOS SDK is no exception. Obviously, picking up this book is an indication that you are ready to start learning all there is to know about iOS 6 SDK, and that is fantastic.

I've personally worked with companies of various sizes around the world and have been developing software pretty much since I was about seven years old. (I started out on my father's Commodore 64 before moving on to an Intel 80186 machine, an 80286, and then Pentium machines.) I did a lot of assembly development as well as some OS programming, including writing a kernel of a toy operating system. I really enjoy software development and have true passion for it. I can express myself using programming, and that's probably the main reason I enjoy writing apps and software in general. Since 2007, I've solely focused on writing iOS apps, and have been working with some really high-profile companies around the world to help them with their projects. I've worked with Scrum Masters (for whom I have much respect), project managers, delivery managers, release managers, testers, and fellow iOS developers—and have done my best to learn as much as possible from them. This edition of the book is the product of all the knowledge that I have gained in many years writing iOS apps.

This edition of the book is especially exciting for me, because of all the modifications and fine-tuning we have done to it as a result of going through the feedback that we received in the last two editions. In this edition, obviously you will learn all about the new features of iOS 6 SDK. On top of that, you will learn about Pass Kit, Auto Layout constraints, file/folder management, customization of UI components, and much more. Of course, you will also learn about all the cool new features that Apple has added to the LLVM compiler and the runtime, such as autosynthesized properties, expression boxing, and collection subscripting.

Audience

I assume you are comfortable with the iOS development environment and know how to create an app for the iPhone or iPad. This book does not get novice programmers started, but presents useful ways to get things done for iOS programmers ranging from novices to experts.

Organization of This Book

In this book, we will discuss frameworks and classes that are available in iOS 6 SDK. This book does its best to teach you the latest and the greatest APIs. As you know, some users of your apps may still be on older versions of iOS, so please consider those users and choose your APIs wisely, depending on the minimum iOS version that you want to target with your apps.

Here is a concise breakdown of the material each chapter covers:

Chapter 1, *The Basics*
> Explains how Objective-C classes are structured and how objects can be instantiated. The chapter talks about properties and delegates as well as memory management in Objective-C. Even if you are competent in Objective-C, I strongly suggest that you read this chapter, even if you only skim through it, to understand the basic material that is used in the rest of the book.

Chapter 2, *Implementing Controllers and Views*
> Describes various approaches to constructing your iOS application's user interface by taking advantage of different tools the SDK provides. This chapter also introduces you to features that are only available on the iPad, such as the popover and split view controllers.

Chapter 3, *Auto Layout and the Visual Format Language*
> Explains how you can take advantage of Auto Layout in the iOS SDK in order to construct your UI in such a way that it can be resized and stretched to pretty much any screen dimension.

Chapter 4, *Constructing and Using Table Views*
> Shows how you can work with table views to create professional-looking iOS applications. Table views are very dynamic in nature, and as a result, programmers sometimes have difficulty understanding how they should work with them. By reading this chapter and trying out the example code, you will gain the knowledge that is required to comfortably work with table views.

Chapter 5, *Storyboards*
> Demonstrates the process of *storyboarding*, the new way to define the connections between different screens in your app. The great thing about storyboarding is that you don't have to know anything about iOS programming to get a simple app running. This helps product analysts, product owners, or designers who work

independently of developers to gain knowledge of the UI components iOS offers and to build more robust products. Programmers can also take advantage of storyboarding to easily create prototypes. Storyboarding is just fun, whether you do it on paper or using Xcode.

Chapter 6, *Concurrency*

As humans, we can do many things simultaneously without thinking much about it. With advances in computer technology, mobile devices are also able to multitask, and provide programmers with tools and mechanisms that can accomplish more than one task at the same time. This is called *concurrency*. In this chapter, you will learn about Grand Central Dispatch, Apple's preferred way of achieving concurrency in iOS. You will also learn about timers, threads, and operations.

Chapter 7, *Core Location and Maps*

Describes how you should use Map Kit and Core Location APIs to develop location-aware iOS applications. First you will learn about maps, and then you will learn how to detect a device's location and tailor your maps with custom annotations. You will also learn about geocoding and reverse geocoding, as well as some of the methods of the Core Location framework, which are only available in the iOS 4 SDK and later.

Chapter 8, *Implementing Gesture Recognizers*

Demonstrates how to use gesture recognizers, which enable your users to easily and intuitively manipulate the graphical interface of your iOS applications. In this chapter, you will learn how to use all available gesture recognizers in the iOS SDK, with working examples tested on iOS 5 on different devices such as the iPhone 3GS, iPhone 4, and iPad.

Chapter 9, *Networking, JSON, XML, and Twitter*

Demonstrates how to download data from a URL and parse XML files. You will learn about synchronous and asynchronous connections and their pros and cons. You will also learn about caching files in memory and on disk to avoid consuming the possibly limited bandwidth of an iOS device on which your application could be running.

Chapter 10, *Audio and Video*

Discusses the AV Foundation and Media Player frameworks that are available on the iOS SDK. You will learn how to play audio and video files and how to handle interruptions, such as a phone call, while the audio or video is being played in iOS 6. This chapter also explains how to record audio using an iOS device's built-in microphone(s). At the end of the chapter, you will learn how to access the iPod Library and play its media content, all from inside your application.

Chapter 11, *Address Book*

Explains the Address Book framework and how to retrieve contacts, groups, and their information from the Address Book database on an iOS device. The Address Book framework is composed entirely of C APIs. Because of this, many Objective-C developers find it difficult to use this framework, as compared to frameworks that provide an Objective-C interface. After reading this chapter and trying the examples for yourself, you will feel much more confident using the Address Book framework.

Chapter 12, *Files and Folder Management*

One of the most important tasks that, as developers, we want to perform in our iOS apps is manipulating files and folders. Whether this means creating, reading from, writing to, or deleting them, this chapter contains enough material to get you up and running with file and folder management in iOS SDK.

Chapter 13, *Camera and the Photo Library*

Demonstrates how you can determine the availability of front- and back-facing cameras on an iOS device. Some of the recipes in this chapter are specific to iOS 4 and above. You will also learn how to access the Photo Library using the Assets Library framework, which is available in iOS 4 and later. At the end of the chapter, you will learn about editing videos right on an iOS device using a built-in view controller.

Chapter 14, *Multitasking*

Explains, with examples, how to create multitasking-aware applications that run beautifully on iOS 4 and above. You will learn about background processing, including how to play audio and retrieve users' locations in the background, as well as how to download content from a URL while your application is running in the background.

Chapter 15, *Core Data*

Describes how to maintain persistent storage for your iOS applications using Core Data. You will learn how to add to, delete from, and edit Core Data objects and how to boost access to data in a table view. In addition, you will learn how to manage relationships between Core Data objects.

Chapter 16, *Dates, Calendars, and Events*

Demonstrates the use of the Event Kit and Event Kit UI frameworks, which are available on iOS 4 and later, in order to manage calendars and events on an iOS device. You will see how to create, modify, save, and delete events. You will also learn, through examples, how to add alarms to calendar events and how to set up CalDAV calendars so that you can share a single calendar among multiple devices.

Chapter 17, *Graphics and Animations*

Introduces the Core Graphics framework. You will learn how to draw images and text on a graphics context, grab the contents of a graphics context and save it as an image, and much more.

Chapter 18, *Core Motion*

Explains the Core Motion framework. Using Core Motion, you will access the accelerometer and the gyroscope on an iOS device. You will also learn how to detect shakes on a device. Of course, not all iOS devices are equipped with an accelerometer and a gyroscope, so you will also learn how to detect the availability of the required hardware.

Chapter 19, *iCloud*

Shows how to use the iCloud service, which ties devices together and allows them to share data to provide a seamless user experience as the user moves from one device to another.

Chapter 20, *Pass Kit*

Perhaps one of the most important updates in iOS 6 is the introduction of Passbook: a virtual wallet, if you will, capable of managing your coupons, boarding passes, rail and bus tickets, and much more. In this chapter, you will learn all there is to know in order to be able to create your own digitally signed passes and distribute them to your users easily.

Additional Resources

From time to time, I refer to official Apple documentation. Some of Apple's descriptions are right on the mark, and there is no point in trying to restate them. Throughout this book, I have listed the most important documents and guides in the official Apple documentation that every professional iOS developer should read.

For starters, I suggest that you have a look at the iOS Human Interface Guidelines (*http://bit.ly/QbdY0B*) for all iOS devices. This document will tell you everything you need to know about developing engaging and intuitive user interfaces for all iOS devices. Every iOS programmer should read this document. In fact, I believe this should be required reading for the product design and development teams of any company that develops iOS applications.

I also suggest that you skim through the "iOS Application Programming Guide" in the iOS Reference Library (*http://bit.ly/Qi7JaZ*) for some tips and advice on how to make great iOS applications:

One of the things you will notice when reading Chapter 14 is the use of block objects. This book concisely explains block objects, but if you require further details on the subject, I suggest you read "A Short Practical Guide to Blocks," available at this URL: *http://bit.ly/TsSMNU*.

Throughout this book, you will see references to "bundles" and loading images and data from bundles. You will read a concise overview about bundles in this book, but if you require further information, head over to the "Bundle Programming Guide," available at this URL: *http://bit.ly/XdLKE6*.

Conventions Used in This Book

The following typographical conventions are used in this book:

Italic

Indicates new terms, URLs, filenames, file extensions, and directories

`Constant width`

Indicates variables and other code elements, the contents of files, and the output from commands

`Constant width bold`

Highlights text in examples that is new or particularly significant in a recipe

`Constant width italic`

Shows text that should be replaced with user-supplied values

 This icon signifies a tip, suggestion, or general note.

Using Code Examples

This book is here to help you get your job done. In general, you may use the code in this book in your programs and documentation. You do not need to contact us for permission unless you're reproducing a significant portion of the code. For example, writing a program that uses several chunks of code from this book does not require permission. Selling or distributing a CD-ROM of examples from O'Reilly books *does* require permission. Answering a question by citing this book and quoting example code does not require permission. Incorporating a significant amount of example code from this book into your product's documentation *does* require permission.

We appreciate, but do not require, attribution. An attribution usually includes the title, author, publisher, and ISBN. For example: "*iOS 6 Programming Cookbook* by Vandad Nahavandipoor (O'Reilly). Copyright 2013 Vandad Nahavandipoor, 978-1-4493-4275-3."

If you feel your use of code examples falls outside fair use or the permission given here, feel free to contact us at *permissions@oreilly.com*.

We'd Like to Hear from You

Every example and code snippet in this book has been tested on the iPhone 3GS, iPhone 4, iPhone 4S, iPhone 5, iPad, and an iPhone/iPad Simulator, but occasionally you may encounter problems—for example, if you have a different version of the SDK than the version on which the example code was compiled and tested. The information in this book has also been verified at each step of the production process. However, mistakes and oversights can occur, and we will gratefully receive details of any you find, as well as any suggestions you would like to make for future editions. You can contact the author and editors at:

O'Reilly Media, Inc.
1005 Gravenstein Highway North
Sebastopol, CA 95472
(800) 998-9938 (in the United States or Canada)
(707) 829-0515 (international or local)
(707) 829-0104 (fax)

We have a web page for this book, where we list errata, examples, and any additional information. You can access this page at:

http://oreil.ly/iOS6_Programming_CB

To access the source codes for this book, please see the author's website at:

https://github.com/vandadnp/ios-6-programming-cookbook-source-codes

To comment or ask technical questions about this book, send email to the following address, mentioning the book's ISBN (9781449342753):

bookquestions@oreilly.com

For more information about our books, conferences, Resource Centers, and the O'Reilly Network, see our website at:

http://www.oreilly.com

Safari® Books Online

Safari Books Online (*www.safaribooksonline.com*) is an on-demand digital library that delivers expert content in both book and video form from the world's leading authors in technology and business.

Technology professionals, software developers, web designers, and business and creative professionals use Safari Books Online as their primary resource for research, problem solving, learning, and certification training.

Safari Books Online offers a range of product mixes and pricing programs for organizations, government agencies, and individuals. Subscribers have access to thousands of books, training videos, and prepublication manuscripts in one fully searchable database from publishers like O'Reilly Media, Prentice Hall Professional, Addison-Wesley Professional, Microsoft Press, Sams, Que, Peachpit Press, Focal Press, Cisco Press, John Wiley & Sons, Syngress, Morgan Kaufmann, IBM Redbooks, Packt, Adobe Press, FT Press, Apress, Manning, New Riders, McGraw-Hill, Jones & Bartlett, Course Technology, and dozens more. For more information about Safari Books Online, please visit us online.

Acknowledgments

I would like to acknowledge Andy Oram, my much-respected editor, and everyone at O'Reilly Media for their continuous support and inspiration, especially Rachel Roumeliotis, Brian Jepson, Rachel B. Steely, and Maria Stallone. Thanks also go to Sarah Schneider for helping me get my repository sorted out.

I am also grateful to my wonderful reviewers, Chris Devers, Mikhail Madnani, and Niklas Saers, for the fantastic job they did reviewing this edition of the book. When I was a kid, I thought I could do everything on my own. But as I've matured, it has become more and more apparent to me that although we humans are limitless in what we can achieve, without a good support system there is just so much we cannot do. Realizing and constantly reminding myself of this when I am surrounded by my friends, I would like to take this opportunity and thank them for their continuous support and unconditional love.

Last, but not least, big thanks to Alina Rizzoni, Bruno, and Tommy Packham for their continuous support and love. Rambo and Professor TJ, I want to say hello to you, too. Good boys!

CHAPTER 1

The Basics

1.0 Introduction

A lot has changed in iPhone, iPad, and iPod touch programming since the introduction of iOS 5. The whole runtime and the way we write Objective-C code have dramatically changed. ARC (Automatic Reference Counting) is now introduced into the LLVM Compiler, which in some ways gives us more flexibility and in other ways makes the runtime more fragile. In this chapter, we will get down and dirty with objects and how we can use them using the modern Objective-C runtime under ARC.

As the name of the language hints at, Objective-C is all about manipulating *objects*. These are containers for all the things you manipulate in the program, ranging from something simple, like a point at the corner of a rectangle, to entire windows containing all kinds of widgets. Apple's Cocoa libraries even define simple values such as integers as objects. Objects are defined according to *classes*, and therefore these two terms are commonly used interchangeably. But actually, a class is just a specification for defining objects; each object is said to be an *instance* of its class. Each class—and therefore the objects that are created from that class—is a set of properties, tasks, methods, enumerations, and much more. In an object-oriented programming language, classes can inherit from each other much like a person can inherit certain traits and characteristics from his parents.

 Objective-C does not allow multiple inheritance. Therefore, every class is the direct descendant of, at most, one other class.

The root class of most Objective-C objects is the NSObject class. This class manages the runtime capabilities offered by iOS; as a result, any class that directly or indirectly inherits from NSObject will inherit these capabilities as well. As we will see later in this chapter, objects that inherit from NSObject can take advantage of Objective-C's distinctive memory management model.

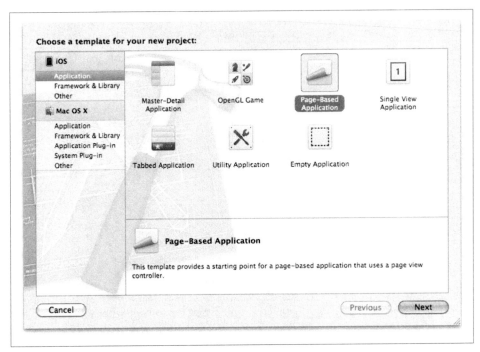

Figure 1-1. The New Project dialog in Xcode

1.1 Creating a Simple iOS App in Xcode

Problem

You've started to learn iOS Programming and you want to create a really simple iOS Project and app in Xcode.

Solution

Create a new iOS Project in Xcode and then run it in the iOS Simulator using Command +Shift+R.

Discussion

I'll assume you have a Mac and you have already installed the Xcode set of tools. Now you want to create an iOS Project and run that app on the iOS Simulator. This process is really straightforward:

1. Open Xcode if you don't have it open yet.
2. Select File on the menu bar, select New, and then select New Project. You will be greeted with a screen similar to that shown in Figure 1-1.

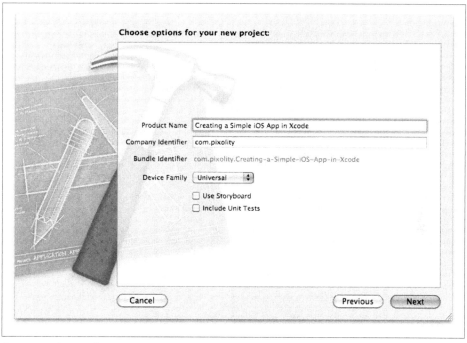

Figure 1-2. Setting the new project's settings

3. In the New Project dialog (Figure 1-1), on the left, make sure the Application category is selected under the iOS main category. Then select Page-Based Application on the right-hand side and press the Next button.

4. You will now need to enter your product name (App Name) and your company identifier. This uniquely identifies your product for your own company. Set your product name to *Creating a Simple iOS App in Xcode*. The company identifier is normally a domain name with the components reversed. My company name is Pixolity, and therefore I will set the Company Name to *com.pixolity* as shown in Figure 1-2. Leave the rest of the values in this screen just the way I've left them in Figure 1-2 and press the Next button.

5. You will now be asked to save your project on a disk. Select your desired location and press the Create button, as shown in Figure 1-3. Xcode will now create your project files and the structure of your project.

6. Now, before running your app, make sure you have unplugged any iPhones or iPads/iPods that you have connected to your computer. The reason behind this is that if a device is connected to your Mac, Xcode will try to run your apps on the device instead of the simulator, and if you haven't configured your device for development, you might get blocked and not be able to run your apps.

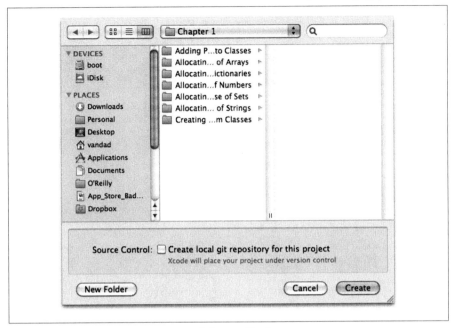

Figure 1-3. Saving a new iOS project on disk using Xcode

Figure 1-4. Running your iOS App on iPad Simulator

7. From the drop-down on the top-left corner of Xcode, make sure iPhone Simulator or iPad Simulator is selected. In this example, I will make sure iPad Simulator is selected, as shown in Figure 1-4.

8. Now that everything is ready, press the Command+Shift+R keys on your keyboard or simply go to the Product menu and then press the Run button as shown in Figure 1-5.

Congratulations. Now you have a simple app running in iOS Simulator. As you saw, there are various different iOS project templates that you can choose from (Figure 1-1). Here is a list of some of the handy project templates that you can use:

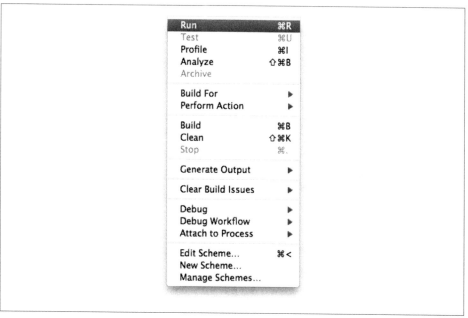

Figure 1-5. The Run menu item in Xcode

Master-Detail Application

This project template will set up a split view controller for your us. Split view controllers are explained in Chapter 2, *Implementing Controllers and Views*.

Page-Based Application

This template will allow your app to have an iBooks user interface, where the user will be able to flip through the pages that are drawn by the app. You'll learn more about this in Chapter 2.

Empty Application

An empty application is simply made out of the most basic components that any iOS app has. I use this template a lot to set up my iOS apps the way I like them to be set up, without any preconfiguration by Xcode.

1.2 Understanding Interface Builder

Problem

You want to start designing a user interface for your iOS apps but don't want to waste time coding.

Solution

Use Interface Builder.

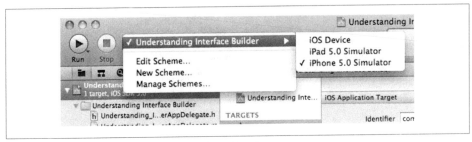

Figure 1-6. Choosing to run your app on iPhone Simulator

Discussion

Interface Builder, or IB, is integrated into Xcode as a tool for creating a user interface for your Mac and iOS apps. IB manipulates *.xib* files, which are sometimes called *nib* files to reflect the file extension they had in past Apple products. A nib file is basically the compiled (binary) version of an XIB file which itself is an XML file that is managed by IB. XIB files are in XML format to make them easier to use with version control systems and text-based tools.

Let's go ahead and start using IB. To do this, first create an iOS App using the Single View Application iOS Project template in Xcode. Follow the instructions in Recipe 1.1, but instead of Page-Based Application template (Figure 1-1), use the Single View Application template and follow it to the last dialog to save your project to disk. I've named the project Understanding Interface Builder.

 Make sure your app is a Universal app, as shown in Figure 1-2.

After your project is created, the first thing you need to do is make sure it is going to run on iPhone Simulator, as shown in Figure 1-6.

Now press Command+Shift+R to run your application. You will then see the iOS Simulator showing your empty application, as shown in Figure 1-7.

Now find the file *Understanding_Interface_BuilderViewController_iPhone.xib* in your project and click on it. Interface Builder will open up within Xcode and will display your user interface to you. Now that you have IB open, select from Xcode menus the View option, and then Utilities, and finally select Show Object Library (Figure 1-8).

Now if you have a look at the Object Library, you can see that you have plenty of choice as to what you want to put on your interface. This includes buttons, on/off switches, progress bars, table views, etc. For now, drag and drop a button on your user interface. It's as simple as that (Figure 1-9).

Figure 1-7. An empty Single View Application running on iOS Simulator

Right after this, from the Xcode menus, select File and then Save to make sure your *Understanding_Interface_BuilderViewController_iPhone.xib* is saved. Then go ahead and run your app on iOS Simulator (Figure 1-10).

You might be surprised, but for now that is *all* that we need to know about Interface Builder.

See Also

Recipe 1.1

1.3 Compiling iOS Apps

Problem

You have learned how to create an iOS app and wonder how it behaves.

Solution

Compile and run your iOS apps using Apple's latest compiler. Then test your app on iOS Simulator and also, preferably, on a device.

Discussion

Creating an iOS App can be categorized under the following tasks:

1. Planning

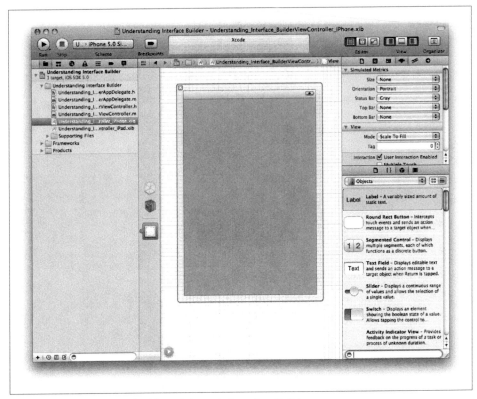

Figure 1-8. UI Objects in the Object Library in Interface Builder

2. Prototyping

3. Designing

4. Implementing and Testing

5. Delivering

During the implementation of an app, you will constantly need to run your app on a simulator or on various devices to make sure it is consistent, adheres to the design guidelines that you or your teammates created for this project, and most importantly, is stable enough for the App Store.

 Crashes provide one of the major reasons for app rejections in the Apple App Store. Apps that are not stable and crash often are not good enough for consumers, and Apple is very likely to reject them. So always make sure that you thoroughly test your apps on iOS Simulator and on devices.

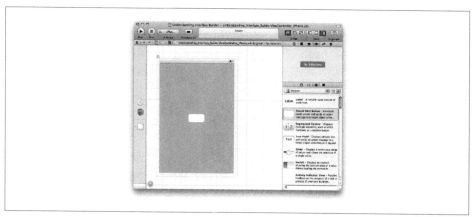

Figure 1-9. A button on a nib

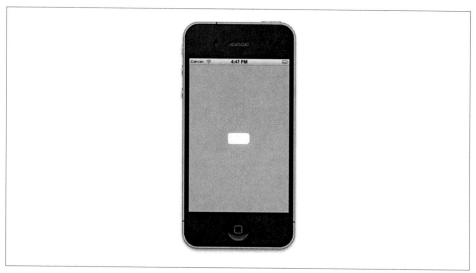

Figure 1-10. A button on the UI of your app

When we write our code, as we will learn very soon, we need to make sure that what we are writing is correct. The process by which Xcode changes our code into executable instructions is called *compilation*. The compiler does the compilation. In Xcode, we use various build commands to compile our apps:

Build for Running
> Use this when you want to debug your applications on the simulator or on a device. Debugging is the process by which you can find mistakes in your code.

Build for Testing

Use this build setting to run unit-tests that you've written for your apps. Unit tests, in short, are a set of instructions that you provide to Xcode. Xcode will run these instructions before it makes the final build. These instructions have one purpose only: to make sure that each part of the app you've written is in full working order.

Build for Profiling

If you want to test the performance of your app, use this setting. Profiling is the process by which you can find bottlenecks, memory leaks, and other quality-related issues not covered by unit testing.

Build for Archiving

When you are sure your app is production quality or simply want to distribute it to testers, use this setting.

To compile your apps in Xcode, simply select the Product menu item, choose Build For, and then choose whichever build setting you believe is relevant to the task you want to accomplish.

What do you think happens if you have an error in your code? In Recipe 1.1 we created a simple Page-Based Application, so let's go back to that app. Now open the *RootViewController.m* file in your project and look for this code:

```
- (void)viewWillAppear:(BOOL)animated
{
  [super viewWillAppear:animated];
}
```

Change this code to the following:

```
- (void)viewWillAppear:(BOOL)animated
{
  [super nonExistentMethod];
  [super viewWillAppear:animated];
}
```

If you now try to use Product menu, Build For, and then Build For Running, you will get the following error from Xcode:

```
error: Automatic Reference Counting Issue: Receiver type 'UIViewController'
for instance message does not declare a method
with selector 'nonExistentMethod'
```

This is what the compiler is telling you: the code that you've written cannot be compiled and translated to proper instructions to the CPU. In this particular case, this is because the compiler doesn't understand what *nonExistentMethod* actually is. This illustrates a good compiler that warns of—and sometimes stops you from making—mistakes that make your apps unstable.

See Also

Recipe 1.1

1.4 Running iOS Apps on the Simulator

Problem

You've prepared an iOS project in Xcode and would like to run it in iOS Simulator to make sure it works.

Solution

You need to use the Scheme breadcrumb button on the top-left corner of Xcode to first select the project that you wish to run on the iOS Simulator and then select the simulator that you wish to run your app on (iPhone/iPad).

Discussion

Follow these steps:

1. Find the Scheme breadcrumb button on the top-left corner of Xcode's window. This button looks like that shown in Figure 1-11.

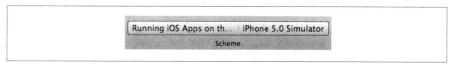

Figure 1-11. The Scheme breadcrumb button in Xcode

2. In Xcode, you can have multiple projects on the same workspace. For example, at the time of writing this recipe, I have one project per recipe, added to one big project that I've created for this book. The left side of the Scheme button shows you the project that's currently selected. So if I click on the left side of the Scheme button, I'll see something similar to Figure 1-12. So go ahead and click on the left side of the Scheme button and select the project that you wish to run on the iOS Simulator.

3. The right side of the Scheme button lets you choose which device/simulator you wish to run your app on. I've selected iPhone Simulator. Go ahead and press the right side of the Scheme button to select which simulator you would like to run your app on (Figure 1-13).

Bear in mind that the options presented to you on the right side of the Scheme button depend entirely on how your project is set up. In the second stage of creating an iOS Project, Xcode asks you which device(s) you would like your app to run on (in the Device Family drop-down). You can see this box in Figure 1-2. A Universal app is an app that runs on both iPad and iPhone. There are also options to select to make your app run only on iPhone or only on the iPad.

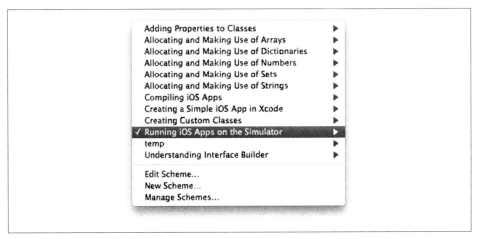

Figure 1-12. The project currently selected

Figure 1-13. Selecting the iPhone Simulator

Now that you have selected which simulator you would like to run your app on, simply go to the Product menu in Xcode and select Run. Xcode will compile your app (Recipe 1.3) if it's not compiled yet and will then run it on your selected simulator.

See Also

Recipe 1.3

1.5 Running iOS Apps on iOS Devices

Problem

You've created an iOS App and now you want to run it on a device.

Solution

Simply plug your device into your computer using the USB cable that comes with your device. Follow the steps in Recipe 1.4 to make sure you have selected the right project in Xcode. Instead of choosing the simulator (as shown in Recipe 1.4) in the Scheme breadcrumb button, choose your device, go to Product, and press Run.

Discussion

Each version of Xcode supports a series of iOS versions. By *support* I mean that the latest version of Xcode, for instance, may not be capable of compiling and running an iOS app on a second-generation iPod touch with iOS 3.0 installed on it. The reason is that the utilities built for each version of Xcode allow you to run your iOS apps on a limited number of versions of iOS on devices. The same is true for iOS Simulator. If you download the latest version of Xcode, you will notice that you might only be able to simulate your apps on iOS Simulator 5.0 and nothing before that.

The way to detect whether Xcode has detected your device is to plug in your device, wait a few seconds for the sync to happen, and see whether the name of your device appears in the right half of the Scheme breadcrumb button.

If you've waited for the device to sync and still the Scheme button is showing *iOS Device* in its list instead of the name of your device, you need to make sure that your device can be used for development purposes. Simply follow these instructions:

1. Select the Window menu.
2. Under the Window menu, select Organizer.
3. On top of Organizer, make sure the Devices item is selected, as shown in Figure 1-14.

Figure 1-14. Selecting the Devices button in Organizer

4. On the left side of Organizer's Devices screen, make sure you've selected your device by clicking on it (Figure 1-15).

5. As you can see, the device has a gray light instead of green. The gray light tells us that this device is not ready for development. After clicking on the device in the list, you will then see a button on the right side of the screen labeled Use for Development. Press that button. Once you press this button, you will see a progress bar appear on the screen and Xcode will start detecting this device.

6. At this stage, Xcode might show a Login screen. This screen asks for your iOS Developer Portal's credentials. This means that Xcode wants to detect whether the UDID (Unique Device ID) of your device has already been added to your portal or not. If it has not been added, Xcode will add it for you. So just go ahead and provide your iOS Portal credentials to Xcode (see Figure 1-16) and then press the Login button.

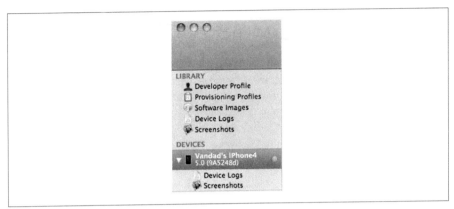

Figure 1-15. A device that is not ready for development

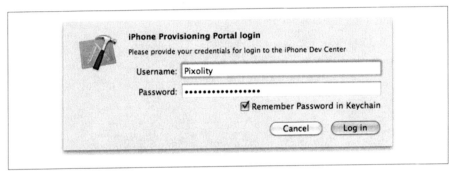

Figure 1-16. Xcode waiting for iOS Portal credentials

7. If everything goes fine and Xcode detects that the iOS version on your device is something that it can support, it will display the green light next to your device on the left-hand side of Organizer's Devices screen, as shown in Figure 1-17.

8. Now close Organizer and come back to Xcode. If you now click on the right side of the Scheme breadcrumb button, you will be able to see your device listed there, as shown in Figure 1-18.

If Xcode cannot detect the version of iOS installed on your device, it will display an amber light next to it. In this case, you either need to get a version of Xcode that does support your device's iOS version, or you need to change the version of iOS on your device to match what Xcode supports. Xcode will display the list of iOS versions that it supports after displaying the amber light next to your device. Xcode, in fact, will give you the reason why it cannot run iOS apps on your device. If the reason stems from the version of iOS on your device, the supported versions of iOS will certainly be displayed in Organizer's Devices section.

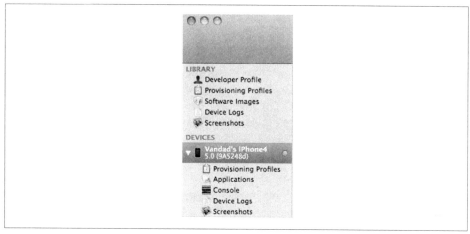

Figure 1-17. An iOS device ready for development

Figure 1-18. An iOS device showing up in the Scheme breadcrumb button in Xcode

See Also

Recipe 1.4

1.6 Packaging iOS Apps for Distribution

Problem

You want to send your iOS app to others so that they can test your app or have a look at it *before* you submit your app to the App Store.

Solution

You need to archive your application.

Discussion

In order to archive an application, you need to follow certain steps:

1. Make sure that you have fully tested the app on the simulator and you are happy that your app is stable.

2. Gather the UDIDs (Unique Device Identifiers) of all those devices on which you want to run your app. You can ask your friends and colleagues for these if the devices belong to them.

3. Add these UDIDs to your iOS Portal.

4. Create an Ad Hoc Distribution provision profile. Provision profiles are a mix of binary and XML content that allow an application to be executed on devices that have been linked to that provision profile.

5. After you have your provision profiles (a file that ends with the *.mobileprovision* extension), tell Xcode to use that provision profile for release purposes, as we will soon see.

6. Within Xcode, select the Product menu and then choose Archive. Xcode will now archive your application and, when that is done, display Organizer to you. Here you can export your archived application as a file (with the *.ipa* extension) that your testers/colleagues/friends can drag and drop into their iTunes or iPhone Configuration Utility to install your app on their iOS devices.

To distribute your iOS app to testers/colleagues and friends, you have to create an Ad Hoc provision profile. Follow these steps to create your Ad Hoc provision profile:

1. Log into the iOS Dev Center (*http://bit.ly/PUtjlY*).

2. Select iOS Provision Portal from the right side of the screen.

3. If you have not created a Distribution certificate yet, follow these steps:
   - On the lefthand side of iOS Provision Profile, select Certificates.
   - On the righthand side, select the Distribution tab on the top of the screen.
   - Follow the instructions on the screen, which will ask you to use Keychain Access to create a new certificate on your computer and then upload that certificate to the portal. After this, you will have your Distribution certificate.
   - Click on the Download button to the right side of your Distribution certificate to download it. After you've downloaded it on your computer, double-click on it to install it in your Keychain Access.

4. Now move to the Devices item on the left side of the screen.

5. Select the Add Devices button on the right side of the screen.

6. Enter the device name and the device UDID in the boxes provided. If entering more than one device, press the + button after every device to make room for a new device. You can add a maximum of 100 devices to each provision portal (except for Enterprise portals, which we won't cover in this book, as they are given only to big organizations).

After a device is added to your iOS portal, it cannot be removed for the period that you hold this portal (which is usually a year). After your portal has expired and when it has been renewed, you will get a chance to delete any unwanted devices, so make sure you are not adding devices to your portal without considering this.

7. Once you are done adding the devices, press the Submit button.

8. Select Provisioning on the left side of the screen.

9. Select the Distribution tab on the righthand side of the screen.

10. Select the New Profile button on the right side of the screen.

11. In the Create iOS Distribution Provisioning Profile screen, make sure the Distribution Method is Ad Hoc (Figure 1-19).

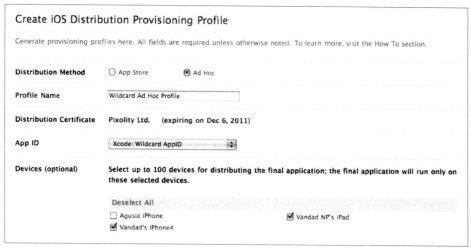

Figure 1-19. Creating a new Ad Hoc provision profile

12. Under Profile Name, give a descriptive name to your provision profile. For instance, something like Wildcard Ad Hoc Profile. Be creative and descriptive.

13. In the App ID drop-down, pick Xcode: Wildcard AppID. This will allow you to provision your apps regardless of their App Identifiers so that you can use the same Ad Hoc provision profile for all your iOS apps.

14. In the Devices section, select all the devices on which you want this provision profile to work. Devices that are not selected in this list will *not* be able to run your apps.

15. After you are done selecting the devices, press the Submit button.

16. Now head back to the Distribution tab of the Provisioning section and press the Download button for the provision profile that you just created. If the status of

this profile is Pending, refresh your page in your browser until the provision profile is created.

17. Now that you have this provision profile downloaded on your computer, drag and drop it into iTunes. iTunes will then install this profile for you.

All done. We are now ready to create an archived app. Follow these steps:

1. Select your profile file in Xcode (this is the file with the blue icon).

2. Now you will see the targets your app supports. Select the desired target.

3. Select Build Settings on the right side of the screen (Figure 1-20).

4. In the Build Settings tab, scroll down until you get to the Code Signing category, as shown in Figure 1-20.

5. Under Code Signing Identity → Release and Code Signing Identity → Release → Any iOS SDK, make sure you pick the provision profile that you created earlier in this recipe.

6. On the Scheme breadcrumb (Figure 1-11), make sure you've chosen iOS Device/ Your Device Name instead of iOS Simulator (iPad or iPhone). Under the simulator, you cannot create an app for distribution.

7. Head over to the Product menu and choose Archive.

Figure 1-20. Xcode Displaying the Build Settings of an iOS App

After the archiving process is finished, Xcode will open Organizer for you and will display the Archives tab, as depicted in Figure 1-21.

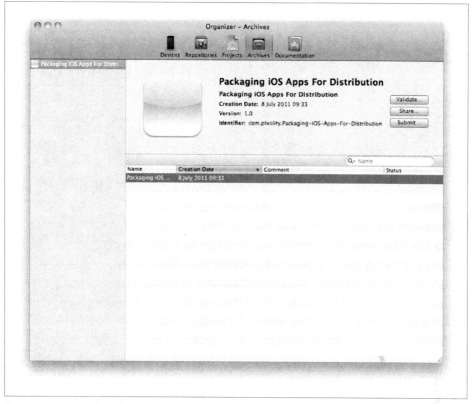

Figure 1-21. An archived application in Organizer

8. Select the Share button on the top-right side of the screen. You will be presented with a dialog similar to that shown in Figure 1-22.

9. Keep the Contents selection as iOS App Store Package (.ipa file), as shown in Figure 1-22.

10. In the Identity drop-down, again, choose the provision profile with which you want to sign your app. We created this provision profile before, remember? Choose the same profile again. Once you are done, press Next.

11. You will now be asked to specify the location where you would like to save this file. Select your desired location and filename, then press Save.

All done. Now you have a file with an *.ipa* extension. When sending this file to your friends/colleagues/etc., make sure you send the provision profile (which you created in the iOS Dev Portal) as well. They will need both of these files (the *.ipa* and the *.mobileprovision* files) in order to install your archived apps on their devices.

A user can use either iTunes or iPhone Configuration Utility (both are free) in order to install your apps on their devices. I personally recommend iPhone Configuration Utility

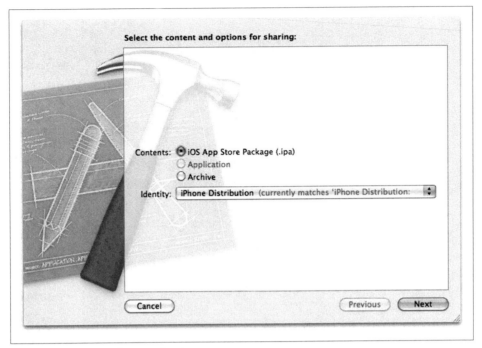

Figure 1-22. Selecting the type of archive we want to create

(or iCU) since it is certainly more robust when it comes to installing Ad Hoc apps on devices. iTunes has some issues when installing archived apps on devices, which I am not going to bore you with. The more you work with these two pieces of software, the more you get to know about their advantages and disadvantages.

1.7 Declaring Variables in Objective-C

Problem

You want to use variables with clear names in your iOS apps.

Solution

Apple conventions dictate certain rules for variable names. Determine the type of the variable (for instance, integer, array, string, etc.) and then a descriptive name for it. In an empty line of code, place the type of your variable first, following by its name. Variable names are advised to follow these rules:

1. Follow the camelCase naming convention. If the variable name is one word, all letters must be lowercase. If the variable name is more than one word, the first word must be entirely lowercase and the subsequent words must have their first letter uppercase and the rest of their letters lowercase. For instance, if you want to

have a counter variable, you can simply name it counter. If you want to call your variable "first counter", declare it firstCounter. The variable name "my very long variable name" would become myVeryLongVariableName. (Names of that length are quite common in iOS programs.)

2. Variables should ideally have no underline in their names. For instance, my_variable_name can and perhaps should be changed to myVariableName.

3. Variable names should contain only letters and numbers (no punctuation such as commas or dashes). This is a restriction in the Objective-C language and many other languages, but this helps keeping variable names tidy.

Let's have a look at a few examples. There are a few primitive data types in Objective-C. A data type is a name that specifies the type of a variable. For instance, you can say that you have an integer variable of type NSInteger or an integer variable of type NSUInteger, where the former is a signed variable and the latter is unsigned (note the "U" after "NS") in the latter example).

 Signed integers *can* contain negative numbers, whereas unsigned integers *cannot*.

We can then define these variables in our source code like so:

```
NSInteger signedInteger = -123;    /* Can take negative numbers */
NSUInteger unsignedInteger = 123; /* Cannot take negative numbers */
```

There are certain rules, as mentioned before, about naming your variables (for instance, the camelCase rule). However, other aspects of your variable naming convention depend entirely on your choice. In general, I advise that you always assume you are working for a big organization (whether it is your own company or somebody else's company) and follow these rules:

1. Give descriptive names to your variables. Avoid names such as "i" or "x." These names will never make any sense to anybody else but yourself and chances are that they won't make sense to you either if you leave the project for some time and come back to it after a few months. The compiler doesn't really care if the variable name is 50 letters long. If that makes your variable name more descriptive and you cannot do without it, then go for it.

2. Avoid creating vague variable names. For instance, if you have a string variable and you want to place the full name of a person in that variable, avoid giving it names such as "theString" or "theGuy" or "theGirl." These make no sense at all. It is best to give a name such as "fullName" or "firstAndLastName" rather than something that confuses everybody who looks at your source code, including yourself!

3. Avoid giving names to your variables that are likely to lead to mistyping. For instance, it is much better to call your variable "fullName" rather than "__full_____name." It is best to avoid underlines in variables all together.

Discussion

Variables are placeholders for data that you want to hold in memory. For instance, if you want to delete 100 files from the disk and those files are named *1.png*, *2.png*, on to *100.png*, it would be best to create a counter variable that starts from 1 and goes all the way to 100 and then use the content of that variable (the number) to delete the files. Programmers use variables to do arithmetic or simple operations, such as prefixing the last name of a person with their first name to create the resulting full name.

Every variable has to have a type. The type of a variable tells the compiler and the machine that runs that program, what type of variable that is and what sort of value it holds. For example, a variable that is an integer can hold the value 123 but cannot hold a value with decimal places such as 123.456. For the latter, we will need a floating-point variable. Integer and floating-point here are the data types and, in Objective-C, are defined with NSInteger and float. Here are some of the commonly used data types in Objective-C:

NSInteger
> Variables of this type can store signed (positive or negative) integer values.

NSUInteger
> Variables of this type can store unsigned (only positive or zero) integer values.

float
> Variables of this type can store floating-point values (values that have decimals in them, such as 1.23 or 73.12).

NSString
> Variables of this type can store strings, such as "my string" or "Mrs Thomson."

NSArray
> Variables of this type can store an array of objects. For instance, if you have read 10 files from the disk, you can store their data in an array. An array can contain more than one instance of the same value.

NSSet
> Variables of this type can store unique instances of variables. Sets are similar to arrays in that they can store multiple value but each value can only appear at most once in a set.

1.8 Allocating and Making Use of Strings

Problem

You want to work with strings in Objective-C

Solution

Use NSString and NSMutableString classes.

Discussion

The NSString and NSMutableString classes allow you to store a string of characters in memory. The NSString class is immutable, meaning that once it is created, its contents cannot be modified. Mutable strings represented with the NSMutableString can be modified once they are created. We will see an example of both of these classes very soon.

Objective-C strings should be placed inside double quotes. The starting double-quote should be prefixed with an at sign (@). For instance, the sentence Hello, World, represented as a string in Objective-C, is written like so:

```
@"Hello, World"
```

There are various ways of placing a string inside an instance of NSString or NSMutable String classes. Here is how:

```
NSString *simpleString = @"This is a simple string";

NSString *anotherString =
  [NSString stringWithString:@"This is another simple string"];

NSString *oneMorestring =
  [[NSString alloc] initWithString:@"One more!"];

NSMutableString *mutableOne =
  [NSMutableString stringWithString:@"Mutable String"];

NSMutableString *anotherMutableOne =
  [[NSMutableString alloc] initWithString:@"A retained one"];

NSMutableString *thirdMutableOne =
  [NSMutableString stringWithString:simpleString];
```

If you are working with strings, you are probably going to need the length of your string objects from time to time to make specific decisions at runtime. Imagine this scenario: you have asked your user to enter her name in a text field. When she presses the button to confirm her name, you would need to check whether she has in fact entered her name. You can do this by calling the length method on an instance of NSString or any of its subclasses, including NSMutableString, as shown here:

```
NSString *userName = ...;

if ([userName length] == 0){
  /* The user didn't enter her name */
} else {
  /* The user did in fact enter her name */
}
```

Another thing that you might want to know about strings is how you can convert a string to its equivalent integral value, i.e., converting a string to an integer, float, or double. You can use the integerValue, floatValue, and doubleValue methods of NSString (or any of its subclasses) to retrieve the integer, float and double values of a string, like so:

```
NSString *simpleString = @"123.456";

NSInteger integerOfString = [simpleString integerValue];
NSLog(@"integerOfString = %ld", (long)integerOfString);

CGFloat floatOfString = [simpleString floatValue];
NSLog(@"floatOfString = %f", floatOfString);

double doubleOfString = [simpleString doubleValue];
NSLog(@"doubleOfString = %f", doubleOfString);
```

The output of this code is:

```
integerOfString = 123
floatOfString = 123.456001
doubleOfString = 123.456000
```

If you would like to work with C Strings, you can! You will use them like NSString *without* the leading at sign, like so:

```
char *cString = "This is a C String";
```

If you want to convert an NSString to a C String, you must use the UTF8String method of NSString, like so:

```
const char *cString = [@"Objective-C String" UTF8String];
NSLog(@"cString = %s", cString);
```

You can use the %s format specifier to print a C String out to the console. In contrast, use the %@ format specifier to print out NSString objects.

To convert a C String to NSString, you must use the stringWithUTF8String: method of the NSString class, as demonstrated here:

```
NSString *objectString = [NSString stringWithUTF8String:"C String"];
NSLog(@"objectString = %@", objectString);
```

In order to find a string inside another string, you can use the rangeOfString: method of NSString. The return value of this method is of type NSRange:

```
typedef struct _NSRange {
  NSUInteger location;
  NSUInteger length;
} NSRange;
```

If the string that you are looking for (needle) is found inside the target string (haystack), the location member of the NSRange structure will be set to the zero-based index of the first character of needle in haystack. If needle cannot be found in haystack, the location member gets set to NSNotFound. Let's have a look at an example:

```
NSString *haystack = @"My Simple String";
NSString *needle = @"Simple";
NSRange  range = [haystack rangeOfString:needle];

if (range.location == NSNotFound){
  /* Could NOT find needle in haystack */
} else {
  /* Found the needle in the haystack */
  NSLog(@"Found %@ in %@ at location %lu",
      needle,
      haystack,
      (unsigned long)range.location);
}
```

The search done by the rangeOfString: method of NSString class is case-sensitive.

In the Platform Dependencies (*http://bit.ly/Ttf8Pf*) section of the String Programming Guide published by Apple, it's been explained why we need to typecast integral values with specifiers such as unsigned long. I highly recommend that you visit the aforementioned guide online.

If you want to have more control over how your search is done on a string, you can use the rangeOfString:options: method, where the options parameter is of type NSString CompareOptions.

```
enum {
    NSCaseInsensitiveSearch = 1,
    NSLiteralSearch = 2,
    NSBackwardsSearch = 4,
    NSAnchoredSearch = 8,
    NSNumericSearch = 64,
    NSDiacriticInsensitiveSearch = 128,
    NSWidthInsensitiveSearch = 256,
    NSForcedOrderingSearch = 512,
```

```
          NSRegularExpressionSearch = 1024
    };
    typedef NSUInteger NSStringCompareOptions;
```

As you can see, the values in this enumeration are multiples of 2. That indicates that you can mix them with the logical OR operator (the | pipe character). Let's say we want to search for a string inside another string but we are not concerned about the case-sensitivity of the search. All we want is to find a string inside another string, whether the case matches or not. Here is how we can do it:

```
NSString *haystack = @"My Simple String";
NSString *needle = @"simple";
NSRange  range = [haystack rangeOfString:needle
                               options:NSCaseInsensitiveSearch];

if (range.location == NSNotFound){
  /* Could NOT find needle in haystack */
} else {
  /* Found the needle in the haystack */
  NSLog(@"Found %@ in %@ at location %lu",
       needle,
       haystack,
       (unsigned long)range.location);
}
```

You can see that we are using the rangeOfString:options: method of NSString with the NSCaseInsensitiveSearch value, which tells the runtime that we want the search to be performed without any regard to case-sensitivity.

Mutable strings are similar to immutable strings. However, they can be modified during runtime. Let's see an example:

```
NSMutableString *mutableString =
  [[NSMutableString alloc] initWithString:@"My MacBook"];

/* Add string to the end of this string */
[mutableString appendString:@" Pro"];

/* Remove the "My " string from the string */
[mutableString
 replaceOccurrencesOfString:@"My "
 withString:[NSString string] /* Empty string */
 options:NSCaseInsensitiveSearch /* Case-insensitive */
 range:NSMakeRange(0, [mutableString length])]; /* All to the end */

NSLog(@"mutableString = %@", mutableString);
```

When the mutableString string gets printed to the console, you will see this:

```
mutableString = MacBook Pro
```

You can see that we started with the string "My MacBook" and then removed the "My " string from that original string. So now we have "MacBook". After this, we appended the string " Pro" to the end of this string to get the final value, which is "MacBook Pro".

1.9 Comparing Values in Objective-C with an if Statement

Problem

You want to compare two values in Objective-C.

Solution

Use if statements. Please refer to the Discussion section of this recipe for more information about different scenarios under which you might want to use if statements.

Discussion

We use if statements in our everyday conversations. For instance, you might say "If I get a hold of him, I'll tell him..." or "I would put the computer to sleep if it didn't take so long to come back up." All these statements have a *condition*. If statements in Objective-C also have a condition. You can even make them more sophisticated, having your app do something if a condition is met and something else if the condition is *not* met. The basic form of an if statement is:

```
if (condition){
  /* Your code to get executed if the condition is met */
}
```

 As long as the condition is a value other than zero/nil/NULL, the code inside the if statement will run.

An if statement that has an "otherwise" clause in it is known as an if-else statement, and its format is:

```
if (condition){
  /* Your code to get executed if the condition is met */
} else {
  /* Code to get executed if condition is not met */
}
```

The else clause of the if-else statement can also contain its own if statement! That might sound strange, but consider this scenario. In real life, you can say something similar to this: "I will go get a cup of coffee. If the place is open, I will get a tall latte; if it's closed and the other place is open, I will get a cappuccino; otherwise, I will just come back home and make tea for myself". The part where we said "...if it's closed and the other place is open..." is an else statement with an if statement embedded in it. Here is how you would implement that in Objective-C:

```
if (Coffee place A is open){
  Get a Tall Latte from coffee place A} else if (Coffee place B is open){
  Get a Cappuccino from coffee place B
} else {
  Come back home and make tea
}
```

The condition for an if statement, regardless of whether it is a standalone if statement (like the first condition in the last example) or embedded inside an else statement, must resolve to a boolean value. A boolean value is either YES or NO. For instance, the following code will *always* get executed, regardless of which condition/device you run it on:

```
if (YES){
  /* This code will get executed whenever the app gets to it */
} else {
  /* The app will NEVER get here */
}
```

The reason behind this is that the condition for the if statement in this example is always met as long as the YES is the condition. To make things more exciting, you can do comparisons in the condition supplied to an if statement, like so:

```
NSInteger integer1 = 123;
NSInteger integer2 = 456;

if (integer1 == integer2){
  NSLog(@"Integers are equal.");
} else {
  NSLog(@"Integers are not equal.");
}
```

Note that a double equal sign is used inside the conditional. A common error is to use a single equal sign, which is a totally different operator. The double equal sign does a comparison and returns a Boolean result, which is what you normally want in a conditional. A single equal sign changes the value of the left-hand variable and returns the value set, which the condition tries to interpret as a Boolean value. Although occasionally appropriate, it's usually a serious error to use a single equal sign.

If you are comparing objects, it is best to use the isEqual: instance method of the NSObject class:

```
NSObject *object1 = [[NSObject alloc] init];
NSObject *object2 = object1;

if ([object1 isEqual:object2]){
  NSLog(@"Both objects are equal.");
} else {
  NSLog(@"Objects are not equal.");
}
```

For now, you don't have to worry about what objects are. This will be explained in detail in other recipes in this chapter.

Some objects such as strings, however, have their own comparison methods, changing the way we compare two strings. For instance, you can have two string objects that contain the same characters. If you compare them using their isEqual: instance method, you will get the result NO, because they are different objects. However, they might still contain the exact same characters. Because of this, different classes expose their own comparison methods in Objective-C. For more information about classes, please refer to Recipe 1.12. To learn more about objects, refer to Recipe 1.15.

An if statement and its else statement can be written with or without curly braces. Using the former syntax (with curly braces), you can execute multiple lines of code after the condition is satisfied. However, without curly braces, you can write only one line of code for each condition. Here is an example of the latter syntax without curly braces:

```
NSString *shortString = @"Hello!";

if ([shortString length] == 0)
  NSLog(@"This is an empty string");
else
  NSLog(@"This is not an empty string.");
```

Be extra careful with logging and if statements without curly braces. Often, when a product goes to production, a production manager might attempt to comment out all your NSLog methods simply by replacing all occurrences of NSLog with //NSLog. If you have if statements without curly braces, as in our last example, the production manager's commented-out code will look like this:

```
NSString *shortString = @"Hello!";

if ([shortString length] == 0)
  //NSLog(@"This is an empty string");
else
  //NSLog(@"This is not an empty string.");
```

This will break the code and people in the company will *not* be happy. It doesn't matter whether they are not happy at you or not happy at the production manager. That would be a team effort gone wrong, so you will all be to blame. To avoid this, make sure that you always write your if statements *with* curly braces.

See Also

Recipe 1.12; Recipe 1.15

1.10 Implementing Loops with for Statements

Problem

You want to implement a code that repeats a certain number of times, perhaps applying the same procedure to every element in an array or some other changing values.

Solution

Use the for statement. The format of this statement is:

```
for (code to execute before loop;
     condition to be met for the loop to terminate;
     code to execute in every iteration of the loop){


}
```

 All three clauses of the for loop are optional. In other words, you can have a for loop that looks like this:

```
for (;;){ YOUR CODE HERE }
```

This is known as an infinite-loop or a loop that has no condition to terminate and will run forever. This is a very bad programming practice indeed and you should avoid using it by all means while developing iOS programs.

Discussion

Loops are useful in programming because you will often need to start a loop from one place to another, from one index to another, or from start to stop. For instance, you might want to loop through all characters inside a string and count how many "A" characters you can find in it. Another example is a loop that finds all files in a directory. This is a loop that finds the number of files and then starts from the first one until it gets to the last one.

Usually, programmers require a counter in their loops. For instance, you might want to read all the characters inside a C-String. For this, you will need the index of each character. If your string is 10 characters long, you will need to go from index 0 to 9. If your string is 20 characters long, you have to read from index 0 to 19. Since the length of your string is a variable, you can put it as the exit-conditional of your loop. Here is an example:

```
char *myString = "This is my string";

NSUInteger counter = 0;
for (counter = 0; /* Start from index 0 */
     counter < strlen(myString); /* Exit loop when we reach last character */
     counter++){ /* Increment the index in every iteration */
```

```
    char character = myString[counter];

    NSLog(@"%c", character);

}
```

The code that gets executed before the loop (as noted in the Solution section of this recipe) is obviously optional. In fact, all three main parts of a for loop are optional, but it is recommended that you think about how you intend to use your loops and use the three main parts of the for statement accordingly.

Let's have a look at where you would want to skip the first statement of your for loop. As you could see in the previous section, our counter variable was set to 0 before we even started our loop. However, we are setting it to 0 again once our loop is about to start. This is unnecessary in this example, but there is nothing wrong with that approach. If you feel you don't need the redundant code, simply remove it:

```
char *myString = "This is my string";

NSUInteger counter = 0;
for (; /* empty section */
     counter < strlen(myString); /* Exit loop when we reach last character */
     counter++){ /* Increment the index in every iteration */

  char character = myString[counter];

  NSLog(@"%c", character);

}
```

The second clause of any for loop is very important because this is the conditional that allows your loop to exit. Having no condition in the second clause is similar to having a never-ending loop, or an infinite loop, as it is known. Therefore, it is best to think about the condition that allows your program to end the loop and continue on its path of execution.

Any variable defined in the first clause of a for loop is accessible inside the loop but not outside it. For instance:

```
for (NSUInteger counter = 0;
     counter < 10;
     counter++){
  NSLog(@"%lu", (unsigned long)counter);
}
/* "counter" is NOT accessible here. This line will throw compile time error */
NSLog(@"%lu", (unsigned long)counter);
```

The third clause inside a for loop is very interesting indeed. This is the statement that gets executed *after* every iteration of your loop. This includes the last iteration. For instance:

```
NSUInteger counter = 0;
for (counter = 0;
     counter < 4;
```

```
      counter++){
    NSLog(@"%lu", (unsigned long)counter);
  }
  NSLog(@"%lu", (unsigned long)counter);
```

This will print the following values to the console:

```
0
1
2
3
4
```

So our counter *did* get to number 4, although in our loop we asked that the counter should be less than 4. This proves the point that when our loop finishes, in the last iteration, the third clause of our for loop gets executed. But the code inside our loop won't be called, since the end-condition (second clause) will not be met and our loop will finish.

1.11 Implementing while Loops

Problem

You want to let a piece of code run over and over again until a certain condition is met.

Solution

Use while loops and specify your exit condition. Here is the format for the while loop:

```
while (condition){
  CODE
}
```

 As long as the condition is a value other than zero/nil/NULL, the while loop will run.

Discussion

The while loop is the arrogant brother of the for loop (see Recipe 1.10) because while loops only take a condition that should be met for the loop to run. If the condition is positive, the loop will always run until the condition becomes negative. For instance, a while loop could be implemented to make an icon in the Dock in Mac OS X jump up and down until the user taps on that icon (this is actually a very bad user experience; icons in the Dock shouldn't jump up and down continuously, but for a short interval, or even a fixed number of times, usually 3). The exit condition for the while loop is the user's tapping on that icon. As long as the user hasn't tapped on the icon, the icon will jump up and down.

A while loop is awkward to use with a counter because of its syntax. If you require a counter to control your loop, it is better to use a for loop. If you do require a while loop but still want to have access to a counter, you will need to manage the counter manually, like so:

```
NSUInteger counter = 0;
while (counter < 10){
  NSLog(@"Counter = %lu", (unsigned long)counter);
  counter++;
}
```

Just as you can have positive conditions for your while loops, you can have negative conditions as well:

```
BOOL shouldExitLoop = NO;
NSUInteger counter = 0;

while (shouldExitLoop == NO){
      counter++;
  if (counter >= 10){
    shouldExitLoop = YES;
  }
}

NSLog(@"Counter = %lu", (unsigned long)counter);
```

The output of this program is:

```
Counter = 10
```

So what we are doing is simply running a loop for as long as our counter is less than 10. If the value of the counter (adjusted inside the loop itself) goes over or becomes equal to 10, then we exit our loop. Just like a for loop, you can create an infinite loop using a while loop, although this is a terrible programming practice and you should avoid it by all means:

```
while (YES){
  /* Infinite loop */
}
```

You must make sure that you have an exit strategy in your while and for loops. For this, you need to keep an eye on the condition for your loops and make sure that the condition will be met at some point without making your loops hog all the memory and/or system resources while they run, while using autorelease objects. As you know, an autorelease object only gets released when the autorelease pool owning that object gets drained or released. If you do not have an autorelease pool inside your loop continuously releasing autorelease objects, your loop might end up consuming too much memory and your app might get terminated by iOS.

Here is another usage of a while loop:

```
char *myString = "Some Random String";
NSUInteger counter = 0;
char character;
```

```
while ((character = myString[counter++]) != 'R' &&
        counter < strlen(myString)){
  /* Empty */
}
NSLog(@"Found the letter R at character #%lu", (unsigned long)counter+1);
```

Here we are searching inside a string for the first occurrence of the letter *R*. As soon as we find it, we exit our while loop. We have included another condition: if we reach the end of the string (`strlen(myString)`), we end the loop, so we don't wander off into undefined memory and cause a crash or a security flaw. (This is called a *buffer overflow*.)

This algorithm has a bug, however: it returns a wrong results when the letter *R* isn't in the string at all. Because the while loop finishes when we get to the end of the string, we always print a message to the console saying that the letter *R* was found at some index. I will leave it up to you to fix this algorithm. As a hint, you might want to use a Boolean value when you do find the letter *R* and then later use that flag to determine whether the letter was found. To use that boolean technique, you might need to change the way the while loop is set up, but I think you get the idea.

A while loop is useful for traversing an array. For instance, a C String is an array of characters ending with a zero byte. If you are searching for a specific character in this array, you can simply write a while loop that starts from the first character and runs until it finds the zero terminator that ends the string. Here is an example:

```
char *cString = "My String";
char *stringPointer = cString;
while (*stringPointer != 0x00){
  NSLog(@"%c", *stringPointer);
  stringPointer++;
}
```

This example will print all the characters inside the string until it gets to the zero terminator of the string. Using a while loop, you can even create a function similar to the `strlen()` function that is able to find the length of a C String, like so:

```
NSUInteger lengthOfCString(const char *paramString){

  NSUInteger result = 0;

  if (paramString == NULL){
    return 0;
  }

  char *stringPointer = (char *)paramString;

  while (*stringPointer != 0x00){
    result++;
    stringPointer++;
  }

  return result;

}
```

It's better to use the built-in strlen for two reasons: it has been optimized to make the best use of the underlying hardware, and it's less likely to contain a bug.

See Also

Recipe 1.10

1.12 Creating Custom Classes

Problem

You want to pack a set of related functionalities into a reusable entity for immediate or later use.

Solution

Create your own classes.

Discussion

Let's say you want to write a calculator program. You are creating the user interface and you want each button on the calculator to have a black background, white text and have a *bump* user interface, just like a real button. Aren't these all common traits among all the buttons you want to place on your UI? You got it! It's best that we create a class to represent all our buttons and write the code once to reuse multiple times.

Classes in objective-C are normally represented with the following code:

Header file
> This is where you define what your class basically does: accept user input, rotate a shape, or whatever. But the header file does *not* implement any of that functionality. Header files have a *.h* extension.

Implementation file
> After defining the functionality of your class in the header file, here you write the actual code for all that functionality. Implementation files have a *.m* extension.

Let's go a bit more into detail by going ahead and creating a class. Follow these steps:

1. In Xcode, go to the File menu and then select New File.

2. A dialog will appear, similar to that shown in Figure 1-23. Here simply select Objective-C class from the list to the right. Make sure iOS is selected on the lefthand side. After this, press the Next button.

3. In the next screen, make sure the Subclass of text box says NSObject. Now press the Next button (Figure 1-24).

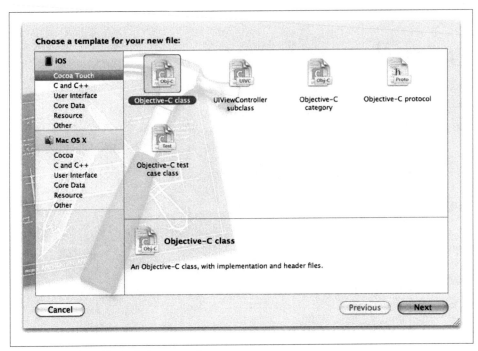

Figure 1-23. The Add File dialog in Xcode

4. In the next screen, as shown in Figure 1-25, make sure that the Save As text box says Person, which is what we'll name our class. On the bottom of this dialog, make sure that you are saving your class in the correct group/folder.

Now two files will get added to your project. One is called *Person.h* and the other *Person.m*. The first one is the header and the second one is the implementation. Let's have a look at the contents of the *Person.h* file:

```
#import <Foundation/Foundation.h>

@interface Person : NSObject

@end
```

How about the contents of *Person.m*?

```
#import "Person.h"

@implementation Person

- (id)init
{
  self = [super init];
  if (self) {
    // Initialization code here.
  }
```

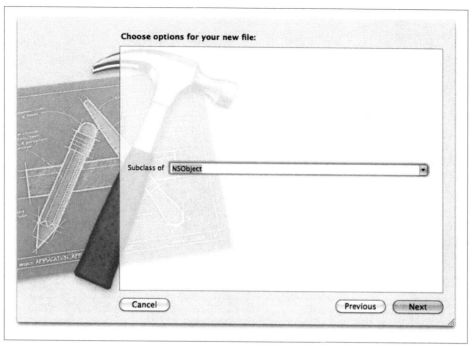

Figure 1-24. Setting the base class of our new class

```
    return self;
}

@end
```

We can see that Xcode has prepopulated these files with some content. We still don't really know what this content is, but it's a start to our code. Now we have a class named Person. Where did we get this name? It's *not* the name of the file itself, but Xcode took the file name in Figure 1-25 and used it as the class name. If you have a look at the contents of the *Person.h* again, you will notice this line of code:

```
@interface Person : NSObject
```

In short, what comes after the `@interface` keyword is your class name in this case. If you don't like this name, simply right-click on it and then select Refactor and then Rename. This will guide you through a refactoring process through which you can rename your class. Xcode will make sure that the name of your class will be changed throughout your code, if you have referred to it anywhere.

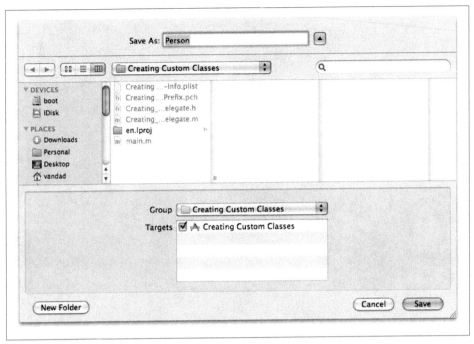

Figure 1-25. Creating a class called Person in Xcode

1.13 Defining Functionality for Classes

Problem

You want to define some functionality for your classes and allow them to be reused later.

Solution

Create instance or class methods for your classes in order to create reusable blocks of code, or simply call a method in your program.

Discussion

Nearly every programming language creates *procedures* and *functions* to encapsulate specific functionality, especially functionality that the programmer uses over and over. Some languages consider "procedure" and "function" just terms for the same thing, while others make a distinction between them. A procedure is a block of code with a name and an optional set of parameters. It does not have a return value. In Objective-C, a procedure returns void to indicate it does not return a value. A function is similar but does have a return value. Here is a simple procedure (with an empty body) written in C:

```
void sendEmailTo(const char *paramTo,
                 const char *paramSubject,
                 const char *paramEmailMessage){

    /* send the email here ... */
}
```

This procedure is named `sendEmailTo` and has three parameters: `paramTo`, `param Subject`, and `paramEmailMessage`. We can then call this procedure as follows:

```
sendEmailTo("somebody@somewhere.com",
            "My Subject",
            "Please read my email");
```

Turning this procedure into a function that returns a Boolean value, we will have code similar to this:

```
BOOL sendEmailTo(const char *paramTo,
                 const char *paramSubject,
                 const char *paramEmailMessage){

    /* send the email here ... */

    if (paramTo == nil ||
        paramSubject == nil ||
        paramEmailMessage == nil){
      /* One or some of the parameters are nil */
      NSLog(@"Nil parameter(s) is/are provided.");
      return NO;
    }

    return YES;
}
```

Calling this function is similar to calling the `sendEmailTo` procedure except that with a function, we can retrieve the return value, like so:

```
BOOL isSuccessful = sendEmailTo("somebody@somewhere.com",
                                "My Subject",
                                "Please read my email");

if (isSuccessful){
  /* Successfully sent the email */
} else {
  /* Failed to send the email. Perhaps we should display
     an error message to the user */
}
```

In Objective-C, each method is created for a class. Creating Objective-C methods is quite different from writing procedures and functions in a programming language such as C. Methods fall into two categories: *instance* or *class*. Instance methods are methods that can be called on an instance of the class (that is, on each object you create based on the class), whereas class methods get called on the class itself and do not require an instance of the class to be created by the programmer. To create a method in Objective-C, follow these steps in the *.m* file of your target class:

1. Type `-` if you want an instance method or `+` if you want a class method.

2. Choose the return type of your method and enclose it within parentheses—for instance, `(void)` for no return value, `(BOOL)` for a Boolean value, `(NSObject *)` to return an instance of `NSObject`, and so on.

3. Choose a name for your method. Start the name with a lowercase letter. It is common in Objective-C to start method names with a lowercase letter—for instance, `sendEmailTo` instead of `SendEmailTo`.

4. If you do not want any parameters for your method, jump to step 9.

5. Choose two names for your parameter. One name becomes a part of the method name and will be used from outside the method (this is optional for all parameters except the first). The other name will be used as a parameter name inside the method. There is an exception to this in which the first name of the first parameter of a method is part of the name of the method that you chose in step 3. For this first parameter, you must only choose a second name, which becomes the parameter name used inside the method itself.

6. Once you are done choosing the name for your parameter, choose the data type of the method and enclose it within parentheses.

7. Put a colon after your parameter's first chosen name (if any), and put the parentheses that carry the data type of your method followed by the second name for your parameter.

8. Repeat steps 5 through 7 for any other parameters that you might have.

9. Insert an open curly brace (`{`) after the method name and parameter names (if you have parameters) and a closing curly brace (`}`) at the end.

Going back to the `sendEmailTo` procedure example that we saw earlier, let's attempt to create the same procedure as a method in Objective-C:

```
- (BOOL) sendEmailTo:(NSString *)paramTo
        withSubject:(NSString *)paramSubject
    andEmailMessage:(NSString *)paramEmailMessage{

    /* Send the email and return an appropriate value */

    if ([paramTo length] == 0 ||
        [paramSubject length] == 0 ||
        [paramEmailMessage length] == 0){
        /* One or some of the parameters are empty */
        NSLog(@"Empty parameter(s) is/are provided.");
        return NO;
    }

    return YES;

}
```

This is an instance method (-) that returns a Boolean value (BOOL). The name of this method is sendEmailTo:withSubject:andEmailMessage: and it has three parameters. We can then call this method in this way:

```
[self sendEmailTo:@"someone@somewhere.com"
      withSubject:@"My Subject"
   andEmailMessage:@"Please read my email."];
```

As mentioned previously, the first name of every parameter (except the first) is optional. In other words, we can construct the sendEmailTo:withSubject:andEmailMessage: method in another way with a different name:

```
- (BOOL) sendEmailTo:(NSString *)paramTo
                    :(NSString *)paramSubject
                    :(NSString *)paramEmailMessage{

   /* Send the email and return an appropriate value */

   if (paramTo length] == 0 ||
       [paramSubject length] == 0 ||
       [paramEmailMessage length] == 0){
     NSLog(@"Empty parameter(s) is/are provided.");
     return NO;
   }

   return YES;

}
```

 I heavily discourage you from writing methods that have no external names for their parameters. This is indeed a very bad programming practice and will confuse you and those whom you work with on the same team, regardless of how well you might have documented your code.

We can call this method like so:

```
[self sendEmailTo:@"someone@somewhere.com"
                 :@"My Subject"
                 :@"Please read my email."];
```

As you can see, the first implementation is easier to understand when you look at the invocation, since you can see the name of each parameter in the call itself.

Declaring and implementing a class method is similar to declaring and implementing an instance method. Here are a couple of things you have to keep in mind when declaring and implementing a class method:

- The method type identifier of a class method is + instead of the - type identifier for instance methods.

- You can access self in a class method.

- Class methods are useful when you want to provide new methods of instantiation for your classes. For example, a class method named `allocAndInit` could both allocate and initialize an object and return the object to its caller.

Suppose we want to create a class named `MyClass`. In this class, we want to implement a class method named `allocAndInit` that will allocate and initialize an instance of `MyClass` and return the result to the caller. The header file of this class will look like this:

```
#import <Foundation/Foundation.h>

@interface MyClass : NSObject

+ (id) allocAndInit;

@end
```

The implementation of this class method will be very straightforward. A simple allocation followed by an initialization:

```
#import "MyClass.h"

@implementation MyClass

+ (id) allocAndInit{
  MyClass *result = [[MyClass alloc] init];
  return result;
}

@end
```

In our app delegate now we can use this class method to allocate and initialize an instance of `MyClass`, like so:

```
#import "AppDelegate.h"
#import "MyClass.h"

@implementation AppDelegate

- (BOOL)            application:(UIApplication *)application
  didFinishLaunchingWithOptions:(NSDictionary *)launchOptions{

    MyClass *instance1 = [MyClass allocAndInit];
    NSLog(@"Instance 1 = %@", instance1);

    self.window = [[UIWindow alloc]
                   initWithFrame:[[UIScreen mainScreen] bounds]];

    self.window.backgroundColor = [UIColor whiteColor];
    [self.window makeKeyAndVisible];
    return YES;
}
```

1.14 Defining Two or More Methods with the Same Name

Problem

You would like to implement two or more methods with the same name in one object. In object-oriented programming, this is called *method overloading*. However, in Objective-C, method overloading does not exist in the same way as it does in other programming languages such as C++.

Solution

Use the same name for your method, but keep the *number* and/or the *names* of your parameters different in every method:

```
- (void) drawRectangle{

    [self drawRectangleInRect:CGRectMake(0.0f, 0.0f, 4.0f, 4.0f)];

}

- (void) drawRectangleInRect:(CGRect)paramInRect{

    [self drawRectangleInRect:paramInRect
                    withColor:[UIColor blueColor]];

}

- (void) drawRectangleInRect:(CGRect)paramInRect
            withColor:(UIColor*)paramColor{

    [self drawRectangleInRect:paramInRect
                    withColor:paramColor
                    andFilled:YES];

}

- (void) drawRectangleInRect:(CGRect)paramInRect
                    withColor:(UIColor*)paramColor
                    andFilled:(BOOL)paramFilled{

    /* Draw the rectangle here */

}
```

This example shows a typical pattern in overloading. Each rectangle can be drawn either filled (solid color) or empty (showing just its boundaries). The first procedure is a "convenience procedure" that allows the caller to avoid specifying how to fill the rectangle. In our implementation of the first procedure, we merely call the second procedure, making the choice for the caller (`andFilled:YES`) The second procedure gives the caller control over filling.

Discussion

You can define two methods with the same name so long as they differ in the parameters they accept. One reasons for doing this is one function offers more customization (through parameterization) than the other function.

Method overloading is a programming language feature supported by Objective-C, C++, Java, and a few other languages. Using this feature, programmers can create different methods with the same name, in the same object. However, method overloading in Objective-C differs from that which can be used in C++. For instance, in C++, to overload a method, the programmer needs to assign a different number of parameters to the same method and/or change a parameter's data type.

In Objective-C, however, you simply change the name of at least one parameter. Changing the type of parameters will not work:

```
- (void) method1:(NSInteger)param1{

  /* We have one parameter only */

}

- (void) method1:(NSString *)param1{

  /* This will not compile as we already have a
    method called [method1] with one parameter */

}
```

Changing the return value of these methods will not work either:

```
- (int) method1:(NSInteger)param1{

  /* We have one parameter only */
  return param1;

}

- (NSString *) method1:(NSString *)param1{

  /* This will not compile as we already have a
    method called [method1] with one parameter */
  return param1;

}
```

As a result, you need to change the *number of parameters* or the *name* of (at least) one parameter that each method accepts. Here is an example where we have changed the number of parameters:

```
- (NSInteger) method1:(NSInteger)param1{

  return param1;
```

```
    }

- (NSString*) method1:(NSString *)param1
          andParam2:(NSString *)param2{

  NSString *result = param1;

  if ([param1 length] > 0 &&
      [param2 length] > 0){
    result = [result stringByAppendingString:param2];
  }

  return result;

}
```

Here is an example of changing the name of a parameter:

```
- (void) drawCircleWithCenter:(CGPoint)paramCenter
                     radius:(CGFloat)paramRadius{

  /* Draw the circle here */

}

- (void) drawCircleWithCenter:(CGPoint)paramCenter
                     Radius:(CGFloat)paramRadius{

  /* Draw the circle here */

}
```

Can you spot the difference between the declarations of these two methods? The first method's second parameter is called **radius** (with a lowercase *r*) whereas the second method's second parameter is called **Radius** (with an uppercase *R*). This will set these two methods apart and allows your program to get compiled. However, Apple has guidelines for choosing method names as well as what to do and what not to do when constructing methods. For more information, please refer to the "Coding Guidelines for Cocoa" Apple documentation available here (*http://bit.ly/XdOvFk*).

Here is another example of two methods that draw a circle but have different names for their second parameter:

```
- (void) drawCircleWithCenter:(CGPoint)paramCenterPoint
             radiusInPoints:(CGFloat)paramRadiusInPoints{
  /* Draw the circle here */
}

- (void) drawCircleWithCenter:(CGPoint)paramCenterPoint
           radiusInMillimeters:(CGFloat)paramRadiusInMillimeters{
  /* Draw the circle here */
}
```

Here is a concise extract of the things to look out for when constructing and working with methods:

- Have your method names describe what the method does clearly, without using too much jargon and abbreviations. A list of acceptable abbreviations is in the Coding Guidelines (*http://bit.ly/Uu1JYx*).
- Have each parameter name describe the parameter and its purpose. On a method with exactly three parameters, you can use the word *and* to start the name of the last parameter if the method is programmed to perform two separate actions. In any other case, refrain from using *and* to start a parameter name. An example of the name of a method that performs two actions and uses the word *and* in its name is `prefixFirstName:withInitials:andMakeInitialsUppercase:`, where the method can prefix a first name (of type `NSString`) with the initials (of type `NSString` again) of that individual. In addition, the method accepts a boolean parameter named `andMakeInitialsUppercase` which, if set to `YES`, will prefix the first name with an uppercase equivalent of the initials passed to the method. If this parameter is set to `NO`, the method will use the initials it is given, without changing their case, to prefix the first name parameter.
- Start method names with a lowercase letter.
- For delegate methods, start the method name with the name of the class that invokes that delegate method.

See Also

Recipe 1.13

1.15 Allocating and Initializing Objects

Problem

You want to create an instance of a new object, but you don't understand the difference between *allocation* and *initialization* and why you should have to both allocate and initialize an object before you can use it.

Solution

You must both allocate and initialize an object before using it. An object can be *allocated* using the `alloc` instance method. This class method will allocate memory to hold the object and its instance variables and methods. However, allocation leaves memory undefined. So in addition, each object must be *initialized*, which sets the values of its data. One initialization method must be the *designated initializer*, which is normally the initialization method with the most parameters. For instance, the `initWithFrame:` method is the designated initializer of objects of type `UIView`. Always allocate and initialize your objects, in that order, before using them.

When implementing a new object, do not override the alloc method. This method is declared in NSObject. Instead, override the init method and create custom initialization methods that handle required parameters for the specific object you are working on.

Discussion

An object that inherits from NSObject must be prepared for use in two steps:

Allocation
> The allocation is done by invoking the alloc method, which is implemented in the NSObject class. This method creates the internal structure of a new object and sets all instance variables' values to zero. After this step is done, the init method takes care of setting up the default values of variables and performing other tasks, such as instantiating other internal objects.

Initialization
> Initialization is the process by which a class prepares each of its instances' storage (variables), required internal data structure and whatnot. Think of allocation as getting inside a car and initialization as switching on the ignition.

Let's look at an example. We are creating a class named MyObject. Here is the *.h* file:

```
#import <Foundation/Foundation.h>

@interface MyObject : NSObject

- (void) doSomething;

@end
```

The implementation of this class is as follows (the *.m* file):

```
#import "MyObject.h"

@implementation MyObject

- (void) doSomething{

  /* Perform a task here */
  NSLog(@"%s", __FUNCTION__);

}

@end
```

the doSomething instance method of the MyObject object will attempt to print the name of the current function to the console window. Now let's go ahead and invoke this method by instantiating an object of type MyObject:

```
MyObject *someObject = [[MyObject alloc] init];
/* Do something with the object, call some methods, etc. */
[someObject doSomething];
```

This code will work absolutely fine. Now try to skip initializing your object:

```
MyObject *someObject = [MyObject alloc];
/* Do something with the object, call some methods, etc. */
[someObject doSomething];
```

If you run this code now, you will realize that it works absolutely fine, too. So, what has happened here? We thought we had to initialize the object before we could use it. Perhaps Apple can explain this behavior better:

> An object isn't ready to be used until it has been initialized. The init method defined in the NSObject class does no initialization; it simply returns self.

Simply put, this means the `init` method is a placeholder for tasks that some classes need to perform before they are used, such as setting up extra data structures or opening files. `NSObject` itself—along with many of the classes you will use—does not have to initialize anything in particular. However, it is a good programming practice to always run the `init` method of an object after allocating it in case the parent of your class has overridden this method to provide a custom initialization. Please bear in mind that the return value for initializer methods of an object is of type `id`, so the initializer method might even return an object that is not the same object that the `alloc` method returned to you. This technique is called *two-stage creation* and is extremely handy. However, discussing this technique is outside the scope of this book. For more information about two-stage creation, please refer to *Cocoa Design Patterns* by Erik M. Buck and Donald A. Yacktman (Addison-Wesley Professional).

1.16 Adding Properties to Classes

Problem

You want to add properties to your classes so that you can take advantage of dot notation to access those values, as opposed to using methods on your classes.

Solution

Define properties in your classes using the `@property` keyword.

Discussion

Anything addressed via dot notation is a property, which is a *shortcut* to a method. What does that mean? Well, let's have a look at an example:

```
NSObject *myObject = [[NSObject alloc] init];
myObject.accessibilityHint = @"Some string";
```

You can see that we allocated and initialized an object of type `NSObject` and used dot notation to access a property called `accessibilityHint` in that object. Where did `accessibilityHint` come from?

It's quite simple. A property is defined using the @property keyword. In fact, if you hold down the Command key on your keyboard in Xcode, and simply click on the accessibilityHint property in the example that we just saw, you will be redirected to the *NSObject.h* file where you will see this:

```
@property(nonatomic, copy) NSString *accessibilityHint;
```

But what *is* a property? It is a high-level language feature—a shortcut, if you will—that allows developers to easily access getters and setter methods on instances of a class without having to refer to the getter and/or the setter method at all. If you want to set a property's value, you simply use the equals sign to do so. If you want to read from the property, you simply point to it using dot notation.

Let's look at this in detail. In Recipe 1.12, we saw how we create classes. We created a class called Person. Then in Recipe 1.13, we learned how to add methods to our classes. Now, by combining the concepts explored in these two recipes, we can learn more about properties. To start, let's go to the *Person.h* file and define a property called firstName:

```
#import <Foundation/Foundation.h>

@interface Person : NSObject

@property (nonatomic, strong) NSString *firstName;

@end
```

 You will learn all about new Automatic Reference Counting keywords, such as strong, in Recipe 1.17.

A nonatomic property is a property that is not meant to be accessed and changed by multiple threads at the same time. Such a property or variable is not thread-safe. A thread-safe (atomic) variable will prevent multiple threads from writing to it at the same time, or a thread from reading it while another thread is writing to it. For performance reasons (as well as the overhead necessary for handling such variables), atomic properties are not by default provided in iOS by the runtime. Only apps developed for the Mac can take advantage of both atomic and nonatomic properties. If you want your properties to be atomic, you will need to handle threading and access on your own using locks or other mechanisms that are outside the scope of this book.

In terms of the setter and the getter methods, fortunately, we don't have to write these two methods for properties manually. The LLVM compiler automatically generates these setter and getter methods by putting a hidden @synthesize in the implementation of our object. This keyword simply creates a getter and a setter method for that property. For instance, if you simply create a property named firstName, the compiler will take the following actions on your behalf:

- Creates an instance method for you named `_firstName`. This rule applies similarly to any other property name.
- Triggers the following synthesize for you in your implementation file without you having to touch it:

  ```
  @synthesize firstName = _firstName
  ```

- Under Automatic Reference Counting, it also takes care of deallocating your properties for you.

Now we can go ahead and use our `Person` class. Here is an example:

```
#import "SomeOtherClass.h"
#import "Person.h"

@implementation SomeOtherClass

- (void) makeNewPerson{

  Person *newPerson = [[Person alloc] init];
  newPerson.firstName = @"Andrew";
  NSLog(@"First name = %@", newPerson.firstName);
  NSLog(@"First name = %@", [newPerson firstName]);

}

@end
```

The example code prints the first name of `newPerson` twice, first using its `firstName` property and then by calling the `firstName` *getter method* on that object. Both will point to the same method, which `@synthesize` created for us in the *Person.m* file.

In an older version of the Objective-C runtime, for `@property` to work, we also had to define an *instance variable*. An instance variable is a variable whose memory management is done by the programmer herself. Instance variables are also not exposed to classes outside the scope of the class that defines them (i.e., they are not exposed to any class that simply imports the class with the instance variable). Instance variables are normally called *ivars* by professional Objective-C developers (ivar is pronounced I-WAR).

With the new runtime, we don't have to define ivars anymore. We simply define the property and the LLVM compiler defines the ivar for us. If you are using the GCC compiler, which is rather unlikely, you will see big differences from how the LLVM compiler treats ivars. For instance, in GCC 4.2, an ivar is not accessible to any subclass of a class, whereas if you are using LLVM Compiler, a subclass of a class can use its superclass's ivars. So make sure you are using Apple's latest compiler, which is LLVM. If a property is read-only, the only way that property's value can change is for the class that defines that property to use the ivar of that property to change the property's value.

If you want to fiddle around with setter and getter methods, you are free to do so. Even if you have used @synthesize to allow the compiler to generate the setter and getter methods of a property for you, you can still go ahead and override those methods. For instance, in this example, I change the setFirstName: setter method of the firstName property of the Person:

```
#import "Person.h"

@implementation Person

- (void) setFirstName:(NSString *)paramFirstName{
  _firstName = [paramFirstName stringByAppendingString:@" Jr"];
}

- (id)init
{
  self = [super init];
  if (self) {
    // Initialization code here.
    _lastName = @"Carnegie";
  }

  return self;
}

@end
```

I have overridden the setter method of my firstName property to add a " Jr" suffix to any string that I am told to assign to the firstName property. So when the setter and getters are invoked, as before:

```
Person *newPerson = [[Person alloc] init];
newPerson.firstName = @"Andrew";
NSLog(@"First name = %@", newPerson.firstName);
NSLog(@"First name = %@", [newPerson firstName]);
NSLog(@"Last name = %@", newPerson.lastName);
```

We will get the following printed out to the console window:

```
First name = Andrew Jr
First name = Andrew Jr
Last name = Carnegie
```

If you want to define a read-only property, all you have to do is to define your property using the @readonly keyword, like so:

```
@property (nonatomic, strong, readonly) NSString *lastName;
```

See Also

Recipe 1.12; Recipe 1.13; Recipe 1.17

1.17 Moving from Manual Reference Counting to Automatic Reference Counting

Problem

You want to learn about Automatic Reference Counting, Apple's new Compiler solution to solving the headache that programmers had to deal with when working with objects and memory management in Objective-C.

 Automatic Reference Counting eliminates many of the manual reference counting issues that ultimately resulted in iOS apps that would crash here and there and would be very unstable when deployed on user devices. ARC removes this headache by leaving most of the memory management complexity to the compiler.

Solution

Study the new storage attributes introduced with the latest LLVM compiler: `strong`, `weak`, and `unsafe_unretained`.

Discussion

To use Automatic Reference Counting (ARC) in the latest LLVM compiler, we need to deal with storage that is strong, weak, or unsafe and unretained. Any object under ARC is managed with one of these storage attributes. Here is a short explanation for each one:

`strong`
An object of this type is automatically retained at runtime and will be valid until the end of its scope, where it will automatically be released. For those familiar with Objective-C's traditional way of memory management, this keyword is similar to the `retain` keyword.

`weak`
This is zeroing weak referencing. If a variable is defined with this keyword, when the object to which this variable points gets deallocated, this value will get set to `nil`. For instance, if you have a strong string property and a weak string property and set the weak property's value to the strong property's value, when the strong property gets deallocated, the weak property's value will get set to `nil`.

`unsafe_unretained`
This is simply pointing one variable to another. This will not retain the object into the new variable, it will simply assign the object to the variable.

By default, all *local* variables are strong variables. In contrast, properties must explicitly specify their storage attribute. In other words, the compiler won't assume that all properties without a storage attribute are by default strong properties. So do make sure that you specify the storage attributes for your properties. Let's have a look at an example of the **strong** storage attribute. Let's assume we have two properties called string1 and string2:

```
#import <UIKit/UIKit.h>

@interface Moving_from_Manual_Reference_Counting_to_ARCAppDelegate
          : UIResponder <UIApplicationDelegate>

@property (strong, nonatomic) UIWindow *window;

@property (nonatomic, strong) NSString *string1;
@property (nonatomic, strong) NSString *string2;

@end
```

Now if we initialize the **string1** property with the string value of *String 1* and assign this property's value to the **string2** property, we will see that with the **strong** storage attribute, the **string2** property will keep its value even after **string1** is deallocated:

```
#import "Moving_from_Manual_Reference_Counting_to_ARCAppDelegate.h"

@implementation Moving_from_Manual_Reference_Counting_to_ARCAppDelegate

- (BOOL)              application:(UIApplication *)application
  didFinishLaunchingWithOptions:(NSDictionary *)launchOptions{
    self.string1 = @"String 1";
    self.string2 = self.string1;
    self.string1 = nil;

    NSLog(@"String 2 = %@", self.string2);

    self.window = [[UIWindow alloc] initWithFrame:
                    [[UIScreen mainScreen] bounds]];

    self.window.backgroundColor = [UIColor whiteColor];
    [self.window makeKeyAndVisible];
    return YES;
}
```

 Memory allocated for an object is disposed of when all strong variables pointing to that memory are deallocated.

The output of this program is this:

```
String 2 = String 1
```

the **strong**, **weak**, and **unsafe_unretained** are most frequently used when declaring properties. You can take advantage of these storage specifiers even when declaring local variables, but you need to change the specifiers a bit. The **strong** specifier's inline equivalent is **__strong**, **weak** specifier's inline equivalent is **__weak**, and **unsafe_unre** tained specifier's inline equivalent is __unsafe_unretained. (Note that each of those keywords begins with two underline characters.) Here is an example:

```
- (BOOL)              application:(UIApplication *)application
  didFinishLaunchingWithOptions:(NSDictionary *)launchOptions{

    /* All local variables are by default strong, so just emphasize that. We
     really don't have to mention __strong for the first variable but
     to make it clear, we will set it. No harm in doing so. */
    __strong NSString *yourString = @"Your String";
    __weak   NSString *myString = yourString;
    yourString = nil;
    __unsafe_unretained NSString *theirString = myString;

    /* All pointers will be nil at this time */
    self.window = [[UIWindow alloc] initWithFrame:
                     [[UIScreen mainScreen] bounds]];

    self.window.backgroundColor = [UIColor whiteColor];
    [self.window makeKeyAndVisible];
    return YES;
}
```

the unsafe_unretained storage specifier is truly unsafe, as its name implies. The reason for it being unsafe is if the object to which an unsafe_unretained variable points gets deallocated, this variable will not get set to nil and will point to a dangling location in the memory. Accessing this location might cause your application to crash. To avoid this, you should be using the zeroing weak referencing storage specifier, weak or its inline equivalent __weak.

Let's see an example for zeroing weak referencing. Let's change our string2 property's storage specifier to weak instead of strong:

```
#import <UIKit/UIKit.h>

@interface Moving_from_Manual_Reference_Counting_to_ARCAppDelegate
          : UIResponder <UIApplicationDelegate>

@property (strong, nonatomic) UIWindow *window;

@property (nonatomic, strong) NSString *string1;
@property (nonatomic, weak) NSString *string2;

@end
```

When our app starts for the first time, we will initialize the strong string1 property and will assign string1 to string2. We will then set the value of the string1 property to nil. Then we will wait. This is absolutely crucial. If immediately after setting the value of string1 to nil, you print out the value of string2, chances are that you will get incorrect results instead of nil. So you need to make sure that your app's run loop has gotten rid of all invalidated objects. In order to achieve this, we will print the value of strong2 when our app gets sent to the background. (This is caused by the user pressing the home button on their iOS device.) Once we're running in the background, we know that the run loop has already gotten rid of invalidated objects in the memory and the results that we will get will be accurate:

```
- (BOOL)              application:(UIApplication *)application
  didFinishLaunchingWithOptions:(NSDictionary *)launchOptions{

  self.string1 = [[NSString alloc] initWithUTF8String:"String 1"];
  self.string2 = self.string1;
  self.string1 = nil;

  /* All pointers will be nil at this time */

  self.window = [[UIWindow alloc] initWithFrame:
                  [[UIScreen mainScreen] bounds]];

  self.window.backgroundColor = [UIColor whiteColor];
  [self.window makeKeyAndVisible];
  return YES;
}

- (void)applicationDidEnterBackground:(UIApplication *)application{
  NSLog(@"String 2 = %@", self.string2);
}
```

Now run this app, wait a second or two, and press the Home button on the device/ simulator. You will notice that the following results will get printed to the console window:

```
String 2 = (null)
```

This easily proved that the zeroing weak references work perfectly under ARC. Now to check how dangerous the unsafe_unretained storage specifier is, let's go ahead and change the string2 property's storage specifier to unsafe_unretained and repeat the exact same practice as we did for the weak property:

```
#import <UIKit/UIKit.h>

@interface Moving_from_Manual_Reference_Counting_to_ARCAppDelegate
        : UIResponder <UIApplicationDelegate>

@property (strong, nonatomic) UIWindow *window;

@property (nonatomic, strong) NSString *string1;
@property (nonatomic, unsafe_unretained) NSString *string2;

@end
```

Now if you leave the implementation of your app delegate as we had implemented it in the previous example (printing the value of string2 property when our app gets sent to the background), and you repeat the same procedure and open your app and send it to the background, you will crash! This means that when our app was sent to the background, we tried to print out the contents of an invalidated memory location that the string2 property was pointing to. Since the string2 property was unsafe and unretained, it didn't know that the object that it was pointing to (in string1) was already deallocated when string1 was set to nil.

In addition to the aforementioned three storage specifiers, we can also use the __auto releasing specifier. This storage specifier is most handy when we want to pass an object by reference to a method. This is required for when you want to call a method and leave that method responsible for allocating, initializing, and returning an instance of a class. The caller method will then have no responsibility at all to release the returned instance and will leave it to the runtime to decide when it is best to release the allocated instance of that class (handled by autorelease pools). For instance, if you have a method that needs to pass an error of type NSError to the caller method, the caller method will pass an uninitialized and unallocated instance of NSError to this method. This means the caller didn't allocate memory for this error variable, so our method should do so. To do this, you must specify that this error parameter needs to be automatically released by the runtime when the right time comes:

```
- (void) generateErrorInVariable:(__autoreleasing NSError **)paramError{

    NSArray *objects = [[NSArray alloc] initWithObjects:@"A simple error", nil];

    NSArray *keys =
    [[NSArray alloc] initWithObjects:NSLocalizedDescriptionKey, nil];

    NSDictionary *errorDictionary = [[NSDictionary alloc] initWithObjects:objects
                                                                   forKeys:keys];

    *paramError = [[NSError alloc] initWithDomain:@"MyApp"
                                             code:1
                                         userInfo:errorDictionary];
}

- (BOOL)            application:(UIApplication *)application
    didFinishLaunchingWithOptions:(NSDictionary *)launchOptions{

    NSError *error = nil;
    [self generateErrorInVariable:&error];

    NSLog(@"Error = %@", error);

    self.window = [[UIWindow alloc] initWithFrame:
                    [[UIScreen mainScreen] bounds]];

    self.window.backgroundColor = [UIColor whiteColor];
    [self.window makeKeyAndVisible];
    return YES;
}
```

In this example, the application:didFinishLaunchingWithOptions: method didn't allocate the instance of NSError; the generateErrorInVariable method did. But for the compiler to understand the scope of the error object, the generateErrorInVariable method mentioned to the compiler that the object which will be created into its error parameter needs to be automatically released if it is no longer needed.

1.18 Typecasting with Automatic Reference Counting

Problem

You want to know how to use the new typecasting facilities under Automatic Reference Counting in order to avoid memory leaks when working with Core Foundation objects inside your Objective-C code.

Solution

Use the __bridge, __bridge_transfer, and __bridge_retained typecasting specifiers.

Discussion

Typecasting is the process of pointing one value of type A to another value of type B. For instance, if you have a Core Foundation string object of type CFStringRef and you would like to place it inside an Objective-C string of type NSString, you can easily create an error:

```
- (BOOL)            application:(UIApplication *)application
  didFinishLaunchingWithOptions:(NSDictionary *)launchOptions{

    CFStringRef coreFoundationString =
    CFStringCreateWithCString(CFAllocatorGetDefault(),
                              "C String",
                              kCFStringEncodingUTF8);

    /* Compile time error!!! */
    NSString *objCString = coreFoundationString;

    self.window = [[UIWindow alloc] initWithFrame:
                     [[UIScreen mainScreen] bounds]];

    self.window.backgroundColor = [UIColor whiteColor];
    [self.window makeKeyAndVisible];
    return YES;
}
```

Here, we are assigning the value of the Core Foundation string coreFoundationString to the Objective-C string of type NSString named objCString. Our compiler will get confused because it doesn't know what we are intending to do with the memory assigned to each one of these objects. Additionally, we will end up with a memory leak because the compiler doesn't know how to get rid of the Core Foundation object for us automatically. Remember that Automatic Reference Counting does *not* work for Core Foundation objects, so we need to assist the compiler. To do this, let's try to understand what each one of these typecasting specifiers does:

`__bridge`
> Simply typecasts the object on the right side of the equation to the left side. This will not modify the retain count on any of the objects; neither the one on the left nor the one on the right side of the equation.

`__bridge_transfer`
> This typecast will assign the object on the right side to the object on the left and will release the object on the right side. So if you have a Core Foundation string, like the one we saw before, that you have just created and want to place it inside a local variable of type `NSString` (local variables are by default strong, see Recipe 1.17), then you should use this typecasting option because then you won't have to release the Core Foundation string after the assignment. We will see an example of this soon.

`__bridge_retained`
> This is similar to the `__bridge_transfer` typecast, but will retain the object on the right side of the equation as well.

Let's try to fix the example code we saw before. Our goal is to place the Core Foundation string into an instance of `NSString` (strong, by default) and then automatically release the Core Foundation string. To do this, we must use the `__bridge_transfer` typecasting option:

```
- (BOOL)                application:(UIApplication *)application
    didFinishLaunchingWithOptions:(NSDictionary *)launchOptions{

    CFStringRef coreFoundationString =
    CFStringCreateWithCString(CFAllocatorGetDefault(),
                              "C String",
                              kCFStringEncodingUTF8);

    /* Compile time error!!! */
    NSString *objCString = (__bridge_transfer NSString *)coreFoundationString;

    NSLog(@"String = %@", objCString);

    self.window = [[UIWindow alloc] initWithFrame:
                    [[UIScreen mainScreen] bounds]];

    self.window.backgroundColor = [UIColor whiteColor];
    [self.window makeKeyAndVisible];
    return YES;
}
```

What happened here was that we created a new Core Foundation object. The retain count on this object is 1 at this time. Then we typecasted and assigned it, using the `__bridge_transfer` typecast option, to a strong local variable of type `NSString`. But this time, because the compiler sees the typecasting, it will retain the Core Foundation string and place it inside the local variable (since the local variable is **strong** by default) and after the assignment, will release the Core Foundation string. Perfect! Exactly what we wanted.

Now let's have a look at when we would use __bridge_retained. This typecasting option is used whenever we would like the object on the right side of the equation to still exist after the assignment. Here is an example:

```
- (BOOL)            application:(UIApplication *)application
  didFinishLaunchingWithOptions:(NSDictionary *)launchOptions{

    CFStringRef coreFoundationString =
    CFStringCreateWithCString(CFAllocatorGetDefault(),
                              "C String",
                              kCFStringEncodingUTF8);

    id unknownObjectType = (__bridge id)coreFoundationString;
    CFStringRef anotherString = (__bridge_retained CFStringRef)unknownObjectType;

    NSString *objCString = (__bridge_transfer NSString *)coreFoundationString;
    NSLog(@"String = %@", objCString);
    objCString = nil;

    CFRelease(anotherString);

    self.window = [[UIWindow alloc] initWithFrame:
                   [[UIScreen mainScreen] bounds]];

    self.window.backgroundColor = [UIColor whiteColor];
    [self.window makeKeyAndVisible];
    return YES;
}
```

Here is what is happening in this code:

1. We allocated a Core Foundation string and placed it inside the coreFoundation String local variable. Since this is a Core Foundation object, ARC will not apply storage attributes to it, so we need to handle its memory manually. Its retain count is 1, as with any newly created variable.

2. Then we typecast this Core Foundation string to a generic object of type id. Note that we didn't retain or release this object, so the retain count on both unknownObjectType and coreFoundationString stays 1. We simply typecasted it to an object of type id.

3. Now we are retaining the generic object of type id and placing the resulting object into another Core Foundation string. At this time, the retain count on the core FoundationString, unknownObjectType, and anotherString variables is 2 and all three of these variables point to the same location in the memory.

4. What we are doing after that is to assign the value inside coreFoundationString to a strong local NSString using the __bridge_transfer typecasting option. This will make sure that the coreFoundationString object will get released after this assignment (the retain count will go from 2 to 1) and it will again be retained (because of the strong NSString variable, shooting the retain count from 1 to 2 again) So now

`coreFoundationString`, `unknownObjectType`, `anotherString` and the `objCString` variables all point to the same string with the retain count of 2.

5. The next stop is setting our strong local variable `objCString` to `nil`. This will release this variable and our string's retain count will go back to 1. All these local variables are still valid and you can read from them because the retain count of the string that all of them point to is still 1.

6. Then we are explicitly releasing the value in the `anotherString` variable. This will set the release count of our object from 1 to 0 and our string object will get deallocated. At this point, you should not use any of these local variables because they are pointing to a deallocated object—except for the `objCString` strong local variable, whose value was set to `nil` by us.

See Also

Recipe 1.17

1.19 Delegating Tasks with Protocols

Problem

You want to make sure a certain object implements a set of methods or properties.

Solution

Use a protocol.

Discussion

A protocol is the declaration (as opposed to implementation) of a set of methods and/or properties in a header file (usually with the extension of *.h*). Any object that you declare to conform to such protocol is responsible for writing the implementation of those methods and properties, depending on whether the protocol specifies them as required or optional.

Think of protocols as sets of rules, with some rules being optional and others mandatory. Any object saying that it conforms to that protocol must follow those rules. Let's see a simple example of this. We will go ahead and define a protocol called `Person` `Protocol`. For this, you need to create a new protocol file, so follow these steps first:

1. In Xcode, while your project is open, go to the File menu and then choose New → New File...

2. Now make sure iOS is the main category on the left side of the New File dialog and then choose the Cocoa Touch subcategory. Once that is done, choose the Objective-C Protocol item and press Next (see Figure 1-26).

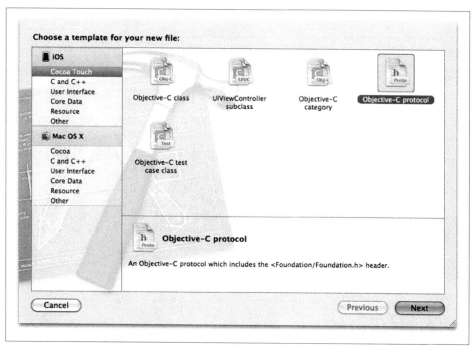

Figure 1-26. Creating a new protocol

3. Now you will be asked to save this file and specify a name for it. Give it the name *PersonProtocol* and press Save (see Figure 1-27).

Now we have our header file. Let's get on with the actual declaration of our protocol. Our objective with this new `PersonProtocol` protocol is to govern the rules on any class that impersonates a "Person," or in other words, says that it is a Person class. For instance, in your application, you can have a class named Infant, Mother, Father, Son, Daughter, Stranger, etc. You can then make all these classes conform to the `Person Protocol` protocol, which will define the types of behavior each of these classes must implement. Let's say that, for every person, we need at least a first name, a last name, and an age:

```
#import <Foundation/Foundation.h>

@protocol PersonProtocol <NSObject>

@property (nonatomic, strong) NSString *firstName;
@property (nonatomic, strong) NSString *lastName;
@property (nonatomic, unsafe_unretained) NSUInteger age;

@end
```

Now let's create a class called Father and make sure that this class conforms to our `PersonProtocol` protocol. To create this class, follow these steps:

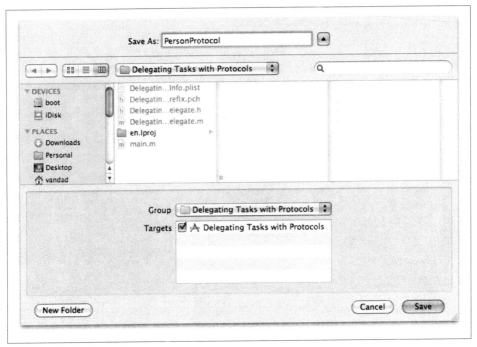

Figure 1-27. Saving the new protocol

1. In Xcode, while in your project, go to the File menu and then select New → New File...

2. In the New File dialog, make sure iOS is the main category and then choose the Cocoa Touch subcategory. After that is done, select the Objective-C class item in the list on the righthand side. Now press the Next button (see Figure 1-28).

3. In this screen (see Figure 1-29), make sure we are creating a subclass of NSObject. Once that is done, press the Next button.

4. Now you are asked to save the new class. Give it the name of Father, and press the Create button (see Figure 1-30).

Fantastic, we now have our Father class and the PersonProtocol protocol. Open the header file of the Father class and make sure that it conforms to the PersonProtocol protocol:

```
#import <Foundation/Foundation.h>
#import "PersonProtocol.h"

@interface Father : NSObject <PersonProtocol>

@end
```

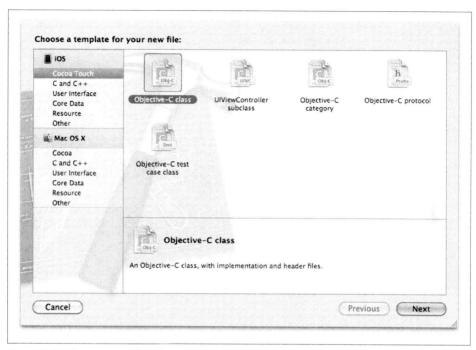

Figure 1-28. Creating a Father class

Now if you attempt to compile your app (by pressing Command+Shift+R simultaneously), you will get warnings from the compiler, similar to those shown in Figure 1-31.

As you can see, the compiler understands that the Father class wants to conform to the PersonProtocol protocol. However, the Father class isn't implementing the required setter and getter methods of the properties defined in the PersonProtocol protocol. We are seeing these warnings because anything defined in a protocol by default is required from its conforming classes. Required methods and properties in a protocol can explicitly be marked with the @required keyword. If you want to specify that followers of a protocol are free to choose to implement or not implement your methods or properties, you can simply tell the compiler that those methods/properties are optional, using the @optional keyword.

Let's go back to *PersonProtocol.h* and mark the firstName, lastName, and age properties as optional, but add a method to the protocol called breathe and make it a required method, because, let's face it, everybody has got to breathe:

```
#import <Foundation/Foundation.h>

@protocol PersonProtocol <NSObject>

@optional
@property (nonatomic, strong) NSString *firstName;
```

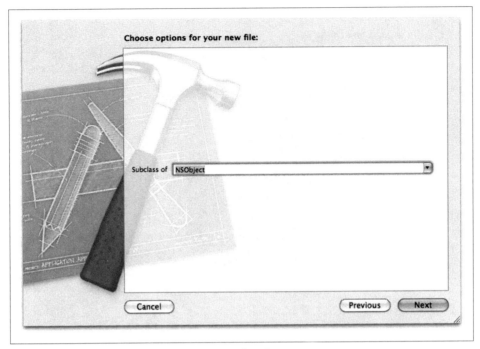

Choose options for your new file:

Subclass of NSObject ▾

Cancel   Previous   Next

Figure 1-29. Subclassing NSObject to create a Father class

```objc
@property (nonatomic, strong) NSString *lastName;
@property (nonatomic, unsafe_unretained) NSUInteger age;

@required
- (void) breathe;

@end
```

Now if you compile your application, you will get completely different warnings (see Figure 1-32).

Now if you go to the Father class and define and implement the breathe method, even if the method implementation is empty, the compiler will be happy with that. Remember, the Father class now doesn't have to implement the three aforementioned properties because they are now defined as optional in the PersonProtocol protocol. Here is now the correct definition of the Father class:

```objc
#import <Foundation/Foundation.h>
#import "PersonProtocol.h"

@interface Father : NSObject <PersonProtocol>

- (void) breathe;

@end
```

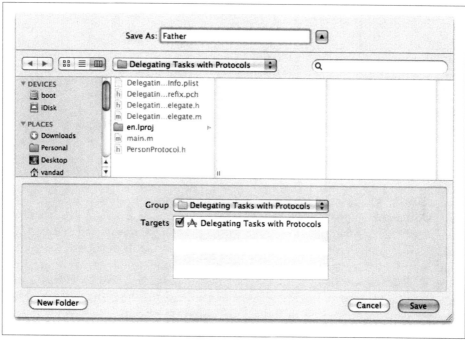

Figure 1-30. Saving the Father class on disk

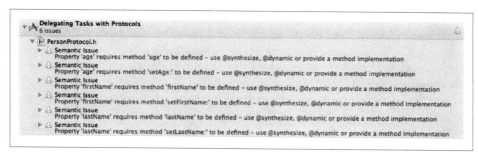

Figure 1-31. Warnings from the compiler related to the protocol we are conforming to

And here is the correct implementation of the Father class:

```
#import "Father.h"

@implementation Father

- (void) breathe{
  /* Implement this method here */
}

@end
```

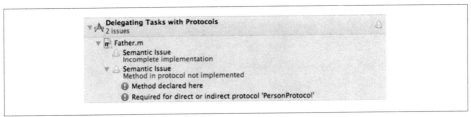

Figure 1-32. The Father class does not implement the breathe method defined in the PersonProtocol protocol

Attempt to compile your app now and you'll notice that the compiler is perfectly happy with our implementation.

Cocoa Touch has given protocols a really nice meaning in Objective-C. In Cocoa Touch, protocols are the perfect means for defining *delegate objects*. A delegate object is an object that another object consults when something happens in that object. For instance, a repairman is the delegate for a broken-down car. If something happens to your car, you go to your repairman and ask him to fix the car for you (although some prefer to repair the car themselves, in which case they are their own delegate for their car). So in Cocoa Touch, many classes expect a delegate object and make sure that whatever object is assigned as their delegate conforms to a certain protocol.

For instance, as we will see in Chapter 4, the UITableView class defines and implements a property called delegate, which is required to conform to the UITableViewDelegate protocol. This protocol simply lays down the law to those objects that want to become the delegate object of a table view. The protocol requires those objects to implement certain methods or in some cases, specifies that some methods/properties are optional so the delegate object is free to implement or not implement them. Now, when a user selects a row in a table, the UITableView can call the tableView:didSelectRowAtIndex Path: method with the assurance that the UITableViewDelegate at least defined the method. The method may be correctly or incorrectly coded, but at least it's present, so the program won't crash at runtime because of a nonexistent method (selector).

1.20 Determining Whether Instance or Class Methods Are Available

Problem

Your development SDK is the newest SDK, but you want to support devices running older iOS versions and APIs.

Solution

Use the `instancesRespondToSelector:` class method of `NSObject` to determine whether a specific selector exists in an instance of that class.

 A selector is the name of your method without the parameter data types. For instance, given the following method declaration:

```
- (BOOL) doesString:(NSString *)paramNeedle
        existInString:(NSString *)paramHaystack;
```

The selector for this method would be `doesString:existInString:`.

To determine whether a class itself responds to a class method, use the `responds ToSelector:` class method of your class. You can use the same method on an instance of a class to determine whether that instance responds to an instance method, as well as the `instancesRespondToSelector:` class method of the `NSObject` class.

Discussion

There are two important concepts with regard to iOS SDK that you need to remember:

Base SDK

The SDK that you use to compile your application. This can be the latest and the greatest SDK with access to all the new APIs available in iOS SDK.

Deployment SDK/Target

This is the SDK that will be used when you compile your app to run on devices.

Because of the fact that you are essentially compiling your apps with two SDKs, one the base and the other the deployment SDK, depending on which profile you are using (device or simulator), your program might be vulnerable to invoking methods in classes that are available only in the latest SDK, but not the deployment SDK. So you might need to check from time to time for the existence of instance or class methods at runtime.

Let me give you an example. The iOS SDK has a class called `NSArray`. As you will see in Recipe 1.23, you can simply allocate and initialize an object of this type and start using its methods. A mutable array (an array that can be changed after it has been constructed) is of type `NSMutableArray` and offers sorting mechanisms that you can use to sort the elements inside the array. There are various sorting methods, some of which are available only in newer SDKs. So what you can do is determine which of the sorting (instance) methods are available at runtime and then use those methods to sort the array:

```
NSMutableArray *array = [[NSMutableArray alloc] initWithObjects:
                            @"Item 1",
                            @"Item 4",
                            @"Item 2",
                            @"Item 5",
                            @"Item 3", nil];

NSLog(@"Array = %@", array);

if ([NSArray instancesRespondToSelector:@selector(sortUsingComparator:)]){

  /* Use the sortUsingComparator: instance method of the array to sort it */

}
else if ([NSArray instancesRespondToSelector:
         @selector(sortUsingFunction:context:)]){

  /* Use the sortUsingFunction:context: instance
    method of the array to sort */

}
else {

  /* Do something else */

}
```

So in this example, we are checking the existence of the specific instance methods using the instancesRespondToSelector: class method of the NSMutableArray class (which itself is a subclass of NSArray). Alternatively, we could use the respondsToSelector: instance method of our array:

```
NSMutableArray *array = [[NSMutableArray alloc] initWithObjects:
                            @"Item 1",
                            @"Item 4",
                            @"Item 2",
                            @"Item 5",
                            @"Item 3", nil];

NSLog(@"Array = %@", array);

if ([array respondsToSelector:@selector(sortUsingComparator:)]){

  /* Use the sortUsingComparator: instance method of the array to sort it */

}
else if ([array respondsToSelector:@selector(sortUsingFunction:context:)]){

  /* Use the sortUsingFunction:context: instance
    method of the array to sort */

}
else {
  /* Do something else */
}
```

Fantastic. We checked the existence of instance methods. How about class methods? The `NSArray` class again has various class methods, two of which are the `array WithObjects:` and the `arrayWithObjects:count:` methods. We can determine their availability at runtime and use them to initialize the array:

```
NSArray *array = nil;

if ([NSArray respondsToSelector:@selector(arrayWithObjects:count:)]){
  NSString *strings[4];
  strings[0] = @"String 1";
  strings[1] = @"String 2";
  strings[2] = @"String 3";
  strings[3] = @"String 4";

  array = [NSArray arrayWithObjects:strings
                              count:4];
}
else if ([NSArray respondsToSelector:@selector(arrayWithObjects:)]){
  array = [NSArray arrayWithObjects:
           @"String 1",
           @"String 2",
           @"String 3",
           @"String 4",
           nil];
}
else {
  /* Do something else */
}

NSLog(@"Array = %@", array);
```

See Also

Recipe 1.23

1.21 Determining Whether a Class Is Available at Runtime

Problem

You are using a few classes that are available in the latest SDK, but you are unsure whether they are available on devices that will be running your app, because your deployment target is earlier than the latest SDK.

Solution

Use the `NSClassFromString` function. Pass the name of your class to this method as a string. If the return value of this function is `nil`, that class is *not* available on the device that runs your app; otherwise, that class is available on the device and you can go ahead and use it as you wish. Here is an example:

```
if (NSClassFromString(@"NSJSONSerialization") != nil){

  /* You can use this class */
  [NSJSONSerialization JSONObjectWithData:...   /* Put data here */
                            options:...   /* Put options here */
                              error:...]; /* Handle errors here */

} else {

  /* That class is not available */

}
```

Discussion

It's no secret that users are slow in upgrading their operating systems. Working for various companies, I can confirm that usually around 30% of iOS devices today are running versions of iOS that are about a year or a year-and-a-half old. For instance, if today we are working with iOS 6, there are still iOS devices out there running iOS 3. Revenue is important to developers, so we need to make sure that we support older devices to some extent, so that we can create a bigger user base than we would by pushing out an app that only runs on iOS 6.

Some of the classes that we use are available only on specific versions of iOS. For instance, the NSJSONSerialization class is available only in iOS 5 SDK and only devices running iOS 5 will be able to run such code. However, if you are planning to support iOS 4 as well as iOS 5, then you can, at runtime, detect the availability of the aforementioned class using the NSClassFromString function, and pass the name of the class that you want to use as a parameter to this function. If the return value of this function is nil, that means the class that you specified cannot be instantiated on the specific device running your app. In this situation, you will need to choose an alternative path and instantiate another class that is available on the device, which carries out similar functionalities as the absent class.

1.22 Allocating and Making Use of Numbers

Problem

You need to use integral values or encapsulate numbers in objects.

Solution

Use NSNumber for an object-oriented approach to handling numbers. If you require simple numbers (nonobjects), use NSInteger to hold signed (positive and negative) values, NSUInteger to hold unsigned (only positive or zero) values, and CGFloat and double to hold floating-point values.

Discussion

Just as we place strings inside instances of NSString, we can place numbers inside instances of NSNumber. "Why?" you might ask. The answer is simple: to allow an object to carry the value of our numbers so that we can save this value to disk easily, load it from disk, and simply allow a single object to carry signed and unsigned integral and floating-point values, without the need for typecasting or defining multiple variables. The possibilities are virtually endless.

Let's have a look at constructing instances of NSNumber:

```
NSNumber *signedNumber = @-123456;
NSNumber *unsignedNumber = @123456;
NSNumber *floatNumber = @123456.123456f;
NSNumber *doubleNumber = @123456.1234567890;
```

Just as we placed signed and unsigned integers and floating-point values into an instance of NSNumber class, we can retrieve those values using some really handy instance methods of NSNumber class, as shown here:

```
NSNumber *signedNumber = @-123456;
NSNumber *unsignedNumber = @123456;
NSNumber *floatNumber = @123.123456f;
NSNumber *doubleNumber = @123.1234567890;

NSInteger signedValue = [signedNumber integerValue];
NSUInteger unsignedValue = [unsignedNumber unsignedIntegerValue];
CGFloat floatValue = [floatNumber floatValue];
double doubleValue = [doubleNumber doubleValue];

NSLog(@"signedValue   = %ld, \n"\
      "unsignedValue = %lu  \n"\
      "floatValue    = %f   \n"\
      "doubleValue   = %f",
      (long)signedValue,
      (unsigned long)unsignedValue,
      floatValue,
      doubleValue);
```

We are using the new features available in the LLVM compiler for iOS 6 SDK to create our numbers. We can simply place our numbers straight after an at sign (@) and our compiler will convert these numbers to instances of the NSNumber class. This technique is called *expression boxing*. If you don't want to use this feature, you can still use the various methods of the NSNumber class to construct instances of this class.

Here are the methods of NSNumber that you can use in your code to actually generate instances of NSNumber class:

numberWithInteger:
> Encapsulates an integer into an instance of NSNumber.

numberWithUnsignedInteger:

Encapsulates an unsigned integer (only positive or zero numbers) into an instance of NSNumber.

numberWithFloat:

Encapsulates a floating-point value into an instance of NSNumber.

numberWithDouble:

Encapsulates a double value into an instance of NSNumber.

And here are the methods that you can use to extract pure numbers from instances of NSNumber:

integerValue

Returns an integer of type NSInteger from the NSNumber on which this method is called.

unsignedIntegerValue

Returns an unsigned integer of type NSUInteger from the NSNumber on which this method is called.

floatValue

Returns a floating-point value of type CGFloat from the NSNumber on which this method is called.

doubleValue

Returns a double value of type double from the NSNumber on which this method is called.

If you want to convert a number to a string, simply convert it to any of the raw integral/float values that you think can contain the whole of that number, and then format your string using a format identifier that suits your data. For instance, to turn an unsigned integer into an instance of NSString, you can use the %lu format specifier, like so:

```
NSNumber *unsignedNumber = @123456;

/* Convert an unsigned integer inside an NSNumber to NSString */
NSString *stringValueOfNumber =
[NSString stringWithFormat:@"%lu",
 (unsigned long)[unsignedNumber unsignedIntegerValue]];

NSLog(@"String from Number = %@", stringValueOfNumber);
```

1.23 Allocating and Making Use of Arrays

Problem

You want to store a series of objects into another object for later use.

Solution

Use NSArray and NSMutableArray classes to store objects into arrays that are fixed and that you can change, respectively.

Discussion

An object of type NSArray or any of its subclasses has the capability to store *n* number of other objects, where *n* will be determined by the runtime and is influenced by how much memory is available at the time. These objects can then be accessed using their index. For instance, let's say you have 10 pairs of socks. Now imagine placing them all on a flat surface from left to right and calling them socks 1, socks 2, socks 3, and so on. So the leftmost pair of socks is now addressed as socks 1, the pair next to it is called socks 2, and the rightmost pair is called socks 10. Isn't that easier than saying something like "the blue socks next to my red socks"? That's exactly what arrays do: they make arranging items much easier.

> You can place any object of type NSObject or any of its subclasses into an array of type NSArray (or subclasses of that type). An array can contain a mix of different types of objects. Not all objects have to be of the same type. In other words, you can have one array with strings, numbers, dictionaries, or even other arrays inside it. Arrays can contain any object as long as those objects can be wrapped in the id data type wrapper.

The primary difference between NSArray and NSMutableArray is that a mutable array can be changed/modified after it has been allocated and initialized, whereas an immutable array, NSArray, cannot.

Let's have a look at an example. First, create an instance of NSString and two instances of NSNumber and place them in an immutable array:

```
NSArray *array = @[@"My String", @123, @-123];
NSLog(@"array = %@", array);
```

When you run this program, the following text is printed to your console:

```
array = (
    "My String",
    123,
    "-123"
)
```

We used the new collection subscripting features of our LLVM compiler to construct the array. These let us construct the array using the @[] collection format and place our objects between the opening and the closing square brackets. This syntax creates an instance of an array for us. When using this method of constructing your arrays, pass your objects that need to be placed inside the array one by one.

We can also use the `arrayWithObjects:` class method of `NSArray` to create an autorelease array, like so:

```
NSArray *array = [NSArray arrayWithObjects:
                  stringObject,
                  signedNumber,
                  unsignedNumber, nil];
```

You can call the `count` method on your array to get the number of objects in that array. You can go through your array using a for loop or using an enumerator. Let's have a look at the solution with a for loop first:

```
NSArray *array = @[@"My String", @123, @-123];

NSUInteger counter = 0;
for (counter = 0;
     counter < [array count];
     counter++){

    id object = array[counter];
    NSLog(@"Object = %@", object);

}
```

And here is the output:

```
Object = My String
Object = -123
Object = 123
```

Aside from the [] syntax to access a specific object in an array, we can also use the `objectAtIndex:` method to get an object at a specific index. Remember that indexes are zero based. In other words, when the counter reaches -1, the loop has to stop because there can be no negative indexes in an array.

As mentioned before, you can also use fast enumeration to go through objects of an array. Fast enumeration is a language feature in Objective-C that allows you to enumerate objects in an array or dictionary (or any other object that supports fast enumeration) without having to use any counter or for loop. The format is as follows:

```
for (Type variableName in array/dictionary/etc){ ... }
```

Suppose we want to code the previous example without the overhead of a counter variable. Here is how we can do it using fast enumeration:

```
for (id object in array){
    NSLog(@"Object = %@", object);
}
```

The results are practically identical to the results we got from the previous version of this code that used a counter variable.

Mutable arrays are very interesting. As you probably have already guessed, immutable arrays cannot be modified once allocated and initialized. Mutable arrays, however, can be modified after their allocation and initialization. Let's have a look at an example:

```
NSArray *anotherArray = @[@"String 1", @"String 2", @"String 3"];

NSMutableArray *mutableArray = [NSMutableArray arrayWithArray:
                               @[@"My String", @123, @-123]];

[mutableArray addObject:@123];
[mutableArray removeObject:@-123];
[mutableArray addObjectsFromArray:anotherArray];

for (id object in mutableArray){
    NSLog(@"Object = %@", object);
}
```

Before we go into analyzing the code, let's have a look at its output:

```
Object = My String
Object = 123
Object = 123
Object = String 1
Object = String 2
Object = String 3
```

You might be wondering what just happened. Well, let's have a look at what methods of the NSMutableArray class we actually used:

addObject:
> This method allows us to add an object to the end of a mutable array.

removeObject:
> Using this method, we can remove a specific object from the array. Remember that we pass an object to this method, not an index of the object. To remove an object using an index into the array, we must use the removeObjectAtIndex: method.

addObjectsFromArray:
> With this method, we can add objects from one array (either mutable or immutable) into our mutable array.

 Bear in mind that during fast enumeration of a mutable array, you must not add to or remove anything from that array or you will get a runtime error. This is the default behavior of mutable arrays during fast enumeration. There are two ways of avoiding this. Either simply follow the rule of not modifying an array while fast enumerating it, or, if you prefer the more proactive approach, you can subclass NSMutableArray and change the behavior for yourself. This topic is outside the scope of this book and will not be discussed.

If you are interested in block objects (and we'll see good reasons to be, later in the book, in Chapter 6), you can also enumerate objects in your arrays using the enumerate ObjectsUsingBlock: method. The block object passed to this method should:

- Return no value.
- Have three parameters:

- First parameter of type id, which will be the object being enumerated at each loop of enumeration.
- Second parameter of type NSUInteger, which will tell you the index of the current object being enumerated.
- Last but not least, a parameter of type *BOOL, which you can use to stop the enumeration. This is a pointer to a boolean variable, which should be NO as long as you want the enumeration to proceed. You can change the value of this pointer to YES in order to stop the enumeration at any time. You would use this if you are looking for an object in an array and you would like to stop the enumeration as soon as you've found that object, since there is no point continuing the enumeration if you've already found your object.

```
NSArray *myArray = @[
@"String 1",
@"String 2",
@"String 3",
@"String 4"];

[myArray enumerateObjectsUsingBlock:
^(__strong id obj, NSUInteger idx, BOOL *stop) {
  NSLog(@"Object = %@", obj);
}];
```

If you need to sort an array, simply use the new block-based sorting methods of NSArray or NSMutableArray. Just remember that the sorting methods of NSArray return a new instance of NSArray and leave the original array intact, since NSArray cannot be modified (sorting can modify an array) after it has been allocated and initialized. This is in comparison to the sorting methods of NSMutableArray, where the original array will be the target of sorting and the sorting methods will not return a new array. Let's look at sorting a mutable array:

```
NSMutableArray *myArray = [NSMutableArray arrayWithArray:@[
                          @"String 2",
                          @"String 4",
                          @"String 1",
                          @"String 3"]];

[myArray sortUsingComparator:
^NSComparisonResult(__strong id obj1, __strong id obj2) {

NSString *string1 = (NSString *)obj1;
NSString *string2 = (NSString *)obj2;
return [string1 compare:string2];

}];

NSLog(@"myArray = %@", myArray);

NSLog(@"%d", [@"String 3" compare:@"String 1"]);
```

The results will then be printed to the console, as follows:

```
myArray = (
    "String 1",
    "String 2",
    "String 3",
    "String 4"
)
```

So, what happened? We simply called the `sortUsingComparator:` method of our array. This method takes in a block object (marked by the initial ^ character) that has to return a value of type `NSComparisonResult`. This value can be any of the following:

`NSOrderedSame`
> The two values being compared are equal.

`NSOrderedAscending`
> The value on the left of the comparison is smaller than the value on the right. Think of it as this: transition from value 1 (left) to value 2 (right) is ascending, meaning that value 1 is smaller.

`NSOrderedDescending`
> The value on the right is smaller than the value on the left. In other words, the transition from value 1 (left) to value 2 (right) is descending, meaning that value 1 is bigger than value 2.

So if we get `String 3` as value 1 (left) and `String 1` as value 2 (right), the sort function compares the two *S* characters and finds them the same, then the two *t* characters, and so on. Finally, when the sort function reaches the 3 and the 1, it finds that 1 is lower than 3 in the UTF-8 string character set, and therefore that the second element is lower than the first.

The block object submitted to the `sortUsingComparator:` method takes two parameters:

First object of type `id`
> This is the first object in the comparison in each iteration.

Second object of type `id`
> This is the second object in the comparison in each iteration.

So when sorting the array, simply use a block-based approach. It's the way Apple is pushing developers to go forward with their implementations, so it's good to know about block objects.

1.24 Allocating and Making Use of Dictionaries

Problem

You want to store key-value data in an object, or you would like to retrieve objects from an array using a key into the array, but arrays won't quite suffice for this purpose, as they do not facilitate finding objects inside the array using a key or a marker for that object.

Solution

Use `NSDictionary` and its mutable counterpart, `NSMutableDictionary`.

Discussion

A dictionary is a special container for objects in which each object is given a key, which itself is an object. That is one of the key differences between dictionaries and arrays. An array has a numeric index into each item/object that it holds, whereas a dictionary holds a key to each item. I'll show you what I mean.

Let's say we want to store a person's first name, last name, and age into an array and then into a dictionary. This is how we would store those values in an array:

```
NSArray *person = @[
@"Anthony",
@"Robbins",
@51];

NSLog(@"First Name = %@", person[0]);
NSLog(@"Last Name = %@", person[1]);
NSLog(@"Age = %@", person[2]);
```

You can see that we are using an index into the array to access each one of these values. With dictionaries, we give each value a *key*, which is an object, and then use that key to access those values. Let's look at the same example but this time using dictionaries. We have a "First Name" key with the value "Anthony" and so on:

```
NSDictionary *person = @{
@"First Name" : @"Anthony",
@"Last Name" : @"Robbins",
@"Age" : @51
};

NSLog(@"First Name = %@", person[@"First Name"]);
NSLog(@"Last Name = %@", person[@"Last Name"]);
NSLog(@"Age = %@", person[@"Age"]);
```

The results will then be printed out as shown here:

```
First Name = Anthony
Last Name = Robbins
Age = 51
```

As you can see, we initialized the dictionary with values and keys. We give a value followed by the key for that value. When we used `NSLog`, we printed out each value by handing the key to the dictionary's `objectForKey:` method.

The mutable version of `NSDictionary`, `NSMutableDictionary`, can be modified after it has been allocated and initialized. For instance, if we want to remove the object associated with the key *Age* from our dictionary after its initialization, we would use a mutable dictionary like so:

```
NSMutableDictionary *person = [@{
                                 @"First Name" : @"Anthony",
                                 @"Last Name" : @"Robbins",
                                 @"Age" : @51
                                 } mutableCopy];

[person removeObjectForKey:@"Age"];

NSLog(@"First Name = %@", person[@"First Name"]);
NSLog(@"Last Name = %@", person[@"Last Name"]);
NSLog(@"Age = %@", person[@"Age"]);
```

We have simply removed the object associated with the key *Age*. The results printed to the console window will be similar to this:

```
First Name = Anthony
Last Name = Robbins
Age = (null)
```

 "Age" is not just empty, but totally missing.

If you want to enumerate all keys with their objects inside a dictionary, you can simply use the enumerateKeysAndObjectsUsingBlock: method of the dictionary. In the previous example, the method would print the "First Name" and "Last Name" elements, but not "Age", because we removed it. The parameter to this method is a block object with no return value and three parameters:

Key
An id that tells you which key is being enumerated at the moment.

Object
An id that gives you the object associated with the key being currently enumerated.

A pointer to a value of type BOOL
At any point during the enumeration, if you want to stop the process, you can simply put the value YES into this pointer's memory address. Keep it untouched if you want to enumerate through all the keys in the dictionary.

Let's see an example:

```
NSDictionary *person = @{
@"First Name" : @"Anthony",
@"Last Name" : @"Robbins",
@"Age" : @51
};
```

```
[person enumerateKeysAndObjectsUsingBlock:
 ^(__strong id key, __strong id obj, BOOL *stop) {

    NSLog(@"Key = %@, Object For Key = %@", key, obj);

}];
```

And the results, which get printed to the console window, are shown here:

```
Key = Last Name, Object For Key = Robbins
Key = First Name, Object For Key = Anthony
Key = Age, Object For Key = 51
```

If you want to do a manual fast enumeration without block objects, you can use the
allKeys method of the dictionary to go through all methods and, once you enumerate
the keys, use the keys to find the objects associated with the keys using the objectFor
Key: method, like so:

```
for (id keyInDictionary in [person allKeys]){

    id objectForKey = [person objectForKey:keyInDictionary];
    NSLog(@"Key = %@, Object For Key = %@", keyInDictionary, objectForKey);

}
```

Bear in mind that you can traverse the keys in a dictionary in various ways. We've just
seen two ways of doing this. There is another method that we can use: calling the
keyEnumerator method of the dictionary to get an object of type NSEnumerator. Here is
an example:

```
NSEnumerator *keys = [person keyEnumerator];
id keyInDictionary = nil;

while ((keyInDictionary = [keys nextObject]) != nil){

    id objectForKey = [person objectForKey:keyInDictionary];
    NSLog(@"Key = %@, Object For Key = %@", keyInDictionary, objectForKey);

}
```

When using the keyEnumerator method of a mutable dictionary, you are
not allowed to change the values inside the dictionary while going
through the keys. The same rule, if you remember, applies to mutable
arrays as well.

1.25 Allocating and Making Use of Sets

Problem

You would like to store an array of objects but you don't want any one object to appear
more than once in the array.

Solution

Use sets instead of arrays.

Discussion

Sets are very similar to arrays. The big difference is that sets allow objects to be added only once. The second time you try to add the same object, it will be rejected by the set. We use NSSet for immutable and NSMutableSet for mutable sets. Let's have a look at an example of an immutable set:

```
NSString *hisName = @"Robert";
NSString *hisLastName = @"Kiyosaki";

NSString *herName = @"Kim";
NSString *herLastName = @"Kiyosaki";

NSSet *setOfNames = [[NSSet alloc] initWithObjects:
                        hisName,
                        hisLastName,
                        herName,
                        herLastName, nil];

NSLog(@"Set = %@", setOfNames);
```

We created an immutable set and passed 4 string objects to its initializer method. So let's see what gets printed out to the console window with our NSLog:

```
Set = {(
    Kim,
    Robert,
    Kiyosaki
)}
```

You can see that the last name *Kiyosaki* was added only once to the list. Our set rejected the second addition of the same object to the list. It is *very* important to understand that a set doesn't just do a comparison on where in memory an object sits, but it actually looks into its contents. hisLastName and herLastName are two separate variables, and they will sit in two different places in the memory. Our set, however, managed to understand that we are passing instances of NSString to it and did a comparison on the *contents* of these strings to find out that we had already added the *Kiyosaki* last name to the set. So only one instance ended up in the set.

Now let's have a look at constructing mutable sets:

```
NSMutableSet *setOfNames = [[NSMutableSet alloc] initWithObjects:
                            hisName,
                            hisLastName, nil];

[setOfNames addObject:herName];
[setOfNames addObject:herLastName];
```

We simply used the addObject: method of NSMutableSet to add new objects to our set. You can also use the removeObject: method to remove an object. Again, remember that the contents of the object matter, not its memory address. So if you want to remove a string from the set, simply pass that string to the removeObject: method, even if your new string is in a different variable or somewhere else in memory. As long as the contents of that string/object are the same, you will get the results you want:

```
NSMutableSet *setOfNames = [[NSMutableSet alloc] initWithObjects:
                            hisName,
                            hisLastName,
                            herName,
                            herLastName, nil];

[setOfNames removeObject:@"Kiyosaki"];

NSLog(@"Set = %@", setOfNames);
```

And the results get printed to the console window:

```
Set = {(
    Kim,
    Robert
)}
```

If you want to fast enumerate all objects in a set, use the enumerateObjectsUsingBlock: method. The block object that you pass to this method should return no value and should have two parameters:

A key of type id
Contains the object in the set that is being currently enumerated.

A pointer to a boolean value of type BOOL
If you want to stop the enumeration at any time, simply place a boolean value of type YES into the memory address of this variable.

Let's have a look at an example. Let's say I want to try to find the string *Kiyosaki* in a set that I have:

```
[setOfNames enumerateObjectsUsingBlock:^(__strong id obj, BOOL *stop) {

  if ([obj isKindOfClass:[NSString class]]){
    NSString *string = (NSString *)obj;
    if ([string isEqualToString:@"Kiyosaki"]){
      NSLog(@"Found %@ in the set", string);
      *stop = YES;
    }
  }

}];
```

If the enumeration can find a string with the value of *Kiyosaki* in the set, we print a string to the console and terminate the enumeration by placing the value of YES into the second parameter of our enumerator block object.

There are other handy methods for sets. Use the count method to get the number of objects currently in a set. You can also use the allObjects method to get an array of all the objects in the set. If you want to extract an object from the set, with no concern for which one, call the anyObject on your set. This method will return, as its name implies, a random object in the set, no matter where in the set it is. You will get nil from this method if the set is empty.

1.26 Creating Bundles

Problem

You want to group your resources into hierarchical structures and be able to access those resources at runtime with ease.

Solution

Follow these steps to successfully create a bundle:

1. Create a root folder on your disk that will later become your bundle. For instance, let's give this folder the name *Resources*.

2. Under the *Resources* folder, create three more folders named *Images*, *Videos*, and *Sounds*.

3. Under the three aforementioned folders, place related resources. For instance, place one or more images in the *Images* folder and one or more video files under the *Videos* folder and so on.

4. Once you are done, rename your *Resources* folder to *Resources.bundle*. Once you add this extension to your folder name, OS X will ask for your confirmation and a dialog similar to that shown in Figure 1-33 will appear on the screen. Press Add on the dialog to add the *.bundle* extension to the *Resources* folder.

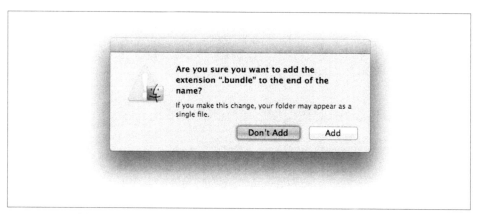

Figure 1-33. Adding a .bundle extension to a folder name in order to turn it into a bundle

Discussion

Bundles are simple folders with a *.bundle* extension. They have two main distinctions from regular folders:

1. Cocoa Touch provides an interface through which you can access bundles and their resources really easily.

2. If a bundle is added to the Navigator on the lefthand side of Xcode, any files added to or removed from the bundle outside Xcode will, respectively, appear in or disappear immediately from Xcode's navigator. In contrast, if you had added a normal folder to Xcode's navigator and then went and deleted a file from that folder on disk, without using Xcode's help, you would see that file marked with red color in Xcode rather than getting deleted immediately. Bundles can be very useful, especially if you want to add files to your folders manually using Finder instead of using Xcode.

Main bundles are flat bundles, in that all files inside the main bundle will be stored in one directory (its root directory). Bundles created by programmers can have subdirectories. Any bundle, including the main bundle, can contain other bundles.

Every iOS application comes with at least one bundle, called the main bundle. The main bundle contains your app's binary code and any other resource you are using inside your application, such as retina images, sounds, HTML files, and whatnot. The main bundle, in other words, contains the resources that get compiled into your final binary that you will submit to the App Store or distribute in your organization. These resources can then be dynamically loaded using the NSBundle class's mainBundle class method.

Although you can add two or more bundles with the same name to one iOS project, it is best not to complicate things like that. The reason this situation could get complicated is that when we start loading resources from our bundles, we will first need to find our bundles by their path. If you have two bundles with the same name, it will become quite difficult to detect which is which. So as a good practice, make sure that your bundles have different names when you add them to your Xcode projects.

1.27 Loading Data from the Main Bundle

Problem

You have added a resource (such as an image) to your Xcode project and now, at runtime, you would like to access that resource.

Solution

Use the `mainBundle` class method of the `NSBundle` class in order to retrieve your main bundle. Once that is done, use the `pathForResource:ofType:` method of your main bundle to retrieve the path for that specific resource. Once the path is detected, depending on the type of resource, you can either pass the path to your file to a class such as `UIImage` or `NSData`, or you can manually access the file using `NSFileManager`.

 It is required that you give a unique name to each resource inside your main bundle. For instance, it is not good practice to have a file named *Default.png* in more than one place inside your main bundle. Different ways of loading a resource from a bundle could then yield different results. As a result, make sure you give unique names to your files inside any bundle, regardless of whether it is the main bundle or a custom bundle that you've created (see Recipe 1.26).

Discussion

To access the main bundle, we can use the `mainBundle` class method of the `NSBundle` class. Bundles are all of type `NSBundle` and once you have an instance of a bundle, you can load resources from that bundle.

 Every app's main bundle has a flat hierarchy on disk when it is compiled for submission to App Store. That means all the files that get wrapped up in your app bundle will be placed on the root folder of the main bundle. In other words, the main bundle has only one folder, the root folder, and all files and resources are stored in that folder. Even if you have a folder on disk with a few files in it and drag and drop it into Xcode, only the files in that folder will be placed in the main bundle's file hierarchy, not the folder itself.

For instance, let's say that you have an image called *AlanSugar.png* sitting on your desktop. Simply drag and drop it into Xcode. At this point, Xcode will display a dialog to you, asking you which project this file has to be added to and whether you want this file to be copied over to the project's folder, if need be. This dialog will look similar to that shown in Figure 1-34.

In this dialog, make sure that the "Copy items into destination group's folder (if needed)" item is selected. This will copy the file that you drop into Xcode to the target app's folder. Now, if you delete the file on your desktop, it won't get deleted from your project because your project has its own copy. It's generally good practice to do this unless, for specific reasons, you decide not to (and I've experienced many of these reasons myself). After you drag and drop the file, the file *AlanSugar.png* is in the project's main bundle and you can retrieve its path in this way:

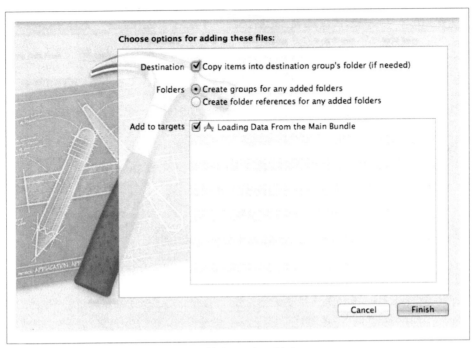

Figure 1-34. Xcode asking which project a file has to be added to

```
- (BOOL)              application:(UIApplication *)application
    didFinishLaunchingWithOptions:(NSDictionary *)launchOptions{

    NSString *alanSugarFilePath =
    [[NSBundle mainBundle] pathForResource:@"AlanSugar"
                                    ofType:@"png"];

    if ([alanSugarFilePath length] > 0){
      UIImage *image = [UIImage imageWithContentsOfFile:alanSugarFilePath];
      if (image != nil){
        NSLog(@"Successfully loaded the file as an image.");
      } else {
        NSLog(@"Failed to load the file as an image.");
      }

    } else {
      NSLog(@"Could not find this file in the main bundle.");
    }

    self.window = [[UIWindow alloc] initWithFrame:
                   [[UIScreen mainScreen] bounds]];

    self.window.backgroundColor = [UIColor whiteColor];
    [self.window makeKeyAndVisible];
    return YES;
}
```

The output of the pathForResource:ofType: method of NSBundle will be either a valid path or nil if the specified resource cannot be found in the target bundle. So after you call this method, it is best to check whether the path could actually be retrieved. If so, the code shown passes the path of the file to the UIImage class in order to load the *AlanSugar.png* file into memory as an image.

Similarly, if you wanted to load the data of that file into memory, instead of retrieving this image as an image object, you could use the NSData class:

```
- (BOOL)            application:(UIApplication *)application
didFinishLaunchingWithOptions:(NSDictionary *)launchOptions{

  NSString *alanSugarFilePath =
  [[NSBundle mainBundle] pathForResource:@"AlanSugar"
                                 ofType:@"png"];

  if ([alanSugarFilePath length] > 0){

    NSError *readError = nil;

    NSData *dataForFile =
    [[NSData alloc] initWithContentsOfFile:alanSugarFilePath
                                   options:NSMappedRead
                                     error:&readError];

    if (readError == nil &&
        dataForFile != nil){
      NSLog(@"Successfully loaded the data.");
    } else if (readError == nil &&
               dataForFile == nil){
      NSLog(@"No data could be loaded.");
    } else {
      NSLog(@"An error occured while loading data. Error = %@", readError);
    }

  } else {
    NSLog(@"Could not find this file in the main bundle.");
  }

  self.window = [[UIWindow alloc] initWithFrame:
                 [[UIScreen mainScreen] bounds]];

  self.window.backgroundColor = [UIColor whiteColor];
  [self.window makeKeyAndVisible];
  return YES;
}
```

See Also

Recipe 1.26

1.28 Loading Data from Other Bundles

Problem

You have included a few images or other resources in a separate bundle inside your main bundle and you would like to access those resources at runtime.

Solution

Find the path to your bundle at runtime using the `pathForResource:ofType:` method of your main bundle. Once you have the path to your bundle, simply access it using the `bundleWithPath:` class method of `NSBundle`.

 Before continuing with this recipe, please follow the instructions in Recipe 1.26 to create a bundle called *Resources.bundle* and place it inside your main bundle.

Discussion

If you have followed the instructions in Recipe 1.26, you now have a bundle called *Resources.bundle* inside this bundle you have a folder called *Images*. Let's now put an image inside this folder. After I placed an image called *AlanSugar.png* into the bundle, Figure 1-35 shows what the bundle contains.

Figure 1-35. Placing an image inside the bundle which we created before

---

Since the *Resources.bundle* is added to our app's main bundle, we will need to use the main bundle in order to find the path to our *Resources.bundle*. Once that is done, we can directly access the files (only *AlanSugar.png* right now) inside this bundle. Since bundles other than the main bundle can have folders embedded inside them, to access files inside folders of a bundle other than the main bundle it is best to use the pathFor Resource:ofType:inDirectory: method of NSBundle to explicitly specify the folder in which a specific file/resource exists.

```
- (BOOL)                application:(UIApplication *)application
  didFinishLaunchingWithOptions:(NSDictionary *)launchOptions{

  NSString *resourcesBundlePath =
  [[NSBundle mainBundle] pathForResource:@"Resources"
                                 ofType:@"bundle"];

  if ([resourcesBundlePath length] > 0){

    NSBundle *resourcesBundle = [NSBundle bundleWithPath:resourcesBundlePath];

    if (resourcesBundle != nil){

      NSString *pathToAlanSugarImage =
      [resourcesBundle pathForResource:@"AlanSugar"
                               ofType:@"png"
                          inDirectory:@"Images"];

      if ([pathToAlanSugarImage length] > 0){

        UIImage *image = [UIImage imageWithContentsOfFile:pathToAlanSugarImage];

        if (image != nil){
          NSLog(@"Successfully loaded the image from the bundle.");
        } else {
          NSLog(@"Failed to load the image.");
        }

      } else {
        NSLog(@"Failed to find the file inside the bundle.");
      }

    } else {
      NSLog(@"Failed to load the bundle.");
    }

  } else {
    NSLog(@"Could not find the bundle.");
  }

  self.window = [[UIWindow alloc] initWithFrame:
                [[UIScreen mainScreen] bounds]];

  self.window.backgroundColor = [UIColor whiteColor];
  [self.window makeKeyAndVisible];
```

```
    return YES;
}
```

If you are attempting to find all the resources which are stored in a specific folder inside a bundle, you can use the pathsForResourcesOfType:inDirectory: method of the NSBundle class. In this code, we will attempt to find the path to all the .png files inside the *Images* folder of our *Resources.bundle* bundle:

```
- (BOOL)              application:(UIApplication *)application
didFinishLaunchingWithOptions:(NSDictionary *)launchOptions{

    NSString *resourcesBundlePath =
    [[NSBundle mainBundle] pathForResource:@"Resources"
                                    ofType:@"bundle"];

    if ([resourcesBundlePath length] > 0){

        NSBundle *resourcesBundle = [NSBundle bundleWithPath:resourcesBundlePath];

        if (resourcesBundle != nil){

            NSArray *PNGPaths = [resourcesBundle pathsForResourcesOfType:@"png"
                                                            inDirectory:@"images"];

            [PNGPaths
              enumerateObjectsUsingBlock:^(id obj, NSUInteger idx, BOOL *stop) {
                NSLog(@"Path %lu = %@", (unsigned long)idx+1, obj);
              }];

        } else {
            NSLog(@"Failed to load the bundle.");
        }

    } else {
        NSLog(@"Could not find the bundle.");
    }

    self.window = [[UIWindow alloc] initWithFrame:
                    [[UIScreen mainScreen] bounds]];

    self.window.backgroundColor = [UIColor whiteColor];
    [self.window makeKeyAndVisible];
    return YES;
}
```

 the enumerateObjectsUsingBlock: method of NSArray accepts a block object as its parameter. For more information about enumerateObjectsUsingBlock: and the block object it accepts, please refer to Recipe 1.25.

See Also

Recipe 1.25; Recipe 1.26

1.29 Sending Notifications with NSNotificationCenter

Problem

You want to broadcast an event in your app and allow any object that is willing to listen to it to take action, depending on the notification that you are broadcasting.

Solution

Use the `postNotificationName:object:userInfo:` method of the default notification center of type `NSNotificationCenter` to post a notification that carries an object (usually the object that fires the notification) and a user-info dictionary that can carry extra information about the notification and/or the object that fires the notification.

Discussion

Notification centers are dispatch centrals for *notification objects*. For instance, when the keyboard pops up anywhere while the user is inside your app, iOS will send a notification to your app. Any object inside your app willing to listen to this notification can add itself to the default notification center as an *observer* for that particular notification. Once your object's lifetime comes to an end, it must remove itself from the notification center's dispatch table. As a result, a notification is a message that gets broadcasted to observers through a notification center. A notification center is an instance of `NSNotificationCenter` class. We retrieve the default notification center object using the `defaultCenter` class method of `NSNotificationCenter`.

Notifications are objects of type `NSNotification`. A notification object has a name (specified as `NSString`) and can carry two key pieces of information:

 You can specify the name of your notifications yourself. You don't have to use an API for that. Just make sure that your notification names are unique enough that they won't clash with a system notification.

Sender Object
> This is the instance of the object that fires the notification. The observer can access this object using the `object` instance method of the `NSNotification` class.

User-Info Dictionary
> This is an optional dictionary that the sender object can create and send alongside a notification object. This dictionary usually contains more information about the notification. For instance, when a keyboard is about to get displayed in iOS for any

component inside your app, iOS sends the UIKeyboardWillShowNotification notification to the default notification center. The user-info dictionary of this notification contains values such as the rectangle of the keyboard before and after animation and the animation duration of the keyboard. Using this data, an observer can make a decision as to, for instance, what to do with UI components that potentially will be obstructed once the keyboard gets displayed on the screen.

Notifications are a great way of implementing decoupled code. By that I mean, using notifications, you can get rid of completion handlers and delegation. However, there is one potential caveat about notifications: they are not delivered immediately. They are dispatched by notification centers, and the implementation of NSNotificationCenter is hidden from application programmers. Delivery might sometimes be delayed by a few milliseconds or, in extreme cases (which I have never encountered), a few seconds. As a result, it is up to you to decide where to and where not to use notifications.

In order to construct a notification of type NSNotification, use the notificationWithName:object:userInfo: class method of the NSNotificationClass, as we will soon see.

It is best to suffix your notification names with the word Notification. For instance, it is permitted to give your notification a name similar to ResultOfAppendingTwoStrings. However, it is better to give the name ResultOfAppendingTwoStringsNotification, as that clearly says what this name belongs to.

Let's have a look at an example. We'll simply take a first name and a last name, append them to create one string (first name + last name) and then broadcast the result using the default notification center. We will do that in the implementation of our app delegate as soon as the user launches our app:

```
#import "AppDelegate.h"

@implementation AppDelegate

/* The notification name */
const NSString *ResultOfAppendingTwoStringsNotification =
                @"ResultOfAppendingTwoStringsNotification";

/* Keys inside the dictionary that our notification sends */
const NSString
  *ResultOfAppendingTwoStringsFirstStringInfoKey = @"firstString";

const NSString
  *ResultOfAppendingTwoStringsSecondStringInfoKey = @"secondString";

const NSString
  *ResultOfAppendingTwoStringsResultStringInfoKey = @"resultString";
```

```
- (BOOL)              application:(UIApplication *)application
  didFinishLaunchingWithOptions:(NSDictionary *)launchOptions{

  NSString *firstName = @"Anthony";
  NSString *lastName = @"Robbins";
  NSString *fullName = [firstName stringByAppendingString:lastName];

  NSArray *objects = [[NSArray alloc] initWithObjects:
                         firstName,
                         lastName,
                         fullName,
                         nil];

  NSArray *keys = [[NSArray alloc] initWithObjects:
                     ResultOfAppendingTwoStringsFirstStringInfoKey,
                     ResultOfAppendingTwoStringsSecondStringInfoKey,
                     ResultOfAppendingTwoStringsResultStringInfoKey,
                     nil];

  NSDictionary *userInfo = [[NSDictionary alloc] initWithObjects:objects
                                                          forKeys:keys];

  NSNotification *notificationObject =
  [NSNotification
   notificationWithName:(NSString *)ResultOfAppendingTwoStringsNotification
   object:self
   userInfo:userInfo];

  [[NSNotificationCenter defaultCenter] postNotification:notificationObject];

  self.window = [[UIWindow alloc] initWithFrame:
                   [[UIScreen mainScreen] bounds]];
  self.window.backgroundColor = [UIColor whiteColor];
  [self.window makeKeyAndVisible];
  return YES;
}
```

Of course, you don't have to specify an object or a user-info dictionary for every notification that you wish to broadcast. However, if you are working with a team of developers on the same app or if you are writing a static library, I suggest that you fully document your notifications and clearly mention whether your notifications carry an object and/or an user-info dictionary with them. If they do, you must say what object each notification carries and what keys and values are inside the user-info dictionary. If you are planning on not sending an object or a user-info dictionary, then I suggest you use the postNotificationName:object: instance method of NSBundle. Specify a string that represents the name of your notification as the first parameter, and nil as the second parameter, which is the object that should be carried with the notification. Here is an example:

```
#import "AppDelegate.h"

@implementation AppDelegate
```

```
/* The notification name */
const NSString *NetworkConnectivityWasFoundNotification =
            @"NetworkConnectivityWasFoundNotification";

- (BOOL)             application:(UIApplication *)application
  didFinishLaunchingWithOptions:(NSDictionary *)launchOptions{

  [[NSNotificationCenter defaultCenter]
   postNotificationName:(NSString *)NetworkConnectivityWasFoundNotification
   object:nil];

  self.window = [[UIWindow alloc] initWithFrame:
                 [[UIScreen mainScreen] bounds]];
  self.window.backgroundColor = [UIColor whiteColor];
  [self.window makeKeyAndVisible];
  return YES;
}
```

1.30 Listening for Notifications Sent from NSNotificationCenter

Problem

You want to listen for different system and custom notifications broadcast using NSNotificationCenter.

Solution

Add your observer object to the notification center using the addObserver:selec tor:name:object: instance method of NSNotificationCenter before a notification is broadcast. To stop observing a notification, use the removeObserver:name:object: instance method of NSNotificationCenter and pass your observer object, then the name of the notification that you want to stop observing and the object that you originally subscribed to (this will be explained in detail in the Discussion section of this recipe).

Discussion

Any object can broadcast a notification and any object within the same app can opt into listening for notifications with specific names. Two notifications with the same name can be broadcast, but they must come from two different objects. For instance, you can have a notification with the name of *DOWNLOAD_COMPLETED* that gets fired from two classes, one being a download manager that downloads images from the Internet and another being a download manager that downloads data from an accessory connected to the iOS device. An observer might be interested only in the notifications of this name coming from a specific object; for instance, the download manager that downloads data from the accessory. You can specify this source object (broadcaster) when you start listening for notifications, using the `object` parameter of the `addObserver:selector:name:object:` method of the notification center.

Here is a brief description of each of the parameters that the `addObserver:selec tor:name:object:` accepts:

`addObserver`
>   The object that will receive the notifications (observer).

`selector`
>   The selector (method) to be called on the observer when the notification is broad-casted and received by the observer. This method takes a single argument of type `NSNotification`.

`name`
>   The name of the notification to observe.

`object`
>   Optionally specifies the source of the broadcast notification. If this parameter is nil, notifications of the specified name will be received by the observer regardless of which object broadcasts them. If this parameter is set, only the notifications of the specified name that are broadcast by the given object will be observed.

In Recipe 1.29 we learned how to post notifications. Let's now try observing the notification that we learned to post there:

```
#import "AppDelegate.h"

@implementation AppDelegate

/* The notification name */
const NSString *ResultOfAppendingTwoStringsNotification =
                @"ResultOfAppendingTwoStringsNotification";

/* Keys inside the dictionary that our notification sends */
const NSString
  *ResultOfAppendingTwoStringsFirstStringInfoKey = @"firstString";

const NSString
  *ResultOfAppendingTwoStringsSecondStringInfoKey = @"secondString";

const NSString
  *ResultOfAppendingTwoStringsResultStringInfoKey = @"resultString";

- (void) broadcastNotification{

  NSString *firstName = @"Anthony";
  NSString *lastName = @"Robbins";
  NSString *fullName = [firstName stringByAppendingString:lastName];

  NSArray *objects = [[NSArray alloc] initWithObjects:
                      firstName,
                      lastName,
                      fullName,
```

```
                        nil]; NSArray *keys = [[NSArray alloc] initWithObjects:
                        ResultOfAppendingTwoStringsFirstStringInfoKey,
                        ResultOfAppendingTwoStringsSecondStringInfoKey,
                        ResultOfAppendingTwoStringsResultStringInfoKey,
                        nil];

    NSDictionary *userInfo = [[NSDictionary alloc] initWithObjects:objects
                                                    forKeys:keys];

    NSNotification *notificationObject =
    [NSNotification
     notificationWithName:(NSString *)ResultOfAppendingTwoStringsNotification
     object:self
     userInfo:userInfo];

    [[NSNotificationCenter defaultCenter] postNotification:notificationObject];

}

- (void) appendingIsFinished:(NSNotification *)paramNotification{

    NSLog(@"Notification is received.");
    NSLog(@"Notification Object = %@", [paramNotification object]);
    NSLog(@"Notification User-Info Dict = %@", [paramNotification userInfo]);

}

- (BOOL)              application:(UIApplication *)application
  didFinishLaunchingWithOptions:(NSDictionary *)launchOptions{


    /* Listen for the notification */
    [[NSNotificationCenter defaultCenter]
     addObserver:self
     selector:@selector(appendingIsFinished:)
     name:(NSString *)ResultOfAppendingTwoStringsNotification
     object:self];

    [self broadcastNotification];

    self.window = [[UIWindow alloc] initWithFrame:
                    [[UIScreen mainScreen] bounds]];
    self.window.backgroundColor = [UIColor whiteColor];
    [self.window makeKeyAndVisible];
    return YES;

}

- (void)applicationWillTerminate:(UIApplication *)application{
    /* We no longer observe ANY notifications */
    [[NSNotificationCenter defaultCenter] removeObserver:self];
}
```

When you run this app, you will see something similar to the following printed to the console window:

```
Notification is received.
Notification Object = <AppDelegate: 0x7408490>
Notification User-Info Dict = {
    firstString = Anthony;
    resultString = AnthonyRobbins;
    secondString = Robbins;
}
```

As you can see, we are using the removeObserver: method of our notification center to remove our object as an observer of all notifications. There are different ways of removing your objects from the chain of observers. Either you can quit cold-turkey, as we have done here—that is, remove your object completely from observing any notification—or you can remove your object from observing specific notifications at any time during the lifetime of your application. If you want to specify the notifications you are removing your object from observing, simply call the removeObserver: name:object: method of your notification center and specify the name of the notification from which you are unsubscribing, as well as (optionally) the object that was sending the notifications.

See Also

Recipe 1.29

CHAPTER 2

Implementing Controllers and Views

2.0 Introduction

All iOS applications essentially use the Model-View-Controller, or MVC architecture. Model, view, and controller are the three main components of an iOS application from an architectural perspective.

The model is the brain of the application. It does the calculations and creates a virtual world for itself that can live without the views and controllers. In other words, think of a model as a virtual copy of your application, without a face!

A view is the window through which your users interact with your application. It displays what's inside the model most of the time, but in addition to that, it accepts users' interactions. Any interaction between the user and your application is sent to a view, which then can be captured by a view controller and sent to the model.

Controllers in iOS programming usually refer to *view controllers*. Think of view controllers as a bridge between the model and your views. They interpret what is happening on one side (what the user does on the view side, or the information provided by the model) and use that information to alter the other side as needed.

In this chapter, you will learn how the structure of an iOS application is created and how to use views and view controllers to create intuitive applications.

In this chapter, for most of the UI (User Interface) components that we create, we are using a Single View Application template in Xcode. To reproduce the examples, follow the instructions in Recipe 1.1 but instead of a Page-Based Application, create a Single View Application. Make sure that your app is Universal, as opposed to an iPhone or iPad app. A Universal app can run on both iPhone and iPad.

2.1 Displaying Alerts with UIAlertView

Problem

You want to display a message to your users in the form of an alert. This could be used to ask them to confirm an action, ask for their username and password, or simply let them enter some simple text that you can use in your app.

Solution

Utilize `UIAlertView`.

Discussion

If you are an iOS user, you have most certainly already seen an alert view. Figure 2-1 depicts an example.

Figure 2-1. An alert view telling the user that she needs an active Internet connection

The best way to initialize an alert view is, of course, by using its designated initializer:

```
UIAlertView *alertView = [[UIAlertView alloc]
                          initWithTitle:@"Title"
                          message:@"Message"
                          delegate:nil
                          cancelButtonTitle:@"Cancel"
                          otherButtonTitles:@"Ok", nil];
[alertView show];
```

When this alert view is displayed to the user, she will see something similar to that shown in Figure 2-2:

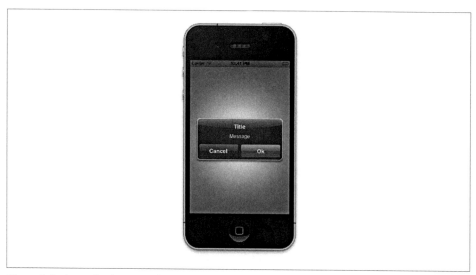

Figure 2-2. A simple alert view displayed to the user

In order to display an alert view to the user, we use the alert view's show method. Let's have a look at the description for each of the parameters that we passed to the initializer of the alert view:

title

> The string that the alert view will display on the top when it is shown to the user. This string is *Title* in Figure 2-2.

message

> The actual message that gets displayed to the user. In Figure 2-2, this message is set to *Message*.

delegate

> The optional delegate object that we pass to the alert view. This object will then get notified whenever the alert's state changes; for instance, when the user taps on a button on the alert view. The object passed to this parameter must conform to the UIAlertViewDelegate protocol.

cancelButtonTitle

> A string that will get assigned to the cancel button on an alert view. An alert view that has a cancel button usually asks the user for an action. If the user isn't comfortable with performing that action, he or she will press the cancel button. This button's title does *not* necessarily have to say *Cancel*. It is up to you to specify a title for this button. This parameter is optional.

otherButtonTitles

> Titles of any other buttons that you want to have appear on the alert view. Separate the titles with commas and make sure you terminate the list of titles with a nil, which is called a *sentinel*. This parameter is optional.

It is possible to create an alert view without any buttons. An alert view without a button cannot be dismissed by the user. If you create such a view, you, as the programmer, need to make sure this alert view will get dismissed automatically; for instance, three seconds after it is displayed. An alert view without any buttons that does not dismiss itself automatically gives a really poor user experience. Not only will your app get low ratings on the App Store for blocking the UI from user access, but chances are that your app will get rejected by Apple.

Alert views can take various styles. The UIAlertView class has a property called alert ViewStyle of type UIAlertViewStyle:

```
typedef enum {
  UIAlertViewStyleDefault = 0,
  UIAlertViewStyleSecureTextInput,
  UIAlertViewStylePlainTextInput,
  UIAlertViewStyleLoginAndPasswordInput
} UIAlertViewStyle;
```

Here is what each of these styles will do:

UIAlertViewStyleDefault
This is the default style of an alert view, as we saw in Figure 2-2.

UIAlertViewStyleSecureTextInput
With this style, the alert view will contain a secure text field, which hides the actual characters typed by the user. For instance, if you are asking the user for her online banking credentials, you might choose this style of alert view.

UIAlertViewStylePlainTextInput
Under this style, the alert view will display a non-secure text field to the user. This style is great if you simply want to ask the user for plain-text entry, such as her phone number.

UIAlertViewStyleLoginAndPasswordInput
With this style, the alert view will display two text fields: a non-secure one for a username and a secure one for a password.

If you need to get notified when the user interacts with the alert view, specify a delegate object to your alert view. This delegate must conform to the UIAlertViewDelegate protocol. The most important method defined in this protocol is the alertView:clicked ButtonAtIndex: method, which gets called as soon as the user taps on one of the buttons in the alert view. The button index is passed to you through the clicked ButtonAtIndex parameter.

As an example, let's display an alert view to the user and ask whether she would like to visit a website in Safari after having pressed a link to that website available in our UI. We will display two buttons on our alert view: Yes and No. In our alert view delegate, we will detect which button she tapped on and will take action accordingly.

Let's first implement two very simple methods that return the title of our two buttons:

```
- (NSString *) yesButtonTitle{
  return @"Yes";
}

- (NSString *) noButtonTitle{
  return @"No";
}
```

Now we need to make sure that we are conforming to the UIAlertViewDelegate protocol in our view controller:

```
#import <UIKit/UIKit.h>

@interface Displaying_Alerts_with_UIAlertViewViewController
          : UIViewController <UIAlertViewDelegate>

@end
```

The next step is to create and display our alert view to the user:

```
- (void)viewDidAppear:(BOOL)animated{
  [super viewDidAppear:animated];

  self.view.backgroundColor = [UIColor whiteColor];

  NSString *message = @"Are you sure you want to open this link in Safari?";
  UIAlertView *alertView = [[UIAlertView alloc]
                            initWithTitle:@"Open Link"
                            message:message
                            delegate:self
                            cancelButtonTitle:[self noButtonTitle]
                            otherButtonTitles:[self yesButtonTitle], nil];
  [alertView show];

}
```

So now, our alert view will look similar to that shown in Figure 2-3.

Now we need a way to know whether the user selected the Yes or the No option in our alert view. For this, we will need to implement the alertView:clickedButtonAtIndex: method of our alert view delegate:

```
- (void)      alertView:(UIAlertView *)alertView
  clickedButtonAtIndex:(NSInteger)buttonIndex{

  NSString *buttonTitle = [alertView buttonTitleAtIndex:buttonIndex];

  if ([buttonTitle isEqualToString:[self yesButtonTitle]]){
    NSLog(@"User pressed the Yes button.");
  }
  else if ([buttonTitle isEqualToString:[self noButtonTitle]]){
    NSLog(@"User pressed the No button.");
  }

}
```

Figure 2-3. An alert view with Yes and No buttons

 Please bear in mind that in big projects where multiple developers work on the same source code, it is usually easier to compare the titles of buttons of alert views to respective strings, rather than picking which button the user selected on an alert view based on the index of that button. For the index solution to work, the programmer has to find out the code that constructed the alert view and, based on the code, find out which button has what index. Whereas, in our solution, any developer, even without any knowledge as to how the alert view was constructed, can tell which if statement does what.

As you can see, we are using the `buttonTitleAtIndex:` method of `UIAlertView`. We pass the zero-based index of a button inside that alert view to this method and will get the string that represents the title of that button, if any. Using this method, we can determine which button the user has tapped on. The index of that button will be passed to us as the `buttonIndex` parameter of the `alertView:clickedButtonAtIndex:` method, but if you need the title of that button, you will then need to use the `buttonTitleAtIndex:` method of `UIAlertView`. That is it; job done!

You can also use an alert view for text entry, such as to ask the user for his credit card number or address. For this, as mentioned before, we need to use the `UIAlert ViewStylePlainTextInput` alert view style. Here is an example:

```
- (void) viewDidAppear:(BOOL)animated{
  [super viewDidAppear:animated];

  UIAlertView *alertView = [[UIAlertView alloc]
                            initWithTitle:@"Credit Card Number"
                            message:@"Please enter your credit card number:"
                            delegate:self
```

```
                    cancelButtonTitle:@"Cancel"
                    otherButtonTitles:@"Ok", nil];
  [alertView setAlertViewStyle:UIAlertViewStylePlainTextInput];

  /* Display a numerical keypad for this text field */
  UITextField *textField = [alertView textFieldAtIndex:0];
  textField.keyboardType = UIKeyboardTypeNumberPad;

  [alertView show];

}
```

If we run our app on the simulator now, we will get a result similar to Figure 2-4.

Figure 2-4. An alert view with plain text input

We did change the alert view's style to `UIAlertViewStylePlainTextInput` in this code, but we did something else as well. We retrieved the reference to the first and the only text field that we knew we would have on the alert view, and used that text field's reference to change the keyboard type of the text field. For more information about text fields, please refer to Recipe 2.19.

In addition to a plain text entry, you can ask the user for secure text. You would normally use this if the text that the user is entering is sensitive, such as a password (see Figure 2-5). Here is an example:

```
- (void) viewDidAppear:(BOOL)animated{
  [super viewDidAppear:animated];

  UIAlertView *alertView = [[UIAlertView alloc]
                            initWithTitle:@"Password"
                            message:@"Please enter your password:"
                            delegate:self
                            cancelButtonTitle:@"Cancel"
                            otherButtonTitles:@"Ok", nil];
```

```
    [alertView setAlertViewStyle:UIAlertViewStyleSecureTextInput];
    [alertView show];

}
```

Figure 2-5. Secure text entry in an alert view

And as you can see, the style we've chosen is `UIAlertViewStyleSecureTextInput`. This
style is very similar to the `UIAlertViewStylePlainTextInput` style, except that the text
field is set to substitute some neutral character for each character of the entered text.

The next style, which is quite useful, displays two text fields, one for a username and
the other for a password. The first is a plain text entry field and the other one is secure:

```
- (void) viewDidAppear:(BOOL)animated{
  [super viewDidAppear:animated];

  UIAlertView *alertView = [[UIAlertView alloc]
                          initWithTitle:@"Password"
                          message:@"Please enter your credentials:"
                          delegate:self
                          cancelButtonTitle:@"Cancel"
                          otherButtonTitles:@"Ok", nil];

  [alertView setAlertViewStyle:UIAlertViewStyleLoginAndPasswordInput];
  [alertView show];

}
```

The results will look similar to that shown in Figure 2-6.

Figure 2-6. Login and password style of alert view

See Also

Recipe 2.19

2.2 Creating and Using Switches with UISwitch

Problem

You would like to give your users the ability to turn an option on or off.

Solution

Use the UISwitch class.

Discussion

The UISwitch class provides an On/Off control like the one shown in Figure 2-7 for Auto-Capitalization, Auto-Correction, and so on.

Figure 2-7. UISwitch used in the Settings app on an iPhone

In order to create a switch, you can either use Interface Builder or simply create your instance in code. Let's do it through code. So next the challenge is to determine which class to place your code in. It needs to be in a View Controller class, which we haven't discussed yet, but for the a Single View Application type of app we're creating in this chapter, you can find the view controller's *.h* (header) file through a name that is based on the name of your project and ends with *ViewController.h*. For instance, I have named my project *Creating and Using Switches with UISwitch*, so the *.h* file of my view controller is called *Creating_and_Using_Switches_with_UISwitchViewController.h*. Open that file now.

 In the latest version of Xcode, creating a Single View Application project will create the header and implementation files of a view controller simply named ViewController. Therefore the header file of your view controller will be in the file named *ViewController.h* and the implementation in a file named *ViewController.m*.

Let's create a property of type UISwitch and call it *mySwitch*:

```
#import <UIKit/UIKit.h>

@interface Creating_and_Using_Switches_with_UISwitchViewController
        : UIViewController

@property (nonatomic, strong) UISwitch *mySwitch;

@end
```

We can go ahead now and create our switch. Find the `viewDidLoad` method in your view controller's implementation file:

```
- (void)viewDidLoad{
    [super viewDidLoad];
}
```

Let's create our switch and place it on our view controller's view:

```
- (void)viewDidLoad{
    [super viewDidLoad];

    /* Make sure our view is white */
    self.view.backgroundColor = [UIColor whiteColor];

    /* Create the switch */
    self.mySwitch = [[UISwitch alloc] initWithFrame:
                    CGRectMake(100, 100, 0, 0)];
    [self.view addSubview:self.mySwitch];

}
```

So we are allocating an object of type `UISwitch` and using the `initWithFrame:` initializer to initialize our switch. Note that the parameter that we have to pass to this method is of type `CGRect`. A `CGRect` denotes the boundaries of a rectangle using the (*x, y*) position of the top-left corner of the rectangle and its width and height. We can construct a `CGRect` using the `CGRectMake` inline method, where the first two parameters passed to this method are the (*x, y*) positions and the next two are the width and height of the rectangle.

After we've created the switch, we simply add it to our view controller's view.

 In this example, we are changing the background color of our view controller's view to white (as opposed to the default Single View Application's gray background color), just to make our app look nicer.

Now let's run our app on iPhone Simulator. Figure 2-8 shows what happens.

As you can see, the switch's default state is off. We can change this by changing the value of the on property of the instance of `UISwitch`. Alternatively, you can call the `setOn:` method on the switch, as shown here:

```
[self.mySwitch setOn:YES];
```

We can also use the `setOn:animated:` method of the switch. The `animated` parameter accepts a Boolean value. If this Boolean value is set to `YES`, the change in the switch's state (from on to off or off to on) will be animated, just as if the user was interacting with it.

Figure 2-8. A switch placed on a view

Obviously, you can read from the on property of the switch to find out whether the switch is on or off at the moment. Alternatively, you can use the isOn method of the switch, as shown here:

```
if ([self.mySwitch isOn]){
  NSLog(@"The switch is on.");
} else {
  NSLog(@"The switch is off.");
}
```

If you want to get notified *when* the switch gets turned on or off, you will need to add your class as the *target* for the switch, using the addTarget:action:forControlEvents: method of UISwitch, as shown here:

```
[self.mySwitch addTarget:self
                action:@selector(switchIsChanged:)
        forControlEvents:UIControlEventValueChanged];
```

Then implement the switchIsChanged: method. When the runtime calls this method for the UIControlEventValueChanged event of the switch, it will pass the switch as the parameter to this method, so you can find out which switch has fired this event:

```
- (void) switchIsChanged:(UISwitch *)paramSender{

  NSLog(@"Sender is = %@", paramSender);

  if ([paramSender isOn]){
    NSLog(@"The switch is turned on.");
  } else {
    NSLog(@"The switch is turned off.");
  }

}
```

Now go ahead and run the app on iOS Simulator. You will see messages similar to this in the console window:

```
Sender is = <UISwitch: 0x6e13500;
            frame = (100 100; 79 27);
            layer = <CALayer: 0x6e13700>>
The switch is turned off.
Sender is = <UISwitch: 0x6e13500;
            frame = (100 100; 79 27);
            layer = <CALayer: 0x6e13700>>
The switch is turned on.
```

2.3 Customizing the UISwitch

Problem

You have placed UISwitch instances on your UI and would now like to customize them to match your UI.

Solution

Simply use one of the tint/image customization properties of the UISwitch such as the tintColor or the onTintColor.

Discussion

In both iOS 5 and iOS 6 SDKs, Apple has done a fantastic job of bringing customization to UI components such as the UISwitch. In previous SDKs, developers were going as far as subclassing UISwitch just to change its appearance and color. Now, iOS 6 SDK makes this much simpler.

There are two main ways of customizing a switch:

Tint Colors

> Tint colors are colors that you can apply to a UI component such as a UISwitch. The tint color will be applied on top of the current color of the component. For instance, in a normal UISwitch, you will be able to see different colors. When you apply the tint color on top, the normal color of the control will be mixed with the tint color, giving a *flavor* of the tint color on the UI control.

Images

> A switch has two images:

> *On Image*

>> The image that represents the *on* state of the switch. The width of this image is 77 points and its height is 22.

> *Off Image*

>> The image that represents the switch in its *off* state. This image, like the *on* state of the switch, is 77 points in width and 22 points in height.

Figure 2-9 shows an example of the on and off image of a switch.

Figure 2-9. The on and off images on a UISwitch

Now that we know the two states (on and off) of a switch, let's get started by learning how we can change the tint color of the switch UI component. This can be achieved by the use of three important properties of the UISwitch class:

tintColor
> This is the tint color that will be applied to the off state of the switch. Unfortunately, Apple has not taken the time to name this property offTintColor instead of tint Color to make it more explicit. This property is of type UIColor.

thumbTintColor
> This is the tint color that will be applied to the little knob on the switch. This property is of type UIColor.

onTintColor
> This tint color will be applied to the switch in its on state. This property is of type UIColor as well.

Here is a simple code snippet that will change the on-mode tint color of the switch to red, the off-mode tint color to brown, and the knob's tint color to green. It is not the best combination of colors, but will demonstrate what this recipe is trying to explain:

```
- (CGRect) roundedValuesInRect:(CGRect)paramRect{
    paramRect.origin.x = round(CGRectGetMinX(paramRect));
    paramRect.origin.y = round(CGRectGetMinY(paramRect));
    paramRect.size.width = round(CGRectGetWidth(paramRect));
    paramRect.size.height = round(CGRectGetHeight(paramRect));
    return paramRect;
}

- (void)viewDidLoad
{
    [super viewDidLoad];

    /* Create the switch */
    self.view.backgroundColor = [UIColor whiteColor];
    self.mainSwitch = [[UISwitch alloc] initWithFrame:CGRectZero];
    self.mainSwitch.center = self.view.center;
    /* Make sure the switch won't appear blurry on iOS Simulator */
    self.mainSwitch.frame = [self roundedValuesInRect:self.mainSwitch.frame];
    [self.view addSubview:self.mainSwitch];

    /* Customize the switch */

    /* Adjust the off-mode tint color */
    self.mainSwitch.tintColor = [UIColor redColor];
    /* Adjust the on-mode tint color */
    self.mainSwitch.onTintColor = [UIColor brownColor];
    /* Also change the knob's tint color */
    self.mainSwitch.thumbTintColor = [UIColor greenColor];

}
```

 In this code snippet, we have coded a method named roundedValuesIn Rect:. The sole purpose of this method is to round the *x, y*, width, and height of a given CGRect structure and return the rounded values as a CGRect. The reason we are doing this is that on iOS Simulator, if any of the *x, y*, width, or height of your UI Components are not round, the controls may appear blurry on the screen. This is just an artifact of the iOS Simulator and does not appear on real iOS devices, so you can code without having to worry about this. But if you really want things to look absolutely great on the simulator, you just need to take this into consideration. Some developers are not really bothered with this as long as the results are great on the device, and that's the approach I also suggest you take.

Now that we are done with the tint colors on a switch, let's move on to customizing the appearance of the switch using its on and off images. As mentioned before, both the on and the off images in a switch should be 77 points wide and 22 points tall. For this, I have prepared a new set of on and off images (in both normal and retina resolutions). I have added them to my Xcode project under the (retina) names of *On@2x.png* and *Off@2x.png* and I've also placed the non-retina flavor of the same images in the project. Now what we have to do is to construct our switch but assign our custom on and off images to the switch, using the following properties on `UISwitch`:

onImage

> As explained before, this will be the image that is displayed when the switch is in its on mode.

offImage

> The image that represents the switch when it is in off mode.

And here is our code snippet to achieve this new look:

```
- (void)viewDidLoad
{
    [super viewDidLoad];

    /* Create the switch */
    self.view.backgroundColor = [UIColor whiteColor];
    self.mainSwitch = [[UISwitch alloc] initWithFrame:CGRectZero];
    self.mainSwitch.center = self.view.center;
    /* Make sure the switch won't appear blurry on iOS Simulator */
    self.mainSwitch.frame = [self roundedValuesInRect:self.mainSwitch.frame];
    [self.view addSubview:self.mainSwitch];

    /* Customize the switch */
    self.mainSwitch.onImage = [UIImage imageNamed:@"On"];
    self.mainSwitch.offImage = [UIImage imageNamed:@"Off"];

}
```

Figure 2-10 shows how the custom switch will look when it's in on-mode:

See Also

Recipe 2.2

2.4 Picking Values with UIPickerView

Problem

You want to allow the users of your app to select from a list of values.

Solution

Use the `UIPickerView` class.

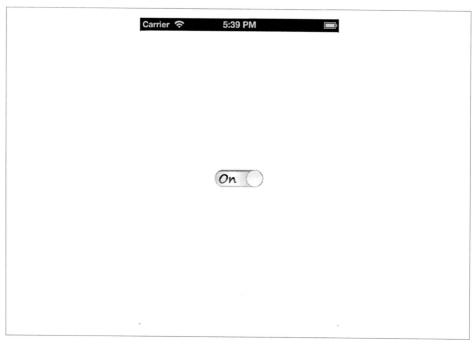

Figure 2-10. A UISwitch with a custom on and off image

Discussion

A picker view is a graphical element that allows you to display series of values to your users and allow them to pick one. The Timer section of the Clock app on the iPhone is a great example of this (Figure 2-11).

As you can see, this specific picker view has two separate and independent visual elements. One is on the left and one is on the right. The left component is displaying hours (such as 0 hours, 1, 2, etc.) and the component on the right is displaying minutes (such as 18, 19, 20 mins, 21, 22, etc.). These two items are called *components*. Each component has rows. Any item in any of the components is in fact represented by a row, as we will soon see. For instance, in the left component, "0 hours" is a row, "1" is a row, etc.

Let's go ahead and create a picker view on our view controller's view. If you don't know where your view controller's source code is, please have a look at Recipe 2.2, where this subject is discussed.

First let's go to the *.h* (header) file of our view controller and define our picker view:

```
#import <UIKit/UIKit.h>

@interface Picking_Values_with_UIPickerViewViewController
            : UIViewController
```

Figure 2-11. A picker view on top of the screen

```
@property (nonatomic, strong) UIPickerView *myPicker;

@end
```

Now let's create the picker view in the viewDidLoad method of our view controller:

```
- (void)viewDidLoad{
  [super viewDidLoad];

  self.view.backgroundColor = [UIColor whiteColor];

  self.myPicker = [[UIPickerView alloc] init];
  self.myPicker.center = self.view.center;
  [self.view addSubview:self.myPicker];

}
```

It's worth noting that in this example, we are centering our picker view at the center of our view so when you run this app, you will see something similar to that shown in Figure 2-12.

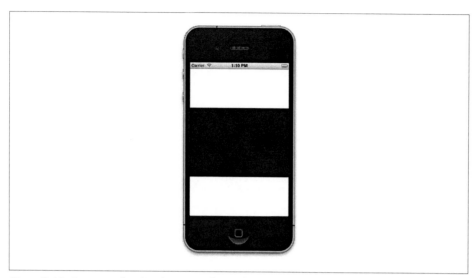

Figure 2-12. An unpopulated and empty picker with its default black color

The reason this picker view is showing up as a plain black color is that we have not yet populated it with any values. Let's do that. We do that by specifying a data source for the picker view and then making sure that our view controller sticks to the protocol that the data source requires. The data source of an instance of `UIPickerView` must conform to the `UIPickerViewDataSource` protocol, so let's go ahead and make our view controller conform to this protocol in the *.h* file:

```
#import <UIKit/UIKit.h>

@interface Picking_Values_with_UIPickerViewViewController
         : UIViewController <UIPickerViewDataSource>

@property (nonatomic, strong) UIPickerView *myPicker;

@end
```

Good. Let's now change our code in the implementation file to make sure we select the current view controller as the data source of the picker view:

```
- (void)viewDidLoad{
  [super viewDidLoad];

  self.view.backgroundColor = [UIColor whiteColor];

  self.myPicker = [[UIPickerView alloc] init];
  self.myPicker.dataSource = self;
  self.myPicker.center = self.view.center;
  [self.view addSubview:self.myPicker];

}
```

After this, if you try to compile your application, you will see that you are getting warnings from the compiler. These warnings are telling you that you have *not* yet implemented some of the methods that the `UIPickerViewDataSource` protocol wants you to implement. The way to fix this is to go back to your *.h* (header) file, hold down the Command key, and then click on the `UIPickerViewDataSource` text. That will send you to the place in your code where this protocol is defined, where you will see something similar to this:

```
@protocol UIPickerViewDataSource<NSObject>
@required

// returns the number of 'columns' to display.
- (NSInteger)numberOfComponentsInPickerView:(UIPickerView *)pickerView;

// returns the # of rows in each component..
- (NSInteger)pickerView:(UIPickerView *)pickerView
numberOfRowsInComponent:(NSInteger)component;
@end
```

Can you see the `@required` keyword there? That is telling us that whichever class wants to become the data source of a picker view *must* implement these methods. Good deal. Let's go implement them in our view controller's implementation file:

```
- (NSInteger)numberOfComponentsInPickerView:(UIPickerView *)pickerView{

  NSInteger result = 0;
  if ([pickerView isEqual:self.myPicker]){
    result = 1;
  }
  return result;

}

- (NSInteger)   pickerView:(UIPickerView *)pickerView
   numberOfRowsInComponent:(NSInteger)component{

  NSInteger result = 0;
  if ([pickerView isEqual:self.myPicker]){
    result = 10;
  }
  return result;

}
```

So what is happening here? Let's have a look at what each one of these data source methods expects:

numberOfComponentsInPickerView:
> This method passes you a picker view object as its parameter and expects you to return an integer, telling the runtime how many components you would like that picker view to render.

`pickerView:numberOfRowsInComponent:`

For each component that gets added to a picker view, you will need to tell the system about the number of rows that you would like to render in that component. This method passes you an instance of picker view and you will need to return an integer to it, telling the runtime how many rows you want the system to render for that component.

So in this case, we are asking the system to display 1 component with 10 rows only for a picker view that we have created before, called `myPicker`.

Compile and run your application on the iPhone Simulator (Figure 2-13). Ewww, what is that?

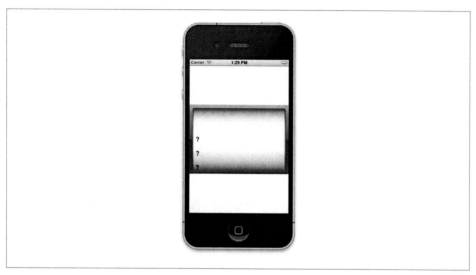

Figure 2-13. A picker view, not knowing what to render

It looks like our picker view knows how many components it should have and how many rows it should render in that component but doesn't know *what text* to display for each row. That is something we need to do now, and we do that by providing a delegate to the picker view. The delegate of an instance of `UIPickerView` has to conform to the `UIPickerViewDelegate` protocol and must implement all the `@required` methods of that protocol. Let's start with our view controller's header file:

```
@interface Picking_Values_with_UIPickerViewViewController
            : UIViewController
            <UIPickerViewDataSource, UIPickerViewDelegate>

@property (nonatomic, strong) UIPickerView *myPicker;

@end
```

There is only one method in the `UIPickerViewDelegate` we are interested in: the `pickerView:titleForRow:forComponent:` method. This method will pass you the index of the current section and the index of the current row in that section for a picker view and it expects you to return an instance of `NSString`. This string will then get rendered for that specific row inside the component. In here, I would simply like to display the first row as Row 1, and then continue to Row 2, Row 3, etc., till the end. Remember, we also have to set the `delegate` property of our picker view:

```
self.myPicker.delegate = self;
```

And now we will handle the delegate method we just learned about:

```
- (NSString *)pickerView:(UIPickerView *)pickerView
             titleForRow:(NSInteger)row
            forComponent:(NSInteger)component{

  NSString *result = nil;
  if ([pickerView isEqual:self.myPicker]){

    /* Row is zero-based and we want the first row (with index 0)
       to be rendered as Row 1 so we have to +1 every row index */
    result = [NSString stringWithFormat:@"Row %ld", (long)row + 1];

  }
  return result;

}
```

Now let's run our app and see what happens (Figure 2-14).

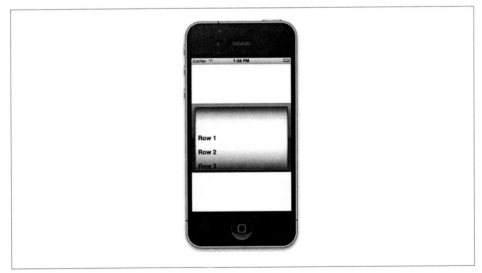

Figure 2-14. A picker view with one section and a few rows

All good? If you now refer back to Figure 2-11, you will notice a horizontal bar running across the picker view. It turns out that `UIPickerView` has a property called `showsSelectionIndicator`, which by default is set to `NO`. You can either directly set the value of this property to YES or use the setShowsSelectionIndicator: method of the picker view to turn this indicator on:

```
self.myPicker.showsSelectionIndicator = YES;
```

And now we will run our app in iOS Simulator and see how it looks (Figure 2-15).

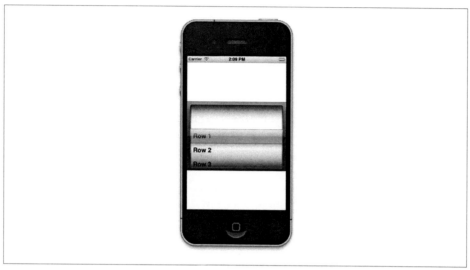

Figure 2-15. A picker view with selection indicator

Now imagine that you have created this picker view in your final application. What is the use of a picker view if we cannot detect what the user has actually selected in each one of its components? Well, it's good that Apple has already thought of that and given us the ability to ask the picker view about this. We can call the selectedRowInComponent: method of a UIPickerView and pass the zero-based index of a component to get an integer back, and this integer will be the zero-based index of the row that is currently selected in that component.

If at runtime, you need to modify the values in your picker view, you need to make sure that your picker view reloads its data from its data source and delegate. To do that, you can either force all the components to reload their data, using the reloadAllCompo nents method, or you can ask a specific component to reload its data, using the reload Component: method and passing the index of the component that has to be reloaded.

See Also

Recipe 2.2

2.5 Picking the Date and Time with UIDatePicker

Problem

You want to allow the users of your app to select a date and time using an intuitive and ready-made user interface.

Solution

Use the `UIDatePicker` class.

Discussion

`UIDatePicker` is very similar to the `UIPickerView` class. The date picker is in fact a pre-populated picker view. A good example of the date picker control is in the Calendar app on the iPhone (Figure 2-16).

Figure 2-16. A date picker shown at the bottom of the screen

Let's get started by first declaring a property of type `UIDatePicker` and then allocating and initializing this property and adding it to the view of our view controller:

```
#import <UIKit/UIKit.h>

@interface Picking_Date_and_Time_with_UIDatePickerViewController
        : UIViewController
```

```
@property (nonatomic, strong) UIDatePicker *myDatePicker;

@end
```

And now let's instantiate the date picker, as planned:

```
- (void)viewDidLoad{
    [super viewDidLoad];
    self.view.backgroundColor = [UIColor whiteColor];
    self.myDatePicker = [[UIDatePicker alloc] init];
    self.myDatePicker.center = self.view.center;
    [self.view addSubview:self.myDatePicker];
}
```

Now let's run the app and see how it looks in Figure 2-17.

Figure 2-17. A simple date picker

You can see that the date picker, by default, has picked today's date. The first thing that we need to know about date pickers is that they can have different styles or modes. This mode can be changed through the datePickerMode property, which is of type UIDatePickerMode:

```
typedef enum {
    UIDatePickerModeTime,
    UIDatePickerModeDate,
    UIDatePickerModeDateAndTime,
    UIDatePickerModeCountDownTimer,
} UIDatePickerMode;
```

Depending on what you need, you can set the mode of your date picker to any of the values listed in the UIDatePickerMode enumeration. I'll show some of these as we go along.

Now that you have successfully displayed a date picker on the screen, you can attempt to retrieve its currently-selected date using its date property. Alternatively, you can call the date method on the date picker, like so:

```
NSDate *currentDate = self.myDatePicker.date;
NSLog(@"Date = %@", currentDate);
```

Just like the UISwitch class, a date picker also sends action messages to its targets whenever the selection of date in it has changed. To respond to these messages, the receiver must add itself as the target of the date picker, using the addTarget:action:for ControlEvents: method, like so:

```
- (void) datePickerDateChanged:(UIDatePicker *)paramDatePicker{

  if ([paramDatePicker isEqual:self.myDatePicker]){
    NSLog(@"Selected date = %@", paramDatePicker.date);
  }

}

- (void)viewDidLoad{
  [super viewDidLoad];
  self.view.backgroundColor = [UIColor whiteColor];
  self.myDatePicker = [[UIDatePicker alloc] init];
  self.myDatePicker.center = self.view.center;
  [self.view addSubview:self.myDatePicker];

  [self.myDatePicker addTarget:self
                        action:@selector(datePickerDateChanged:)
              forControlEvents:UIControlEventValueChanged];

}
```

Now, every time the user changes the date, you will get a message from the date picker.

With a date picker, you also have the ability to set the minimum and the maximum dates that it can display. For this, let's first switch our date picker mode to UIDatePickerModeDate and then, using the maximumDate and the minimumDate properties, adjust this range:

```
- (void)viewDidLoad{
  [super viewDidLoad];
  self.view.backgroundColor = [UIColor whiteColor];
  self.myDatePicker = [[UIDatePicker alloc] init];
  self.myDatePicker.center = self.view.center;
  self.myDatePicker.datePickerMode = UIDatePickerModeDate;
  [self.view addSubview:self.myDatePicker];

  NSTimeInterval oneYearTime = 365 * 24 * 60 * 60;
  NSDate *todayDate = [NSDate date];

  NSDate *oneYearFromToday = [todayDate
                              dateByAddingTimeInterval:oneYearTime];
```

```
NSDate *twoYearsFromToday = [todayDate
                             dateByAddingTimeInterval:2 * oneYearTime];

self.myDatePicker.minimumDate = oneYearFromToday;
self.myDatePicker.maximumDate = twoYearsFromToday;
}
```

With these two properties, we can then limit the user's selection on the date to a specific range, as shown in Figure 2-18. In this example code, we have limited the user's input of dates to the range of a year to two years from now.

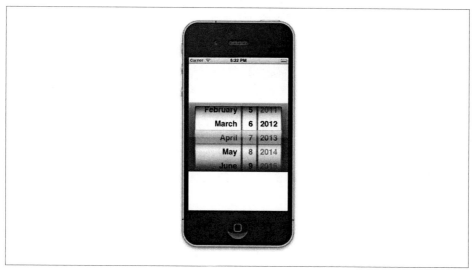

Figure 2-18. Minimum and maximum dates applied to a date picker

If you want to use the date picker as a countdown timer, you must set your date picker mode to UIDatePickerModeCountDownTimer and use the countDownDuration property of the date picker to specify the default countdown duration. For instance, if you want to present a countdown picker to the user and set the default countdown duration to two minutes, you would write your code like this:

```
- (void)viewDidLoad{
  [super viewDidLoad];
  self.view.backgroundColor = [UIColor whiteColor];
  self.myDatePicker = [[UIDatePicker alloc] init];
  self.myDatePicker.center = self.view.center;
  self.myDatePicker.datePickerMode = UIDatePickerModeCountDownTimer;
  [self.view addSubview:self.myDatePicker];

  NSTimeInterval twoMinutes = 2 * 60;
  [self.myDatePicker setCountDownDuration:twoMinutes];
}
```

The results are shown in Figure 2-19.

Figure 2-19. A two-minute countdown duration set on a date picker

2.6 Implementing Range Pickers with UISlider

Problem

You would like to allow your users to specify a value within a range, using an easy-to-use and intuitive UI.

Solution

Use the UISlider class.

Discussion

You've certainly seen sliders before. Figure 2-20 shows an example.

To create a slider, instantiate an object of type UISlider. Let's dive right in and create a slider and place it on our view controller's view. We'll start with our view controller's header file:

```
#import <UIKit/UIKit.h>

@interface Implementing_Range_Pickers_with_UISliderViewController
        : UIViewController

@property (nonatomic, strong) UISlider *mySlider;

@end
```

Figure 2-20. The volume slider at the bottom of the screen

And now let's go to the `viewDidLoad` method and create our slider component. In this code, we are going to give our slider a range between 0 to 100 and set its default position to be halfway between start and end.

 The range of a slider has *nothing* to do with its appearance. We use the range specifiers of a slider to tell the slider to calculate its value based on the relative position within the range. For instance, if the range of a slider is provided as 0 to 100, when the knob on the slider is on the leftmost part, the `value` property of the slider is 0, and if the knob is to the rightmost side of the slider, the `value` property would be 100.

```
- (void)viewDidLoad{
  [super viewDidLoad];
  self.view.backgroundColor = [UIColor whiteColor];
  self.mySlider = [[UISlider alloc] initWithFrame:CGRectMake(0.0f,
                                                             0.0f,
                                                             200.0f,
                                                             23.0f)];
  self.mySlider.center = self.view.center;
  self.mySlider.minimumValue = 0.0f;
  self.mySlider.maximumValue = 100.0f;
  self.mySlider.value = self.mySlider.maximumValue / 2.0;
  [self.view addSubview:self.mySlider];
}
```

What do the results look like? You can now run the app on the simulator and you'll get results like those shown in Figure 2-21.

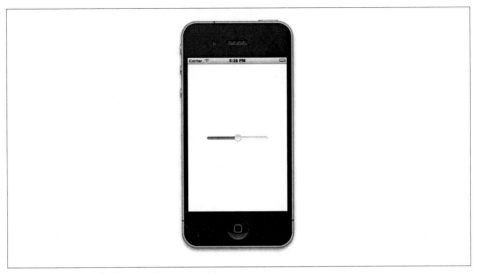

Figure 2-21. A simple slider at the center of the screen

We used a few properties of the slider to get the results we wanted. What were they?

minimumValue
> Specifies the minimum value of the range that the slider should support.

maximumValue
> Specifies the maximum value that the slider should support.

value
> The current value of the slider. This is a read/write property, meaning that you can both read from it and write to it. If you want the slider's knob to be moved to this value in an animated mode, you can call the setValue:animated: method of the slider and pass YES as the animated parameter.

 The little knob on a slider is called the *thumb*. We will soon see how we can customize the slider and I will be using the term *thumb* to describe the knob on the slider, so please keep that in mind.

If you wish to receive an event whenever the slider's thumb has moved, you must add your object as the target of the slider, using the slider's addTarget:action:forControl Events: method:

```
- (void) sliderValueChanged:(UISlider *)paramSender{

    if ([paramSender isEqual:self.mySlider]){
```

```
        NSLog(@"New value = %f", paramSender.value);
    }

}- (void)viewDidLoad{
    [super viewDidLoad];
    self.view.backgroundColor = [UIColor whiteColor];
    self.mySlider = [[UISlider alloc] initWithFrame:CGRectMake(0.0f,
                                                               0.0f,
                                                               200.0f,
                                                               23.0f)];
    self.mySlider.center = self.view.center;
    self.mySlider.minimumValue = 0.0f;
    self.mySlider.maximumValue = 100.0f;
    self.mySlider.value = self.mySlider.maximumValue / 2.0;
    [self.view addSubview:self.mySlider];

    [self.mySlider addTarget:self
                      action:@selector(sliderValueChanged:)
            forControlEvents:UIControlEventValueChanged];
}
```

If you run the application on the simulator now, you will notice that the sliderValue
Changed: target method gets called *whenever and as soon as* the slider's thumb moves.
This might be what you want, but in some cases, you might need to get notified only
after the user has let go of the thumb on the slider and let it settle. If you want to wait
to be notified, set the continuous property of the slider to NO. This property, when set
to YES (its default value), will call the slider's targets continuously *while* the thumb
moves.

The iOS SDK also gives us the ability to modify how a slider looks. For instance, the
thumb on the slider can have a different image. To change the image of the thumb,
simply use the setThumbImage:forState: method and pass an image along with a second
parameter that can take any of these values:

UIControlStateNormal
> The normal state of the thumb, with no user finger on this component.

UIControlStateHighlighted
> The image that has to be displayed for the thumb while the user is moving her
> finger on this component.

I have prepared two images: one for the normal state of the thumb and the other one
for the highlighted (touched) state of the thumb. Let's go ahead and add them to the
slider:

```
[self.mySlider setThumbImage:[UIImage imageNamed:@"ThumbNormal.png"]
                    forState:UIControlStateNormal];
[self.mySlider setThumbImage:[UIImage imageNamed:@"ThumbHighlighted.png"]
                    forState:UIControlStateHighlighted];
```

And now let's have a look and see how our normal thumb image looks in the simulator
(Figure 2-22).

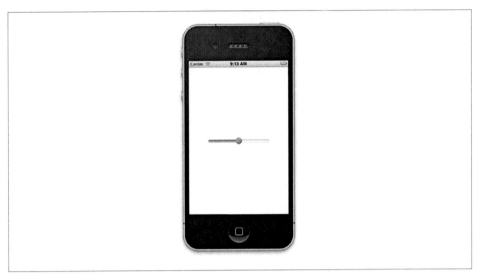

Figure 2-22. A slider with a custom thumb image

2.7 Customizing the UISlider

Problem

You are using the default appearance of the UISlider UI component and now you want to be able to customize this look and feel.

Solution

Either modify the tint colors of the different parts of the slider, or provide your own images for the parts.

Discussion

Apple has done a great job giving us methods to customize UI components in iOS 6 SDK. One customization is to modify the tint colors of various parts of the UI component. Let's take a simple UISlider as an example. I have broken it down into its different UI components in Figure 2-23.

A method and property exists for each of these components in UISlider that allow you to change the appearance of the slider. The easiest of these properties to use are the ones that modify the tint color of these components. The properties are:

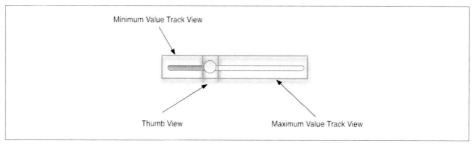

Figure 2-23. *Different components of a UISlider*

minimumTrackTintColor
> This property changes the tint color of the minimum value track view of the slider.

thumbTintColor
> This property, as its name shows, changes the tint color of the thumb view of the slider.

maximumTrackTintColor
> This property changes the tint color of the maximum value track view of the slider.

  All these properties are of type UIColor.

The following sample code instantiates a UISlider and places it at the center of the view of the view controller. It also sets the tint color of the minimum value tracking view of the slider to red, the tint color of the thumb view of the slider to black, and the tint color of the maximum value tracking view of the slider to green:

```
#import "ViewController.h"

@interface ViewController ()
@property (nonatomic, strong) UISlider *slider;
@end

@implementation ViewController

- (void)viewDidLoad{
    [super viewDidLoad];

    /* Create  the slider */
    self.slider = [[UISlider alloc] initWithFrame:CGRectMake(0.0f,
                                                             0.0f,
                                                             118.0f,
                                                             23.0f)];
    self.slider.value = 0.5;
    self.slider.minimumValue = 0.0f;
    self.slider.maximumValue = 1.0f;
```

```
        self.slider.center = self.view.center;
        [self.view addSubview:self.slider];

        /* Set the tint color of the minimum value */
        self.slider.minimumTrackTintColor = [UIColor redColor];

        /* Set the tint color of the thumb */
        self.slider.maximumTrackTintColor = [UIColor greenColor];

        /* Set the tint color of the maximum value */
        self.slider.thumbTintColor = [UIColor blackColor];

    }

    - (void)didReceiveMemoryWarning{
        [super didReceiveMemoryWarning];
    }

    @end
```

If you run the app now, you will see something similar to what is shown in Figure 2-24.

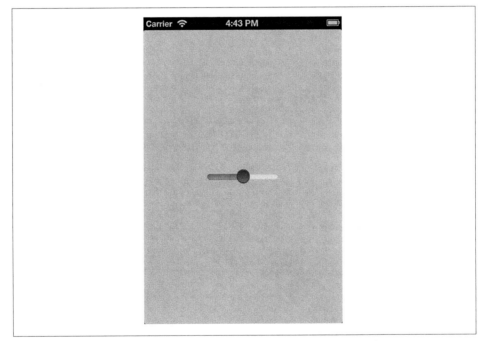

Figure 2-24. The tint color of all the different components of a slider are modified

Sometimes you may want to have more control over how a slider looks on the screen. For this, tint colors may not be sufficient. That's why Apple has provided other ways of modifying the look and feel of a slider, allowing you to provide images for different components in the slider. These images are:

Minimum value image

This is the image that will be displayed to the outer-left side of the slider. By default, no image is provided for the minimum value image, so you cannot really see this if you create a new slider on a view. You can use this image to give your users an indication of what the minimum value in your slider may mean in the context of your app. For instance, in an app where the user is allowed to increase or decrease the brightness of the screen, the minimum value image may display a dim lightbulb, suggesting to users that moving the thumb in the slider to the left (toward the minimum value) will reduce the brightness of the screen further. To change this image, use the `setMinimumValueImage:` instance method of the slider. The image needs to be 23 points wide and 23 points tall. Obviously, for retina displays, simply provide the same image but twice as big.

Minimum track image

This is the image that will be displayed for the track of the slider on the left side of the thumb. To change this image, use the `setMinimumTrackImage:forState:` instance method of the slider. The image needs to be 11 points wide and 9 points tall, and be constructed as a resizable image (see Recipe 17.5). Obviously, you need to provide a 46x46 image for retina displays.

Thumb image

The image for the thumb; the only moving component in the slider. To change this image, use the `setThumbImage:forState:` instance method of the slider. The image needs to be 23 points wide and 23 points tall.

Maximum track image

The image for the track of the slider to the right of the thumb. To change this image, use the `setMaximumTrackImage:forState:` instance method of the slider. The image needs to be 11 points wide and 9 points tall, and be constructed as a resizable image (see Recipe 17.5).

Maximum value image

The maximum value image is the image that gets displayed on the outer-right side of the slider. This is similar to the minimum value image, but of course depicts the maximum value of the slider instead. To continue the example that we read about for the minimum value image, the image for the maximum value can be a bright light with rays emitting from it, suggesting to the user that the further they move the slider to the right, the brighter the display gets. To change this image, use the `setMaximumValueImage:` instance method of the slider. The image needs to be 23 points wide and 23 points tall.

The images that you provide for the minimum and the maximum track need to be resizable. For more information about resizable images, see Recipe 17.5.

For the sake of this exercise, I have created five unique images for each one of the components of the slider. I've made sure that the minimum and the maximum track images are resizable images. What I am trying to achieve with the customization of this slider component is to make the user think that they are changing the temperature settings of a room, where moving the slider to the left means less heat and moving to the right means more heat. So here is the code that creates a slider and skins its various components:

```
#import "ViewController.h"

@interface ViewController ()
@property (nonatomic, strong) UISlider *slider;
@end

@implementation ViewController

/*
 This method returns a resizable image for the
 minimum track component of the slider
 */
- (UIImage *) minimumTrackImage{
    UIImage *result = [UIImage imageNamed:@"MinimumTrack"];
    UIEdgeInsets edgeInsets;
    edgeInsets.left = 4.0f;
    edgeInsets.top = 0.0f;
    edgeInsets.right = 0.0f;
    edgeInsets.bottom = 0.0f;
    result = [result resizableImageWithCapInsets:edgeInsets];
    return result;
}

/*
 Similar to the previous method, this one returns the resizable maximum
 track image for the slider
 */
- (UIImage *) maximumTrackImage{
    UIImage *result = [UIImage imageNamed:@"MaximumTrack"];
    UIEdgeInsets edgeInsets;
    edgeInsets.left = 0.0f;
    edgeInsets.top = 0.0f;
    edgeInsets.right = 3.0f;
    edgeInsets.bottom = 0.0f;
    result = [result resizableImageWithCapInsets:edgeInsets];
    return result;
}

- (void)viewDidLoad{
    [super viewDidLoad];

    /* Create  the slider */
    self.slider = [[UISlider alloc] initWithFrame:CGRectMake(0.0f,
                                                             0.0f,
                                                             218.0f,
                                                             23.0f)];
```

```
    self.slider.value = 0.5;
    self.slider.minimumValue = 0.0f;
    self.slider.maximumValue = 1.0f;
    self.slider.center = self.view.center;
    [self.view addSubview:self.slider];

    /* Change the minimum value image */
    [self.slider setMinimumValueImage:[UIImage imageNamed:@"MinimumValue"]];

    /* Change the minimum track image */
    [self.slider setMinimumTrackImage:[self minimumTrackImage]
                             forState:UIControlStateNormal];

    /* Change the thumb image for both untouched and touched states */
    [self.slider setThumbImage:[UIImage imageNamed:@"Thumb"]
                      forState:UIControlStateNormal];
    [self.slider setThumbImage:[UIImage imageNamed:@"Thumb"]
                      forState:UIControlStateHighlighted];

    /* Change the maximum track image */
    [self.slider setMaximumTrackImage:[self maximumTrackImage]
                             forState:UIControlStateNormal];

    /* Change the maximum value image */
    [self.slider setMaximumValueImage:[UIImage imageNamed:@"MaximumValue"]];

}

- (void)didReceiveMemoryWarning{
    [super didReceiveMemoryWarning];
}

@end
```

The results are shown in Figure 2-25.

See Also

Recipe 2.6

2.8 Grouping Compact Options with UISegmentedControl

Problem

You would like to present a few options to your users from which they can pick, through a UI that is compact, simple, and easy to understand.

Solution

Use the UISegmentedControl class, an example of which is shown in Figure 2-26.

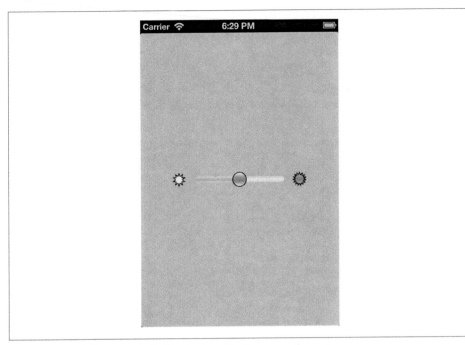

Figure 2-25. A fully customized slider is placed in the center of our view

Discussion

A segmented control is a UI component that allows you to display, in a compact UI, series of options for the user to choose from. To show a segmented control, create an instance of UISegmentedControl. Let's start with our view controller's *.h* file:

```
#import <UIKit/UIKit.h>

@interface Grouping_Compact_Options_with_UISegmentedControlViewController
            : UIViewController
@property (nonatomic, strong) UISegmentedControl *mySegmentedControl;

@end
```

And create the segmented control in the viewDidLoad method of your view controller:

```
- (void)viewDidLoad{
  [super viewDidLoad];
  self.view.backgroundColor = [UIColor whiteColor];
  NSArray *segments = [[NSArray alloc] initWithObjects:
                        @"iPhone",
                        @"iPad",
                        @"iPod",
                        @"iMac", nil];

  self.mySegmentedControl = [[UISegmentedControl alloc]
                             initWithItems:segments];
  self.mySegmentedControl.center = self.view.center;
```

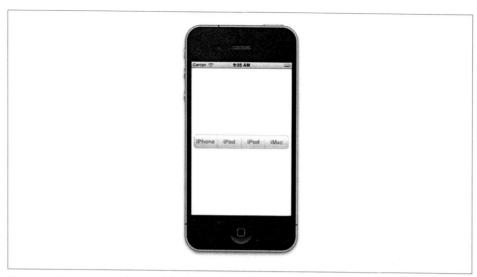

Figure 2-26. A segmented control displaying four options

```
[self.view addSubview:self.mySegmentedControl];

}
```

We are simply using an array of strings to provide the different options that our segmented control has to display. We initialize our segmented control using the `initWithObjects:` initializer and pass the array of strings and images to the segmented control. The results will look like what we saw in Figure 2-26.

Now the user can pick *one* of the options in the segmented control. Let's say she has picked *iPad*. The segmented control will then change its user interface to show the user what option she has selected, as depicted in Figure 2-27.

Now the question is, how do you recognize when the user selects a new option in a segmented control? The answer is simple. Just as with a `UISwitch` or a `UISlider`, use the `addTarget:action:forControlEvents:` method of the segmented control to add a target to it. Provide the value of `UIControlEventValueChanged` for the `forControlEvents` parameter, because that is the event that gets fired when the user selects a new option in a segmented control:

```
- (void) segmentChanged:(UISegmentedControl *)paramSender{
  if ([paramSender isEqual:self.mySegmentedControl]){
    NSInteger selectedSegmentIndex = [paramSender selectedSegmentIndex];

    NSString  *selectedSegmentText =
      [paramSender titleForSegmentAtIndex:selectedSegmentIndex];

    NSLog(@"Segment %ld with %@ text is selected",
          (long)selectedSegmentIndex,
          selectedSegmentText);
```

Figure 2-27. User has selected one of the items in a segmented control

```
    }
}

- (void)viewDidLoad{
    [super viewDidLoad];
        self.view.backgroundColor = [UIColor whiteColor];
    NSArray *segments = [[NSArray alloc] initWithObjects:
                            @"iPhone",
                            @"iPad",
                            @"iPod",
                            @"iMac", nil];

    self.mySegmentedControl = [[UISegmentedControl alloc]
                            initWithItems:segments];
    self.mySegmentedControl.center = self.view.center;
    [self.view addSubview:self.mySegmentedControl];

    [self.mySegmentedControl addTarget:self
                            action:@selector(segmentChanged:)
                  forControlEvents:UIControlEventValueChanged];
}
```

If the user starts from the left side and selects each of the options in Figure 2-26, all the way to the right side of the control, the following text will print out to the console:

```
Segment 0 with iPhone text is selected
Segment 1 with iPad text is selected
Segment 2 with iPod text is selected
Segment 3 with iMac text is selected
```

As you can see, we used the `selectedSegmentIndex` method of the segmented control to find the index of the currently selected item. If no item is selected, this method returns the value −1. We also used the `titleForSegmentAtIndex:` method. Simply pass the index of an option in the segmented control to this method, and the segmented control will return the text for that item. Simple, isn't it?

As you might have noticed, once the user selects an option in a segmented control, that option will get selected and will *remain* selected, as shown in Figure 2-27. If you want the user to be able to select an option but you would like the button for that option to bounce back to its original shape once it has been selected (just like a normal button that bounces back up once it is tapped), you need to set the `momentary` property of the segmented control to `YES`:

```
self.mySegmentedControl.momentary = YES;
```

One of the really neat features of segmented controls is that they can contain images instead of text. To do this, simply use the `initWithObjects:` initializer method of the `UISegmentedControl` class and pass the strings and images that will be used to initialize the segmented UI control:

```
- (void)viewDidLoad{
  [super viewDidLoad];
  self.view.backgroundColor = [UIColor whiteColor];
  NSArray *segments = [[NSArray alloc] initWithObjects:
                        @"iPhone",
                        [UIImage imageNamed:@"iPad.png"],
                        @"iPod",
                        @"iMac", nil];

  self.mySegmentedControl = [[UISegmentedControl alloc]
                              initWithItems:segments];

  CGRect segmentedFrame = self.mySegmentedControl.frame;
  segmentedFrame.size.height = 64.0f;
  segmentedFrame.size.width = 300.0f;
  self.mySegmentedControl.frame = segmentedFrame;

  self.mySegmentedControl.center = self.view.center;

  [self.view addSubview:self.mySegmentedControl];
}
```

 In this example, the *iPad.png* file is simply an image of an iPad, with a resolution of 36×47 pixels.

The results are shown in Figure 2-28.

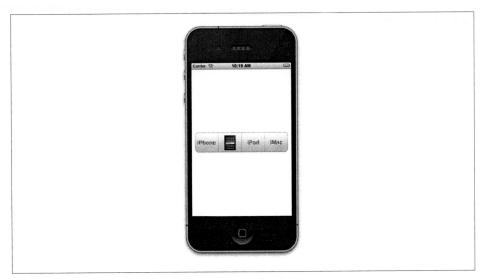

Figure 2-28. A segmented control with an option displayed as an image

One of the features of segmented controls is that we can select their style using the segmentedControlStyle property. This property is of type UISegmentedControlStyle:

```
typedef enum {
  UISegmentedControlStylePlain,
  UISegmentedControlStyleBordered,
  UISegmentedControlStyleBar,
  UISegmentedControlStyleBezeled,
} UISegmentedControlStyle;
```

The default style of a segmented control is UISegmentedControlStylePlain. You can change the style of your segmented controls to any of the values listed in the UISegmentedControlStyle enumeration. Figure 2-29 is an example of a bezeled segmented control.

2.9 Customizing the UISegmentedControl

Problem

You have already placed a segmented control or two on your UI, and now want to be able to customize them to match your UI's theme.

Solution

Either apply tint color to the segmented control or create your own images and apply them to this component.

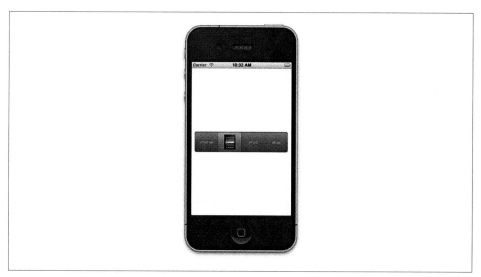

Figure 2-29. A bezeled segmented control

Discussion

Tint colors are the easiest way of applying new colors to your UI components. The
UISegmentedControl class has a property named tintColor that you can utilize to change
the tint color of your segmented control. There is one important thing that you have
to bear in mind before attempting to change the value of the aforementioned property:
the style of your segmented control has to be set to UISegmentedControlStyleBar. You
can change the style of your segmented control by changing the value of the segmented
ControlStyle property of your control. Here is an example:

```objc
#import "ViewController.h"

@interface ViewController ()
@property (nonatomic, strong) UISegmentedControl *segmentedControl;
@end

@implementation ViewController

- (void)viewDidLoad{
    [super viewDidLoad];

    NSArray *items = @[@"Item 1", @"Item 2", @"Item 3"];
    self.segmentedControl = [[UISegmentedControl alloc] initWithItems:items];
    /* We have to do this if we want to change the tint color */
    self.segmentedControl.segmentedControlStyle = UISegmentedControlStyleBar;
    [self.view addSubview:self.segmentedControl];
    self.segmentedControl.center = CGPointMake(self.view.center.x + 25.0f,
                                               self.view.center.y);

    /* Change the tint color now */
    self.segmentedControl.tintColor = [UIColor blueColor];
```

```
}

- (void)didReceiveMemoryWarning{
    [super didReceiveMemoryWarning];
}

@end
```

And the output of this program is shown in Figure 2-30.

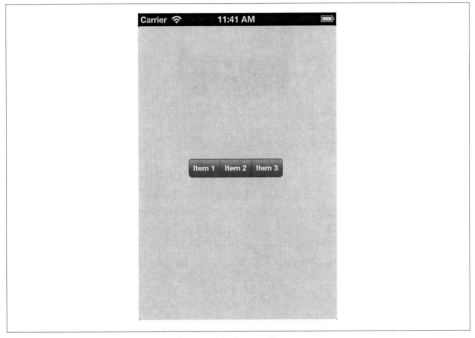

Figure 2-30. A segmented control with a modified tint color

Even though changing the tint color of the segmented control gives you some control over how you customize its appearance, some may say that is not enough. For this reason, you can also set custom images for different components of the segmented control through the following methods:

setBackgroundImage:forState:barMetrics:
    This method can set the background images of the segmented control. The for State parameter defines which state of the component should have the background image you specify. There are two states: selected (after the user has pressed that item down) and unselected (the initial state, when the user has not selected the control yet). Pass UIControlStateNormal to change the unselected mode and UICon trolStateSelected to change the selected mode.

```
setDividerImage:forLeftSegmentState:rightSegmentState:barMetrics:
```
This method can set the image of the divider that is visible between the different items in the segmented control. You have to provide three images for the divider:

- Divider that sits between two unselected segmented items.
- Divider that sits between a selected (on the left) and an unselected (on the right) item.
- Divider that sits between an unselected (on the left) and a selected (on the right) item.

I have created all these images in retina and non-retina modes for the project that I am going to demonstrate to you right now. Let's take it one step at a time. Since we need three divider images, it's best to create some sort of convenient methods to create the images for the three states for us. I have created an enumeration of strings that list the image names that a method can use for the divider images. Here is the top of the implementation of our view controller:

```
#import "ViewController.h"

@interface ViewController ()
@property (nonatomic, strong) UISegmentedControl *segmentedControl;
@end

NSString *const DividerImageTypeUnselectedUnselected = @"Unselected-Unselected";
NSString *const DividerImageTypeSelectedUnselected =  @"Selected-Unselected";
NSString *const DividerImageTypeUnselectedSelected =  @"Unselected-Selected";
typedef NSString *DividerImageType;

@implementation ViewController
```

Since the selected/unselected background images are similar in size and differ only in filenames, it's best to create just one method that can return one of these images to us, choosing the image based on a parameter that can take a Boolean value indicating whether an item was selected or unselected. Also, we have three divider images, which can all be returned by a single method. We will pass one of the previously defined DividerImageType strings to this method as a parameter. And since these image types are defined as strings containing the actual filenames, the method can consume the filenames and create images from the filenames, like so:

```
- (UIImage *) segmentImageInSelectedMode:(BOOL)paramInSelectedMode{

    UIImage *result;
    if (paramInSelectedMode){
        result = [UIImage imageNamed:@"Selected"];
    } else {
        result = [UIImage imageNamed:@"Unselected"];
    }
    UIEdgeInsets edgeInsets;
    edgeInsets.left = 8.0f;
    edgeInsets.top = 0.0f;
    edgeInsets.right = 8.0f;
```

```
        edgeInsets.bottom = 0.0f;
        result = [result resizableImageWithCapInsets:edgeInsets];
        return result;

    }

    - (UIImage *) dividerImageOfType:(DividerImageType)paramType{

        UIImage *result = [UIImage imageNamed:paramType];
        UIEdgeInsets edgeInsets;
        edgeInsets.left = 25.0f;
        edgeInsets.top = 0.0f;
        edgeInsets.right = 25.0f;
        edgeInsets.bottom = 0.0f;
        result = [result resizableImageWithCapInsets:edgeInsets];
        return result;

    }
```

Now we will just utilize these methods to get our images:

```
    - (UIImage *) normalImage{
        return [self segmentImageInSelectedMode:NO];
    }

    - (UIImage *) selectedImage{
        return [self segmentImageInSelectedMode:YES];
    }

    - (UIImage *) dividerUnselectedUnselected{
        return [self dividerImageOfType:DividerImageTypeUnselectedUnselected];
    }

    - (UIImage *) dividerSelectedUnselected{
        return [self dividerImageOfType:DividerImageTypeSelectedUnselected];
    }

    - (UIImage *) dividerUnselectedSelected{
        return [self dividerImageOfType:DividerImageTypeUnselectedSelected];
    }
```

Using these methods that we just wrote, we will now write other methods that will change the background and divider images of our segmented control. We will use the following methods in the viewDidLoad method of our view controller:

```
    - (void) setBackgroundImages{
        [self.segmentedControl setBackgroundImage:[self normalImage]
                                forState:UIControlStateNormal
                                barMetrics:UIBarMetricsDefault];

        [self.segmentedControl setBackgroundImage:[self selectedImage]
                                forState:UIControlStateSelected
                                barMetrics:UIBarMetricsDefault];
    }
```

```
- (void) setDividerImages{
    [self.segmentedControl setDividerImage:[self dividerUnselectedUnselected]
                       forLeftSegmentState:UIControlStateNormal
                         rightSegmentState:UIControlStateNormal
                                barMetrics:UIBarMetricsDefault];

    [self.segmentedControl setDividerImage:[self dividerSelectedUnselected]
                       forLeftSegmentState:UIControlStateSelected
                         rightSegmentState:UIControlStateNormal
                                barMetrics:UIBarMetricsDefault];

    [self.segmentedControl setDividerImage:[self dividerUnselectedSelected]
                       forLeftSegmentState:UIControlStateNormal
                         rightSegmentState:UIControlStateSelected
                                barMetrics:UIBarMetricsDefault];
}
```

And here is our viewDidLoad method:

```
- (void)viewDidLoad{
    [super viewDidLoad];

    NSArray *items = @[@"Item 1", @"Item 2", @"Item 3"];
    self.segmentedControl = [[UISegmentedControl alloc] initWithItems:items];
    [self.view addSubview:self.segmentedControl];
    self.segmentedControl.center = CGPointMake(self.view.center.x - 50.0f,
                                               self.view.center.y);


    [self setBackgroundImages];
    [self setDividerImages];

    /* Make sure in the normal state of the control that the text is light
     gray color and there is no shadow for the font */
    [self.segmentedControl
     setTitleTextAttributes:
     @{
     UITextAttributeTextColor:[UIColor lightGrayColor],
     UITextAttributeTextShadowColor: [UIColor clearColor],
     }
     forState:UIControlStateNormal];


    /* In the selected state of the segmented control, make sure the text
     is rendered in white */
    [self.segmentedControl
     setTitleTextAttributes:@{UITextAttributeTextColor:[UIColor whiteColor]}
     forState:UIControlStateSelected];

}

- (void)didReceiveMemoryWarning{
    [super didReceiveMemoryWarning];
}

@end
```

In this method, we are doing the following:

1. Instantiating the segmented control.
2. Setting the background images of selected/unselected modes.
3. Setting the divider images.
4. Changing the font color and the shadow settings of the font in unselected mode of the segmented control.
5. Changing the font color of the segmented control in selected mode.

Figure 2-31 shows how our segmented control will look once rendered on the screen.

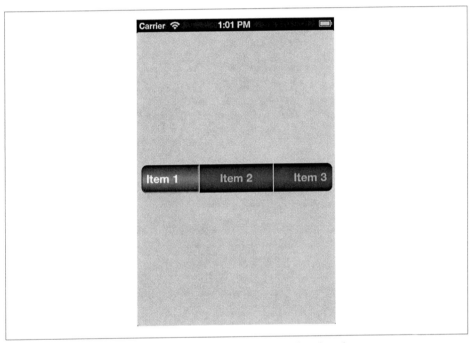

Figure 2-31. The finished customized segmented control is displayed on the screen

See Also

Recipe 2.8

2.10 Presenting and Managing Views with UIViewController

Problem

You want to switch between different views in your application.

Solution

Use the `UIViewController` class.

Discussion

Apple's strategy for iOS development was to use the Model-View-Controller (MVC) division of labor. Views are what get displayed to users, while the model is the data that the app manages, or the engine of the app. The controller is the bridge between the model and the view. The controller, or in this case, view controller, manages the relationship between the view and the model. Why doesn't the view do that instead? Well, the answer is quite simple: the view's code would get messy and that design choice would tightly couple our views with the model, which is not a good practice.

 Before running this recipe, you need to have an Xcode project already created. Follow the instructions in Recipe 1.1, but instead of a Pages-Based Application, create an Empty Application.

View controllers can be loaded from *.xib* files (for use with Interface Builder), or simply be created programmatically. We will first have a look at creating a view controller *without* a *.xib* file.

Xcode helps us create view controllers. Now that you have created an application using the Empty Application template in Xcode, follow these steps to create a new view controller for your app:

1. In Xcode, select the File menu and then choose New → New File...

2. In the New File dialog, make sure iOS is the selected category on the left and that Cocoa Touch is the chosen subcategory. Once you've done that, select the `UIView Controller` subclass from the righthand side of the dialog and then press Next, as shown in Figure 2-32.

3. In the next screen, make sure that the Subclass of text field says `UIView Controller` and also make sure that neither the "Targeted for iPad" nor "With XIB for user interface" checkboxes are selected, as shown in Figure 2-33. Press Next.

4. On the next screen (Save As), give your view controller's file the name of *Root-ViewController* and press the Save button, as shown in Figure 2-34.

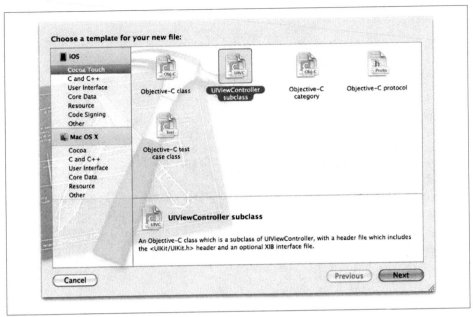

Figure 2-32. New view controller subclass

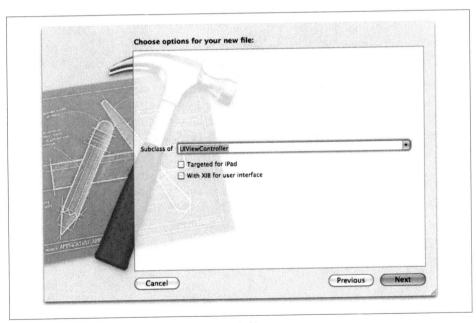

Figure 2-33. A custom view controller with no .xib file

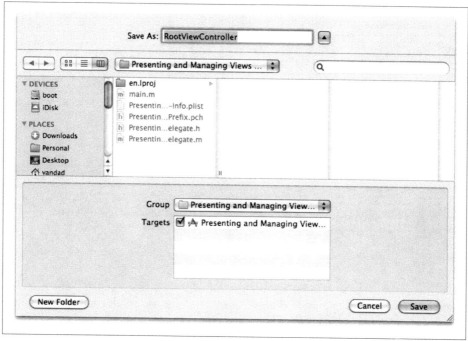

Figure 2-34. Saving a view controller without an xib file

5. Now find your application delegate's *.h* file. I have named my project *Presenting and Managing Views with UIViewController* and because of this, my application delegate's class is called `Presenting_and_Managing_Views_with_UIViewController AppDelegate`. The *.h* file of my app delegate is therefore *Presenting_and_Managing_Views_with_UIViewControllerAppDelegate.h*. In this file, declare a property of type `RootViewController`:

```
#import <UIKit/UIKit.h>

@class RootViewController;

@interface Presenting_and_Managing_Views_with_UIViewControllerAppDelegate :
        UIResponder <UIApplicationDelegate>

@property (nonatomic, strong) UIWindow *window;
@property (nonatomic, strong) RootViewController *rootViewController;

@end
```

6. Now find the `application:didFinishLaunchingWithOptions:` method of the app delegate inside the implementation (*.m*) file, and instantiate the view controller and add it to your window:

```
- (BOOL)          application:(UIApplication *)application
  didFinishLaunchingWithOptions:(NSDictionary *)launchOptions{
```

```
self.window = [[UIWindow alloc]
                initWithFrame:[[UIScreen mainScreen] bounds]];

[self.window makeKeyAndVisible];

self.rootViewController = [[RootViewController alloc]
                            initWithNibName:nil
                            bundle:NULL];
[self.window addSubview:self.rootViewController.view];

return YES;

}
```

 We add the *view of the view controller* to the window, *not* the view
controller itself.

Now if you run your app on the simulator, you will see a black screen. The reason is
that our view controller's view doesn't have a background color yet. So go to the
RootViewController.m file and find the `viewDidLoad` method, which is in a state similar
to this:

```
/*
- (void)viewDidLoad
{
  [super viewDidLoad];
}
*/
```

Remove the comment lines from around this method:

```
- (void)viewDidLoad{
  [super viewDidLoad];
}
```

Now let's set the background color of our view controller's view to white:

```
- (void)viewDidLoad{
  [super viewDidLoad];

  self.view.backgroundColor = [UIColor whiteColor];

}
```

Go ahead and run the app on the simulator. You will now see a plain white view on
the screen. Congratulations! You just created a view controller and now you have access
to the view controller and its view object.

While creating the view controller (Figure 2-33), if you had selected the "With XIB for
user interface" checkbox, Xcode would have also generated a *.xib* file for you. In that

case, you would have to load your view controller *from* that *.xib* file by passing the *.xib* file's full name to the `initWithNibName` parameter of the `initWithNibName:bun dle:` method of the view controller, like so:

```
- (BOOL)              application:(UIApplication *)application
   didFinishLaunchingWithOptions:(NSDictionary *)launchOptions{

   self.window = [[UIWindow alloc]
                   initWithFrame:[[UIScreen mainScreen] bounds]];

   [self.window makeKeyAndVisible];

   self.rootViewController = [[RootViewController alloc]
                               initWithNibName:@"RootViewController"
                               bundle:NULL];
   [self.window addSubview:self.rootViewController.view];

   return YES;

}
```

If you *did* create a *.xib* file while creating your view controller, you can now select that file in Xcode and design your user interface with Interface Builder.

See Also

Recipe 1.1

2.11 Presenting Sharing Options with UIActivityViewController

Problem

You want to be able to allow your users to share content inside your apps with their friends, through an interface similar to that shown in Figure 2-35, using different sharing options available in iOS, such as Facebook and Twitter.

Solution

Create an instance of the `UIActivityViewController` class and share your content through this class, as we will see in the Discussion section of this recipe.

 The instances of `UIActivityViewController` must be presented modally on the iPhone and inside a popover on an iPad. For more information about popovers, refer to Recipe 2.27.

Figure 2-35. The activity view controller displayed on an iOS device

Discussion

There are many sharing options inside iOS 6, and all are built into the core of the OS. For instance, Facebook and Twitter integration is now an integral part of the core of iOS and you can share pretty much any content from anywhere you want. Third-party apps like ours can also use all the sharing functionalities available in iOS without having to think about the low-level details of these services and how iOS provides these sharing options. The beauty of this whole thing is that you mention *what* you want to share and iOS will pick the sharing options that are capable of handling the items that you want to share. For instance, if you want to share images and text, iOS will display many more items to you than if you want to share an audio file.

Sharing data is very easy in iOS. All you have to do is instantiate the UIActivityView Controller class using its initWithActivityItems:applicationActivities: initializer. The parameters to this method are:

initWithActivityItems
> The array of items that you want to share. These can be instances of NSString, UIImage, or instances of any of your custom classes that conform to the UIActivi tyItemSource protocol. We will talk about this protocol later in detail.

applicationActivities
> This is an array of instances of UIActivity that represent the activities that your own application supports. For instance, you can indicate here whether your ap-

plication can handle its own sharing of images and strings. We will not go into detail about this parameter and will simply pass nil as its value, telling iOS that we want to stick to the system sharing options.

So let's say that you have a text field where the user can enter text to be shared, and a Share button right near it. When the user presses the Share button, you will simply pass the text of the text field to your instance of the UIActivityViewController class. Here is our code now. We are writing this code for iPhone, so we will present our activity view controller as a modal view controller:

 Now let's discuss what to do if you want sharing options to be displayed as soon as your view controller is displayed on the screen. The viewDi dAppear method of your view controller will be called when the view of your view controller is displayed on the screen and is guaranteed to be in the view hierarchy of your app, meaning that you can now display other views on top of your view controller's view. Do not attempt to present the activity view controller in the viewDidLoad method of your view controller. At that stage in the app, your view controller's view is still not attached to the view hierarchy of the application, so attempting to present a view controller on the view will not work. Your view must be present in the hierarchy of the views for your modal views to work. For this reason, you need to present the sharing view controller in the viewDidAppear method of your view controller.

Since we are putting a text field on our view controller, we need to make sure that we are handling its delegate messages, especially the textFieldShouldReturn: method of the UITextFieldDelegate protocol. Therefore, we are going to elect our view controller as the delegate of the text field. Also, we are going to attach an action method to our Share button. Once the button is tapped, we want to make sure there is something in the text field to share. If there isn't, we will simply display an alert to the user telling them why we cannot share the content of the text field. If there is some text in the text field, we will pop up an instance of the UIActivityViewController class. So let's begin with the header file of our view controller:

```
#import <UIKit/UIKit.h>

@interface ViewController : UIViewController <UITextFieldDelegate>

@end
```

The next thing is to go to the implementation file of our view controller and define our UI components:

```
#import "ViewController.h"

@interface ViewController ()
@property (nonatomic, strong) UITextField *textField;
@property (nonatomic, strong) UIButton *buttonShare;
```

```
@property (nonatomic, strong) UIActivityViewController *activityViewController;
@end

@implementation ViewController

...
```

After this, we will simply write two methods for our view controller, each of which is able to create one of our UI components and place it on our view controller's view. One will create the text field, and the other will create the button next to it:

```
- (void) createTextField{
    self.textField = [[UITextField alloc] initWithFrame:CGRectMake(20.0f,
                                                                    35.0f,
                                                                    280.0f,
                                                                    30.0f)];
    self.textField.translatesAutoresizingMaskIntoConstraints = NO;
    self.textField.borderStyle = UITextBorderStyleRoundedRect;
    self.textField.placeholder = @"Enter text to share...";
    self.textField.delegate = self;
    [self.view addSubview:self.textField];
}

- (void) createButton{
    self.buttonShare = [UIButton buttonWithType:UIButtonTypeRoundedRect];
    self.buttonShare.translatesAutoresizingMaskIntoConstraints = NO;
    self.buttonShare.frame = CGRectMake(20.0f, 80.0f, 280.0f, 44.0f);
    [self.buttonShare setTitle:@"Share" forState:UIControlStateNormal];

    [self.buttonShare addTarget:self
                         action:@selector(handleShare:)
               forControlEvents:UIControlEventTouchUpInside];

    [self.view addSubview:self.buttonShare];
}
```

Once we are done with that, we just have to call these two methods in the viewDid Load method of our view controller. This will allow the UI components to be placed on the view of our view controller:

```
- (void)viewDidLoad{

    [super viewDidLoad];
    [self createTextField];
    [self createButton];

}

- (void)didReceiveMemoryWarning{
    [super didReceiveMemoryWarning];
}
```

In the textFieldShouldReturn:, all we do is dismiss the keyboard in order to resign the text field's active state. This simply means that when a user has been editing the text field and then presses the Return/Enter button on the keyboard, the keyboard should be dismissed. Bear in mind that the `createTextField` method that we just coded has set our view controller as the delegate of the text field. So we have to implement the afore-mentioned method as follows:

```
- (BOOL) textFieldShouldReturn:(UITextField *)textField{
    [textField resignFirstResponder];
    return YES;
}
```

Last but not least is the handler method of our button. As you saw, the `createButton` method creates the button for us and elects the `handleShare:` method to handle the touch down inside action of the button. So let's code this method:

```
- (void) handleShare:(id)paramSender{

    if ([self.textField.text length] == 0){
        NSString *message = @"Please enter a text and then press Share";
        UIAlertView *alertView = [[UIAlertView alloc] initWithTitle:nil
                                                           message:message
                                                          delegate:nil
                                                 cancelButtonTitle:@"OK"
                                                 otherButtonTitles:nil];
        [alertView show];
        return;
    }

    self.activityViewController = [[UIActivityViewController alloc]
                        initWithActivityItems:@[self.textField.text]
                          applicationActivities:nil];
    [self presentViewController:self.activityViewController
                       animated:YES
                     completion:^{
                        /* Nothing for now */
                     }];

}
```

Now if you run the app, enter some text in the text field, and then press the Share button, you will see something similar to Figure 2-36.

See Also

Recipe 2.27

2.12 Implementing Navigation with UINavigationController

Problem

You would like to allow your users to move from one view controller to the other with a smooth and built-in animation.

Figure 2-36. Sharing options displayed for the instance of string that we are trying to share

Solution

Use a `UINavigationController` widget.

Discussion

If you've used an iPhone, iPod touch, or iPad before, chances are that you have already seen a navigation controller in action. For instance, if you go to the Settings app on your phone and then press an option such as Wallpaper (Figure 2-37), you will see the Settings' main screen get pulled out of the screen from the left and the Wallpaper screen pushing its way into the screen from the right. That is the magic of navigation controllers. They allow you to *push* view controllers onto a stack and *pop* them from the stack. The view controller on top of the stack is the top view controller and is the one seen by the user at that moment. So only the top view controller gets displayed to the user, and is changed either by popping (removing) it or by pushing another view controller onto the stack.

Now we are going to add a navigation controller to our project, but we need a project first. Please follow the instructions in Recipe 2.10 to create an empty application with a simple view controller. In this recipe, we will expand on Recipe 2.10. Let's start with the *.h* file of our app delegate:

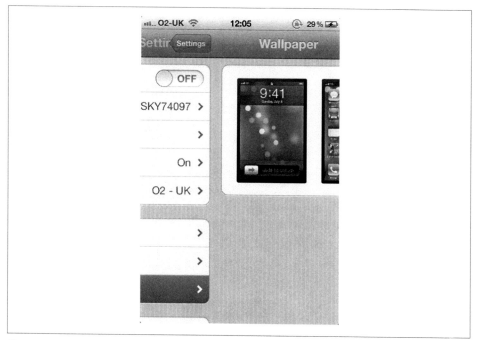

Figure 2-37. Settings view controller pushing the Wallpaper view controller

```
#import <UIKit/UIKit.h>

@class RootViewController;

@interface Implementing_Navigation_with_UINavigationControllerAppDelegate
        : UIResponder <UIApplicationDelegate>

@property (nonatomic, strong) UIWindow *window;
@property (nonatomic, strong) UINavigationController *navigationController;
@property (nonatomic, strong) RootViewController *rootViewController;

@end
```

Now we have to initialize our navigation controller using its `initWithRootViewControl ler:` method and pass our root view controller as its parameter. Then we will add the navigation controller's view to the window:

```
- (BOOL)              application:(UIApplication *)application
  didFinishLaunchingWithOptions:(NSDictionary *)launchOptions{

    self.window = [[UIWindow alloc]
                initWithFrame:[[UIScreen mainScreen] bounds]];

    [self.window makeKeyAndVisible];

    self.rootViewController = [[RootViewController alloc]
                        initWithNibName:nil
```

```
                    bundle:NULL];

    self.navigationController =
    [[UINavigationController alloc]
     initWithRootViewController:self.rootViewController];

    [self.window addSubview:self.navigationController.view];

    return YES;
}
```

Now let's run our app in the simulator, as shown in Figure 2-38.

The first thing you might notice in Figure 2-38 is the bar on top of the screen. The screen isn't plain white anymore. What's the new widget? A navigation bar. We will be using that bar a lot for navigation, placing buttons there, and so forth. That bar is also capable of displaying a title. Each view controller specifies a title for itself, and the navigation controller will automatically display that title once the view controller is pushed into the stack.

Figure 2-38. An empty view controller displayed inside a navigation controller

Let's go to our root view controller's implementation file, inside the viewDidLoad method, and set the title property of our view controller to *First Controller*:

```
- (void)viewDidLoad{
    [super viewDidLoad];
    self.view.backgroundColor = [UIColor whiteColor];
    self.title = @"First Controller";
}
```

Run the app again and you will see something similar to that shown in Figure 2-39.

Figure 2-39. A view controller with title

Now let's go and create a second view controller, *without* a *.xib* file, and call it *Second ViewController*. Follow the same process that you learned in Recipe 2.10. Once you are done creating this view controller, give it a title of *Second Controller*.

```
#import "SecondViewController.h"

@implementation SecondViewController

- (void)viewDidLoad{
  [super viewDidLoad];
  self.view.backgroundColor = [UIColor whiteColor];
  self.title = @"Second Controller";
}

...
```

Our plan is to *push* the second view controller on top of the first view controller five seconds after the first view controller appears on the screen. So let's first import the second view controller into the first one:

```
#import "RootViewController.h"
#import "SecondViewController.h"

@implementation RootViewController

...
```

Now go back to the implementation of the root view controller and code the view DidAppear: method like this:

```
- (void) pushSecondController{
  SecondViewController *secondController = [[SecondViewController alloc]
```

```
                                    initWithNibName:nil
                                    bundle:NULL];
    [self.navigationController pushViewController:secondController
                                    animated:YES];
}

- (void) viewDidAppear:(BOOL)paramAnimated{
    [super viewDidAppear:paramAnimated];
    [self performSelector:@selector(pushSecondController)
              withObject:nil
              afterDelay:5.0f];
}
```

We are using the performSelector:withObject:afterDelay: method of NSObject to call our new method, pushSecondController, five seconds after our first view controller successfully displays its view. In the pushSecondController method, we are simply using the navigationController property of our view controller (this is built into UIView Controller and is *not* something that we coded) to push an instance of SecondView Controller into the stack of view controllers. The result is similar to what you can see in Figure 2-40.

Figure 2-40. A view controller is pushed on top of another one

You can see that the navigation bar is displaying the title of the top view controller and even sports a back button that will take the user back to the previous view controller. You can push as many view controllers as you like into the stack and the navigation controller will work the navigation bar to display the relevant back buttons that allow the user to back through your application's UI, all the way to the first screen.

We learned about pushing a view controller. How about popping or removing a view controller from the stack of the navigation controller? The answer is straightforward:

using the `popViewControllerAnimated:` method of the navigation controller. Let's make our second view controller pop itself off of the stack automatically five seconds after it is displayed on the screen:

```
- (void) goBack{
  [self.navigationController popViewControllerAnimated:YES];
}- (void) viewDidAppear:(BOOL)paramAnimated{
  [super viewDidAppear:paramAnimated];
  [self performSelector:@selector(goBack)
            withObject:nil
            afterDelay:5.0f];
}
```

So if you open the app in the simulator now and wait five seconds after the first view controller is displayed, you will see that the second view controller will automatically get displayed on the screen. Wait another five seconds now and the second view controller will automatically go back to the first view controller.

See Also

Recipe 2.10

2.13 Manipulating a Navigation Controller's Array of View Controllers

Problem

You would like to directly manipulate the array of view controllers associated with a specific navigation controller.

Solution

Use the `viewControllers` property of the `UINavigationController` class to access and modify the array of view controllers associated with a navigation controller:

```
- (void) goBack{
  /* Get the current array of View Controllers */
  NSArray *currentControllers = self.navigationController.viewControllers;

  /* Create a mutable array out of this array */
  NSMutableArray *newControllers = [NSMutableArray
                            arrayWithArray:currentControllers];

  /* Remove the last object from the array */
  [newControllers removeLastObject];

  /* Assign this array to the Navigation Controller */
  self.navigationController.viewControllers = newControllers
}
```

You can call this method inside any view controller in order to pop the last view controller from the hierarchy of the navigation controller associated with the current view controller.

Discussion

An instance of the `UINavigationController` class holds an array of `UIViewController` objects. After retrieving this array, you can manipulate it in any way you wish. For instance, you can remove a view controller from an arbitrary place in the array.

Manipulating the view controllers of a navigation controller directly by assigning an array to the `viewControllers` property of the navigation controller will commit the operation without a transition/animation. If you wish this operation to be animated, use the `setViewControllers:animated:` method of the `UINavigationController` class, as shown in the following snippet:

```
- (void) goBack{
  /* Get the current array of View Controllers */
  NSArray *currentControllers = self.navigationController.viewControllers;

  /* Create a mutable array out of this array */
  NSMutableArray *newControllers = [NSMutableArray
                            arrayWithArray:currentControllers];

  /* Remove the last object from the array */
  [newControllers removeLastObject];

  /* Assign this array to the Navigation Controller with animation */
  [self.navigationController setViewControllers:newControllers
                                animated:YES];

}
```

2.14 Displaying an Image on a Navigation Bar

Problem

You want to display an image instead of text as the title of the current view controller on the navigation controller.

Solution

Use the `titleView` property of the view controller's navigation item:

```
- (void)viewDidLoad{
  [super viewDidLoad];
  self.view.backgroundColor = [UIColor whiteColor];

  /* Create an Image View to replace the Title View */
  UIImageView *imageView =
  [[UIImageView alloc]
   initWithFrame:CGRectMake(0.0f, 0.0f, 100.0f, 40.0f)];
```

```
imageView.contentMode = UIViewContentModeScaleAspectFit;

/* Load an image. Be careful, this image will be cached */
UIImage *image = [UIImage imageNamed:@"FullSizeLogo.png"];

/* Set the image of the Image View */
[imageView setImage:image];

/* Set the Title View */
self.navigationItem.titleView = imageView;

}
```

 The preceding code must be executed in a view controller that is placed inside a navigation controller.

Discussion

The navigation item of every view controller can display two different types of content in the title area of the view controller to which it is assigned:

- Simple text
- A view

If you want to use text, you can use the `title` property of the navigation item. However, if you want more control over the title or if you simply want to display an image or any other view up on the navigation bar, you can use the `titleView` property of the navigation item of a view controller. You can assign any object that is a subclass of the `UIView` class. In our example, we created an image view and assigned an image to it. Then we displayed it as the title of the current view controller on the navigation controller.

2.15 Adding Buttons to Navigation Bars Using UIBarButtonItem

Problem

You want to add buttons to a navigation bar.

Solution

Use the `UIBarButtonItem` class.

Discussion

A navigation bar can contain different items. Buttons are often displayed on the left and the right sides. These buttons are of class `UIBarButtonItem` and can take many different shapes and forms. Let's have a look at an example in Figure 2-41.

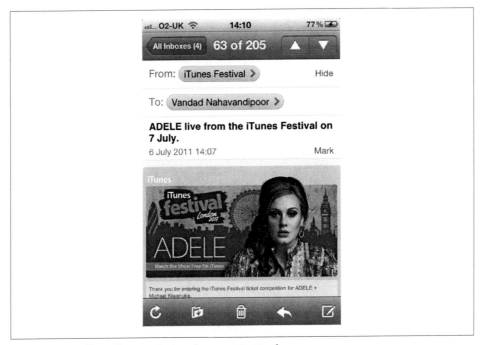

Figure 2-41. Different buttons displayed on a navigation bar

You might be surprised that the bar on the *bottom* of Figure 2-41 is also a navigation bar! Navigation bars are of class `UINavigationBar` and can be created at any time and added to any view. So just look at all the different buttons with different shapes that have been added to the navigation bars in Figure 2-41. The ones on the top right have up and down arrows, the one on the top left has an arrow pointing to the left, and the ones on the bottom navigation bar have all sorts of shapes. We will have a look at creating some of these buttons in this recipe.

 For this recipe, you must follow the instructions in Recipe 1.1 to create an Empty application. Then follow the instructions in Recipe 2.12 to add a navigation controller to your app delegate.

In order to create a navigation button, we must:

1. Create an instance of `UIBarButtonItem`.

2. Add that button to the navigation bar of a view controller using the view controller's `navigationItem` property. The `navigationItem` property allows us to interact with the navigation bar. This property has two others on itself: `rightBarButton Item` and `leftBarButtonItem`. Both these properties are of type `UIBarButtonItem`.

Let's then have a look at an example where we add a button to the right side of our navigation bar. In this button we will display the text `Add`:

```
- (void) performAdd:(id)paramSender{
  NSLog(@"Action method got called.");
}

- (void)viewDidLoad{
  [super viewDidLoad];
  self.view.backgroundColor = [UIColor whiteColor];
  self.title = @"First Controller";

  self.navigationItem.rightBarButtonItem =
  [[UIBarButtonItem alloc] initWithTitle:@"Add"
                             style:UIBarButtonItemStylePlain
                             target:self
                             action:@selector(performAdd:)];
}
```

When we run our app now, we will see something similar to Figure 2-42.

Figure 2-42. A navigation button added to a navigation bar

That was easy. But if you are an iOS user, you probably have noticed that the system apps that come preconfigured on iOS have a different Add button. Figure 2-43 shows an example in the Alarm section of the Clock app on the iPhone (notice the + button on the top right of the navigation bar).

Figure 2-43. The proper way of creating an Add button

It turns out that the iOS SDK allows us to create *system* buttons on the navigation bar. We do that by using the initWithBarButtonSystemItem:target:action: initializer of the UIBarButtonItem class:

```
- (void) performAdd:(id)paramSender{
  NSLog(@"Action method got called.");
}

- (void)viewDidLoad{
  [super viewDidLoad];
  self.view.backgroundColor = [UIColor whiteColor];
  self.title = @"First Controller";

  self.navigationItem.rightBarButtonItem =
  [[UIBarButtonItem alloc]
   initWithBarButtonSystemItem:UIBarButtonSystemItemAdd
                        target:self
                        action:@selector(performAdd:)];
}
```

And the results are exactly what we were looking for (Figure 2-44).

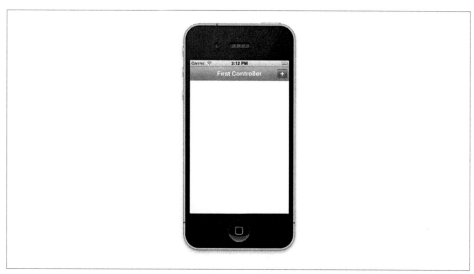

Figure 2-44. A system Add button

The first parameter of the `initWithBarButtonSystemItem:target:action:` initializer method of the navigation button can have any of the values listed in the `UIBarButton SystemItem` enumeration:

```
typedef enum {
    UIBarButtonSystemItemDone,
    UIBarButtonSystemItemCancel,
    UIBarButtonSystemItemEdit,
    UIBarButtonSystemItemSave,
    UIBarButtonSystemItemAdd,
    UIBarButtonSystemItemFlexibleSpace,
    UIBarButtonSystemItemFixedSpace,
    UIBarButtonSystemItemCompose,
    UIBarButtonSystemItemReply,
    UIBarButtonSystemItemAction,
    UIBarButtonSystemItemOrganize,
    UIBarButtonSystemItemBookmarks,
    UIBarButtonSystemItemSearch,
    UIBarButtonSystemItemRefresh,
    UIBarButtonSystemItemStop,
    UIBarButtonSystemItemCamera,
    UIBarButtonSystemItemTrash,
    UIBarButtonSystemItemPlay,
    UIBarButtonSystemItemPause,
    UIBarButtonSystemItemRewind,
    UIBarButtonSystemItemFastForward,
    UIBarButtonSystemItemUndo,
    UIBarButtonSystemItemRedo,
    UIBarButtonSystemItemPageCurl,
} UIBarButtonSystemItem;
```

One of the really great initializers of the `UIBarButtonItem` class is the `initWithCustomView:` method. As its parameter, this method accepts any view. This means we can even add a `UISwitch` (see Recipe 2.2) as a button on the navigation bar. This won't look very good, but let's give it a try:

```
- (void) switchIsChanged:(UISwitch *)paramSender{
  if ([paramSender isOn]){
    NSLog(@"Switch is on.");
  } else {
    NSLog(@"Switch is off.");
  }
}

- (void)viewDidLoad{
  [super viewDidLoad];
  self.view.backgroundColor = [UIColor whiteColor];
  self.title = @"First Controller";

  UISwitch *simpleSwitch = [[UISwitch alloc] init];
  simpleSwitch.on = YES;
  [simpleSwitch addTarget:self
                   action:@selector(switchIsChanged:)
         forControlEvents:UIControlEventValueChanged];

  self.navigationItem.rightBarButtonItem =
  [[UIBarButtonItem alloc] initWithCustomView:simpleSwitch];
}
```

And Figure 2-45 shows the results.

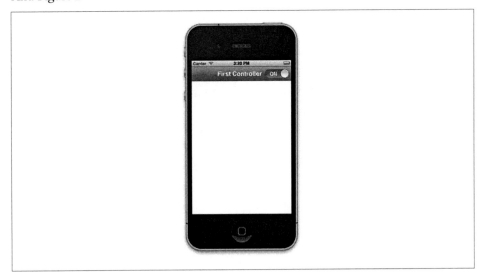

Figure 2-45. A switch added to a navigation bar

You can create pretty amazing navigation bar buttons. Just take a look at what Apple has done with the up and down arrows on the top-right corner of Figure 2-41. Let's do the same thing, shall we? Well, it looks like the button actually contains a segmented control (see Recipe 2.8). So we should create a segmented control with two segments, add it to a navigation button, and finally place the navigation button on the navigation bar. Let's get started:

```
- (void) segmentedControlTapped:(UISegmentedControl *)paramSender{

  if ([paramSender selectedSegmentIndex] == 0){
    /* Up button */
    NSLog(@"Up");
  } else  if ([paramSender selectedSegmentIndex] == 1){
    /* Down button */
    NSLog(@"Down");
  }

}

- (void)viewDidLoad{
  [super viewDidLoad];
  self.view.backgroundColor = [UIColor whiteColor];
  self.title = @"First Controller";

  NSArray *items = [[NSArray alloc] initWithObjects:
                    [UIImage imageNamed:@"UpArrow.png"],
                    [UIImage imageNamed:@"DownArrow.png"], nil];

  UISegmentedControl *segmentedControl = [[UISegmentedControl alloc]
                                          initWithItems:items];

  segmentedControl.segmentedControlStyle = UISegmentedControlStyleBar;
  segmentedControl.momentary = YES;

  [segmentedControl addTarget:self
                    action:@selector(segmentedControlTapped:)
             forControlEvents:UIControlEventValueChanged];

  self.navigationItem.rightBarButtonItem =
  [[UIBarButtonItem alloc] initWithCustomView:segmentedControl];
}
```

 I manually created the arrow images. They are not present in the iOS SDK. Creating these images is quite easy, though. They are simple triangles: one pointing up and the other pointing down. If you are graphically challenged, maybe you could find some images using a search engine?

And Figure 2-46 shows what the output looks like.

Figure 2-46. A segmented control inside a navigation button

The `navigationItem` of every view controller also has two very interesting methods:

`setRightBarButtonItem:animated:`
    Sets the navigation bar's right button.

`setLeftBarButtonItem:animated:`
    Sets the navigation bar's left button.

Both methods allow you to specify whether you want the placement to be animated. Pass the value of `YES` to the `animated` parameter if you want the placement to be animated. Here is an example:

```
UIBarButtonItem *rightBarButton =
[[UIBarButtonItem alloc] initWithCustomView:segmentedControl];

[self.navigationItem setRightBarButtonItem:rightBarButton
                                  animated:YES];
```

See Also

Recipe 1.1; Recipe 2.2; Recipe 2.8; Recipe 2.12

2.16 Presenting Multiple View Controllers with UITabBarController

Problem

You would like to give your users the option to switch from one section of your app to another, with ease.

Solution

Use the UITabBarController class.

Discussion

If you use your iPhone as an alarm clock, you have certainly seen a tab bar. Have a look at Figure 2-43. The bottom icons labeled World Clock, Alarm, Stopwatch, and Timer are parts of a tab bar. The whole black bar at the bottom of the screen is a tab bar and the aforementioned icons are tab bar items.

A tab bar is a container controller. In other words, we create instances of UITabBarController and add them to the window of our application. For each tab bar item, we add a navigation controller or a view controller to the tab bar, and those items will appear as tab bar items. A tab bar controller contains a tab bar of type UITabBar. We don't create this object manually. We create the tab bar controller, and that will create the tab bar object for us. To make things simple, remember that we instantiate a tab bar controller and set the view controllers of that tab bar to instances of either UIView Controller or UINavigationController if we intend to have navigation controllers for each of the tab bar items (aka, the view controllers set for the tab bar controller). Navigation controllers are of type UINavigationController that are subclasses of UIView Controller. Therefore, a navigation controller is a view controller, but view controllers of type UIViewController are not navigation controllers.

So let's assume we have two view controllers with class names FirstViewController and SecondViewController. We now go into our app delegate and define our view controllers and our tab bar:

```
#import <UIKit/UIKit.h>

@class FirstViewController;
@class SecondViewController;

@interface Presenting_Multiple_View_Controllers_with_UITabBarControllerAppDelegate
         : UIResponder <UIApplicationDelegate>

@property (nonatomic, strong) UIWindow *window;
@property (nonatomic, strong) FirstViewController *firstViewController;
@property (nonatomic, strong) SecondViewController *secondViewController;
@property (nonatomic, strong) UITabBarController *tabBarController;
```

@end

Now let's go and instantiate our view controllers and tab bar controller:

```objc
#import "Presenting_Multiple_View_Controllers_with_UITabBarControllerAppDelegate.h"
#import "FirstViewController.h"
#import "SecondViewController.h"

@implementation Presenting_Multiple_View_Controllers_with_UITabBarControllerAppDelegate

- (BOOL)              application:(UIApplication *)application
  didFinishLaunchingWithOptions:(NSDictionary *)launchOptions{

    // Override point for customization after application launch.
    self.window = [[UIWindow alloc] initWithFrame:
                   [[UIScreen mainScreen] bounds]];

    [self.window makeKeyAndVisible];

    self.firstViewController = [[FirstViewController alloc]
                               initWithNibName:nil
                               bundle:NULL];
    self.secondViewController = [[SecondViewController alloc]
                                initWithNibName:nil
                                bundle:NULL];

    NSArray *twoViewControllers = [[NSArray alloc]
                                   initWithObjects:
                                   self.firstViewController,
                                   self.secondViewController, nil];

    self.tabBarController = [[UITabBarController alloc] init];
    [self.tabBarController setViewControllers:twoViewControllers];

    [self.window addSubview:self.tabBarController.view];

    return YES;

}
```

A tab bar, when displayed on the screen, will display tab bar items just like those we saw in Figure 2-43. The name of each of these tab bar items comes from the title of the view controller that is representing that tab bar item, so let's go ahead and set the title for both our view controllers.

When a tab bar loads up, it loads only the view of the first view controller in its items. All other view controllers will be initialized, but their views won't be loaded. This means that any code that you have written in the viewDidLoad of the second view controller will *not* get executed until after the user taps on the second tab bar item for the first time. So if you assign a title to the second view controller in its viewDidLoad and run your app, you will find that the title in the tab bar item is still empty.

For the first view controller, we choose the title *First*:

```
#import "FirstViewController.h"

@implementation FirstViewController

- (id)initWithNibName:(NSString *)nibNameOrNil
              bundle:(NSBundle *)nibBundleOrNil{

  self = [super initWithNibName:nibNameOrNil
                         bundle:nibBundleOrNil];
  if (self != nil) {
    self.title = @"First";
  }
  return self;

}

- (void)viewDidLoad{
  [super viewDidLoad];
  self.view.backgroundColor = [UIColor whiteColor];
}

...
```

And for the second view controller, we pick the title *Second*:

```
#import "SecondViewController.h"

@implementation SecondViewController

- (id)initWithNibName:(NSString *)nibNameOrNil
              bundle:(NSBundle *)nibBundleOrNil{

  self = [super initWithNibName:nibNameOrNil
                         bundle:nibBundleOrNil];
  if (self != nil) {
    self.title = @"Second";
  }
  return self;

}

- (void)viewDidLoad{
  [super viewDidLoad];
  self.view.backgroundColor = [UIColor whiteColor];}

...
```

Now let's run our app and see what happens (Figure 2-47).

Figure 2-47. A very simple tab bar populated with two view controllers

You can see that our view controllers do *not* have a navigation bar. What should we do? It's easy. Remember that a UINavigationController is actually a subclass of UIView Controller. So, we can add instances of navigation controllers to a tab bar, and inside each navigation controller, we can load a view controller. What are we waiting for, then? Let's start with the header file of our app delegate:

```
#import <UIKit/UIKit.h>

@class FirstViewController;
@class SecondViewController;

@interface Presenting_Multiple_View_Controllers_with_UITabBarControllerAppDelegate
        : UIResponder <UIApplicationDelegate>

@property (nonatomic, strong) UIWindow *window;

@property (nonatomic, strong) FirstViewController *firstViewController;
@property (nonatomic, strong)
  UINavigationController *firstNavigationController;

@property (nonatomic, strong) SecondViewController *secondViewController;
@property (nonatomic, strong)
  UINavigationController *secondNavigationController;

@property (nonatomic, strong) UITabBarController *tabBarController;

@end
```

Now that we have the declaration in place, let's implement the tab bar controller in the implementation file of our app delegate:

```
- (BOOL)              application:(UIApplication *)application
  didFinishLaunchingWithOptions:(NSDictionary *)launchOptions{

    // Override point for customization after application launch.
    self.window = [[UIWindow alloc] initWithFrame:
                   [[UIScreen mainScreen] bounds]];

    [self.window makeKeyAndVisible];

    self.firstViewController = [[FirstViewController alloc]
                                initWithNibName:nil
                                bundle:NULL];
    self.firstNavigationController =
      [[UINavigationController alloc]
        initWithRootViewController:self.firstViewController];

    self.secondViewController = [[SecondViewController alloc]
                                 initWithNibName:nil
                                 bundle:NULL];
    self.secondNavigationController =
      [[UINavigationController alloc]
        initWithRootViewController:self.secondViewController];

    NSArray *twoNavControllers = [[NSArray alloc]
                                  initWithObjects:
                                  self.firstNavigationController,
                                  self.secondNavigationController, nil];

    self.tabBarController = [[UITabBarController alloc] init];
    [self.tabBarController setViewControllers:twoNavControllers];

    [self.window addSubview:self.tabBarController.view];

    return YES;

}
```

And the results? Exactly what we wanted (Figure 2-48).

As we can see in Figure 2-43, each tab bar item can have text and an image. We've learned that, using the `title` property of a view controller, we can specify this text, but what about the image? It turns out that every view controller has a property called `tabItem`. This property is the tab item for the current view controller, and you can use this property to set the image of the tab bar item through the `image` property of the tab item. I've already designed two images, a rectangle and a circle. I'm going to display them as the tab bar item image for each of my view controllers. Here is code for the first view controller:

```
#import "FirstViewController.h"

@implementation FirstViewController

- (id)initWithNibName:(NSString *)nibNameOrNil
               bundle:(NSBundle *)nibBundleOrNil{
```

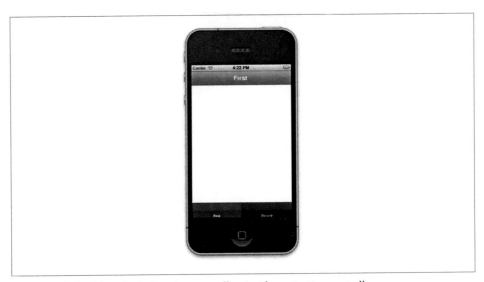

Figure 2-48. A tab bar displaying view controllers inside navigation controllers

```
    self = [super initWithNibName:nibNameOrNil
                           bundle:nibBundleOrNil];
    if (self != nil) {
      self.title = @"First";
      self.tabBarItem.image = [UIImage imageNamed:@"FirstTab.png"];
    }
    return self;

}

...
```

And here it is for the second view controller:

```
#import "SecondViewController.h"

@implementation SecondViewController

- (id)initWithNibName:(NSString *)nibNameOrNil
              bundle:(NSBundle *)nibBundleOrNil{

    self = [super initWithNibName:nibNameOrNil
                           bundle:nibBundleOrNil];
    if (self != nil) {
      self.title = @"Second";
      self.tabBarItem.image = [UIImage imageNamed:@"SecondTab.png"];
    }
    return self;

}

...
```

Running the app in the simulator, we will see that the images are displayed properly (Figure 2-49).

Figure 2-49. Tab bar items with images

2.17 Displaying Static Text with UILabel

Problem

You want to display text to your users. You would also like to control the text's font and color.

 A static text is text that is not directly changeable by the user at runtime.

Solution

Use the UILabel class.

Discussion

Labels are everywhere in iOS. You can see them in practically every application, except for games where the content is usually rendered with OpenGL ES instead of the core drawing frameworks in iOS. Figure 2-50 shows several labels in the Settings app on the iPhone.

Figure 2-50. Labels as titles of each one of the settings

You can see that the labels are displaying text in the Settings app, such as General, iCloud, Twitter, Phone, FaceTime, etc.

To create a label, instantiate an object of type UILabel. Setting or getting the text of a label can be done through its text property. So let's define a label in our view controller's header file:

```
#import <UIKit/UIKit.h>

@interface Displaying_Static_Text_with_UILabelViewController
         : UIViewController

@property (nonatomic, strong) UILabel *myLabel;

@end
```

Now in the viewDidLoad method, instantiate the label and tell the runtime where the label has to be positioned (through its frame property) on the view to which it will be added (in this case, our view controller's view):

```
- (void)viewDidLoad{
  [super viewDidLoad];

  self.view.backgroundColor = [UIColor whiteColor];
  CGRect labelFrame = CGRectMake(0.0f,
                                 0.0f,
```

```
                           100.0f,
                           23.0f);
    self.myLabel = [[UILabel alloc] initWithFrame:labelFrame];
    self.myLabel.text = @"iOS 6 Programming Cookbook";
    self.myLabel.font = [UIFont boldSystemFontOfSize:14.0f];
    self.myLabel.center = self.view.center;
    [self.view addSubview:self.myLabel];

}
```

Now let's run our app and see what happens (see Figure 2-51).

Figure 2-51. A label that is too small in width to contain its contents

You can see that the contents of the label are truncated, with trailing full stops, because the width of the label isn't enough to contain the whole contents. One solution would be to make the width longer, but how about the height? What if we wanted the text to wrap to the next line? OK, go ahead and change the height from 23.0f to 50.0f:

```
CGRect labelFrame = CGRectMake(0.0f,
                               0.0f,
                               100.0f,
                               50.0f);
```

If you run your app now, you will get *exactly* the same results that you got in Figure 2-51. You might ask, "I increased the height, so why didn't the content wrap to the next line?" It turns out that UILabel class has a property called numberOfLines that needs to be adjusted to the number of lines the label has to wrap the text to, in case it runs out of horizontal space. If you set this value to 3, it tells the label that you want the text to wrap to a maximum of three lines if it cannot fit the text into one line:

```
self.myLabel.numberOfLines = 3;
```

If you run the app now, you will get the desired results (see Figure 2-52).

Figure 2-52. A label wrapping its contents to three lines

 In some situations, you might not know how many lines are required to display a certain text in a label. In those instances, you need to set the numberOfLines property of your label to 0.

If you want your label's frame to stay static and you want the font inside your label to adjust itself to fit into the boundaries of the label, you need to set the adjustsFontSize ToFitWidth property of your label to YES. For instance, if the height of our label was 23.0f, as we see in Figure 2-51, we could adjust the font of the label to fit into the boundaries. Here is how it works:

```
- (void)viewDidLoad{
    [super viewDidLoad];

    self.view.backgroundColor = [UIColor whiteColor];
    CGRect labelFrame = CGRectMake(0.0f,
                                   0.0f,
                                   100.0f,
                                   23.0f);
    self.myLabel = [[UILabel alloc] initWithFrame:labelFrame];
    self.myLabel.adjustsFontSizeToFitWidth = YES;
    self.myLabel.text = @"iOS 6 Programming Cookbook";
    self.myLabel.font = [UIFont boldSystemFontOfSize:14.0f];  self.myLabel.center =
    self.view.center;
    [self.view addSubview:self.myLabel];

}
```

2.18 Customizing the UILabel

Problem

You want to be able to customize the appearance of your labels, from shadow settings to alignment settings.

Solution

Use the following properties of the UILabel class, depending on your requirements:

shadowColor

> This property is of type UIColor and, as its name shows, it specifies the color of the dropshadow to render for your label. If you are setting this property, you should also set the shadowOffset property.

shadowOffset

> This property is of type CGSize and it specifies the offset of the dropshadow from the text. For instance, if you set this property to (1, 0), the dropshadow will appear 1 point to the right of the text. If you set this property to (1, 2), the dropshadow will appear 1 point to the right and 2 points down from the text. If you set this property to (-2, -10), the dropshadow will render 2 points to the left and 10 points above the text.

numberOfLines

> This property is an integer that specifies how many lines of text the label is able to render. By default, this property's value is set to 1, meaning any label that you create by default can handle 1 line of text. If you want 2 lines of text, for instance, set this property to 2. If you want unlimited lines of text to be rendered in your text field or you simply don't know how many lines of text you will end up displaying, set this property to 0. (I know, it's really strange. Instead of NSInteger Max or something similar, Apple has decided that 0 means unlimited!)

lineBreakMode

> This property is of type NSLineBreakMode and specifies how you want to line-wrap the text inside your text field. For instance, if you set this property to NSLineBreak ByWordWrapping, words will be kept together, but the string will be wrapped to the next line if there is not enough space to display it. Alternatively, if you set this property to NSLineBreakByCharWrapping, words may be broken across lines when text is wrapped. You would probably use NSLineBreakByCharWrapping only if the space is very tight and you need to fit as much information as possible on the screen. I personally do not recommend using this option if you want to keep a consistent and clear user interface.

textAlignment

This property is of type NSTextAlignment and sets the horizontal alignment of the text in your label. For instance, you can set the value of this property to NSText AlignmentCenter to horizontally center-align your text.

textColor

This property is of type UIColor and defines the color of the text inside the label.

font

This property of type UIFont specifies the font with which the text inside your label will get rendered.

adjustsFontSizeToFitWidth

This property is of type BOOL. When set to YES, it will change the size of the font to fit your label. For instance, if you have a small label and the text you are trying to set in it is too big to fit, if this property is set to YES, the runtime will automatically reduce the font size of your label to make sure the text will fit into the label. In contrast, if this property is set to NO, the current line/word/character wrapping option is taken into account and your text will be rendered in an incomplete manner with just a few words being displayed.

Discussion

Labels are one of the easiest UI components we can utilize in our applications. Although labels are simple, they are really powerful. Customization of labels is therefore very important in order to deliver the best user experience. For this reason, Apple has given us plenty of ways to customize the instances of UILabel. Let us have a look at an example. We'll create a simple Single View Application with one view controller, place a simple label at the center of the screen with a huge font, and write "iOS SDK" in it. We will set the background color of our view to white, the text color of our label to black, and the shadow color of our label to light gray. We will make sure a dropshadow appears at the bottom righthand side of our label. Figure 2-53 shows the effect our app should produce.

And here is our code to achieve this:

```
#import "ViewController.h"

@interface ViewController ()
@property (nonatomic, strong) UILabel *label;
@end

@implementation ViewController

- (void)viewDidLoad{
    [super viewDidLoad];
    self.view.backgroundColor = [UIColor whiteColor];
    self.label = [[UILabel alloc] init];
    self.label.backgroundColor = [UIColor clearColor];
    self.label.text = @"iOS SDK";
    self.label.font = [UIFont boldSystemFontOfSize:70.0f];
```

Figure 2-53. How our label is customized and rendered on the screen

```
self.label.textColor = [UIColor blackColor];
self.label.shadowColor = [UIColor lightGrayColor];
self.label.shadowOffset = CGSizeMake(2.0f, 2.0f);
[self.label sizeToFit];
self.label.center = self.view.center;
[self.view addSubview:self.label];

}

@end
```

See Also

Recipe 2.17; Recipe 2.30

2.19 Accepting User Text Input with UITextField

Problem

You want to accept text input in your user interface.

Solution

Use the UITextField class.

Discussion

A text field is very much like a label in that it can display text, but a text field can also accept text entry at runtime. Figure 2-54 shows two text fields in the Twitter section of the Settings app on an iPhone.

Figure 2-54. Username and password text fields allowing text entry

 A text field allows only a single line of text to be input/displayed. As a result, the default height of a text field is only 31 points. In Interface Builder, this height cannot be modified, but if you are creating your text field in code, you can change the text field's height. A change in height, though, will *not* change the number of lines you can render in a text field, which is always 1.

Let's start with the header file of our view controller to define our text field:

```
#import <UIKit/UIKit.h>

@interface Accepting_User_Text_Input_with_UITextFieldViewController
        : UIViewController

@property (nonatomic, strong) UITextField *myTextField;

@end
```

And then let's create the text field:

```
- (void)viewDidLoad{
  [super viewDidLoad];

  self.view.backgroundColor = [UIColor whiteColor];
  CGRect textFieldFrame = CGRectMake(0.0f,
                                     0.0f,
                                     200.0f,
                                     31.0f);

  self.myTextField = [[UITextField alloc]
                        initWithFrame:textFieldFrame];
  self.myTextField.borderStyle = UITextBorderStyleRoundedRect;

  self.myTextField.contentVerticalAlignment =
    UIControlContentVerticalAlignmentCenter;

  self.myTextField.textAlignment = UITextAlignmentCenter;

  self.myTextField.text = @"Sir Richard Branson";
  self.myTextField.center = self.view.center;
  [self.view addSubview:self.myTextField];

}
```

Before looking at the details of the code, let's first have a look at the results (Figure 2-55).

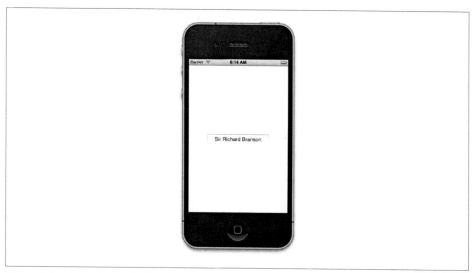

Figure 2-55. A simple text field with center aligned text

In order to create this text field, we used various properties of UITextField. These are:

borderStyle

> This property is of type UITextBorderStyle and specifies how the text field should render its borders.

contentVerticalAlignment

> This value is of type UIControlContentVerticalAlignment and tells the text field how the text should appear, vertically, in the boundaries of the control. If we didn't center the text vertically, it would appear on the top-left corner of the text field by default.

textAlignment

> This property is of type UITextAlignment and specifies the horizontal alignment of the text in a text field. In this example, we have centered the text horizontally (as well as vertically).

text

> This is a read/write property: you can both read from it and write to it. Reading from it will return the text field's current text and writing to it will set the text field's text to the value that you specify.

A text field sends delegate messages to its delegate object. These messages get sent, for instance, when the user starts editing the text inside a text field, when the user enters any character into the text field (changing its contents in any way), and when the user finishes editing the field (by leaving the field). To get notified of these events, set the delegate property of the text field to your object. The delegate of a text field must conform to the UITextFieldDelegate protocol, so let's first take care of this:

```
#import <UIKit/UIKit.h>

@interface Accepting_User_Text_Input_with_UITextFieldViewController
        : UIViewController <UITextFieldDelegate>

@property (nonatomic, strong) UITextField *myTextField;

@end
```

Hold down the Command key on your computer and click on the UITextFieldDelegate protocol in Xcode. You will see all the methods that this protocol gives you control over. Here are those methods with description of when they get called:

textFieldShouldBeginEditing:

> A method that returns a BOOL telling the text field (the parameter to this method) whether it should start getting edited by the user or not. Return NO if you don't want the user to edit your text field. This method gets fired as soon as the user taps on the text field with the goal of editing its content (assuming the text field allows editing).

textFieldDidBeginEditing:

> Gets called when the text field starts to get edited by the user. This method gets called when the user has already tapped on the text field and the textFieldShould

BeginEditing: delegate method of the text field returned YES, telling the text field it is OK for the user to edit the content of the text field.

textFieldShouldEndEditing:

Returns a BOOL telling the text field whether it should end its current editing session or not. This method gets called when the user is about to leave the text field or the first responder is switching to another data entry field. If you return NO from this method, the user will not be able to switch to another text entry field, and the keyboard will stay on the screen.

textFieldDidEndEditing:

Gets called when the editing session of the text field ends. This happens when the user decides to edit some other data entry field or uses a button provided by the supplier of the app to dismiss the keyboard shown for the text field.

textField:shouldChangeCharactersInRange:replacementString:

Gets called whenever the text inside the text field is modified. The return value of this method is a Boolean. If you return YES, you say that you allow the text to be changed. If you return NO, the change in the text of the text field will *not* be confirmed and will not happen.

textFieldShouldClear:

Each text field has a *clear* button that is usually a circular X button. When the user presses this button, the contents of the text field will automatically get erased. We need to manually enable the clear button, though. If you have enabled the clear button and you return NO to this method, that gives the user the impression that your app isn't working, so make sure you know what you are doing. It is a very poor user experience if the user sees a clear button and presses it, but doesn't see the text in the text field get erased.

textFieldShouldReturn:

Gets called when the user has pressed the Return/Enter key on the keyboard, trying to dismiss the keyboard. You should assign the text field as the first responder in this method.

Let's mix this recipe with Recipe 2.17 and create a dynamic text label under our text field. We'll also display the total number of characters entered in our text field in the label. Let's start with our header file:

```
#import <UIKit/UIKit.h>

@interface Accepting_User_Text_Input_with_UITextFieldViewController
        : UIViewController <UITextFieldDelegate>

@property (nonatomic, strong) UITextField *myTextField;
@property (nonatomic, strong) UILabel *labelCounter;

@end
```

Now for the creation of the text field along with the label and the text field delegate methods we require. We skip implementing many of the UITextFieldDelegate methods, because we don't need all of them in this example:

```
- (void) calculateAndDisplayTextFieldLengthWithText:(NSString *)paramText{

  NSString *characterOrCharacters = @"Characters";
  if ([paramText length] == 1){
    characterOrCharacters = @"Character";
  }

  self.labelCounter.text = [NSString stringWithFormat:@"%lu %@",
                          (unsigned long)[paramText length],
                          characterOrCharacters];
}

- (BOOL)                  textField:(UITextField *)textField
    shouldChangeCharactersInRange:(NSRange)range
                replacementString:(NSString *)string{

  BOOL result = YES;

  if ([textField isEqual:self.myTextField]){
    NSString *wholeText =
    [textField.text stringByReplacingCharactersInRange:range
                                      withString:string];
    [self calculateAndDisplayTextFieldLengthWithText:wholeText];
  }

  return result;

}

- (BOOL)textFieldShouldReturn:(UITextField *)textField{
  [textField resignFirstResponder];
  return YES;
}

- (void)viewDidLoad{
  [super viewDidLoad];

  self.view.backgroundColor = [UIColor whiteColor];
  CGRect textFieldFrame = CGRectMake(38.0f,
                                     30.0f,
                                     220.0f,
                                     31.0f);

  self.myTextField = [[UITextField alloc]
                      initWithFrame:textFieldFrame];

  self.myTextField.delegate = self;

  self.myTextField.borderStyle = UITextBorderStyleRoundedRect;

  self.myTextField.contentVerticalAlignment =
```

```
        UIControlContentVerticalAlignmentCenter;

    self.myTextField.textAlignment = UITextAlignmentCenter;

    self.myTextField.text = @"Sir Richard Branson";
    [self.view addSubview:self.myTextField];

    CGRect labelCounterFrame = self.myTextField.frame;
    labelCounterFrame.origin.y += textFieldFrame.size.height + 10;
    self.labelCounter = [[UILabel alloc] initWithFrame:labelCounterFrame];
    [self.view addSubview:self.labelCounter];

    [self calculateAndDisplayTextFieldLengthWithText:self.myTextField.text];

}
```

One important calculation we are doing is in the textField:shouldChangeCharactersIn
Range:replacementString: method. There, we declare and use a variable called whole
Text. When this method gets called, the replacementString parameter specifies the
string that the user has entered into the text field. You might be thinking that the user
can enter only one character at a time, so why can't this field be a char? But don't forget
that the user can paste a whole chunk of text into a text field, so this parameter needs
to be a string. The shouldChangeCharactersInRange parameter specifies where, in terms
of location inside the text field's text, the user is entering the text. So using these two
parameters, we will create a string that first reads the whole text inside the text field
and then uses the given range to place the new text inside the old text. With this, we
will come up with the text that will appear in the text field *after* the textField:should
ChangeCharactersInRange:replacementString: method returns YES. Figure 2-56 shows
how our app looks when it gets run on the simulator.

Figure 2-56. Responding to delegate messages of a text field

In addition to displaying text, a text field can also display a *placeholder*. A placeholder is the text displayed *before* the user has entered any text in the text field, while the text field's text property is empty. This can be any string that you wish, and setting it will help give the user an indication as to what this text field is for. Many use this placeholder to tell the user what type of value she can enter in that text field. For instance, in Figure 2-54, the two text fields (username and password) have placeholders that say "Required". You can use the `placeholder` property of the text field to set or get the current placeholder. Here is an example:

```
self.myTextField = [[UITextField alloc]
                        initWithFrame:textFieldFrame];

self.myTextField.delegate = self;

self.myTextField.borderStyle = UITextBorderStyleRoundedRect;

self.myTextField.contentVerticalAlignment =
   UIControlContentVerticalAlignmentCenter;

self.myTextField.textAlignment = UITextAlignmentCenter;

self.myTextField.placeholder = @"Enter text here...";
[self.view addSubview:self.myTextField];
```

The results are shown in Figure 2-57.

Figure 2-57. A placeholder is shown when the user has not entered any text in a text field

Text fields have two really neat properties called `leftView` and `rightView`. These two properties are of type `UIView` and are read/write. They appear, as their names imply, on the left and the right side of a text field if you assign a view to them. One place you might use a left view, for instance, is if you are displaying a currency text field where you would like to display the currency of the user's current country in the left view, as a UILabel. Here is how we can accomplish that:

```
UILabel *currencyLabel = [[UILabel alloc] initWithFrame:CGRectZero];
currencyLabel.text = [[[NSNumberFormatter alloc] init] currencySymbol];
currencyLabel.font = self.myTextField.font;
[currencyLabel sizeToFit];
self.myTextField.leftView = currencyLabel;
self.myTextField.leftViewMode = UITextFieldViewModeAlways;
```

If we simply assign a view to the leftView or to the rightView properties of a text field, those views will not appear automatically by default. When they show up on the screen depends on the mode that governs their appearance, and you can control that mode using the leftViewMode and rightViewMode properties, respectively. These modes are of type UITextFieldViewMode:

```
typedef enum {
  UITextFieldViewModeNever,
  UITextFieldViewModeWhileEditing,
  UITextFieldViewModeUnlessEditing,
  UITextFieldViewModeAlways
} UITextFieldViewMode;
```

So if, for instance, you set the left view mode to UITextFieldViewModeWhileEditing and assign a value to it, it will appear only while the user is editing the text field. Conversely, if you set this value to UITextFieldViewModeUnlessEditing, the left view will appear only while the user is *not* editing the text field. As soon as editing starts, the left view will disappear. Let's have a look at our code now in the simulator (Figure 2-58).

Figure 2-58. A text field with a left view

See Also

Recipe 2.17

2.20 Displaying Long Lines of Text with UITextView

Problem

You want to display multiple lines of text in your UI inside one scrollable view.

Solution

Use the UITextView class.

Discussion

The UITextView class can display multiple lines of text and contain scrollable content, meaning that if the contents run off the boundaries of the text view, the text view's internal components allow the user to scroll the text up and down to see different parts of the text. An example of a text view in an iOS app is the Notes app on the iPhone (Figure 2-59).

Figure 2-59. Notes app on the iPhone uses a text view to render text

Let's create a text view and see how it works. We start off by declaring the text view in our view controller's header file:

```
#import <UIKit/UIKit.h>

@interface Displaying_Long_Lines_of_Text_with_UITextViewViewController
          : UIViewController

@property (nonatomic, strong) UITextView *myTextView;

@end
```

Now it's time to create the text view itself. We will make the text view as big as the view controller's view:

```
- (void)viewDidLoad{
  [super viewDidLoad];

  self.view.backgroundColor = [UIColor whiteColor];

  self.myTextView = [[UITextView alloc] initWithFrame:self.view.bounds];
  self.myTextView.text = @"Some text here...";
  self.myTextView.font = [UIFont systemFontOfSize:16.0f];
  [self.view addSubview:self.myTextView];

}
```

Now let's run the app in iOS Simulator and see how it looks (Figure 2-60).

Figure 2-60. A text view consuming the entire boundary of the screen

If you tap on the text field, you will notice a keyboard pop up from the bottom of the screen, concealing almost half the entire area of the text view. That means if the user starts typing text and gets to the middle of the text view, the rest of the text that she types will *not* be visible to her (Figure 2-61).

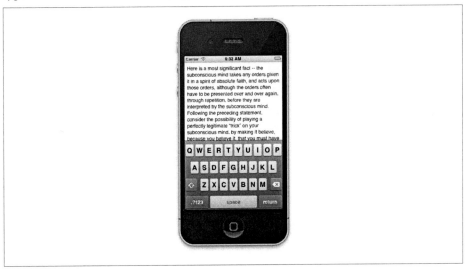

Figure 2-61. Keyboard concealing half the size of a text view

To remedy this, we have to listen for certain notifications:

UIKeyboardWillShowNotification
> Gets sent by the system whenever the keyboard is brought up on the screen for any component, be it a text field, a text view, etc.

UIKeyboardDidShowNotification
> Gets sent by the system when the keyboard has already been displayed.

UIKeyboardWillHideNotification
> Gets sent by the system when the keyboard is about to hide.

UIKeyboardDidHideNotification
> Gets sent by the system when the keyboard is now fully hidden.

 The keyboard notifications contain a dictionary, accessible through the userInfo property, that specifies the boundaries of the keyboard on the screen. This property is of type NSDictionary. One of the keys in this dictionary is UIKeyboardFrameEndUserInfoKey, which contains an object of type NSValue that itself contains the rectangular boundaries of the keyboard when it is fully shown. This rectangular area is denoted with a CGRect.

So our strategy is to find out when the keyboard is getting displayed and then somehow resize our text view. For this, we will use the contentInset property of UITextView to specify the margins of contents in the text view from top, left, bottom, and right:

```objc
- (void) handleKeyboardDidShow:(NSNotification *)paramNotification{

  /* Get the frame of the keyboard */
  NSValue *keyboardRectAsObject =
    [[paramNotification userInfo]
     objectForKey:UIKeyboardFrameEndUserInfoKey];

  /* Place it in a CGRect */
  CGRect keyboardRect;

  [keyboardRectAsObject getValue:&keyboardRect];

  /* Give a bottom margin to our text view that makes it
   reach to the top of the keyboard */
  self.myTextView.contentInset =
    UIEdgeInsetsMake(0.0f,
                     0.0f,
                     keyboardRect.size.height,
                     0.0f);
}

- (void) handleKeyboardWillHide:(NSNotification *)paramNotification{
  /* Make the text view as big as the whole view again */
  self.myTextView.contentInset = UIEdgeInsetsZero;
}

- (void) viewWillAppear:(BOOL)paramAnimated{
  [super viewWillAppear:paramAnimated];

  [[NSNotificationCenter defaultCenter]
    addObserver:self
      selector:@selector(handleKeyboardDidShow:)
         name:UIKeyboardDidShowNotification
       object:nil];

  [[NSNotificationCenter defaultCenter]
    addObserver:self
      selector:@selector(handleKeyboardWillHide:)
         name:UIKeyboardWillHideNotification
       object:nil];

  self.view.backgroundColor = [UIColor whiteColor];

  self.myTextView = [[UITextView alloc] initWithFrame:self.view.bounds];
  self.myTextView.text = @"Some text here...";
  self.myTextView.font = [UIFont systemFontOfSize:16.0f];
  [self.view addSubview:self.myTextView];

}

- (void) viewWillDisappear:(BOOL)paramAnimated{
  [super viewWillDisappear:paramAnimated];

  [[NSNotificationCenter defaultCenter] removeObserver:self];
}
```

In this code, we start looking for keyboard notifications in `viewWillAppear:` and we stop listening to keyboard notifications in `viewWillDisappear:`. Removing your view controller as the listener is important, because when your view controller is no longer displayed, you probably don't want to receive keyboard notifications fired by any other view controller. There may be times when a view controller in the background needs to receive notifications, but these are rare and you must normally make sure to stop listening for notifications in `viewWillDisappear:`. I've seen many applications programmers break their apps by not taking care of this simple logic.

 If you intend to change your UI structure when the keyboard gets displayed and when the keyboard is dismissed, the only method that you can rely on is to use the keyboard notifications. Delegate messages of `UITextField` get fired when the text field is getting edited, whether there is a soft keyboard on the screen or not. Remember, a user can have a Bluetooth keyboard connected to his iOS device and use it to edit the content of text fields and any other data entry in your apps. In the case of a Bluetooth keyboard, no soft keyboard will be displayed on the screen—and if you change your UI when your text fields start to get edited, you might unnecessarily change the UI while the Bluetooth keyboard user is editing text.

Now, if the user tries to enter some text into the text view, the keyboard will pop up, and we take the height of the keyboard and assign that value as the bottom margin of the contents inside the text view. This makes our text view's contents smaller in size and allows the user to enter as much text as she wishes without the keyboard blocking her view.

2.21 Adding Buttons to the User Interface with UIButton

Problem

You want to display a button on your UI and handle the touch events for that button.

Solution

Use the `UIButton` class.

Discussion

Buttons allow users to initiate an action in your apps. For instance, the iCloud Settings bundle in the Settings app presents a Delete Account button in Figure 2-62. If you press this button, the iCloud app will take action. The action depends on the app. Not all apps act the same when a Delete button is pressed by the user. Buttons can have images in them as well as text, as we will soon see.

Figure 2-62. A Delete Account button

A button can assign actions to different triggers. For instance, a button can fire one action when the user puts her finger down on the button and another action when she lifts her finger off the button. These become actions and the objects implementing the actions become targets. Let's go ahead and define a button in our view controller's header file:

```
#import <UIKit/UIKit.h>

@interface Adding_Buttons_to_the_User_Interface_with_UIButtonViewController
        : UIViewController

@property (nonatomic, strong) UIButton *myButton;

@end
```

The default height of UIButton is 37.0f points.

Next, we move on to the implementation of the button (Figure 2-63):

```
- (void) buttonIsPressed:(UIButton *)paramSender{
  NSLog(@"Button is pressed.");
```

```
}- (void) buttonIsTapped:(UIButton *)paramSender{
  NSLog(@"Button is tapped.");
}

- (void)viewDidLoad{
  [super viewDidLoad];
      self.view.backgroundColor = [UIColor whiteColor];

  self.myButton = [UIButton buttonWithType:UIButtonTypeRoundedRect];

  self.myButton.frame = CGRectMake(110.0f,
                                   200.0f,
                                   100.0f,
                                   37.0f);

  [self.myButton setTitle:@"Press Me"
                 forState:UIControlStateNormal];

  [self.myButton setTitle:@"I'm Pressed"
                 forState:UIControlStateHighlighted];

  [self.myButton addTarget:self
                    action:@selector(buttonIsPressed:)
          forControlEvents:UIControlEventTouchDown];

  [self.myButton addTarget:self
                    action:@selector(buttonIsTapped:)
          forControlEvents:UIControlEventTouchUpInside];

  [self.view addSubview:self.myButton];

}
```

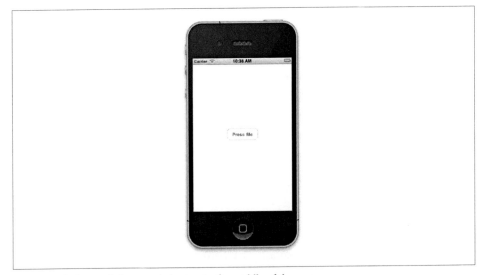

Figure 2-63. A rounded rectangle button in the middle of the screen

In this example code, we are using the `setTitle:forState:` method of our button to set two different titles for the button. The title is the text that gets displayed on the button. A button can be in different states at different times—such as normal and highlighted (pressed down)—and can display a different title in each state. So in this case, when the user sees the button for the first time, he will read *Press Me*. Once he presses the button, the title of the button will change to *I'm Pressed*.

We did a similar thing with the actions that the button fires. We used the `addTarget:action:forControlEvents:` method to specify two actions for our button:

1. An action to be fired when the user presses the button down.
2. Another action to be fired when the user has pressed the button and has lifted his finger off the button. This completes a *touch-up-inside* action.

The other thing that you need to know about `UIButton` is that it must always be assigned a type, which you do by initializing it with a call to the class method `buttonWithType`, as shown in the example code. As the parameter to this method, pass a value of type `UIButtonType`:

```
typedef enum {
    UIButtonTypeCustom = 0,
    UIButtonTypeRoundedRect,
    UIButtonTypeDetailDisclosure,
    UIButtonTypeInfoLight,
    UIButtonTypeInfoDark,
    UIButtonTypeContactAdd,
} UIButtonType;
```

A button can also render an image. An image will replace the default look and feel of the button. When you have an image or series of images that you want to assign to different states of a button, make sure your button is of type `UIButtonTypeCustom`. I have prepared two images here: one for the normal state of the button and the other for the highlighted (pressed) state. I will now create my custom button and assign two images to it. One image is for the normal state of the button, and the other for the highlighted state:

```
UIImage *normalImage = [UIImage imageNamed:@"NormalBlueButton.png"];
UIImage *highlightedImage = [UIImage imageNamed:@"HighlightedBlueButton"];

self.myButton = [UIButton buttonWithType:UIButtonTypeCustom];

self.myButton.frame = CGRectMake(110.0f,
                                 200.0f,
                                 100.0f,
                                 37.0f);

[self.myButton setBackgroundImage:normalImage
                         forState:UIControlStateNormal];
[self.myButton setTitle:@"Normal"
               forState:UIControlStateNormal];

[self.myButton setBackgroundImage:highlightedImage
```

```
                                  forState:UIControlStateHighlighted];
        [self.myButton setTitle:@"Pressed"
                        forState:UIControlStateHighlighted];
```

Figure 2-64 shows what the app looks like when we run it in the iOS Simulator. We
are using the setBackgroundImage:forState: method of the button to set a background
image. With a background image, we can still use the setTitle:forState: methods to
render text on top of the background image. If your images contain text and you don't
need the title for a button, you can instead use the setImage:forState: method or simply
remove the titles from the button.

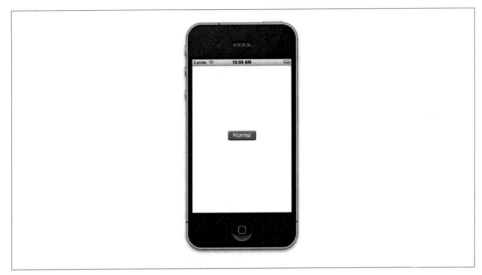

Figure 2-64. A button with a background image

2.22 Displaying Images with UIImageView

Problem

You would like to display images to your users on your app's UI.

Solution

Use the UIImageView class.

Discussion

The UIImageView is one of the least complicated classes in the iOS SDK. As you know,
an image view is responsible for displaying images. There are no tips or tricks involved.
All you have to do is to instantiate an object of type UIImageView and add it to your

views. Now, I have a picture of Apple MacBook Air and I would like to display it in an image view. Let's start with our view controller's header file:

```
#import <UIKit/UIKit.h>

@interface Displaying_Images_with_UIImageViewViewController
          : UIViewController

@property (nonatomic, strong) UIImageView *myImageView;

@end
```

Go ahead and instantiate the image view and place the image in it:

```
- (void)viewDidLoad{
  [super viewDidLoad];

  self.view.backgroundColor = [UIColor whiteColor];

  UIImage *macBookAir = [UIImage imageNamed:@"MacBookAir.png"];
  self.myImageView = [[UIImageView alloc] initWithImage:macBookAir];
  self.myImageView.center = self.view.center;
  [self.view addSubview:self.myImageView];

}
```

Now if we run the app, we will see something similar to Figure 2-65.

Figure 2-65. An image view that is too big to fit on the screen

I should mention that the MacBook Air image that I'm loading into this image view is 980×519 pixels and as you can see, it certainly doesn't fit into the iPhone screen. So how do we solve this problem? First, we need to make sure that we are initializing our image view using the `initWithFrame:` method, instead of the `initWithImage:` method as the latter will set the width and height of the image view to the exact width and height of the image. So let's remedy that first:

```
- (void)viewDidLoad{
  [super viewDidLoad];

  self.view.backgroundColor = [UIColor whiteColor];

  UIImage *macBookAir = [UIImage imageNamed:@"MacBookAir.png"];
  self.myImageView = [[UIImageView alloc] initWithFrame:self.view.bounds];
  self.myImageView.image = macBookAir;
  self.myImageView.center = self.view.center;
  [self.view addSubview:self.myImageView];

}
```

So how does the app look now? See Figure 2-66.

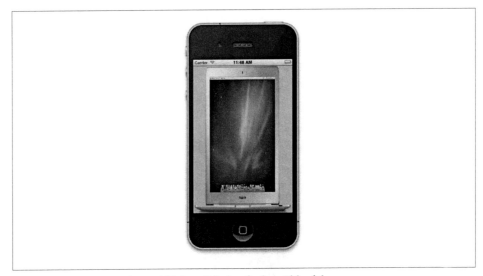

Figure 2-66. An image whose width is squished to fit the width of the screen

This isn't really what we wanted to do, is it? Of course, we got the frame of the image view right, but the way the image is rendered in the image view isn't quite right. So what can we do? We can rectify this by setting the contentMode property of the image view. This property is of type UIContentMode:

```
typedef enum {
  UIViewContentModeScaleToFill,
  UIViewContentModeScaleAspectFit,
  UIViewContentModeScaleAspectFill,
  UIViewContentModeRedraw,
  UIViewContentModeCenter,
  UIViewContentModeTop,
  UIViewContentModeBottom,
```

```
    UIViewContentModeLeft,
    UIViewContentModeRight,
    UIViewContentModeTopLeft,
    UIViewContentModeTopRight,
    UIViewContentModeBottomLeft,
    UIViewContentModeBottomRight,
} UIViewContentMode;
```

Here is an explanation of some of the most useful values in the UIViewContentMode enumeration:

UIViewContentModeScaleToFill

This will scale the image inside the image view to fill the entire boundaries of the image view.

UIViewContentModeScaleAspectFit

This will make sure the image inside the image view will have the right aspect ratio and fits inside the image view's boundaries.

UIViewContentModeScaleAspectFill

This will makes sure the image inside the image view will have the right aspect ratio and fills the entire boundaries of the image view. For this value to work properly, make sure that you have set the clipsToBounds property of the image view to YES.

 The clipsToBounds property of UIView denotes whether the subviews of that view should be clipped if they go outside the boundaries of the view. You use this property if you want to be absolutely certain that the subviews of a specific view will not get rendered outside the boundaries of that view (or that they do get rendered outside the boundaries, depending on your requirements).

So to make sure the image fits into the image view's boundaries and that the aspect ratio of the image is right, we need to use the UIViewContentModeScaleAspectFit content mode:

```
- (void)viewDidLoad{
  [super viewDidLoad];

  self.view.backgroundColor = [UIColor whiteColor];

  UIImage *macBookAir = [UIImage imageNamed:@"MacBookAir.png"];
  self.myImageView = [[UIImageView alloc] initWithFrame:self.view.bounds];
  self.myImageView.contentMode = UIViewContentModeScaleAspectFit;
  self.myImageView.image = macBookAir;
  self.myImageView.center = self.view.center;
  [self.view addSubview:self.myImageView];
}
```

And the results will be exactly what we expected (Figure 2-67).

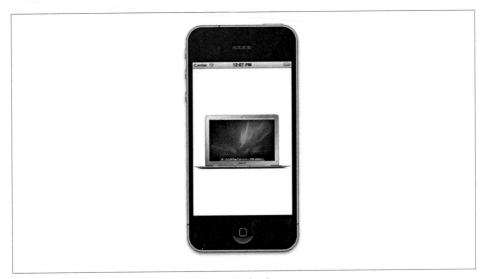

Figure 2-67. The aspect ratio of image view is absolutely spot on

2.23 Creating Scrollable Content with UIScrollView

Problem

You have content that needs to get displayed on the screen, but it requires more real estate than what the device's screen allows for.

Solution

Use the `UIScrollView` class.

Discussion

Scroll views are one of the features that make iOS a really neat operating system. They are practically everywhere. You've been to the Clock or the Contacts apps, haven't you? Have you seen how the content can be scrolled up and down? Well that's the magic of scroll views.

There really is one basic concept you need to learn about scroll views: the *content size*, which lets the scroll view conform to the size of what it's displaying The content size is a value of type `CGSize` that specifies the width and the height of the contents of a scroll view. A scroll view, as its name implies, is a subclass of `UIView`, so you can simply add your views to a scroll view using its `addSubview:` method. However, you need to make sure that the scroll view's content size is set properly, otherwise, the contents inside the scroll view *won't* scroll.

As an example, let's find a big image and load it to an image view. I will add the same image that I used in Recipe 2.22: a MacBook Air image. I will add it to an image view and place it in a scroll view. Then I will use the contentSize of the scroll view to make sure this content size is equal to the size of the image (width and height). First, let's start with the header file of our view controller:

```
#import <UIKit/UIKit.h>

@interface Creating_Scrollable_Content_with_UIScrollViewViewController
        : UIViewController

@property (nonatomic, strong) UIImageView *myImageView;
@property (nonatomic, strong) UIScrollView *myScrollView;

@end
```

And let's place the image view inside the scroll view:

```
- (void)viewDidLoad{
  [super viewDidLoad];

  self.view.backgroundColor = [UIColor whiteColor];

  UIImage *imageToLoad = [UIImage imageNamed:@"MacBookAir.png"];
  self.myImageView = [[UIImageView alloc] initWithImage:imageToLoad];
  self.myScrollView = [[UIScrollView alloc] initWithFrame:self.view.bounds];
  [self.myScrollView addSubview:self.myImageView];
  self.myScrollView.contentSize = self.myImageView.bounds.size;
  [self.view addSubview:self.myScrollView];

}
```

If you now load up the app in iOS Simulator, you will see that you can scroll the image horizontally and vertically. The challenge here, of course, is to provide an image that is bigger than the screen's boundaries. For example, if you provide an image that is 20×20 pixels, the scroll view won't be of much use to you. In fact, it would be wrong to place such an image into a scroll view, as the scroll view would practically be useless in that scenario. There would be nothing to scroll because the image is smaller than the screen size.

One of the handy features of UIScrollView is support for delegation, so that it can report really important events to the app through a delegate. A delegate for a scroll view must conform to the UIScrollViewDelegate protocol. Some of the methods defined in this protocol are:

scrollViewDidScroll:
    Gets called whenever the contents of a scroll view get scrolled.

scrollViewWillBeginDecelerating:
    Gets called when the user scrolls the contents of a scroll view and lifts his finger off of the screen, as the scroll view scrolls.

`scrollViewDidEndDecelerating:`

Gets called when the scroll view has finished scrolling its contents.

`scrollViewDidEndDragging:willDecelerate:`

Gets called when the user finishes dragging the contents of the scroll view. This method is very similar to the `scrollViewDidEndDecelerating:` method *but* you need to bear in mind that the user can drag the contents of a scroll view without scrolling the contents. She can simply put her finger on the content, move her finger to any location on the screen and lift her finger without giving the contents any momentum to move. This is dragging as opposed to scrolling. Scrolling is similar to dragging, but the user will give momentum to the contents' movement by lifting her finger off the screen while the content is being dragged around, and not waiting for the content to stop before lifting the finger off the screen. Dragging is comparable to holding down the accelerator in a car or pedaling on a bicycle, whereas scrolling is comparable to coasting in a car or on a bicycle.

So let's add some fun to our previous app. Now the goal is to set the alpha level of the image inside our image view to 0.50f (half transparent) when the user starts to scroll the scroll view and set this alpha back to 1.0f (opaque) when the user finishes scrolling. Let's begin by conforming to the `UIScrollViewDelegate` protocol:

```
#import <UIKit/UIKit.h>

@interface Creating_Scrollable_Content_with_UIScrollViewViewController
            : UIViewController <UIScrollViewDelegate>

@property (nonatomic, strong) UIImageView *myImageView;
@property (nonatomic, strong) UIScrollView *myScrollView;

@end
```

Then let's implement this functionality:

```
- (void)scrollViewDidScroll:(UIScrollView *)scrollView{
  /* Gets called when user scrolls or drags */
  self.myScrollView.alpha = 0.50f;
}

- (void)scrollViewDidEndDecelerating:(UIScrollView *)scrollView{
  /* Gets called only after scrolling */
  self.myScrollView.alpha = 1.0f;
}

- (void)scrollViewDidEndDragging:(UIScrollView *)scrollView
                  willDecelerate:(BOOL)decelerate{
  /* Make sure the alpha is reset even if the user is dragging */
  self.myScrollView.alpha = 1.0f;
}

- (void)viewDidLoad{
  [super viewDidLoad];

  self.view.backgroundColor = [UIColor whiteColor];
```

```
UIImage *imageToLoad = [UIImage imageNamed:@"MacBookAir.png"];
self.myImageView = [[UIImageView alloc] initWithImage:imageToLoad];
self.myScrollView = [[UIScrollView alloc] initWithFrame:self.view.bounds];
[self.myScrollView addSubview:self.myImageView];
self.myScrollView.contentSize = self.myImageView.bounds.size;
self.myScrollView.delegate = self;
[self.view addSubview:self.myScrollView];

}
```

As you might have noticed, scroll views have *indicators*. An indicator is the little tracking line that appears on the sides of a scroll view when its contents are getting scrolled and moved. Figure 2-68 shows an example.

Figure 2-68. Black indicators appearing on the right and bottom of a scroll view

Indicators simply show the user where the current view is in relation to the content (top, halfway down, etc.). You can control what the indicators look like by changing the value of the `indicatorStyle` property. For instance, here I have changed the indicator style of my scroll view to white:

```
self.myScrollView.indicatorStyle = UIScrollViewIndicatorStyleWhite;
```

One of the great features of scroll views is that they allow pagination. Pagination is the same as scrolling, but locks the scrolling when the user moves to the next *page*. You have perhaps already seen this if you've ever used the Photos app on the iPhone or iPad. When you are looking at photos, you can swipe between them. Each swipe brings the next or previous photo onto the screen. Your swiping never scrolls all the way to the end or all the way to the start. When the scrolling starts, the scroll view detects the next image to display, scrolls and bounces to that image, and stops the scrolling animation.

That's pagination. If you haven't tried it already, I urge you to do so, because otherwise I could go on and on and none of this would make sense unless you looked at an app that supports pagination.

For this example code, I've prepared three images: an iPhone, iPad, and a MacBook Air. I've placed them in their individual image views and added them to a scroll view. Then we can enable pagination by setting the value of the pagingEnabled property of the scroll view to YES:

```
- (void)viewDidLoad{
  [super viewDidLoad];

  self.view.backgroundColor = [UIColor whiteColor];

  UIImage *iPhone = [UIImage imageNamed:@"iPhone.png"];
  UIImage *iPad = [UIImage imageNamed:@"iPad.png"];
  UIImage *macBookAir = [UIImage imageNamed:@"MacBookAir.png"];

  CGRect scrollViewRect = self.view.bounds;

  self.myScrollView = [[UIScrollView alloc] initWithFrame:scrollViewRect];
  self.myScrollView.pagingEnabled = YES;
  self.myScrollView.contentSize = CGSizeMake(scrollViewRect.size.width * 3.0f,
                                             scrollViewRect.size.height);
  [self.view addSubview:self.myScrollView];

  CGRect imageViewRect = self.view.bounds;
  UIImageView *iPhoneImageView = [self newImageViewWithImage:iPhone
                                                       frame:imageViewRect];
  [self.myScrollView addSubview:iPhoneImageView];

  /* Go to next page by moving the x position of the next image view */
  imageViewRect.origin.x += imageViewRect.size.width;
  UIImageView *iPadImageView = [self newImageViewWithImage:iPad
                                                     frame:imageViewRect];
  [self.myScrollView addSubview:iPadImageView];

  /* Go to next page by moving the x position of the next image view */
  imageViewRect.origin.x += imageViewRect.size.width;
  UIImageView *macBookAirImageView =
    [self newImageViewWithImage:macBookAir
                          frame:imageViewRect];
  [self.myScrollView addSubview:macBookAirImageView];

}
```

Now we have three pages of scrollable content (Figure 2-69).

Figure 2-69. Scrolling through pages in a page-enabled scroll view

2.24 Loading Web Pages with UIWebView

Problem

You want to load a web page dynamically right inside your iOS app.

Solution

Use the UIWebView class.

Discussion

A web view is what the Safari browser uses on iOS to load web content. You have the whole power of Safari in your iOS apps through the UIWebView class. All you have to do is to place a web view on your UI and use one of its loading methods:

loadData:MIMEType:textEncodingName:baseURL:
    Loads an instance of NSData into the web view.

loadHTMLString:baseURL:
    Loads an instance of NSString into the web view. The string should be a valid HTML, or in other words, something that a web browser can render.

loadRequest:
    Loads an instance of NSURLRequest. This is useful when you want to load the contents of a remote URL into a web view inside your application.

Let's see an example. We'll start with the header file of our view controller:

```
#import <UIKit/UIKit.h>

@interface Loading_Web_Pages_with_UIWebViewViewController
           : UIViewController

@property (nonatomic, strong) UIWebView *myWebView;

@end
```

Now I would like to load the string *iOS 6 Programming Cookbook* into the web view. To prove things are working as expected and that our web view is capable of rendering rich text, I will go ahead and make the *Programming* part bold while leaving the rest of the text intact (Figure 2-70):

```
- (void)viewDidLoad{
  [super viewDidLoad];

  self.view.backgroundColor = [UIColor whiteColor];

  self.myWebView = [[UIWebView alloc] initWithFrame:self.view.bounds];
  [self.view addSubview:self.myWebView];

  NSString *htmlString = @"iOS 6 Programming <strong>Cookbook</strong>";
  [self.myWebView loadHTMLString:htmlString
                        baseURL:nil];
}
```

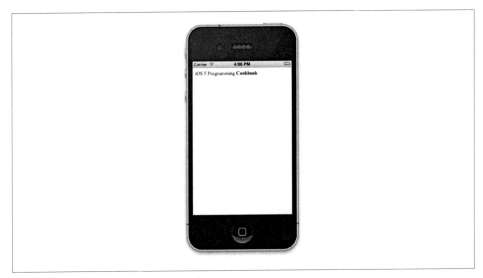

Figure 2-70. Loading rich text into a web view

Another way to use a web view is to load a remote URL into it. For this purpose, we can use the loadRequest: method. Let's go ahead and look at an example where we will load Apple's main page into a web view in our iOS app (Figure 2-71):

```
- (void)viewDidLoad{
  [super viewDidLoad];

  self.view.backgroundColor = [UIColor whiteColor];

  self.myWebView = [[UIWebView alloc] initWithFrame:self.view.bounds];
  self.myWebView.scalesPageToFit = YES;
  [self.view addSubview:self.myWebView];

  NSURL *url = [NSURL URLWithString:@"http://www.apple.com"];
  NSURLRequest *request = [NSURLRequest requestWithURL:url];

  [self.myWebView loadRequest:request];

}
```

Figure 2-71. Apple's home page loaded into a web view

It might take quite a while for a web view to load the contents that you pass to it. You might have noticed that when loading content in Safari, you get a little activity indicator in the top-left corner of the screen telling you that the device is busy loading the contents. Figure 2-72 shows an example.

Figure 2-72. A progress bar indicating a loading process

iOS accomplishes this through delegation. We will subscribe as the delegate of a web view, and the web view will notify us when it starts to load content. When the content is fully loaded, we get a message from the web view informing us about this. We do this through the delegate property of the web view. A delegate of a web view must conform to the UIWebViewDelegate protocol.

Let's go ahead and implement the little activity indicator in our view controller. Please bear in mind that the activity indicator is already a part of the application and we don't have to create it. We can control it using the setNetworkActivityIndicatorVisible: method of UIApplication. So let's start with the header file of our view controller:

```
#import <UIKit/UIKit.h>

@interface Loading_Web_Pages_with_UIWebViewViewController
          : UIViewController <UIWebViewDelegate>

@property (nonatomic, strong) UIWebView *myWebView;

@end
```

Then, do the implementation. Here we will use three of the methods declared in the UIWebViewDelegate protocol:

webViewDidStartLoad:
> This method gets called as soon as the web view starts loading content.

webViewDidFinishLoad:
> This method gets called as soon as the web view finishes loading content.

webView:didFailLoadWithError:
> This method gets called when the web view stops loading content, for instance because of an error or a broken network connection.

```
- (void)webViewDidStartLoad:(UIWebView *)webView{
  [[UIApplication sharedApplication] setNetworkActivityIndicatorVisible:YES];
}

- (void)webViewDidFinishLoad:(UIWebView *)webView{
  [[UIApplication sharedApplication] setNetworkActivityIndicatorVisible:NO];
}

- (void)webView:(UIWebView *)webView didFailLoadWithError:(NSError *)error{
  [[UIApplication sharedApplication] setNetworkActivityIndicatorVisible:NO];
}

- (void)viewDidLoad{
  [super viewDidLoad];

  self.view.backgroundColor = [UIColor whiteColor];

  self.myWebView = [[UIWebView alloc] initWithFrame:self.view.bounds];
  self.myWebView.delegate = self;
  self.myWebView.scalesPageToFit = YES;
  [self.view addSubview:self.myWebView];
```

```
    NSURL *url = [NSURL URLWithString:@"http://www.apple.com"];
    NSURLRequest *request = [NSURLRequest requestWithURL:url];

    [self.myWebView loadRequest:request];

}
```

2.25 Presenting Master-Detail Views with UISplitViewController

Problem

You want to take maximum advantage of iPad's relatively large screen by presenting two side-by-side view controllers.

Solution

Use the `UISplitViewController` class.

Discussion

Split view controllers are present only on the iPad. If you've used an iPad, you've probably already seen them. Just open the Settings app in landscape mode and have a look. Can you see the split view controller there in Figure 2-73?

A split view controller has left and right sides. The left side displays the main settings, and tapping on each one of those settings shows the details of that setting item on the right side of the split view controller.

 Never attempt to instantiate an object of type `UISplitViewController` on a device other than an iPad. This will raise an exception.

Apple has made it extremely easy to create split view controller based applications. Simply follow these steps to create your app based on split view controllers:

1. In Xcode, navigate to the File menu and choose New → New Project...

2. In the New Project screen, pick iOS → Application on the left side and then pick Master-Detail Application (as shown in Figure 2-74) and press Next.

3. In this screen, pick your Product Name and make sure your Device Family is Universal. We want to make sure our app runs both on the iPhone and the iPad. Once you are done, press Next (see Figure 2-75).

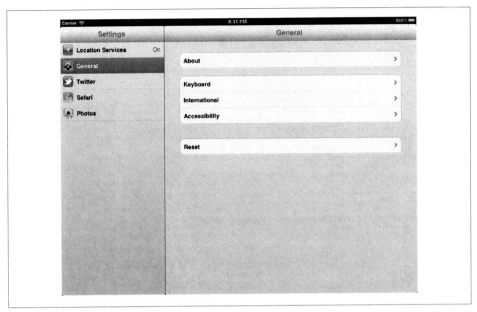

Figure 2-73. Split view controller in the Settings app on the iPad

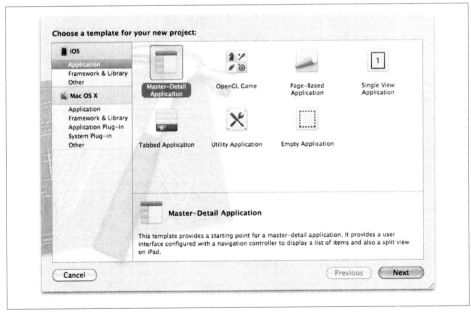

Figure 2-74. Picking the Master-Detail Application project template in Xcode

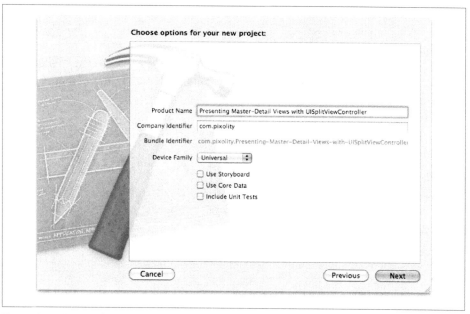

Figure 2-75. Setting the master-detail project settings in Xcode

4. Now pick where you would like to save your project. Once done, press the Create button (see Figure 2-76).

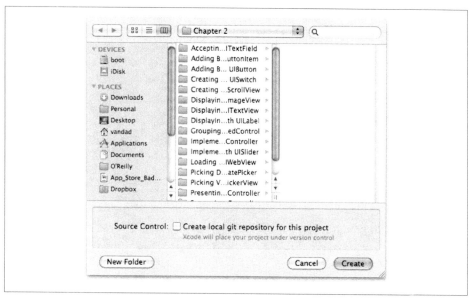

Figure 2-76. Saving the new master-detail application on disk

Now the project is created. In the Scheme breadcrumb button on the top-left corner of Xcode, make sure your app is set to run on the iPad Simulator instead of the iPhone Simulator. If you create a universal master-detail app in Xcode, Xcode makes sure that your app runs on the iPhone as well, but when you run your app on the iPhone, the structure of the app will be different. It will have a navigation controller with a view controller inside it, whereas running the same app on the iPad will use a split view controller with two view controllers inside it.

There are two files that are very important to note in the split view controller project template:

RootViewController
> The master view controller that appears on the left side of the split view controller on the iPad. On the iPhone, it is the first view controller that the user sees.

DetailViewController
> The detail view controller that appears on the right side of the split view controller on the iPad. On the iPhone, it is the view controller that gets pushed onto the stack once the user taps on any of the items on the root (first, master) view controller.

Now you need to think about communication between the master and the detail view controller. Do you want the communication to be done through the app delegate, or do you want the master view controller to send messages to the detail view controller directly? That's really up to you.

If you run the app in iPad Simulator, you'll notice that in landscape mode, you can see our master and detail view controllers in the split view controller, but as soon as you rotate the orientation to portrait, your master view controller is gone and is replaced with a Master navigation button on the top-left side of the navigation bar of the detail view controller. Although this is good, we weren't expecting it, since we were comparing it with the Settings app on the iPad. If you rotate the settings app to portrait on an iPad, you can still see both the master and the detail view controllers. How can we accomplish this? It turns out Apple has exposed an API to us through which we can do it. Simply go to the *DetailViewController.m* file and implement this method:

```
- (BOOL) splitViewController:(UISplitViewController *)svc
    shouldHideViewController:(UIViewController *)vc
               inOrientation:(UIInterfaceOrientation)orientation{
    return NO;
}
```

 This method is available only in iOS 5.0 SDK and above.

If you return NO from this method, iOS will *not* hide the master view controller in either orientation and both the master and the detail view controllers will be visible in both

---

landscape and portrait orientations. Now that we have implemented this method, we won't need those two methods anymore:

```
- (void)splitViewController:(UISplitViewController *)svc
    willHideViewController:(UIViewController *)aViewController
        withBarButtonItem:(UIBarButtonItem *)barButtonItem
      forPopoverController: (UIPopoverController *)pc{
  barButtonItem.title = @"Master";
  NSMutableArray *items = [[self.toolbar items] mutableCopy];
  [items insertObject:barButtonItem atIndex:0];
  [self.toolbar setItems:items animated:YES];
  self.popoverController = pc;
}

- (void)splitViewController:(UISplitViewController *)svc
    willShowViewController:(UIViewController *)aViewController
  invalidatingBarButtonItem:(UIBarButtonItem *)barButtonItem{
  NSMutableArray *items = [[self.toolbar items] mutableCopy];
  [items removeObjectAtIndex:0];
  [self.toolbar setItems:items animated:YES];
  self.popoverController = nil;
}
```

These methods were there simply to manage the navigation bar button for us, but now that we are not using that button any more, we can get rid of the methods. You can comment them out, or just remove them from the *DetailViewController.m* file.

At the moment, communication between the master and the detail view controller through messaging seems impossible, because the master doesn't have a reference to the detail view controller. Let's remedy that, shall we? The app delegate is the object that created both these view controllers, so we can keep the reference to the detail view controller in app delegate and read it in the master view controller. Let's add a property to our app delegate and call it detailViewController:

```
#import <UIKit/UIKit.h>

@class DetailViewController;

@interface Presenting_Master_Detail_Views_with_UISplitViewControllerAppDelegate
        : UIResponder <UIApplicationDelegate>

@property (nonatomic, strong) UIWindow *window;
@property (nonatomic, strong) UINavigationController *navigationController;
@property (nonatomic, strong) UISplitViewController *splitViewController;

@property (nonatomic, strong)
  DetailViewController *detailViewController;

@end
```

In the app delegate's implementation file, we can see the application:didFinishLaun chingWithOptions: selector. Find this line of code in that method:

```
DetailViewController *detailViewController =
  [[DetailViewController alloc] initWithNibName:@"DetailViewController_iPad"
                                    bundle:nil];
```

There, the app will instantiate an object of type DetailViewController and will place it inside the split view controller. However, as you can see, detailViewController in this code is a local variable. It shadows our property that has the same name, so we need to remove the local variable declaration and change it to this:

```
detailViewController =
  [[DetailViewController alloc] initWithNibName:@"DetailViewController_iPad"
                                    bundle:nil];
```

Now in the root view controller (master), find this method:

```
- (void)          tableView:(UITableView *)tableView
  didSelectRowAtIndexPath:(NSIndexPath *)indexPath{

  if ([[UIDevice currentDevice] userInterfaceIdiom]
      == UIUserInterfaceIdiomPhone) {

    DetailViewController *detailViewController =
      [[DetailViewController alloc]
        initWithNibName:@"DetailViewController_iPhone"
              bundle:nil];
    [self.navigationController pushViewController:detailViewController
                                  animated:YES];

  } else {
    /* iPad */
  }
}
```

This method gets called whenever the user taps on one of the items in the master view controller. As you can see, the logic is empty if the device is an iPad, so let's go ahead and retrieve the reference to the detail view controller through the app delegate:

```
- (void)          tableView:(UITableView *)tableView
  didSelectRowAtIndexPath:(NSIndexPath *)indexPath{

  if ([[UIDevice currentDevice] userInterfaceIdiom]
      == UIUserInterfaceIdiomPhone) {

    DetailViewController *detailViewController =
    [[DetailViewController alloc]
      initWithNibName:@"DetailViewController_iPhone"
      bundle:nil];
    [self.navigationController pushViewController:detailViewController
                                  animated:YES];

  } else {
    /* iPad */

    Presenting_Master_Detail_Views_with_UISplitViewControllerAppDelegate
    *appDelegate = [[UIApplication sharedApplication] delegate];
```

```
        NSLog(@"%@", appDelegate.detailViewController);

    }
}
```

Great. Now we have a reference to the detail view controller. Using this reference, you can now send messages to the detail view controller and ask it to perform various tasks based on the user's selection on the master view controller.

2.26 Enabling Paging with UIPageViewController

Problem

You want to create an app that works similarly to iBooks, where the user can flip through the pages of a book as if it were a real book, to provide an intuitive and real user experience.

Solution

Use UIPageViewController.

Discussion

Xcode has a template for page view controllers. It's best to first see how they look before reading an explanation of what they actually are. So follow these steps to create your app to use page view controllers:

 Page view controllers work both on the iPhone and the iPad.

1. In Xcode, go to the File menu and then choose New → New Project...
2. On the lefthand side of the New Project window, make sure you've selected iOS and then Application. Once that is done, pick the Page-Based Application template from the right side and press Next, as shown in Figure 2-78.
3. Now, select a product name and make sure the Device Family that you've chosen is Universal, as you normally would want your app to run on both the iPhone and the iPad (see Figure 2-77). Once you are done, press Next.
4. Select where you want to save your project. Once you are done, press the Create button. You have now successfully created your project.

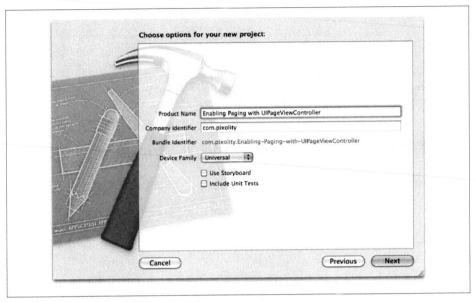

Figure 2-77. Setting the project settings of a page-based app

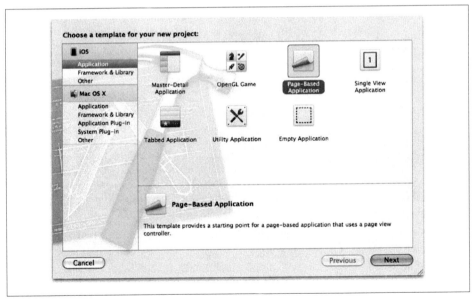

Figure 2-78. Creating a Page-Based Application in Xcode

You can now see that Xcode has created quite a few classes in your project. Let's have a quick look at what each one of these classes does:

Delegate Class

The app delegate simply creates an instance of the RootViewController class and presents it to the user. There is one *.xib* for iPad and another one of iPhone, but both are using the aforementioned class.

RootViewController

Creates an instance of UIPageViewController and adds that view controller to itself. So the UI of this view controller is actually a mix of two view controllers: the RootViewController itself and a UIPageViewController.

DataViewController

For every page in the page view controller, an instance of this class gets presented to this user. This class is a subclass of UIViewController.

ModelController

This is simply a subclass of NSObject that conforms to the UIPageViewController DataSource protocol. This class is the data source of the page view controller.

So you can see that a page view controller has both a delegate and a data source. With Xcode's default page-based application template, the root view controller becomes the delegate and the model controller becomes the data source of the page view controller. In order to understand how a page view controller really works, we need to understand its delegation and data source protocols. Let's start with the delegate, UIPageViewCon trollerDelegate. This protocol has two important methods:

```
- (void)pageViewController:(UIPageViewController *)pageViewController
        didFinishAnimating:(BOOL)finished
   previousViewControllers:(NSArray *)previousViewControllers
       transitionCompleted:(BOOL)completed;

- (UIPageViewControllerSpineLocation)
    pageViewController:(UIPageViewController *)pageViewController
    spineLocationForInterfaceOrientation:(UIInterfaceOrientation)orientation;
```

The first method gets called when the user turns to the next or the previous page, *or* if the user initiates the movement from one page to the other but decides against it while the page is moving (in which case, the user gets sent back to the page she was in before). The transitionCompleted will get set to YES if this was a successful page animation, or set to NO if the user decided against the movement and cancelled it in the middle of the animation.

The second method gets called whenever the device orientation changes. You can use this method to specify the location of the spine for the pages by returning a value of type UIPageViewControllerSpineLocation:

```
enum {
  UIPageViewControllerSpineLocationNone = 0,
  UIPageViewControllerSpineLocationMin = 1,
  UIPageViewControllerSpineLocationMid = 2,
  UIPageViewControllerSpineLocationMax = 3
};
typedef NSInteger UIPageViewControllerSpineLocation;
```

This might be a bit confusing to you, but let me demonstrate. If we are using a UIPage ViewControllerSpineLocationMin spine location, the page view controller will require only one view controller to present to the user, and when the user goes to the next page, a new view controller will be presented to him. However, if we set the spine location to UIPageViewControllerSpineLocationMid, we will be required to display 2 view controllers at the same time: one on the left and another on the right, with the spine sitting between them. Let me show you what I mean. In Figure 2-79 you can see an example of a page view controller in landscape mode, with the spine location set to UIPageView ControllerSpineLocationMin.

Figure 2-79. One view controller presented in a page view controller in landscape mode

Now if we return the spine location of UIPageViewControllerSpineLocationMid, we will get results similar to Figure 2-80.

As you can see in that image, the spine is located exactly in the center of the screen between two view controllers. Once the user flips a page from right to the left, the page rests on the left and the page view controller reveals a new view controller on the right side. This whole logic is in this delegate method:

```
- (UIPageViewControllerSpineLocation)pageViewController
    :(UIPageViewController *)pageViewController
    spineLocationForInterfaceOrientation:(UIInterfaceOrientation)orientation;
```

We've now covered the delegate of the page view controller, but how about the data source? The data source of a page view controller must conform to the UIPage ViewControllerDataSource. Two important methods that this protocol exposes are:

```
- (UIViewController *)
    pageViewController:(UIPageViewController *)pageViewController
```

Figure 2-80. Two view controllers displayed in a page view controller in landscape mode

```
    viewControllerBeforeViewController:(UIViewController *)viewController;

  - (UIViewController *)
    pageViewController:(UIPageViewController *)pageViewController
    viewControllerAfterViewController:(UIViewController *)viewController;
```

The first method gets called when the page view controller already has a view controller on the screen and needs to know which previous view controller to render. This happens when the user decides to flip to the next page. The second method is called when the page view controller needs to figure out which view controller to display after the view controller that is being flipped.

Xcode, as you've already seen, has greatly simplified setting up a page-based application. All you really need to do now is to provide content to the data model (`ModelController`) and off you go. If you need to customize the colors and images in your view controllers, do so by either using the Interface Builder to modify the *.xib* files directly or write your own code in the implementation of each of the view controllers.

2.27 Displaying Popovers with UIPopoverController

Problem

You want to display content on an iPad without blocking the whole screen.

Solution

Use popovers.

Discussion

Popovers are used to display additional information on the iPad screen. An example can be seen in the Safari app on the iPad. When the user taps on the Bookmarks button, she will see a popover displaying the bookmarks content on the screen (see Figure 2-81).

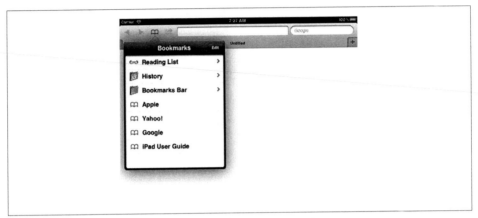

Figure 2-81. The bookmarks popover in the Safari app on an iPad

The default behavior of popovers is that when the user taps somewhere outside the region of the popover, the popover will automatically get dismissed. You can ask the popover to not get dismissed if the user taps on specific parts of the screen, as we will see later. Popovers present their content by using a view controller. Note that you can also present navigation controllers inside popovers, because navigation controllers are a subclass of `UIViewController`.

 Popovers can be used only on iPad devices. If you have a view controller whose code runs both on an iPad and on an iPhone, you need to make sure that you are not instantiating the popover on a device other than the iPad.

Popovers can be presented to the user in two ways:

1. From inside a navigation button, an instance of `UIBarButtonItem`
2. From inside a rectangular area in a view

When a device orientation is changed (the device is rotated), popovers are either dismissed or hidden temporarily. You need to make sure that you give your users a good experience by redisplaying the popover after the orientation change has settled, if possible. In certain cases, your popover might get dismissed automatically after an orientation change. For instance, if the user taps on a navigation button in landscape mode you might display a popover on the screen. Suppose your app is designed so that when the orientation changes to portrait, the navigation button is removed from the navigation bar for some reason. Now, the correct user experience would be to hide the popover associated with that navigation bar after the orientation of the device is changed to portrait. In some instances, though, you will need to play with popovers a bit to give your users a good experience, because handling device orientation is not always as straightforward as in the aforementioned scenario.

To create the demo popover app, we need to first come up with a strategy based on our requirements. For this example, we want to build an app with a view controller loaded inside a navigation controller. The root view controller will display a + button on the right corner of its navigation bar. When the + button is tapped on an iPad device, it will display a popover with two buttons on it. The first button will say "Photo" and the second button will say "Audio." When the same navigation button is tapped on an iPhone device, we will display an alert view with three buttons: the two aforementioned buttons, and a cancel button so that the user can cancel the alert view if he wishes to. When these buttons are tapped (whether on the alert view on an iPhone or the popover on an iPad), we won't really do anything. We will simply dismiss the alert view or the popover.

Go ahead and create a Single View universal project in Xcode and name the project *Displaying_Popovers_with_UIPopoverControllerViewController*. Then go to your app delegate's header file and define a navigation controller:

```
#import <UIKit/UIKit.h>

@class Displaying_Popovers_with_UIPopoverControllerViewController;

@interface Displaying_Popovers_with_UIPopoverControllerAppDelegate
        : UIResponder <UIApplicationDelegate>

@property (nonatomic, strong) UIWindow *window;

@property (nonatomic, strong)
  Displaying_Popovers_with_UIPopoverControllerViewController *viewController;

@property (nonatomic, strong) UINavigationController *navigationController;

@end
```

Next, instantiate your navigation controller in the app delegate's implementation file, but instead of the view controller, display the navigation controller to the user:

```
#import "Displaying_Popovers_with_UIPopoverControllerAppDelegate.h"

#import "Displaying_Popovers_with_UIPopoverControllerViewController.h"

@implementation Displaying_Popovers_with_UIPopoverControllerAppDelegate

- (BOOL)            application:(UIApplication *)application
  didFinishLaunchingWithOptions:(NSDictionary *)launchOptions{

  self.window = [[UIWindow alloc] initWithFrame:
                [[UIScreen mainScreen] bounds]];
```

```
UIUserInterfaceIdiom uiIdiom = [[UIDevice currentDevice] userInterfaceIdiom];

NSString *viewControllerClass =
  @"Displaying_Popovers_with_UIPopoverControllerViewController_iPad";

if (uiIdiom == UIUserInterfaceIdiomPhone) {
  viewControllerClass =
    @"Displaying_Popovers_with_UIPopoverControllerViewController_iPhone";
}

self.viewController =
[[Displaying_Popovers_with_UIPopoverControllerViewController alloc]
 initWithNibName:viewControllerClass
 bundle:nil];

self.navigationController = [[UINavigationController alloc]
                             initWithRootViewController:self.viewController];

self.window.rootViewController = self.navigationController;
[self.window makeKeyAndVisible];
return YES;
}
```

After this, we need to go into the definition file of our view controller and define a property of type UIPopoverController:

```
#import <UIKit/UIKit.h>
@interface Displaying_Popovers_with_UIPopoverControllerViewController
        : UIViewController <UIAlertViewDelegate>

@property (nonatomic, strong) UIPopoverController *popoverController;
@property (nonatomic, strong) UIBarButtonItem *barButtonAdd;

@end
```

You can see that we are also defining a property called barButtonAdd in our view controller. This is the navigation button that we will add on our navigation bar. Our plan is to display our popover when the user taps on this button (you can read more about navigation buttons in Recipe 2.15). However, we need to make sure we instantiate the popover only if the device is an iPad. Before we go ahead and implement our root view controller with the navigation button, let's go ahead and create a subclass of UIView Controller and name it *PopoverContentViewController*. We will display the contents of this view controller inside our popover later. See Recipe 2.10 for information about view controllers and ways of creating them.

The content view controller displayed inside the popover will have two buttons (as per our requirements). However, this view controller will need to have a reference to the popover controller in order to dismiss the popover when the user taps on any of the buttons. For this, we need to define a property in our content view controller to refer to the popover:

```
#import <UIKit/UIKit.h>

@interface PopoverContentViewController : UIViewController

@property (nonatomic, strong) UIButton *buttonPhoto;
@property (nonatomic, strong) UIButton *buttonAudio;

/* We shouldn't define this as strong. That will create a retain cycle
  between the popover controller and the content view controller, since the
  popover controller retains the content view controller and the view controller
  retains the popover controller */
@property (nonatomic, weak) UIPopoverController *popoverController;

@end
```

Now we will go and synthesize the popover controller in the implementation file of our content view controller:

```
#import "PopoverContentViewController.h"

@implementation PopoverContentViewController

@synthesize popoverController;

...
```

After this, we'll create our two buttons in the content view controller and link them to their action methods. These methods will take care of dismissing the popover that is displaying this view controller. Remember, the popover controller will be responsible for assigning itself to the popoverController property of the content view controller:

```
#import "PopoverContentViewController.h"

@implementation PopoverContentViewController

@synthesize popoverController;

- (BOOL) isInPopover{

  Class popoverClass = NSClassFromString(@"UIPopoverController");

  if (popoverClass != nil &&
      UI_USER_INTERFACE_IDIOM() == UIUserInterfaceIdiomPad &&
      self.popoverController != nil){
    return YES;
  } else {
    return NO;
  }

}

- (void) gotoAppleWebsite:(id)paramSender{

  if ([self isInPopover]){
    /* Go to website and then dismiss popover */
```

```
    [self.popoverController dismissPopoverAnimated:YES];
  } else {
    /* Handle case for iPhone */
  }

}

- (void) gotoAppleStoreWebsite:(id)paramSender{

  if ([self isInPopover]){
    /* Go to website and then dismiss popover */
    [self.popoverController dismissPopoverAnimated:YES];
  } else {
    /* Handle case for iPhone */
  }

}


- (void)viewDidLoad{
  [super viewDidLoad];

  self.view.backgroundColor = [UIColor whiteColor];

  self.contentSizeForViewInPopover = CGSizeMake(200.0f, 125.0f);

  CGRect buttonRect = CGRectMake(20.0f,
                                 20.0f,
                                 160.0f,
                                 37.0f);

  self.buttonPhoto = [UIButton buttonWithType:UIButtonTypeRoundedRect];
  [self.buttonPhoto setTitle:@"Photo"
                   forState:UIControlStateNormal];
  [self.buttonPhoto addTarget:self
                       action:@selector(gotoAppleWebsite:)
              forControlEvents:UIControlEventTouchUpInside];

  self.buttonPhoto.frame = buttonRect;

  [self.view addSubview:self.buttonPhoto];


  buttonRect.origin.y += 50.0f;
  self.buttonAudio = [UIButton buttonWithType:UIButtonTypeRoundedRect];

  [self.buttonAudio setTitle:@"Audio"
                   forState:UIControlStateNormal];
  [self.buttonAudio addTarget:self
                       action:@selector(gotoAppleStoreWebsite:)
              forControlEvents:UIControlEventTouchUpInside];

  self.buttonAudio.frame = buttonRect;

  [self.view addSubview:self.buttonAudio];
```

```
    }

    - (BOOL)shouldAutorotateToInterfaceOrientation
          :(UIInterfaceOrientation)interfaceOrientation{
      return YES;
    }

    @end
```

Now in the viewDidLoad method of our root view controller, we will create our navigation button. Based on the device type, when the navigation bar is tapped, we will display either a popover (on the iPad) or an alert view (on the iPhone):

```
    - (void)viewDidLoad{
      [super viewDidLoad];

      /* See if this class exists on the iOS running the app */
      Class popoverClass = NSClassFromString(@"UIPopoverController");

      if (popoverClass != nil &&
          UI_USER_INTERFACE_IDIOM() == UIUserInterfaceIdiomPad){

        PopoverContentViewController *content =
        [[PopoverContentViewController alloc]  initWithNibName:nil
                                                        bundle:nil];

        self.popoverController = [[UIPopoverController alloc]
                              initWithContentViewController:content];

        content.popoverController = self.popoverController;

        self.barButtonAdd = [[UIBarButtonItem alloc]
                        initWithBarButtonSystemItem:UIBarButtonSystemItemAdd
                        target:self
                        action:@selector(performAddWithPopover:)];

      } else {

        self.barButtonAdd = [[UIBarButtonItem alloc]
                        initWithBarButtonSystemItem:UIBarButtonSystemItemAdd
                        target:self
                        action:@selector(performAddWithAlertView:)];

      }

      [self.navigationItem setRightBarButtonItem:self.barButtonAdd
                                        animated:NO];


    }

    - (BOOL)shouldAutorotateToInterfaceOrientation
          :(UIInterfaceOrientation)interfaceOrientation{
```

```
    return YES;
}
```

 The popover controller sets a reference to itself in the content view controller after its initialization. This is very important. A popover controller *cannot* be initialized without a content view controller. Once the popover is initialized with a content view controller, you can go ahead and change the content view controller in the popover controller, but not during the initialization.

We have elected the `performAddWithPopover:` method to be invoked when the + navigation bar button is tapped on an iPad device. If the device isn't an iPad, we've asked the + navigation bar button to invoke the `performAddWithAlertView:` method. Let's go ahead and implement these methods and also take care of the delegate methods of our alert view, so that we know what alert view button the user tapped on an iPhone:

```
- (NSString *) photoButtonTitle{
  return @"Photo";
}

- (NSString *) audioButtonTitle{
  return @"Audio";
}

- (void)           alertView:(UIAlertView *)alertView
  didDismissWithButtonIndex:(NSInteger)buttonIndex{

  NSString *buttonTitle = [alertView buttonTitleAtIndex:buttonIndex];

  if ([buttonTitle isEqualToString:[self photoButtonTitle]]){
    /* Adding a photo ... */
  }
  else if ([buttonTitle isEqualToString:[self audioButtonTitle]]){
    /* Adding an audio... */
  }

}

- (void) performAddWithAlertView:(id)paramSender{

  [[[UIAlertView alloc] initWithTitle:nil
                              message:@"Add..."
                             delegate:self
                    cancelButtonTitle:@"Cancel"
                    otherButtonTitles:
     [self photoButtonTitle],
     [self audioButtonTitle], nil] show];

}

- (void) performAddWithPopover:(id)paramSender{
```

```
[self.popoverController
 presentPopoverFromBarButtonItem:self.barButtonAdd
 permittedArrowDirections:UIPopoverArrowDirectionAny
 animated:YES];

}
```

If you now run your app on iPad Simulator and tap the + button on the navigation bar, you will see an interface similar to Figure 2-82:

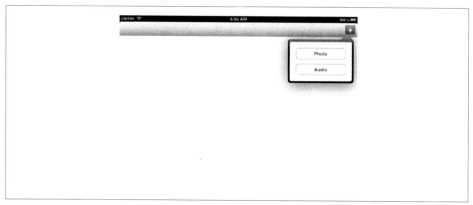

Figure 2-82. Our simple popover displayed when a navigation button was tapped

If you run the same universal app on the iPhone Simulator and tap the + button on the navigation bar, you will see results similar to Figure 2-83.

Figure 2-83. Popovers are replaced by alert view in a universal app

We used an important property of our content view controller: `contentSizeForView InPopover`. The popover, when displaying its content view controller, will read the value of this property automatically and will adjust its size (width and height) to thissize. Also, we used the `presentPopoverFromBarButtonItem:permittedArrowDirections:anima ted:` method of our popover in our root view controller to display the popover over a navigation bar button. The first parameter to this method is the navigation bar button from which the popover controller has to be displayed. The second parameter specifies the direction of the popover when it appears, in relation to the object from which it appears. For example, in Figure 2-82, you can see that our popover's arrow is pointing up towards the navigation bar button. The value that you pass to this parameter must be of type `UIPopoverArrowDirection`:

```
enum {
  UIPopoverArrowDirectionUp = 1UL << 0,
  UIPopoverArrowDirectionDown = 1UL << 1,
  UIPopoverArrowDirectionLeft = 1UL << 2,
  UIPopoverArrowDirectionRight = 1UL << 3,
  UIPopoverArrowDirectionAny = UIPopoverArrowDirectionUp |
                               UIPopoverArrowDirectionDown |
                               UIPopoverArrowDirectionLeft |
                               UIPopoverArrowDirectionRight,
                               UIPopoverArrowDirectionUnknown = NSUIntegerMax
};
typedef NSUInteger UIPopoverArrowDirection;
```

See Also

Recipe 2.10; Recipe 2.15

2.28 Displaying Progress with UIProgressView

Problem

You want to display a progress bar on the screen, depicting the progress of a certain task; for instance, the progress of downloading a file from a URL.

Solution

Instantiate a view of type `UIProgressView` and place it on another view.

Discussion

A progress view is what programmers generally call a progress bar. An example of a progress view is depicted in Figure 2-84.

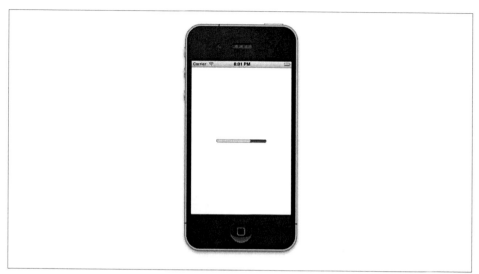

Figure 2-84. A simple progress view

Progress views are generally displayed to users to show them the progress of a task that has a well-defined starting and ending point. For instance, downloading 30 files is a well-defined task with a specific starting and ending point. This task obviously finishes when all 30 files have been downloaded. A progress view is an instance of `UIProgress View` and is initialized using the designated initializer of this class, the `initWithProg ressViewStyle:` method. This method takes in the style of the progress bar to be created as a parameter. This parameter is of type `UIProgressViewStyle` and can therefore be one of the following values:

`UIProgressViewStyleDefault`

This is the default style of the progress view. An example of this is the progress view shown in Figure 2-84.

`UIProgressViewStyleBar`

This is similar to the `UIProgressViewStyleDefault` but is meant to be used for progress views that are to be added to a toolbar.

An instance of `UIProgressView` defines a property called `progress` (of type `float`). This property tells iOS how the bar inside the progress view should be rendered. This value must be in the range +0 to +1.0. If the value of +0 is given, the progress bar won't appear to have started yet. A value of +1.0 shows the progress of 100%. The progress depicted in Figure 2-84 is 0.5 (or 50%).

To get used to creating progress views, let's create one similar to what we saw in Figure 2-84. First things first: define a property for your progress view:

```
#import <UIKit/UIKit.h>

@interface ViewController : UIViewController
```

```
@property (nonatomic, strong) UIProgressView *progressView;

@end
```

Then instantiate an object of type UIProgressView:

```
- (void)viewDidLoad{

    [super viewDidLoad];
    self.view.backgroundColor = [UIColor whiteColor];

    self.progressView = [[UIProgressView alloc]
                            initWithProgressViewStyle:UIProgressViewStyleBar];
    self.progressView.center = self.view.center;
    self.progressView.progress = 0.5f;

    [self.view addSubview:self.progressView];

}
```

Obviously, creating a progress view is very straightforward. All you really need to do is to display your progress correctly, because the progress property of a progress view should be in the range +0 to +1.0, which is a normalized value. So if you have 30 tasks to take care of and you have completed 20 of them so far, you need to assign the result of the following equation to the progress property of your progress view:

```
self.progressView.progress = 20.0f / 30.0f;
```

 The reason the values 20 and 30 are passed to the equation as floating-point values is to tell the compiler that the division has to happen on floating-point values, producing a value with decimal numbers. If you provided the integer division 20/30 to the compiler to place inside the progress property of your progress view, you would get the integral value of 0 out of the division, because the compiler will perform integer division that truncates the result to the next lower integer. In short, your progress view would show zero progress all the way to the end, when 30/30 produces the result of 1; not of much value to the user.

2.29 Listening and Reacting to Keyboard Notifications

Problem

You are allowing the user to enter some text in your UI, using some component such as a text field or text view that requires the keyboard's presence. However, when the keyboard pops up on the screen, it obstructs a good half of your UI, rendering it useless. You want to avoid this situation.

Solution

Listen to keyboard notifications and move your UI components up/down or completely reshuffle your components, so that with the keyboard obstructing the screen, what is essential to the user is still visible to him. For more information about the actual notifications sent by the keyboard, please refer to the Discussion section of this recipe.

Discussion

iOS devices do not have a physical keyboard. They have a software keyboard that pops up whenever the user has to enter some text into something like a text field (UIText Field, see Recipe 2.19 for more information) or a text view (UITextView, see Recipe 2.20 for more information). On the iPad, the user can even split the keyboard and move it up and down. These are some of the edge cases that you might want to take care of when designing your user interface. You can work with the UI designers in your company (if you have access to such experts) and let them know about the possibility of the user splitting the keyboard on the iPad. They will need to know about that before making the art and creatives. We will discuss that edge case in this recipe.

Let's have a look at the keyboard on the iPhone first. The keyboard can get displayed in portrait and landscape mode. In portrait, the keyboard on an iPhone looks like Figure 2-85.

Figure 2-85. Portrait-mode keyboard on an iPhone

The keyboard in landscape mode on an iPhone will look similar to that shown in Figure 2-86.

Figure 2-86. The keyboard in landscape mode on an iPhone

On the iPad, however, the keyboard is a bit different. The most obvious difference is that the keyboard is actually much bigger in size than the one on the iPhone, since the iPad screen is physically bigger. Also, the user can split the keyboard if she wants to. Figure 2-87 shows an example of the iPad keyboard in portrait mode. The landscape keyboard on an iPad is obviously wider, but contains the same keys as the portrait-mode keyboard does (Figure 2-88). Finally, Figure 2-89 shows an example of the split keyboard on the iPad, in landscape mode (the keyboard can be split in both landscape mode and portrait mode).

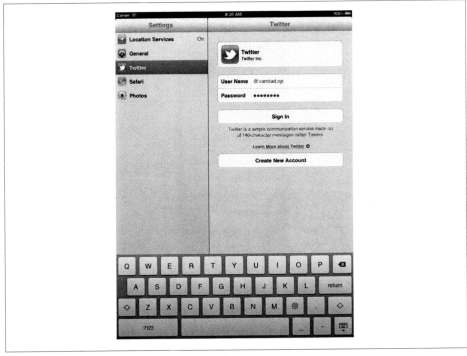

Figure 2-87. The iPad keyboard in portrait mode

Figure 2-88. The iPad keyboard in landscape mode

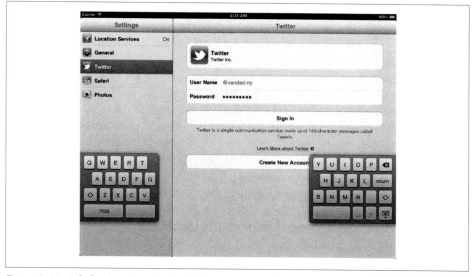

Figure 2-89. Split keyboard on the iPad in landscape mode

iOS broadcasts various notifications related to the display of the keyboard on the screen. Here is a list of these notifications and a brief explanation for each one:

UIKeyboardWillShowNotification

> This notification gets broadcast when the keyboard is about to get displayed on the screen. This notification carries with it a user-info dictionary that contains

various information about the keyboard, the animation that the keyboard will use to get displayed on the screen, and more.

UIKeyboardDidShowNotification

This notification gets broadcast when the keyboard gets displayed on the screen.

UIKeyboardWillHideNotification

This notification gets broadcast when the keyboard is about to get removed from the screen. This notification will carry with it a user-info dictionary that contains various bits and pieces of information about the keyboard, the keyboard's animation when it is hiding, the duration of the animation, etc.

UIKeyboardDidHideNotification

This notification gets broadcast when the keyboard gets fully hidden after it was being shown on the screen.

As already mentioned, only the UIKeyboardWillShowNotification and the UIKeyboardWillHideNotification notifications carry a user-info dictionary with them with valid keys and values in those dictionaries. Here are the keys in those dictionaries that you might be interested in:

UIKeyboardAnimationCurveUserInfoKey

The value of this key specifies the type of animation curve the keyboard is using to show or hide itself. This key contains a value (encapsulated in an object of type NSValue) of type NSNumber that itself contains an unsigned integer of type NSUInteger.

UIKeyboardAnimationDurationUserInfoKey

The value of this key specifies the duration of animation the keyboard is using to show or hide itself, in seconds. This key contains a value (encapsulated in an object of type NSValue) of type NSNumber that itself contains a double value of type double.

UIKeyboardFrameBeginUserInfoKey

The value of this key specifies the frame of the keyboard before the animation happens. If the keyboard is about to get displayed, this will be the frame before the keyboard appears. If the keyboard is already displayed and is about to hide, this will be the frame of the keyboard as it is on the screen, before it animates out of the screen. This key contains a value (encapsulated in an object of type NSValue) of type CGRect.

UIKeyboardFrameEndUserInfoKey

The value of this key specifies the frame of the keyboard after the animation happens. If the keyboard is about to get displayed, this will be the frame after the keyboard animates up and is fully displayed. If the keyboard is already displayed and is about to hide, this will be the frame of the keyboard after it is fully hidden. This key contains a value (encapsulated in an object of type NSValue) of type CGRect.

The frames that get reported by iOS as the beginning and ending frames of the keyboard do not take into account the orientation of the device. You need to convert the reported CGRect values to a relevant orientation-aware coordinate, as we will see soon in this recipe.

Let's have a look at an example, shall we? Let's create a simple table view on our view controller's view and change its content inset (the margins from top, right, bottom, and left side of the table view) when the keyboard gets displayed. We will populate this table view with 100 cells, enough to fill the entire screen on both the iPhone and the iPad (in a Universal app), so let's start with the header file of our view controller:

The CGRectIntersection function that we are going to use in this recipe is defined and implemented in the CoreGraphics framework. To be able to compile this code, you will need to make sure that you have linked your app against the aforementioned framework. You can do so by selecting your project's icon in Xcode, then selecting your target from the list that appears on the righthand side. Now you need to select the Build Phases tab. In the Link Binary With Libraries box, make sure that your target is linked against this framework. If not, you can press the + button in that box and simply add that framework to the list of frameworks your app links against.

```
#import <UIKit/UIKit.h>

@interface ViewController : UIViewController
        <UITableViewDelegate, UITableViewDataSource, UITextFieldDelegate>

@property (nonatomic, strong) UITableView *myTableView;

@end
```

Next, we will instantiate the table view when our view loads:

```
- (void)viewDidLoad{
  [super viewDidLoad];

  self.myTableView = [[UITableView alloc]
                      initWithFrame:self.view.bounds
                      style:UITableViewStyleGrouped];

  self.myTableView.delegate = self;
  self.myTableView.dataSource = self;
  self.myTableView.autoresizingMask = UIViewAutoresizingFlexibleWidth |
                                      UIViewAutoresizingFlexibleHeight;
  [self.view addSubview:self.myTableView];

}
```

After this, we will need to populate our table view with 100 cells and in each cell, create a text field as the accessory view. We do this to allow the user to trigger the keyboard to pop up. If we don't have a text field or some means for the user to enter text, we will never be able to get the keyboard on the screen, so let's do that now:

```
- (BOOL)textFieldShouldReturn:(UITextField *)textField{
  /* Make sure the Done button on the keyboard for each text field
   (accessory views of each cell) dismisses the keyboard */
  [textField resignFirstResponder];
  return YES;
}

- (NSInteger) numberOfSectionsInTableView:(UITableView *)tableView{
  return 1;
}

- (NSInteger) tableView:(UITableView *)tableView
  numberOfRowsInSection:(NSInteger)section{
  return 100;
}

- (UITableViewCell *) tableView:(UITableView *)tableView
         cellForRowAtIndexPath:(NSIndexPath *)indexPath{

  UITableViewCell *result = nil;

  static NSString *CellIdentifier = @"CellIdentifier";

  result = [tableView dequeueReusableCellWithIdentifier:CellIdentifier];

  if (result == nil){
    result = [[UITableViewCell alloc] initWithStyle:UITableViewCellStyleDefault
                              reuseIdentifier:CellIdentifier];
    result.selectionStyle = UITableViewCellSelectionStyleNone;
  }

  result.textLabel.text = [NSString stringWithFormat:
                       @"Cell %ld", (long)indexPath.row];

  CGRect accessoryRect = CGRectMake(0.0f,
                                    0.0f,
                                    150.0f,
                                    31.0f);

  UITextField *accesssory = [[UITextField alloc] initWithFrame:accessoryRect];
  accesssory.borderStyle = UITextBorderStyleRoundedRect;
  accesssory.contentVerticalAlignment = UIControlContentVerticalAlignmentCenter;
  accesssory.placeholder = @"Enter Text";
  accesssory.delegate = self;
  result.accessoryView = accesssory;

  return result;

}
```

Fantastic. If you now run your app on iPhone Simulator, you will see something similar to Figure 2-90.

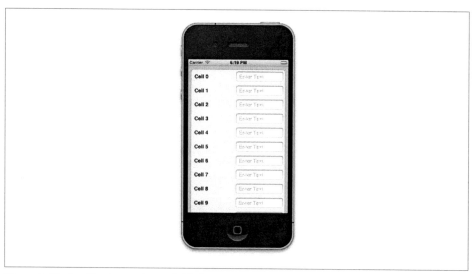

Figure 2-90. A table view with text fields for accessory view of each cell

Go ahead now and tap on the first text field (in the first cell). Now scroll the table view all the way down to the last cell and see what happens, You can't see the last 5-6 cells, can you? What you can see in portrait mode on an iPhone will be similar to that shown in Figure 2-91.

Figure 2-91. Keyboard obstructing the bottom half of a table view

What we can now do is to listen for the UIKeyboardWillShowNotification and the UIKey
boardWillHideNotification notifications and adjust our table view's content inset accordingly:

```
- (void) viewDidAppear:(BOOL)paramAnimated{
  [super viewDidAppear:paramAnimated];

  NSNotificationCenter *center = [NSNotificationCenter defaultCenter];

  [center addObserver:self
             selector:@selector(handleKeyboardWillShow:)
                 name:UIKeyboardWillShowNotification
               object:nil];
  [center addObserver:self
             selector:@selector(handleKeyboardWillHide:)
                 name:UIKeyboardWillHideNotification
               object:nil];

}

- (void) viewDidDisappear:(BOOL)paramAnimated{
  [super viewDidDisappear:paramAnimated];
  [[NSNotificationCenter defaultCenter] removeObserver:self];
}
```

 A common mistake programmers make is to keep listening for keyboard
notifications even if their view controller's view is not on the screen.
They start listening for notifications in the viewDidLoad method and
remove themselves as the observer in viewDidUnload or the dealloc
method if they don't have ARC enabled. This is a problematic approach
because when your view is off the screen and the keyboard is getting
displayed on some other view, you should not be adjusting any components on your hidden view controller. Keep in mind that keyboard
notifications, just like any other notification, are broadcast to all observer objects, so you need to take extra care that you do not react to
keyboard notifications while your view is offscreen.

Now that we have started listening for keyboard notifications, we can implement the
observer methods that we submitted to NSNotificationCenter. The handleKeyboard
WillShow: method will be responsible for setting the content inset of our table view:

```
- (void) handleKeyboardWillShow:(NSNotification *)paramNotification{

  NSDictionary *userInfo = [paramNotification userInfo];

  NSValue *animationCurveObject =
    [userInfo valueForKey:UIKeyboardAnimationCurveUserInfoKey];

  NSValue *animationDurationObject =
    [userInfo valueForKey:UIKeyboardAnimationDurationUserInfoKey];

  NSValue *keyboardEndRectObject =
```

```
        [userInfo valueForKey:UIKeyboardFrameEndUserInfoKey];

NSUInteger animationCurve = 0;
double animationDuration = 0.0f;
CGRect keyboardEndRect = CGRectMake(0, 0, 0, 0);

[animationCurveObject getValue:&animationCurve];
[animationDurationObject getValue:&animationDuration];
[keyboardEndRectObject getValue:&keyboardEndRect];

[UIView beginAnimations:@"changeTableViewContentInset"
                context:NULL];
[UIView setAnimationDuration:animationDuration];
[UIView setAnimationCurve:(UIViewAnimationCurve)animationCurve];

UIWindow *window = [[[UIApplication sharedApplication] delegate] window];

CGRect intersectionOfKeyboardRectAndWindowRect =
  CGRectIntersection(window.frame, keyboardEndRect);

CGFloat bottomInset = intersectionOfKeyboardRectAndWindowRect.size.height;

self.myTableView.contentInset = UIEdgeInsetsMake(0.0f,
                                                 0.0f,
                                                 bottomInset,
                                                 0.0f);

NSIndexPath *indexPathOfOwnerCell = nil;
/* Also, make sure the selected text field is visible on the screen */
NSInteger numberOfCells = [self.myTableView.dataSource
                           tableView:self.myTableView
                           numberOfRowsInSection:0];

/* So let's go through all the cells and find their accessory text fields.
 Once we have the reference to those text fields, we can see which one of
 them is the first responder (has the keyboard) and we will make a call
 to the table view to make sure that, after the keyboard is displayed,
 that specific cell is NOT obstructed by the keyboard */
for (NSInteger counter = 0;
     counter < numberOfCells;
     counter++){
  NSIndexPath *indexPath = [NSIndexPath indexPathForRow:counter
                                              inSection:0];
  UITableViewCell *cell = [self.myTableView cellForRowAtIndexPath:indexPath];
  UITextField *textField = (UITextField *)cell.accessoryView;
  if ([textField isKindOfClass:[UITextField class]] == NO){
    continue;
  }
  if ([textField isFirstResponder]){
    indexPathOfOwnerCell = indexPath;
    break;
  }
}

[UIView commitAnimations];
```

```
    if (indexPathOfOwnerCell != nil){
      [self.myTableView scrollToRowAtIndexPath:indexPathOfOwnerCell
                         atScrollPosition:UITableViewScrollPositionMiddle
                                 animated:YES];
    }

  }
```

So here is what we are doing in this method, in that order:

1. Retrieve the different animation properties of the keyboard, including its animation time, its animation curve, and the frame that the keyboard will have once its animation finished. We do this using the user-info dictionary of the UIKeyboardWill ShowNotification notification.

2. We then start an animation block that will change the content inset of our table view. Before we do this, we need to know how much of the area of our table view the keyboard will be obstructing.

3. Using the CGRectIntersection function, we retrieve the intersection between our window's frame and the frame of the keyboard when it has finished its animation. Using this technique, we can find out how much of the area of our window will be obstructed by the keyboard after its animation, so that we can set the bottom content inset of the table view accordingly.

4. We set the properties of our animation block, such as its curve and duration, and commit the animation. The animation block, as mentioned before, will simply change the content inset of our table view to fit the whole content into the visible area of the screen after the keyboard pops up.

Now we need to move on to the implementation of the handleKeyboardWillHide: method:

```
- (void) handleKeyboardWillHide:(NSNotification *)paramNotification{

  if (UIEdgeInsetsEqualToEdgeInsets(self.myTableView.contentInset,
                                    UIEdgeInsetsZero)){
    /* Our table view's content inset is intact so no need to reset it */
    return;
  }

  NSDictionary *userInfo = [paramNotification userInfo];

  NSValue *animationCurveObject =
  [userInfo valueForKey:UIKeyboardAnimationCurveUserInfoKey];

  NSValue *animationDurationObject =
  [userInfo valueForKey:UIKeyboardAnimationDurationUserInfoKey];

  NSValue *keyboardEndRectObject =
  [userInfo valueForKey:UIKeyboardFrameEndUserInfoKey];

  NSUInteger animationCurve = 0;
```

```
    double animationDuration = 0.0f;
    CGRect keyboardEndRect = CGRectMake(0, 0, 0, 0);

    [animationCurveObject getValue:&animationCurve];
    [animationDurationObject getValue:&animationDuration];
    [keyboardEndRectObject getValue:&keyboardEndRect];
    [UIView beginAnimations:@"changeTableViewContentInset"
                    context:NULL];
    [UIView setAnimationDuration:animationDuration];
    [UIView setAnimationCurve:(UIViewAnimationCurve)animationCurve];

    self.myTableView.contentInset = UIEdgeInsetsZero;

    [UIView commitAnimations];

}
```

In the handleKeyboardWillHide: method, we are doing the following, in this order:

1. Find out whether the content inset of our table view has already been changed. If our table view's content inset wasn't changed, we shouldn't take any further action. We will just assume that we received this notification by mistake or that some other object on another view on our view controller caused this notification to get broadcast.

2. Using the user-info dictionary of the UIKeyboardWillHideNotification notification, we get the duration and curve of the keyboard's animation while it is tucking away. Using this information, we will create an animation block.

3. We set our table view's content inset to UIEdgeInsetsZero and commit our animation.

As mentioned before, when the keyboard notifications are broadcast, the current orientation of the device is *not* taken into account to construct the starting and ending frames of our table view. For instance, if we log the ending frame of our keyboard in the handleKeyboardWillShow: method of our view controller on an iPhone in portrait mode, we will get the following values:

```
{{0, 264}, {320, 216}}
```

If you now rotate the orientation to landscape and log the values again, you will see the following value printed out to the console window:

```
{{0, 0}, {162, 480}}
```

It is immediately obvious that the values are incorrect. As you can see, the Y position of the keyboard is reported as 0—but we know that when the keyboard is displayed in landscape mode on an iPhone, the Y position is certainly not at 0. Furthermore, the width is the width of the whole screen, which obviously is not 162.0 in landscape mode, and the height is almost half of the screen, which makes the value of 480 incorrect. The reason for the incorrect values is that iOS doesn't take the orientation of the device into account when reporting these values to your apps. The frames reported to your app are in the app's main window's coordinate system. Therefore, to convert these reported frames from the window's coordinate system to your view's coordinate system, use the convertRect:fromView: method of your view and pass your app's window as the from View parameter.

So let's modify the implementation of the handleKeyboardWillShow: method slightly to take the conversion of coordinate systems into account, from the window's to our view's coordinate system.

 The implementation of the handleKeyboardWillHide: method does not use the rectangles in the user-info dictionary. In this method we always assume that the keyboard is hiding and that its rectangle is (0, 0, 0, 0).

```
- (void) handleKeyboardWillShow:(NSNotification *)paramNotification{

    NSDictionary *userInfo = [paramNotification userInfo];

    NSValue *animationCurveObject =
    [userInfo valueForKey:UIKeyboardAnimationCurveUserInfoKey];

    NSValue *animationDurationObject =
    [userInfo valueForKey:UIKeyboardAnimationDurationUserInfoKey];

    NSValue *keyboardEndRectObject =
    [userInfo valueForKey:UIKeyboardFrameEndUserInfoKey];

    NSUInteger animationCurve = 0;
    double animationDuration = 0.0f;
    CGRect keyboardEndRect = CGRectMake(0, 0, 0, 0);

    [animationCurveObject getValue:&animationCurve];
    [animationDurationObject getValue:&animationDuration];
    [keyboardEndRectObject getValue:&keyboardEndRect];

    UIWindow *window = [[[UIApplication sharedApplication] delegate] window];

    /* Convert the frame from window's coordinate system to
     our view's coordinate system */
    keyboardEndRect = [self.view convertRect:keyboardEndRect
                                    fromView:window];

    [UIView beginAnimations:@"changeTableViewContentInset"
                    context:NULL];
    [UIView setAnimationDuration:animationDuration];
    [UIView setAnimationCurve:(UIViewAnimationCurve)animationCurve];

    CGRect intersectionOfKeyboardRectAndWindowRect =
    CGRectIntersection(window.frame, keyboardEndRect);

    CGFloat bottomInset = intersectionOfKeyboardRectAndWindowRect.size.height;
```

```
self.myTableView.contentInset = UIEdgeInsetsMake(0.0f,
                                                 0.0f,
                                                 bottomInset,
                                                 0.0f);
NSIndexPath *indexPathOfOwnerCell = nil;
/* Also, make sure the selected text field is visible on the screen */
NSInteger numberOfCells = [self.myTableView.dataSource
                             tableView:self.myTableView
                             numberOfRowsInSection:0];

/* So let's go through all the cells and find their accessory text fields.
 Once we have the reference to those text fields, we can see which one of
 them is the first responder (has the keyboard) and we will make a call
 to the table view to make sure after the keyboard is displayed,
 that specific cell is NOT obstructed by the keyboard */
for (NSInteger counter = 0;
     counter < numberOfCells;
     counter++){
  NSIndexPath *indexPath = [NSIndexPath indexPathForRow:counter
                                            inSection:0];
  UITableViewCell *cell = [self.myTableView cellForRowAtIndexPath:indexPath];
  UITextField *textField = (UITextField *)cell.accessoryView;
  if ([textField isKindOfClass:[UITextField class]] == NO){
    continue;
  }
  if ([textField isFirstResponder]){
    indexPathOfOwnerCell = indexPath;
    break;
  }
}

[UIView commitAnimations];

if (indexPathOfOwnerCell != nil){
  [self.myTableView scrollToRowAtIndexPath:indexPathOfOwnerCell
                           atScrollPosition:UITableViewScrollPositionMiddle
                                   animated:YES];
}

}
```

Brilliant. Now run the app on iPhone Simulator and rotate the simulator's orientation to landscape and tap on one of the text fields. When the keyboard is displayed, scroll all the way down to the end of the table view's content to make sure that we have given the right content inset, taking into account the coordinate system conversion to our table view (Figure 2-92).

Figure 2-92. Calculating the correct edge inset by taking the coordinate system of the keyboard into account

See Also

Recipe 2.19; Recipe 2.20

2.30 Constructing and Displaying Styled Texts

Problem

You want to be able to be able to display rich formatted text in your UI components without having to create a separate UI component per attribute. For instance, you may want to display one sentence that contains only one of its words written in bold, inside a UILabel.

Solution

Construct an instance of the NSAttributedString or the mutable variant of it, the NSMutableAttributedString, and either set it as the text of a UI component like the UILabel component through its special attributed string property, or simply use the attributed string's built-in methods to draw the text on a canvas.

Discussion

Rich text is a thing of legend! A lot of us programmers have had the requirement to display mixed-style strings in one line of text on our UI. For instance, in one line of text you may have to display straight and italic text together, where one word is italic and the rest of the words are regular text. Or you may have had to underline a word inside a sentence. For this, some of us had to use Web Views, but that is not the optimal solution because Web Views are quite slow in rendering their content, and that will definitely impact the performance of your app. In iOS 6, finally, we can start using attributed strings. I don't know what took Apple so long to introduce this feature to iOS, as Mac developers have been using attributed strings for a long time now!

Before we begin, I want to clearly show you what I mean by attributed strings, using Figure 2-93. Then we will set out on the journey to write the program to achieve exactly this.

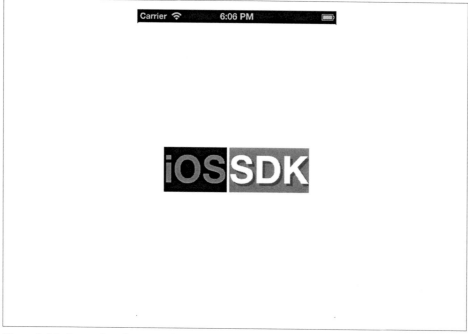

Figure 2-93. An attributed string is displayed on the screen inside a simple label

 Just to be explicit, this text is rendered inside a *single* instance of the UILabel class.

So what do we see in this example? I'll list the pieces:

The text "iOS" with the following attributes:
- Bold font with size of 60 points
- Background color of black
- Font color of red

The text "SDK" with the following attributes:
- Bold font with size of 60 points
- White text color
- Light gray shadow

The best way to construct attributed strings is to use the initWithString: method of the mutable variant of the NSMutableAttributedString class and pass an instance of the NSString to this method. This will create our attributed string without any attributes. Then, to assign attributes to different parts of the string, we will use the setAttributes:range: method of the NSMutableAttributedString class. This method takes in two parameters:

setAttributes

A dictionary whose keys are character attributes and the value of each key depends on the key itself. Here are the most important keys that you can set in this dictionary:

NSFontAttributeName

The value of this key is an instance of UIFont and defines the font for the specific range of your string.

NSForegroundColorAttributeName

The value for this key is of type UIColor and defines the color for your text for the specific range of your string.

NSBackgroundColorAttributeName

The value of this key is of type UIColor and defines the background color on which the specific range of your string has to be drawn.

NSShadowAttributeName

The value of this key must be an instance of the NSShadow and defines the shadow that you want to use under the specific range of your string.

range

A value of type NSRange that defines the starting point and the length of characters to which you want to apply the attributes.

To see all the different keys that you can pass to this method, simply browse the Apple documentation online for the NSMutableAttributed String class. I will not put the direct URL to this documentation here as Apple may change the URL at some point, but a simple search online will do the trick.

We'll break our example down into two dictionaries of attributes. The dictionary of attributes for the word "iOS" can be constructed in this way in code:

```
NSDictionary *attributesForFirstWord = @{
    NSFontAttributeName : [UIFont boldSystemFontOfSize:60.0f],
    NSForegroundColorAttributeName : [UIColor redColor],
    NSBackgroundColorAttributeName : [UIColor blackColor]
};
```

And the word "SDK" will be constructed using the following attributes:

```
NSShadow *shadow = [[NSShadow alloc] init];
shadow.shadowColor = [UIColor darkGrayColor];
shadow.shadowOffset = CGSizeMake(4.0f, 4.0f);

NSDictionary *attributesForSecondWord = @{
    NSFontAttributeName : [UIFont boldSystemFontOfSize:60.0f],
    NSForegroundColorAttributeName : [UIColor whiteColor],
    NSBackgroundColorAttributeName : [UIColor redColor],
    NSShadowAttributeName : shadow
};
```

Putting it together, we will get the following code that not only creates our label, but also sets its attributed text:

```
#import "ViewController.h"

@interface ViewController ()
@property (nonatomic, strong) UILabel *label;
@end

@implementation ViewController

- (NSAttributedString *) attributedText{

    NSString *string = @"iOS SDK";

    NSMutableAttributedString *result = [[NSMutableAttributedString alloc]
                                         initWithString:string];

    NSDictionary *attributesForFirstWord = @{
    NSFontAttributeName : [UIFont boldSystemFontOfSize:60.0f],
    NSForegroundColorAttributeName : [UIColor redColor],
    NSBackgroundColorAttributeName : [UIColor blackColor]
    };

    NSShadow *shadow = [[NSShadow alloc] init];
    shadow.shadowColor = [UIColor darkGrayColor];
    shadow.shadowOffset = CGSizeMake(4.0f, 4.0f);

    NSDictionary *attributesForSecondWord = @{
    NSFontAttributeName : [UIFont boldSystemFontOfSize:60.0f],
    NSForegroundColorAttributeName : [UIColor whiteColor],
    NSBackgroundColorAttributeName : [UIColor redColor],
    NSShadowAttributeName : shadow
    };

    /* Find the string "iOS" in the whole string and sets its attribute */
    [result setAttributes:attributesForFirstWord
                    range:[string rangeOfString:@"iOS"]];

    /* Do the same thing for the string "SDK" */
    [result setAttributes:attributesForSecondWord
                    range:[string rangeOfString:@"SDK"]];

    return [[NSAttributedString alloc] initWithAttributedString:result];
```

```
}

- (void)viewDidLoad{
    [super viewDidLoad];
    self.view.backgroundColor = [UIColor whiteColor];
    self.label = [[UILabel alloc] init];
    self.label.backgroundColor = [UIColor clearColor];
    self.label.attributedText = [self attributedText];
    [self.label sizeToFit];
    self.label.center = self.view.center;
    [self.view addSubview:self.label];

}

@end
```

See Also

Recipe 2.17; Recipe 2.18

CHAPTER 3

Auto Layout and the Visual Format Language

3.0 Introduction

Aligning UI components has always been a big headache for programmers. Most of the view controllers in complex iOS apps contain a lot of code just to set the frame of UI components on the screen, align components horizontally/vertically, and make sure the components look good on different iOS versions. Not only that, but some programmers want to also use the same view controllers across various devices such as iPhones and iPads. This adds a lot of complexity to the code. Apple has made it easier for us in iOS 6. They have brought Auto Layout from OS X over to iOS. We will be talking about the details of Auto Layout in a moment, but let me just give you a brief introduction to it and explain what it is for.

Let's say you have a button that you want to keep at the center of the screen. The relation between the center of the button and the center of the view on which it resides can be simply described like so:

- Button's center.x is equal to view's center.x
- Button's center.y is equal to view's center.y

Apple noticed that a lot of the positioning of UI components can be solved with a simple formula:

```
object1.property1 = (object2.property2 * multiplier) + constant value
```

For instance, using this formula, I could simply center a button on its superview like so:

```
button.center.x = (button.superview.center.x * 1) + 0
button.center.y = (button.superview.center.y * 1) + 0
```

Using this formula, you can do some really funky things during the UI development of your iOS apps that you could not do before. The aforementioned formula is wrapped inside a class in the iOS SDK called NSLayoutConstraint. Every constraint that you create (i.e., every instance of this class) represents only one constraint. For instance, if you want to center your button on the view that owns the button, you have to center the *x* and the *y* position of the button. That means you have to create two constraints. Centering simply cannot be expressed by one constraint. However, later in this chapter we will learn about the Visual Format Language, which is a great addition to the iOS language and simplifies things even further in terms of UI layouts.

Constraints can be created by cross views. For instance, if you have two buttons on one view and you want them to be 100 points apart vertically, you need to create the constraint for this rule but add it to the common ancestor of both the buttons, which is perhaps the view that owns both of them. These are the rules:

- If the constraint is between two views that sit on a common immediate parent view, meaning that both these views have the same superview, add the constraints to the parent view.
- If the constraint is between a view and its parent view, add the constraint to the parent view.
- If the constraint is between two views that do not share the same parent view, add the constraint to the common ancestor of the views.

Figure 3-1 is a graphical demonstration of how these constraints actually work.

Constraints are created using the `constraintWithItem:attribute:relatedBy:toItem :attribute:multiplier:constant:` class method of the `NSLayoutConstraint` class. The different parameters to this method are:

constraintWithItem
: This is a parameter of type `id` and represents *object1* in the formula that I mentioned before.

attribute
: This represents *property1* in our formula and should be of type `NSLayoutAttribute`.

relatedBy
: This represents the *equals sign* in our formula. The value of this parameter is of type `NSLayoutRelation` and, as you will soon see, you can specify not only an equals sign, but a greater-than or less-than sign here. We will talk about this in detail in this chapter.

toItem
: This parameter is of type `id` and represents *object2* in our formula.

attribute
: This parameter is of type `NSLayoutAttribute` and represents *property2* in our formula.

multiplier
: This parameter is of type `CGFloat` and represents *multiplier* in our formula.

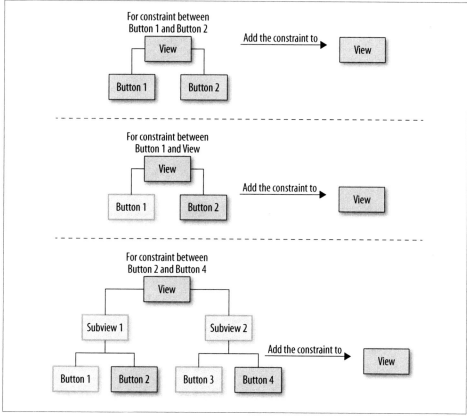

Figure 3-1. The relationship between constraints and the views they should be added to

constant

This parameter is also of type CGFloat and represents *constant value* in our formula.

After you create your constraints, you can simply add them to the appropriate view (see Figure 3-1) using either one of these methods of the UIView class:

addConstraint:

This method can add a single constraint of type NSLayoutConstraint to the view.

addConstraints:

This method allows you to add an array of constraints to the view. The constraints again have to be of type NSLayoutConstraint wrapped inside an array of type NSArray.

There are many things that you can achieve with Auto Layout, as you will see in the rest of this chapter. However, the more you dive in, the more you'll realize that the setting of layout automatically will mean creating more and more constraints of type NSLayoutConstraint. You will notice that your code size keeps growing and becomes more difficult to maintain. For this reason, Apple has created the Visual Format

Language by which you can express your constraints using simply ASCII characters. For instance, if you have two buttons and you want the buttons to always be 100 points apart from each other horizontally, you would express it using the Visual Format Language code written like this:

```
[button1]-100-[button2]
```

Constraints with the Visual Format Language are created using the `constraintsWith VisualFormat:options:metrics:views:` class method of the `NSLayoutConstraint` class. Here is a brief explanation of each one of the parameters to this method:

constraintsWithVisualFormat
> The Visual Format Language expression, written as `NSString`.

options
> A parameter of type `NSLayoutFormatOptions`. For Visual Format Language, we usually pass 0 to this parameter.

metrics
> A dictionary of constant values that you use in your Visual Format Language expression. For the sake of simplicity, we will pass nil to this method for now.

views
> This is a dictionary of views that you have written the constraint for in the first parameter of this method. To construct this dictionary, simply use the `NSDictio naryOfVariableBindings` C function and pass your view objects to this method. It will then construct the dictionary for you. The keys in this dictionary are the view names that you should be using in the first parameter to this method. Don't worry if this all is a bit strange right now and doesn't make sense. Soon it will! Once you see a few examples of this, it will all click.

With this basic information in hand, and without bloating our heads with too much information, I believe it is time to dive straight into this chapter's recipes and flex our muscles with constraints a little bit. Are you ready? I know I am!

3.1 Placing UI Components in the Center of the Screen

Problem

You want to be able to place a UI component in the center of the screen. In other words, you want to place a view at the center of its superview, using constraints.

Solution

Create two constraints: one to align the center.x position of the target view on its superview's center.x position, and the other to align the center.y position of the target view on its superview's center.y position.

Discussion

Let's get started by first creating a simple button, which we will align at the center of the screen. As mentioned in the Solution section of this recipe, all we have to do is make sure the x and the y of the center of our button is the same as the x and y of the center of the view on which the button resides. So for this, we will create two constraints and add them to the view that owns the button, called the superview of the button. Here is the simple code that will achieve this:

```
#import "ViewController.h"

@interface ViewController ()
@property (nonatomic, strong) UIButton *button;
@end

@implementation ViewController

- (void)viewDidLoad{
    [super viewDidLoad];

    /* 1) Create our button */
    self.button = [UIButton buttonWithType:UIButtonTypeRoundedRect];
    self.button.translatesAutoresizingMaskIntoConstraints = NO;
    [self.button setTitle:@"Button" forState:UIControlStateNormal];
    [self.view addSubview:self.button];

    UIView *superview = self.button.superview;

    /* 2) Create the constraint to put the button horizontally in the center */
    NSLayoutConstraint *centerXConstraint =
    [NSLayoutConstraint constraintWithItem:self.button
                                 attribute:NSLayoutAttributeCenterX
                                 relatedBy:NSLayoutRelationEqual
                                    toItem:superview
                                 attribute:NSLayoutAttributeCenterX
                                multiplier:1.0f
                                  constant:0.0f];

    /* 3) Create the constraint to put the button vertically in the center */
    NSLayoutConstraint *centerYConstraint =
    [NSLayoutConstraint constraintWithItem:self.button
                                 attribute:NSLayoutAttributeCenterY
                                 relatedBy:NSLayoutRelationEqual
                                    toItem:superview
                                 attribute:NSLayoutAttributeCenterY
                                multiplier:1.0f
                                  constant:0.0f];

    /* Add the constraints to the superview of the button */
    [superview addConstraints:@[centerXConstraint, centerYConstraint]];

}

/* Suport rotation of device to all orientations */
```

```
- (NSUInteger) supportedInterfaceOrientations{
    return UIInterfaceOrientationMaskAll;
}

- (void)didReceiveMemoryWarning{
    [super didReceiveMemoryWarning];
}

@end
```

 This view controller is trying to tell iOS that it supports all interface orientations that the device supports, to demonstrate that the button will indeed be placed in the center of the screen regardless of the type of device and its orientation. However, before this method takes over, you need to make sure you have enabled all required orientations inside your project itself. To do this, navigate in Xcode to your target properties, go to the Summary tab, find the Supported Interface Orientations section, and enable all the available orientations, as shown in Figure 3-2.

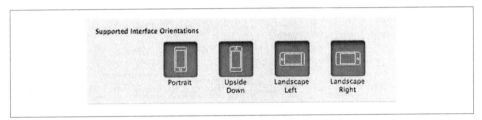

Figure 3-2. Enabling all supported interface orientation in Xcode for your target

Now if you run this app on the device or in the simulator, you will notice that a simple button is displayed on the screen. Now rotate the device and note how the button stays at the center of the screen. All of this was achieved without having to write a single line of code for setting the frame of the button or listening to any type of orientation change notification and adjusting the position of the button, thanks to Auto Layout. See Figure 3-3. This approach is better simply because our code now will work on any device in any orientation with any resolution. In contrast, if we were to set the frame of our UI components, we would have to set the frame for each orientation on each device we would want to support, because different iOS devices can have different screen resolutions. For instance, our app now will happily be able to run on an iPad or an iPhone and will retain the button in the center of the screen, regardless of the orientation or the resolution of the device and its display.

See Also

Recipe 3.2; Recipe 3.0

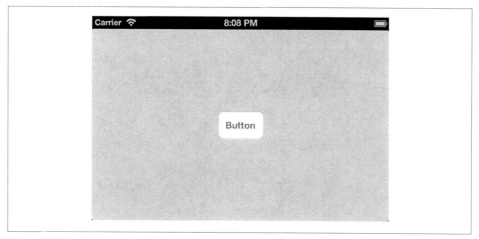

Figure 3-3. The button is at the center of the screen in every orientation

3.2 Defining Horizontal and Vertical Constraints with the Visual Format Language

Problem

You want to be able to define constraints that change the way a UI component is horizontally or vertically aligned on its superview.

Solution

Use the H: orientation specifier in the formatting string for your constraint to dictate horizontal alignment, and the V: orientation specifier to dictate vertical alignment.

Discussion

I won't pretend the Visual Format Language is easy to understand. It is indeed very cryptic. For this reason, I will give you a few examples that hopefully will clear things up. All of these examples will change the horizontal alignment of a button on the screen (Figure 3-4).

As you can see, the formatting might take you some time to get used to. However, once you get the hang of the basics of it, it will slowly start to make sense. The same rules apply for vertical alignment, which uses the V: orientation specifier. Figure 3-5 shows an example.

Let's put the things that we have learned so far into practice. How about writing constraints using the Visual Format Language that represent a UI similar to that depicted in Figure 3-6?

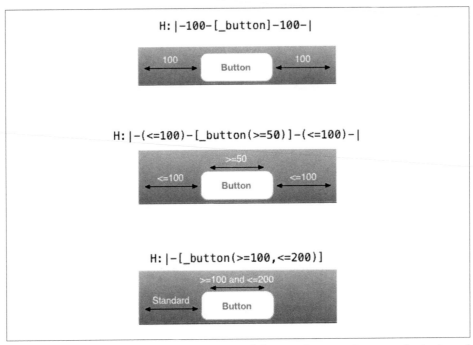

Figure 3-4. Three simple examples of the usage of the Visual Format Language for horizontal constraints

 To help apps look consistent and make decisions easier for the designers of apps, Apple has designed standard distances or spaces between UI components. The standards are described in Apple's iOS Human Interface Guidelines (*http://bit.ly/QkQrtU*).

Before we dive into coding, let's put down the constraints as we can see them in the figure:

- The email field has standard vertical distance to the top of the view.
- The confirm email field has standard vertical distance to the email field.
- The Register button has standard vertical distance to the confirm email field.
- All components are horizontally centered in relation to the parent (super) view.
- Both the email and the conform email fields have standard horizontal distance from the left and the righthand side of the super view.
- The width of the button is fixed at 128 points.

Shall we dig into the code now to achieve this? Let's start by actually defining our constraints in plain Visual Format Language on top of our view controller:

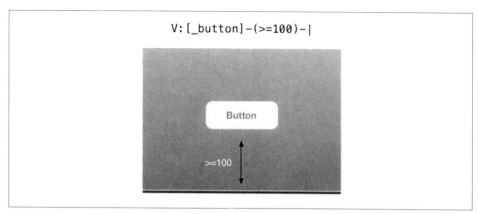

Figure 3-5. An example of setting vertical alignment using the Visual Format Language

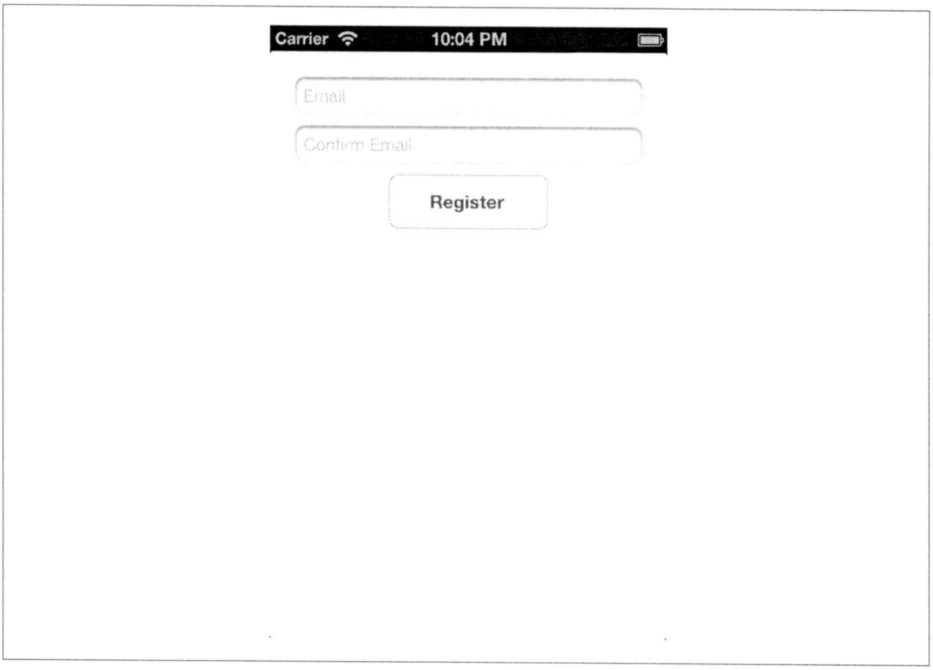

Figure 3-6. The UI that we want to achieve using constraints and the Visual Format Language

```
/* Email text field constraints */
NSString *const kEmailTextFieldHorizontal = @"H:|-[_textFieldEmail]-|";
NSString *const kEmailTextFieldVertical = @"V:|-[_textFieldEmail]";

/* Confirm email text field constraints */
NSString *const kConfirmEmailHorizontal = @"H:|-[_textFieldConfirmEmail]-|";
NSString *const kConfirmEmailVertical =
              @"V:[_textFieldEmail]-[_textFieldConfirmEmail]";
```

```
/* Register button constraint */
NSString *const kRegisterVertical =
            @"V:[_textFieldConfirmEmail]-[_registerButton]";
```

It is immediately obvious that both text fields have both their horizontal and vertical constraints defined in the Visual Format Language, but the Register button has only its vertical constraint defined as a Visual Format Language expression. Why is that? It turns out center aligning a UI component horizontally is not possible with the Visual Format Language. For this, we are going to have to use the same technique that we learned in Recipe 3.1. But that's OK. Don't let that stop you from enjoying the Visual Format Language and finding out how powerful it truly is. Obviously nothing is perfect, but that doesn't mean we shouldn't use it.

Now let's define our UI components as private properties of our view controller in the implementation file of the view controller:

```
@interface ViewController ()
@property (nonatomic, strong) UITextField *textFieldEmail;
@property (nonatomic, strong) UITextField *textFieldConfirmEmail;
@property (nonatomic, strong) UIButton *registerButton;
@end
```

What's next? We need to actually construct our UI components in the implementation file of the view controller. So we will write two handy methods that will help us do this. Again, remember, we are not going to set the frame of these UI components. Auto Layout will later help us with this:

```
- (UITextField *) textFieldWithPlaceholder:(NSString *)paramPlaceholder{

    UITextField *result = [[UITextField alloc] init];
    result.translatesAutoresizingMaskIntoConstraints = NO;
    result.borderStyle = UITextBorderStyleRoundedRect;
    result.placeholder = paramPlaceholder;
    return result;

}

- (void) constructUIComponents{

    self.textFieldEmail =
        [self textFieldWithPlaceholder:@"Email"];

    self.textFieldConfirmEmail =
        [self textFieldWithPlaceholder:@"Confirm Email"];

    self.registerButton = [UIButton buttonWithType:UIButtonTypeRoundedRect];
    self.registerButton.translatesAutoresizingMaskIntoConstraints = NO;
    [self.registerButton setTitle:@"Register" forState:UIControlStateNormal];

}
```

The textFieldWithPlaceholder: method simply creates text fields that contain a given placeholder text and the constructUIComponents method creates the two text fields using the previously mentioned method and the button. You have probably noticed that we are setting the `translatesAutoresizingMaskIntoConstraints` property of all our UI components to `NO`. This will force UIKit not to think that autoresizing masks have something to do with Auto Layout constraints. As you know, you can set autoresizing masks for your UI components and view controllers in code and interface builder, as we learned in Chapter 2. Setting this property to `NO` makes sure that UIKit won't mix things up and won't automatically translate autoresizing masks to Auto Layout constraints. Setting this option is required if you are mixing Auto Layout properties of your components with layout constraints. It is generally a good idea to set this property of all your UI components to `NO` whenever you are working with Auto Layout constraints, unless you explicitly want UIKit to translate autoresizing masks to Auto Layout constraints.

We are constructing our UI components, but the `viewDidLoad` method of our view controller obviously needs to add all three UI components to our view, so why not have a little method that will help us with this?

```
- (void) addUIComponentsToView:(UIView *)paramView{

    [paramView addSubview:self.textFieldEmail];
    [paramView addSubview:self.textFieldConfirmEmail];
    [paramView addSubview:self.registerButton];

}
```

We are almost there. The next big task is to create methods that allow us to construct and collect all the constraints into an array. For this, we have three methods that return the constraints of each one of our UI components as an array. We also have a handy fourth method that collects all the constraints from all three UI components and puts them into one big array. Here is how we have implemented it:

```
- (NSArray *) emailTextFieldConstraints{

    NSMutableArray *result = [[NSMutableArray alloc] init];

    NSDictionary *viewsDictionary =
        NSDictionaryOfVariableBindings(_textFieldEmail);

    [result addObjectsFromArray:
     [NSLayoutConstraint constraintsWithVisualFormat:kEmailTextFieldHorizontal
                                             options:0
                                             metrics:nil
                                               views:viewsDictionary]
     ];

    [result addObjectsFromArray:
     [NSLayoutConstraint constraintsWithVisualFormat:kEmailTextFieldVertical
                                             options:0
                                             metrics:nil
                                               views:viewsDictionary]
     ];
```

```
    return [NSArray arrayWithArray:result];

}

- (NSArray *) confirmEmailTextFieldConstraints{

    NSMutableArray *result = [[NSMutableArray alloc] init];

    NSDictionary *viewsDictionary =
        NSDictionaryOfVariableBindings(_textFieldConfirmEmail, _textFieldEmail);

    [result addObjectsFromArray:
     [NSLayoutConstraint constraintsWithVisualFormat:kConfirmEmailHorizontal
                                             options:0
                                             metrics:nil
                                               views:viewsDictionary]
     ];

    [result addObjectsFromArray:
     [NSLayoutConstraint constraintsWithVisualFormat:kConfirmEmailVertical
                                             options:0
                                             metrics:nil
                                               views:viewsDictionary]
     ];

    return [NSArray arrayWithArray:result];

}

- (NSArray *) registerButtonConstraints{

    NSMutableArray *result = [[NSMutableArray alloc] init];

    NSDictionary *viewsDictionary =
        NSDictionaryOfVariableBindings(_registerButton, _textFieldConfirmEmail);

    [result addObject:

     [NSLayoutConstraint constraintWithItem:self.registerButton
                                  attribute:NSLayoutAttributeCenterX
                                  relatedBy:NSLayoutRelationEqual
                                     toItem:self.view
                                  attribute:NSLayoutAttributeCenterX
                                 multiplier:1.0f
                                   constant:0.0f]
     ];

    [result addObjectsFromArray:
     [NSLayoutConstraint constraintsWithVisualFormat:kRegisterVertical
                                             options:0
                                             metrics:nil
                                               views:viewsDictionary]
     ];
```

```
    return [NSArray arrayWithArray:result];
}

- (NSArray *) constraints{

    NSMutableArray *result = [[NSMutableArray alloc] init];

    [result addObjectsFromArray:[self emailTextFieldConstraints]];
    [result addObjectsFromArray:[self confirmEmailTextFieldConstraints]];
    [result addObjectsFromArray:[self registerButtonConstraints]];
    return [NSArray arrayWithArray:result];

}
```

It's in fact the constraints instance method of our view controller that collects all the constraints for all three UI components and returns it as one big array. Now for the main part of the controller, the viewDidLoad method:

```
- (void)viewDidLoad{

    [super viewDidLoad];

    [self constructUIComponents];
    [self addUIComponentsToView:self.view];
    [self.view addConstraints:[self constraints]];

}

- (NSUInteger) supportedInterfaceOrientations{

    return UIInterfaceOrientationMaskAll;

}
```

This method simply constructs the UI, adding the UI components and their constraints to itself using the methods we wrote before. Great stuff, but how does it look on the screen when we run the program? We have already seen how it looks in the portrait mode of the device (see Figure 3-6) but let's see how it will look once we rotate the device's orientation to landscape (Figure 3-7).

See Also

Recipe 3.0; Recipe 3.1

3.3 Utilizing Cross View Constraints

Problem

You want to align a UI component in relation to another UI component, but these UI components have different parents.

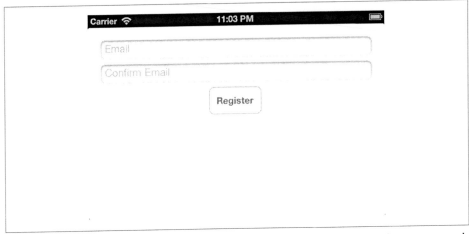

Figure 3-7. The constraints seem to be working just as fine in landscape as they work in portrait mode

Solution

Utilizing Figure 3-1, make sure that you find the common UI superview between the two UI components and add your constraint to that superview.

Discussion

Before going into too much detail, let's first see what cross view constraints are all about. I believe I can demonstrate it to you in a picture better than it can be explained in words, so check out Figure 3-8.

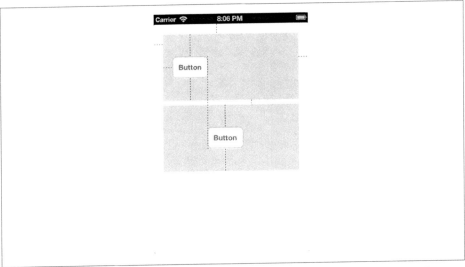

Figure 3-8. The important cross view constraints between two buttons are depicted in this photo

Many constraints have been applied to the views in this figure, but let's start one by one and break it down into small chunks:

- We have two gray views on the main view of our view controller. Both should have standard space from the left and the right side of the view of the view controller. There must be standard space from the top of the view to the top of the view on top. There should be standard vertical space between the two gray views.
- There must be a button vertically centered in both gray views.
- The button on the top gray view should have standard space to the left of its superview.
- The button on the bottom gray view should have its lefthand side aligned with the righthand side of the button in the top gray view. This is the cross view constraint that is very important to us.
- The gray views should be able to get resized as the view of the view controller changes orientation.
- The height of both gray views must be 100 points.

OK, let's begin. We are going to do all this by starting from the `viewDidLoad` method of our view controller. It's always best to think of a clean way of putting all your methods together. Obviously, in this example, we are working with quite a few constraints and views, so how can we make the `viewDidLoad` method of our view controller clean? Like this:

```
- (void)viewDidLoad{
    [super viewDidLoad];

    [self createGrayViews];

    [self createButtons];

    [self applyConstraintsToTopGrayView];
    [self applyConstraintsToButtonOnTopGrayView];

    [self applyConstraintsToBottomGrayView];
    [self applyConstraintsToButtonOnBottomGrayView];

}
```

We have simply broken our tasks down into different methods, which we are soon going to implement. Let's go ahead and define our views in the implementation file of our view controller as an extension to our interface:

```
#import "ViewController.h"

@interface ViewController ()

@property (nonatomic, strong) UIView *topGrayView;
@property (nonatomic, strong) UIButton *topButton;

@property (nonatomic, strong) UIView *bottomGrayView;
```

```
@property (nonatomic, strong) UIButton *bottomButton;

@end

@implementation ViewController

...
```

The next step is to implement the `createGrayViews` method. As its name shows, this method is responsible for creating our gray views on the screen:

```
- (UIView *) newGrayView{

    UIView *result = [[UIView alloc] init];
    result.backgroundColor = [UIColor lightGrayColor];
    result.translatesAutoresizingMaskIntoConstraints = NO;
    [self.view addSubview:result];
    return result;

}

- (void) createGrayViews{

    self.topGrayView = [self newGrayView];
    self.bottomGrayView = [self newGrayView];

}
```

Simple enough? Both gray views are getting added to the view of our view controller. Great stuff. What's next? We now need to implement the `createButtons` method, because it is getting called in the `viewDidLoad` method of our view controller. This method should simply create our buttons and place them on their associated gray views:

```
- (UIButton *) newButtonPlacedOnView:(UIView *)paramView{

    UIButton *result = [UIButton buttonWithType:UIButtonTypeRoundedRect];
    result.translatesAutoresizingMaskIntoConstraints = NO;
    [result setTitle:@"Button" forState:UIControlStateNormal];
    [paramView addSubview:result];
    return result;

}

- (void) createButtons{
    self.topButton = [self newButtonPlacedOnView:self.topGrayView];
    self.bottomButton = [self newButtonPlacedOnView:self.bottomGrayView];
}
```

Again, as you can see in the `createButtons` method, after the creation of our gray views and the buttons, we need to start applying the constraints to the gray views and the buttons. We will start by applying the constraints to the top gray view. These constraints must cover the following conditions:

- The top view has to have standard space from the left and the top of the view of the view controller.

- The height of this gray view has to be 100 points.

```
- (void) applyConstraintsToTopGrayView{

    NSDictionary *views = NSDictionaryOfVariableBindings(_topGrayView);

    NSMutableArray *constraints = [[NSMutableArray alloc] init];

    NSString *const kHConstraint = @"H:|-[_topGrayView]-|";
    NSString *const kVConstraint = @"V:|-[_topGrayView(==100)]";

    /* Horizontal constraint(s) */
    [constraints addObjectsFromArray:
     [NSLayoutConstraint constraintsWithVisualFormat:kHConstraint
                                             options:0
                                             metrics:nil
                                               views:views]
     ];

    /* Vertical constraint(s) */
    [constraints addObjectsFromArray:
     [NSLayoutConstraint constraintsWithVisualFormat:kVConstraint
                                             options:0
                                             metrics:nil
                                               views:views]
     ];

    [self.topGrayView.superview addConstraints:constraints];

}
```

It's important to note how we are constructing the vertical constraint of the top gray view. You can see that we are using the (==100) format to specify that the height of the top gray view has to be 100 points. The reason that the runtime is interpreting this value as the height is because of the V: specifier that tells the runtime that the numbers we are feeding into the system have something to do with the height and the vertical alignment of the target view, rather than the width or the horizontal alignment.

The next thing that we need to take care of is to set the constraints for the button on the top gray view. This is done through the applyConstraintsToButtonOnTopGrayView method. This button will have the following constraints, as specified before:

- It should sit vertically in the center of the top gray view.
- It should have standard distance from the left of the top gray view.
- It should have no specific height or width defined and should fit its content, aka the *Button* text that we've decided to put in it.

```
- (void) applyConstraintsToButtonOnTopGrayView{

    NSDictionary *views = NSDictionaryOfVariableBindings(_topButton);

    NSMutableArray *constraints = [[NSMutableArray alloc] init];
```

```
    NSString *const kHConstraint = @"H:|-[_topButton]";

    /* Horizontal constraint(s) */
    [constraints addObjectsFromArray:
     [NSLayoutConstraint constraintsWithVisualFormat:kHConstraint
                                             options:0
                                             metrics:nil
                                               views:views]
     ];

    /* Vertical constraint(s) */
    [constraints addObject:
     [NSLayoutConstraint constraintWithItem:self.topButton
                                  attribute:NSLayoutAttributeCenterY
                                  relatedBy:NSLayoutRelationEqual
                                     toItem:self.topGrayView
                                  attribute:NSLayoutAttributeCenterY
                                 multiplier:1.0f
                                   constant:0.0f]
     ];

    [self.topButton.superview addConstraints:constraints];

}
```

We are all done with the top gray view and the button inside it. Time to move on to the bottom gray view and its button. The method we should take care of now is the applyConstraintsToBottomGrayView method. This method will be setting the constraints for the bottom gray view. Just to recap, the constraints that we have to create for this view are:

- Must have standard distance from the left of the view of the view controller.
- Must have standard distance from the bottom of the top gray view.
- Must have the height of 100 points.

```
- (void) applyConstraintsToBottomGrayView{

    NSDictionary *views = NSDictionaryOfVariableBindings(_topGrayView,
                                                         _bottomGrayView);

    NSMutableArray *constraints = [[NSMutableArray alloc] init];

    NSString *const kHConstraint = @"H:|-[_bottomGrayView]-|";
    NSString *const kVConstraint =
        @"V:|-[_topGrayView]-[_bottomGrayView(==100)]";

    /* Horizontal constraint(s) */
    [constraints addObjectsFromArray:
     [NSLayoutConstraint constraintsWithVisualFormat:kHConstraint
                                             options:0
                                             metrics:nil
                                               views:views]
     ];
```

```
/* Vertical constraint(s) */
[constraints addObjectsFromArray:
 [NSLayoutConstraint constraintsWithVisualFormat:kVConstraint
                                         options:0
                                         metrics:nil
                                           views:views]
 ];

[self.bottomGrayView.superview addConstraints:constraints];
}
```

The vertical constraints for the bottom gray view may look a bit long in Visual Format Language, but it's very simple indeed. If you have a close look, you'll notice that the constraints are just aligning the top and the bottom gray view on the view of the view controller using standard distance specifiers and the constant height of 100 points.

The next and perhaps the last UI component for which we have to write constraints is the button on the bottom gray view. The method that will take care of this is called applyConstraintsToButtonOnBottomGrayView. Before we implement this method, let's talk about the constraint requirements for the bottom button:

- It should be vertically aligned at the center of the bottom gray view.
- Its left side should be aligned with the right side of the button on the top gray view.
- It should have no specific height or width defined and should fit its content, aka the *Button* text that we've decided to put in it.

```
- (void) applyConstraintsToButtonOnBottomGrayView{

    NSDictionary *views = NSDictionaryOfVariableBindings(_topButton,
                                                         _bottomButton);

    NSString *const kHConstraint = @"H:[_topButton][_bottomButton]";

    /* Horizontal constraint(s) */
    [self.bottomGrayView.superview addConstraints:
     [NSLayoutConstraint constraintsWithVisualFormat:kHConstraint
                                             options:0
                                             metrics:nil
                                               views:views]
     ];

    /* Vertical constraint(s) */
    [self.bottomButton.superview addConstraint:
     [NSLayoutConstraint constraintWithItem:self.bottomButton
                                  attribute:NSLayoutAttributeCenterY
                                  relatedBy:NSLayoutRelationEqual
                                     toItem:self.bottomGrayView
                                  attribute:NSLayoutAttributeCenterY
                                 multiplier:1.0f
                                   constant:0.0f]
     ];
```

```
    }
```
Last but not least, we need to make sure our view controller tells the runtime that it is able to handle all orientations, just to demonstrate the point of this recipe, so we should override the supportedInterfaceOrientations method of UIViewController:

```
- (NSUInteger) supportedInterfaceOrientations{
    return UIInterfaceOrientationMaskAll;
}
```

We are done with this view controller now. Let's run our app and see how it behaves in portrait mode (see Figure 3-9).

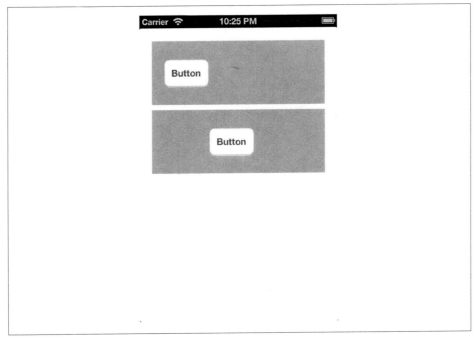

Figure 3-9. Our app renders the UI components in portrait mode according to the requirements that we set

The moment of truth! How about in landscape mode? Do we dare run the app in landscape and see whether it behaves as expected? Let's give it a go (see Figure 3-10).

Perfect. I think we nailed it.

See Also

Recipe 3.0

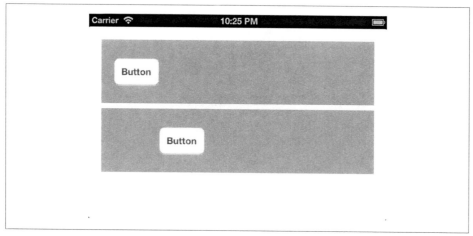

Figure 3-10. The same code behaves as expected in landscape mode

3.4 Configuring Auto Layout Constraints in Interface Builder

Problem

You want to be able to utilize Interface Builder's power in order to create your UI constraints.

Solution

Follow these steps:

1. Open the XIB that you want to edit in Interface Builder.
2. In Interface Builder, make sure that you have selected the view object on which you want to enable Auto Layout, simply by clicking on that view object.
3. Click on the View → Utilities → Show File Inspector menu item.
4. In the File Inspector, under the Interface Builder Document section, make sure that the *Use Auto Layout* check is enabled, as shown in Figure 3-11.

Discussion

Interface Builder can help us programmers a lot in creating constraints without much involvement from us. Normally, before the introduction of Auto Layout to iOS, the guideline bars that appeared on the screen while you moved UI components around on a view were related to Autosizing masks that you could also create in code, just like Constraints. However, after switching on the Use Auto Layout option in Interface Builder, the guidelines tell you something else. They are telling you about the constraints that Interface Builder is creating for you in the background.

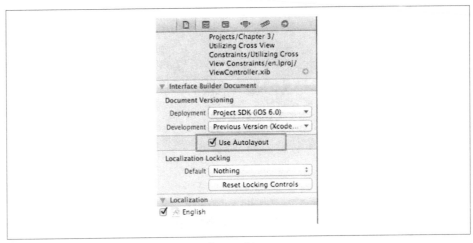

Figure 3-11. Enabling Auto Layout in Interface Builder

Let's do a little experiment. Create a new Single View Application project in Xcode. This will create an application with a single view controller for you. The class for your view controller will be `ViewController` and the XIB file for this view controller will be *ViewController.xib*. Simply click on this file to let Interface Builder open it for you. Make sure that the Use Auto Layout option is ticked in the File Inspector, as explained in the Solution section of this recipe.

Now from the Object Library, simply drag and drop a *Round Rect Button* onto the center of the screen until Interface Builder guidelines appear on the screen, telling you that now the center of the button is aligned with the center of the screen. From the Edit menu, now choose the Show Document Outline. If you already have the Document Outline section of Interface Builder open, this menu item will read Hide Document Outline, in which case you don't have to take any action. Now in the Document Outline, have a look under a new blue-colored section that has been created for you, named Constraints. Expand the constraints that Interface Builder has created for you for this button. What you see now is quite similar to what is shown in Figure 3-12.

As you can see, Interface Builder created two constraints for you. One of the constraints is saying that the X position of the center point of our button has to be aligned with the X position of the center point of the view on which the button resides. In other words, this means that the button has to be horizontally centered on its superview. The other constraint is saying that the button has to always have a distance of 208 points from the top of its superview. Now if you run this app in portrait mode, you will see the button at the center of screen, as shown in Figure 3-13.

Now rotate the device to landscape mode and you will see that the button stays horizontally centered, but the vertical alignment is not centered, which is again what we

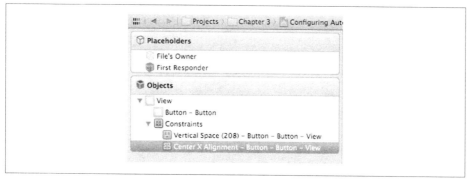

Figure 3-12. *Interface Builder created Layout Constraints for us*

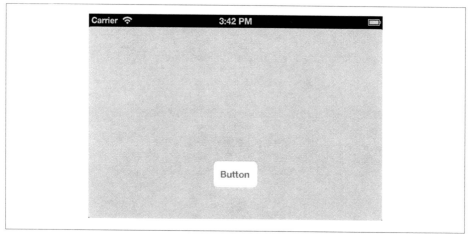

Figure 3-13. *The button appears to be centered on its superview in portrait mode*

expected. The constraint that Xcode created is for the button to maintain a distance of 208 points from the top point of its superview (see Figure 3-14).

> Constraints that are created using the Visual Format Language or through Interface Builder do not have the ability to vertically center-align a component on its superview. To be able to do this, simply create a constraint using the `constraintWithItem:attribute:related By:toItem:attribute:multiplier:constant:` class method of the class `NSLayoutConstraint`, as discussed before.

It is worth noting that you can actually modify the layout constraints that Interface Builder has created for you. Simply click on one of the constraints and then pop open the Attributes Inspector of Interface Builder. You shall now be able to see the different

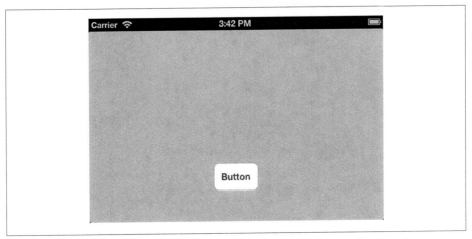

Figure 3-14. The button maintains a vertical distance of 208 from the top of its superview

properties that are available for modification, right in Interface Builder, as shown in Figure 3-15.

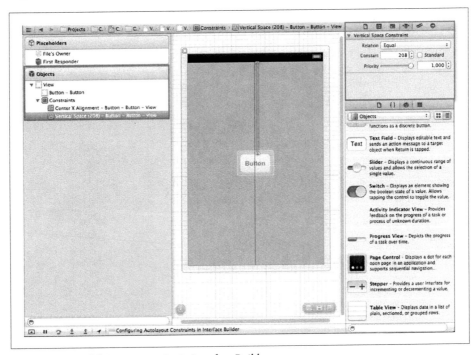

Figure 3-15. Modifying a constraint in Interface Builder

See Also

Recipe 3.0

CHAPTER 4

Constructing and Using Table Views

4.0 Introduction

A table view is simply a scrolling view that is separated into sections, each of which is further separated into rows. Each row is an instance of the `UITableViewCell` class, and you can create custom table view rows by *subclassing* this class.

Using table views is an ideal way to present a list of items to users. You can embed images, text, and other objects into your table view cells; you can customize their height, shape, grouping, and much more. The simplicity of the structure of table views is what makes them highly customizable.

A table view can be fed with data using a table view data source, and you can receive various events and control the physical appearance of table views using a table view delegate object. These are defined, respectively, in the `UITableViewDataSource` and `UITableViewDelegate` protocols.

Although an instance of `UITableView` subclasses `UIScrollView`, table views can only scroll vertically. This is more a feature than a limitation. In this chapter, we will discuss the different ways of creating, managing, and customizing table views.

4.1 Instantiating a Table View

Problem

You want to place a table view on your UI.

Solution

Instantiate an object of type `UITableView` and add it as a subview of any of your views.

Discussion

There are two ways of instantiating a table view:

1. Through code
2. Using Interface Builder

If you are using Interface Builder, creating a table view is as simple as dragging and dropping a table view from the object library into your .xib file. If you are more comfortable creating your components using code, then that is no problem either. All you have to do is to instantiate an object of type UITableView. Let's start by defining our table view in our view controller's header file:

```
#import <UIKit/UIKit.h>

@interface Instantiating_a_Table_ViewViewController : UIViewController

@property (nonatomic, strong) UITableView *myTableView;

@end
```

And creating the view controller is as easy as just allocating and initializing an instance of UITableView:

```
- (void)viewDidLoad{
  [super viewDidLoad];

  self.view.backgroundColor = [UIColor whiteColor];

  self.myTableView =
    [[UITableView alloc] initWithFrame:self.view.bounds
                                style:UITableViewStylePlain];

  [self.view addSubview:self.myTableView];

}
```

The style parameter of the initWithFrame:style: initializer of the view controller allows us to specify what type of table view we need. There are two styles that we can choose from:

UITableViewStylePlain
> Creates a plain table view with no background images.

UITableViewStyleGrouped
> Creates a table view with a background image and rounded group borders, similar to the Settings app.

If you run your app right now on the iPhone Simulator, you will see the table view sitting there with no table view cells populated inside it (Figure 4-1).

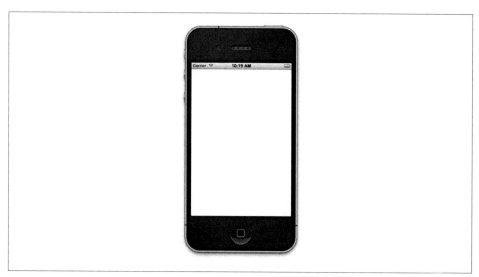

Figure 4-1. A plain table view with no content

4.2 Assigning a Delegate to a Table View

Problem

You have decided to assign a delegate to a table view.

Solution

Assign an object that conforms to the UITableViewDelegate protocol to the delegate property of your table view:

```
- (void)viewDidLoad{
  [super viewDidLoad];

  /* We want a full-screen Table View which is as
   big as the View attached to the current
   View Controller */
  CGRect tableViewFrame = self.view.bounds;

  self.myTableView = [[UITableView alloc]
                        initWithFrame:tableViewFrame
                        style:UITableViewStylePlain];

  self.myTableView.delegate = self;

  /* Add this Table View to our View */
  [self.view addSubview:self.myTableView];

}
```

This code assigns the current object as the delegate of the table view. `myTableView` is a property of type `UITableView` belonging to the calling view controller. The statement is embedded in the `viewDidLoad` method, because the calling object here is an instance of `UIViewController`, and this method is the right place to put the statement so that the association is made just once.

Discussion

The `UITableView` class defines a property called `delegate`. The table view should assign to this property an object that conforms to the `UITableViewDelegate` protocol. In other words, this delegate must *promise* to reply to the messages defined in this protocol, which are sent to the delegate object by the table view itself. Think of the delegate of a table view as an object that listens to various events sent by the table view, such as when a cell is selected or when the table view wants to figure out the height of each of its cells. We can modify the visual appearance of a table and its cells (to some extent) using Interface Builder, too. Just open Interface Builder and select a table view that you previously created, and then select Tools → Size Inspector. In the Size Inspector panel, you can modify the visual appearance of the table view by changing values such as the height of the table view's cells.

To make the delegate object that you choose for a table view conform to the `UITable ViewDelegate` protocol, you need to add that protocol to that object's interface declaration in this way:

```
#import <UIKit/UIKit.h>

@interface Assigning_a_Delegate_to_a_Table_ViewViewController
        : UIViewController <UITableViewDelegate>

@property (nonatomic, strong) UITableView *myTableView;

@end
```

 It is mandatory for the delegate object to respond to messages that are marked as `@required` by the `UITableViewDelegate` protocol. Responding to other messages is optional, but the delegate must respond to any messages you want to affect the table view.

Messages sent to the delegate object of a table view carry a parameter that tells the delegate object which table view has fired that message in its delegate. This is very important to note because you might, under certain circumstances, require more than one table view to be placed on one object (usually a view). Because of this, it is highly recommended that you make your decisions based on which table view has actually sent that specific message to your delegate object, like so:

```
- (CGFloat)     tableView:(UITableView *)tableView
  heightForRowAtIndexPath:(NSIndexPath *)indexPath{
```

```
CGFloat result = 20.0f;

if ([tableView isEqual:self.myTableView]){
  result = 40.0f;
}

return result;

}
```

It is worth noting that the location of a cell in a table view is represented by its index path. An index path is the combination of the section and the row index, where the section index is the zero-based index specifying which grouping or section each cell belongs to, and the cell index is the zero-based index of that particular cell in its section.

4.3 Populating a Table View with Data

Problem

You would like to populate your table view with data.

Solution

Conform to the UITableViewDataSource protocol in an object and assign that object to the dataSource property of a table view.

Discussion

Create an object that conforms to the UITableViewDataSource protocol and assign it to a table view instance. Then, by responding to the data source messages, provide information to your table view. For this example, let's go ahead and declare the .h file of our view controller, which will later create a table view on its own view, in code:

```
#import <UIKit/UIKit.h>

@interface Populating_a_Table_View_with_DataViewController
           : UIViewController <UITableViewDataSource>

@property (nonatomic, strong) UITableView *myTableView;

@end
```

In the viewDidLoad method of our view controller, we will create the table view and will assign our view controller as its data source:

```
- (void)viewDidLoad{
  [super viewDidLoad];

  self.view.backgroundColor = [UIColor whiteColor];

  self.myTableView =
```

```
    [[UITableView alloc] initWithFrame:self.view.bounds
                          style:UITableViewStylePlain];

self.myTableView.dataSource = self;

/* Make sure our table view resizes correctly */
self.myTableView.autoresizingMask =
  UIViewAutoresizingFlexibleWidth |
  UIViewAutoresizingFlexibleHeight;

[self.view addSubview:self.myTableView];

}
```

Now we need to make sure our table view responds to the @required methods of the
UITableViewDataSource protocol. Hold down the Command key on your keyboard and
click on the UITableViewDataSource protocol's mention in your view controller's .*h* file.
This will show you the required methods for this protocol.

The UITableView class defines a property called dataSource. This is an untyped object
that must conform to the UITableViewDataSource protocol. Every time a table view is
refreshed and reloaded using the reloadData method, the table view will call various
methods in its data source to find out about the data you intend to populate it with. A
table view data source can implement three important methods, two of which are
mandatory for every data source:

numberOfSectionsInTableView:
> This method allows the data source to inform the table view of the number of
> sections that must be loaded into the table.

tableView:numberOfRowsInSection:
> This method tells the view controller how many cells or rows have to be loaded for
> each section. The section number is passed to the data source in the numberOfRows
> InSection parameter. The implementation of this method is mandatory in the data
> source object.

tableView:cellForRowAtIndexPath:
> This method is responsible for returning instances of the UITableViewCell class as
> rows that have to be populated into the table view. The implementation of this
> method is mandatory in the data source object.

So let's go ahead and implement these methods in our view controller, one by one.
First, let's tell the table view that we want it to render three sections:

```
- (NSInteger)numberOfSectionsInTableView:(UITableView *)tableView{

NSInteger result = 0;
```

```
if ([tableView isEqual:self.myTableView]){
   result = 3;
  }
  return result;

}
```

Then we tell the table view how many rows we want it to render, for each section:

```
- (NSInteger)tableView:(UITableView *)tableView
 numberOfRowsInSection:(NSInteger)section{

  NSInteger result = 0;
  if ([tableView isEqual:self.myTableView]){
    switch (section){
      case 0:{
        result = 3;
        break;
      }
      case 1:{
        result = 5;
        break;
      }
      case 2:{
        result = 8;
        break;
      }
    }
  }
  return result;

}
```

So up to now, we have asked the table view to render three sections with three rows in the first, five rows in the second, and eight rows in the third section. What's next? We have to return instances of UITableViewCell to the table view—the cells that we want the table view to render:

```
- (UITableViewCell *)      tableView:(UITableView *)tableView
              cellForRowAtIndexPath:(NSIndexPath *)indexPath{

  UITableViewCell *result = nil;

  if ([tableView isEqual:self.myTableView]){

    static NSString *TableViewCellIdentifier = @"MyCells";

    result = [tableView
            dequeueReusableCellWithIdentifier:TableViewCellIdentifier];

    if (result == nil){
      result = [[UITableViewCell alloc]
               initWithStyle:UITableViewCellStyleDefault
               reuseIdentifier:TableViewCellIdentifier];
    }
```

```
        result.textLabel.text = [NSString stringWithFormat:@"Section %ld, Cell %ld",
                                  (long)indexPath.section,
                                  (long)indexPath.row];

    }

    return result;

}
```

Now if we run our app in iPhone Simulator, we will see the results of our work (Figure 4-2).

Figure 4-2. A plain table view with three sections

When a table view is reloaded or refreshed, it queries its data source through the UITableViewDataSource protocol, asking for various bits of information. Among the important methods previously mentioned, the table view will first ask for the number of sections. Each section is responsible for holding rows or cells. After the data source specifies the number of sections, the table view will ask for the number of rows that have to be loaded into each section. The data source gets the zero-based index of each section and, based on this, can decide how many cells have to be loaded into each section.

The table view, after determining the number of cells in the sections, will continue to ask the data source about the view that will represent each cell in each section. You can allocate instances of the UITableViewCell class and return them to the table view. There are, of course, properties that can be set for each cell, including the title, subtitle, and color of each cell, among other properties.

4.4 Receiving and Handling Table View Events

Problem

You would like to respond to various events that a table view can generate.

Solution

Provide your table view with a delegate object.

Here is an excerpt of the *.h* file of a view controller with a table view:

```
#import <UIKit/UIKit.h>

@interface Receiving_and_Handling_Table_View_EventsViewController
        : UIViewController <UITableViewDelegate, UITableViewDataSource>

@property (nonatomic, strong) UITableView *myTableView;

@end
```

The *.m* file of the same view controller implements a method defined in the UITable
ViewDelegate protocol:

```
- (void)         tableView:(UITableView *)tableView
  didSelectRowAtIndexPath:(NSIndexPath *)indexPath{

  if ([tableView isEqual:self.myTableView]){

    NSLog(@"%@",
    [NSString stringWithFormat:@"Cell %ld in Section %ld is selected",
      (long)indexPath.row, (long)indexPath.section]);
  }

}

- (void)viewDidLoad {
  [super viewDidLoad];

  self.myTableView = [[UITableView alloc]
                      initWithFrame:self.view.bounds
                      style:UITableViewStylePlain];

  self.myTableView.autoresizingMask =
    UIViewAutoresizingFlexibleHeight |
    UIViewAutoresizingFlexibleWidth;

  self.myTableView.dataSource = self;
  self.myTableView.delegate = self;

  [self.view addSubview:self.myTableView];

}
```

Discussion

While a data source is responsible for providing data to the table view, the table view consults the delegate whenever an event occurs, or if the table view needs further information before it can complete a task. For instance, the table view invokes a delegate's method:

- When and before a cell is selected or deselected
- When the table view needs to find the height of each cell
- When the table view needs to construct the header and footer of every section

As you can see in the example code in this recipe's Solution, the current object is set as the delegate of a table view. The delegate implements the `tableView:didSelect RowAtIndexPath:` selector in order to get notified when the user selects a cell or a row on a table view. The documentation for the `UITableViewDelegate` protocol in the SDK shows you all the methods that the delegate can define and the view can invoke.

See Also

UITableViewDelegate Protocol Reference (*http://bit.ly/Uvtvnw*)

4.5 Using Different Types of Accessories in a Table View Cell

Problem

You want to grab users' attention in a table view by displaying accessories, and offer different ways to interact with each cell in your table view.

Solution

Use the `accessoryType` of the `UITableViewCell` class, instances of which you provide to your table view in its data source object:

```
- (UITableViewCell *)tableView:(UITableView *)tableView
        cellForRowAtIndexPath:(NSIndexPath *)indexPath{

  UITableViewCell* result = nil;

  if ([tableView isEqual:self.myTableView]){

    static NSString *MyCellIdentifier = @"SimpleCell";

    /* We will try to retrieve an existing cell
     with the given identifier */
    result = [tableView
            dequeueReusableCellWithIdentifier:MyCellIdentifier];

    if (result == nil){
      /* If a cell with the given identifier does not
```

```
        exist, we will create the cell with the identifier
        and hand it to the table view */

    result = [[UITableViewCell alloc]
             initWithStyle:UITableViewCellStyleDefault
             reuseIdentifier:MyCellIdentifier];
  }

  result.textLabel.text =
  [NSString stringWithFormat:@"Section %ld, Cell %ld",
   (long)indexPath.section,
   (long)indexPath.row];

  result.accessoryType = UITableViewCellAccessoryDetailDisclosureButton;

  }

  return result;

}

- (NSInteger) tableView:(UITableView *)tableView
  numberOfRowsInSection:(NSInteger)section{
  return 10;
}

- (void)viewDidLoad{
  [super viewDidLoad];

  self.myTableView = [[UITableView alloc] initWithFrame:self.view.bounds
                                            style:UITableViewStylePlain];

  self.myTableView.dataSource = self;
  self.myTableView.delegate = self;

  self.myTableView.autoresizingMask =
    UIViewAutoresizingFlexibleWidth |
    UIViewAutoresizingFlexibleHeight;

  [self.view addSubview:self.myTableView];

}
```

Discussion

You can assign any of the values defined in the UITableViewCellAccessoryType enumeration to the accessoryType property of an instance of the UITableViewCell class. Two very useful accessories are the *disclosure indicator* and the *detail disclosure button*. They both display a chevron indicating to users that if they tap on the associated table view cell, a new view or view controller will be displayed. In other words, the users will be taken to a new screen with further information about their current selector. The difference between these two accessories is that the disclosure indicator produces no event, whereas the detail disclosure button fires an event to the delegate when pressed. In other words, pressing the button has a different effect from pressing the cell itself. Thus, the detail disclosure button allows the user to perform two separate but related actions on the same row.

Figure 4-3 shows these two different accessories on a table view. The first row has a disclosure indicator and the second row has a detail disclosure button.

Figure 4-3. Two table view cells with different accessories

If you tap any detail disclosure button assigned to a table view cell, you will immediately realize that it truly is a separate button. Now the question is: how does the table view know when the user taps this button?

Table views, as explained before, fire events on their delegate object. The detail disclosure button on a table view cell also fires an event that can be captured by the delegate object of a table view:

```
- (void)                           tableView:(UITableView *)tableView
  accessoryButtonTappedForRowWithIndexPath:(NSIndexPath *)indexPath{

    /* Do something when the accessory button is tapped */
    NSLog(@"Accessory button is tapped for cell at index path = %@", indexPath);

    UITableViewCell *ownerCell = [tableView cellForRowAtIndexPath:indexPath];

    NSLog(@"Cell Title = %@", ownerCell.textLabel.text);

}
```

This code finds the table view cell whose detail disclosure button has been tapped and prints the contents of the text label of that cell into the console screen. As a reminder, you can display the console screen in Xcode by selecting Run → Console.

4.6 Creating Custom Table View Cell Accessories

Problem

The accessories provided to you by the iOS SDK are not sufficient, and you would like to create your own accessories.

Solution

Assign an instance of the UIView class to the accessoryView property of any instance of the UITableViewCell class:

```
- (UITableViewCell *)tableView:(UITableView *)tableView
        cellForRowAtIndexPath:(NSIndexPath *)indexPath{

    UITableViewCell* result = nil;

    static NSString *MyCellIdentifier = @"SimpleCell";

    /* We will try to retrieve an existing cell
     with the given identifier */
    result = [tableView dequeueReusableCellWithIdentifier:MyCellIdentifier];

    if (result == nil){
      result = [[UITableViewCell alloc] initWithStyle:UITableViewCellStyleDefault
                                      reuseIdentifier:MyCellIdentifier];
    }

    result.textLabel.text = [NSString stringWithFormat:@"Section %ld, Cell %ld",
                            (long)indexPath.section,
                            (long)indexPath.row];

    UIButton *button = [UIButton buttonWithType:UIButtonTypeRoundedRect];
    button.frame = CGRectMake(0.0f, 0.0f, 150.0f, 25.0f);

    [button setTitle:@"Expand"
          forState:UIControlStateNormal];

    [button addTarget:self
             action:@selector(performExpand:)
     forControlEvents:UIControlEventTouchUpInside];

    result.accessoryView = button;

    return result;

}
```

As you can see, this code uses the performExpand: method as the selector for each button. Here is the definition of this method:

```
- (void) performExpand:(id)paramSender{
  /* Take an action here */
}
```

This example code snippet assigns a custom button to the accessory view of every row in the targeted table. The result is shown in Figure 4-4.

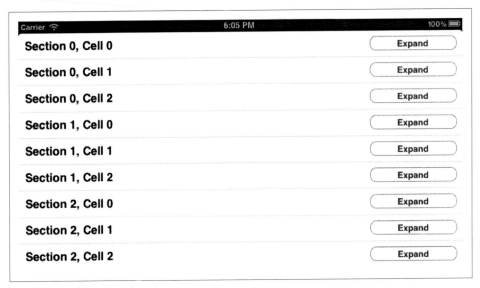

Figure 4-4. Table view cells with custom accessory views

Discussion

An object of type UITableViewCell retains a property named accessoryView. This is the view you can assign a value to if you are not completely happy with the built-in iOS SDK table view cell accessories. After this property is set, Cocoa Touch will ignore the value of the accessoryType property and will use the view assigned to the accessory View property as the accessory assigned to the cell.

The code listed in this recipe's Solution creates buttons for all the cells populated into the table view. When a button is pressed in any cell, the performExpand: method gets called, and if you are like me, you have probably already started thinking about how you can determine which cell the sender button belongs to. So, now we have to some-how link our buttons with the cells to which they belong.

One way to handle this situation is to retrieve the superview of the button that fires the event. Since the accessory view of the cells of a table view adds the cells' accessory views as their subviews, retrieving the superview of the button will return the table view cell that owns the button as its accessory view:

```
- (void) performExpand:(UIButton *)paramSender{

    UITableViewCell *ownerCell = (UITableViewCell*)paramSender.superview;

    if (ownerCell != nil){

        /* Now we will retrieve the index path of the cell
        which contains the section and the row of the cell */

        NSIndexPath *ownerCellIndexPath =
```

```
    [self.myTableView indexPathForCell:ownerCell];

    NSLog(@"Accessory in index path is tapped. Index path = %@",
        ownerCellIndexPath);

    /* Now we can use these two values to truly determine that
     the accessory button of which cell was the sender of this event:

     OwnerCellIndexPath.section
     OwnerCellIndexPath.row

    */

    if (ownerCellIndexPath.section == 0 &&
        ownerCellIndexPath.row == 1){
      /* This is the second row in the first section */
    }

    /* And so forth with the other checks ... */

  }

}
```

4.7 Displaying Hierarchical Data in Table Views

Problem

You want to be able to display hierarchical data in a table view.

Solution

Use the indentation functionality of table view cells:

```
- (UITableViewCell *)tableView:(UITableView *)tableView
        cellForRowAtIndexPath:(NSIndexPath *)indexPath{
  UITableViewCell* result = nil;

  static NSString *MyCellIdentifier = @"SimpleCells";

  result = [tableView dequeueReusableCellWithIdentifier:MyCellIdentifier];

  if (result == nil){
    result = [[UITableViewCell alloc] initWithStyle:UITableViewCellStyleDefault
                                  reuseIdentifier:MyCellIdentifier];
  }

  result.textLabel.text = [NSString stringWithFormat:@"Section %ld, Cell %ld",
                          (long)indexPath.section,
                          (long)indexPath.row];

  result.indentationLevel = indexPath.row;
  result.indentationWidth = 10.0f;
```

```
    return result;

}
```

The indentation level is simply multiplied by the indentation width in order to give a margin to the content view of each cell. Figure 4-5 depicts how these cells look when displayed inside a table view.

Discussion

Although you might rarely find it useful, you can apply indentation to table view cells in the iOS SDK. Each cell can have two properties related to indentation: *indentation level* and *indentation width*. The indentation level is simply multiplied by the indentation width, and the resultant value is the offset by which the table view cell's content is shifted to the right or left.

For instance, if the indentation level of a cell is set to 2 and its indentation width is set to 3, the resultant value is 6. This means the content view of the cell is shifted to the right by six pixels when displayed in a table view.

 The indentation level is defined as a signed integer value, making it possible for you to assign negative values to it. This will obviously shift the content view of your cells to the left.

The indentation level assigned to table view cells enables programmers to present hierarchical data, and it is up to the programmer to determine the indentation level and the indentation width of each cell.

4.8 Enabling Swipe Deletion of Table View Cells

Problem

You want your application users to be able to delete rows from a table view easily.

Solution

Implement the `tableView:editingStyleForRowAtIndexPath:` selector in the delegate and the `tableView:commitEditingStyle:forRowAtIndexPath:` selector in the data source of your table view:

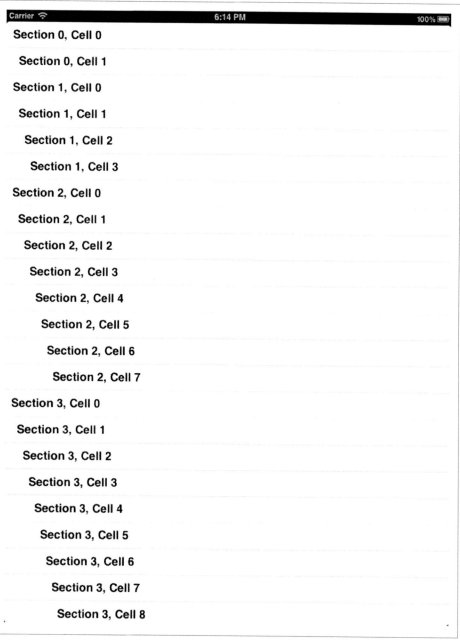

Figure 4-5. Table view cells with indentation

```
- (UITableViewCellEditingStyle)tableView:(UITableView *)tableView
           editingStyleForRowAtIndexPath:(NSIndexPath *)indexPath{

  UITableViewCellEditingStyle result = UITableViewCellEditingStyleNone;

  if ([tableView isEqual:self.myTableView]){
    result = UITableViewCellEditingStyleDelete;
  }

  return result;

}

- (void) setEditing:(BOOL)editing
           animated:(BOOL)animated{

  [super setEditing:editing
           animated:animated];

  [self.myTableView setEditing:editing
                      animated:animated];


}

- (void)  tableView:(UITableView *)tableView
  commitEditingStyle:(UITableViewCellEditingStyle)editingStyle
   forRowAtIndexPath:(NSIndexPath *)indexPath{

  if (editingStyle == UITableViewCellEditingStyleDelete){

    if (indexPath.row < [self.arrayOfRows count]){

      /* First remove this object from the source */
      [self.arrayOfRows removeObjectAtIndex:indexPath.row];

      /* Then remove the associated cell from the Table View */
      [tableView deleteRowsAtIndexPaths:[NSArray arrayWithObject:indexPath]
                       withRowAnimation:UITableViewRowAnimationLeft];

    }
  }

}
```

The tableView:editingStyleForRowAtIndexPath: method can enable deletions. It is called by the table view and its return value determines what the table view allows the user to do (insertion, deletion, etc.). The tableView:commitEditingStyle:forRowAtIndex Path: method carries out the user's requested deletion. The latter method is defined in the delegate, but its functionality is a bit overloaded: not only do you use the method to delete data, but you also have to delete rows from the table here.

Discussion

The table view responds to the swipe by showing a button on the right side of the targeted row (Figure 4-6). As you can see, the table view is *not* in editing mode, but the button allows the user to delete the row.

This mode is enabled by implementing the `tableView:editingStyleForRowAtIndex Path:` method (declared in the `UITableViewDelegate` protocol), whose return value indicates whether the table should allow insertions, deletions, both, or neither. By implementing the `tableView:commitEditingStyle:forRowAtIndexPath:` method in the data source of a table view, you can then get notified if a user has performed an insertion or deletion.

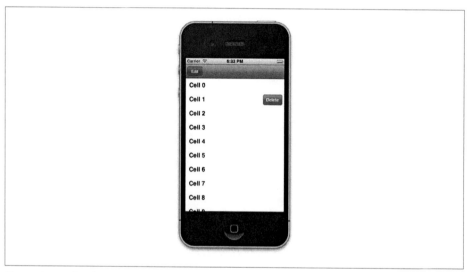

Figure 4-6. Delete button appearing on a table view cell

The second parameter of the `deleteRowsAtIndexPaths:withRowAnimation:` method allows you to specify an animation method that will be performed when rows are deleted from a table view. Our example specifies that we want rows to disappear by moving from right to left when deleted.

4.9 Constructing Headers and Footers in Table Views

Problem

You want to create a header and/or a footer for a table view.

Solution

Create a view (could be a label, image view, etc., anything that directly or indirectly subclasses UIView), and assign that view to the header and/or the footer of a section of a table view. You can also allocate specific number of points in height for a header or a footer, as we will soon see.

Discussion

A table view can have multiple headers and footers. Each section in a table view can have its own header and footer, so if you have three sections in a table view, you can have a maximum of three headers and maximum of three footers. You are *not* obliged to provide headers and footers for any of these sections. It is up to you to tell the table view whether you want a header and/or a footer for a section and you pass these views to the table view through its delegate, should you wish to provide header(s)/footer(s) for section(s) of your table view. Headers and footers in a table view become a part of the table view, meaning that when the table view's contents scroll, so do the header(s) and footer(s) inside that table view. Let's have a look at a sample header and footer in a table view (Figure 4-7).

Figure 4-7. A footer for the top section and the Shortcuts header for the last section of a table view

As you can see, the top section (with items such as "Check Spelling" and "Enable Caps Lock") has a footer that says "Double tapping the space bar will insert a period followed by a space." That is the footer of the top section of that table view. The reason why it is a footer rather than a header is because it is attached to the bottom of that section rather than the top. The last section in this table view also has a header that reads "Shortcuts." The reason why this is a header rather than a footer is because it appears on the top of the section rather than the bottom.

Specifying the height of a header and footer in a section inside a table view is done through methods defined in the UITableViewDataSource. Specifying the actual view that has to be displayed for the header/footer of a section in a table view is done through methods defined in the UITableViewDelegate protocol.

Let's go ahead and create a simple app with one table view in it. Then let's provide two labels, of type UILabel, one as the header and the other as the footer of the only section in our table view, and populate this one section with only three cells. In the header we will place the text "Section 1 Header," and in the footer label we will place the text "Section 1 Footer." Starting with the header file of our root view controller, we will define a table view:

```
#import <UIKit/UIKit.h>

@interface Constructing_Headers_and_Footers_in_Table_ViewsViewController
        : UIViewController <UITableViewDataSource, UITableViewDelegate>

@property (nonatomic, strong) UITableView *myTableView;

@end
```

Now we will create a grouped table view and load three cells into it:

```
- (UITableViewCell *) tableView:(UITableView *)tableView
        cellForRowAtIndexPath:(NSIndexPath *)indexPath{

  UITableViewCell *result = nil;

  static NSString *CellIdentifier = @"CellIdentifier";

  result = [tableView dequeueReusableCellWithIdentifier:CellIdentifier];

  if (result == nil){
    result = [[UITableViewCell alloc] initWithStyle:UITableViewCellStyleDefault
                                reuseIdentifier:CellIdentifier];
  }

  result.textLabel.text = [[NSString alloc] initWithFormat:@"Cell %ld",
                          (long)indexPath.row];

  return result;

}

- (NSInteger) tableView:(UITableView *)tableView
  numberOfRowsInSection:(NSInteger)section{
  return 3;
}

- (void)viewDidLoad{
  [super viewDidLoad];
```

```
        self.myTableView =
        [[UITableView alloc] initWithFrame:self.view.bounds
                                     style:UITableViewStyleGrouped];

        self.myTableView.dataSource = self;
        self.myTableView.delegate = self;
        self.myTableView.autoresizingMask = UIViewAutoresizingFlexibleWidth |
                                 UIViewAutoresizingFlexibleHeight;

        [self.view addSubview:self.myTableView];

}

- (BOOL)shouldAutorotateToInterfaceOrientation
        :(UIInterfaceOrientation)interfaceOrientation{
   return YES;
}
```

Here is the exciting part. We can now use two important methods (which are defined in UITableViewDelegate) to provide a label for the header and another label for the footer of the one section that we have loaded into our table view. These methods are:

tableView:viewForHeaderInSection:
> This method expects a return value of type UIView. The view returned from this method will be displayed as the header of the section specified by the viewForHea derInSection parameter.

tableView:viewForFooterInSection:
> This method expects a return value of type UIView. The view returned from this method will be displayed as the footer of the section specified by the viewForFoo terInSection parameter.

Our task now is to implement these methods and return an instance of UILabel. On the header label we will enter the text "Section 1 Header," and on the footer label the text "Section 1 Footer," as we had planned:

```
- (UIView *)  tableView:(UITableView *)tableView
  viewForHeaderInSection:(NSInteger)section{

  UILabel *result = nil;

  if ([tableView isEqual:self.myTableView] &&
      section == 0){
    result = [[UILabel alloc] initWithFrame:CGRectZero];
    result.text = @"Section 1 Header";
    result.backgroundColor = [UIColor clearColor];
    [result sizeToFit];
  }

  return result;

}

- (UIView *)  tableView:(UITableView *)tableView
```

```
viewForFooterInSection:(NSInteger)section{

  UILabel *result = nil;

  if ([tableView isEqual:self.myTableView] &&
      section == 0){
    result = [[UILabel alloc] initWithFrame:CGRectZero];
    result.text = @"Section 1 Footer";
    result.backgroundColor = [UIColor clearColor];
    [result sizeToFit];
  }

  return result;

}
```

If you run your app on the iPhone Simulator now, you will certainly see something strange, as shown in Figure 4-8.

Figure 4-8. The header and footer labels of a table view are not aligned properly

The reason for this misalignment of the labels is because the table view doesn't really know the height of these views. To specify the height of the header and footer views, we need to use the following two methods which are defined in the UITableViewDele gate protocol:

tableView:heightForHeaderInSection:
  The return value of this method is of type CGFloat, and it specifies the height of the header for a section in a table view. The section's index is passed through the heightForHeaderInSection parameter.

`tableView:heightForFooterInSection:`

The return value of this method is of type `CGFloat`, and it specifies the height of the footer for a section in a table view. The section's index is passed through the `heightForHeaderInSection` parameter.

```
- (CGFloat)      tableView:(UITableView *)tableView
  heightForHeaderInSection:(NSInteger)section{

    CGFloat result = 0.0f;

    if ([tableView isEqual:self.myTableView] &&
        section == 0){
      result = 30.0f;
    }

    return result;

}

- (CGFloat)      tableView:(UITableView *)tableView
  heightForFooterInSection:(NSInteger)section{

    CGFloat result = 0.0f;

    if ([tableView isEqual:self.myTableView] &&
        section == 0){
      result = 30.0f;
    }

    return result;

}
```

Running the app, you can see that the height of the header and the footer labels is fixed. There is still something wrong with the code we've written—the left margin of our header and footer labels. Take a look for yourself in Figure 4-9.

The reason for this is that the table view, by default, places header and footer views at *x* point `0.0f`. You might think that changing the frame of your header and footer labels will fix this issue, but unfortunately it doesn't. The solution to this problem is creating a generic `UIView` and placing your header and footer labels on that view. Return the generic view as the header/footer, but change the *x* position of your labels within the generic view. We now need to modify our implementation of the `tableView:view ForHeaderInSection:` and the `tableView:viewForFooterInSection:` methods:

```
- (UIView *)  tableView:(UITableView *)tableView
  viewForHeaderInSection:(NSInteger)section{

    UIView *result = nil;

    if ([tableView isEqual:self.myTableView] &&
        section == 0){
```

Figure 4-9. The left margin of our header and footer labels is not correct

```
    UILabel *label = [[UILabel alloc] initWithFrame:CGRectZero];
    label.text = @"Section 1 Header";
    label.backgroundColor = [UIColor clearColor];
    [label sizeToFit];

    /* Move the label 10 points to the right */
    label.frame = CGRectMake(label.frame.origin.x + 10.0f,
                            5.0f, /* Go 5 points down in y axis */
                            label.frame.size.width,
                            label.frame.size.height);

    /* Give the container view 10 points more in width than our label
      because the label needs a 10 extra points left-margin */
    CGRect resultFrame = CGRectMake(0.0f,
                                    0.0f,
                                    label.frame.size.width + 10.0f,
                                    label.frame.size.height);
    result = [[UIView alloc] initWithFrame:resultFrame];
    [result addSubview:label];

  }

  return result;

}

- (UIView *) tableView:(UITableView *)tableView
 viewForFooterInSection:(NSInteger)section{

  UIView *result = nil;

  if ([tableView isEqual:self.myTableView] &&
      section == 0){
```

```
UILabel *label = [[UILabel alloc] initWithFrame:CGRectZero];
label.text = @"Section 1 Footer";
label.backgroundColor = [UIColor clearColor];
[label sizeToFit];

/* Move the label 10 points to the right */
label.frame = CGRectMake(label.frame.origin.x + 10.0f,
                         5.0f, /* Go 5 points down in y axis */
                         label.frame.size.width,
                         label.frame.size.height);

/* Give the container view 10 points more in width than our label
   because the label needs a 10 extra points left-margin */
CGRect resultFrame = CGRectMake(0.0f,
                                0.0f,
                                label.frame.size.width + 10.0f,
                                label.frame.size.height);
result = [[UIView alloc] initWithFrame:resultFrame];
[result addSubview:label];

}

return result;

}
```

Now if you run your app, you will get results similar to Figure 4-10.

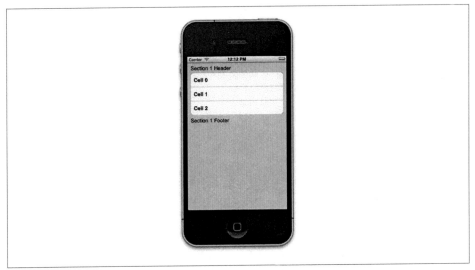

Figure 4-10. Our header and footer labels displayed in a table view

With the methods you just learned, you can even place images as the header/footer of your table views. Instances of UIImageView have UIView as their superclass, so you can easily place your images in image views and return them as headers/footers of a table view. If all you want to place is text as the header/footer of table views, you can use two handy methods defined in the UITableViewDataSource protocol, which will save you a lot of hassle. Instead of creating your own labels and returning them as headers/footers of your table view, you can simply use these methods:

tableView:titleForHeaderInSection:

> The return value of this method is of type NSString. This string will automatically be placed inside a label by the table view and will be displayed as the header of the section, which is specified in the titleForHeaderInSection parameter.

tableView:titleForFooterInSection:

> The return value of this method is of type NSString. This string will automatically be placed inside a label by the table view and will be displayed as the footer of the section, which is specified in the titleForFooterInSection parameter.

So to make our app's code simpler, let's get rid of our implementation of the table View:viewForHeaderInSection: and the tableView:viewForFooterInSection: methods, and replace them with the implementation of the tableView:titleForHeaderInSec tion: and the tableView:titleForFooterInSection: methods:

```
- (NSString *) tableView:(UITableView *)tableView
  titleForHeaderInSection:(NSInteger)section{

  NSString *result = nil;

  if ([tableView isEqual:self.myTableView] &&
      section == 0){
    result = @"Section 1 Header";
  }

  return result;

}


- (NSString *) tableView:(UITableView *)tableView
  titleForFooterInSection:(NSInteger)section{

  NSString *result = nil;

  if ([tableView isEqual:self.myTableView] &&
      section == 0){
    result = @"Section 1 Footer";
  }

  return result;

}
```

Now run your app in the iPhone Simulator, and you will see that the table view has automatically created a left-aligned label for the header and a center-aligned label for the footer of the only section in our table view. The alignment of these labels is the default alignment that every table view creates its header/footer labels with (see Figure 4-11).

Figure 4-11. A table view rendering text in headers and footers

4.10 Displaying Context Menus on Table View Cells

Problem

You want to give your users the ability to use copy/paste options among other operations that they can choose, by holding down one of their fingers on a table view cell in your app.

Solution

Implement the following three methods of the `UITableViewDelegate` protocol in the delegate object of your table view:

`tableView:shouldShowMenuForRowAtIndexPath:`
> The return value of this method is of type `BOOL`. If you return `YES` from this method, iOS will display the context menu for the table view cell whose index gets passed to you through the `shouldShowMenuForRowAtIndexPath` parameter.

`tableView:canPerformAction:forRowAtIndexPath:withSender:`
> The return value of this method is also of type `BOOL`. Once you allow iOS to display a context menu for a table view cell, iOS will call this method multiple times and pass you the selector of the action that you can choose to display in the context menu or not. So, if iOS wants to ask you whether you would like to show the Copy menu to be displayed to the user, this method will get called in your table view's

delegate object and the `canPerformAction` parameter of this method will be equal to `@selector(copy:)`. We will read more information about this in this recipe's Discussion.

`tableView:performAction:forRowAtIndexPath:withSender:`

Once you allow a certain action to be displayed in the context menu of a table view cell, when the user picks that action from the menu, this method will get called in your table view's delegate object. In here, you must do whatever needs to be done to satisfy the user's request. For instance, if it is the Copy menu that the user has selected, you will need to use a pasteboard to place the chosen table view cell's content into the pasteboard.

Discussion

A table view can give a yes/no answer to iOS, allowing or disallowing the display of available system menu items for a table view cell. iOS attempts to display a context menu on a table view cell when the user has held down his finger on the cell for a certain period of time, roughly about one second. iOS then asks the table view whose cell was the source of the trigger for the menu. If the table view gives a yes answer, iOS will then tell the table view what options can be displayed in the context menu, and the table view will be able to say yes or no to any of those items. If there are five menu items available, for instance, and the table view says yes to only two of them, then only those two items will be displayed.

After the menu items are displayed to the user, the user can either tap on one of the items or tap outside the context menu to cancel it. Once the user taps on one of the menu items, iOS will send a delegate message to the table view informing it of the menu item that the user has picked. Based on this information, the table view can make a decision as to what to do with the selected action.

I suggest that we first see what actions are actually available for a context menu on a table view cell, so let's create our table view and then display a few cells inside it:

```
- (NSInteger) tableView:(UITableView *)tableView
  numberOfRowsInSection:(NSInteger)section{
  return 3;
}

- (UITableViewCell *) tableView:(UITableView *)tableView
        cellForRowAtIndexPath:(NSIndexPath *)indexPath{

  UITableViewCell *result = nil;

  static NSString *CellIdentifier = @"CellIdentifier";

  result = [tableView dequeueReusableCellWithIdentifier:CellIdentifier];

  if (result == nil){
    result = [[UITableViewCell alloc] initWithStyle:UITableViewCellStyleDefault
                                    reuseIdentifier:CellIdentifier];
```

```
    }

    result.textLabel.text = [[NSString alloc]
                             initWithFormat:@"Section %ld Cell %ld",
                             (long)indexPath.section,
                             (long)indexPath.row];

    return result;

}

- (void)viewDidLoad{
    [super viewDidLoad];

    self.view.backgroundColor = [UIColor whiteColor];

    self.myTableView = [[UITableView alloc]
                        initWithFrame:self.view.bounds
                        style:UITableViewStylePlain];

    self.myTableView.autoresizingMask = UIViewAutoresizingFlexibleWidth |
                                        UIViewAutoresizingFlexibleHeight;

    self.myTableView.dataSource = self;
    self.myTableView.delegate = self;

    [self.view addSubview:self.myTableView];

}
```

Now we will implement the three aforementioned methods defined in the UITableView
Delegate protocol and simply convert the available actions (of type SEL) to strings and
print them out to the console:

```
- (BOOL)                    tableView:(UITableView *)tableView
  shouldShowMenuForRowAtIndexPath:(NSIndexPath *)indexPath{

    /* Allow the context menu to be displayed on every cell */
    return YES;

}

- (BOOL) tableView:(UITableView *)tableView
  canPerformAction:(SEL)action
 forRowAtIndexPath:(NSIndexPath *)indexPath
        withSender:(id)sender{

    NSLog(@"%@", NSStringFromSelector(action));

    /* Allow every action for now */
    return YES;
}

- (void) tableView:(UITableView *)tableView
      performAction:(SEL)action
```

```
forRowAtIndexPath:(NSIndexPath *)indexPath
        withSender:(id)sender{

    /* Empty for now */

}
```

Now run your app in the simulator or on the device. You will then see three cells loaded into the table view. Hold down your finger (if on a device) or your pointer (if using iOS Simulator) on one of the cells and observe what gets printed out to the console window:

```
cut:
copy:
select:
selectAll:
paste:
delete:
_promptForReplace:
_showTextStyleOptions:
_define:
_accessibilitySpeak:
_accessibilityPauseSpeaking:
makeTextWritingDirectionRightToLeft:
makeTextWritingDirectionLeftToRight:
cut:
copy:
select:
selectAll:paste:
delete:
_promptForReplace:
_showTextStyleOptions:
_define:
_accessibilitySpeak:
_accessibilityPauseSpeaking:
makeTextWritingDirectionRightToLeft:
makeTextWritingDirectionLeftToRight:
```

These are all the actions that iOS will allow you to show your users, should you need them. So for instance, if you would like to allow your users to have the Copy option, in the `tableView:canPerformAction:forRowAtIndexPath:withSender:` method, simply find out which action iOS is asking your permission for before displaying it, and either return YES or NO:

```
- (BOOL) tableView:(UITableView *)tableView
  canPerformAction:(SEL)action
forRowAtIndexPath:(NSIndexPath *)indexPath
        withSender:(id)sender{

    if (action == @selector(copy:)){
      return YES;
    }

    return NO;
}
```

The next step is to intercept what menu item the user actually selected from the context menu. Based on this information, we can then take appropriate action. For instance, if the user selected the Copy item in the context menu (see Figure 4-12), then we can use UIPasteBoard to copy that cell into the pasteboard for later use:

Figure 4-12. The Copy action displayed inside a context menu on a table view cell

```
- (void) tableView:(UITableView *)tableView
      performAction:(SEL)action
 forRowAtIndexPath:(NSIndexPath *)indexPath
         withSender:(id)sender{

  if (action == @selector(copy:)){

    UITableViewCell *cell = [tableView cellForRowAtIndexPath:indexPath];
    UIPasteboard *pasteBoard = [UIPasteboard generalPasteboard];
    [pasteBoard setString:cell.textLabel.text];

  }

}
```

4.11 Moving Cells and Sections in Table Views

Problem

You want to move and shuffle cells and sections inside a table view, with smooth and intuitive animations.

Solution

Use the `moveSection:toSection:` method of the table view to move a section to a new position. You can also use the `moveRowAtIndexPath:toIndexPath:` method to move a table view cell from its current place to a new place.

Discussion

Moving table view cells and sections differs from exchanging them. Let's have a look at an example that will make this easier to understand. Let's say you have three sections in your table view: Sections A, B, and C. If you move Section A to Section C, the table view will notice this move and will then shift Section B to the previous position of Section A, and will move Section B to the previous position of Section B. However, if Section B is moved to Section C, the table view will not have to move Section A at all, as it is sitting on top and doesn't interfere with the repositioning of Section B and C. In this case, Section B will be moved to Section C and Section C to Section B. The same logic will be used by the table view when moving cells.

To demonstrate this, let's create a table view and preload it with three sections, each of which contains three cells of its own. Let's start with the header file of our view controller:

```
#import <UIKit/UIKit.h>

@interface Moving_Cells_and_Sections_in_Table_ViewsViewController
            : UIViewController <UITableViewDelegate, UITableViewDataSource>

@property (nonatomic, strong) UITableView *myTableView;

/* Each section is an array on its own, containing objects of type NSString */
@property (nonatomic, strong) NSMutableArray *arrayOfSections;

@end
```

Our view controller will become the data source of the table view. The table view has sections and each section has rows. We will keep an array of arrays; the first array is our array of sections, which will itself contain other arrays that contain our cells. The **arrayOfSections** defined in the header file of our view controller will bear that responsibility. Let's go ahead and populate this array in the implementation of our view controller:

```
#import "Moving_Cells_and_Sections_in_Table_ViewsViewController.h"

@implementation Moving_Cells_and_Sections_in_Table_ViewsViewController

- (NSMutableArray *) newSectionWithIndex:(NSUInteger)paramIndex
                        withCellCount:(NSUInteger)paramCellCount{

  NSMutableArray *result = [[NSMutableArray alloc] init];

  NSUInteger counter = 0;
```

```
for (counter = 0;
     counter < paramCellCount;
     counter++){
    [result addObject:[[NSString alloc] initWithFormat:@"Section %lu Cell %lu",
                        (unsigned long)paramIndex,
                        (unsigned long)counter+1]];

}

return result;

}

- (id) initWithNibName:(NSString *)nibNameOrNil
            bundle:(NSBundle *)nibBundleOrNil{

    self = [super initWithNibName:nibNameOrNil
                    bundle:nibBundleOrNil];

    if (self != nil){

        arrayOfSections = [[NSMutableArray alloc] init];

        NSMutableArray *section1 = [self newSectionWithIndex:1
                                            withCellCount:3];
        NSMutableArray *section2 = [self newSectionWithIndex:2
                                            withCellCount:3];
        NSMutableArray *section3 = [self newSectionWithIndex:3
                                            withCellCount:3];
        [arrayOfSections addObject:section1];
        [arrayOfSections addObject:section2];
        [arrayOfSections addObject:section3];

    }

    return self;

}
```

We shall then instantiate our table view and implement the necessary methods in the UITableViewDataSource protocol to populate our table view with data:

```
- (NSInteger) numberOfSectionsInTableView:(UITableView *)tableView{

    NSInteger result = 0;

    if ([tableView isEqual:self.myTableView]){
        result = (NSInteger)[self.arrayOfSections count];
    }

    return result;

}

- (NSInteger) tableView:(UITableView *)tableView
    numberOfRowsInSection:(NSInteger)section{
```

```
    NSInteger result = 0;

    if ([tableView isEqual:self.myTableView]){

      if ([self.arrayOfSections count] > section){

        NSMutableArray *sectionArray = [self.arrayOfSections
                                        objectAtIndex:section];
        result = (NSInteger)[sectionArray count];

      }

    }

    return result;

}

- (UITableViewCell *)tableView:(UITableView *)tableView
         cellForRowAtIndexPath:(NSIndexPath *)indexPath{

  UITableViewCell *result = nil;

  if ([tableView isEqual:self.myTableView]){

    static NSString *CellIdentifier = @"CellIdentifier";

    result = [tableView dequeueReusableCellWithIdentifier:CellIdentifier];

    if (result == nil){
      result = [[UITableViewCell alloc]
                initWithStyle:UITableViewCellStyleDefault
                reuseIdentifier:CellIdentifier];
    }

    NSMutableArray *sectionArray = [self.arrayOfSections
                                    objectAtIndex:indexPath.section];

    result.textLabel.text = [sectionArray objectAtIndex:indexPath.row];

  }

  return result;

}

- (void)viewDidLoad{
  [super viewDidLoad];

  self.myTableView =
  [[UITableView alloc] initWithFrame:self.view.bounds
                             style:UITableViewStyleGrouped];

  self.myTableView.autoresizingMask = UIViewAutoresizingFlexibleWidth |
```

```
                                                UIViewAutoresizingFlexibleHeight;

    self.myTableView.delegate = self;

    self.myTableView.dataSource = self;

    [self.view addSubview:self.myTableView];

}
```

Show time! Shall we first have a look at how sections can be moved to a new position? Let's write a method that will move Section 1 to 3:

```
- (void) moveSection1ToSection3{

    NSMutableArray *section1 = [self.arrayOfSections objectAtIndex:0];
    [self.arrayOfSections removeObject:section1];
    [self.arrayOfSections addObject:section1];

    [self.myTableView moveSection:0
                        toSection:2];

}
```

I will leave it up to you to decide when you would like to invoke this method, as we don't have a button on our UI at the moment. You can simply create a navigation controller, place a navigation button on it, and then invoke this method.

Once you run the app normally, you will see the sections lined up from 1 to 3, as in Figure 4-13.

Figure 4-13. A table view with three sections, each containing three cells

After you invoke the `moveSection1ToSection3` method, you will see that Section 1 gets moved to Section 3, Section 3 moves to Section 2's previous position, and finally Section 2 moves to Section 1's previous position (Figure 4-14).

Figure 4-14. Section 1 is moved to Section 3, and other sections are subsequently moved as well

Moving cells is very similar to moving sections. To move cells, all we have to do is to use the `moveRowAtIndexPath:toIndexPath:` method. Remember that you can move a cell from one section to the same section, or to a new section. Let's make it easy and move Cell 1 in Section 1 to Cell 2 in the same section and see what happens:

```
- (void) moveCell1InSection1ToCell2InSection1{

    NSMutableArray *section1 = [self.arrayOfSections objectAtIndex:0];
    NSString *cell1InSection1 = [section1 objectAtIndex:0];
    [section1 removeObject:cell1InSection1];
    [section1 insertObject:cell1InSection1
                   atIndex:1];

    NSIndexPath *sourceIndexPath = [NSIndexPath indexPathForRow:0
                                                      inSection:0];
    NSIndexPath *destinationIndexPath = [NSIndexPath indexPathForRow:1
                                                           inSection:0];

    [self.myTableView moveRowAtIndexPath:sourceIndexPath
                             toIndexPath:destinationIndexPath];

}
```

So what is going on in this code? Well, we need to make sure our data source holds the correct data that needs to be displayed in our table view after we have moved the cells around, so we remove Cell 1 in Section 1 first. That moves Cell 2 to Cell 1, and Cell 3 to Cell 2, with a total of 2 cells in the array. Then we will insert Cell 1 into Index 1 (second object) of the array. That will make our array contain Cell 2, Cell 1, and then Cell 3. After that is done, we have actually moved the cells in our table view.

Let's make this a bit more difficult. How about moving Cell 2 in Section 1 to Cell 1 in Section 2?

```
- (void) moveCell2InSection1ToCell1InSection2{

    NSMutableArray *section1 = [self.arrayOfSections objectAtIndex:0];
    NSMutableArray *section2 = [self.arrayOfSections objectAtIndex:1];

    NSString *cell2InSection1 = [section1 objectAtIndex:1];
    [section1 removeObject:cell2InSection1];

    [section2 insertObject:cell2InSection1
                atIndex:0];

    NSIndexPath *sourceIndexPath = [NSIndexPath indexPathForRow:1
                                                      inSection:0];
    NSIndexPath *destinationIndexPath = [NSIndexPath indexPathForRow:0
                                                           inSection:1];

    [self.myTableView moveRowAtIndexPath:sourceIndexPath
                             toIndexPath:destinationIndexPath];

}
```

The results of this transition are shown in Figure 4-15.

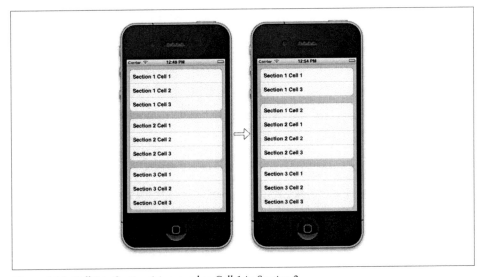

Figure 4-15. Cell 2 in Section 1 is moved to Cell 1 in Section 2

4.12 Deleting Cells and Sections from Table Views

Problem

You want to delete sections and/or cells from table views using animations.

Solution

In order to delete sections from a table view, follow these steps:

1. First delete the section(s) in your data source, whether you are using a data model like Core Data or a dictionary/array.

2. Invoke the `deleteSections:withRowAnimation:` instance method of `UITableView` on your table view. The first parameter that you need to pass to this method is of type `NSIndexSet` and this object can be instantiated using the `indexSetWithIndex:` class method of `NSIndexSet` class, where the given index is an unsigned integer. Using this approach, you will be able to delete only one section at a time. If you intend to delete more than one section at a time, use the `indexSetWithIndexesInRange:` class method of `NSIndexSet` to create the index set using a range and pass that index set to the aforementioned instance method of `UITableView`.

If you want to delete cells from your table view, follow these steps:

1. First, delete the cell(s) from your data source. Again, it doesn't matter if you are using Core Data, a simple dictionary, array, or anything else. The important thing is to delete the objects that represent the table view cells from your data source.

2. Now, in order to delete the cells that correspond to your data objects, invoke the `deleteRowsAtIndexPaths:withRowAnimation:` instance method of your table view. The first parameter that you have to pass to this method is an array of type `NSArray` that must contain objects of type `NSIndexPath`, with each index path representing one cell in the table view. Each index path has a section and a row, and can be constructed using the `indexPathForRow:inSection:` class method of `NSIndexPath` class.

Discussion

In your UI code, sometimes you might need to delete cells and/or sections. For instance, you might have a switch (of type `UISwitch`; see Recipe 2.2), and when the switch is turned on by the user, you might want to insert a few rows into your table view. After the switch is turned off by the user, you will then want to delete those rows. It's not always table view cells (rows) that you have to delete. Sometimes you might need to delete a whole section or a few sections simultaneously from your table view. The key for deleting cells and sections from table views is to first delete the data corresponding to those cells/sections from your data source, and then call the appropriate deletion method on the table view. After the deletion method finishes, the table view will refer back to its data source object. If the number of cells/sections in the data source doesn't match the number of cells/sections in the table view after the deletion is complete, your app will crash. But don't worry—if you ever do make this mistake, the debug text that gets printed to the console is descriptive enough to point you in the right direction.

Let's have a look at how we can delete sections from a table view. For this recipe, we will display a table view on a view controller that is displayed inside a navigation controller. Inside the table view, we will display two sections, one for odd numbers and another for even numbers. We will only display 1, 3, 5, and 7 for odd numbers and 0, 2, 4, and 6 for even numbers. For the first exercise, we are going to place a navigation bar button on our navigation bar and make that button responsible for deleting the section with odd numbers in it. Figure 4-16 shows what we want the results to look like.

Figure 4-16. The user interface to display two sections in a table view and a button that will delete the Odd Numbers section

First things first. Let's define our view controller:

```
#import <UIKit/UIKit.h>

@interface ViewController : UIViewController <UITableViewDelegate,
                                              UITableViewDataSource>

@property (nonatomic, strong) UITableView *tableViewNumbers;
@property (nonatomic, strong) NSMutableDictionary *dictionaryOfNumbers;
@property (nonatomic, strong) UIBarButtonItem *barButtonAction;

@end
```

The tableViewNumbers property is our table view. The barButtonAction property is the bar button that we'll display on the navigation bar. Last but not least, the dictionary

OfNumbers property is our data source for the table view. In this dictionary, we will place two values of type NSMutableArray that contain our numbers of type NSNumber. They are mutable arrays, so that, later in this chapter, we will be able to delete them individually from the arrays in the dictionary. We will keep the keys for these arrays in our dictionary as static values in the implementation file of our view controller, so that we can later simply extract them from the dictionary using the static keys (if the keys were not static, finding our arrays in the dictionary would have to be done with string comparison, which is slightly more time-consuming than simply associating the object with a static key that doesn't change during the lifetime of our view controller). Now let's define the static string keys for our arrays inside the data source dictionary:

```
#import "ViewController.h"

@implementation ViewController

static NSString *SectionOddNumbers = @"Odd Numbers";
static NSString *SectionEvenNumbers = @"Even Numbers";
...
```

We now need to populate our data source dictionary with values before we create our table view. Here is the simple method that will take care of populating the dictionary for us:

```
#pragma mark - Populating the Data Source Dictionary
- (void) constructDictionaryOfNumbers{

  self.dictionaryOfNumbers = [[NSMutableDictionary alloc] init];

  NSMutableArray *arrayOfEvenNumbers = [[NSMutableArray alloc] initWithObjects:
                                        [NSNumber numberWithUnsignedInteger:0],
                                        [NSNumber numberWithUnsignedInteger:2],
                                        [NSNumber numberWithUnsignedInteger:4],
                                        [NSNumber numberWithUnsignedInteger:6],
                                        nil];

  NSMutableArray *arrayOfOddNumbers = [[NSMutableArray alloc] initWithObjects:
                                       [NSNumber numberWithUnsignedInteger:1],
                                       [NSNumber numberWithUnsignedInteger:3],
                                       [NSNumber numberWithUnsignedInteger:5],
                                       [NSNumber numberWithUnsignedInteger:7],
                                       nil];

  [self.dictionaryOfNumbers setObject:arrayOfEvenNumbers
                              forKey:SectionEvenNumbers];

  [self.dictionaryOfNumbers setObject:arrayOfOddNumbers
                              forKey:SectionOddNumbers];

}
```

So far so good? As you can see, we have two arrays, each of which contains some numbers (one odd and the other even numbers) and we associate them with the

SectionEvenNumbers and SectionOddNumbers keys that we declared before in the imple-mentation file of our view controller. Now let's go ahead and instantiate our table view:

```
- (void)viewDidLoad
{
  [super viewDidLoad];

  [self constructDictionaryOfNumbers];

  self.barButtonAction =
  [[UIBarButtonItem alloc] initWithTitle:@"Delete Odd Numbers"
                                   style:UIBarButtonItemStylePlain
                                  target:self
                                  action:@selector(deleteOddNumbersSection:)];
  [self.navigationItem setRightBarButtonItem:self.barButtonAction animated:NO];

  self.tableViewNumbers = [[UITableView alloc]
                            initWithFrame:self.view.frame
                                    style:UITableViewStyleGrouped];
  self.tableViewNumbers.autoresizingMask = UIViewAutoresizingFlexibleWidth |
                                           UIViewAutoresizingFlexibleHeight;
  self.tableViewNumbers.delegate = self;
  self.tableViewNumbers.dataSource = self;
  [self.view addSubview:self.tableViewNumbers];

}
```

The next thing we need to do is to populate our table view with data inside our data source dictionary:

```
#pragma mark - Table View Data Source
- (NSInteger) numberOfSectionsInTableView:(UITableView *)tableView{

  NSInteger result = 0;
  result = [[self.dictionaryOfNumbers allKeys] count];
  return result;

}

- (NSInteger) tableView:(UITableView *)tableView
  numberOfRowsInSection:(NSInteger)section{

  NSInteger result = 0;
  NSString *sectionNameInDictionary = [[self.dictionaryOfNumbers allKeys]
                                        objectAtIndex:section];
  NSArray *sectionArray = [self.dictionaryOfNumbers objectForKey:
                            sectionNameInDictionary];
  result = [sectionArray count];
  return result;

}

- (UITableViewCell *) tableView:(UITableView *)tableView
         cellForRowAtIndexPath:(NSIndexPath *)indexPath{

  UITableViewCell *result = nil;
```

```
    static NSString *CellIdentifier = @"NumbersCellIdentifier";

    result = [tableView dequeueReusableCellWithIdentifier:CellIdentifier];

    if (result == nil){
      result = [[UITableViewCell alloc] initWithStyle:UITableViewCellStyleDefault
                                      reuseIdentifier:CellIdentifier];
    }

    NSString *sectionNameInDictionary = [[self.dictionaryOfNumbers allKeys]
                                       objectAtIndex:indexPath.section];
    NSArray *sectionArray = [self.dictionaryOfNumbers objectForKey:
                            sectionNameInDictionary];
    NSNumber *number = [sectionArray objectAtIndex:indexPath.row];

    result.textLabel.text = [NSString stringWithFormat:@"%lu",
                            (unsigned long)[number unsignedIntegerValue]];

    return result;

}

- (NSString *) tableView:(UITableView *)tableView
 titleForHeaderInSection:(NSInteger)section{

  NSString *result = nil;
  result = [[self.dictionaryOfNumbers allKeys] objectAtIndex:section];
  return result;

}
```

Our navigation button is linked to the deleteOddNumbersSection: selector. This is a method we are going to code now. The purpose of this method, as its name implies, is to find the section that corresponds to all odd numbers in our data source and the table view, and remove that section from both of these. Here is how we will do it:

```
- (void) deleteOddNumbersSection:(id)paramSender{

  /* First remove the section from our data source */
  NSString *key = SectionOddNumbers;
  NSInteger indexForKey = [[self.dictionaryOfNumbers allKeys]
                          indexOfObject:key];
  if (indexForKey == NSNotFound){
    NSLog(@"Could not find the section in the data source.");
    return;
  }
  [self.dictionaryOfNumbers removeObjectForKey:key];

  /* Then delete the section from the table view */
  NSIndexSet *sectionToDelete = [NSIndexSet indexSetWithIndex:indexForKey];
  [self.tableViewNumbers deleteSections:sectionToDelete
                      withRowAnimation:UITableViewRowAnimationAutomatic];

  /* Finally, remove the button from the navigation bar
```

```
    as it is not useful any longer */
    [self.navigationItem setRightBarButtonItem:nil animated:YES];

}
```

Simple enough. Now, when the user presses the navigation bar button, the Odd Numbers section will disappear from the table view. You can note that there is an animation that gets committed on the table view while the section is being deleted. This is because of the UITableViewRowAnimationAutomatic animation type that we are passing to the withRowAnimation: parameter of the deleteSections:withRowAnimation: method of our table view. Now run the app in iOS Simulator and select Debug → Toggle Slow Animations. Then attempt to press the navigation bar button and see what happens. You can see the deletion animation in slow motion. It's neat, isn't it? After the deletion is completed, our app will look similar to Figure 4-17.

Figure 4-17. The section containing odd numbers is removed from the table view

We now know how to delete sections from table views. Let's move to deleting cells. We are going to change the functionality of our navigation bar button so that when it is pressed, it will delete all cells in all sections of our table view with a numerical value greater than 2. That includes all odd and even numbers greater than 2. So let's change our navigation bar button item in the viewDidLoad method of our view controller:

```
- (void)viewDidLoad
{
    [super viewDidLoad];

    [self constructDictionaryOfNumbers];

    self.barButtonAction =
    [[UIBarButtonItem alloc] initWithTitle:@"Delete Numbers > 2"
```

```
                              style:UIBarButtonItemStylePlain
                              target:self
                              action:@selector(deleteNumbersGreaterThan2:)];
    [self.navigationItem setRightBarButtonItem:self.barButtonAction animated:NO];

    self.tableViewNumbers = [[UITableView alloc]
                             initWithFrame:self.view.frame
                             style:UITableViewStyleGrouped];
    self.tableViewNumbers.autoresizingMask = UIViewAutoresizingFlexibleWidth |
    UIViewAutoresizingFlexibleHeight;
    self.tableViewNumbers.delegate = self;
    self.tableViewNumbers.dataSource = self;
    [self.view addSubview:self.tableViewNumbers];

}
```

Figure 4-18 shows the results of our app running in iPhone Simulator.

Figure 4-18. A button that will delete all cells containing a number greater than 2

The navigation bar button is now connected to the `deleteNumbersGreaterThan2:` selector. This is a method that we have to implement in our view controller, but before jumping into coding it straightaway, let's first define what this method should do:

1. Find both arrays of odd and even numbers in our data source and grab the index paths (of type `NSIndexPath`) of those numbers that are greater than 2. We will use these index paths to later delete the corresponding cells from the table view.

2. Delete all the numbers greater than 2 from our data source, in both the even and odd number dictionaries.

3. Delete the relevant cells from the table view. We collected the index paths of these cells in the first step.

4. Remove the navigation bar button, since it won't be of any use after the relevant cells have been deleted from the data source and the table view. Alternatively, if you want, you could just disable this button—but I think removing that button provides a better user experience, since a disabled button is really of no use to the user.

```
- (void) deleteNumbersGreaterThan2:(id)paramSender{

  NSMutableArray *arrayOfIndexPathsToDelete = [[NSMutableArray alloc] init];
  NSMutableArray *arrayOfNumberObjectsToDelete = [[NSMutableArray alloc] init];

  /* Step 1: gather the objects we have to delete from our data source
   and their index paths */
  __block NSUInteger keyIndex = 0;
  [self.dictionaryOfNumbers enumerateKeysAndObjectsUsingBlock:
   ^(NSString *key, NSMutableArray *object, BOOL *stop) {

     [object enumerateObjectsUsingBlock:
      ^(NSNumber *number, NSUInteger numberIndex, BOOL *stop) {

        if ([number unsignedIntegerValue] > 2){
          NSIndexPath *indexPath = [NSIndexPath indexPathForRow:numberIndex
                                                      inSection:keyIndex];
          [arrayOfIndexPathsToDelete addObject:indexPath];
          [arrayOfNumberObjectsToDelete addObject:number];
        }

      }];

     keyIndex++;
   }];

  /* Step 2: delete the objects from the data source */
  if ([arrayOfNumberObjectsToDelete count] > 0){
    NSMutableArray *arrayOfOddNumbers = [self.dictionaryOfNumbers
                                          objectForKey:SectionOddNumbers];
    NSMutableArray *arrayOfEvenNumbers = [self.dictionaryOfNumbers
                                           objectForKey:SectionEvenNumbers];
    [arrayOfNumberObjectsToDelete enumerateObjectsUsingBlock:
     ^(NSNumber *numberToDelete, NSUInteger idx, BOOL *stop) {
       if ([arrayOfOddNumbers indexOfObject:numberToDelete] != NSNotFound){
         [arrayOfOddNumbers removeObject:numberToDelete];
       }
       if ([arrayOfEvenNumbers indexOfObject:numberToDelete] != NSNotFound){
         [arrayOfEvenNumbers removeObject:numberToDelete];
       }
       [arrayOfEvenNumbers removeObject:numberToDelete];
     }];
  }  /* Step 3: delete the cells that correspond to the objects */
  NSArray *arrayOfPaths = [[NSArray alloc]
                            initWithArray:arrayOfIndexPathsToDelete];
  [self.tableViewNumbers
   deleteRowsAtIndexPaths:arrayOfPaths
   withRowAnimation:UITableViewRowAnimationAutomatic];
```

```
        [self.navigationItem setRightBarButtonItem:nil animated:YES];

    }
```

After the user presses the button on the navigation bar, all cells containing a number greater than 2 will be deleted from our data source, and the table view and our app will look like Figure 4-19.

Figure 4-19. We have deleted all cells with a value greater than 2

See Also

Recipe 2.2

4.13 Utilizing the UITableViewController for Easy Creation of Table Views

Problem

You want to be able to create table views quickly.

Solution

Use the `UITableViewController` view controller, which by default comes with a table view controller.

Discussion

The iOS SDK contains a really handy class called `UITableViewController` that comes predefined with a table view instance inside it. In order to take advantage of this class, all you have to really do is create a new class that subclasses the aforementioned class. Here, I will walk you through the steps necessary to create a new Xcode project that utilizes the table view controller:

1. In Xcode, from the menu bar, choose File → New → Project...

2. On the lefthand side of the screen, make sure the iOS category is selected. Then choose the Application subcategory. On the righthand side, choose the Empty Application template and then press the Next button, as shown in Figure 4-20.

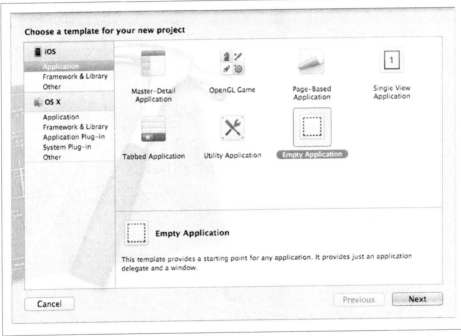

Figure 4-20. Creating a new empty application that will later contain our table view controller

3. In the next screen, simply choose a name for your project and make sure that you are using Automatic Reference Counting. Also make sure everything except for the Organization Name and the Company Identifier in your dialog is the same as the one that I am demonstrating to you in Figure 4-21. Once you are done, press the Next button.

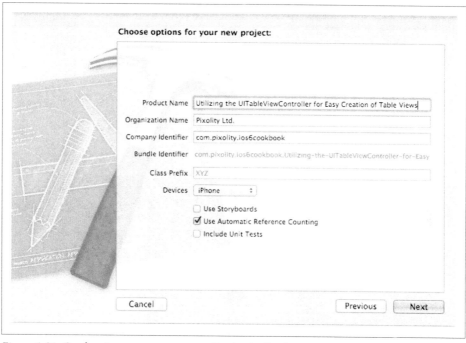

Choose options for your new project:

Product Name   Utilizing the UITableViewController for Easy Creation of Table Views

Organization Name   Pixolity Ltd.

Company Identifier   com.pixolity.ios6cookbook

Bundle Identifier   com.pixolity.ios6cookbook.Utilizing-the-UITableViewController-for-Easy

Class Prefix   XYZ

Devices   iPhone

☐ Use Storyboards
☑ Use Automatic Reference Counting
☐ Include Unit Tests

Cancel   Previous   Next

Figure 4-21. Configuring our new empty application in Xcode

4. In the next screen, you are given the opportunity to save your application to disk. Simply save the application in a place that makes sense to you and press the Create button.

5. In Xcode, choose the File → New → File... menu.

6. In the dialog, make sure iOS is the main category on the lefthand side and that Cocoa Touch is the subcategory that is selected. Then on the righthand side of the dialog, choose the Objective-C class as shown in Figure 4-22.

7. In the next screen, you get to choose the superclass of your new class. This step is very important. Make sure that you set your superclass to UITableView Controller. Also make sure the rest of your settings are the same as those that I am demonstrating in Figure 4-23. After you are done, press the Next button.

8. In the next screen, you get the chance to save your table view controller in your project. Go on, save it as the ViewController class and press the Create button.

9. In the implementation file of your app delegate, remember to import this view controller's header file and then create an instance of this class and set it as the root view controller of your application, as shown here:

```
#import "AppDelegate.h"
#import "ViewController.h"

@implementation AppDelegate

- (BOOL)                application:(UIApplication *)application
  didFinishLaunchingWithOptions:(NSDictionary *)launchOptions{

    self.window = [[UIWindow alloc]
                   initWithFrame:[[UIScreen mainScreen] bounds]];

    self.window.backgroundColor = [UIColor whiteColor];
    [self.window makeKeyAndVisible];

    self.window.rootViewController =
    [[ViewController alloc] initWithStyle:UITableViewStylePlain];

    return YES;
}
```

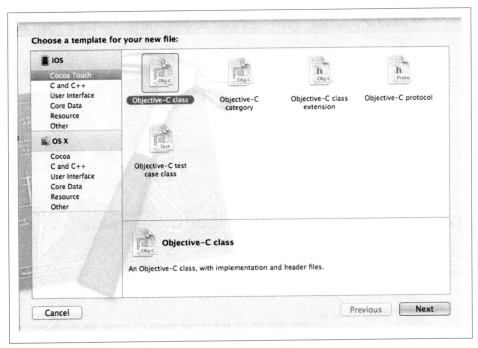

Figure 4-22. Creating a new class for our table view controller

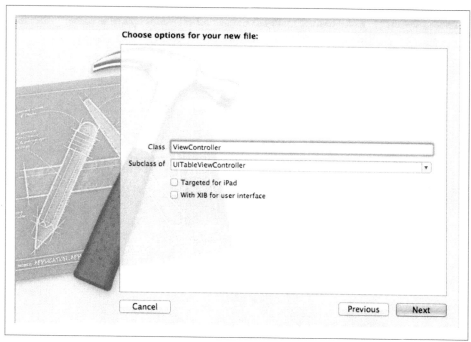

Figure 4-23. Setting the superclass of our new object that will become the table view controller

Now if you try to compile your project, you will see that the compiler will give you the following warnings:

```
ViewController.m:47:2: Potentially incomplete method implementation.
ViewController.m:54:2: Incomplete method implementation.
```

This simply tells you that there are warnings that you have to take care of in the implementation file of your view controller. If you open this file, you will see that Apple has inserted #warning macros in the table view controller class template, which are causing these warnings to be displayed on your screen. One warning is placed inside the numberOfSectionsInTableView: method and the other one is inside the table View:numberOfRowsInSection: method. The reason we are seeing these warnings is that we have not coded the logic for these methods. The minimum information that the table view controller must have is the number of sections to display, the number of rows to display, and the cell object to be displayed for each row. The reason you are not seeing any warnings for the lack of cell object implementation is that Apple by default provides a dummy implementation of this method that creates empty cells for you.

The table view controller by default is the data source and the delegate of the table view. You do not have to specify a delegate or a data source separately to the table view.

Now let's go into the implementation of our table view controller and make sure that we have an array of strings (just as an example) that we can feed into our table view:

```
#import "ViewController.h"

@interface ViewController ()
@property (nonatomic, strong) NSArray *items;
@end

@implementation ViewController

- (id)initWithStyle:(UITableViewStyle)style
{
    self = [super initWithStyle:style];
    if (self) {
        // Custom initialization
        self.items = @[
            @"Anthony Robbins",
            @"Steven Paul Jobs",
            @"Paul Gilbert",
            @"Yngwie Malmsteen"
        ];
    }
    return self;
}

- (void) viewDidLoad{
    [super viewDidLoad];
}

- (NSInteger)numberOfSectionsInTableView:(UITableView *)tableView{
    return 1;
}

- (NSInteger)tableView:(UITableView *)tableView
  numberOfRowsInSection:(NSInteger)section{
    return self.items.count;
}

- (UITableViewCell *)tableView:(UITableView *)tableView
        cellForRowAtIndexPath:(NSIndexPath *)indexPath{

    static NSString *CellIdentifier = @"Cell";
    UITableViewCell *cell =
    [tableView dequeueReusableCellWithIdentifier:CellIdentifier];
    if (cell == nil) {
        cell = [[UITableViewCell alloc]
                initWithStyle:UITableViewCellStyleDefault
                reuseIdentifier:CellIdentifier];
```

```
    }

    cell.textLabel.text = self.items[indexPath.row];

    return cell;
}

@end
```

Now if we run our app, we will see something similar to what is shown in Figure 4-24.

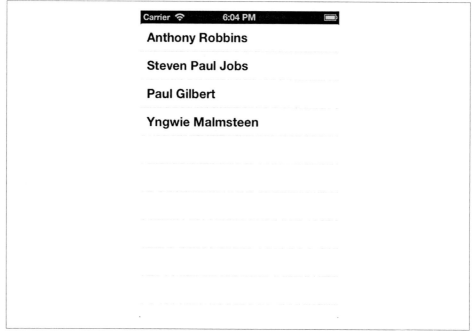

Figure 4-24. Our strings are properly displayed in the table view

That's pretty much all there is to know about table view controllers. Remember, as mentioned before, that your table view controller is the delegate *and* the data source of your table view now. So you can implement the methods in the UITableViewData Source protocol as well as the UITableViewDelegate protocol's methods right in the implementation of your table view controller.

See Also

Recipe 4.1; Recipe 4.2; Recipe 4.3

4.14 Displaying a Refresh Control for Table Views

Problem

You want to display a nice refresh UI control on top of your table views that allows your users to intuitively pull down the table view in order to update its contents. Examples of a refresh control in two of its different states are shown in Figure 4-25.

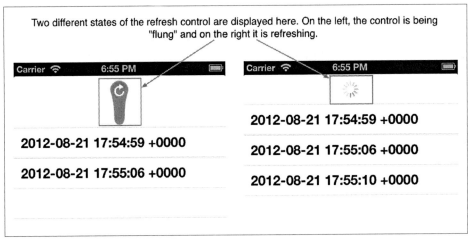

Figure 4-25. Two different states of the refresh control

Solution

Simply create a table view controller (as discussed in Recipe 4.13) and set its refresh Control property to a new instance of UIRefreshControl class, as shown here:

```
- (id)initWithStyle:(UITableViewStyle)style{
    self = [super initWithStyle:style];
    if (self) {

        /* Create the refresh control */
        self.refreshControl = [[UIRefreshControl alloc] init];
        self.refreshControl = self.refreshControl;
        [self.refreshControl addTarget:self
                            action:@selector(handleRefresh:)
                    forControlEvents:UIControlEventValueChanged];

    }
    return self;
}
```

Discussion

Refresh controls are a new UI component added to the iOS 6 SDK. They are simple visual indicators that appear on top of table views and tell the user that something is about to get updated. For instance, prior to iOS 6, in order to refresh your mailbox in the Mail app, you had to press a refresh button. In iOS 6, now you can simply drag the list of your emails down, as if you wanted to see what's above there in the list that you haven't read already. Once iOS detects this gesture of yours, it will trigger a refresh. Isn't that cool? Twitter's iPhone app started this whole thing when they added a refresh control to their apps, so kudos to them for this. Apple has realized this is in fact a really nice and intuitive way of updating table views and has since added a dedicated component to the SDK to implement it. The class name for this component is UIRefresh Control.

Create a new instance of this class simply by calling its `init` method. Once you are done, add this instance to your table view controller, as described in the Solution section of this recipe.

Now you'll want to know when the user has triggered a refresh on your table view. To do this, simply call the `addTarget:action:forControlEvents:` instance method of your refresh control and pass the target object and a selector on that object that takes care of the refresh for you. Pass `UIControlEventValueChanged` to the `forControlEvents` parameter of this method.

Here—I want to demonstrate this to you. In this example, we will have a table view controller that displays date and time formatted as strings. Once the user refreshes the list by pulling it down, we will add the current date and time again to the list and refresh our table view. This way, every time the user pulls the list down, it triggers a refresh that will allow us to add the current date and time to the list and refresh the table view to display the new date and time. So let's start in the implementation file of our table view controller and define our refresh control and our data source:

```
#import "ViewController.h"

@interface ViewController ()
@property (nonatomic, strong) NSMutableArray *times;
@property (nonatomic, strong) UIRefreshControl *refreshControl;
@end

@implementation ViewController

...
```

The `times` property is a simple mutable array that will contain all the instances of NSDate in it as the user refreshes the table view. We have already seen the initialization of our table view controller in the Solution section of this recipe, so I won't write it again here. But as you saw there, we have hooked the `UIControlEventValueChanged` event of our refresh control to a method called `handleRefresh:`. In this method, all we are going to do is add the current date and time to our array of date and times and then refresh the table view:

```
- (void) handleRefresh:(id)paramSender{

    /* Put a bit of delay between when the refresh control is released
```

```
    and when we actually do the refreshing to make the UI look a bit
    smoother than just doing the update without the animation */
    int64_t delayInSeconds = 1.0f;
    dispatch_time_t popTime =
        dispatch_time(DISPATCH_TIME_NOW, delayInSeconds * NSEC_PER_SEC);
    dispatch_after(popTime, dispatch_get_main_queue(), ^(void){

        /* Add the current date to the list of dates that we have
        so that when the table view is refreshed, a new item will appear
        on the screen so that the user will see the difference between
        the before and the after of the refresh */
        [self.times addObject:[NSDate date]];

        [self.refreshControl endRefreshing];
        [self.tableView reloadData];
    });

}
```

Last but not least, we will provide the date to our table view through the table view's delegate and data source methods:

```
- (id)initWithStyle:(UITableViewStyle)style{
    self = [super initWithStyle:style];
    if (self) {
        self.times = [NSMutableArray arrayWithObject:[NSDate date]];

        /* Create the refresh control */
        self.refreshControl = [[UIRefreshControl alloc] init];
        self.refreshControl = self.refreshControl;
        [self.refreshControl addTarget:self
                                action:@selector(handleRefresh:)
                      forControlEvents:UIControlEventValueChanged];

    }
    return self;
}

- (NSInteger)numberOfSectionsInTableView:(UITableView *)tableView{
    return 1;
}

- (NSInteger)tableView:(UITableView *)tableView
 numberOfRowsInSection:(NSInteger)section{
    return self.times.count;
}

- (UITableViewCell *)tableView:(UITableView *)tableView
         cellForRowAtIndexPath:(NSIndexPath *)indexPath{

    static NSString *CellIdentifier = @"Cell";
    UITableViewCell *cell =
    [tableView dequeueReusableCellWithIdentifier:CellIdentifier];
    if (cell == nil) {
        cell = [[UITableViewCell alloc]
                initWithStyle:UITableViewCellStyleDefault
```

```
                    reuseIdentifier:CellIdentifier];
    }

    cell.textLabel.text = [NSString stringWithFormat:@"%@",
                           self.times[indexPath.row]];

    return cell;
}
```

Give this a go in either the simulator or the device. Once you open the app, at first you will see only one date/time added to the list. Keep dragging the table view down to get more items in the list (see Figure 4-26).

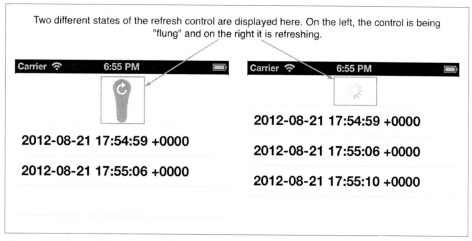

Figure 4-26. Our table view controller is populated by a new item every time it is refreshed

See Also

Recipe 4.13

CHAPTER 5

Storyboards

5.0 Introduction

iOS programmers are all used to view controllers by now. We know how to use navigation controllers in order to push and pop view controllers. But Apple believes this can be done more easily, and that's the whole story behind storyboards. *Storyboarding* is the new way of defining the connections between different screens in your app. For instance, if you have 20 unique view controllers in your app that you coded a year ago and are looking at the source code again *now*, you will need to find your way around the connections between these view controllers, and to try to remember what view controller is pushed when a certain action is taken by the user. This can be very difficult, especially if you have not documented your code. Storyboards come to the rescue. With storyboards, you can now view/create your entire app's UI and the connections between view controllers in one screen. It's that simple.

To take advantage of storyboarding, you need to get acquainted with Interface Builder. Don't worry; it's all covered in this chapter.

With storyboards, one screen's worth of content is called a *scene*. The relation between a scene and a storyboard on the iPhone can be compared to a view and a view controller. In a scene, you put all your content on the screen to be presented to the user at the same time. On the iPad, more than one scene can be presented to the user at the same time because of the bigger screen.

Storyboarding supports transitioning from one scene to another. The equivalent of a navigation controller pushing one view controller on top of another is a *segue* in storyboarding. Another type of transition is a modal view controller that slides a scene from the bottom of the screen up to fill the screen temporarily. On the iPad, modal screens usually appear in the center of the screen and dim the rest of the screen, to point out that they are the main input at that moment.

5.1 Creating a Project with Storyboards

Problem

In Xcode, you want to create a project that uses Storyboards.

Solution

Choose the Use Storyboard option in the New Project setting dialog (Figure 5-1) and make your app a universal app.

Figure 5-1. The Use Storyboard option of New Project dialog

Discussion

If you want to create a project that uses storyboards, simply follow these steps:

1. In Xcode, select the File menu and then New → New Project...
2. In the New Project dialog, make sure the iOS main category is selected and select the Application subcategory under iOS. Once that is done, on the right side, select Single View Application and press Next, as shown in Figure 5-2.
3. Now select a product name and make sure your app is a Universal app. Apple wants developers to start writing universal apps whenever they can, in order for iPad users to also enjoy the same apps that iPhone and iPod touch users have access to. In this dialog, make sure you have checked the User Storyboards checkbox, as shown in Figure 5-3. After you are done, press Next.
4. You will now be asked to save your project in a folder. Once you are done, press the Create button (see Figure 5-4) and now you have a project that uses storyboards.

Now if you have a look at the files that Xcode has created for you (see Figure 5-5), you'll notice two files whose names end with *.storyboard*. Xcode, because this is a universal app, created a storyboard for iPhone and another storyboard for iPad, so you can dictate how you want your app to look on each device family.

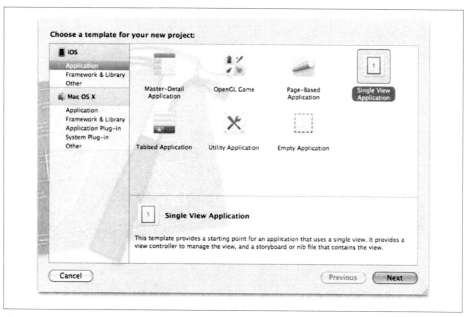

Figure 5-2. Creating a new application to use storyboards

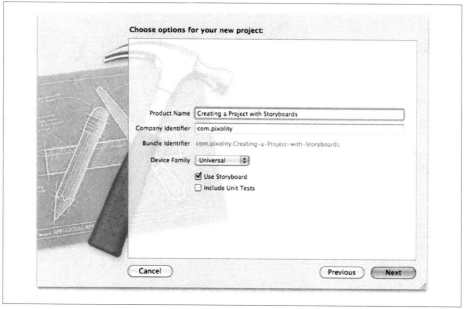

Figure 5-3. Using storyboards for a new project

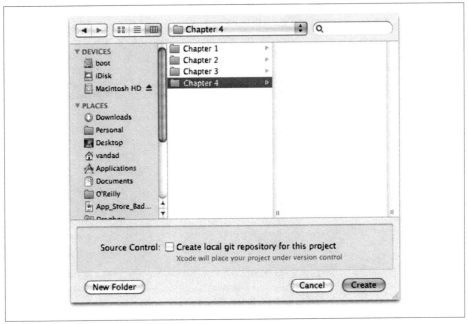

Figure 5-4. Saving the storyboard app on disk

Figure 5-5. Two storyboard files in a universal app

5.2 Adding a Navigation Controller to a Storyboard

Problem

You want to be able to manage multiple view controllers inside a storyboard-based application.

Solution

Set a navigation controller as the initial view controller of your storyboard file.

Discussion

If you followed the instructions in Recipe 5.1 and are now running your app on the iPhone Simulator, you'll see just a white screen with no navigation bar across the top. The reason is that the initial view controller of our storyboard file is a view controller, as opposed to a navigation controller. In order to add a navigation controller to your storyboard-based app, simply follow these steps:

1. Click on the iPhone storyboard that Xcode created for you. I have named my project *Adding a Navigation Bar to a Storyboard*. My iPhone storyboard file is *Main-Storyboard_iPhone.storyboard* (the name of the default storyboard file created by Xcode, depending on the version of Xcode you are using, does not have to have any connection to the name of your project). Once you click on this file, Interface Builder will display its contents.

2. Once the storyboard file is open in IB (Interface Builder), simply double-click on an empty space on the storyboard's canvas and you will see the content shrink in size and give you more free space to play with, as you can see in Figure 5-6.

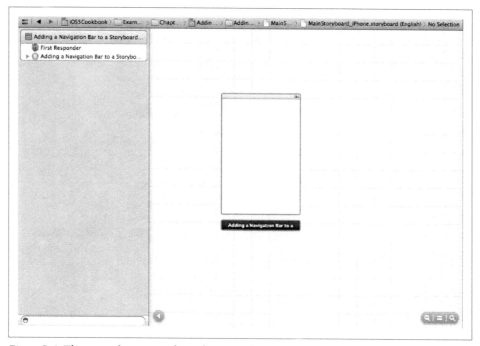

Figure 5-6. The zoomed out view of an iPhone storyboard

3. Under the View menu, select Utilities → Show Object Library.

4. In the Object Library, find the Navigation Controller object (see Figure 5-7) and drag and drop it into the storyboard, to the *left* side of your existing view controller (Figure 5-6). Now you will see something similar to Figure 5-8.

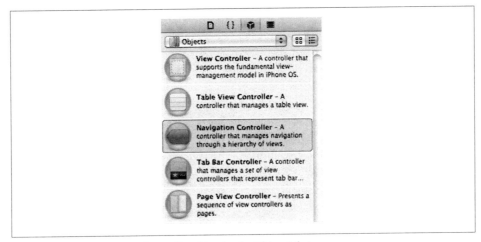

Figure 5-7. The Navigation Controller object in the Object Library

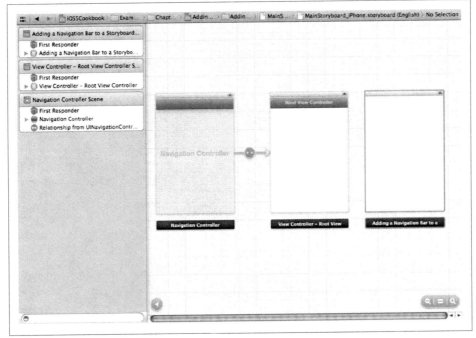

Figure 5-8. A navigation controller comes with its own root view controller

5. As you can see in Figure 5-8, the navigation controller has now added another view controller to our UI. What you need to do is to simply delete this view controller. Do so by selecting it and then pressing the Delete button on the keyboard. Now you are left with the navigation controller and your original view controller, as you can see in Figure 5-9.

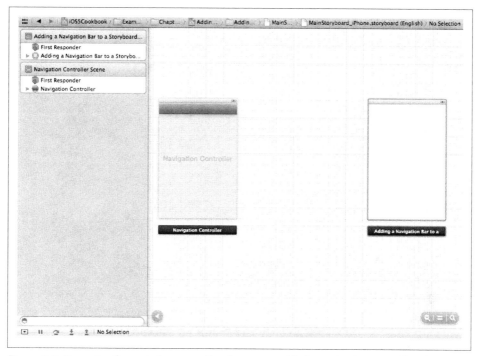

Figure 5-9. Removing the root view controller that comes with the navigation controller object

 The project that we set up in Recipe 5.1 is a Single View Application. This type of application does *not* come with a navigation controller by default, for the obvious reason that it is a Single View Application. Therefore, to change this structure, we will need to add the navigation controller to our storyboard file manually.

6. Now click once on the navigation controller object on the storyboard. Once the navigation controller object is selected, *hold down the Control key on your keyboard and the left button on your mouse* and drag your mouse over to the view controller (on the right) that was originally on your storyboard. This will draw a line from the navigation controller all the way to the view controller, as you can see in Figure 5-10.

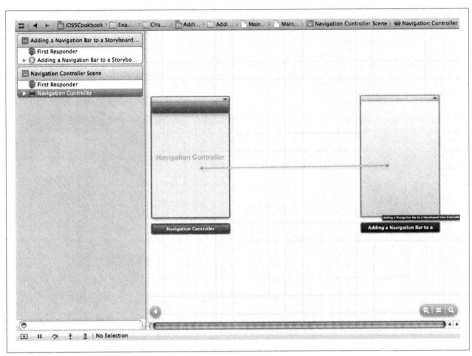

Figure 5-10. Connecting the navigation controller to the initial view controller

7. Now release your mouse button, at which point you will be presented with a dialog asking you what type of connection you want to create between the navigation and the view controller. Select the `rootViewController` item from the list by simply clicking on it (see Figure 5-11).

8. After this is done, the storyboard will show that your navigation controller is connected to the original view controller, as you can see in Figure 5-12.

Figure 5-11. Setting a view controller as the root of a navigation controller

9. The last but perhaps *most important* step is to make your navigation controller the initial/root view controller. If you don't do this, the storyboard will use the view controller that it initially assigned as the initial view controller. Have another look at Figure 5-12. Can you see that the view controller on the right side has a colorful border around it? That indicates an initial view controller. To make your navigation the initial view controller, simply select the Navigation Controller under the Navigation Controller Scene panel in Interface Builder, as you can see in Figure 5-13.

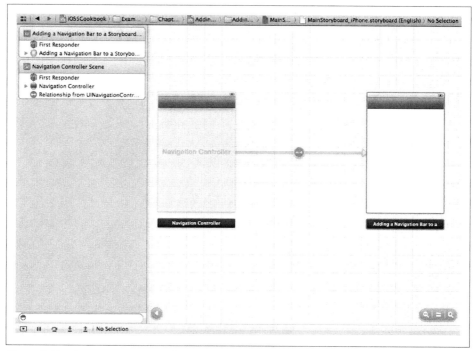

Figure 5-12. The navigation controller is connected to the initial view controller

Now select the View menu in Xcode and choose View → Show Attributes Inspector. Once the attributes inspector is opened, under the View Controller category, check the Is Initial View Controller checkbox (see Figure 5-14).

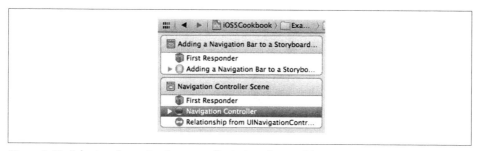

Figure 5-13. Selecting the navigation controller in Interface Builder

As you can see, your navigation controller now has a border around it instead of the righthand view controller. Now if you run your application, you will notice that the initial view controller has a navigation bar on top, indicating that this view controller now has a navigation controller (Figure 5-15). In the next recipes, we will see how we can make use of the navigation controller to display new scenes on the screen.

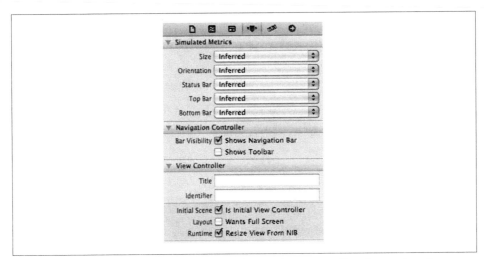

Figure 5-14. Selecting a navigation controller as the initial view controller of a storyboard

Figure 5-15. The navigation bar on a view controller created with a storyboard

We now have a navigation controller with a view controller inside it, but our objective now is to trigger an action and then move from one view controller to another—what Apple calls a segue. All right then; let's place a button on our view controller and push a view controller into the stack once the user presses the button. Sounds good? Do it as follows:

1. Go back to your *.storyboard* file.
2. In the Object Library, find the View Controller object (see Figure 5-16) and drag and drop it onto the storyboard, on the right side of your existing view controller, as shown in Figure 5-17.

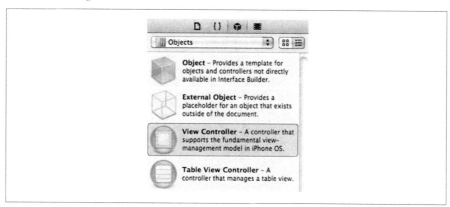

Figure 5-16. A view controller object in the Object Library

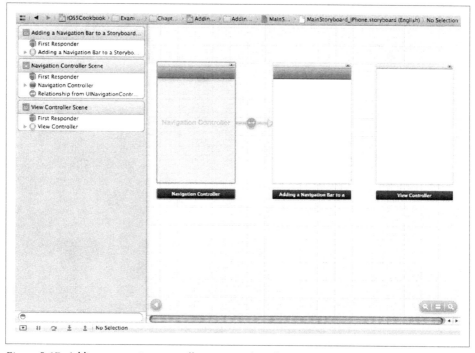

Figure 5-17. Adding a new view controller to a storyboard

3. In Object Library, find the Button object (see Figure 5-18) and drag and drop it into the first view controller (see Figure 5-19). Note that if you are zoomed out,

Interface Builder will not allow you to drop a button onto a view controller. You need to double-click on an empty space on your storyboard to zoom into it before Interface Builder allows you to drop UI components onto your view controllers.

4. Now, to select the button, hold down the Control key on your keyboard and the left mouse button over the button, and drag it all the way to the second view controller (see Figure 5-20).

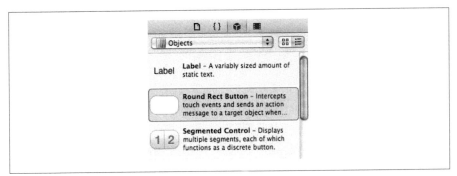

Figure 5-18. Selecting the Button object in the Object Library

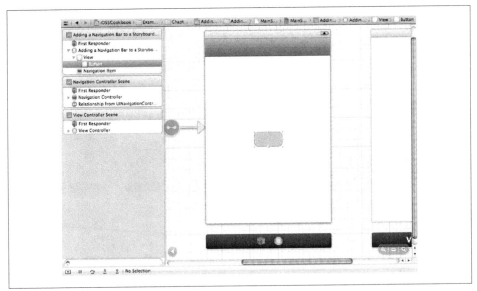

Figure 5-19. Dropping a button on the first view controller in our storyboard

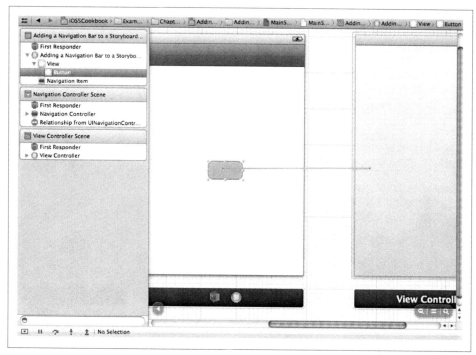

Figure 5-20. Connecting a button to another view controller in a storyboard

5. Now lift your fingers off the mouse button and the Control key on your keyboard. You will now be presented with a dialog similar to that shown in Figure 5-21. Click on the `performSegueWithIdentifier:sender:` item.

Figure 5-21. Making a button perform a segue

Now if you have a look at your storyboard, you will see that the first view controller is connected to the second view controller, as shown in Figure 5-22.

Now if you run your app and tap on the button on the first view controller, you'll see that the second view controller will automatically get pushed onto the stack of view controllers. Once the second view controller is presented, you will see a back button on the navigation bar. If you press that button, you will be sent back to the first view controller.

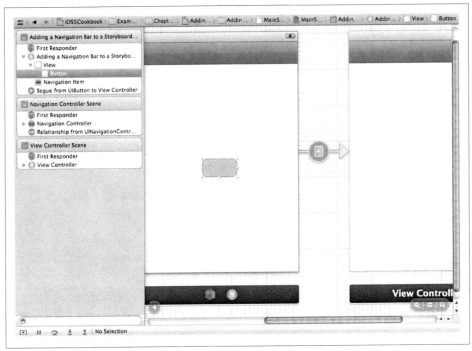

Figure 5-22. The first view controller is connected to the second view controller through a segue

See Also

Recipe 5.1

5.3 Passing Data From One Screen to Another

Problem

You want to pass data from one scene to another using storyboards.

Solution

Use segue objects.

Discussion

A segue is an object, just like any other object in Objective-C. To carry out a transition from one scene to another, the storyboard runtime creates a segue object for that transition. A segue is an instance of class `UIStoryboardSegue`. To start a transition, the current view controller (which will get pushed out of the screen after the segue) receives the `prepareForSegue:sender:` message, where the `prepareForSegue` parameter will be an object of type `UIStoryboardSegue`. If you want to pass any data from the current view controller to the view controller that is about to appear on the screen, you need to do that in the `prepareForSegue:sender:` method.

 For this recipe to make sense, you need to have followed the instructions in Recipe 5.2 and created two view controllers inside a navigation controller on your storyboard.

Let's implement the `prepareForSegue:sender:` method in the first view controller:

```
- (void) prepareForSegue:(UIStoryboardSegue *)segue sender:(id)sender{

    NSLog(@"Source Controller = %@", [segue sourceViewController]);
    NSLog(@"Destination Controller = %@", [segue destinationViewController]);
    NSLog(@"Segue Identifier = %@", [segue identifier]);

}
```

If you run this app now, you will see the results in the console window. However, you might note that the identifier is `nil`. Each segue has an identifier that uniquely identifies it. Since one scene can have more than one segue associated with it, it's a good idea to give your segues identifiers that you can then detect in your view controllers and take action accordingly.

A segue object in Interface Builder is the connection between two scenes. Figure 5-23 shows the segue as an arrow between my first view controller on the left and the second view controller on the right.

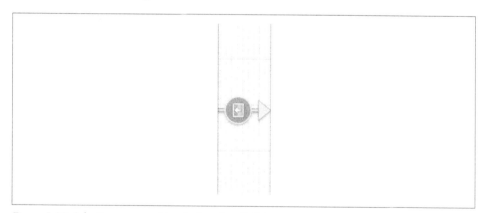

Figure 5-23. Selecting a segue object in Interface Builder

Follow these steps to give your segue an identifier:

1. Select your segue object in Interface Builder by clicking on it.
2. From the View menu, select Utilities → Show Attributes Inspector.

3. In the Attributes Inspector, in the Identifier text field, simply write the identifier that you would like this segue to carry with itself.

When the storyboard runtime calls the prepareForSegue:sender: method in the current view controller to prepare it for the segue, the destination view controller has already been initialized in the segue object. Now this is your chance to pass any required data to the destination view controller. You can either set the data directly into a property of the destination view controller, or pass your data by calling a method on that view controller; it is really up to you. In this code, my second view controller is of class SecondViewController and I've given my segue the identifier of *SimpleSegueToSecond ViewController*:

```
- (void) prepareForSegue:(UIStoryboardSegue *)segue sender:(id)sender{

    NSLog(@"Source Controller = %@", [segue sourceViewController]);
    NSLog(@"Destination Controller = %@", [segue destinationViewController]);
    NSLog(@"Segue Identifier = %@", [segue identifier]);

    if ([[segue identifier]
        isEqualToString:@"SimpleSegueToSecondViewController"]){

      SecondViewController *viewController = [segue destinationViewController];
      viewController.dataModel = ...; /* Write the code here */

    }

}
```

In this example code, the dataModal property is a hypothetical property declared and implemented in the view controller that is the target of our segue. This view controller is an instance of the SecondViewController that we have created for this project. The purpose of this example is to show how you can prepare your view controllers for a segue and populate necessary data into the target view controller.

See Also

Recipe 5.2

5.4 Adding a Storyboard to an Existing Project

Problem

You have already coded your app without storyboards and now you would like to start using storyboards instead of handling the flow of your app manually.

Solution

Follow these steps to allow your non-storyboard apps to take advantage of storyboards:

1. From the File menu, choose New → New File...

2. In the New File dialog, make sure you have selected the Resource subcategory of the iOS category on the left. Then choose the Storyboard item on the right and press Next (see Figure 5-24).

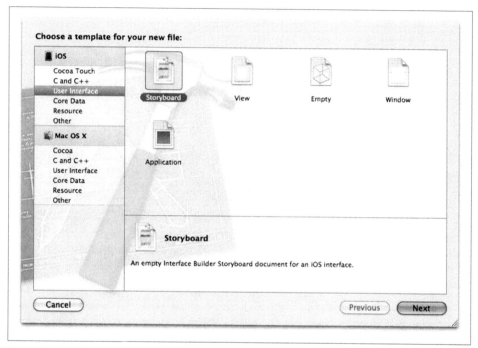

Figure 5-24. Adding a storyboard to an existing application

3. In this screen, pick the Device Family for which you want to create your storyboard. If your app is an iPhone- or iPad-only app, pick the appropriate device family. If your app is universal, you will need to select one device family now, create the storyboard file, and then come back and create another one for your other device family. Once you are done, press the Next button.

4. Now select where to save your storyboard. I had a universal app based on the Single View Application template, so I have now created two storyboard files under the names *StoryboardiPhone.storyboard* and *StoryboardiPad.storyboard*.

5. In your project structure, find the *Info.plist* file. Note that this *.plist* file might have been stored under a different name. For instance, I have named my project *Adding a Storyboard to an Existing Project* and my *Info.plist* is stored under the name *Adding a Storyboard to an Existing Project-Info.plist*. Once you click on this file, the property list editor will open automatically.

6. If you have any of these keys, delete them from the *.plist* file, because storyboarding renders them superfluous:

- NSMainNibFile (might appear as *Main nib file base name*).
- NSMainNibFile~ipad (might appear as *Main nib file base name (iPad)*).

7. If you have an iPhone or iPad only app, create a new key called UIMainStoryboard File for iPhone or UIMainStoryboardFile~ipad for iPad. If you have a universal app, create both these keys.

8. For the values of these keys, provide the filenames of the storyboards that you created *without* the *.storyboard* extension.

9. Make sure to save the *.plist* file.

10. Last, but perhaps most important, remove the code that set up the view controllers from the application:didFinishLaunchingWithOptions: method in your app delegate's implementation. With storyboards, you will no longer need to set up view controllers manually in your app delegate, so have a look at the aforementioned method and remove the unnecessary setup.

Discussion

Apps created without storyboards (either on older versions of Xcode or using the new versions without storyboarding) have a different structure from apps that use storyboards. For one thing, the storyboard-based apps no longer use a main nib file for their windows. So this file needs to be removed from the *.plist* of our app. The other thing to do, as we saw in the Solution section, is to make our app understand what our storyboard files are by setting them in the *.plist*.

Once all that is done, we need to make sure that our app delegate is not messing with how we intend to load our storyboards. Every project is different, and you need to make sure that the app delegate is *not* assigning any object to the rootViewController property of the window. If it does, your storyboards will not be displayed and you will spend hours and hours trying to find out what the issue is. The easiest solution is to simply comment out the entire application:didFinishLaunchingWithOptions: method and consider putting your initialization (for instance, initializing any data models) in other places in your app. An alternative is to simply leave this method as it is but comment out any lines that might be changing the window's root view controller object.

CHAPTER 6

Concurrency

6.0 Introduction

Concurrency is achieved when two or more tasks are executed at the same time. Modern operating systems have the ability to run tasks concurrently, even on one CPU. They achieve this by giving every task a certain time slice from the CPU. For instance, if there are 10 tasks to be executed in one second, all with the same priority, the operating system will divide 1000 milliseconds by 10 (tasks) and will give each task 100 milliseconds of the CPU time. That means all these tasks will then be executed in the same second and they will appear to have been executed concurrently.

However, with advances in technology, now we have CPUs with more than one core. This means that the CPU is truly capable of executing tasks at the same time. The operating system will dispatch the tasks to the CPU and will wait until they are done. It's that simple!

Grand Central Dispatch, or GCD for short, is a low-level C API that works with block objects. The real use for GCD is to dispatch tasks to multiple cores without making you, the programmer, worry about which core is executing which task. On Mac OS X, multicore devices, including laptops, have been available to users for quite some time. With the introduction of multicore devices such as the new iPad, programmers can write amazing multicore-aware multithreaded apps for iOS.

At the heart of GCD are dispatch queues. Dispatch queues, as we will soon see, are pools of threads managed by GCD on the host operating system, whether iOS or Mac OS X. You will not be working with these threads directly. You will just work with dispatch queues, dispatching *tasks* to these queues and asking the queues to invoke your tasks. GCD offers several options for running tasks: synchronously, asynchronously, after a certain delay, etc.

To start using GCD in your apps, you don't have to import any special library into your project. Apple has already incorporated GCD into various frameworks, including Core Foundation and Cocoa/Cocoa Touch. All methods and data types available in GCD start with a *dispatch_* keyword. For instance, `dispatch_async` allows you to dispatch a task on a queue for asynchronous execution, whereas `dispatch_after` allows you to run a block of code after a given delay.

Before GCD and operations, programmers had to create their own threads to perform tasks in parallel. For instance, an iOS developer would create a thread similar to this to perform an operation 1000 times:

```
- (void) doCalculation{
  /* Do your calculation here */
}

- (void) calculationThreadEntry{

  @autoreleasepool {
    NSUInteger counter = 0;
    while ([[NSThread currentThread] isCancelled] == NO){
      [self doCalculation];
      counter++;
      if (counter >= 1000){
        break;
      }
    }
  }

}

- (BOOL)             application:(UIApplication *)application
    didFinishLaunchingWithOptions:(NSDictionary *)launchOptions{

  /* Start the thread */
  [NSThread detachNewThreadSelector:@selector(calculationThreadEntry)
                          toTarget:self
                        withObject:nil];

  self.window = [[UIWindow alloc] initWithFrame:
                  [[UIScreen mainScreen] bounds]];
  self.window.backgroundColor = [UIColor whiteColor];
  [self.window makeKeyAndVisible];
  return YES;
}
```

The programmer has to start the thread manually and then create the required structure for the thread (entry point, autorelease pool, and thread's main loop). When we write the same code with GCD, we really won't have to do much. We will simply place our code in a block object and dispatch that block object to GCD for execution. Whether that code gets executed on the main thread or any other thread depends on us. Here is an example:

```
dispatch_queue_t queue =
  dispatch_get_global_queue(DISPATCH_QUEUE_PRIORITY_DEFAULT, 0);

size_t numberOfIterations = 1000;dispatch_async(queue, ^(void) {
  dispatch_apply(numberOfIterations, queue, ^(size_t iteration){
    /* Perform the operation here */
```

```
    });
  });
```

In this chapter, you will learn all there is to know about GCD and how to use it to write modern multithreaded apps for iOS and Mac OS X that will achieve blazing performance on multicore devices such as the iPad 2.

We will be working with dispatch queues a lot, so please make sure that you fully understand the concept behind them. There are three types of dispatch queues:

Main queue

> This queue performs all its tasks on the main thread, which is where Cocoa and Cocoa Touch require programmers to call all UI-related methods. Use the `dispatch_get_main_queue` function to retrieve the handle to the main queue.

Concurrent queues

> These are queues that you can retrieve from GCD in order to execute asynchronous or synchronous tasks. Multiple concurrent queues can be executing multiple tasks in parallel, without breaking a sweat. No more thread management, yippee! Use the `dispatch_get_global_queue` function to retrieve the handle to a concurrent queue.

Serial queues

> These are queues that, no matter whether you submit synchronous or asynchronous tasks to them, will always execute their tasks in a first-in-first-out (FIFO) fashion, meaning that they can only execute one block object at a time. However, they do *not* run on the main thread and therefore are perfect for a series of tasks that have to be executed in strict order without blocking the main thread. Use the `dispatch_queue_create` function to create a serial queue. Once you are done with the queue, you must release it using the `dispatch_release` function.

At any moment during the lifetime of your application, you can use multiple dispatch queues at the same time. Your system has only one main queue, but you can create as many serial dispatch queues as you want (within reason, of course), for whatever functionality you require for your app. You can also retrieve multiple concurrent queues and dispatch your tasks to them. Tasks can be handed to dispatch queues in two forms: block objects or C functions, as we will see in Recipe 6.4.

Block objects are *packages* of code that usually appear in the form of methods in Objective-C. Block objects, together with Grand Central Dispatch (GCD), create a harmonious environment in which you can deliver high-performance multithreaded apps in iOS and Mac OS X. What's so special about block objects and GCD, you might ask? It's simple: no more threads! All you have to do is to put your code in block objects and ask GCD to take care of the execution of that code for you.

Perhaps the most important difference between block objects and traditional function pointers is that block objects copy the values of local variables accessed inside the block objects and keep those copies for local use. If the values of those variables change outside the scope of the block object, you can be sure that the block object still keeps its own copy of the variable. We will discuss this in more detail soon.

Block objects in Objective-C are what the programming field calls *first-class objects*. This means you can build code dynamically, pass a block object to a method as a parameter, and return a block object from a method. All of these things make it easier to choose what you want to do at runtime and change the activity of a program. In particular, block objects can be run in individual threads by GCD. Being Objective-C objects, block objects can be treated like any other object.

 Block objects are sometimes referred to as *closures*.

Constructing block objects is similar to constructing traditional C functions, as we will see in Recipe 6.1. Block objects can have return values and can accept parameters. Block objects can be defined inline or treated as a separate block of code, similar to a C function. When created inline, the scope of variables accessible to block objects is considerably different from when a block object is implemented as a separate block of code.

GCD works with block objects. When performing tasks with GCD, you can pass a block object whose code can get executed synchronously or asynchronously, depending on which methods you use in GCD. Thus, you can create a block object that is responsible for downloading a URL passed to it as a parameter. That single block object can then be used in various places in your app synchronously or asynchronously, depending on how you would like to run it. You don't have to make the block object synchronous or asynchronous per se; you will simply call it with synchronous or asynchronous GCD methods and the block object will *just work*.

Block objects are quite new to programmers writing iOS and OS X apps. In fact, block objects are not as popular as threads yet, perhaps because their syntax is a bit different from pure Objective-C methods and more complicated. Nonetheless, block objects are enormously powerful and Apple is making a big push toward incorporating them into Apple libraries. You can already see these additions in classes such as NSMutableArray, where programmers can sort the array using a block object.

This chapter is dedicated entirely to constructing and using block objects in iOS and Mac OS X apps, using GCD for dispatching tasks to the operating system, threads and timers. I would like to stress that the only way to get used to block objects' syntax is to write a few of them for yourself. Have a look at the sample code in this chapter and try implementing your own block objects.

Here, you will learn the basics of block objects, followed by some more advanced subjects, such as Grand Central Dispatch, Threads, Timers, Operations, and Operation Queues. You will understand everything you need to know about block objects before moving to the Grand Central Dispatch material. From my experience, the best way to learn block objects is through examples, so you will see a lot of them in this chapter. Make sure you try the examples for yourself in Xcode to really *get* the syntax of block objects.

Operations can be configured to run a block of code synchronously or asynchronously. You can manage operations manually or place them on *operation queues*, which facilitate concurrency so that you do not need to think about the underlying thread management. In this chapter, you will see how to use operations and operation queues, as well as basic threads and timers, to synchronously and asynchronously execute tasks in applications.

Cocoa provides three different types of operations:

Block operations
> These facilitate the execution of one or more block objects.

Invocation operations
> These allow you to invoke a method in another, currently existing object.

Plain operations
> These are plain operation classes that need to be subclassed. The code to be executed will be written inside the `main` method of the operation object.

Operations, as mentioned before, can be managed with operation queues, which have the data type `NSOperationQueue`. After instantiating any of the aforementioned operation types (block, invocation, or plain operation), you can add them to an operation queue and have the queue manage the operation.

An operation object can have dependencies on other operation objects and be instructed to wait for the completion of one or more operations before executing the task associated with it. Unless you add a dependency, you have no control over the order in which operations run. For instance, adding them to a queue in a certain order does not guarantee that they will execute in that order, despite the use of the term *queue*.

There are a few important things to bear in mind while working with operation queues and operations:

- Operations, by default, run on the thread that starts them, using their `start` instance method. If you want the operations to work asynchronously, you will have to use either an operation queue or a subclass `NSOperation` and detach a new thread on the `main` instance method of the operation.

- An operation can wait for the execution of another operation to finish before it starts itself. Be careful not to create interdependent operations, a common mistake known as a *deadlock*. In other words, do not tell operation A to depend on operation B if B already depends on A; this will cause both to wait forever, taking up memory and possibly hanging your application.

- Operations can be cancelled. So, if you have subclassed NSOperation to create custom operation objects, you have to make sure to use the isCancelled instance method to check whether the operation has been cancelled before executing the task associated with the operation. For instance, if your operation's task is to check for the availability of an Internet connection every 20 seconds, it must call the isCancelled instance method at the beginning of each run to make sure it has not been cancelled before attempting to check for an Internet connection again. If the operation takes more than a few seconds (such as when you download a file), you should also check isCancelled periodically while running the task.

- Operation objects are key-value observing (KVO) compliant on various key paths such as isFinished, isReady, and isExecuting. We will be discussing Key Value Coding and Key Value Observing in a later chapter.

- If you plan to subclass NSOperation and provide a custom implementation for the operation, you must create your own autorelease pool in the main method of the operation, which gets called from the start method. We will discuss this in detail later in this chapter.

- Always keep a reference to the operation objects you create. The concurrent nature of operation queues might make it impossible for you to retrieve a reference to an operation after it has been added to the queue.

Threads and timers are objects, subclassing NSObject. Spawning a thread requires more work than creating timers, and setting up a thread loop itself is more difficult than simply listening for a timer firing on a selector. When an application runs under iOS, the operating system creates at least one thread for that application, called the main thread. Every thread and timer must be added to a run loop. A run loop, as its name implies, is a loop during which different events can occur, such as a timer firing or a thread running. Discussion of run loops is beyond the scope of this chapter, but we will refer to them here and there in recipes.

Think of a run loop as a kind of loop that has a starting point, a condition for finishing, and a series of events to process during its lifetime. A thread or timer is attached to a run loop, and in fact requires a run loop to function.

The main thread of an application is the thread that handles the UI events. If you perform a long-running task on the main thread, you will notice that the UI of your application will become unresponsive or slow to respond. To avoid this, you can create separate threads and/or timers, each of which performs its own task (even if it is a long-running task) but will not block the main thread.

6.1 Constructing Block Objects

Problem

You want to be able to write your own block objects or use block objects with iOS SDK classes.

Solution

You just need to understand the basic differences between the syntax of block objects and classic C functions. These differences are explained in the Discussion section.

Discussion

Block objects can either be inline or coded as independent blocks of code. Let's start with the latter type. Suppose you have a method in Objective-C that accepts two integer values of type NSInteger and returns the difference of the two values, by subtracting one from the other, as an NSInteger:

```
- (NSInteger) subtract:(NSInteger)paramValue
                  from:(NSInteger)paramFrom{

  return paramFrom - paramValue;

}
```

That was very simple, wasn't it? Now let's translate this Objective-C code to a pure C function that provides the same functionality to get one step closer to learning the syntax of block objects:

```
NSInteger subtract(NSInteger paramValue, NSInteger paramFrom){

  return paramFrom - paramValue;

}
```

You can see that the C function is quite different in syntax from its Objective-C counterpart. Now let's have a look at how we could code the same function as a block object:

```
NSInteger (^subtract)(NSInteger, NSInteger) =
  ^(NSInteger paramValue, NSInteger paramFrom){

  return paramFrom - paramValue;

};
```

Before I go into details about the syntax of block objects, let me show you a few more examples. Suppose we have a function in C that takes a parameter of type NSUInteger (an unsigned integer) and returns it as a string of type NSString. Here is how we implement this in C:

```
NSString* intToString (NSUInteger paramInteger){

    return [NSString stringWithFormat:@"%lu",
            (unsigned long)paramInteger];

}
```

 To learn about formatting strings with system-independent format specifiers in Objective-C, please refer to the String Programming Guide in the iOS Developer Library (*https://developer.apple.com/library/ios/ #documentation/Cocoa/Conceptual/Strings/Articles/formatSpecifiers .html*) on Apple's website.

The block object equivalent of this C function is shown in Example 6-1.

Example 6-1. Example block object defined as function

```
NSString* (^intToString)(NSUInteger) = ^(NSUInteger paramInteger){
  NSString *result = [NSString stringWithFormat:@"%lu",
                        (unsigned long)paramInteger];

  return result;
};
```

The simplest form of an independent block object would be a block object that returns void and does not take in any parameters:

```
void (^simpleBlock)(void) = ^{
  /* Implement the block object here */
};
```

Block objects can be invoked in the exact same way as C functions. If they have any parameters, you pass those as you would for a C function, and any return value can be retrieved exactly as you would retrieve a C function's return value. Here is an example:

```
NSString* (^intToString)(NSUInteger) = ^(NSUInteger paramInteger){
    NSString *result = [NSString stringWithFormat:@"%lu",
                        (unsigned long)paramInteger];
    return result;
};

- (void) callIntToString{

    NSString *string = intToString(10);
    NSLog(@"string = %@", string);

}
```

The callIntToString Objective-C method is calling the intToString block object by passing the value 10 as the only parameter to this block object and placing the return value of this block object in the string local variable.

Now that we know how to write block objects as independent blocks of code, let's have a look at passing block objects as parameters to Objective-C methods. We will have to think a bit abstractly to understand the goal of the following example.

Suppose we have an Objective-C method that accepts an integer and performs some kind of transformation on it, which may change depending on what else is happening in the program. We know that we'll have an integer as input and a string as output, but we'll leave the exact transformation up to a block object that can be different each time the method runs. This method, therefore, will accept as parameters both the integer to be transformed and the block that will transform it.

For the block object, we'll use the same intToString block object that we implemented earlier in Example 6-1. Now we need an Objective-C method that will accept an unsigned integer parameter and a block object as its parameter. The unsigned integer parameter is easy, but how do we tell the method that it has to accept a block object *of the same type* as the intToString block object? First we typedef the signature of the intToString block object, which tells the compiler what parameters the block object should accept:

```
typedef NSString* (^IntToStringConverter)(NSUInteger paramInteger);
```

This typedef just tells the compiler that block objects that accept an integer parameter and return a string can simply be represented by an identifier named IntToString Converter. Now let's go ahead and write the Objective-C method that accepts both an integer and a block object of type IntToStringConverter:

```
- (NSString *) convertIntToString:(NSUInteger)paramInteger
              usingBlockObject:(IntToStringConverter)paramBlockObject{

    return paramBlockObject(paramInteger);

}
```

All we have to do now is call the convertIntToString: method with the block object of choice (Example 6-2).

Example 6-2. Calling the block object in another method

```
- (void) doTheConversion{

  NSString *result = [self convertIntToString:123
                        usingBlockObject:intToString];

  NSLog(@"result = %@", result);

}
```

Now that we know something about independent block objects, let's turn to inline block objects. In the doTheConversion method we just saw, we passed the intTo String block object as the parameter to the convertIntToString:usingBlockObject: method. What if we didn't have a block object ready to be passed to this method? Well, that wouldn't be a problem. As mentioned before, block objects are first-class functions and can be constructed at runtime. Let's have a look at an alternative implementation of the doTheConversion method (Example 6-3).

Example 6-3. Example block object defined as a function

```
- (void) doTheConversion{

  IntToStringConverter inlineConverter = ^(NSUInteger paramInteger){
    NSString *result = [NSString stringWithFormat:@"%lu",
                        (unsigned long)paramInteger];
    return result;
  };

  NSString *result = [self convertIntToString:123
                            usingBlockObject:inlineConverter];

  NSLog(@"result = %@", result);

}
```

Compare Example 6-3 to Example 6-1. I have removed the initial code that provided the block object's signature, which consisted of a name and argument, (^intToString) (NSUInteger). I left the rest of the block object intact; it is now an anonymous object. But this doesn't mean I have no way to refer to the block object. I assign it using an equal sign to a type and a name: IntToStringConverter inlineConverter. Now I can use the data type to enforce proper use in methods, and use the name to actually pass the block object.

In addition to constructing block objects inline as just shown, we can construct a block object *while* passing it as a parameter:

```
    - (void) doTheConversion{

      NSString *result =
      [self convertIntToString:123
              usingBlockObject:^NSString *(NSUInteger paramInteger) {

        NSString *result = [NSString stringWithFormat:@"%lu",
                            (unsigned long)paramInteger];
        return result;

      }];

      NSLog(@"result = %@", result);

    }
```

Compare this example with Example 6-2. Both methods use a block object through the usingBlockObject syntax. But whereas the earlier version referred to a previously declared block object by name (intToString), this one simply creates a block object on the fly. In this code, we constructed an inline block object that gets passed to the `convertIntToString:usingBlockObject:` method as the second parameter.

6.2 Accessing Variables in Block Objects

Problem

You want to understand the difference between accessing variables in Objective-C methods and accessing those variables in block objects.

Solution

Here is a brief summary of what you must know about variables in block objects:

- Local variables in block objects work exactly the same as in Objective-C methods.
- For inline block objects, local variables constitute not only variables defined within the block, but also the variables that have been defined in the method that implements that block object. (Examples will come shortly.)
- You *cannot* refer to `self` in independent block objects implemented in an Objective-C class. If you need to access `self`, you must pass that object to the block object as a parameter. We will see an example of this soon.
- You can refer to `self` in an inline block object only if `self` is present in the lexical scope inside which the block object is created.
- For inline block objects, local variables that are defined *inside* the block object's implementation can be read from and written to. In other words, the block object has read-write access to variables defined inside the block object's body.
- For inline block objects, variables local to the Objective-C method that implements that block can only be read from, not written to. There is an exception, though: a block object can write to such variables if they are defined with the `__block` storage type. We will see an example of this as well.
- Suppose you have an object of type `NSObject` and inside that object's implementation you are using a block object in conjunction with GCD. Inside this block object, you will have read-write access to declared properties of that `NSObject` inside which your block is implemented.
- You can access declared properties of your `NSObject` inside independent block objects *only if* you use the setter and getter methods of these properties. You cannot access declared properties of an object using dot notation inside an independent block object.

Discussion

Let's first see how we can use variables that are local to the implementation of two block objects. One is an inline block object and the other an independent block object:

```
void (^independentBlockObject)(void) = ^(void){

    NSInteger localInteger = 10;

    NSLog(@"local integer = %ld", (long)localInteger);

    localInteger = 20;

    NSLog(@"local integer = %ld", (long)localInteger);

};
```

Invoking this block object, the values we assigned are printed to the console window:

```
local integer = 10
local integer = 20
```

So far, so good. Now let's have a look at inline block objects and variables that are local to them:

```
- (void) simpleMethod{

    NSUInteger outsideVariable = 10;

    NSMutableArray *array = [[NSMutableArray alloc]
                             initWithObjects:@"obj1",
                             @"obj2", nil];

    [array sortUsingComparator:^NSComparisonResult(id obj1, id obj2) {
      NSUInteger insideVariable = 20;

      NSLog(@"Outside variable = %lu", (unsigned long)outsideVariable);
      NSLog(@"Inside variable = %lu", (unsigned long)insideVariable);

      /* Return value for the block object */
      return NSOrderedSame;

    }];

}
```

 The sortUsingComparator: instance method of NSMutableArray attempts to sort a mutable array. The goal of this example code is just to demonstrate the use of local variables, so you don't have to know what this method actually does.

The block object can read and write its own insideVariable local variable. However, the block object has read-only access to the outsideVariable variable by default. In order to allow the block object to write to outsideVariable, we must prefix outside Variable with the __block storage type:

```
- (void) simpleMethod{
```

```
    __block NSUInteger outsideVariable = 10;

    NSMutableArray *array = [[NSMutableArray alloc]
                               initWithObjects:@"obj1",
                               @"obj2", nil];


    [array sortUsingComparator:^NSComparisonResult(id obj1, id obj2) {

        NSUInteger insideVariable = 20;
        outsideVariable = 30;

        NSLog(@"Outside variable = %lu", (unsigned long)outsideVariable);
        NSLog(@"Inside variable = %lu", (unsigned long)insideVariable);

        /* Return value for the block object */
        return NSOrderedSame;

    }];

}
```

Accessing self in inline block objects is fine as long as self is defined in the lexical scope inside which the inline block object is created. For instance, in this example, the block object will be able to access self, since simpleMethod is an instance method of an Objective-C class:

```
- (void) simpleMethod{

    NSMutableArray *array = [[NSMutableArray alloc]
                               initWithObjects:@"obj1",
                               @"obj2", nil];

    [array sortUsingComparator:^NSComparisonResult(id obj1, id obj2) {

        NSLog(@"self = %@", self);

        /* Return value for the block object */
        return NSOrderedSame;

    }];

}
```

You cannot, without a change in your block object's implementation, access self in an independent block object. Attempting to compile this code will give you a compile-time error:

```
void (^incorrectBlockObject)(void) = ^{
    NSLog(@"self = %@", self); /* self is undefined here */
};
```

If you want to access self in an independent block object, simply pass the object that self represents as a parameter to your block object:

```
void (^correctBlockObject)(id) = ^(id self){

  NSLog(@"self = %@", self);

};

- (void) callCorrectBlockObject{

  correctBlockObject(self);

}
```

 You don't have to assign the name self to this parameter. You can simply call this parameter anything else. However, if you call this parameter self, you can simply grab your block object's code later and place it in an Objective-C method's implementation without having to change every instance of your variable's name to self for it to be understood by the compiler.

Let's have a look at declared properties and how block objects can access them. For inline block objects, you can use dot notation to read from or write to declared properties of self. For instance, let's say we have a declared property of type NSString called stringProperty in the class:

```
#import <UIKit/UIKit.h>

@interface GCDAppDelegate : NSObject <UIApplicationDelegate>

@property (nonatomic, strong) NSString    *stringProperty;

@end
```

Now we can simply access this property in an inline block object like so:

```
#import "GCDAppDelegate.h"

@implementation GCDAppDelegate

- (void) simpleMethod{

  NSMutableArray *array = [[NSMutableArray alloc]
                     initWithObjects:@"obj1",
                     @"obj2", nil];

  [array sortUsingComparator:^NSComparisonResult(id obj1, id obj2) {

    NSLog(@"self = %@", self);

    self.stringProperty = @"Block Objects";

    NSLog(@"String property = %@", self.stringProperty);

    /* Return value for the block object */
```

```
    return NSOrderedSame;

  }];

}

@end
```

In an independent block object, however, you cannot use dot notation to read from or write to a declared property:

```
void (^correctBlockObject)(id) = ^(id self){

  NSLog(@"self = %@", self);

  /* Should use setter method instead of this */
  self.stringProperty = @"Block Objects"; /* Compile-time Error */

  /* Should use getter method instead of this */
  NSLog(@"self.stringProperty = %@",
        self.stringProperty); /* Compile-time Error */

};
```

Instead of dot notation in this scenario, use the getter and the setter methods of this property:

```
void (^correctBlockObject)(id) = ^(id self){

  NSLog(@"self = %@", self);

  /* This will work fine */
  [self setStringProperty:@"Block Objects"];

  /* This will work fine as well */
  NSLog(@"self.stringProperty = %@",
        [self stringProperty]);

};
```

When it comes to inline block objects, there is one *very* important rule that you have to remember: inline block objects copy the value for the variables in their lexical scope. If you don't understand what that means, don't worry. Let's have a look at an example:

```
typedef void (^BlockWithNoParams)(void);

- (void) scopeTest{

  NSUInteger integerValue = 10;

  /*************** Definition of internal block object ***************/
  BlockWithNoParams myBlock = ^{
    NSLog(@"Integer value inside the block = %lu",
          (unsigned long)integerValue);
  };
  /*************** End definition of internal block object ***************/
```

```
integerValue = 20;

/* Call the block here after changing the
   value of the integerValue variable */
myBlock();

NSLog(@"Integer value outside the block = %lu",
      (unsigned long)integerValue);

}
```

We are declaring an integer local variable and initially assigning the value of 10 to it. We then implement the block object, but *don't call the block object yet*. After the block object is *implemented*, we simply change the value of the local variable that the block object will later try to read when we call it. Right after changing the local variable's value to 20, we call the block object. You would expect the block object to print the value 20 for the variable, but it won't. It will print 10, as you can see here:

```
Integer value inside the block = 10
Integer value outside the block = 20
```

What's happening here is that the block object is keeping a read-only copy of the integerValue variable for itself right where the block is implemented. You might be thinking: why is the block object capturing a *read-only* value of the local variable integerValue? The answer is simple, and we've already learned it in this section. Unless prefixed with storage type __block, local variables in the lexical scope of a block object are just passed to the block object as read-only variables. Therefore, to change this behavior, we could change the implementation of the scopeTest method to prefix the integerValue variable with __block storage type, like so:

```
- (void) scopeTest{

  __block NSUInteger integerValue = 10;

  /*************** Definition of internal block object **************/
  BlockWithNoParams myBlock = ^{
    NSLog(@"Integer value inside the block = %lu",
          (unsigned long)integerValue);
  };
  /*************** End definition of internal block object **************/

  integerValue = 20;

  /* Call the block here after changing the
     value of the integerValue variable */
  myBlock();

  NSLog(@"Integer value outside the block = %lu",
        (unsigned long)integerValue);

}
```

Now if we get the results from the console window after the `scopeTest` method is called, we will see this:

```
Integer value inside the block = 20
Integer value outside the block = 20
```

This section should have given you sufficient information about using variables with block objects. I suggest that you write a few block objects and use variables inside them, assigning to them and reading from them, to get a better understanding of how block objects use variables. Keep coming back to this section if you forget the rules that govern variable access in block objects.

6.3 Invoking Block Objects

Problem

You've learned how to construct block objects, and now you want to execute your block objects to get results.

Solution

Execute your block objects the same way you execute a C function, as shown in the Discussion section.

Discussion

We've seen examples of invoking block objects in Recipes 6.1 and 6.2. This section contains more concrete examples.

If you have an independent block object, you can simply invoke it just like you would invoke a C function:

```
void (^simpleBlock)(NSString *) = ^(NSString *paramString){
  /* Implement the block object here and use the
   paramString parameter */
};

- (void) callSimpleBlock{

  simpleBlock(@"O'Reilly");

}
```

If you want to invoke an independent block object within another independent block object, follow the same instructions by invoking the new block object just as you would invoke a C method:

```
/************** Definition of first block object **************/
NSString *(^trimString)(NSString *) = ^(NSString *inputString){

  NSString *result = [inputString stringByTrimmingCharactersInSet:
```

```
                                      [NSCharacterSet whitespaceCharacterSet]];
        return result;

      };
      /************** End definition of first block object **************/

      /************** Definition of second block object **************/
      NSString *(^trimWithOtherBlock)(NSString *) = ^(NSString *inputString){
        return trimString(inputString);
      };
      /************** End definition of second block object **************/

      - (void) callTrimBlock{

        NSString *trimmedString = trimWithOtherBlock(@"   O'Reilly   ");
        NSLog(@"Trimmed string = %@", trimmedString);

      }
```

In this example, go ahead and invoke the `callTrimBlock` Objective-C method:

```
[self callTrimBlock];
```

The `callTrimBlock` method will call the `trimWithOtherBlock` block object, and the `trimWithOtherBlock` block object will call the `trimString` block object in order to trim the given string. Trimming a string is easy and can be done in one line of code, but this example code shows how you can call block objects within block objects.

See Also

Recipe 6.1; Recipe 6.2

6.4 Dispatching Tasks to Grand Central Dispatch

Problem

You want to learn how to create a block of code that can be executed by GCD.

Solution

There are two ways to submit tasks to dispatch queues:

- Block Objects (see Recipe 6.1)
- C functions

Discussion

Block objects are the best way of utilizing GCD and its enormous power. Some GCD functions have been extended to allow programmers to use C functions instead of block objects. However, the truth is that only a limited set of GCD functions allow programmers to use C functions, so please do read the recipe about block objects (Recipe 6.1) before proceeding any further.

C functions that have to be supplied to various GCD functions should be of type dispatch_function_t, which is defined as follows in the Apple libraries:

```
typedef void (*dispatch_function_t)(void *);
```

So if we want to create a function named, for instance, myGCDFunction, we would have to implement it in this way:

```
void myGCDFunction(void * paraContext){

  /* Do the work here */

}
```

 The paraContext parameter refers to the context that GCD allows programmers to pass to their C functions when they dispatch tasks to them. We will learn about this shortly.

Block objects that get passed to GCD functions don't always follow the same structure. Some must accept parameters and some shouldn't, but none of the block objects submitted to GCD return a value.

In the next three sections, you will learn how to submit tasks to GCD for execution whether they are in the form of block objects or C functions.

See Also

Recipe 6.1

6.5 Performing UI-Related Tasks with GCD

Problem

You are using GCD for concurrency and you would like to know what the best way of working with UI-related APIs is.

Solution

Use the dispatch_get_main_queue function.

Discussion

UI-related tasks have to be performed on the main thread, so the main queue is the only candidate for UI task execution in GCD. We can use the dispatch_get_main_queue function to get the handle to the main dispatch queue.

There are two ways of dispatching tasks to the main queue. Both are asynchronous, letting your program continue even when the task is not yet executed:

dispatch_async *function*
> Executes a block object on a dispatch queue.

dispatch_async_f *function*
> Executes a C function on a dispatch queue.

> The dispatch_sync method *cannot* be called on the main queue because it will block the thread indefinitely and cause your application to deadlock. All tasks submitted to the main queue through GCD must be submitted asynchronously.

Let's have a look at using the dispatch_async function. It accepts two parameters:

Dispatch queue handle
> The dispatch queue on which the task has to be executed.

Block object
> The block object to be sent to the dispatch queue for asynchronous execution.

Here is an example. This code will display an alert in iOS to the user, using the main queue:

```
dispatch_queue_t mainQueue = dispatch_get_main_queue();

dispatch_async(mainQueue, ^(void) {

    [[[UIAlertView alloc] initWithTitle:@"GCD"
                                message:@"GCD is amazing!"
                               delegate:nil
                      cancelButtonTitle:@"OK"
                      otherButtonTitles:nil, nil] show];

});
```

> As you've noticed, the dispatch_async GCD function has no parameters or return value. The block object that is submitted to this function must gather its own data in order to complete its task. In the code snippet that we just saw, the alert view has all the values that it needs to finish its task. However, this might not always be the case. In such instances, you must make sure the block object submitted to GCD has access in its scope to all the values that it requires.

Running this app in iOS Simulator, the user will get results similar to those shown in Figure 6-1.

Figure 6-1. An alert displayed using asynchronous GCD calls

This might not seem very impressive, if you think about it. So what makes the main queue truly interesting? The answer is simple: when you are getting the maximum performance from GCD to do some heavy calculation on concurrent or serial threads, you might want to display the results to your user or move a component on the screen. For that, you *must* use the main queue, because it is UI-related work. The functions shown in this section are the *only* ways to get out of a serial or a concurrent queue while still utilizing GCD to update your UI, so you can imagine how important they are.

Instead of submitting a block object for execution on the main queue, you can submit a C function object. Submit all UI-related C functions for execution in GCD to the dispatch_async_f function. We can get the same results as we got in Figure 6-1, using C functions instead of block objects, with a few adjustments to the code.

As mentioned before, with the dispatch_async_f function, we can submit a pointer to an application-defined context, which can then be used by the C function that gets called. So, let's create a structure that holds values such as an alert view's title, message, and cancel-button's title. When the app starts, we will put all the values in this structure and pass it to the C function to display. Here is how we define the structure:

```
typedef struct{
  char *title;
  char *message;
  char *cancelButtonTitle;
} AlertViewData;
```

Now let's go and implement a C function that we will later call with GCD. This C function should expect a parameter of type void *, which we will then typecast to AlertViewData *. In other words, we expect the caller of this function to pass us a reference to the data for the alert view, encapsulated inside the AlertViewData structure:

```
void displayAlertView(void *paramContext){

  AlertViewData *alertData = (AlertViewData *)paramContext;

  NSString *title =
    [NSString stringWithUTF8String:alertData->title];

  NSString *message =
    [NSString stringWithUTF8String:alertData->message];

  NSString *cancelButtonTitle =
    [NSString stringWithUTF8String:alertData->cancelButtonTitle];

  [[[UIAlertView alloc] initWithTitle:title
                              message:message
                             delegate:nil
                    cancelButtonTitle:cancelButtonTitle
                    otherButtonTitles:nil, nil] show];

  free(alertData);

}
```

 The reason we are freeing the context passed to us in here instead of in the caller is that the caller is going to execute this C function asynchronously and cannot know when the C function will finish executing. Therefore, the caller has to `malloc` enough space for the `AlertViewData` context and the `displayAlertView` C function has to free that space.

And now let's call the `displayAlertView` function on the main queue and pass the context (the structure that holds the alert view's data) to it:

```
- (BOOL)             application:(UIApplication *)application
  didFinishLaunchingWithOptions:(NSDictionary *)launchOptions{

  dispatch_queue_t mainQueue = dispatch_get_main_queue();

  AlertViewData *context = (AlertViewData *)
  malloc(sizeof(AlertViewData));

  if (context != NULL){
    context->title = "GCD";
    context->message = "GCD is amazing.";
    context->cancelButtonTitle = "OK";

    dispatch_async_f(mainQueue,
                     (void *)context,
                     displayAlertView);
  }

  self.window = [[UIWindow alloc] initWithFrame:
                 [[UIScreen mainScreen] bounds]];
```

```
    self.window.backgroundColor = [UIColor whiteColor];
    [self.window makeKeyAndVisible];
    return YES;
}
```

If you invoke the currentThread class method of the NSThread class, you will find out that the block objects or the C functions you dispatch to the main queue are indeed running on the main thread:

```
- (BOOL)             application:(UIApplication *)application
  didFinishLaunchingWithOptions:(NSDictionary *)launchOptions{

  dispatch_queue_t mainQueue = dispatch_get_main_queue();

  dispatch_async(mainQueue, ^(void) {
    NSLog(@"Current thread = %@", [NSThread currentThread]);
    NSLog(@"Main thread = %@", [NSThread mainThread]);
  });

  self.window = [[UIWindow alloc] initWithFrame:
                  [[UIScreen mainScreen] bounds]];
  self.window.backgroundColor = [UIColor whiteColor];
  [self.window makeKeyAndVisible];
  return YES;
}
```

The output of this code would be similar to that shown here:

```
Current thread = <NSThread: 0x4b0e4e0>{name = (null), num = 1}
Main thread = <NSThread: 0x4b0e4e0>{name = (null), num = 1}
```

Now that you know how to perform UI-related tasks using GCD, it is time we moved to other subjects, such as performing tasks in parallel using concurrent queues (see Recipes 6.6 and Recipe 6.7) and mixing the code with UI-related code if need be.

6.6 Executing Non-UI Related Tasks Synchronously with GCD

Problem

You want to perform synchronous tasks that do not involve any UI-related code.

Solution

Use the dispatch_sync function.

Discussion

There are times when you want to perform tasks that have nothing to do with the UI or interact with the UI as well as doing other tasks that take up a lot of time. For instance, you might want to download an image and display it to the user after it is downloaded. The downloading process has absolutely nothing to do with the UI.

For any task that doesn't involve the UI, you can use global concurrent queues in GCD. These allow either synchronous or asynchronous execution. But synchronous execution does *not* mean your program waits for the code to finish before continuing. It simply means that the concurrent queue will wait until your task has finished before it continues to the next block of code on the queue. When you put a block object on a concurrent queue, your own program *always* continues right away without waiting for the queue to execute the code. This is because concurrent queues, as their name implies, run their code on threads other than the main thread. (There is one exception to this: when a task is submitted to a concurrent or a serial queue using the `dispatch_sync` function, iOS will, if possible, run the task on the *current* thread, which *might* be the main thread, depending on where the code path is at the moment. This is an optimization that has been programmed on GCD, as we shall soon see.)

If you submit a task to a concurrent queue synchronously, and at the same time submit another synchronous task to *another* concurrent queue, these two synchronous tasks will run asynchronously in relation to each other because they are running two *different concurrent queues*. It's important to understand this because sometimes, as we'll see, you want to make sure task A finishes before task B starts. To ensure that, submit them synchronously to the *same* queue.

You can perform synchronous tasks on a dispatch queue using the `dispatch_sync` function. All you have to do is to provide it with the handle of the queue that has to run the task and a block of code to execute on that queue.

Let's look at an example. It prints the integers 1 to 1000 twice, one complete sequence after the other, without blocking the main thread. We can create a block object that does the counting for us and synchronously call the same block object twice:

```
void (^printFrom1To1000)(void) = ^{

  NSUInteger counter = 0;
  for (counter = 1;
       counter <= 1000;
       counter++){

    NSLog(@"Counter = %lu - Thread = %@",
          (unsigned long)counter,
          [NSThread currentThread]);

  }

};
```

Now let's go and invoke this block object using GCD:

```
dispatch_queue_t concurrentQueue =
  dispatch_get_global_queue(DISPATCH_QUEUE_PRIORITY_DEFAULT, 0);

dispatch_sync(concurrentQueue, printFrom1To1000);
dispatch_sync(concurrentQueue, printFrom1To1000);
```

If you run this code, you might notice the counting taking place on the main thread, even though you've asked a concurrent queue to execute the task. It turns out this is an optimization by GCD. The `dispatch_sync` function will use the current thread—the thread you're using when you dispatch the task—whenever possible, as a part of an optimization that has been programmed into GCD. Here is what Apple says about it:

> As an optimization, this function invokes the block on the current thread when possible.
>
> —Grand Central Dispatch (GCD) Reference

To execute a C function instead of a block object, synchronously, on a dispatch queue, use the `dispatch_sync_f` function. Let's simply translate the code we've written for the `printFrom1To1000` block object to its equivalent C function, like so:

```
void printFrom1To1000(void *paramContext){

  NSUInteger counter = 0;
  for (counter = 1;
       counter <= 1000;
       counter++){

    NSLog(@"Counter = %lu - Thread = %@",
          (unsigned long)counter,
          [NSThread currentThread]);

  }

}
```

And now we can use the `dispatch_sync_f` function to execute the `printFrom1To1000` function on a concurrent queue, as demonstrated here:

```
dispatch_queue_t concurrentQueue =
  dispatch_get_global_queue(DISPATCH_QUEUE_PRIORITY_DEFAULT, 0);

dispatch_sync_f(concurrentQueue,
                NULL,
                printFrom1To1000);

dispatch_sync_f(concurrentQueue,
                NULL,
                printFrom1To1000);
```

The first parameter of the `dispatch_get_global_queue` function specifies the priority of the concurrent queue that GCD has to retrieve for the programmer. The higher the priority, the more CPU timeslices will be provided to the code getting executed on that queue. You can use any of these values for the first parameter to the `dispatch_get_global_queue` function:

DISPATCH_QUEUE_PRIORITY_LOW
    Fewer timeslices will be applied to your task than normal tasks.

DISPATCH_QUEUE_PRIORITY_DEFAULT
    The default system priority for code execution will be applied to your task.

```
DISPATCH_QUEUE_PRIORITY_HIGH
```
   More timeslices will be applied to your task than normal tasks.

 The second parameter of the `dispatch_get_global_queue` function is reserved and you should always pass the value 0 to it.

In this section you saw how you can dispatch tasks to concurrent queues for synchronous execution. The next section shows asynchronous execution on concurrent queues, while Recipe 6.11 will show you how to execute tasks synchronously and asynchronously on serial queues that you create for your applications.

See Also

Recipe 6.7; Recipe 6.11

6.7 Executing Non-UI Related Tasks Asynchronously with GCD

Problem

You want to be able to execute non-UI related tasks asynchronously, with the help of GCD.

Solution

This is where GCD can show its true power: executing blocks of code asynchronously on the main, serial, or concurrent queues. I promise that, by the end of this section, you will be completely convinced GCD is the future of multithread applications, completely replacing threads in modern apps.

In order to execute asynchronous tasks on a dispatch queue, you must use one of these functions:

`dispatch_async`
   Submits a block object to a dispatch queue (both specified by parameters) for asynchronous execution.

`dispatch_async_f`
   Submits a C function to a dispatch queue, along with a context reference (all three specified by parameters), for asynchronous execution.

Discussion

Let's have a look at a real example. We'll write an iOS app that is able to download an image from a URL on the Internet. After the download is finished, the app should display the image to the user. Here is the plan and how we will use what we've learned so far about GCD in order to accomplish it:

1. We are going to launch a block object asynchronously on a concurrent queue.

2. Once in this block, we will launch another block object *synchronously*, using the `dispatch_sync` function, to download the image from a URL. We do this because we want the rest of the code in this concurrent queue to wait until the image is downloaded. Therefore, we are only making the concurrent queue wait; not the rest of the queues. Synchronously downloading a URL from an asynchronous code block holds up just the queue running the synchronous function, not the main thread. The whole operation is still asynchronous when we look at it from the main thread's perspective. All we care about is that we are not blocking the main thread while downloading the image.

3. Right after the image is downloaded, we will synchronously execute a block object on the *main queue* (see Recipe 6.5) in order to display the image to the user on the UI.

The skeleton for the plan is as simple as this:

```
dispatch_queue_t concurrentQueue =
  dispatch_get_global_queue(DISPATCH_QUEUE_PRIORITY_DEFAULT, 0);

dispatch_async(concurrentQueue, ^{

  __block UIImage *image = nil;

  dispatch_sync(concurrentQueue, ^{
    /* Download the image here */
  });

  dispatch_sync(dispatch_get_main_queue(), ^{
    /* Show the image to the user here on the main queue*/
  });

});
```

The second `dispatch_sync` call, which displays the image, will be executed on the queue after the first synchronous call, which downloads the image. That's exactly what we want, because we *have* to wait for the image to be fully downloaded before we can display it to the user. So after the image is downloaded, we execute the second block object, but this time on the main queue.

Let's download the image and display it to the user now. We will do this in the `viewDidAppear:` instance method of a view controller displayed in an iPhone app:

```
- (void) viewDidAppear:(BOOL)paramAnimated{

  dispatch_queue_t concurrentQueue =
  dispatch_get_global_queue(DISPATCH_QUEUE_PRIORITY_DEFAULT, 0);

  dispatch_async(concurrentQueue, ^{
```

```objc
__block UIImage *image = nil;

dispatch_sync(concurrentQueue, ^{
  /* Download the image here */

  /* iPad's image from Apple's website. Wrap it into two
   lines as the URL is too long to fit into one line */
  NSString *urlAsString = @"http://images.apple.com/mobileme/features"\
                          "/images/ipad_findyouripad_20100518.jpg";

  NSURL *url = [NSURL URLWithString:urlAsString];

  NSURLRequest *urlRequest = [NSURLRequest requestWithURL:url];

  NSError *downloadError = nil;
  NSData *imageData = [NSURLConnection
                        sendSynchronousRequest:urlRequest
                        returningResponse:nil
                        error:&downloadError];

  if (downloadError == nil &&
      imageData != nil){

    image = [UIImage imageWithData:imageData];
    /* We have the image. We can use it now */

  }
  else if (downloadError != nil){
    NSLog(@"Error happened = %@", downloadError);
  } else {
    NSLog(@"No data could get downloaded from the URL.");
  }

});

dispatch_sync(dispatch_get_main_queue(), ^{
  /* Show the image to the user here on the main queue*/

  if (image != nil){
    /* Create the image view here */
    UIImageView *imageView = [[UIImageView alloc]
                              initWithFrame:self.view.bounds];

    /* Set the image */
    [imageView setImage:image];

    /* Make sure the image is not scaled incorrectly */
    [imageView setContentMode:UIViewContentModeScaleAspectFit];

    /* Add the image to this view controller's view */
    [self.view addSubview:imageView];

  } else {
    NSLog(@"Image isn't downloaded. Nothing to display.");
```

```
            }
        });

    });

}
```

As you can see in Figure 6-2, we have successfully downloaded the image and also created an image view to display the image to the user on the UI.

Figure 6-2. Downloading and displaying images to users, using GCD

Let's move on to another example. Let's say that we have an array of 10,000 random numbers that have been stored in a file on disk and we want to load this array into memory, sort the numbers in an ascending fashion (with the smallest number appearing first in the list), and then display the list to the user. The control used for the display depends on whether you are coding this for iOS (ideally, you'd use an instance of UITableView) or Mac OS X (NSTableView would be a good candidate). Since we don't have an array, why don't we create the array first, then load it, and finally display it?

Here are two methods that will help us find the location where we want to save the array of 10,000 random numbers on disk on the device:

```
- (NSString *) fileLocation{

    /* Get the document folder(s) */
    NSArray *folders =
    NSSearchPathForDirectoriesInDomains(NSDocumentDirectory,
                                        NSUserDomainMask,
                                        YES);
```

```
/* Did we find anything? */
if ([folders count] == 0){
  return nil;
}

/* Get the first folder */
NSString *documentsFolder = [folders objectAtIndex:0];

/* Append the file name to the end of the documents path */
return [documentsFolder
        stringByAppendingPathComponent:@"list.txt"];

}

- (BOOL) hasFileAlreadyBeenCreated{

  BOOL result = NO;

  NSFileManager *fileManager = [[NSFileManager alloc] init];
  if ([fileManager fileExistsAtPath:[self fileLocation]]){
    result = YES;
  }

  return result;
}
```

Now the important part: we want to save an array of 10,000 random numbers to disk *if and only if* we have not created this array before on disk. If we have, we will load the array from disk immediately. If we have not created this array before on disk, we will first create it and then move on to loading it from disk. At the end, if the array was successfully read from disk, we will sort the array in an ascending fashion and finally display the results to the user on the UI. I will leave displaying the results to the user up to you:

```
dispatch_queue_t concurrentQueue =
  dispatch_get_global_queue(DISPATCH_QUEUE_PRIORITY_DEFAULT, 0);

/* If we have not already saved an array of 10,000
 random numbers to the disk before, generate these numbers now
 and then save them to the disk in an array */
dispatch_async(concurrentQueue, ^{

  NSUInteger numberOfValuesRequired = 10000;

  if ([self hasFileAlreadyBeenCreated] == NO){
    dispatch_sync(concurrentQueue, ^{

      NSMutableArray *arrayOfRandomNumbers =
      [[NSMutableArray alloc] initWithCapacity:numberOfValuesRequired];

      NSUInteger counter = 0;
      for (counter = 0;
           counter < numberOfValuesRequired;
           counter++){
```

```
      unsigned int randomNumber =
      arc4random() % ((unsigned int)RAND_MAX + 1);

      [arrayOfRandomNumbers addObject:
       [NSNumber numberWithUnsignedInt:randomNumber]];
    }

    /* Now let's write the array to disk */
    [arrayOfRandomNumbers writeToFile:[self fileLocation]
                          atomically:YES];

  });
}

__block NSMutableArray *randomNumbers = nil;

/* Read the numbers from disk and sort them in an
 ascending fashion */
dispatch_sync(concurrentQueue, ^{

  /* If the file has now been created, we have to read it */
  if ([self hasFileAlreadyBeenCreated]){
    randomNumbers = [[NSMutableArray alloc]
                     initWithContentsOfFile:[self fileLocation]];

    /* Now sort the numbers */
    [randomNumbers sortUsingComparator:
     ^NSComparisonResult(id obj1, id obj2) {

        NSNumber *number1 = (NSNumber *)obj1;
        NSNumber *number2 = (NSNumber *)obj2;
        return [number1 compare:number2];

     }];
  }
});


dispatch_async(dispatch_get_main_queue(), ^{
  if ([randomNumbers count] > 0){
    /* Refresh the UI here using the numbers in the
     randomNumbers array */
  }
});

});
```

There is a lot more to GCD than synchronous and asynchronous block or function execution. In Recipe 6.10, you will learn how to group block objects together and prepare them for execution on a dispatch queue. I also suggest that you have a look at Recipes 6.8 and 6.9 to learn about other functionalities that GCD can provide to programmers.

See Also

Recipe 6.5; Recipe 6.8; Recipe 6.9

6.8 Performing Tasks After a Delay with GCD

Problem

You want to be able to execute code, but after a certain amount of delay, which you would like to specify using GCD.

Solution

Use the dispatch_after and dispatch_after_f functions.

Discussion

With Core Foundation, you can invoke a selector in an object after a given period of time, using the performSelector:withObject:afterDelay: method of the NSObject class. Here is an example:

```
- (void) printString:(NSString *)paramString{
  NSLog(@"%@", paramString);
}

- (BOOL)             application:(UIApplication *)application
  didFinishLaunchingWithOptions:(NSDictionary *)launchOptions{

  [self performSelector:@selector(printString:)
             withObject:@"Grand Central Dispatch"
             afterDelay:3.0];

  self.window = [[UIWindow alloc] initWithFrame:
                 [[UIScreen mainScreen] bounds]];

  // Override point for customization after application launch.
  self.window.backgroundColor = [UIColor whiteColor];
  [self.window makeKeyAndVisible];
  return YES;
}
```

In this example, we are asking the runtime to call the printString: method after three seconds of delay. We can do the same thing in GCD using the dispatch_after and dispatch_after_f functions, each of which is described here:

dispatch_after
   Dispatches a block object to a dispatch queue after a given period of time, specified in nanoseconds. These are the parameters that this function requires:

Delay in nanoseconds

The number of nanoseconds GCD has to wait on a given dispatch queue (specified by the second parameter) before it executes the given block object (specified by the third parameter).

Dispatch queue

The dispatch queue on which the block object (specified by the third parameter) has to be executed after the given delay (specified by the first parameter).

Block object

The block object to be invoked after the specified number of nanoseconds on the given dispatch queue. This block object should have no return value and should accept no parameters (see Recipe 6.1).

`dispatch_after_f`

Dispatches a C function to GCD for execution after a given period of time, specified in nanoseconds. This function accepts four parameters:

Delay in nanoseconds

The number of nanoseconds GCD has to wait on a given dispatch queue (specified by the second parameter) before it executes the given function (specified by the fourth parameter).

Dispatch queue

The dispatch queue on which the C function (specified by the fourth parameter) has to be executed after the given delay (specified by the first parameter).

Context

The memory address of a value in the heap to be passed to the C function (for an example, see Recipe 6.5).

C function

The address of the C function that has to be executed after a certain period of time (specified by the first parameter) on the given dispatch queue (specified by the second parameter).

 Although the delays are in nanoseconds, it is up to iOS to decide the granularity of dispatch delay, and this delay might not be as precise as what you hope when you specify a value in nanoseconds.

Let's have a look at an example for `dispatch_after` first:

```
double delayInSeconds = 2.0;

dispatch_time_t delayInNanoSeconds =
  dispatch_time(DISPATCH_TIME_NOW, delayInSeconds * NSEC_PER_SEC);

dispatch_queue_t concurrentQueue =
  dispatch_get_global_queue(DISPATCH_QUEUE_PRIORITY_DEFAULT, 0);
```

```
dispatch_after(delayInNanoSeconds, concurrentQueue, ^(void){
  /* Perform your operations here */
});
```

As you can see, the nanoseconds delay parameter for both the dispatch_after and dispatch_after_f functions has to be of type dispatch_time_t, which is an abstract representation of absolute time. To get the value for this parameter, you can use the dispatch_time function as demonstrated in this sample code. Here are the parameters that you can pass to the dispatch_time function:

Base time
> If this value was denoted with *B* and the delta parameter was denoted with *D*, the resulting time from this function would be equal to *B* + *D*. You can set this parameter's value to DISPATCH_TIME_NOW to denote *now* as the base time and then specify the delta from now using the delta parameter.

Delta to add to base time
> This parameter is the nanoseconds that will get added to the base time parameter to create the result of this function.

For example, to denote a time 3 seconds from now, you could write your code like so:

```
dispatch_time_t delay =
dispatch_time(DISPATCH_TIME_NOW, 3.0f * NSEC_PER_SEC);
```

Or to denote half a second from now:

```
dispatch_time_t delay =
dispatch_time(DISPATCH_TIME_NOW, (1.0 / 2.0f) * NSEC_PER_SEC);
```

Now let's have a look at how we can use the dispatch_after_f function:

```
void processSomething(void *paramContext){
  /* Do your processing here */
  NSLog(@"Processing...");
}

- (BOOL)            application:(UIApplication *)application
  didFinishLaunchingWithOptions:(NSDictionary *)launchOptions{

  double delayInSeconds = 2.0;

  dispatch_time_t delayInNanoSeconds =
    dispatch_time(DISPATCH_TIME_NOW, delayInSeconds * NSEC_PER_SEC);

  dispatch_queue_t concurrentQueue =
    dispatch_get_global_queue(DISPATCH_QUEUE_PRIORITY_DEFAULT, 0);

  dispatch_after_f(delayInNanoSeconds,
                   concurrentQueue,
                   NULL,
                   processSomething);

  self.window = [[UIWindow alloc] initWithFrame:
                  [[UIScreen mainScreen] bounds]];
```

```
    // Override point for customization after application launch.
    self.window.backgroundColor = [UIColor whiteColor];
    [self.window makeKeyAndVisible];
    return YES;
}
```

See Also

Recipe 6.1; Recipe 6.5

6.9 Performing a Task Only Once with GCD

Problem

You want to make sure a piece of code gets executed only once during the lifetime of your application, even if it gets called more than once from different places in your code (such as the initializer for a singleton).

Solution

Use the dispatch_once function.

Discussion

Allocating and initializing a singleton is one of the tasks that has to happen exactly once during the lifetime of an app. I am sure you know of other scenarios where you had to make sure a piece of code was executed only once during the lifetime of your application.

GCD lets you specify an identifier for a piece of code when you attempt to execute it. If GCD detects that this identifier has been passed to the framework before, it won't execute that block of code again. The function that allows you to do this is dis patch_once, which accepts two parameters:

Token
> A token of type dispatch_once_t that holds the token generated by GCD when the block of code is executed for the first time. If you want a piece of code to be executed at most once, you must specify the same token to this method whenever it is invoked in the app. We will see an example of this soon.

Block object
> The block object to get executed at most once. This block object returns no values and accepts no parameters.

dispatch_once always executes its task on the current queue being used by the code that issues the call, be it a serial queue, a concurrent queue, or the main queue.

Here is an example:

```
static dispatch_once_t onceToken;

void (^executedOnlyOnce)(void) = ^{

  static NSUInteger numberOfEntries = 0;
  numberOfEntries++;
  NSLog(@"Executed %lu time(s)", (unsigned long)numberOfEntries);

};


- (BOOL)              application:(UIApplication *)application
    didFinishLaunchingWithOptions:(NSDictionary *)launchOptions{

  dispatch_queue_t concurrentQueue =
    dispatch_get_global_queue(DISPATCH_QUEUE_PRIORITY_DEFAULT, 0);

  dispatch_once(&onceToken, ^{
    dispatch_async(concurrentQueue,
                   executedOnlyOnce);
  });

  dispatch_once(&onceToken, ^{
    dispatch_async(concurrentQueue,
                   executedOnlyOnce);
  });

  self.window = [[UIWindow alloc] initWithFrame:
                    [[UIScreen mainScreen] bounds]];

  self.window.backgroundColor = [UIColor whiteColor];
  [self.window makeKeyAndVisible];
  return YES;

}
```

As you can see, although we are attempting to invoke the executedOnlyOnce block object twice, using the dispatch_once function, in reality GCD is only executing this block object once, since the identifier passed to the dispatch_once function is the same both times.

Apple, in its Cocoa Fundamentals Guide (*http://bit.ly/TOj3IU*), shows programmers how to create a singleton. This source code is quite old and has *not yet been updated* to use GCD and Automatic Reference Counting. We can change this model to make use of GCD and the dispatch_once function in order to initialize a shared instance of an object, like so:

```
#import "MySingleton.h"

@implementation MySingleton

- (id) sharedInstance{
  static MySingleton *SharedInstance = nil;
  static dispatch_once_t onceToken;
  dispatch_once(&onceToken, ^{
    SharedInstance = [MySingleton new];
  });
  return SharedInstance;
}

@end
```

6.10 Grouping Tasks Together with GCD

Problem

You want to group blocks of code together and ensure that all of them get executed by GCD one by one, as dependencies of one another.

Solution

Use the `dispatch_group_create` function to create groups in GCD.

Discussion

GCD lets us create *groups*, which allow you to place your tasks in one place, run all of them, and get a notification at the end from GCD. This has many valuable applications. For instance, suppose you have a UI-based app and want to reload the components on your UI. You have a table view, a scroll view, and an image view. You want to reload the contents of these components using these methods:

```
- (void) reloadTableView{
  /* Reload the table view here */
  NSLog(@"%s", __FUNCTION__);
}

- (void) reloadScrollView{
  /* Do the work here */
  NSLog(@"%s", __FUNCTION__);
}

- (void) reloadImageView{
  /* Reload the image view here */
  NSLog(@"%s", __FUNCTION__);
}
```

At the moment these methods are empty, but you can put the relevant UI code in them later. Now we want to call these three methods, one after the other, and we want to know when GCD has finished calling these methods so that we can display a message to the user. For this, we should be using a group. You should know about four functions when working with groups in GCD:

dispatch_group_create

    Creates a group handle. Once you are done with this group handle, you should dispose of it using the `dispatch_release` function.

dispatch_group_async

    Submits a block of code for execution on a group. You must specify the dispatch queue on which the block of code has to be executed *as well as* the group to which this block of code belongs.

dispatch_group_notify

    Allows you to submit a block object that should be executed once all tasks added to the group for execution have finished their work. This function also allows you to specify the dispatch queue on which that block object has to be executed.

dispatch_release

    Use this function to dispose of any dispatch groups that you create using the `dispatch_group_create` function.

Let's have a look at an example. As explained, in the example we want to invoke the `reloadTableView`, `reloadScrollView`, and `reloadImageView` methods one after the other and then display a message to the user once we are done. We can utilize GCD's powerful grouping facilities in order to accomplish this:

```
dispatch_group_t taskGroup = dispatch_group_create();
dispatch_queue_t mainQueue = dispatch_get_main_queue();

/* Reload the table view on the main queue */
dispatch_group_async(taskGroup, mainQueue, ^{
  [self reloadTableView];
});

/* Reload the scroll view on the main queue */
dispatch_group_async(taskGroup, mainQueue, ^{
  [self reloadScrollView];
});

/* Reload the image view on the main queue */
dispatch_group_async(taskGroup, mainQueue, ^{
  [self reloadImageView];
});

/* At the end when we are done, dispatch the following block */
dispatch_group_notify(taskGroup, mainQueue, ^{
  /* Do some processing here */
  [[[UIAlertView alloc] initWithTitle:@"Finished"
                              message:@"All tasks are finished"
                             delegate:nil
                    cancelButtonTitle:@"OK"
                    otherButtonTitles:nil, nil] show];
```

```
  });

  /* We are done with the group */
  dispatch_release(taskGroup);
```

In addition to dispatch_group_async, you can also dispatch asynchronous C functions to a dispatch group using the dispatch_group_async_f function.

 GCDAppDelegate is simply the name of the class from which this example is taken. We have to use this class name in order to typecast a context object so that the compiler will understand the commands.

Like so:

```
void reloadAllComponents(void *context){

  Grouping_Tasks_Together_with_GCDAppDelegate *self =
    (__bridge Grouping_Tasks_Together_with_GCDAppDelegate *)context;

  [self reloadTableView];
  [self reloadScrollView];
  [self reloadImageView];

}

- (BOOL)               application:(UIApplication *)application
    didFinishLaunchingWithOptions:(NSDictionary *)launchOptions{

  dispatch_group_t taskGroup = dispatch_group_create();
  dispatch_queue_t mainQueue = dispatch_get_main_queue();

  dispatch_group_async_f(taskGroup,
                         mainQueue,
                         (__bridge void *)self,
                         reloadAllComponents);

  /* At the end when we are done, dispatch the following block */
  dispatch_group_notify(taskGroup, mainQueue, ^{
    /* Do some processing here */
    [[[UIAlertView alloc] initWithTitle:@"Finished"
                                message:@"All tasks are finished"
                               delegate:nil
                      cancelButtonTitle:@"OK"
                      otherButtonTitles:nil, nil] show];

  });

  /* We are done with the group */
  dispatch_release(taskGroup);

  self.window = [[UIWindow alloc] initWithFrame:
                 [[UIScreen mainScreen] bounds]];
```

```
    self.window.backgroundColor = [UIColor whiteColor];
    [self.window makeKeyAndVisible];
    return YES;
}
```

 Since the dispatch_group_async_f function accepts a C function as the block of code to be executed, the C function must have a reference to self to be able to invoke instance methods of the current object in which the C function is implemented. That is the reason behind passing self as the context pointer in the dispatch_group_async_f function. For more information about contexts and C functions, please refer to Recipe 6.5.

Once all the given tasks are finished, the user will see a result similar to that shown in Figure 6-3.

Figure 6-3. Managing a group of tasks with GCD

See Also

Recipe 6.5

6.11 Constructing Your Own Dispatch Queues with GCD

Problem

You want to create your own uniquely named dispatch queues.

Solution

Use the `dispatch_queue_create` function.

Discussion

With GCD, you can create your own serial dispatch queues (see Recipe 6.0 to read about serial queues). Serial dispatch queues run their tasks in a first-in-first-out (FIFO) fashion. The asynchronous tasks on serial queues will *not* be performed on the main thread, however, making serial queues highly desirable for concurrent FIFO tasks.

All synchronous tasks submitted to a serial queue will be executed on the current thread being used by the code that is submitting the task, whenever possible. But asynchronous tasks submitted to a serial queue will always be executed on a thread other than the main thread.

We'll use the `dispatch_queue_create` function to create serial queues. The first parameter in this function is a C string (`char *`) that will uniquely identify that serial queue in the *system*. The reason I am emphasizing *system* is because this identifier is a system-wide identifier, meaning that if your app creates a new serial queue with the identifier of *serialQueue1* and somebody else's app does the same, the results of creating a new serial queue with the same name are undefined by GCD. Because of this, Apple strongly recommends that you use a reverse DNS format for identifiers. Reverse DNS identifiers are usually constructed in this way: com.*COMPANY*. *PRODUCT*. *IDENTIFIER*. For instance, I could create two serial queues and assign these names to them:

```
com.pixolity.GCD.serialQueue1
com.pixolity.GCD.serialQueue2
```

After you've created your serial queue, you can start dispatching tasks to it using the various GCD functions you've learned in this book. Once you are done with the serial dispatch queue that you've just created, you *must* dispose of it using the `dispatch_release` function.

Would you like to see an example? I thought so!

```
dispatch_queue_t firstSerialQueue =
dispatch_queue_create("com.pixolity.GCD.serialQueue1", 0);

dispatch_async(firstSerialQueue, ^{
  NSUInteger counter = 0;
  for (counter = 0;
       counter < 5;
       counter++){
    NSLog(@"First iteration, counter = %lu", (unsigned long)counter);
  }
});

dispatch_async(firstSerialQueue, ^{
  NSUInteger counter = 0;
  for (counter = 0;
```

```
            counter < 5;
            counter++){
        NSLog(@"Second iteration, counter = %lu", (unsigned long)counter);
      }
});

dispatch_async(firstSerialQueue, ^{
  NSUInteger counter = 0;
  for (counter = 0;
       counter < 5;
       counter++){
      NSLog(@"Third iteration, counter = %lu", (unsigned long)counter);
    }
});

dispatch_release(firstSerialQueue);
```

If you run this code and have a look at the output printed to the console window, you will see results similar to these:

```
First iteration, counter = 0
First iteration, counter = 1
First iteration, counter = 2
First iteration, counter = 3
First iteration, counter = 4
Second iteration, counter = 0
Second iteration, counter = 1
Second iteration, counter = 2
Second iteration, counter = 3
Second iteration, counter = 4
Third iteration, counter = 0
Third iteration, counter = 1
Third iteration, counter = 2
Third iteration, counter = 3
Third iteration, counter = 4
```

It's obvious that, although we dispatched the block objects asynchronously to the serial queue, the queue has executed their code in a FIFO fashion. We can modify the same sample code to make use of dispatch_async_f function instead of the dispatch_async function, like so:

```
void firstIteration(void *paramContext){

  NSUInteger counter = 0;
  for (counter = 0;
       counter < 5;
       counter++){
    NSLog(@"First iteration, counter = %lu", (unsigned long)counter);
  }
}

void secondIteration(void *paramContext){

  NSUInteger counter = 0;
  for (counter = 0;
```

```
      counter < 5;
      counter++){
    NSLog(@"Second iteration, counter = %lu", (unsigned long)counter);
  }
}

void thirdIteration(void *paramContext){

  NSUInteger counter = 0;
  for (counter = 0;
      counter < 5;
      counter++){
    NSLog(@"Third iteration, counter = %lu", (unsigned long)counter);
  }
}

- (BOOL)              application:(UIApplication *)application
  didFinishLaunchingWithOptions:(NSDictionary *)launchOptions{

  dispatch_queue_t firstSerialQueue =
  dispatch_queue_create("com.pixolity.GCD.serialQueue1", 0);

  dispatch_async_f(firstSerialQueue, NULL, firstIteration);
  dispatch_async_f(firstSerialQueue, NULL, secondIteration);
  dispatch_async_f(firstSerialQueue, NULL, thirdIteration);

  dispatch_release(firstSerialQueue);

  self.window = [[UIWindow alloc] initWithFrame:
                [[UIScreen mainScreen] bounds]];
  self.window.backgroundColor = [UIColor whiteColor];
  [self.window makeKeyAndVisible];
  return YES;
}
```

6.12 Running Tasks Synchronously with Operations

Problem

You want to run a series of tasks synchronously.

Solution

Create operations and start them manually:

```
#import <UIKit/UIKit.h>

@interface Running_Tasks_Synchronously_with_OperationsAppDelegate
          : UIResponder <UIApplicationDelegate>
```

```
@property (strong, nonatomic) UIWindow *window;
@property (nonatomic, strong) NSInvocationOperation *simpleOperation;

@end
```

The implementation of the application delegate is as follows:

```
- (void) simpleOperationEntry:(id)paramObject{

    NSLog(@"Parameter Object = %@", paramObject);
    NSLog(@"Main Thread = %@", [NSThread mainThread]);
    NSLog(@"Current Thread = %@", [NSThread currentThread]);

}

- (BOOL)              application:(UIApplication *)application
    didFinishLaunchingWithOptions:(NSDictionary *)launchOptions{

    NSNumber *simpleObject = [NSNumber numberWithInteger:123];

    self.simpleOperation = [[NSInvocationOperation alloc]
                            initWithTarget:self
                            selector:@selector(simpleOperationEntry:)
                            object:simpleObject];

    [self.simpleOperation start];

    self.window = [[UIWindow alloc] initWithFrame:
                   [[UIScreen mainScreen] bounds]];
    self.window.backgroundColor = [UIColor whiteColor];
    [self.window makeKeyAndVisible];
    return YES;
}
```

The output of this program (in the console window) will be similar to this:

```
Parameter Object = 123
Main Thread = <NSThread: 0x6810280>{name = (null), num = 1}
Current Thread = <NSThread: 0x6810280>{name = (null), num = 1}
```

As the name of this class implies (NSInvocationOperation), the main responsibility of an object of this type is to invoke a method in an object. This is the most straightforward way to invoke a method inside an object using operations.

Discussion

An invocation operation, as described in this chapter's Introduction, is able to invoke a method inside an object. "What is so special about this?" you might ask. The invocation operation's power can be demonstrated when it is added to an operation queue. With an operation queue, an invocation operation can invoke a method in a target object asynchronously and in parallel to the thread that started the operation. If you have a look at the output printed to the console (in this recipe's Solution), you will notice that the current thread inside the method invoked by the invocation operation is the same as the main thread since the main thread in the `application:didFin` `ishLaunchingWithOptions:` method started the operation using its `start` method. In Recipe 6.13, we will learn how to take advantage of operation queues to run tasks asynchronously.

In addition to invocation operations, you can use block or plain operations to perform tasks synchronously. Here is an example using a block operation to count numbers from zero to 999 (inside the *.h* file of the application delegate):

```
#import <UIKit/UIKit.h>

@interface Running_Tasks_Synchronously_with_OperationsAppDelegate
        : UIResponder <UIApplicationDelegate>

@property (strong, nonatomic) UIWindow *window;
@property (nonatomic, strong) NSBlockOperation *simpleOperation;

@end
```

Here is the implementation of the application delegate (*.m* file):

```
- (BOOL)               application:(UIApplication *)application
  didFinishLaunchingWithOptions:(NSDictionary *)launchOptions{

  self.simpleOperation = [NSBlockOperation blockOperationWithBlock:^{
    NSLog(@"Main Thread = %@", [NSThread mainThread]);
    NSLog(@"Current Thread = %@", [NSThread currentThread]);
    NSUInteger counter = 0;
    for (counter = 0;
         counter < 1000;
         counter++){
      NSLog(@"Count = %lu", (unsigned long)counter);
    }
  }];

  /* Start the operation */
  [self.simpleOperation start];
  /* Print something out just to test if we have to wait
   for the block to execute its code or not */
  NSLog(@"Main thread is here");

  self.window = [[UIWindow alloc] initWithFrame:
                 [[UIScreen mainScreen] bounds]];
  self.window.backgroundColor = [UIColor whiteColor];
  [self.window makeKeyAndVisible];
  return YES;
}
```

If we run the application, we will see the values 0 to 999 printed out to the screen followed by the "Main thread is here" message, like this:

```
Main Thread = <NSThread: 0x6810280>{name = (null), num = 1}
Current Thread = <NSThread: 0x6810280>{name = (null), num = 1}
...
Count = 991
```

```
Count = 992
Count = 993
Count = 994
Count = 995
Count = 996
Count = 997
Count = 998
Count = 999
Main thread is here
```

This proves that since the block operation was started in the `application:didFinish` `LaunchingWithOptions:` method, which itself runs on the main thread, the code inside the block was also running on the main thread. The main point to take from the log messages is that the operation blocked the main thread and the main thread's code continued to be executed after the work for the block operation was done. This is a very bad programming practice. In fact, iOS developers must perform any trick and use any technique that they know of to keep the main thread responsive so that it can do the key job of processing users' input. Here is what Apple has to say about this:

> You should be careful what work you perform from the main thread of your application. The main thread is where your application handles touch events and other user input. To ensure that your application is always responsive to the user, you should never use the main thread to perform long-running tasks or to perform tasks with a potentially unbounded end, such as tasks that access the network. Instead, you should always move those tasks onto background threads. The preferred way to do so is to wrap each task in an operation object and add it to an operation queue, but you can also create explicit threads yourself.

To read more about this subject, browse through the "Performance Tuning" document in the iOS Reference Library, available at this URL (*http://bit.ly/RGuYIJ*).

In addition to invocation and block operations, you can also subclass `NSOperation` and perform your task in that class. Before getting started, you must keep a few things in mind while subclassing `NSOperation`:

- If you are not planning on using an operation queue, you have to detach a new thread of your own in the **start** method of the operation. If you do not want to use an operation queue and you do not want your operation to run asynchronously from other operations that you start manually, you can simply call the `main` method of your operation inside the **start** method.

- Two important methods in an instance of `NSOperation` must be overridden by your own implementation of the operation: `isExecuting` and `isFinished`. These can be called from any other object. In these methods, you must return a thread-safe value that you can manipulate from inside the operation. As soon as your operation starts, you must, through KVO, inform any listeners that you are changing the values that these two methods return. We will see how this works in the example code.

- You must provide your own autorelease pool inside the main method of the operation in case your operation will be added to an operation queue at some point in the future. You must make sure your operations work in both ways: whether you start them manually or they get started by an operation queue.
- You must have an initialization method for your operations. There must be only one designated initializer method per operation. All other initializer methods, including the default init method of an operation, must call the designated initializer that has the most number of parameters. Other initializer methods must make sure they pass appropriate parameters (if any) to the designated initializer.

Here is the declaration of the operation object (.h file):

```
#import <Foundation/Foundation.h>

@interface CountingOperation : NSOperation

/* Designated Initializer */
- (id) initWithStartingCount:(NSUInteger)paramStartingCount
              endingCount:(NSUInteger)paramEndingCount;

@end
```

The implementation (.m file) of the operation might be a bit long, but hopefully it's easy to understand:

```
#import "CountingOperation.h"

@implementation CountingOperation

NSUInteger    startingCount;
NSUInteger    endingCount;
BOOL          finished;
BOOL          executing;

- (id) init {
  return([self initWithStartingCount:0
                         endingCount:1000]);
}

- (id) initWithStartingCount:(NSUInteger)paramStartingCount
              endingCount:(NSUInteger)paramEndingCount{

  self = [super init];

  if (self != nil){

    /* Keep these values for the main method */
    startingCount = paramStartingCount;
    endingCount = paramEndingCount;

  }

  return(self);
```

```objc
}

- (void) start {

  /* If we are cancelled before starting, then
   we have to return immediately and generate the
   required KVO notifications */
  if ([self isCancelled]){
    /* If this operation *is* cancelled */
    /* KVO compliance */
    [self willChangeValueForKey:@"isFinished"];
    finished = YES;
    [self didChangeValueForKey:@"isFinished"];
    return;

  } else {
    /* If this operation is *not* cancelled */
    /* KVO compliance */
    [self willChangeValueForKey:@"isExecuting"];
    executing = YES;
    /* Call the main method from inside the start method */
    [self didChangeValueForKey:@"isExecuting"];
    [self main];

  }

}

- (void) main {

  @try {
    /* Here is the autorelease pool */
    @autoreleasepool {
      /* Keep a local variable here that must get set to YES
             whenever we are done with the task */
      BOOL taskIsFinished = NO;

      /* Create a while loop here that only exists
       if the taskIsFinished variable is set to YES or
       the operation has been cancelled */
      while (taskIsFinished == NO &&
             [self isCancelled] == NO){

        /* Perform the task here */
        NSLog(@"Main Thread = %@", [NSThread mainThread]);
        NSLog(@"Current Thread = %@", [NSThread currentThread]);
        NSUInteger counter = startingCount;
        for (counter = startingCount;
             counter < endingCount;
             counter++){
          NSLog(@"Count = %lu", (unsigned long)counter);
        }
```

```
              /* Very important. This way we can get out of the
               loop and we are still complying with the cancellation
               rules of operations */
              taskIsFinished = YES;

          }

          /* KVO compliance. Generate the
           required KVO notifications */
          [self willChangeValueForKey:@"isFinished"];
          [self willChangeValueForKey:@"isExecuting"];
          finished = YES;
          executing = NO;
          [self didChangeValueForKey:@"isFinished"];
          [self didChangeValueForKey:@"isExecuting"];
        }
      }
      @catch (NSException * e) {
        NSLog(@"Exception %@", e);
      }

  }

  - (BOOL)  isFinished{
    /* Simply return the value */
    return(finished);
  }

  - (BOOL)  isExecuting{
    /* Simply return the value */
    return(executing);
  }

  @end
```

We can start this operation like so:

```
#import "Running_Tasks_Synchronously_with_OperationsAppDelegate.h"
#import "CountingOperation.h"

@implementation Running_Tasks_Synchronously_with_OperationsAppDelegate

- (BOOL)              application:(UIApplication *)application
  didFinishLaunchingWithOptions:(NSDictionary *)launchOptions{

  self.simpleOperation = [[CountingOperation alloc] initWithStartingCount:0
                                                           endingCount:1000];

  [self.simpleOperation start];

  NSLog(@"Main thread is here");

  self.window = [[UIWindow alloc] initWithFrame:
               [[UIScreen mainScreen] bounds]];
  self.window.backgroundColor = [UIColor whiteColor];
```

```
    [self.window makeKeyAndVisible];
    return YES;
}

@end
```

If we run the code, we will see the following results in the console window, just as we did when we used a block operation:

```
Main Thread = <NSThread: 0x6810260>{name = (null), num = 1}
Current Thread = <NSThread: 0x6810260>{name = (null), num = 1}
...
Count = 993
Count = 994
Count = 995
Count = 996
Count = 997
Count = 998
Count = 999
Main thread is here
```

See Also

Recipe 6.13

6.13 Running Tasks Asynchronously with Operations

Problem

You want to execute operations concurrently.

Solution

Use operation queues. Alternatively, subclass NSOperation and detach a new thread on the main method.

Discussion

As mentioned in Recipe 6.12, operations, by default, run on the thread that calls the start method. Usually we start operations on the main thread, but at the same time we expect the operations to run on their own threads and not take the main thread's time slice. The best solution for us would be to use operation queues. However, if you want to manage your operations manually, which I do not recommend, you can subclass NSOperation and detach a new thread on the main method. Please refer to Recipe 6.16 for more information about detached threads.

Let's go ahead and use an operation queue and add two simple invocation operations to it. (For more information about invocation operations, please refer to this chapter's Introduction. For additional example code on invocation operations, please refer to

---

Recipe 6.12.) Here is the declaration (.*h* file) of the application delegate that utilizes an operation queue and two invocation operations:

```objc
#import <UIKit/UIKit.h>

@interface Running_Tasks_Asynchronously_with_OperationsAppDelegate
          : UIResponder <UIApplicationDelegate>

@property (nonatomic, strong) UIWindow *window;
@property (nonatomic, strong) NSOperationQueue      *operationQueue;
@property (nonatomic, strong) NSInvocationOperation *firstOperation;
@property (nonatomic, strong) NSInvocationOperation *secondOperation;

@end
```

The implementation (.*m* file) of the application delegate is as follows:

```objc
#import "Running_Tasks_Asynchronously_with_OperationsAppDelegate.h"

@implementation Running_Tasks_Asynchronously_with_OperationsAppDelegate

- (void) firstOperationEntry:(id)paramObject{

  NSLog(@"%s", __FUNCTION__);
  NSLog(@"Parameter Object = %@", paramObject);
  NSLog(@"Main Thread = %@", [NSThread mainThread]);
  NSLog(@"Current Thread = %@", [NSThread currentThread]);

}

- (void) secondOperationEntry:(id)paramObject{

  NSLog(@"%s", __FUNCTION__);
  NSLog(@"Parameter Object = %@", paramObject);
  NSLog(@"Main Thread = %@", [NSThread mainThread]);
  NSLog(@"Current Thread = %@", [NSThread currentThread]);

}

- (BOOL)              application:(UIApplication *)application
  didFinishLaunchingWithOptions:(NSDictionary *)launchOptions{

  NSNumber *firstNumber = [NSNumber numberWithInteger:111];
  NSNumber *secondNumber = [NSNumber numberWithInteger:222];

  self.firstOperation =[[NSInvocationOperation alloc]
                        initWithTarget:self
                        selector:@selector(firstOperationEntry:)
                        object:firstNumber];

  self.secondOperation = [[NSInvocationOperation alloc]
                          initWithTarget:self
                          selector:@selector(secondOperationEntry:)
                          object:secondNumber];

  self.operationQueue = [[NSOperationQueue alloc] init];
```

```
/* Add the operations to the queue */
[self.operationQueue addOperation:self.firstOperation];
[self.operationQueue addOperation:self.secondOperation];

NSLog(@"Main thread is here");

self.window = [[UIWindow alloc] initWithFrame:
               [[UIScreen mainScreen] bounds]];
self.window.backgroundColor = [UIColor whiteColor];
[self.window makeKeyAndVisible];
return YES;
}

@end
```

Here is what is happening in the implementation of the code:

- We have two methods: `firstOperationEntry:` and `secondOperationEntry:`. Each method accepts an object as a parameter and prints out the current thread, the main thread, and the parameter to the console window. These are the entry methods of the invocation operations that will be added to an operation queue.

- We initialize two objects of type `NSInvocationOperation` and set the target selector to each operation entry point described previously.

- We then initialize an object of type `NSOperationQueue`. (It could also be created before the entry methods.) The queue object will be responsible for managing the concurrency in the operation objects.

- We invoke the `addOperation:` instance method of `NSOperationQueue` to add each invocation operation to the operation queue. At this point, the operation queue may or may not immediately start the invocation operations through their `start` methods. However, it is very important to bear in mind that after adding operations to an operation queue, you must not start the operations manually. You must leave this to the operation queue.

Now let's run the example code once and see the results in the console window:

```
[Running_Tasks_Asynchronously_with_OperationsAppDelegate firstOperationEntry:]
Main thread is here
Parameter Object = 111
[Running_Tasks_Asynchronously_with_OperationsAppDelegate secondOperationEntry:]
Main Thread = <NSThread: 0x6810260>{name = (null), num = 1}
Parameter Object = 222
Current Thread = <NSThread: 0x6805c20>{name = (null), num = 3}
Main Thread = <NSThread: 0x6810260>{name = (null), num = 1}
Current Thread = <NSThread: 0x6b2d1d0>{name = (null), num = 4}
```

Brilliant! This proves that the invocation operations are running on their own threads in parallel to the main thread without blocking the main thread at all. Now let's run the same code a couple more times and observe the output in the console window. If you do this, chances are that you will get a completely different result, such as this:

```
Main thread is here
[Running_Tasks_Asynchronously_with_OperationsAppDelegate firstOperationEntry:]
[Running_Tasks_Asynchronously_with_OperationsAppDelegate secondOperationEntry:]
Parameter Object = 111
Main Thread = <NSThread: 0x6810260>{name = (null), num = 1}
Current Thread = <NSThread: 0x68247c0>{name = (null), num = 3}
Parameter Object = 222
Main Thread = <NSThread: 0x6810260>{name = (null), num = 1}
Current Thread = <NSThread: 0x6819b00>{name = (null), num = 4}
```

You can clearly observe that the main thread is not blocked and that both invocation operations are running in parallel with the main thread. This just proves the concurrency in the operation queue when two nonconcurrent operations are added to it. The operation queue manages the threads required to run the operations.

If we were to subclass NSOperation and add the instances of the new class to an operation queue, we would do things slightly differently. Keep a few things in mind:

- Plain operations that subclass NSOperation, when added to an operation queue, will run asynchronously. For this reason, you must override the isConcurrent instance method of NSOperation and return the value YES.

- You must prepare your operation for cancellation by checking the value of the isCancelled method periodically while performing the main task of the operation and in the start method before you even run the operation. The start method will get called by the operation queue in this case after the operation is added to the queue. In this method, check whether the operation is cancelled using the isCancelled method. If the operation is cancelled, simply return from the start method. If not, call the main method from inside the start method.

- Override the main method with your own implementation of the main task that is to be carried out by the operation. Make sure to allocate and initialize your own autorelease pool in this method and to release the pool just before returning.

- Override the isFinished and isExecuting methods of your operation and return appropriate BOOL values to reveal whether the operation is finished or is executing at the time.

Here is the declaration (.h file) of the operation:

```
#import <Foundation/Foundation.h>

@interface SimpleOperation : NSOperation

/* Designated Initializer */
- (id) initWithObject:(NSObject *)paramObject;

@end
```

The implementation of the operation is as follows:

```
#import "SimpleOperation.h"

@implementation SimpleOperation
```

```
NSObject       *givenObject;
BOOL           finished;
BOOL           executing;

- (id) init {
  NSNumber *dummyObject = [NSNumber numberWithInteger:123];
  return([self initWithObject:dummyObject]);
}

- (id) initWithObject:(NSObject *)paramObject{
  self = [super init];
  if (self != nil){
    /* Keep these values for the main method */
    givenObject = paramObject;
  }
  return(self);
}

- (void) start {

  /* If we are cancelled before starting, then
   we have to return immediately and generate the
   required KVO notifications */
  if ([self isCancelled]){
    /* If this operation *is* cancelled */
    /* KVO compliance */
    [self willChangeValueForKey:@"isFinished"];
    finished = YES;
    [self didChangeValueForKey:@"isFinished"];
    return;

  } else {
    /* If this operation is *not* cancelled */
    /* KVO compliance */
    [self willChangeValueForKey:@"isExecuting"];
    executing = YES;
    /* Call the main method from inside the start method */
    [self didChangeValueForKey:@"isExecuting"];
    [self main];
  }

}

- (void) main {

  @try {
    @autoreleasepool {
      /* Keep a local variable here that must get set to YES
       whenever we are done with the task */
      BOOL taskIsFinished = NO;

      /* Create a while loop here that only exists
       if the taskIsFinished variable is set to YES or
       the operation has been cancelled */
```

```objectivec
    while (taskIsFinished == NO &&
           [self isCancelled] == NO){

      /* Perform the task here */
      NSLog(@"%s", __FUNCTION__);
      NSLog(@"Parameter Object = %@", givenObject);
      NSLog(@"Main Thread = %@", [NSThread mainThread]);
      NSLog(@"Current Thread = %@", [NSThread currentThread]);

      /* Very important. This way we can get out of the
       loop and we are still complying with the cancellation
       rules of operations */
      taskIsFinished = YES;

    }

    /* KVO compliance. Generate the
     required KVO notifications */
    [self willChangeValueForKey:@"isFinished"];
    [self willChangeValueForKey:@"isExecuting"];
    finished = YES;
    executing = NO;
    [self didChangeValueForKey:@"isFinished"];
    [self didChangeValueForKey:@"isExecuting"];
    }
  }
  @catch (NSException * e) {
    NSLog(@"Exception %@", e);
  }

}

- (BOOL)  isConcurrent{
  return YES;
}

- (BOOL)  isFinished{
  /* Simply return the value */
  return finished;
}

- (BOOL)  isExecuting{
  /* Simply return the value */
  return executing;
}

@end
```

You can now use this operation class in any other class, such as your application delegate. Here is the declaration of the application delegate to utilize this new operation class and add it in an operation queue:

```objectivec
#import <UIKit/UIKit.h>

@class SimpleOperation;
```

```
@interface Running_Tasks_Asynchronously_with_OperationsAppDelegate
          : UIResponder <UIApplicationDelegate>

@property (nonatomic, strong) UIWindow *window;
@property (nonatomic, strong) NSOperationQueue *operationQueue;
@property (nonatomic, strong) SimpleOperation  *firstOperation;
@property (nonatomic, strong) SimpleOperation  *secondOperation;

@end
```

The implementation of the application delegate is as follows:

```
#import "Running_Tasks_Asynchronously_with_OperationsAppDelegate.h"
#import "SimpleOperation.h"

@implementation Running_Tasks_Asynchronously_with_OperationsAppDelegate

- (BOOL)              application:(UIApplication *)application
  didFinishLaunchingWithOptions:(NSDictionary *)launchOptions{

  NSNumber *firstNumber = [NSNumber numberWithInteger:111];
  NSNumber *secondNumber = [NSNumber numberWithInteger:222];

  self.firstOperation = [[SimpleOperation alloc]
                          initWithObject:firstNumber];

  self.secondOperation = [[SimpleOperation alloc]
                          initWithObject:secondNumber];

  self.operationQueue = [[NSOperationQueue alloc] init];

  /* Add the operations to the queue */
  [self.operationQueue addOperation:self.firstOperation];
  [self.operationQueue addOperation:self.secondOperation];

  NSLog(@"Main thread is here");

  self.window = [[UIWindow alloc] initWithFrame:
                  [[UIScreen mainScreen] bounds]];
  self.window.backgroundColor = [UIColor whiteColor];
  [self.window makeKeyAndVisible];
  return YES;
}

@end
```

The results printed to the console window will be similar to what we saw earlier when we used concurrent invocation operations:

```
Main thread is here
-[SimpleOperation main]
-[SimpleOperation main]
Parameter Object = 222
Parameter Object = 222
Main Thread = <NSThread: 0x6810260>{name = (null), num = 1}
```

```
Main Thread = <NSThread: 0x6810260>{name = (null), num = 1}
Current Thread = <NSThread: 0x6a10b90>{name = (null), num = 3}
Current Thread = <NSThread: 0x6a13f50>{name = (null), num = 4}
```

See Also

Recipe 6.12; Recipe 6.16

6.14 Creating Dependency Between Operations

Problem

You want to start a certain task only after another task has finished executing.

Solution

If operation B has to wait for operation A before it can run the task associated with it, operation B has to add operation A as its dependency using the addDependency: instance method of NSOperation, as shown here:

```
[self.firstOperation addDependency:self.secondOperation];
```

Both the firstOperation and the secondOperation properties are of type NSInvoca tionOperation, as we will see in this recipe's Discussion. In this example code, the first operation will not be executed by the operation queue until after the second operation's task is finished.

Discussion

An operation will not start executing until all the operations on which it depends have successfully finished executing the tasks associated with them. By default, an operation, after initialization, has no dependency on other operations.

If we want to introduce dependencies to the example code described in Recipe 6.13, we can slightly modify the application delegate's implementation and use the add Dependency: instance method to have the first operation wait for the second operation:

```
#import "Creating_Dependency_Between_OperationsAppDelegate.h"

@implementation Creating_Dependency_Between_OperationsAppDelegate

- (void) firstOperationEntry:(id)paramObject{

  NSLog(@"First Operation - Parameter Object = %@",
      paramObject);

  NSLog(@"First Operation - Main Thread = %@",
      [NSThread mainThread]);

  NSLog(@"First Operation - Current Thread = %@",
      [NSThread currentThread]);
```

```
}

- (void) secondOperationEntry:(id)paramObject{

  NSLog(@"Second Operation - Parameter Object = %@",
        paramObject);

  NSLog(@"Second Operation - Main Thread = %@",
        [NSThread mainThread]);

  NSLog(@"Second Operation - Current Thread = %@",
        [NSThread currentThread]);

}

- (BOOL)              application:(UIApplication *)application
  didFinishLaunchingWithOptions:(NSDictionary *)launchOptions{

  NSNumber *firstNumber = [NSNumber numberWithInteger:111];
  NSNumber *secondNumber = [NSNumber numberWithInteger:222];

  self.firstOperation = [[NSInvocationOperation alloc]
                          initWithTarget:self
                          selector:@selector(firstOperationEntry:)
                          object:firstNumber];

  self.secondOperation = [[NSInvocationOperation alloc]
                           initWithTarget:self
                           selector:@selector(secondOperationEntry:)
                           object:secondNumber];

  [self.firstOperation addDependency:self.secondOperation];

  self.operationQueue = [[NSOperationQueue alloc] init];

  /* Add the operations to the queue */
  [self.operationQueue addOperation:self.firstOperation];
  [self.operationQueue addOperation:self.secondOperation];

  NSLog(@"Main thread is here");

  self.window = [[UIWindow alloc] initWithFrame:
                  [[UIScreen mainScreen] bounds]];
  self.window.backgroundColor = [UIColor whiteColor];
  [self.window makeKeyAndVisible];
  return YES;
}

@end
```

Now if you execute the program, you will see a result similar to this in the console window:

```
Second Operation - Parameter Object = 222
Main thread is here
```

```
Second Operation - Main Thread = <NSThread: 0x6810250>{name = (null), num = 1}
Second Operation - Current Thread = <NSThread: 0x6836ab0>{name = (null), num = 3}
First Operation - Parameter Object = 111
First Operation - Main Thread = <NSThread: 0x6810250>{name = (null), num = 1}
First Operation - Current Thread = <NSThread: 0x6836ab0>{name = (null), num = 3}
```

It's quite obvious that although the operation queue attempted to run both operations in parallel, the first operation had a dependency on the second operation, and therefore the second operation had to finish before the first operation could run.

If at any time you want to break the dependency between two operations, you can use the `removeDependency:` instance method of an operation object.

See Also

Recipe 6.13

6.15 Creating Timers

Problem

You would like to perform a specific task repeatedly with a certain delay. For instance, you want to update a view on your screen every second that your application is running.

Solution

Use a timer:

```
- (void) paint:(NSTimer *)paramTimer{
  /* Do something here */
  NSLog(@"Painting");
}

- (void) startPainting{

  self.paintingTimer = [NSTimer
                        scheduledTimerWithTimeInterval:1.0
                        target:self
                        selector:@selector(paint:)
                        userInfo:nil
                        repeats:YES];

}

- (void) stopPainting{
  if (self.paintingTimer != nil){
    [self.paintingTimer invalidate];
  }
}

- (void)applicationWillResignActive:(UIApplication *)application{
  [self stopPainting];
```

```
}

- (void)applicationDidBecomeActive:(UIApplication *)application{
  [self startPainting];
}
```

The `invalidate` method will also release the timer, so that we don't have to do that manually. As you can see, we have defined a property called `paintingTimer` that is declared in this way in the header file (*.h* file):

```
#import <UIKit/UIKit.h>

@interface Creating_TimersAppDelegate : UIResponder <UIApplicationDelegate>

@property (nonatomic, strong) UIWindow *window;
@property (nonatomic, strong) NSTimer *paintingTimer;

@end
```

Discussion

A timer is an object that fires an event at specified intervals. A timer must be scheduled in a run loop. Defining an `NSTimer` object creates a nonscheduled timer that does nothing but is available to the program when you want to schedule it. Once you issue a call, e.g. `scheduledTimerWithTimeInterval:target:selector:userInfo:repeats:`, the time becomes a scheduled timer and will fire the event you request. A scheduled timer is a timer that is added to a run loop. To get any timer to fire its target event, we must schedule that timer on a run loop. This is demonstrated in a later example where we create a nonscheduled timer and then manually schedule it on the main run loop of the application.

Once a timer is created and added to a run loop, either explicitly or implicitly, the timer will start calling a method in its target object (as specified by the programmer) every *n* seconds (*n* is specified by the programmer as well). Because *n* is floating-point, you can specify a fraction of a second.

There are various ways to create, initialize, and schedule timers. One of the easiest ways is through the `scheduledTimerWithTimeInterval:target:selector:userInfo:repeats:` class method of `NSTimer`. Here are the different parameters of this method:

`scheduledTimerWithTimeInterval`
This is the number of seconds the timer has to wait before it fires an event. For example, if you want the timer to call a method in its target object twice per second, you have to set this parameter to 0.5 (1 second divided by 2); if you want the target method to be called four times per second, this parameter should be set to 0.25 (1 second divided by 4).

`target`
This is the object that will receive the event.

selector

This is the method signature in the target object that will receive the event.

userInfo

This is the object that will be retained in the timer for later reference (in the target method of the target object).

repeats

This specifies whether the timer must call its target method repeatedly (in which case this parameter has to be set to YES), or just once and then stop (in which case this parameter has to be set to NO).

 Once a timer is created and added to a run loop, you can stop and release that timer using the invalidate instance method of the NSTimer class. This not only will release the timer, but also will release the object, if any, that was passed for the timer to retain during its lifetime (e.g., the object passed to the userInfo parameter of the scheduledTimerWith TimeInterval:target:selector:userInfo:repeats: class method of NSTimer). If you pass NO to the repeats parameter, the timer will invalidate itself after the first pass and subsequently will release the object it had retained (if any).

There are other methods you can use to create a scheduled timer. One of them is the scheduledTimerWithTimeInterval:invocation:repeats: class method of NSTimer:

```
- (void) paint:(NSTimer *)paramTimer{
  /* Do something here */
  NSLog(@"Painting");
}

- (void) startPainting{

  /* Here is the selector that we want to call */
  SEL selectorToCall = @selector(paint:);

  /* Here we compose a method signature out of the selector.
   We know that the selector is in the current class so it is easy
   to construct the method signature */
  NSMethodSignature *methodSignature =
    [[self class] instanceMethodSignatureForSelector:selectorToCall];

  /* Now base the invocation on the method signature. We need this
   invocation to schedule a timer */
  NSInvocation *invocation =
    [NSInvocation invocationWithMethodSignature:methodSignature];
  [invocation setTarget:self];
  [invocation setSelector:selectorToCall];

  /* Start a scheduled timer now */
  self.paintingTimer = [NSTimer scheduledTimerWithTimeInterval:1.0
                                                    invocation:invocation
```

```
                                                repeats:YES];

  }

  - (void) stopPainting{
    if (self.paintingTimer != nil){
      [self.paintingTimer invalidate];
    }
  }

  - (void)applicationWillResignActive:(UIApplication *)application{
    [self stopPainting];
  }

  - (void)applicationDidBecomeActive:(UIApplication *)application{
    [self startPainting];
  }
```

Scheduling a timer can be compared to starting a car's engine. A scheduled timer is a running car engine. A nonscheduled timer is a car engine that is ready to be started, but is not running yet. We can schedule and unschedule timers whenever we want in the application, just like we might need the engine of a car to be on or off depending on the situation we are in. If you want to schedule a timer manually at a certain time in your application, you can use the timerWithTimeInterval:target:selector:userInfo:repeats: class method of NSTimer, and when you are ready, you can add the timer to your run loop of choice:

```
  - (void) startPainting{

    self.paintingTimer = [NSTimer timerWithTimeInterval:1.0
                                                 target:self
                                               selector:@selector(paint:)
                                               userInfo:nil
                                                repeats:YES];

    /* Do your processing here and, whenever you are ready,
       use the addTimer:forMode instance method of the NSRunLoop class
       in order to schedule the timer on that run loop */

    [[NSRunLoop currentRunLoop] addTimer:self.paintingTimer
                                 forMode:NSDefaultRunLoopMode];

  }
```

 The currentRunLoop and mainRunLoop class methods of NSRunLoop return the current and main run loops of the application, respectively, as their names imply.

Just like you can use the scheduledTimerWithTimeInterval:invocation:repeats: variant of creating scheduled timers using invocations, you can also use the timerWith

TimeInterval:invocation:repeats: class method of NSTimer to create an unscheduled timer using an invocation:

```
- (void) paint:(NSTimer *)paramTimer{
  /* Do something here */
  NSLog(@"Painting");
}

- (void) startPainting{

  /* Here is the selector that we want to call */
  SEL selectorToCall = @selector(paint:);
  /* Here we compose a method signature out of the selector. We
   know that the selector is in the current class so it is easy
   to construct the method signature */
  NSMethodSignature *methodSignature =
  [[self class] instanceMethodSignatureForSelector:selectorToCall];

  /* Now base the invocation on the method signature. We need this
   invocation to schedule a timer */
  NSInvocation *invocation =
  [NSInvocation invocationWithMethodSignature:methodSignature];

  [invocation setTarget:self];
  [invocation setSelector:selectorToCall];

  self.paintingTimer = [NSTimer timerWithTimeInterval:1.0
                                           invocation:invocation
                                              repeats:YES];;

  /* Do your processing here and, whenever you are ready,
   use the addTimer:forMode instance method of the NSRunLoop class
   in order to schedule the timer on that run loop */

  [[NSRunLoop currentRunLoop] addTimer:self.paintingTimer
                               forMode:NSDefaultRunLoopMode];

}

- (void) stopPainting{
  if (self.paintingTimer != nil){
    [self.paintingTimer invalidate];
  }
}

- (void)applicationWillResignActive:(UIApplication *)application{
  [self stopPainting];
}

- (void)applicationDidBecomeActive:(UIApplication *)application{
  [self startPainting];
}
```

The target method of a timer receives the instance of the timer that calls it as its parameter. For instance, the paint: method introduced initially in this recipe demonstrates how the timer gets passed to its target method, by default, as the target method's one and only parameter:

```
- (void) paint:(NSTimer *)paramTimer{
  /* Do something here */
  NSLog(@"Painting");
}
```

This parameter provides you with a reference to the timer that is firing this method. You can, for instance, prevent the timer from running again using the `invalidate` method, if needed. You can also invoke the `userInfo` method of the `NSTimer` instance in order to retrieve the object being retained by the timer (if any). This object is just an object passed to the initialization methods of `NSTimer`, and it gets directly passed to the timer for future reference.

6.16 Creating Concurrency with Threads

Problem

You would like to have maximum control over how separate tasks run in your application. For instance, you would like to run a long calculation requested by the user while freeing the main UI thread to interact with the user and do other things.

Solution

Utilize threads in your application, like so:

```
- (void) downloadNewFile:(id)paramObject{

  @autoreleasepool {
    NSString *fileURL = (NSString *)paramObject;

    NSURL    *url = [NSURL URLWithString:fileURL];

    NSURLRequest *request = [NSURLRequest requestWithURL:url];

    NSURLResponse *response = nil;
    NSError       *error = nil;

    NSData *downloadedData =
    [NSURLConnection sendSynchronousRequest:request
                          returningResponse:&response
                                      error:&error];

    if ([downloadedData length] > 0){
      /* Fully downloaded */
    } else {
      /* Nothing was downloaded. Check the Error value */
    }
  }
}
```

```
    }

- (void)viewDidLoad {
    [super viewDidLoad];

    NSString *fileToDownload = @"http://www.OReilly.com";

    [NSThread detachNewThreadSelector:@selector(downloadNewFile:)
                             toTarget:self
                           withObject:fileToDownload];

}
```

Discussion

Any iOS application is made out of one or more threads. In iOS, a normal application with one view controller could initially have up to four or five threads created by the system libraries to which the application is linked. At least one thread will be created for your application whether you use multiple threads or not. It is called the "main UI thread" attached to the main run loop.

To understand how useful threads are, let's do an experiment. Suppose we have three loops:

```
- (void) firstCounter{

    NSUInteger counter = 0;
    for (counter = 0;
         counter < 1000;
         counter++){
      NSLog(@"First Counter = %lu", (unsigned long)counter);
    }

}

- (void) secondCounter{

    NSUInteger counter = 0;
    for (counter = 0;
         counter < 1000;
         counter++){
      NSLog(@"Second Counter = %lu", (unsigned long)counter);
    }

}

- (void) thirdCounter{

    NSUInteger counter = 0;
```

```
    for (counter = 0;
         counter < 1000;
         counter++){
      NSLog(@"Third Counter = %lu", (unsigned long)counter);
    }

  }
```

Very simple, aren't they? All they do is go from zero to 1,000, printing their counter numbers. Now suppose you want to run these counters as we would normally do:

```
- (void) viewDidLoad{
  [super viewDidLoad];
  [self firstCounter];
  [self secondCounter];
  [self thirdCounter];
}
```

 This code does not necessarily have to be in a view controller's viewDid Load method.

Now open the console window and run this application. You will see the first counter's complete run, followed by the second counter and then the third counter. This means these loops are being run on the same thread. Each one blocks the rest of the thread's code from being executed until it finishes its loop.

What if we wanted all these counters to run at the same time? Of course, we would have to create separate threads for each one. But wait a minute! We already learned that the application creates threads for us when it loads and that whatever code we have been writing so far in the application, wherever it was, was being executed in a thread. So, we just have to create two threads for the first and second counters and leave the third counter to do its job in the main thread:

```
- (void) firstCounter{

  @autoreleasepool {
    NSUInteger counter = 0;
    for (counter = 0;
         counter < 1000;
         counter++){
      NSLog(@"First Counter = %lu", (unsigned long)counter);
    }
  }

}

- (void) secondCounter{

  @autoreleasepool {
    NSUInteger counter = 0;
```

```
    for (counter = 0;
         counter < 1000;
         counter++){
      NSLog(@"Second Counter = %lu", (unsigned long)counter);
    }
  }

}

- (void) thirdCounter{

  NSUInteger counter = 0;
  for (counter = 0;
       counter < 1000;
       counter++){
    NSLog(@"Third Counter = %lu", (unsigned long)counter);
  }

}

- (void)viewDidLoad {

  [super viewDidLoad];

  [NSThread detachNewThreadSelector:@selector(firstCounter)
                           toTarget:self
                         withObject:nil];


  [NSThread detachNewThreadSelector:@selector(secondCounter)
                           toTarget:self
                         withObject:nil];

  /* Run this on the main thread */
  [self thirdCounter];

}
```

 The thirdCounter method does not have an autorelease pool since it is not run in a new detached thread. This method will be run in the application's main thread, which has an autorelease pool created for it automatically at the startup of every Cocoa Touch application.

The calls to detachNewThreadSelector near the end of the code run the first and second counters as separate threads. Now if you run the application, you will notice output such as the following, in the console window:

```
Second Counter = 921
Third Counter = 301
Second Counter = 922
Second Counter = 923
Second Counter = 924
First Counter = 956
```

```
Second Counter = 925
First Counter = 957
Second Counter = 926
First Counter = 958
Third Counter = 302
Second Counter = 927
Third Counter = 303
Second Counter = 928
```

In other words, all three counters run at once, and interleave their output randomly.

Every thread must create an autorelease pool. An autorelease pool internally keeps a reference to objects that are being autoreleased before the pool itself is released. This is a very important mechanism in a reference-counted memory management environment such as Cocoa Touch, where objects can be autoreleased. Whenever we allocate instances of objects, the retain count of the objects gets set to 1. If we mark the objects as autorelease, the retain count remains at 1, but when the autorelease pool in which the object was created is released, the autorelease object is also sent a **release** message. If its retain count is still 1 at that point, the object gets deallocated.

Every thread requires an autorelease pool to be created for it as the first object that is allocated in that thread. If you don't do this, any object that you allocate in your thread will leak when the thread exists. To understand this better, let's have a look at the following code:

```
- (void) autoreleaseThread:(id)paramSender{

    NSBundle *mainBundle = [NSBundle mainBundle];
    NSString *filePath = [mainBundle pathForResource:@"AnImage"
                                              ofType:@"png"];

    UIImage *image = [UIImage imageWithContentsOfFile:filePath];

    /* Do something with the image */
    NSLog(@"Image = %@", image);

}

- (void)viewDidLoad {

    [super viewDidLoad];

    [NSThread detachNewThreadSelector:@selector(autoreleaseThread:)
                            toTarget:self
                          withObject:self];

}
```

If you run this code and keep an eye on the console window, you will receive a message similar to this:

```
*** __NSAutoreleaseNoPool(): Object 0x5b2c990 of
class NSCFString autoreleased with no pool in place - just leaking
*** __NSAutoreleaseNoPool(): Object 0x5b2ca30 of
```

```
class NSPathStore2 autoreleased with no pool in place - just leaking
*** __NSAutoreleaseNoPool(): Object 0x5b205c0 of
class NSPathStore2 autoreleased with no pool in place - just leaking
*** __NSAutoreleaseNoPool(): Object 0x5b2d650 of
class UIImage autoreleased with no pool in place - just leaking
```

This shows that the autorelease UIImage instance we created is creating a memory leak —and, in addition, so is the NSString instance called FilePath and other objects that would normally "magically" get deallocated. This is because in the thread, we forgot to allocate and initialize an autorelease pool as the first thing we did. The following is the correct code, which you can test for yourself to make sure it doesn't leak:

```
- (void) autoreleaseThread:(id)paramSender{

  @autoreleasepool {
    NSBundle *mainBundle = [NSBundle mainBundle];
    NSString *filePath = [mainBundle pathForResource:@"AnImage"
                                              ofType:@"png"];

    UIImage *image = [UIImage imageWithContentsOfFile:filePath];

    /* Do something with the image */
    NSLog(@"Image = %@", image);
  }

}
```

6.17 Invoking Background Methods

Problem

You want to know an easy way to create threads without having to deal with threads directly.

Solution

Use the performSelectorInBackground:withObject: instance method of NSObject:

```
- (BOOL)             application:(UIApplication *)application
  didFinishLaunchingWithOptions:(NSDictionary *)launchOptions{

  [self performSelectorInBackground:@selector(firstCounter)
                         withObject:nil];

  [self performSelectorInBackground:@selector(secondCounter)
                         withObject:nil];

  [self performSelectorInBackground:@selector(thirdCounter)
                         withObject:nil];

  self.window = [[UIWindow alloc] initWithFrame:
                [[UIScreen mainScreen] bounds]];
```

```
      self.window.backgroundColor = [UIColor whiteColor];
      [self.window makeKeyAndVisible];
      return YES;
  }
```

The counter methods are implemented in this way:

```
- (void) firstCounter{

  @autoreleasepool {
    NSUInteger counter = 0;
    for (counter = 0;
         counter < 1000;
         counter++){
      NSLog(@"First Counter = %lu", (unsigned long)counter);
    }
  }

}

- (void) secondCounter{

  @autoreleasepool {
    NSUInteger counter = 0;
    for (counter = 0;
         counter < 1000;
         counter++){
      NSLog(@"Second Counter = %lu", (unsigned long)counter);
    }
  }

}

- (void) thirdCounter{

  @autoreleasepool {
    NSUInteger counter = 0;
    for (counter = 0;
         counter < 1000;
         counter++){
      NSLog(@"Third Counter = %lu", (unsigned long)counter);
    }
  }

}
```

Discussion

The performSelectorInBackground:withObject: method creates a new thread in the background for us. This is equivalent to the creating a new thread for the selectors. The most important thing we have to keep in mind is that since this method creates a thread on the given selector, the selector must have an autorelease pool just like any other thread in a reference-counted memory environment.

6.18 Exiting Threads and Timers

Problem

You would like to stop a thread or a timer, or prevent one from firing again.

Solution

For timers, use the `invalidate` instance method of `NSTimer`. For threads, use the `can cel` method. Avoid using the `exit` method of threads, as it does not give the thread a chance to clean up after itself and your application will end up leaking resources:

```
NSThread *thread = /* Get the reference to your thread here */;
[thread cancel];

NSTimer *timer = /* Get the reference to your timer here */;
[timer invalidate];
```

Discussion

Exiting a timer is quite straightforward; you can simply call the timer's `invalidate` instance method. After you call that method, the timer will not fire any more events to its target object.

However, threads are a bit more complicated to exit. When a thread is sleeping and its `cancel` method is called, the thread's loop will still perform its task fully before exiting. Let me demonstrate this for you:

```
- (void) threadEntryPoint{

  @autoreleasepool {
    NSLog(@"Thread Entry Point");
    while ([[NSThread currentThread] isCancelled] == NO){
      [NSThread sleepForTimeInterval:4];
      NSLog(@"Thread Loop");
    }
    NSLog(@"Thread Finished");
  }

}

- (void) stopThread{

  NSLog(@"Cancelling the Thread");
  [self.myThread cancel];
  NSLog(@"Releasing the thread");
  self.myThread = nil;

}

- (BOOL)            application:(UIApplication *)application
  didFinishLaunchingWithOptions:(NSDictionary *)launchOptions{
```

```
self.myThread = [[NSThread alloc]
                    initWithTarget:self
                    selector:@selector(threadEntryPoint)
                    object:nil];  [self performSelector:@selector(stopThread)
               withObject:nil
               afterDelay:3.0f];

[self.myThread start];

self.window = [[UIWindow alloc] initWithFrame:
               [[UIScreen mainScreen] bounds]];
self.window.backgroundColor = [UIColor whiteColor];
[self.window makeKeyAndVisible];
return YES;
}
```

This code creates an instance of NSThread and starts the thread immediately. The thread
sleeps for four seconds in every loop before performing its task. However, before the
thread is started, we are calling the stopThread method of the view controller (which
we have written) with a three-second delay. This method calls the cancel method of
the thread in an attempt to make the thread exit its loop. Now let's run the application
and see what gets printed to the console screen:

```
...
Thread Entry Point
Cancelling the Thread
Releasing the thread
Thread Loop
Thread Finished
```

You can clearly see that the thread finished its current loop before exiting, even though
the request to cancel it was fired in the middle of the loop. This is a very common pitfall
that can be avoided simply by checking whether the thread is cancelled before attempting to perform a task with external side effects inside the thread's loop. We can
rewrite the example as follows so that the operation with an external effect (writing to
the log) checks first to make sure the thread hasn't been cancelled:

```
- (void) threadEntryPoint{

  @autoreleasepool {
    NSLog(@"Thread Entry Point");
    while ([[NSThread currentThread] isCancelled] == NO){
      [NSThread sleepForTimeInterval:4];
      if ([[NSThread currentThread] isCancelled] == NO){
        NSLog(@"Thread Loop");
      }
    }
    NSLog(@"Thread Finished");
  }

}

- (void) stopThread{
```

```
    NSLog(@"Cancelling the Thread");
    [self.myThread cancel];
    NSLog(@"Releasing the thread");
    self.myThread = nil;

}

- (BOOL)              application:(UIApplication *)application
  didFinishLaunchingWithOptions:(NSDictionary *)launchOptions{

    self.myThread = [[NSThread alloc]
                    initWithTarget:self
                    selector:@selector(threadEntryPoint)
                    object:nil];

    [self performSelector:@selector(stopThread)
            withObject:nil
            afterDelay:3.0f];

    [self.myThread start];

    self.window = [[UIWindow alloc] initWithFrame:
                    [[UIScreen mainScreen] bounds]];
    self.window.backgroundColor = [UIColor whiteColor];
    [self.window makeKeyAndVisible];
    return YES;
}
```

6.18 Exiting Threads and Timers | 427

CHAPTER 7

Core Location and Maps

7.0 Introduction

The Core Location and Map Kit frameworks can be used to create location-aware and map-based applications. The Core Location framework uses the device's internal hardware to determine the current location of the device. The Map Kit framework enables your application to display maps to your users, put custom annotations on the maps, and so on. The availability of location services from the pure programming perspective depends on the availability of hardware on the device; if the hardware is there, it must be enabled and switched on for the Map Kit and Core Location frameworks to work. An iOS device with GPS services can use 2G, EDGE, 3G, 4G, and other technologies to determine the user's location. Presently, almost all iOS devices support location services, but it is good programming practice to check the availability of location services before starting to use them, as we cannot predict whether in the future Apple will release a device with all hardware required to support location services.

To use the Core Location and Map Kit frameworks, you need to first add them to your project and make sure appropriate header files are imported. Follow these steps to add these two frameworks to your project:

1. Click on your project icon in Xcode.
2. Select the target to which you want to add the frameworks, as shown in Figure 7-1.
3. Select the Build Phases tab on the top (Figure 7-1).
4. Expand the Link Binary With Libraries box and press the + button.
5. In the dialog, you will see the list of all available frameworks and static libraries. Find and select both `CoreLocation.framework` and `MapKit.framework` and then press Add, as shown in Figure 7-2.

After adding these two frameworks, you will need to add two header files to your *.m* file (or to your *.h* file, if you are referring to any entity that is included in either of the two aforementioned frameworks):

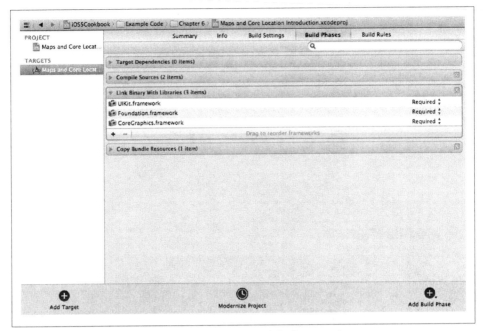

Figure 7-1. Selecting the target to which we want to add the frameworks

```
#import <CoreLocation/CoreLocation.h>
#import <MapKit/MapKit.h>
```

7.1 Creating a Map View

Problem

You want to instantiate and display a map on a view.

Solution

Create an instance of the MKMapView class and add it to a view or assign it as a subview of your view controller. Here is the sample *.h* file of a view controller that creates an instance of MKMapView and displays it full-screen on its view:

```
#import <UIKit/UIKit.h>
#import <MapKit/MapKit.h>

@interface Creating_a_Map_ViewViewController : UIViewController

@property (nonatomic, strong) MKMapView *myMapView;

@end
```

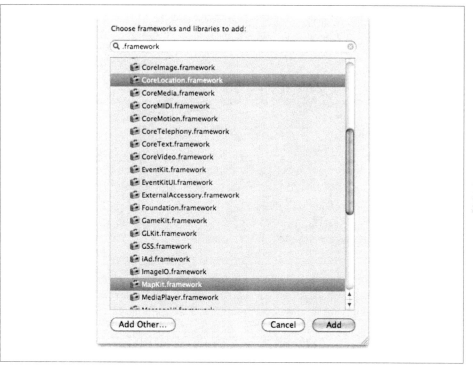

Choose frameworks and libraries to add:

🔍 .framework

- CoreImage.framework
- CoreLocation.framework
- CoreMedia.framework
- CoreMIDI.framework
- CoreMotion.framework
- CoreTelephony.framework
- CoreText.framework
- CoreVideo.framework
- EventKit.framework
- EventKitUI.framework
- ExternalAccessory.framework
- Foundation.framework
- GameKit.framework
- GLKit.framework
- GSS.framework
- iAd.framework
- ImageIO.framework
- MapKit.framework
- MediaPlayer.framework

Add Other...   Cancel   Add

Figure 7-2. Adding the CoreLocation and the MapKit frameworks to a project

This is a simple root view controller with a variable of type MKMapView. Later in the implementation of this view controller (.*m* file), we will initialize the map and set its type to Satellite, like so:

```
#import "Creating_a_Map_ViewViewController.h"

@implementation Creating_a_Map_ViewViewController

- (void)didReceiveMemoryWarning{
  [super didReceiveMemoryWarning];
}

- (void)viewDidLoad{
  [super viewDidLoad];

  self.view.backgroundColor = [UIColor whiteColor];

  self.myMapView = [[MKMapView alloc]
                    initWithFrame:self.view.bounds];
  /* Set the map type to Satellite */
  self.myMapView.mapType = MKMapTypeSatellite;

  self.myMapView.autoresizingMask =
    UIViewAutoresizingFlexibleWidth |
```

```
        UIViewAutoresizingFlexibleHeight;

    /* Add it to our view */
    [self.view addSubview:self.myMapView];

}

- (BOOL)shouldAutorotateToInterfaceOrientation
        :(UIInterfaceOrientation)interfaceOrientation{
    return YES;
}

@end
```

Discussion

Creating an instance of the `MKMapView` class is quite straightforward. We can simply assign a frame to it using its constructor, and after the map is created, add it as a subview of the view on the screen just so that we can see it.

> `MKMapView` is a subclass of `UIView`, so you can manipulate any map view the way you manipulate an instance of `UIView`. We use a `UIView` property, for instance, insetting the `backgroundColor` property of our view.

If you haven't already noticed, the `MKMapView` class has a property called `mapType` that can be set to satellite, standard, or hybrid. In this example, we are using the satellite map type (see Figure 7-3).

You can change the visual representation type of a map view using the `mapType` property of the `MKMapView` instance. Here are the different values you can use for this property:

`MKMapTypeStandard`
   Use this map type to display a standard map (this is the default).

`MKMapTypeSatellite`
   Use this map type to display a satellite image map (as depicted in Figure 7-3).

`MKMapTypeHybrid`
   Use this map type to display a standard map overlaid on a satellite image map.

7.2 Handling the Events of a Map View

Problem

You want to handle various events that a map view can send to its delegate.

Figure 7-3. A satellite map view

Solution

Assign a delegate object that conforms to the `MKMapViewDelegate` protocol to the `dele gate` property of an instance of the `MKMapView` class:

```
/* Create a map as big as our view */
self.myMapView = [[MKMapView alloc]
                  initWithFrame:self.view.bounds];

/* Set the map type to Satellite */
self.myMapView.mapType = MKMapTypeSatellite;

self.myMapView.delegate = self;

self.myMapView.autoresizingMask =
  UIViewAutoresizingFlexibleWidth |
  UIViewAutoresizingFlexibleHeight;

/* Add it to our view */
[self.view addSubview:self.myMapView];
```

This code can easily run in the `viewDidLoad` method of a view controller object that has a property named `MapView` of type `MKMapView`:

```
#import <UIKit/UIKit.h>
#import <MapKit/MapKit.h>

@interface Handling_the_Events_of_a_Map_ViewViewController
```

```
                : UIViewController <MKMapViewDelegate>

    @property (nonatomic, strong) MKMapView *myMapView;

    @end
```

Discussion

The delegate object of an instance of the `MKMapView` class must implement the methods defined in the `MKMapViewDelegate` protocol in order to receive various messages from the map view and, as we will see later, to provide information to the map view. Various methods are defined in the `MKMapViewDelegate` protocol, such as the `mapViewWill StartLoadingMap:` method that will get called in the delegate object whenever the map loading process starts. Bear in mind that a delegate for a map view is not a required object, meaning that you can create map views without assigning delegates to them; these views simply won't respond to user manipulation.

Here is a list of some of the methods declared in the `MKMapViewDelegate` protocol and what they are meant to report to the delegate object of an instance of `MKMapView`:

`mapViewWillStartLoadingMap:`
: This method is called on the delegate object whenever the map view starts to load the data that visually represents the map to the user.

`mapView:viewForAnnotation:`
: This method is called on the delegate object whenever the map view is asking for an instance of `MKAnnotationView` to visually represent an annotation on the map. For more information about this, please refer to Recipe 7.4.

`mapViewWillStartLocatingUser:`
: This method, as its name implies, gets called on the delegate object whenever the map view starts to detect the user's location. For information about finding a user's location, please refer to Recipe 7.3.

`mapView:regionDidChangeAnimated:`
: This method gets called on the delegate object whenever the region displayed by the map changes.

See Also

Recipe 7.3; Recipe 7.4

7.3 Pinpointing the Location of a Device

Problem

You want to find the latitude and longitude of a device.

Solution

Use the `CLLocationManager` class:

```
if ([CLLocationManager locationServicesEnabled]){
  self.myLocationManager = [[CLLocationManager alloc] init];
  self.myLocationManager.delegate = self;

  self.myLocationManager.purpose =
  @"To provide functionality based on user's current location.";

  [self.myLocationManager startUpdatingLocation];
} else {
  /* Location services are not enabled.
   Take appropriate action: for instance, prompt the
   user to enable location services */
  NSLog(@"Location services are not enabled");
}
```

In this code, `myLocationManager` is a property of type `CLLocationManager`. The current class is also the delegate of the location manager in this sample code.

Discussion

The Core Location framework in the SDK provides functionality for programmers to detect the current spatial location of an iOS device. Because in iOS, the user is allowed to disable location services using Settings, before instantiating an object of type `CLLocationManager`, it is best to first determine whether location services are enabled on the device.

 The delegate object of an instance of `CLLocationManager` must conform to the `CLLocationManagerDelegate` protocol.

This is how we will declare our location manager object in the *.h* file of a view controller (the object creating an instance of `CLLocationManager` does not necessarily have to be a view controller):

```
#import <UIKit/UIKit.h>
#import <CoreLocation/CoreLocation.h>

@interface Pinpointing_the_Location_of_a_DeviceViewController
          : UIViewController <CLLocationManagerDelegate>

@property (nonatomic, strong) CLLocationManager *myLocationManager;

@end
```

The implementation of our view controller is as follows:

```
#import "Pinpointing_the_Location_of_a_DeviceViewController.h"

@implementation Pinpointing_the_Location_of_a_DeviceViewController

- (void)didReceiveMemoryWarning{
  [super didReceiveMemoryWarning];
}

- (void)locationManager:(CLLocationManager *)manager
    didUpdateToLocation:(CLLocation *)newLocation
           fromLocation:(CLLocation *)oldLocation{

  /* We received the new location */

  NSLog(@"Latitude = %f", newLocation.coordinate.latitude);
  NSLog(@"Longitude = %f", newLocation.coordinate.longitude);

}

- (void)locationManager:(CLLocationManager *)manager
       didFailWithError:(NSError *)error{

  /* Failed to receive user's location */

}

- (void)viewDidLoad {
  [super viewDidLoad];  if ([CLLocationManager locationServicesEnabled]){
    self.myLocationManager = [[CLLocationManager alloc] init];
    self.myLocationManager.delegate = self;

    self.myLocationManager.purpose =
    @"To provide functionality based on user's current location.";

    [self.myLocationManager startUpdatingLocation];
  } else {
    /* Location services are not enabled.
     Take appropriate action: for instance, prompt the
     user to enable location services */
    NSLog(@"Location services are not enabled");
  }

}

- (BOOL)shouldAutorotateToInterfaceOrientation
        :(UIInterfaceOrientation)interfaceOrientation{
  return YES;
}

@end
```

The `startUpdateLocation` instance method of `CLLocationManager` reports the success or failure of retrieving the user's location to its delegate through the `locationMan ager:didUpdateToLocation:fromLocation:` method and the `locationManager:didFailWi thError:` method of its delegate object, in that order.

The `locationServicesEnabled` class method of `CLLocationManager` is available in SDK 4.0 and later.

The `CLLocationManager` class implements a property named `purpose`. This property allows us to customize the message that is shown to the users of our application, asking whether they will allow the use of location services for our application using Core Location functionalities. A good practice is to use localized strings for the value of this property.

7.4 Displaying Pins on a Map View

Problem

You want to point out a specific location on a map to the user.

Solution

Use built-in map view annotations. Follow these steps:

1. Create a new class and call it `MyAnnotation`.
2. Make sure this class conforms to the `MKAnnotation` protocol.
3. Define a property for this class of type `CLLocationCoordinate2D` and name it `coordinate`. Make sure you set it as a `readonly` property since the `coordinate` property is defined as `readonly` in the `MKAnnotation` protocol.
4. Optionally, define two properties of type `NSString`, namely `title` and `subtitle`, which will be able to carry the title and the subtitle information for your annotation view. Both of these properties are `readonly` as well.
5. Create an initializer method for your class that will accept a parameter of type `CLLocationCoordinate2D`. In this method, assign the passed location parameter to the property that we defined in step 3. Since this property is `readonly`, it cannot be assigned by code outside the scope of this class. Therefore, the initializer of this class acts as a bridge here and allows us to indirectly assign a value to this property. We will do the same thing for the `title` and `subtitle` properties.
6. Instantiate the `MyAnnotation` class and add it to your map using the `addAnnotation:` method of the `MKMapView` class.

Discussion

As explained in this recipe's Solution, we must create an object that conforms to the `MKAnnotation` protocol, and later instantiate this object and pass it to the map to be displayed. We will write the *.h* file of this object like so:

```
#import <Foundation/Foundation.h>
#import <MapKit/MapKit.h>

@interface MyAnnotation : NSObject <MKAnnotation>

@property (nonatomic, readonly) CLLocationCoordinate2D coordinate;
@property (nonatomic, copy, readonly) NSString *title;
@property (nonatomic, copy, readonly) NSString *subtitle;

- (id) initWithCoordinates:(CLLocationCoordinate2D)paramCoordinates
                     title:(NSString *)paramTitle
                  subTitle:(NSString *)paramSubTitle;

@end
```

The *.m* file of the `MyAnnotation` class sets up the class to display location information as follows:

```
#import "MyAnnotation.h"

@implementation MyAnnotation

- (id) initWithCoordinates:(CLLocationCoordinate2D)paramCoordinates
                     title:(NSString *)paramTitle
                  subTitle:(NSString *)paramSubTitle{

  self = [super init];

  if (self != nil){
    _coordinate = paramCoordinates;
    _title = paramTitle;
    _subtitle = paramSubTitle;
  }

  return(self);

}

@end
```

Later, we will instantiate this class and add it to our map, for instance, in the *.m* file of a view controller that creates and displays a map view:

```
#import "Displaying_Pins_on_a_Map_ViewViewController.h"
#import "MyAnnotation.h"

@implementation Displaying_Pins_on_a_Map_ViewViewController

- (void)didReceiveMemoryWarning
{
  [super didReceiveMemoryWarning];
  // Release any cached data, images, etc that aren't in use.
}

- (void)viewDidLoad {
  [super viewDidLoad];
```

```
/* Create a map as big as our view */
self.myMapView = [[MKMapView alloc]
                  initWithFrame:self.view.bounds];

self.myMapView.delegate = self;

/* Set the map type to Standard */
self.myMapView.mapType = MKMapTypeStandard;

self.myMapView.autoresizingMask =
  UIViewAutoresizingFlexibleWidth |
  UIViewAutoresizingFlexibleHeight;

/* Add it to our view */
[self.view addSubview:self.myMapView];

/* This is just a sample location */
CLLocationCoordinate2D location =
  CLLocationCoordinate2DMake(50.82191692907181, -0.13811767101287842);

/* Create the annotation using the location */
MyAnnotation *annotation =
[[MyAnnotation alloc] initWithCoordinates:location
                                    title:@"My Title"
                                 subTitle:@"My Sub Title"];

/* And eventually add it to the map */
[self.myMapView addAnnotation:annotation];

}

- (BOOL)shouldAutorotateToInterfaceOrientation
        :(UIInterfaceOrientation)interfaceOrientation{
  return YES;
}

@end
```

Figure 7-4 depicts the output of the program when run in iPhone Simulator.

7.5 Displaying Pins with Different Colors on a Map View

Problem

The default color for pins dropped on a map view is red. You want to be able to display pins in different colors in addition to the default color.

Solution

Return instances of MKPinAnnotationView to your map view through the mapView:view ForAnnotation: delegate method.

Figure 7-4. A built-in pin dropped on a map

Every annotation that is added to an instance of MKMapView has a corresponding view that gets displayed on the map view. These views are called *annotation views*. An annotation view is an object of type MKAnnotationView, which is a subclass of UIView. If the delegate object of a map view implements the mapView:viewForAnnotation: delegate method, the delegate object will have to return instances of the MKAnnotationView class to represent (and optionally, customize) the annotation views to be displayed on a map view.

Discussion

To set up our program so we can customize the color (choosing from the default SDK pin colors) of the annotation view that gets dropped on a map view to represent the annotation, we must return an instance of the MKPinAnnotationView class instead of an instance of MKAnnotationView in the mapView:viewForAnnotation: delegate method. Bear in mind that the MKPinAnnotationView class is a subclass of the MKAnnotationView class.

```
- (MKAnnotationView *)mapView:(MKMapView *)mapView
          viewForAnnotation:(id <MKAnnotation>)annotation{

  MKAnnotationView *result = nil;

  if ([annotation isKindOfClass:[MyAnnotation class]] == NO){
    return result;
  }
```

```
if ([mapView isEqual:self.myMapView] == NO){
  /* We want to process this event only for the Map View
   that we have created previously */
  return result;
}

/* First, typecast the annotation for which the Map View has
 fired this delegate message */
MyAnnotation *senderAnnotation = (MyAnnotation *)annotation;

/* Using the class method we have defined in our custom
 annotation class, we will attempt to get a reusable
 identifier for the pin we are about
 to create */
NSString *pinReusableIdentifier =
[MyAnnotation
 reusableIdentifierforPinColor:senderAnnotation.pinColor];

/* Using the identifier we retrieved above, we will
 attempt to reuse a pin in the sender Map View */
MKPinAnnotationView *annotationView = (MKPinAnnotationView *)
[mapView
 dequeueReusableAnnotationViewWithIdentifier:pinReusableIdentifier];

if (annotationView == nil){
  /* If we fail to reuse a pin, then we will create one */
  annotationView = [[MKPinAnnotationView alloc]
                    initWithAnnotation:senderAnnotation
                    reuseIdentifier:pinReusableIdentifier];

  /* Make sure we can see the callouts on top of
   each pin in case we have assigned title and/or
   subtitle to each pin */
  [annotationView setCanShowCallout:YES];
}

/* Now make sure, whether we have reused a pin or created a new one,
 that the color of the pin matches the color of the annotation */
annotationView.pinColor = senderAnnotation.pinColor;

result = annotationView;

return result;
}
```

An annotation view must be reused by giving it an identifier (an NSString). By determining which type of pin you would like to display on a map view and setting a unique identifier for each type of pin (e.g., blue pins can be treated as one type of pin and red pins as another), you must reuse the proper type of pin using the dequeueReusableAnnotationViewWithIdentifier: instance method of MKMapView as demonstrated in the code.

We have set the mechanism of retrieving the unique identifiers of each pin in our custom MyAnnotation class. Here is the .h file of the MyAnnotation class:

```
#import <Foundation/Foundation.h>
#import <MapKit/MapKit.h>

/* These are the standard SDK pin colors. We are setting
 unique identifiers per color for each pin so that later we
 can reuse the pins that have already been created with the same
 color */

#define REUSABLE_PIN_RED      @"Red"
#define REUSABLE_PIN_GREEN    @"Green"
#define REUSABLE_PIN_PURPLE   @"Purple"

@interface MyAnnotation : NSObject <MKAnnotation>

/* unsafe_unretained since this is not an object. We can skip this and leave
 it to the compiler to decide. weak or strong won't work as this is not
 an object */
@property (nonatomic, unsafe_unretained, readonly)
  CLLocationCoordinate2D coordinate;

@property (nonatomic, copy) NSString  *title;
@property (nonatomic, copy) NSString  *subtitle;

/* unsafe_unretained for the same reason as the coordinate property */
@property (nonatomic, unsafe_unretained) MKPinAnnotationColor  pinColor;

- (id) initWithCoordinates:(CLLocationCoordinate2D)paramCoordinates
                    title:(NSString*)paramTitle
                 subTitle:(NSString*)paramSubTitle;

+ (NSString *)   reusableIdentifierforPinColor
                 :(MKPinAnnotationColor)paramColor;

@end
```

Annotations are not the same as annotation views. An annotation is the location that you want to show on a map, and an annotation view is the view that represents that annotation on the map. The MyAnnotation class is the annotation, not the annotation view. When we create an annotation by instantiating the MyAnnotation class, we can assign a color to it using the pinColor property that we have defined and implemented. When the time comes for a map view to display an annotation, the map view will call the mapView:viewForAnnotation: delegate method and ask its delegate for an annotation view. The forAnnotation parameter of this method passes the annotation that needs to be displayed. By getting a reference to the annotation, we can type-cast the annotation to an instance of MyAnnotation, retrieve its pinColor property, and based on that, create an instance of MKPinAnnotationView with the given pin color and return it to the map view.

This is the .m file of MyAnnotation:

```
#import "MyAnnotation.h"

@implementation MyAnnotation
```

```
+ (NSString *)  reusableIdentifierforPinColor
                :(MKPinAnnotationColor)paramColor{

  NSString *result = nil;

  switch (paramColor){
    case MKPinAnnotationColorRed:{
      result = REUSABLE_PIN_RED;
      break;
    }
    case MKPinAnnotationColorGreen:{
      result = REUSABLE_PIN_GREEN;
      break;
    }
    case MKPinAnnotationColorPurple:{
      result = REUSABLE_PIN_PURPLE;
      break;
    }
  }

  return result;
}

- (id) initWithCoordinates:(CLLocationCoordinate2D)paramCoordinates
                     title:(NSString*)paramTitle
                  subTitle:(NSString*)paramSubTitle{

  self = [super init];

  if (self != nil){
    _coordinate = paramCoordinates;
    _title = paramTitle;
    _subtitle = paramSubTitle;
    _pinColor = MKPinAnnotationColorGreen;
  }

  return self;

}

@end
```

After implementing the MyAnnotation class, it's time to use it in our application (in this example, we will use it in a view controller). Here is the .h file of the view controller:

```
#import <UIKit/UIKit.h>
#import <MapKit/MapKit.h>

@interface Displaying_Pins_with_Different_Colors_on_a_Map_ViewViewController
        : UIViewController <MKMapViewDelegate>

@property (nonatomic, strong) MKMapView *myMapView;

@end
```

The implementation is in the *.m* file like so:

```objc
#import "Displaying_Pins_with_Different_Colors_on_a_Map_ViewViewController.h"
#import "MyAnnotation.h"

@implementation
  Displaying_Pins_with_Different_Colors_on_a_Map_ViewViewController

- (void)didReceiveMemoryWarning{
  [super didReceiveMemoryWarning];
}

- (MKAnnotationView *)mapView:(MKMapView *)mapView
            viewForAnnotation:(id <MKAnnotation>)annotation{

  MKAnnotationView *result = nil;

  if ([annotation isKindOfClass:[MyAnnotation class]] == NO){
    return result;
  }

  if ([mapView isEqual:self.myMapView] == NO){
    /* We want to process this event only for the Map View
     that we have created previously */
    return result;
  }

  /* First typecast the annotation for which the Map View has
   fired this delegate message */
  MyAnnotation *senderAnnotation = (MyAnnotation *)annotation;

  /* Using the class method we have defined in our custom
   annotation class, we will attempt to get a reusable
   identifier for the pin we are about
   to create */  NSString *pinReusableIdentifier =
  [MyAnnotation
   reusableIdentifierforPinColor:senderAnnotation.pinColor];

  /* Using the identifier we retrieved above, we will
   attempt to reuse a pin in the sender Map View */
  MKPinAnnotationView *annotationView = (MKPinAnnotationView *)
  [mapView
   dequeueReusableAnnotationViewWithIdentifier:pinReusableIdentifier];

  if (annotationView == nil){
    /* If we fail to reuse a pin, then we will create one */
    annotationView = [[MKPinAnnotationView alloc]
                      initWithAnnotation:senderAnnotation
                      reuseIdentifier:pinReusableIdentifier];

    /* Make sure we can see the callouts on top of
     each pin in case we have assigned title and/or
     subtitle to each pin */
    [annotationView setCanShowCallout:YES];
  }
```

```objc
    /* Now make sure, whether we have reused a pin or not, that
     the color of the pin matches the color of the annotation */
    annotationView.pinColor = senderAnnotation.pinColor;

    result = annotationView;

    return result;
}

- (void)viewDidLoad {
    [super viewDidLoad];

    /* Create a map as big as our view */
    self.myMapView = [[MKMapView alloc]
                        initWithFrame:self.view.bounds];

    self.myMapView.delegate = self;

    /* Set the map type to Standard */
    self.myMapView.mapType = MKMapTypeStandard;

    self.myMapView.autoresizingMask =
      UIViewAutoresizingFlexibleWidth |
      UIViewAutoresizingFlexibleHeight;

    /* Add it to our view */
    [self.view addSubview:self.myMapView];

    /* This is just a sample location */
    CLLocationCoordinate2D location;
    location.latitude = 50.82191692907181;
    location.longitude = -0.13811767101287842;

    /* Create the annotation using the location */
    MyAnnotation *annotation =
    [[MyAnnotation alloc] initWithCoordinates:location
                                        title:@"My Title"
                                     subTitle:@"My Sub Title"];

    annotation.pinColor = MKPinAnnotationColorPurple;

    /* And eventually add it to the map */
    [self.myMapView addAnnotation:annotation];

}

- (BOOL)shouldAutorotateToInterfaceOrientation
        :(UIInterfaceOrientation)interfaceOrientation{
    return YES;
}

@end
```

The results are shown in Figure 7-5.

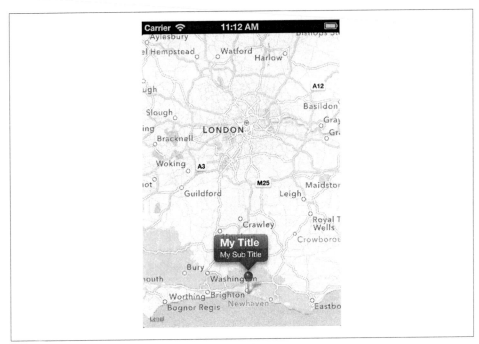

Figure 7-5. A pin with an alternative color displayed on a map view

7.6 Displaying Custom Pins on a Map View

Problem

Instead of the default iOS SDK pins, you would like to display your own images as pins on a map view.

Solution

Load an arbitrary image into an instance of the UIImage class and assign it to the image property of the MKAnnotationView instance that you return to your map view as a pin:

```
- (MKAnnotationView *)mapView:(MKMapView *)mapView
          viewForAnnotation:(id <MKAnnotation>)annotation{

  MKAnnotationView *result = nil;

  if ([annotation isKindOfClass:[MyAnnotation class]] == NO){
    return result;
  } if ([mapView isEqual:self.myMapView] == NO){
    /* We want to process this event only for the Map View
     that we have created previously */
    return result;
  }
```

```
/* First typecast the annotation for which the Map View has
   fired this delegate message */
MyAnnotation *senderAnnotation = (MyAnnotation *)annotation;

/* Using the class method we have defined in our custom
   annotation class, we will attempt to get a reusable
   identifier for the pin we are about to create */
NSString *pinReusableIdentifier =
[MyAnnotation
 reusableIdentifierforPinColor:senderAnnotation.pinColor];

/* Using the identifier we retrieved above, we will
   attempt to reuse a pin in the sender Map View */
MKPinAnnotationView *annotationView = (MKPinAnnotationView *)
[mapView
 dequeueReusableAnnotationViewWithIdentifier:
 pinReusableIdentifier];

if (annotationView == nil){
  /* If we fail to reuse a pin, then we will create one */
  annotationView =
  [[MKPinAnnotationView alloc]  initWithAnnotation:senderAnnotation
                                 reuseIdentifier:pinReusableIdentifier];

  /* Make sure we can see the callouts on top of
   each pin in case we have assigned title and/or
   subtitle to each pin */
  annotationView.canShowCallout = YES;

}

UIImage *pinImage = [UIImage imageNamed:@"BluePin.png"];
if (pinImage != nil){
  annotationView.image = pinImage;
}

result = annotationView;

return result;
}
```

In this code, we are displaying an image named *BluePin.png* (in our application bundle) for any pin that is dropped on the map. For the definition and the implementation of the MyAnnotation class, refer to Recipe 7.5.

Discussion

The delegate object of an instance of the MKMapView class must conform to the MKMap ViewDelegate protocol and implement the mapView:viewForAnnotation: method. The return value of this method is an instance of the MKAnnotationView class. Any object that subclasses the aforementioned class, by default, inherits a property called image.

Assigning a value to this property will replace the default image provided by the Map Kit framework, as shown in Figure 7-6.

See Also

Recipe 7.5

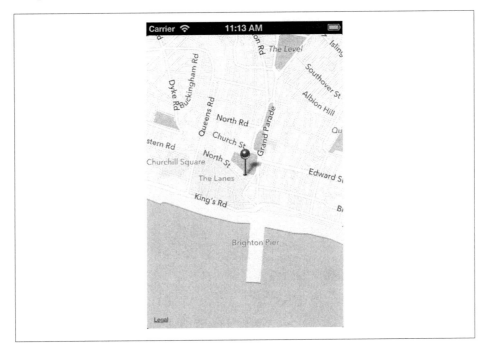

Figure 7-6. A custom image displayed on a map view

7.7 Converting Meaningful Addresses to Longitude and Latitude

Problem

You have an address of a location and you want to find the spatial location (*longitude, latitude*) of that address.

Solution

Use the geocodeAddressString:completionHandler: method of the CLGeocoder class.

Discussion

Reverse geocoding is the process of retrieving a meaningful address, city and country, and so on, using spatial locations (*Longitude, Latitude*). *Geocoding*, on the other hand, is the process of finding the spatial locations of a given address. Both geocoding and reverse geocoding facilities are encapsulated into the `CLGeocoder` class in the Core Location framework.

We geocode spatial locations by passing the address as `NSString` to the `geocodeAddressString:completionHandler:` method of the `CLGeocoder` class. The `completionHandler` parameter of this method accepts a block object that returns no value and has two parameters:

1. A placemarks array (of type `NSArray`), which will be set to the locations that matched your search.

2. An error (of type `NSError`), which will get set to an error code if the geocoding fails.

Let's go ahead and declare a property of type `CLGeocoder` first:

```
#import <UIKit/UIKit.h>
#import <CoreLocation/CoreLocation.h>

@interface
  Converting_Meaningful_Addresses_to_Longitude_and_LatitudeViewController
  : UIViewController

@property (nonatomic, strong) CLGeocoder *myGeocoder;

@end
```

Now, let's go ahead and implement the code to geocode an address:

```
- (void)didReceiveMemoryWarning{
  [super didReceiveMemoryWarning];
  // Release any cached data, images, etc that aren't in use.
}

- (void)viewDidLoad{
  [super viewDidLoad];  /* We have our address */
  NSString *oreillyAddress =
    @"1005 Gravenstein Highway North, Sebastopol, CA 95472, USA";

  self.myGeocoder = [[CLGeocoder alloc] init];

  [self.myGeocoder
   geocodeAddressString:oreillyAddress
   completionHandler:^(NSArray *placemarks, NSError *error) {

     if ([placemarks count] > 0 &&
         error == nil){
       NSLog(@"Found %lu placemark(s).", (unsigned long)[placemarks count]);
       CLPlacemark *firstPlacemark = [placemarks objectAtIndex:0];
       NSLog(@"Longitude = %f", firstPlacemark.location.coordinate.longitude);
       NSLog(@"Latitude = %f", firstPlacemark.location.coordinate.latitude);
```

```
    }
    else if ([placemarks count] == 0 &&
             error == nil){
      NSLog(@"Found no placemarks.");
    }
    else if (error != nil){
      NSLog(@"An error occurred = %@", error);
    }

  }];

}
```

Once the program is run, even in the simulator, you will get the following values printed to the console window if you have a working and active network connection:

```
Found 1 placemark(s).
Longitude = -122.841135
Latitude = 38.410373
```

7.8 Converting Longitude and Latitude to a Meaningful Address

Problem

You have the latitude and longitude of a spatial location and you want to retrieve the address of this location.

Solution

Retrieving a meaningful address using spatial x and y coordinates is called *reverse geocoding*. To do this, create and use an instance of the CLGeocoder class and provide a completion block object, making sure that the block object has no return value and accepts two parameters:

1. A placemarks array (of type NSArray), which will be set to the locations which matched your search.

2. An error (of type NSError), which will get set to an error code if the reverse geocoding fails.

After instantiating an object of type CLGeocoder, we will use its reverseGeocodeLocation:completionHandler: method to do the reverse geocoding.

The *.h* file of a simple view controller for this purpose is defined like so:

```
#import <UIKit/UIKit.h>
#import <CoreLocation/CoreLocation.h>

@interface
  Converting_Longitude_and_Latitude_to_a_Meaningful_AddressViewController
```

```
     : UIViewController

@property (nonatomic, strong) CLGeocoder *myGeocoder;

@end
```

You can do the reverse geocoding when your view loads:

```
- (void)viewDidLoad{
  [super viewDidLoad];

  CLLocation *location = [[CLLocation alloc]
                            initWithLatitude:+38.4112810
                            longitude:-122.8409780f];

  self.myGeocoder = [[CLGeocoder alloc] init];

  [self.myGeocoder
   reverseGeocodeLocation:location
   completionHandler:^(NSArray *placemarks, NSError *error) {

     if (error == nil &&
         [placemarks count] > 0){

       CLPlacemark *placemark = [placemarks objectAtIndex:0];
       /* We received the results */
       NSLog(@"Country = %@", placemark.country);
       NSLog(@"Postal Code = %@", placemark.postalCode);
       NSLog(@"Locality = %@", placemark.locality);
     }
     else if (error == nil &&
              [placemarks count] == 0){
       NSLog(@"No results were returned.");
     }
     else if (error != nil){
       NSLog(@"An error occurred = %@", error);
     }

   }];
}
```

The placemarks array, if the operation is successful, will contain objects of type CLPlacemark, which mark the addresses that match the longitude and latitude we passed to the reverseGeocodeLocation:completionHandler: method. So all we have to do is make sure that there were no errors, and that the array of placemarks contains at least one placemark.

The NSLog methods in the preceding code write the reverse geocoded address to the console window:

```
Country = United States
Postal Code = 95472
Locality = Sebastopol
```

Discussion

Each application has a limit on the number of reverse geocoding requests that it can make each day. The amount depends on the backend provider for the location services in iOS. There are various paid online services that expose third party APIs to developers. I cannot promote any of these services, but feel free to browse the Internet for them if you would like to get rid of limitations that currently exist in iOS SDK for reverse geocoding spatial coordinates. To perform a reverse geocoding request, you must create an instance of the `CLGeocoder` class. This class requires an active network connection in order to process requests successfully. The reverse geocoded values are reported to the completion handler block that is passed to the `reverseGeocodeLocation:completion Handler:` method.

CHAPTER 8

Implementing Gesture Recognizers

8.0 Introduction

Gestures are a combination of touch events. An example of a gesture can be found in the default iOS Photo application, which allows the user to zoom into and out of a photo while "pinching" the photo in and out using two fingers. Some of the most common gesture event detection code is encapsulated into reusable classes built into the iOS SDK. These classes can be used to detect swipe, pinch, pan, tap, drag, long press, and rotation gestures.

Gesture recognizers must be added to instances of the `UIView` class. A single view can have more than one gesture recognizer. Once a view catches the gesture, that view will be responsible for passing down the same gesture to other views in the hierarchy, if needed.

Some touch events required by an application might be complicated to process and might require the same event to be detectable in other views in the same application. This introduces the requirements for reusable gesture recognizers. There are six gesture recognizers in iOS SDK 5 and above:

- Swipe
- Rotation
- Pinch
- Pan
- Long press
- Tap

The basic framework for handling a gesture through a built-in gesture recognizer is as follows:

1. Create an object of the right data type for the gesture recognizer you want.
2. Add this object as a gesture recognizer to the view that will receive the gesture.
3. Write a method that is called when the gesture occurs and that takes the action you want.

The method associated as the target method of any gesture recognizer must follow these rules:

- It must return void.
- It must either accept no parameters, or accept a single parameter of type UIGesture Recognizer in which the system will pass the gesture recognizer that calls this method.

Here are two examples:

```
- (void) tapRecognizer:(UITapGestureRecognizer *)paramSender{
    /* */
}

- (void) tapRecognizer{
    /* */
}
```

Gesture recognizers are divided into two categories: *discrete* and *continuous*. Discrete gesture recognizers detect their gesture events and, once detected, call a method in their respective owners. Continuous gesture recognizers keep their owner objects informed of the events as they happen, and will call the method in their target object repeatedly as the event happens and until it ends.

For instance, a double-tap event is discrete. Even though it consists of two taps, the system recognizes that the taps occurred close enough together to be treated as a single event. The double-tap gesture recognizer calls the method in its target object once the double-tap event is detected.

An example of a continuous gesture recognizer is rotation. This gesture starts as soon as the user starts the rotation and only finishes when the user lifts his fingers off the screen. The method provided to the rotation gesture recognizer class gets called at short intervals until the event is finished.

Gesture recognizers can be added to any instance of the UIView class using the addGes tureRecognizer: method of the view, and when needed, they can be removed from the view using the removeGestureRecognizer: method.

The UIGestureRecognizer class has a property named state. The state property represents the different states the gesture recognizer can have throughout the recognition process. Discrete and continuous gesture recognizers go through different sets of states.

Discrete gesture recognizers can pass through the following states:

1. `UIGestureRecognizerStatePossible`

2. `UIGestureRecognizerStateRecognized`

3. `UIGestureRecognizerStateFailed`

Depending on the situation, a discrete gesture recognizer might send the `UIGestureRe cognizerStateRecognized` state to its target, or it might send the `UIGestureRecognizer StateFailed` state if an error occurs during the recognition process.

Continuous gesture recognizers take a different path in the states they send to their targets:

1. `UIGestureRecognizerStatePossible`

2. `UIGestureRecognizerStateBegan`

3. `UIGestureRecognizerStateChanged`

4. `UIGestureRecognizerStateEnded`

5. `UIGestureRecognizerStateFailed`

 A gesture recognizer's state is changed to `UIGestureRecognizerStatePos sible` when it is gathering information about touch events on a view and *might* at any point detect the relevant gesture. In addition to the afore-mentioned states of a continuous gesture recognizer, the `UIGestureRe cognizerStateCancelled` state can also be generated if anything inter-rupts the gesture. For instance, an incoming phone call can interrupt a pan gesture. In that case, the state of the gesture recognizer will be changed to `UIGestureRecognizerStateCancelled` and no further messag-es will be called on the receiver object by that gesture recognizer unless the user restarts the gesture sequence.

Again, if the continuous gesture recognizer stumbles upon a situation that cannot be fixed internally, it will end with the `UIGestureRecognizerStateFailed` state instead of `UIGestureRecognizerStateEnded`.

8.1 Detecting Swipe Gestures

Problem

You want to be able to detect when the user performs a swipe gesture on a view—for instance, swiping a picture out of the window.

Solution

Instantiate an object of type `UISwipeGestureRecognizer` and add it to an instance of `UIView`:

```
- (void)viewDidLoad {
  [super viewDidLoad];

  /* Instantiate the object */
  self.swipeGestureRecognizer = [[UISwipeGestureRecognizer alloc]
                                 initWithTarget:self
                                 action:@selector(handleSwipes:)];

  /* Swipes that are performed from right to
   left are to be detected */
  self.swipeGestureRecognizer.direction =
    UISwipeGestureRecognizerDirectionLeft;

  /* Just one finger needed */
  self.swipeGestureRecognizer.numberOfTouchesRequired = 1;

  /* Add it to the view */
  [self.view addGestureRecognizer:self.swipeGestureRecognizer];

}
```

A gesture recognizer could be created as a standalone object, but here, because we are using it just for one view, we have created it as a property of the view controller that will receive the gesture (`self.swipeGestureRecognizer`). This recipe's Discussion shows the `handleSwipes:` method used in this code as the target for the swipe gesture recognizer.

Discussion

The swipe gesture is one of the most straightforward motions that built-in iOS SDK gesture recognizers will register. It is a simple movement of one or more fingers on a view from one direction to another. The `UISwipeGestureRecognizer`, like other gesture recognizers, inherits from the `UIGestureRecognizer` class and adds various functionalities to this class, such as properties that allow us to specify the direction in which the swipe gestures have to be performed in order to be detected, or how many fingers the user has to hold on the screen to be able to perform a swipe gesture. Please bear in mind that swipe gestures are discrete gestures.

The `handleSwipes:` method that we used for the gesture recognizer instance can be implemented in this way:

```
- (void) handleSwipes:(UISwipeGestureRecognizer *)paramSender{

  if (paramSender.direction & UISwipeGestureRecognizerDirectionDown){
    NSLog(@"Swiped Down.");
  }
  if (paramSender.direction & UISwipeGestureRecognizerDirectionLeft){
    NSLog(@"Swiped Left.");
  }
  if (paramSender.direction & UISwipeGestureRecognizerDirectionRight){
    NSLog(@"Swiped Right.");
  }
```

```
if (paramSender.direction & UISwipeGestureRecognizerDirectionUp){
  NSLog(@"Swiped Up.");
}

}
```

 You can combine more than one direction in the direction property of an instance of the UISwipeGestureRecognizer class by using the bitwise OR operand. In Objective-C, this is done with the pipe (|) character. For instance, to detect diagonal swipes to the bottom-left corner of the screen, you can combine the UISwipeGestureRecognizerDirectionLeft and UISwipeGestureRecognizerDirectionDown values using the pipe character when constructing your swipe gesture recognizer. In the example, we are attempting to detect only swipes from the right side to the left.

Although swipe gestures are usually performed with one finger, the number of fingers required for the swipe gesture to be recognized can also be specified with the number OfTouchesRequired property of the UISwipeGestureRecognizer class.

8.2 Detecting Rotation Gestures

Problem

You want to detect when a user is attempting to rotate an element on the screen using her fingers.

Solution

Create an instance of the UIRotationGestureRecognizer class and attach it to your target view:

```
- (void)viewDidLoad {
[super viewDidLoad];

self.view.backgroundColor = [UIColor whiteColor];
self.helloWorldLabel = [[UILabel alloc] initWithFrame:CGRectZero];
self.helloWorldLabel.text = @"Hello, World!";
self.helloWorldLabel.font = [UIFont systemFontOfSize:16.0f];
[self.helloWorldLabel sizeToFit];
self.helloWorldLabel.center = self.view.center;
[self.view addSubview:self.helloWorldLabel];

self.rotationGestureRecognizer = [[UIRotationGestureRecognizer alloc]
                                  initWithTarget:self
                                  action:@selector(handleRotations:)];

[self.view addGestureRecognizer:self.rotationGestureRecognizer];

}
```

Discussion

The `UIRotationGestureRecognizer`, as its name implies, is the perfect candidate among gesture recognizers to detect rotation gestures and to help you build more intuitive graphical user interfaces. For instance, when the user encounters an image on the screen in your application in full-screen mode, it is quite intuitive for him to attempt to correct the orientation by rotating the image.

The `UIRotationGestureRecognizer` class implements a property named `rotation` that specifies the total amount and direction of rotation requested by the user's gesture, in radians. The rotation is determined from the fingers' initial position (`UIGestureRecognizerStateBegan`) and final position (`UIGestureRecognizerStateEnded`).

To rotate UI elements that inherit from `UIView` class, you can pass the `rotation` property of the rotation gesture recognizer to the `CGAffineTransformMakeRotation` function to make an affine transform, as shown in the example.

The code in this recipe's Solution passes the current object, in this case a view controller, to the target of the rotation gesture recognizer. The target selector is specified as `handleRotations:`, a method we have to implement. But before we do that, let's have a look at the header file of the view controller:

```
#import <UIKit/UIKit.h>

@interface Detecting_Rotation_GesturesViewController : UIViewController

@property (nonatomic, strong)
  UIRotationGestureRecognizer *rotationGestureRecognizer;

@property (nonatomic, strong)
  UILabel *helloWorldLabel;

/* We can remove the nonatomic and the unsafe_unretained marks from this
 property declaration. On a float value, the compiler will generate both
 these for us automatically */
@property (nonatomic, unsafe_unretained)
  CGFloat rotationAngleInRadians;

@end
```

Before we carry on, let's have a look at what each one of these properties does and why they are declared:

`helloWorldLabel`

This is a label we must create on the view of the view controller. Then we will write the code to rotate this label whenever the user attempts to perform rotation gestures on the view that owns this label (in this case, the view of the view controller).

`rotationGestureRecognizer`

This is the instance of the rotation gesture recognizer that we will later allocate and initialize.

`rotationAngleInRadians`

This is the value we will query as the exact rotation angle of our label. Initially we will set this to zero. Since the rotation angles reported by a rotation gesture recognizer are reset every time the rotation gesture is started again, we can keep the value of the rotation gesture recognizer whenever it goes into the `UIGestureRecognizer` `StateEnded` state. The next time the gesture is started, we will add the previous value to the new value to get an overall rotation angle.

The size and the origin of the label does not matter much. Even the position of the label isn't that important, as we will only attempt to rotate the label around its center, no matter where on the view the label is positioned. The only important thing to remember is that in universal applications, the position of a label on a view controller used in different targets (devices) must be calculated dynamically using the size of its parent view. Otherwise, on different devices such as the iPad or the iPhone, it might appear in different places on the screen.

Using the `center` property of the label, and setting that center location to the center of the containing view, we will center-align the contents of the label. The rotation transformation that we will apply to this label rotates the label around its center—and left-aligned or right-aligned labels whose actual frame is bigger than the minimum frame required to hold their contents without truncation will appear to be rotating in an unnatural way and not on the center. If you are curious, go ahead and left- or right-align the contents of the label and see what happens.

As we saw in this recipe's Solution, the rotation gesture recognizer that we created will send its events to a method called `handleRotations:`. Here is the implementation for this method:

```
- (void) handleRotations:(UIRotationGestureRecognizer *)paramSender{

  if (self.helloWorldLabel == nil){
    return;
  }

  /* Take the previous rotation and add the current rotation to it */
  self.helloWorldLabel.transform =
  CGAffineTransformMakeRotation(self.rotationAngleInRadians +
                           paramSender.rotation);

  /* At the end of the rotation, keep the angle for later use */
  if (paramSender.state == UIGestureRecognizerStateEnded){
    self.rotationAngleInRadians += paramSender.rotation;
  }

}
```

The way a rotation gesture recognizer sends us the rotation angles is very interesting. This gesture recognizer is continuous, which means it starts finding the angles as soon as the user begins her rotation gesture, and sends updates to the handler method at frequent intervals until the user is done. Each message treats the starting angle as zero and reports the difference between the message's starting point (which is the angle where the previous message left off) and its ending point. Thus, the complete effect of the gesture can be discovered only by adding up the angles reported by the different events. Clockwise movement produces a positive angular value, whereas counterclockwise movement produces a negative value.

 If you are using iPhone Simulator instead of a real device, you can still simulate the rotation gesture by holding down the Option key in the simulator. You will see two circles appear on the simulator at the same distance from the center of the screen, representing two fingers. If you want to shift these fingers from the center to another location while holding down the Alt key, press the Shift key and point somewhere else on the screen. Where you leave your pointer will become the new center for these two fingers.

Now we will simply assign this angle to the rotation angle of the label. But can you imagine what will happen once the rotation is finished and another one starts? The second rotation gesture's angle will replace that of the first rotation in the rotation value reported to the handler. For this reason, whenever a rotation gesture is finished, we must keep the current rotation of the label. The value in each rotation gesture's angle must be added in turn, and we must assign the result to the label's rotation transformation as we saw before.

As we saw earlier, we used the CGAffineTransformMakeRotation function to create an affine transformation. Functions in the iOS SDK that start with "CG" refer to the Core Graphics framework. For programs that use Core Graphics to compile and link successfully, you must make sure the Core Graphics framework is added to the list of frameworks. New versions of Xcode link a default project against the CoreGraphics framework automatically, so you don't really have to worry about that.

Now that we are sure Core Graphics is added to the target, we can compile and run the app.

See Also

Recipe 8.6

8.3 Detecting Panning and Dragging Gestures

Problem

You want the users of your application to be able to move GUI elements around using their fingers.

Pan gestures are continuous movements of fingers on the screen; recall that swipe gestures were discrete gestures. This means the method set as the target method of a pan gesture recognizer gets called repeatedly from the beginning to the end of the recognition process.

Solution

Use the `UIPanGestureRecognizer` class:

```
- (void)viewDidLoad {
[super viewDidLoad];

self.view.backgroundColor = [UIColor whiteColor];

/* Let's first create a label */
CGRect labelFrame = CGRectMake(0.0f,     /* X */
                               0.0f,     /* Y */
                               150.0f,   /* Width */
                               100.0f);  /* Height */

self.helloWorldLabel = [[UILabel alloc] initWithFrame:labelFrame];
self.helloWorldLabel.text = @"Hello World";
self.helloWorldLabel.backgroundColor = [UIColor blackColor];
self.helloWorldLabel.textColor = [UIColor whiteColor];
self.helloWorldLabel.textAlignment = UITextAlignmentCenter;

/* Make sure to enable user interaction; otherwise, tap events
 won't be caught on this label */
self.helloWorldLabel.userInteractionEnabled = YES;

/* And now make sure this label gets displayed on the view */
[self.view addSubview:self.helloWorldLabel];

/* Create the Pan Gesture Recognizer */
self.panGestureRecognizer = [[UIPanGestureRecognizer alloc]
                             initWithTarget:self
                             action:@selector(handlePanGestures:)];

/* At least and at most we need only one finger to activate
 the pan gesture recognizer */
self.panGestureRecognizer.minimumNumberOfTouches = 1;
self.panGestureRecognizer.maximumNumberOfTouches = 1;

/* Add it to the view */
[self.helloWorldLabel addGestureRecognizer:self.panGestureRecognizer];

}
```

The pan gesture recognizer will call the `handlePanGestures:` method as its target method. This method is described in this recipe's Discussion.

Discussion

The UIPanGestureRecognizer, as its name implies, can detect *pan gestures*. The pan gesture recognizer will go through the following states while recognizing the pan gesture:

1. UIGestureRecognizerStateBegan
2. UIGestureRecognizerStateChanged
3. UIGestureRecognizerStateEnded

We can implement the gesture recognizer target method as follows. The code will continuously move the center of the label along with the user's finger as UIGestureRecognizerStateChanged events are reported:

```
- (void) handlePanGestures:(UIPanGestureRecognizer*)paramSender{

  if (paramSender.state != UIGestureRecognizerStateEnded &&
      paramSender.state != UIGestureRecognizerStateFailed){
    CGPoint location = [paramSender locationInView:paramSender.view.superview];
    paramSender.view.center = location;
  }

}
```

 To be able to move the label on the view of the view controller, we need the position of the finger on the view, not the label. For this reason, we are calling the locationInView: method of the pan gesture recognizer and passing the superview of the label as the target view.

Use the locationInView: method of the pan gesture recognizer to find the point of the current panning finger(s). To detect multiple finger locations, use the locationOfTouch:inView: method. Using the minimumNumberOfTouches and maximumNumberOfTouches properties of the UIPanGestureRecognizer, you can detect more than one panning touch at a time. In the example, for the sake of simplicity, we are trying to detect only one finger.

 During the UIGestureRecognizerStateEnded state, the reported *x* and *y* values might not be a number; in other words, they could be equal to NAN. That is why we need to avoid using the reported values during this particular state.

8.4 Detecting Long Press Gestures

Problem

You want to be able to detect when the user taps and holds his finger on a view for a certain period of time.

Solution

Create an instance of the UILongPressGestureRecognizer class and add it to the view that has to detect long tap gestures. The *.h* file of the view controller is defined in this way:

```
#import <UIKit/UIKit.h>

@interface Detecting_Long_Press_GesturesViewController : UIViewController

@property (nonatomic, strong)
  UILongPressGestureRecognizer *longPressGestureRecognizer;

@property (nonatomic, strong) UIButton *dummyButton;

@end
```

Here is the viewDidLoad instance method of the view controller that uses the long press gesture recognizer that we defined in the *.m* file:

```
- (void)viewDidLoad {
  [super viewDidLoad];

  self.view.backgroundColor = [UIColor whiteColor];

  self.dummyButton = [UIButton buttonWithType:UIButtonTypeRoundedRect];
  self.dummyButton.frame = CGRectMake(0.0f,
                                      0.0f,
                                      72.0f,
                                      37.0f);
  self.dummyButton.center = self.view.center;
  [self.view addSubview:self.dummyButton];

  /* First create the gesture recognizer */
  self.longPressGestureRecognizer =
  [[UILongPressGestureRecognizer alloc]
   initWithTarget:self
   action:@selector(handleLongPressGestures:)];

  /* The number of fingers that must be present on the screen */
  self.longPressGestureRecognizer.numberOfTouchesRequired = 2;

  /* Maximum 100 points of movement allowed before the gesture
   is recognized */
  self.longPressGestureRecognizer.allowableMovement = 100.0f;
```

```
/* The user must press two fingers (numberOfTouchesRequired) for
 at least one second for the gesture to be recognized */
self.longPressGestureRecognizer.minimumPressDuration = 1.0;

/* Add this gesture recognizer to the view */
[self.view addGestureRecognizer:self.longPressGestureRecognizer];

}
```

 If the long-press gesture recognizer is firing events to the receiver object while the gesture is continuing on the user's end, and a phone call or any other interruption comes in, the state of the gesture recognizer will be changed to UIGestureRecognizerStateCancelled. No further messages will be sent to the receiver object from that gesture recognizer until the user initiates the actions required to start the recognition process again; in this example, holding two fingers for at least one second on the view of our view controller.

 Our code runs on a view controller with a property named longPress GestureRecognizer of type UILongPressGestureRecognizer. For more information, refer to this recipe's Discussion.

Discussion

The iOS SDK comes with a long tap gesture recognizer class named UILongTapGes tureRecognizer. A long tap gesture is triggered when the user presses one or more fingers (configurable by the programmer) on a UIView and holds the finger(s) for a specific amount of time. Furthermore, you can narrow the detection of gestures down to only those long tap gestures that are performed after a certain number of fingers are tapped on a view for a certain number of times and are then kept on the view for a specified number of seconds. Bear in mind that long taps are continuous events.

Four important properties can change the way the long tap gesture recognizer performs. These are:

numberOfTapsRequired
> This is the number of taps the user has to perform on the target view, before the gesture can be triggered. Bear in mind that a tap is *not* merely a finger positioned on a screen. A tap is the movement of putting a finger down on the screen and lifting the finger off. The default value of this property is 0.

numberOfTouchesRequired
> This property specifies the number of fingers that must be touching the screen before the gesture can be recognized. You must specify the same number of fingers to detect the taps, if the numberOfTapsRequired property is set to a value larger than 0.

allowableMovement

This is the maximum number of pixels that the fingers on the screen can be moved before the gesture recognition is aborted.

minimumPressDuration

This property dictates how long, measured in seconds, the user must press his finger(s) on the screen before the gesture event can be detected.

In the example, these properties are set as follows:

- numberOfTapsRequired: Default (we are not changing this value)
- numberOfTouchesRequired: 2
- allowableMovement: 100
- minimumPressDuration: 1

With these values, the long tap gesture will be recognized only if the user presses on the screen and holds both fingers for one second (minimumPressDuration) without moving her fingers more than 100 pixels around (allowableMovement).

Now when the gesture is recognized, it will call the handleLongPressGestures: method, which we can implement in this way:

```
- (void) handleLongPressGestures:(UILongPressGestureRecognizer *)paramSender{

  /* Here we want to find the midpoint of the two fingers
     that caused the long press gesture to be recognized. We configured
     this number using the numberOfTouchesRequired property of the
     UILongPressGestureRecognizer that we instantiated in the
     viewDidLoad instance method of this View Controller. If we
     find that another long press gesture recognizer is using this
     method as its target, we will ignore it */

  if ([paramSender isEqual:self.longPressGestureRecognizer]){

    if (paramSender.numberOfTouchesRequired == 2){

      CGPoint touchPoint1 =
      [paramSender locationOfTouch:0
                           inView:paramSender.view];

      CGPoint touchPoint2 =
      [paramSender locationOfTouch:1
                           inView:paramSender.view];

      CGFloat midPointX = (touchPoint1.x + touchPoint2.x) / 2.0f;
      CGFloat midPointY = (touchPoint1.y + touchPoint2.y) / 2.0f;

      CGPoint midPoint = CGPointMake(midPointX, midPointY);

      self.dummyButton.center = midPoint;
```

```
        } else {
          /* This is a long press gesture recognizer with more
             or less than 2 fingers */

        }
      }

    }
```

 One of the applications in iOS that uses long tap gesture recognizers is the Maps application. In this application, when you are looking at different locations, press your finger on a specific location and hold it for a while without lifting it off the screen. This will drop a pin on that specific location.

8.5 Detecting Tap Gestures

Problem

You want to be able to detect when users tap on a view.

Solution

Create an instance of the UITapGestureRecognizer class and add it to the target view, using the addGestureRecognizer: instance method of the UIView class. Let's have a look at the definition of the view controller (the *.h* file):

```
#import <UIKit/UIKit.h>

@interface Detecting_Tap_GesturesViewController : UIViewController

@property (nonatomic, strong)
  UITapGestureRecognizer *tapGestureRecognizer;

@end
```

The implementation of the viewDidLoad instance method of the view controller is as follows:

```
- (void)viewDidLoad {
  [super viewDidLoad];

  self.view.backgroundColor = [UIColor whiteColor];

  /* Create the Tap Gesture Recognizer */
  self.tapGestureRecognizer = [[UITapGestureRecognizer alloc]
                                 initWithTarget:self
                                 action:@selector(handleTaps:)];

  /* The number of fingers that must be on the screen */
```

```
self.tapGestureRecognizer.numberOfTouchesRequired = 2;

/* The total number of taps to be performed before the
 gesture is recognized */
self.tapGestureRecognizer.numberOfTapsRequired = 3;

/* Add this gesture recognizer to the view */
[self.view addGestureRecognizer:self.tapGestureRecognizer];

}
```

Discussion

The tap gesture recognizer is the best candidate among gesture recognizers to detect plain tap gestures. A tap event is the event triggered by the user touching and lifting his finger(s) off the screen. A tap gesture is a discrete gesture.

The locationInView: method of the UITapGestureRecognizer class can be used to detect the location of the tap event. If the tap gesture requires more than one touch, the locationOfTouch:inView: method of the UITapGestureRecognizer class can be called to determine individual touch points. In the code, we have set the numberOf TouchesRequired property of the tap gesture recognizer to 2. With this value set, the gesture recognizer will require two fingers to be on the screen on each tap event. The number of taps that are required for the gesture recognizer to recognize this gesture is set to 3, using the numberOfTapsRequired property. We have provided the handleTaps: method as the target method of the tap gesture recognizer:

```
- (void) handleTaps:(UITapGestureRecognizer*)paramSender{

    NSUInteger touchCounter = 0;
    for (touchCounter = 0;
         touchCounter < paramSender.numberOfTouchesRequired;
         touchCounter++){
      CGPoint touchPoint =
      [paramSender locationOfTouch:touchCounter
                            inView:paramSender.view];
        NSLog(@"Touch #%lu: %@",
              (unsigned long)touchCounter+1,
              NSStringFromCGPoint(touchPoint));
    }

}
```

In this code, we are going through the number of touches that the tap gesture recognizer was asked to look for. Based on that number, we are finding the location of each tap. Depending on where you tap on the view on your simulator, you will get results similar to this in the console window:

```
Touch #1: {107, 186}
Touch #2: {213, 254}
```

If you are using the simulator, you can simulate two touches at the same time by holding down the Option key and moving your mouse on the simulator's screen. You will now have two concentric touch points on the screen.

One function worth noting is the NSStringFromCGPoint method, which, as its name implies, can convert a CGPoint structure to NSString. We use this function to convert the CGPoint of each touch on the screen to an NSString, so that we can log it to the console window using NSLog. You can bring up the console window with Run → Console.

8.6 Detecting Pinch Gestures

Problem

You want your users to be able to perform a pinch gesture on a view.

Solution

Create an instance of the UIPinchGestureRecognizer class and add it to your target view, using the addGestureRecognizer: instance method of the UIView class:

```
- (void)viewDidLoad {
  [super viewDidLoad];

  self.view.backgroundColor = [UIColor whiteColor];

  CGRect labelRect = CGRectMake(0.0f,    /* X */
                                0.0f,    /* Y */
                                200.0f,  /* Width */
                                200.0f); /* Height */

  self.myBlackLabel = [[UILabel alloc] initWithFrame:labelRect];
  self.myBlackLabel.center = self.view.center;
  self.myBlackLabel.backgroundColor = [UIColor blackColor];

  /* Without this line, the pinch gesture recognizer will not work */
  self.myBlackLabel.userInteractionEnabled = YES;
  [self.view addSubview:self.myBlackLabel];

  /* Create the Pinch Gesture Recognizer */
  self.pinchGestureRecognizer = [[UIPinchGestureRecognizer alloc]
                                 initWithTarget:self
                                 action:@selector(handlePinches:)];

  /* Add this gesture recognizer to the view */
  [self.myBlackLabel
   addGestureRecognizer:self.pinchGestureRecognizer];

}
```

The .h file of the view controller is defined in this way:

```
#import <UIKit/UIKit.h>

@interface Detecting_Pinch_GesturesViewController : UIViewController

@property (nonatomic, strong)
  UIPinchGestureRecognizer *pinchGestureRecognizer;

@property (nonatomic, strong) UILabel *myBlackLabel;

@property (nonatomic, unsafe_unretained) CGFloat currentScale;

@end
```

Discussion

Pinching allows users to scale GUI elements up and down easily. For instance, the Safari web browser on iOS allows users to pinch on a web page in order to zoom into the contents being displayed. Pinching works in two ways: scaling up and scaling down. It is a continuous gesture that must always be performed using two fingers on the screen.

The state of this gesture recognizer changes in this order:

1. UIGestureRecognizerStateBegan
2. UIGestureRecognizerStateChanged
3. UIGestureRecognizerStateEnded

Once the pinch gesture is recognized, the action method in the target object will be called (and will continue to be called until the pinch gesture ends). Inside the action method you can access two very important properties of the pinch gesture recognizer: scale and velocity. scale is the factor by which you should scale the x- and y-axes of a GUI element to reflect the size of the user's gesture. velocity is the velocity of the pinch in pixels per second. The velocity is a negative value if the touch points are getting closer to each other, and a positive value if they are getting farther away from each other.

The value of the scale property can be provided to the CGAffineTransformMakeScale Core Graphics function in order to retrieve an affine transformation. This affine transformation can be applied to the transform property of any instance of the UIView class in order to change its transformation. We are using this function in this way:

```
- (void) handlePinches:(UIPinchGestureRecognizer*)paramSender{

    if (paramSender.state == UIGestureRecognizerStateEnded){
      self.currentScale = paramSender.scale;
    } else if (paramSender.state == UIGestureRecognizerStateBegan &&
            self.currentScale != 0.0f){
      paramSender.scale = self.currentScale;
    }

    if (paramSender.scale != NAN &&
        paramSender.scale != 0.0){
```

```
        paramSender.view.transform =
        CGAffineTransformMakeScale(paramSender.scale,
                                   paramSender.scale);
    }

}
```

Since the scale property of a pinch gesture recognizer is reset every time a new pinch gesture is recognized, we are storing the last value of this property in an instance property of the view controller called currentScale. The next time a new gesture is recognized, we start the scale factor from the previously reported scale factor, as demonstrated in the code.

CHAPTER 9

Networking, JSON, XML, and Twitter

9.0 Introduction

iOS apps, when connected to the Internet, become more lively. For example, imagine an app that brings high-quality wallpapers to its users. The user can pick from a big list of wallpapers and assign any of those images as his iOS background. Now consider an app that does the same thing, but adds to its list of wallpapers every day, week, or month. The user comes back to the app, and voilá! Tons of new wallpapers are dynamically added to the app. That is the magic of web services and the Internet. This can easily be achieved with basic knowledge of networking, XML, JSON, and Twitter connectivity along with some creativity on the app developer's part.

The iOS SDK allows us to connect to the Internet and retrieve and send data using the `NSURLConnection` class. JSON serialization and deserialization will all be done using the `NSJSONSerialization` class. XML parsing will be done using `NSXMLParser`, and the Twitter connectivity will be done using the Twitter framework.

9.1 Downloading Asynchronously with NSURLConnection

Problem

You want to download a file from a URL, asynchronously.

Solution

Use the `NSURLConnection` class with an asynchronous request.

Discussion

There are two ways of using the `NSURLConnection` class. One is asynchronous and the other is synchronous. Asynchronous connection will create a new thread and does its downloading process on the new thread. Synchronous connection will block the *calling thread* while downloading content and doing its communication.

Many developers think that a synchronous connection blocks the *main thread*, but that is incorrect. A synchronous connection will always block the thread from which it is fired. If you fire a synchronous connection from the main thread, yes, the main thread will be blocked. But if you fire a synchronous connection from a thread other than the main thread, it will be like an asynchronous connection in that it won't block your main thread. In fact, the only difference between a synchronous and an asynchronous connection is that the runtime will create a thread for the asynchronous connection, while it won't do such thing for a synchronous connection.

In order to create an asynchronous connection, we need to:

1. Have our URL in an instance of `NSString`.
2. Convert our string to an instance of `NSURL`.
3. Place our URL in a URL Request of type `NSURLRequest`, or in case of mutable URLs, in an instance of `NSMutableURLRequest`.
4. Create an instance of `NSURLConnection` and pass the URL request to it.

We can create an asynchronous URL connection using the `sendAsynchronousRequest:queue:completionHandler:` class method of `NSURLConnection`. The parameters to this method are:

`sendAsynchronousRequest`
> A request of type `NSURLRequest`, as we already discussed.

`queue`
> An operation queue. We can simply allocate and initialize a new operation queue and pass it to this method, if we wish.

`completionHandler`
> A block object to be executed when the asynchronous connection finishes its work either successfully or unsuccessfully. This block object should accept three parameters:
>
> 1. An object of type `NSURLResponse` which encapsulates the response that the server sent us, if any.
> 2. Data of type `NSData` if any. This data will be the data that the connection fetched from the URL.
> 3. Error of type `NSError` if an error occurs.

The `sendAsynchronousRequest:queue:completionHandler:` method doesn't get called on the main thread, so make sure that if you want to perform a UI-related task, that you are back on the main thread.

Enough talk and let's have a look at an example. In this example, we will try to fetch the HTML contents of Apple's home page and then print the contents as a string to the console window:

```
NSString *urlAsString = @"http://www.apple.com";
NSURL *url = [NSURL URLWithString:urlAsString];
NSURLRequest *urlRequest = [NSURLRequest requestWithURL:url];
NSOperationQueue *queue = [[NSOperationQueue alloc] init];

[NSURLConnection
 sendAsynchronousRequest:urlRequest
 queue:queue
 completionHandler:^(NSURLResponse *response,
                     NSData *data,
                     NSError *error) {

   if ([data length] >0  &&
       error == nil){
     NSString *html = [[NSString alloc] initWithData:data
                                    encoding:NSUTF8StringEncoding];
     NSLog(@"HTML = %@", html);
   }
   else if ([data length] == 0 &&
            error == nil){
     NSLog(@"Nothing was downloaded.");
   }
   else if (error != nil){
     NSLog(@"Error happened = %@", error);
   }

 }];
```

It's as simple as that. If you wanted to save the data that the connection downloaded
for us to the disk, you could simply do so using the appropriate methods of the
NSData that we get from the completion block:

```
NSString *urlAsString = @"http://www.apple.com";
NSURL *url = [NSURL URLWithString:urlAsString];
NSURLRequest *urlRequest = [NSURLRequest requestWithURL:url];
NSOperationQueue *queue = [[NSOperationQueue alloc] init];

[NSURLConnection
 sendAsynchronousRequest:urlRequest
 queue:queue
 completionHandler:^(NSURLResponse *response,
                     NSData *data,
                     NSError *error) {

   if ([data length] >0  &&
       error == nil){

     /* Get the documents directory */
     NSString *documentsDir =
     [NSSearchPathForDirectoriesInDomains(NSDocumentDirectory,
                                 NSUserDomainMask,
                                 YES) objectAtIndex:0];
     /* Append the file name to the documents directory */
     NSString *filePath = [documentsDir
                   stringByAppendingPathComponent:@"apple.html"];
```

```
/* Write the data to the file */
[data writeToFile:filePath
        atomically:YES];

NSLog(@"Successfully saved the file to %@", filePath);

}
else if ([data length] == 0 &&
        error == nil){
  NSLog(@"Nothing was downloaded.");
}
else if (error != nil){
  NSLog(@"Error happened = %@", error);
}

}];
```

It's that simple, really. In older versions of iOS SDK, URL connections used the delegation model, but now it's all simply block-based and you no longer have to worry about implementing delegate methods.

9.2 Handling Timeouts in Asynchronous Connections

Problem

You want to set a wait limit—in other words, a timeout—on an asynchronous connection.

Solution

Set the timeout on the URL request that you pass to the NSURLConnection class.

Discussion

When instantiating an object of type NSURLRequest to pass to your URL connection, you can use its requestWithURL:cachePolicy:timeoutInterval: class method and pass the desired number of seconds of your timeout as the timeoutInterval parameter.

For instance, if you want to wait a maximum of 30 seconds to download the contents of Apple's home page using a synchronous connection, create your URL request like so:

```
NSString *urlAsString = @"http://www.apple.com";
NSURL *url = [NSURL URLWithString:urlAsString];

NSURLRequest *urlRequest =
[NSURLRequest
 requestWithURL:url cachePolicy:NSURLRequestReloadIgnoringLocalAndRemoteCacheData
 timeoutInterval:30.0f];

NSOperationQueue *queue = [[NSOperationQueue alloc] init];
```

```
[NSURLConnection
 sendAsynchronousRequest:urlRequest
 queue:queue
 completionHandler:^(NSURLResponse *response,
                     NSData *data,
                     NSError *error) {

  if ([data length] >0  &&
      error == nil){
    NSString *html = [[NSString alloc] initWithData:data
                                        encoding:NSUTF8StringEncoding];
    NSLog(@"HTML = %@", html);
  }
  else if ([data length] == 0 &&
          error == nil){
    NSLog(@"Nothing was downloaded.");
  }
  else if (error != nil){
    NSLog(@"Error happened = %@", error);
  }

}];
```

What will happen here is that the runtime will try to retrieve the contents of the provided URL. If this can be done before 30 seconds have elapsed and the connection is established before the timeout occurs, then fine. If not, the runtime will provide you with a timeout error in the error parameter of the completion block.

9.3 Downloading Synchronously with NSURLConnection

Problem

You want to download the contents of a URL, synchronously.

Solution

Use the sendSynchronousRequest:returningResponse:error: class method of NSURLConnection. The return value of this method is data of type NSData.

Discussion

Using the sendSynchronousRequest:returningResponse:error: class method of NSURLConnection, we can send a synchronous request to a URL. Now, remember: synchronous connections do *not* necessarily block the main thread! Synchronous connections block the *current thread* and if the current thread is the main thread, then the main thread will be blocked. If you go on a global concurrent queue with GCD and then initiate a synchronous connection, then you are *not* blocking the main thread.

Let's go ahead and initiate our first synchronous connection and see what happens. In this example, we will try to retrieve the home page of Yahoo!'s US website:

```
- (BOOL)           application:(UIApplication *)application
  didFinishLaunchingWithOptions:(NSDictionary *)launchOptions{

    NSLog(@"We are here...");

    NSString *urlAsString = @"http://www.yahoo.com";
    NSURL *url = [NSURL URLWithString:urlAsString];

    NSURLRequest *urlRequest = [NSURLRequest requestWithURL:url];

    NSURLResponse *response = nil;
    NSError *error = nil;

    NSLog(@"Firing synchronous url connection...");
    NSData *data = [NSURLConnection sendSynchronousRequest:urlRequest
                                        returningResponse:&response
                                                    error:&error];

    if ([data length] > 0 &&
        error == nil){
      NSLog(@"%lu bytes of data was returned.", (unsigned long)[data length]);
    }
    else if ([data length] == 0 &&
             error == nil){
      NSLog(@"No data was returned.");
    }
    else if (error != nil){
      NSLog(@"Error happened = %@", error);
    }

    NSLog(@"We are done.");

    self.window = [[UIWindow alloc] initWithFrame:
                    [[UIScreen mainScreen] bounds]];

    self.window.backgroundColor = [UIColor whiteColor];
    [self.window makeKeyAndVisible];
    return YES;
}
```

If you run this app and then look at the console window, you will see something similar to this printed out:

```
We are here...
Firing synchronous url connection...
194472 bytes of data was returned.
We are done.
```

So it's obvious that the current thread printed the string *We are here...* to the console window, waited for the connection to finish (as it was a synchronous connection that blocks the current thread), and then printed the *We are done.* text to the console window. Now let's do an experiment. Let's place the same exact synchronous connection inside a global concurrent queue in GCD, which guarantees concurrency, and see what happens:

```
- (BOOL)              application:(UIApplication *)application
  didFinishLaunchingWithOptions:(NSDictionary *)launchOptions{

  NSLog(@"We are here...");

  NSString *urlAsString = @"http://www.yahoo.com";

  NSLog(@"Firing synchronous url connection...");

  dispatch_queue_t dispatchQueue =
    dispatch_get_global_queue(DISPATCH_QUEUE_PRIORITY_DEFAULT, 0);

  dispatch_async(dispatchQueue, ^(void) {

    NSURL *url = [NSURL URLWithString:urlAsString];
    NSURLRequest *urlRequest = [NSURLRequest requestWithURL:url];
    NSURLResponse *response = nil;
    NSError *error = nil;

    NSData *data = [NSURLConnection sendSynchronousRequest:urlRequest
                                        returningResponse:&response
                                                    error:&error];

    if ([data length] > 0 &&
        error == nil){
      NSLog(@"%lu bytes of data was returned.", (unsigned long)[data length]);
    }
    else if ([data length] == 0 &&
             error == nil){
      NSLog(@"No data was returned.");
    }
    else if (error != nil){
      NSLog(@"Error happened = %@", error);
    }
  });


  NSLog(@"We are done.");

  self.window = [[UIWindow alloc] initWithFrame:
                  [[UIScreen mainScreen] bounds]];

  self.window.backgroundColor = [UIColor whiteColor];
  [self.window makeKeyAndVisible];
  return YES;
}
```

The output will be similar to this:

```
We are here...
Firing synchronous url connection...
We are done.
194326 bytes of data was returned.
```

So in this example, the current thread carried on to print the `We are done.` text to the console window without having to wait for the synchronous connection to finish reading from its URL. That is interesting, isn't it? So this proves that a synchronous URL connection won't necessarily block the main thread, if managed properly. Synchronous connections are guaranteed to block the *current thread*, though.

9.4 Modifying a URL Request with NSMutableURLRequest

Problem

You want to adjust various HTTP headers and settings of a URL request before passing it to a URL connection.

Solution

This technique is the basis of many useful recipes shown later in this chapter. Use `NSMutableURLRequest` instead of `NSURLRequest`.

Discussion

A URL request can be either *mutable* or *immutable*. A mutable URL request can be changed after it has been allocated and initialized, whereas an immutable URL request cannot. Mutable URL requests are the target of this recipe. You can create them using the `NSMutableURLRequest` class.

Let's have a look at an example where we will change the timeout interval of a URL request *after* we have allocated and initialized it:

```
NSString *urlAsString = @"http://www.apple.com";
NSURL *url = [NSURL URLWithString:urlAsString];
NSMutableURLRequest *urlRequest = [NSMutableURLRequest requestWithURL:url];
[urlRequest setTimeoutInterval:30.0f];
```

Now let's have a look at another example where we set the URL and the timeout of a URL request after it has been allocated and initialized:

```
NSString *urlAsString = @"http://www.apple.com";
NSURL *url = [NSURL URLWithString:urlAsString];
NSMutableURLRequest *urlRequest = [NSMutableURLRequest new];
[urlRequest setTimeoutInterval:30.0f];
[urlRequest setURL:url];
```

In other recipes in this chapter, we will have a look at some of the really neat tricks that we can perform using mutable URL requests.

9.5 Sending HTTP GET Requests with NSURLConnection

Problem

You want to send a GET request over the HTTP protocol and perhaps pass parameters along your request to the receiver.

Solution

By convention, GET requests allow parameters through query strings of the familiar form:

```
http://example.com/?param1=value1&param2=value2...
```

You can use strings to provide the parameters in the conventional format.

Discussion

A GET request is a request to a web server to retrieve data. The request usually carries some parameters, which are sent in a query string as part of the URL.

To let you test parameter passing, I have prepared a simple GET web service at the following address: *http://pixolity.com/get.php*. If you open this URL in your browser, you will see something similar to Figure 9-1.

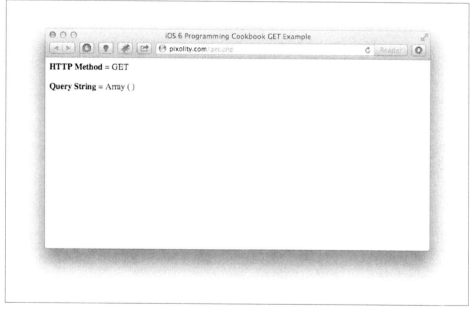

Figure 9-1. The example GET web service opened in a web browser

So our web browser is able to open this URL just fine, and you can see that the web service is able to detect query string parameters and GET parameters. Now if you open the following URL (*http://pixolity.com/get.php?param1=First&param2=Second*) in your browser, you will see results similar to those shown in Figure 9-2.

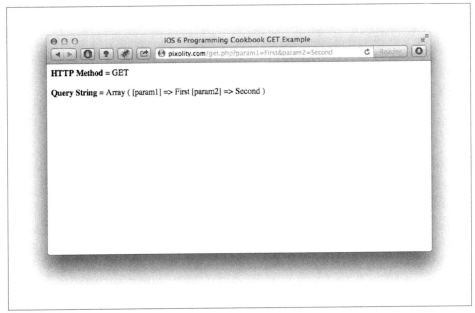

Figure 9-2. Query string parameters sent to the GET web service

To simulate sending query string parameters in a GET request to the same web service using NSURLConnection, use a mutable URL request and explicitly specify your HTTP method to GET using the setHTTPMethod: method of NSMutableURLRequest and put your parameters as part of the URL, like so:

```
/* URL = http://pixolity.com/get.php?param1=First&param2=Second */
NSString *urlAsString = @"http://pixolity.com/get.php";
urlAsString = [urlAsString stringByAppendingString:@"?param1=First"];
urlAsString = [urlAsString stringByAppendingString:@"&param2=Second"];

NSURL *url = [NSURL URLWithString:urlAsString];

NSMutableURLRequest *urlRequest = [NSMutableURLRequest requestWithURL:url];
[urlRequest setTimeoutInterval:30.0f];
[urlRequest setHTTPMethod:@"GET"];

NSOperationQueue *queue = [[NSOperationQueue alloc] init];

[NSURLConnection
 sendAsynchronousRequest:urlRequest
 queue:queue
 completionHandler:^(NSURLResponse *response,
```

```
                    NSData *data,
                    NSError *error) {

    if ([data length] >0  &&
        error == nil){
      NSString *html = [[NSString alloc] initWithData:data
                                       encoding:NSUTF8StringEncoding];
      NSLog(@"HTML = %@", html);
    }
    else if ([data length] == 0 &&
             error == nil){
      NSLog(@"Nothing was downloaded.");
    }
    else if (error != nil){
      NSLog(@"Error happened = %@", error);
    }

  }];
```

What gets printed to the console window now is the data that comes back from the web service:

```
HTML =
<html>
    <head>
        <title>iOS 6 Programming Cookbook GET Example</title>
    </head>
    <body>

<b>HTTP Method</b> = GET<br/><br/><b>Query String</b> = Array
(
    [param1] => First
    [param2] => Second
)

    </body>
</html>
```

The only thing that you have to bear in mind is that the first parameter is prefixed with a question mark and any subsequent parameter is prefixed with an ampersand. That's really about it! Now you are using the HTTP GET method and you know how to send parameters as a query string.

9.6 Sending HTTP POST Requests with NSURLConnection

Problem

You want to call a web service using HTTP POST method, and perhaps pass parameters (as part of the HTTP body or in the query string) to the web service.

Solution

Just as with the GET method, we can use the POST method using `NSURLConnection`. We must explicitly set our URL's method to POST.

Discussion

I have set up a dummy web service at the following address: *http://pixolity.com/post .php*. If you open this URL in your browser, you will see something similar to the screen shown in Figure 9-3.

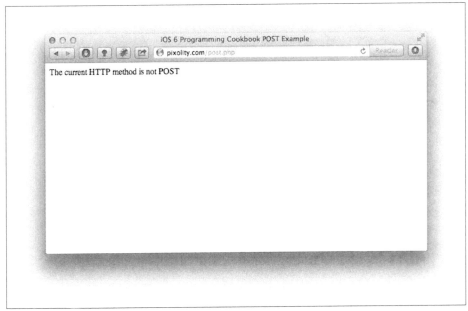

Figure 9-3. The POST web service opened in a web browser

This web service expects POST requests and is able to print out parameters that are sent as part of the query string and as part of the HTTP body. You can send both, if you want to. Let's write a simple app that can create an asynchronous connection and send a few parameters as a query string and a few parameters in the HTTP body to the aforementioned URL:

```
NSString *urlAsString = @"http://pixolity.com/post.php";
urlAsString = [urlAsString stringByAppendingString:@"?param1=First"];
urlAsString = [urlAsString stringByAppendingString:@"&param2=Second"];

NSURL *url = [NSURL URLWithString:urlAsString];

NSMutableURLRequest *urlRequest = [NSMutableURLRequest requestWithURL:url];
[urlRequest setTimeoutInterval:30.0f];
[urlRequest setHTTPMethod:@"POST"];
```

```
NSString *body = @"bodyParam1=BodyValue1&bodyParam2=BodyValue2";
[urlRequest setHTTPBody:[body dataUsingEncoding:NSUTF8StringEncoding]];

NSOperationQueue *queue = [[NSOperationQueue alloc] init];

[NSURLConnection
 sendAsynchronousRequest:urlRequest
 queue:queue
 completionHandler:^(NSURLResponse *response,
                     NSData *data,
                     NSError *error) {

   if ([data length] >0  &&
       error == nil){
     NSString *html = [[NSString alloc] initWithData:data
                                         encoding:NSUTF8StringEncoding];
     NSLog(@"HTML = %@", html);
   }
   else if ([data length] == 0 &&
            error == nil){
     NSLog(@"Nothing was downloaded.");
   }
   else if (error != nil){
     NSLog(@"Error happened = %@", error);
   }

}];
```

 The first parameter sent in the HTTP body does not have to be prefixed with a question mark, unlike the first parameter in a query string.

If you now look at the output printed to the console window, you will see something similar to this:

```
HTML =
<html>
    <head>
        <title>iOS 6 Programming Cookbook POST Example</title>
    </head>
    <body>

<b>HTTP Method</b> = POST<br/><br/><b>Query String</b> = Array
(
    [param1] => First
    [param2] => Second
)
<br/><br/><b>Body Parameters</b> = Array
(
    [bodyParam1] => BodyValue1
    [bodyParam2] => BodyValue2
)
```

```
        </body>
    </html>
```

9.7 Sending HTTP DELETE Requests with NSURLConnection

Problem

You want to call a web service using the HTTP DELETE method to delete a resource from a URL, and perhaps pass parameters, as part of the HTTP body or in the query string, to the web service.

Solution

Just as with the GET and POST methods, you can use the DELETE method using NSURLConnection. You must explicitly set your URL's method to DELETE.

Discussion

I have set up a dummy web service at the following address: *http://pixolity.com/delete .php*. If you open this URL in your browser, you will see something similar to the screen shown in Figure 9-4.

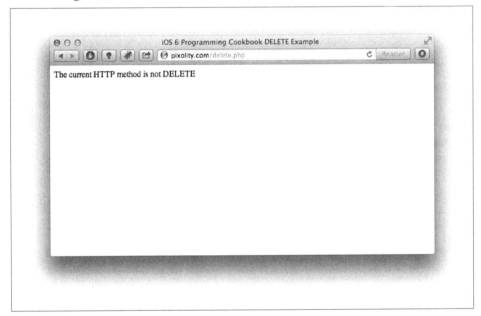

Figure 9-4. The DELETE web service opened in a web browser

This web service expects DELETE requests (but it's just a dummy service, so it doesn't delete any resources). It can print out parameters that are sent as part of the query string

---

and as part of the HTTP body, so you can send both types in the same request. Let's write a simple app that can create an asynchronous connection and send a few parameters as a query string and a few parameters in the HTTP body to the aforementioned URL, using the DELETE HTTP method:

```
NSString *urlAsString = @"http://pixolity.com/delete.php";
urlAsString = [urlAsString stringByAppendingString:@"?param1=First"];
urlAsString = [urlAsString stringByAppendingString:@"&param2=Second"];

NSURL *url = [NSURL URLWithString:urlAsString];

NSMutableURLRequest *urlRequest = [NSMutableURLRequest requestWithURL:url];
[urlRequest setTimeoutInterval:30.0f];
[urlRequest setHTTPMethod:@"DELETE"];

NSString *body = @"bodyParam1=BodyValue1&bodyParam2=BodyValue2";
[urlRequest setHTTPBody:[body dataUsingEncoding:NSUTF8StringEncoding]];

NSOperationQueue *queue = [[NSOperationQueue alloc] init];

[NSURLConnection
 sendAsynchronousRequest:urlRequest
 queue:queue
 completionHandler:^(NSURLResponse *response,
                     NSData *data,
                     NSError *error) {

   if ([data length] >0  &&
       error == nil){
     NSString *html = [[NSString alloc] initWithData:data
                                        encoding:NSUTF8StringEncoding];
     NSLog(@"HTML = %@", html);
   }
   else if ([data length] == 0 &&
            error == nil){
     NSLog(@"Nothing was downloaded.");
   }
   else if (error != nil){
     NSLog(@"Error happened = %@", error);
   }

}];
```

And if you now look at the output printed to the console window, you will see something similar to this:

```
HTML =
<html>
    <head>
        <title>iOS 6 Programming Cookbook DELETE Example</title>
    </head>
    <body>

<b>HTTP Method</b> = DELETE<br/><br/><b>Query String</b> = Array
(
```

```
    [param1] => First
    [param2] => Second
)
<br/><br/><b>Body Parameters</b> = Array
(
    [bodyParam1] => BodyValue1
    [bodyParam2] => BodyValue2
)

    </body>
</html>
```

9.8 Sending HTTP PUT Requests with NSURLConnection

Problem

You want to call a web service using the HTTP PUT method to place a resource into the web server, and perhaps pass parameters as part of the HTTP body or in the query string, to the web service.

Solution

Just as with the GET, POST, and DELETE methods, we can use the PUT method using NSURLConnection. We must explicitly set our URL's method to PUT.

Discussion

I have set up a dummy web service at the following address: *http://pixolity.com/put .php*. If you open this URL in your browser, you will see something similar to the screen shown in Figure 9-5:

This web service expects PUT requests and is able to print out parameters that are sent as part of the query string and as part of the HTTP body. So you can send both types of parameters in the same request. Let's write a simple app that can create an asynchronous connection and send a few parameters as a query string, and a few parameters in the HTTP body to the aforementioned URL using the PUT method:

```
NSString *urlAsString = @"http://pixolity.com/put.php";
urlAsString = [urlAsString stringByAppendingString:@"?param1=First"];
urlAsString = [urlAsString stringByAppendingString:@"&param2=Second"];

NSURL *url = [NSURL URLWithString:urlAsString];

NSMutableURLRequest *urlRequest = [NSMutableURLRequest requestWithURL:url];
[urlRequest setTimeoutInterval:30.0f];
[urlRequest setHTTPMethod:@"PUT"];

NSString *body = @"bodyParam1=BodyValue1&bodyParam2=BodyValue2";
[urlRequest setHTTPBody:[body dataUsingEncoding:NSUTF8StringEncoding]];

NSOperationQueue *queue = [[NSOperationQueue alloc] init];
```

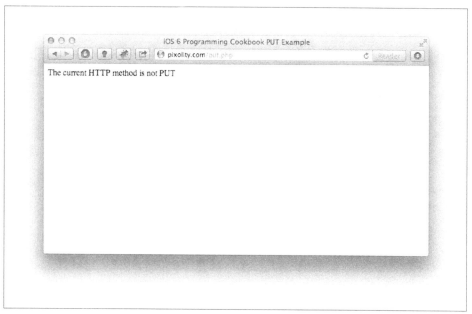

Figure 9-5. The PUT web service opened in a web browser

```
[NSURLConnection
 sendAsynchronousRequest:urlRequest
 queue:queue
 completionHandler:^(NSURLResponse *response,
                     NSData *data,
                     NSError *error) {

  if ([data length] >0  &&
      error == nil){
    NSString *html = [[NSString alloc] initWithData:data
                                        encoding:NSUTF8StringEncoding];
    NSLog(@"HTML = %@", html);
  }
  else if ([data length] == 0 &&
           error == nil){
    NSLog(@"Nothing was downloaded.");
  }
  else if (error != nil){
    NSLog(@"Error happened = %@", error);
  }

}];
```

  The first parameter sent in the HTTP body does not have to be prefixed with a question mark, unlike the first parameter in a query string.

And if you now look at the output printed to the console window, you will see something similar to this:

```
HTML =
<html>
    <head>
        <title>iOS 6 Programming Cookbook PUT Example</title>
    </head>
    <body>

<b>HTTP Method</b> = PUT<br/><br/><b>Query String</b> = Array
(
    [param1] => First
    [param2] => Second
)
<br/><br/><b>Body Parameters</b> = Array
(
    [bodyParam1] => BodyValue1
    [bodyParam2] => BodyValue2
)

    </body>
</html>
```

9.9 Serializing Arrays and Dictionaries into JSON

Problem

You want to serialize a dictionary or an array into a JSON object that you can transfer over the network or simply save to disk.

Solution

Use the `dataWithJSONObject:options:error:` method of the `NSJSONSerialization` class.

Discussion

The `dataWithJSONObject:options:error:` method of the `NSJSONSerialization` class can serialize dictionaries and arrays that contain only instances of `NSString`, `NSNumber`, `NSArray`, `NSDictionary` variables, or `NSNull` for nil values. As mentioned, the object that you pass to this method should either be an array or a dictionary.

Now let's go ahead and create a simple dictionary with a few keys and values:

```
NSMutableDictionary *dictionary =
[NSMutableDictionary dictionaryWithDictionary:@{
 @"First Name" : @"Anthony",
 @"Last Name" : @"Robbins",
 @"Age" : @51
 }];
```

```
NSArray *arrayOfAnthonysChildren = @[
@"Anthony's Son 1",
@"Anthony's Daughter 1",
@"Anthony's Son 2",
@"Anthony's Son 3",
@"Anthony's Daughter 2"
];

[dictionary setValue:arrayOfAnthonysChildren forKey:@"children"];
```

As you can see, this dictionary contains the first name, last name, and age of Anthony Robbins. A key in the dictionary named *children* contains the names of Anthony's children. This is an array of strings with each string representing one child. So by this time, the `dictionary` variable contains all the values that we want it to contain. It is now time to serialize it into a JSON object:

```
NSError *error = nil;
NSData *jsonData = [NSJSONSerialization
                    dataWithJSONObject:dictionary
                    options:NSJSONWritingPrettyPrinted
                    error:&error];

if ([jsonData length] > 0 &&
    error == nil){

    NSLog(@"Successfully serialized the dictionary into data = %@",
        jsonData);

}
else if ([jsonData length] == 0 &&
        error == nil){

    NSLog(@"No data was returned after serialization.");

}
else if (error != nil){

    NSLog(@"An error happened = %@", error);

}
```

The return value of the `dataWithJSONObject:options:error:` method is data of type `NSData`. However, you can simply turn this data into a string and print it to the console using the `initWithData:encoding:` initializer of `NSString`. Here is the complete example that serializes a dictionary into a JSON object, converts that object into a string, and prints the string out to the console window:

```
NSMutableDictionary *dictionary =
[NSMutableDictionary dictionaryWithDictionary:@{
@"First Name" : @"Anthony",
@"Last Name" : @"Robbins",
@"Age" : @51
}];
```

```
NSArray *arrayOfAnthonysChildren = @[
@"Anthony's Son 1",
@"Anthony's Daughter 1",
@"Anthony's Son 2",
@"Anthony's Son 3",
@"Anthony's Daughter 2"
];

[dictionary setValue:arrayOfAnthonysChildren forKey:@"children"];

NSError *error = nil;
NSData *jsonData = [NSJSONSerialization
                    dataWithJSONObject:dictionary
                    options:NSJSONWritingPrettyPrinted
                    error:&error];

if ([jsonData length] > 0 &&
    error == nil){

    NSLog(@"Successfully serialized the dictionary into data.");
    NSString *jsonString =
    [[NSString alloc] initWithData:jsonData
                          encoding:NSUTF8StringEncoding];
    NSLog(@"JSON String = %@", jsonString);

}
else if ([jsonData length] == 0 &&
         error == nil){

    NSLog(@"No data was returned after serialization.");

}
else if (error != nil){

    NSLog(@"An error happened = %@", error);

}
```

When you run this app, the following results will get printed to the console window:

```
Successfully serialized the dictionary into data.
JSON String = {
  "Last Name" : "Robbins",
  "First Name" : "Anthony",
  "children" : [
    "Anthony's Son 1",
    "Anthony's Daughter 1",     "Anthony's Son 2",
    "Anthony's Son 3",
    "Anthony's Daughter 2"
  ],
  "Age" : 51
}
```

9.10 Deserializing JSON into Arrays and Dictionaries

Problem

You have JSON data and you want to deserialize it into a dictionary or an array.

Solution

Use the `JSONObjectWithData:options:error:` method of the `NSJSONSerialization` class.

Discussion

If you already have serialized your dictionary or array into a JSON object (encapsulated inside an instance of `NSData`, see Recipe 9.9), you should be able to deserialize them back into a dictionary or an array, using the `JSONObjectWithData:options:error:` method of the `NSJSONSerialization` class. The object that is returned back by this method will either be a dictionary or an array, depending on the data that we pass to it. Here is an example:

```
/* Now try to deserialize the JSON object into a dictionary */
error = nil;
id jsonObject = [NSJSONSerialization
                 JSONObjectWithData:jsonData
                 options:NSJSONReadingAllowFragments
                 error:&error];

if (jsonObject != nil &&
    error == nil){

  NSLog(@"Successfully deserialized...");

  if ([jsonObject isKindOfClass:[NSDictionary class]]){

    NSDictionary *deserializedDictionary = (NSDictionary *)jsonObject;
    NSLog(@"Deserialized JSON Dictionary = %@", deserializedDictionary);

  }
  else if ([jsonObject isKindOfClass:[NSArray class]]){

    NSArray *deserializedArray = (NSArray *)jsonObject;
    NSLog(@"Deserialized JSON Array = %@", deserializedArray);

  } else {
    /* Some other object was returned. We don't know how to deal
      with this situation, as the deserializer returns only dictionaries
      or arrays */
  }

}
else if (error != nil){
  NSLog(@"An error happened while deserializing the JSON data.");
}
```

If now we mix this code with the code from Recipe 9.9, we can first serialize our dictionary into a JSON object, deserialize that JSON object back into a dictionary, and print out the results to make sure things went fine:

```
NSMutableDictionary *dictionary = [[NSMutableDictionary alloc] init];

[dictionary setValue:@"Anthony"
              forKey:@"First Name"];

[dictionary setValue:@"Robbins"
              forKey:@"Last Name"];

[dictionary setValue:[NSNumber numberWithUnsignedInteger:51]
              forKey:@"Age"];

NSArray *arrayOfAnthonysChildren = [[NSArray alloc]
                                    initWithObjects:
                                    @"Anthony's Son 1",
                                    @"Anthony's Daughter 1",
                                    @"Anthony's Son 2",
                                    @"Anthony's Son 3",
                                    @"Anthony's Daughter 2",
                                    nil];

[dictionary setValue:arrayOfAnthonysChildren
              forKey:@"children"];

NSError *error = nil;
NSData *jsonData = [NSJSONSerialization
                    dataWithJSONObject:dictionary
                    options:NSJSONWritingPrettyPrinted
                    error:&error];

if ([jsonData length] > 0 &&
    error == nil){

  NSLog(@"Successfully serialized the dictionary into data.");

  /* Now try to deserialize the JSON object into a dictionary */
  error = nil;
  id jsonObject = [NSJSONSerialization
                   JSONObjectWithData:jsonData
                   options:NSJSONReadingAllowFragments
                   error:&error];

  if (jsonObject != nil &&
      error == nil){

    NSLog(@"Successfully deserialized...");

    if ([jsonObject isKindOfClass:[NSDictionary class]]){

      NSDictionary *deserializedDictionary = (NSDictionary *)jsonObject;
      NSLog(@"Deserialized JSON Dictionary = %@", deserializedDictionary);
```

```
    }
    else if ([jsonObject isKindOfClass:[NSArray class]]){

      NSArray *deserializedArray = (NSArray *)jsonObject;
      NSLog(@"Deserialized JSON Array = %@", deserializedArray);

    }
    else {
      /* Some other object was returned. We don't know how to deal
         with this situation as the deserializer only returns dictionaries
         or arrays */
    }

  }
  else if (error != nil){
    NSLog(@"An error happened while deserializing the JSON data.");
  }

}
else if ([jsonData length] == 0 &&
         error == nil){

  NSLog(@"No data was returned after serialization.");

}
else if (error != nil){

  NSLog(@"An error happened = %@", error);

}
```

The options parameter of the JSONObjectWithData:options:error: method accepts one or a mixture of the following values:

NSJSONReadingMutableContainers

> The dictionary or the array returned by the JSONObjectWithData:options:error: method will be mutable. In other words, this method will return either an instance of NSMutableArray or NSMutableDictionary, as opposed to an immutable array or dictionary.

NSJSONReadingMutableLeaves

> Leaf values will be encapsulated into instances of NSMutableString.

NSJSONReadingAllowFragments

> Allows the deserialization of JSON data whose root top-level object is not an array or a dictionary.

See Also

Recipe 9.9

9.11 Integrating Twitter Functionality into Your Apps

Problem

You want to integrate Twitter functionality into your iOS apps.

Solution

Use the Twitter framework.

Discussion

To be able to integrate Twitter functionality into our iOS apps, we need to use the Twitter framework. So first we need to add this framework to our app. Follow these steps to add the Twitter framework to your app:

1. Click on your project icon in Xcode.
2. Select the target to which you want to add the Twitter framework.
3. On the top, select Build Phases.
4. Expand the Link Binary with Libraries box to see all the frameworks that are currently linked to your target.
5. Click on the little + button at the bottom-left corner of the "Link Binary with Libraries" box.
6. Select *Twitter.framework* from the list and then press the Add button.

Good! Now you have the Twitter framework linked to your app. The next thing you need to do is import the appropriate header file into your view controller's header file:

```
#import <UIKit/UIKit.h>
#import <Twitter/Twitter.h>

@interface Integrating_Twitter_Functionality_Into_Your_AppsViewController
        : UIViewController

@end
```

The next step is to instantiate an object of type `TWTweetComposeViewController`, which will take care of tweeting for you. This is just a view controller that you can display on top of your view controller. I have defined a property for our view controller for this:

```
#import <UIKit/UIKit.h>
#import <Twitter/Twitter.h>

@interface Integrating_Twitter_Functionality_Into_Your_AppsViewController
        : UIViewController

@property (nonatomic, strong) TWTweetComposeViewController *twitterController;

@end
```

Then, in the `viewDidLoad` method of your view controller, initialize your Twitter composer controller. You can then use the `setInitialText:` method of `TWTweetComposeView Controller` to set the text that will appear in the Twitter composer controller initially, before the user enters anything:

```
- (void)viewDidLoad{
  [super viewDidLoad];

  self.twitterController = [[TWTweetComposeViewController alloc] init];
  [self.twitterController setInitialText:@"Your Tweet Goes Here"];
  [self.navigationController presentModalViewController:self.twitterController
                                              animated:YES];

}
```

Now if you open your app in the simulator, you will notice that the Twitter composer is displayed for a second (see Figure 9-6). Next, you will probably just see the Twitter credentials screen in the Settings app, as shown in Figure 9-7.

Figure 9-6. Twitter composer shown as a modal controller

The reason for the Twitter login screen being displayed is that the user has not yet logged into Twitter on that iOS device. Go ahead and enter your Twitter credentials in the login screen (see Figure 9-7). Once you enter your credentials and press the Sign In button, you will be presented with a dialog asking you whether you want the Twitter app on your device or not. Press *Later*. We don't want to be bothered with installing that app at the moment. I've also noticed that trying to install the Twitter app on the simulator is problematic; you will get an icon on your simulator saying *Waiting* and the wait will never be over. So we are better off without the Twitter app on the simulator. On a real device, though, this works just fine (Figure 9-8).

Figure 9-7. The Twitter login screen is displayed if the user has not yet logged into Twitter

Figure 9-8. Installing the Twitter app

After the user has entered her Twitter credentials, launching your app again will simply display the Twitter composer (see Figure 9-6).

Aside from the main text that you add to the composer controller, you can also add images using the `addImage:` method of the composer controller. You can also attach a URL to your tweets using the `addURL:` method of the composer controller. Here is an example:

```
- (void)viewDidLoad{
  [super viewDidLoad];

  self.twitterController = [[TWTweetComposeViewController alloc] init];

  NSString *text =
  @"Anthony Robbins at Unleash the Power Within (UPW) in London";

  [self.twitterController setInitialText:text];

  UIImage *anthonyRobbins = [UIImage imageNamed:@"Anthony Robbins.jpg"];
  [self.twitterController addImage:anthonyRobbins];

  NSURL *url = [NSURL URLWithString:@"http://www.tonyrobbins.com"];
  [self.twitterController addURL:url];


  [self.navigationController presentModalViewController:self.twitterController
                                               animated:YES];

}
```

 The URL that you add to a tweet will *not* be displayed as part of your tweet in the Twitter controller, although it will be sent as part of your tweet to your Twitter timeline.

The results that your users will now see on their devices will be similar to Figure 9-9.

Figure 9-9. A simple tweet with image and URL

The Twitter composer controller does *not* work with delegates. It works with completion handler blocks, like all modern components in the iOS SDK. So if you want to get updates from this controller after you have displayed it to the user, add a completion handler block object to the composer, using its setCompletionHandler: method. This method requires a block object that should have not a return value and must accept a parameter of type TWTweetComposeViewControllerResult that will have one of the following values:

TWTweetComposeViewControllerResultCancelled

The result that gets sent to our completion block when the user cancels the Twitter composer controller. In this case, we must dismiss the Twitter composer controller.

TWTweetComposeViewControllerResultDone

The result that gets sent to our completion block when the Twitter composer controller has successfully sent the tweet to the user's timeline. If you get this result, you don't have to dismiss the controller, because it gets dismissed automatically.

Here is an example:

```
- (void)viewDidLoad{
[super viewDidLoad];

self.twitterController = [[TWTweetComposeViewController alloc] init];

__weak
  Integrating_Twitter_Functionality_Into_Your_AppsViewController
    *weakSelf = self;

[self.twitterController setCompletionHandler:
 ^(TWTweetComposeViewControllerResult result){

   Integrating_Twitter_Functionality_Into_Your_AppsViewController
    *strongSelf = weakSelf;

   switch (result){
     case TWTweetComposeViewControllerResultDone:{
       /* The tweet was submitted successfully.
        Will be dismissed automatically */
       break;
     }
     case TWTweetComposeViewControllerResultCancelled:{
       if (strongSelf != nil){
         [strongSelf.twitterController
          dismissModalViewControllerAnimated:YES];
       }
       break;
     }
   }
 }];

NSString *text =
@"Anthony Robbins at Unleash the Power Within (UPW) in London";
```

```
    [self.twitterController setInitialText:text];

    UIImage *anthonyRobbins = [UIImage imageNamed:@"Anthony Robbins.jpg"];
    [self.twitterController addImage:anthonyRobbins];

    NSURL *url = [NSURL URLWithString:@"http://www.tonyrobbins.com"];
    [self.twitterController addURL:url];


    [self.navigationController presentModalViewController:self.twitterController
                                                animated:YES];

}
```

9.12 Parsing XML with NSXMLParser

Problem

You want to parse an XML snippet or document.

Solution

Use the NSXMLParser class.

Discussion

The NSXMLParser uses a delegate model to parse XML content. Let's go ahead and create
a simple XML file that contains the following data (save this file as *MyXML.xml* in your
project):

```
<?xml version="1.0" encoding="UTF-8"?>
<root>

  <person id="1">
    <firstName>Anthony</firstName>
    <lastName>Robbins</lastName>
    <age>51</age>
  </person>

  <person id="2">
    <firstName>Richard</firstName>
    <lastName>Branson</lastName>
    <age>61</age>
  </person>

</root>
```

Now define a property of type NSXMLParser:

```
#import <UIKit/UIKit.h>

@interface Parsing_XML_with_NSXMLParserAppDelegate
```

```
                : UIResponder <UIApplicationDelegate, NSXMLParserDelegate>

@property (nonatomic, strong) UIWindow *window;
@property (nonatomic, strong) NSXMLParser *xmlParser;

@end
```

You can also see that I have defined my app delegate as an XML parser delegate by conforming to the NSXMLParserDelegate protocol, which is required for a delegate object of an XML parser of type NSXMLParser. Now let's read the *MyXML.xml* file from the disk and pass it to your XML parser:

```
- (BOOL)            application:(UIApplication *)application
  didFinishLaunchingWithOptions:(NSDictionary *)launchOptions{

  NSString *xmlFilePath = [[NSBundle mainBundle] pathForResource:@"MyXML"
                                       ofType:@"xml"];

  NSData *xml = [[NSData alloc] initWithContentsOfFile:xmlFilePath];

  self.xmlParser = [[NSXMLParser alloc] initWithData:xml];
  self.xmlParser.delegate = self;
  if ([self.xmlParser parse]){
    NSLog(@"The XML is parsed.");
  } else{
    NSLog(@"Failed to parse the XML");
  }

  self.window = [[UIWindow alloc] initWithFrame:
                  [[UIScreen mainScreen] bounds]];

  self.window.backgroundColor = [UIColor whiteColor];
  [self.window makeKeyAndVisible];
  return YES;
}
```

We first read the contents of our file into an instance of NSData and then initialize our XML parser with the initWithData:, using the data that we read from the XML file. We then call the parse method of the XML parser to start the parsing process. This method will block the current thread until the parsing process is finished. If you have big XML files to parse, it is highly recommended that you use a global dispatch queue to do the parsing.

To parse the XML file, we need to know the delegate methods defined in the NSXMLParserDelegate protocol and their responsibilities:

parserDidStartDocument:
    Called when the parsing starts.

parserDidEndDocument:
    Called when the parsing ends.

```
parser:didStartElement:namespaceURI:qualifiedName:attributes:
```
Called when the parser encounters and parses a new element in the XML document.

```
parser:didEndElement:namespaceURI:qualifiedName:
```
Called when the parser has finished parsing the current element.

```
parser:foundCharacters:
```
Called when the parser parses string contents of elements.

Using these delegate methods, we can go ahead and define an object model for our XML objects. Let's first define an object to represent an XML element, in a class called XMLElement:

```
#import <Foundation/Foundation.h>

@interface XMLElement : NSObject

@property (nonatomic, strong) NSString *name;
@property (nonatomic, strong) NSString *text;
@property (nonatomic, strong) NSDictionary *attributes;
@property (nonatomic, strong) NSMutableArray *subElements;
@property (nonatomic, weak) XMLElement *parent;

@end
```

Now let's implement our XMLElement class:

```
#import "XMLElement.h"

@implementation XMLElement

- (NSMutableArray *) subElements{
  if (_subElements == nil){
    _subElements = [[NSMutableArray alloc] init];
  }
  return _subElements;
}

@end
```

We want the subElements mutable array to be created only if it is nil when it is accessed, so we place our allocation and initialization code for the subElements property of the XMLElement class in its own getter method. If an XML element doesn't have subelements and we never use that property, there is no point allocating and initializing a mutable array for that element. This technique is known as lazy allocation.

So now let's go ahead and define an instance of XMLElement and call it *rootElement*. Our plan is to start the parsing process and drill down the XML file as we parse it with our delegate methods, until we have successfully parsed the whole file:

```
#import <UIKit/UIKit.h>

@class XMLElement;
```

```
@interface Parsing_XML_with_NSXMLParserAppDelegate
            : UIResponder <UIApplicationDelegate, NSXMLParserDelegate>
@property (nonatomic, strong) UIWindow *window;
@property (nonatomic, strong) NSXMLParser *xmlParser;
@property (nonatomic, strong) XMLElement *rootElement;
@property (nonatomic, strong) XMLElement *currentElementPointer;

@end
```

The currentElementPointer will be the XML element that we are parsing at the moment in our XML structure, so it can move up and down the structure as we parse the file. Unlike the constantly changing currentElementPointer pointer, the rootElement pointer will always be the root element of our XML and its value will not change during the course of parsing the XML file.

Let's start the parsing process. The first method we want to take care of is the parser DidStartDocument: method. In this method, we will simply reset everything:

```
- (void)parserDidStartDocument:(NSXMLParser *)parser{
    self.rootElement = nil;
    self.currentElementPointer = nil;
}
```

The next method is the parser:didStartElement:namespaceURI:qualifiedName: attributes: method. In this method, we will create the root element (if it has not been created already). If any new element in the XML file is getting parsed, we will calculate where in the structure of the XML we are and then add a new element object to our current element object:

```
- (void)          parser:(NSXMLParser *)parser
       didStartElement:(NSString *)elementName
          namespaceURI:(NSString *)namespaceURI
         qualifiedName:(NSString *)qName
            attributes:(NSDictionary *)attributeDict{

  if (self.rootElement == nil){
    /* We don't have a root element. Create it and point to it */
    self.rootElement = [[XMLElement alloc] init];
    self.currentElementPointer = self.rootElement;
  } else {
    /* Already have root. Create new element and add it as one of
     the subelements of the current element */
    XMLElement *newElement = [[XMLElement alloc] init];
    newElement.parent = self.currentElementPointer;
    [self.currentElementPointer.subElements addObject:newElement];
    self.currentElementPointer = newElement;
  }

  self.currentElementPointer.name = elementName;
  self.currentElementPointer.attributes = attributeDict;

}
```

Next up is the `parser:foundCharacters:` method. This method can get called multiple times for the current element, so you need to make sure we are ready for multiple entries into this method. For instance, if the text of an element is 4000 characters long, the parser might parse a maximum of 1000 characters in the first go, then the next 1000, and so on. In that case, the parser would call your `parser:foundCharacters:` method for the current element four times. You probably want to just accumulate the results that get returned into a string:

```
- (void)          parser:(NSXMLParser *)parser
        foundCharacters:(NSString *)string{

  if ([self.currentElementPointer.text length] > 0){
    self.currentElementPointer.text =
      [self.currentElementPointer.text stringByAppendingString:string];
  } else {
    self.currentElementPointer.text = string;
  }

}
```

The next method to take care of is the `parser:didEndElement:namespaceURI:qualified Name:` method, which gets called when the parser encounters the end of an element. Here you just need to point our XML element pointer back one level to the parent of the current element—it's as simple as this:

```
- (void)          parser:(NSXMLParser *)parser
        didEndElement:(NSString *)elementName
         namespaceURI:(NSString *)namespaceURI
        qualifiedName:(NSString *)qName{

  self.currentElementPointer = self.currentElementPointer.parent;

}
```

Last but not least, you need to handle the `parserDidEndDocument:` method and dispose of your `currentElementPointer` property:

```
- (void)parserDidEndDocument:(NSXMLParser *)parser{
  self.currentElementPointer = nil;
}
```

That is all. Now let's go ahead and parse our document:

```
- (BOOL)          application:(UIApplication *)application
  didFinishLaunchingWithOptions:(NSDictionary *)launchOptions{

  NSString *xmlFilePath = [[NSBundle mainBundle] pathForResource:@"MyXML"
                                                          ofType:@"xml"];

  NSData *xml = [[NSData alloc] initWithContentsOfFile:xmlFilePath];

  self.xmlParser = [[NSXMLParser alloc] initWithData:xml];
  self.xmlParser.delegate = self;
  if ([self.xmlParser parse]){
    NSLog(@"The XML is parsed.");
```

```
    /* self.rootElement is now the root element in the XML */

  } else{
    NSLog(@"Failed to parse the XML");
  }

  self.window = [[UIWindow alloc] initWithFrame:
                    [[UIScreen mainScreen] bounds]];

  self.window.backgroundColor = [UIColor whiteColor];
  [self.window makeKeyAndVisible];
  return YES;
}
```

Now you can use the rootElement property to traverse the structure of our XML.

CHAPTER 10

Audio and Video

10.0 Introduction

The AV Foundation framework in the iOS SDK allows developers to play and/or record audio and video with ease. In addition, the Media Player framework allows developers to play audio and video files.

Before you can run the code in this chapter, you must add the *AVFoundation.framework* and *MediaPlayer.framework* frameworks to your Xcode project. You can do this by following these steps:

1. In Xcode, click on your project's icon (a blue icon).
2. Select the target to which you want to add the framework.
3. On the top, select Build Phases.
4. Select the + button in the bottom-left corner of the Link Binaries with Libraries box.
5. Hold down the Command key and choose *AVFoundation.framework* and *Media-Player.framework* from the list.
6. Select Add.

10.1 Playing Audio Files

Problem

You want to be able to play an audio file in your application.

Solution

Use the AV Foundation (Audio and Video Foundation) framework's `AVAudioPlayer` class.

Discussion

The AVAudioPlayer class in the AV Foundation framework can play back all audio formats supported by iOS. The delegate property of an instance of AVAudioPlayer allows you to get notified by events, such as when the audio playback is interrupted or an error occurs as a result of playing an audio file. Let's have a look at a simple example that demonstrates how we can play an audio file from the application's bundle:

```
- (void)viewDidLoad {
  [super viewDidLoad];

  self.view.backgroundColor = [UIColor whiteColor];

  dispatch_queue_t dispatchQueue =
    dispatch_get_global_queue(DISPATCH_QUEUE_PRIORITY_DEFAULT, 0);

  dispatch_async(dispatchQueue, ^(void) {
    NSBundle *mainBundle = [NSBundle mainBundle];

    NSString *filePath = [mainBundle pathForResource:@"MySong"
                                              ofType:@"mp3"];

    NSData   *fileData = [NSData dataWithContentsOfFile:filePath];

    NSError  *error = nil;

    /* Start the audio player */
    self.audioPlayer = [[AVAudioPlayer alloc] initWithData:fileData
                                                     error:&error];

    /* Did we get an instance of AVAudioPlayer? */
    if (self.audioPlayer != nil){
      /* Set the delegate and start playing */
      self.audioPlayer.delegate = self;
      if ([self.audioPlayer prepareToPlay] &&
          [self.audioPlayer play]){
        /* Successfully started playing */
      } else {
        /* Failed to play */
      }
    } else {
      /* Failed to instantiate AVAudioPlayer */
    }
  });

}
```

As you can see, the file's data is loaded into an instance of NSData and then passed on to AVAudioPlayer 's initWithData:error: method. Because we need the actual, absolute path of the MP3 file to extract the data from that file, we invoke the mainBundle class method of NSBundle to retrieve the information from the application's configuration. The pathForResource:ofType: instance method of NSBundle can then be used to retrieve the absolute path to a resource of a specific type, as demonstrated in the example code.

In the `viewDidLoad` method, we are using GCD to asynchronously load the song's data into an instance of `NSData` and use that as a feed to the audio player. We do this because loading the data of an audio file can take a long time (depending on the length of the audio file), and if we do this on the main thread, we run the risk of stalling the UI experience. Because of this, we are using a global concurrent queue to ensure that the code does *not* run on the main thread.

Since we are assigning the instance of `AVAudioPlayer` to a property named `audio Player`, we must also see how this property is defined:

```
#import <UIKit/UIKit.h>
#import <AVFoundation/AVFoundation.h>

@interface Playing_Audio_FilesViewController
          : UIViewController <AVAudioPlayerDelegate>

@property (nonatomic, strong) AVAudioPlayer *audioPlayer;

@end
```

As you can see, we have made the view controller the delegate of the audio player. This way, we can receive messages from the system whenever the audio player, for instance, is interrupted or has finished playing the song. With this information in hand, we can make appropriate decisions in the application, such as starting to play another audio file.

See Also

Recipe 10.2; Recipe 10.5; Chapter 6

10.2 Handling Interruptions while Playing Audio

Problem

You want your `AVAudioPlayer` instance to resume playing after an interruption on an iOS device, such as an incoming call.

Solution

Implement the `audioPlayerBeginInterruption:` and `audioPlayerEndInterruption:with Flags:` methods of the `AVAudioPlayerDelegate` protocol in the delegate object of your `AVAudioPlayer` instance:

```
- (void)audioPlayerBeginInterruption:(AVAudioPlayer *)player{

  /* Audio Session is interrupted. The player will be paused here */

}- (void)audioPlayerEndInterruption:(AVAudioPlayer *)player
                    withFlags:(NSUInteger)flags{
```

```
    if (flags == AVAudioSessionInterruptionFlags_ShouldResume &&
        player != nil){
      [player play];
    }

  }
```

Discussion

On an iOS device, such as an iPhone, a phone call could interrupt the execution of the foreground application. In that case, the audio session(s) associated with the application will be deactivated, and audio files will not be played until the interruption has ended. At the beginning and the end of an interruption, we receive delegate messages from the AVAudioPlayer informing us of the different states the audio session is passing through. After the end of an interruption, we can simply resume the playback of audio.

> Incoming phone calls cannot be simulated with iPhone Simulator. You must always test your applications on a real device.

When an interruption occurs, the audioPlayerBeginInterruption: delegate method of an AVAudioPlayer instance will be called. Here, your audio session has been deactivated. In case of a phone call, the user can just hear his ringtone. When the interruption ends (the phone call is finished or the user rejects the call), the audioPlayerEndInterruption:withFlags: delegate method of your AVAudioPlayer will be invoked. If the withFlags parameter contains the value AVAudioSessionInterruptionFlags_ShouldResume, you can immediately resume the playback of your audio player using the play instance method of AVAudioPlayer.

> The playback of audio files using AVAudioPlayer might show memory leaks in Instruments when the application is being run on iPhone Simulator. Testing the same application on an iOS device proves that the memory leaks are unique to the simulator, not the device. I strongly suggest that you run, test, debug, and optimize your applications on real devices before releasing them to the App Store.

10.3 Recording Audio

Problem

You want to be able to record audio files on an iOS device.

Solution

Make sure you have added the CoreAudio.framework framework to your target file, and use the `AVAudioRecorder` class in the AV Foundation framework:

```
NSError    *error = nil;

NSString *pathAsString = [self audioRecordingPath];

NSURL *audioRecordingURL = [NSURL fileURLWithPath:pathAsString];

self.audioRecorder = [[AVAudioRecorder alloc]
                          initWithURL:audioRecordingURL
                          settings:[self audioRecordingSettings]
                          error:&error];
```

For information about the `audioRecordingSettings` and `audioRecordingPath` methods used in this example, refer to this recipe's Discussion.

Discussion

The `AVAudioRecorder` class in the AV Foundation framework facilitates audio recording in iOS applications. To start a recording, you need to pass various pieces of information to the `initWithURL:settings:error:` instance method of `AVAudioRecorder`:

The URL of the file where the recording should be saved
This is a local URL. The AV Foundation framework will decide which audio format should be used for the recording based on the file extension provided in this URL, so choose the extension carefully.

The settings that must be used before and while recording
Examples include the sampling rate, channels, and other information that will help the audio recorder start the recording. This is a dictionary object.

The address of an instance of `NSError` *where any initialization errors should be saved to*
The error information could be valuable later, and you can retrieve it from this instance method in case something goes wrong.

The `settings` parameter of the `initWithURL:settings:error:` method is particularly interesting. There are many keys that could be saved in the `settings` dictionary, but we will discuss only some of the most important ones in this recipe:

AVFormatIDKey
The format of the recorded audio. Some of the values that can be specified for this key are:

- `kAudioFormatLinearPCM`
- `kAudioFormatAppleLossless`

AVSampleRateKey
The sample rate that needs to be used for the recording.

AVNumberOfChannelsKey

The number of channels that must be used for the recording.

AVEncoderAudioQualityKey

The quality with which the recording must be made. Some of the values that can be specified for this key are:

- AVAudioQualityMin

- AVAudioQualityLow

- AVAudioQualityMedium

- AVAudioQualityHigh

- AVAudioQualityMax

With all this information in hand, we can go on and write an application that can record audio input into a file and then play it using AVAudioPlayer. What we want to do, specifically, is:

1. Start recording audio in Apple Lossless format.

2. Save the recording into a file named *Recording.m4a* in the application's *Documents* directory.

3. Five seconds after the recording starts, finish the recording process and immediately start playing the file into which we recorded the audio input.

We will start by declaring the required properties in the *.h* file of a simple view controller:

```
#import <UIKit/UIKit.h>
#import <CoreAudio/CoreAudioTypes.h>
#import <AVFoundation/AVFoundation.h>

@interface Recording_AudioViewController : UIViewController
        <AVAudioPlayerDelegate, AVAudioRecorderDelegate>

@property (nonatomic, strong) AVAudioRecorder *audioRecorder;
@property (nonatomic, strong) AVAudioPlayer *audioPlayer;

- (NSString *)      audioRecordingPath;
- (NSDictionary *)  audioRecordingSettings;

@end
```

When the view inside the view controller is loaded for the first time, we will attempt to start the recording process and then stop the process, if successfully started, after five seconds:

```
- (void)viewDidLoad {
  [super viewDidLoad];

  NSError    *error = nil;

  NSString *pathAsString = [self audioRecordingPath];
```

```
    NSURL *audioRecordingURL = [NSURL fileURLWithPath:pathAsString];

    self.audioRecorder = [[AVAudioRecorder alloc]
                            initWithURL:audioRecordingURL
                            settings:[self audioRecordingSettings]
                            error:&error];

    if (self.audioRecorder != nil){

      self.audioRecorder.delegate = self;
      /* Prepare the recorder and then start the recording */

      if ([self.audioRecorder prepareToRecord] &&
         [self.audioRecorder record]){
        NSLog(@"Successfully started to record.");

        /* After five seconds, let's stop the recording process */
        [self performSelector:@selector(stopRecordingOnAudioRecorder:)
                  withObject:self.audioRecorder
                  afterDelay:5.0f];

      } else {
        NSLog(@"Failed to record.");
        self.audioRecorder = nil;
      }

    } else {
      NSLog(@"Failed to create an instance of the audio recorder.");
    }

  }
```

In the viewDidLoad method of the view controller, we attempt to instantiate an object of type AVAudioRecorder and assign it to the audioRecorder property that we declared in the *.h* file of the same view controller earlier.

We are using an instance method called audioRecordingPath to determine the NSString representation of the local URL where we want to store the recording. This method is implemented like so:

```
- (NSString *) audioRecordingPath{

  NSString *result = nil;

  NSArray *folders =
  NSSearchPathForDirectoriesInDomains(NSDocumentDirectory,
                                      NSUserDomainMask,
                                      YES);

  NSString *documentsFolder = [folders objectAtIndex:0];

  result = [documentsFolder
            stringByAppendingPathComponent:@"Recording.m4a"];
```

```
    return result;

}
```

The return value of this function is the document path of your application with the name of the destination file appended to it. For instance, if the document path of your application is:

```
/var/mobile/Applications/ApplicationID/Documents/
```

the destination audio recording path will be:

```
/var/mobile/Applications/ApplicationID/Documents/Recording.m4a
```

When instantiating the AVAudioRecorder, we are using a dictionary for the settings parameter of the initialization method of the audio recorder, as explained before. This dictionary is constructed using the audioRecordingSettings instance method, implemented in this way:

```
- (NSDictionary *) audioRecordingSettings{

NSDictionary *result = nil;

/* Let's prepare the audio recorder options in the dictionary.
 Later we will use this dictionary to instantiate an audio
 recorder of type AVAudioRecorder */

NSMutableDictionary *settings = [[NSMutableDictionary alloc] init];

[settings
 setValue:[NSNumber numberWithInteger:kAudioFormatAppleLossless]
 forKey:AVFormatIDKey];

[settings
 setValue:[NSNumber numberWithFloat:44100.0f]
 forKey:AVSampleRateKey];

[settings
 setValue:[NSNumber numberWithInteger:1]
 forKey:AVNumberOfChannelsKey];

[settings
 setValue:[NSNumber numberWithInteger:AVAudioQualityLow]
 forKey:AVEncoderAudioQualityKey];

result = [NSDictionary dictionaryWithDictionary:settings];

return result;

}
```

You can see that five seconds after the recording successfully starts in the viewDid Load method of the view controller, we call the stopRecordingOnAudioRecorder method, implemented like so:

```
- (void) stopRecordingOnAudioRecorder
        :(AVAudioRecorder *)paramRecorder{

  /* Just stop the audio recorder here */
  [paramRecorder stop];

}
```

Now that we have asked the audio recorder to stop recording, we will wait for its delegate messages to tell us when the recording has actually stopped. You shouldn't assume that the stop instance method of AVAudioRecorder instantly stops the recording. Instead, I recommend that you wait for the audioRecorderDidFinishRecording:success fully: delegate method (declared in the AVAudioRecorderDelegate protocol) before proceeding.

When the audio recording has actually stopped, we will attempt to play what was recorded:

```
- (void)audioRecorderDidFinishRecording:(AVAudioRecorder *)recorder
                        successfully:(BOOL)flag{

  if (flag){

    NSLog(@"Successfully stopped the audio recording process.");

    /* Let's try to retrieve the data for the recorded file */
    NSError *playbackError = nil;

    NSError *readingError = nil;
    NSData  *fileData =
    [NSData dataWithContentsOfFile:[self audioRecordingPath]
                          options:NSDataReadingMapped
                            error:&readingError];

    /* Form an audio player and make it play the recorded data */
    self.audioPlayer = [[AVAudioPlayer alloc] initWithData:fileData
                                                    error:&playbackError];

    /* Could we instantiate the audio player? */
    if (self.audioPlayer != nil){
      self.audioPlayer.delegate = self;

      /* Prepare to play and start playing */
      if ([self.audioPlayer prepareToPlay] &&
          [self.audioPlayer play]){
        NSLog(@"Started playing the recorded audio.");
      } else {
        NSLog(@"Could not play the audio.");
      }

    } else {
      NSLog(@"Failed to create an audio player.");
    }
```

```
  } else {
    NSLog(@"Stopping the audio recording failed.");
  }

  /* Here we don't need the audio recorder anymore */
  self.audioRecorder = nil;

}
```

After the audio player is finished playing the song (if it does so successfully), the audio PlayerDidFinishPlaying:successfully: delegate method will be called in the delegate object of the audio player. We will implement this method like so (this method is defined in the AVAudioPlayerDelegate protocol):

```
- (void)audioPlayerDidFinishPlaying:(AVAudioPlayer *)player
                     successfully:(BOOL)flag{

  if (flag){
    NSLog(@"Audio player stopped correctly.");
  } else {
    NSLog(@"Audio player did not stop correctly.");
  }

  if ([player isEqual:self.audioPlayer]){
    self.audioPlayer = nil;
  } else {
    /* This is not the player */
  }

}
```

As explained in Recipe 10.2, when playing audio files using AVAudioPlayer, we also need to handle interruptions (such as incoming phone calls) when deploying the application on an iOS device and before releasing the application to the App Store:

```
- (void)audioPlayerBeginInterruption:(AVAudioPlayer *)player{

  /* The audio session has been deactivated here */

}

- (void)audioPlayerEndInterruption:(AVAudioPlayer *)player
                          withFlags:(NSUInteger)flags{

  if (flags == AVAudioSessionInterruptionFlags_ShouldResume){
    [player play];
  }

}
```

Instances of AVAudioRecorder must also handle interruptions, just like instances of AVAudioPlayer. These interruptions can be handled as explained in Recipe 10.4.

See Also

Recipe 10.2; Recipe 10.4

10.4 Handling Interruptions while Recording Audio

Problem

You want your AVAudioRecorder instance to be able to resume recording after an interruption, such as an incoming phone call.

Solution

Implement the audioRecorderBeginInterruption: and audioRecorderEndInterruption:withFlags: methods of the AVAudioRecorderDelegate protocol in the delegate object of your audio recorder, and resume the recording process by invoking the record instance method of your AVAudioRecorder when the interruption has ended:

```
- (void)audioRecorderBeginInterruption:(AVAudioRecorder *)recorder{

  NSLog(@"Recording process is interrupted");

}

- (void)audioRecorderEndInterruption:(AVAudioRecorder *)recorder
                      withFlags:(NSUInteger)flags{

  if (flags == AVAudioSessionInterruptionFlags_ShouldResume){
    NSLog(@"Resuming the recording...");
    [recorder record];
  }

}
```

Discussion

Just like audio players (instances of AVAudioPlayer), audio recorders of type AVAudioRecorder also receive delegate messages whenever the audio session associated with them is deactivated because of an interruption. The two methods mentioned in this recipe's Solution are the best places to handle such interruptions. In the case of an interruption to the audio recorder, you can invoke the record instance method of AVAudioRecorder after the interruption to continue the recording process. However, the recording will overwrite the previous recording, and all data recorded before the interruption will be lost.

It is very important to bear in mind that when the delegate of your audio recorder receives the `audioRecorderBeginInterruption:` method, the audio session has already been deactivated, and invoking the `resume` instance method will not work on your audio recorder. After the interruption has ended, you must invoke the `record` instance method of your `AVAudioRecorder` to resume recording.

10.5 Playing Audio over Other Active Sounds

Problem

You either want to put other applications in silent mode while you play audio or play audio on top of other applications' audio playback (if any).

Solution

Use audio sessions to set the type of audio category your application uses.

Discussion

The `AVAudioSession` class was introduced in the AV Foundation framework. Every iOS application has one audio session. This audio session can be accessed using the `sharedInstance` class method of the `AVAudioSession` class, like so:

```
AVAudioSession *audioSession = [AVAudioSession sharedInstance];
```

After retrieving an instance of the `AVAudioSession` class, you can invoke the `setCategory:error:` instance method of the audio session object to choose among the different categories available to iOS applications. Different values that can be set as the audio session category of an application are listed here:

AVAudioSessionCategoryAmbient
    This category will not stop the audio from other applications, but it will allow you to play audio over the audio being played by other applications, such as the Music app. The main UI thread of your application will function normally. The `prepareToPlay` and `play` instance methods of `AVAudioPlayer` will return with the value YES. The audio being played by your application will stop when the user locks the screen. The silent mode silences the audio playback of your application only if your application is the only application playing an audio file. If you start playing audio while the Music app is playing a song, putting the device in silent mode does not stop your audio playback.

AVAudioSessionCategorySoloAmbient
    This category is exactly like the `AVAudioSessionCategoryAmbient` category, except that this category will stop the audio playback of all other applications, such as the Music app. When the device is put into silent mode, your audio playback will be

paused. This also happens when the screen is locked. This is the default category that iOS chooses for an application.

AVAudioSessionCategoryRecord

This stops other applications' audio (e.g., the music) and also will not allow your application to initiate an audio playback (e.g., using AVAudioPlayer). You can only record audio in this mode. Using this category, calling the prepareToPlay instance method of AVAudioPlayer will return YES and the play instance method will return NO. The main UI interface will function as usual. The recording of your application will continue even if the iOS device's screen is locked by the user.

AVAudioSessionCategoryPlayback

This category will silence other applications' audio playback (such as the audio playback of music applications). You can then use the prepareToPlay and play instance methods of AVAudioPlayer to play a sound in your application. The main UI thread will function as normal. The audio playback will continue even if the screen is locked by the user or if the device is in silent mode.

AVAudioSessionCategoryPlayAndRecord

This category allows audio to be played and recorded at the same time in your application. This will stop the audio playback of other applications when your audio recording or playback begins. The main UI thread of your application will function as normal. The playback and the recording will continue even if the screen is locked or the device is in silent mode.

AVAudioSessionCategoryAudioProcessing

This category can be used for applications that do audio processing, but not audio playback or recording. By setting this category, you cannot play or record any audio in your application. Calling the prepareToPlay and play instance methods of AVAudioPlayer will return NO. Audio playback of other applications, such as the Music app, will also stop if this category is set.

To give you an example of using AVAudioSession, let's start an audio player that will play its audio file over other applications' audio playback. We will begin with the *.h* file of a view controller:

```
#import <UIKit/UIKit.h>
#import <AVFoundation/AVFoundation.h>

@interface Playing_Audio_over_Other_Active_SoundsViewController
        : UIViewController <AVAudioPlayerDelegate>

@property (nonatomic, strong) AVAudioPlayer *audioPlayer;

@end
```

Here is how we will alter the audio session and then load a song into the memory and into an audio player for playing. We will do this in the viewDidLoad method of the view controller:

```objective-c
- (void)viewDidLoad {
  [super viewDidLoad];

  NSError *audioSessionError = nil;
  AVAudioSession *audioSession = [AVAudioSession sharedInstance];
  if ([audioSession setCategory:AVAudioSessionCategoryAmbient
                          error:&audioSessionError]){
    NSLog(@"Successfully set the audio session.");
  } else {
    NSLog(@"Could not set the audio session");
  }

  dispatch_queue_t dispatchQueue =
    dispatch_get_global_queue(DISPATCH_QUEUE_PRIORITY_DEFAULT, 0);

  dispatch_async(dispatchQueue, ^(void) {
    NSBundle *mainBundle = [NSBundle mainBundle];

    NSString *filePath = [mainBundle pathForResource:@"MySong"
                                              ofType:@"mp3"];

    NSData *fileData = [NSData dataWithContentsOfFile:filePath];

    NSError *audioPlayerError = nil;

    self.audioPlayer = [[AVAudioPlayer alloc] initWithData:fileData
                                                    error:&audioPlayerError];

    if (self.audioPlayer != nil){

      self.audioPlayer.delegate = self;

      if ([self.audioPlayer prepareToPlay] &&
          [self.audioPlayer play]){
        NSLog(@"Successfully started playing.");

      } else {
        NSLog(@"Failed to play the audio file.");
        self.audioPlayer = nil;
      }    } else {
        NSLog(@"Could not instantiate the audio player.");
    }
  });

}
```

Next, we will move on to handling the `AVAudioPlayerDelegate` protocol's methods:

```objective-c
- (void)audioPlayerBeginInterruption:(AVAudioPlayer *)player{
  /* The audio session has been deactivated here */
}

- (void)audioPlayerEndInterruption:(AVAudioPlayer *)player
                         withFlags:(NSUInteger)flags{
  if (flags == AVAudioSessionInterruptionFlags_ShouldResume){
    [player play];
```

```
    }
  }

- (void)audioPlayerDidFinishPlaying:(AVAudioPlayer *)player
                     successfully:(BOOL)flag{

  if (flag){
    NSLog(@"Audio player stopped correctly.");
  } else {
    NSLog(@"Audio player did not stop correctly.");
  }

  if ([player isEqual:self.audioPlayer]){
    self.audioPlayer = nil;
  } else {
    /* This is not the audio player */
  }

}
```

You can see that we are using the shared instance of the `AVAudioSession` class in the `viewDidLoad` instance method of the view controller to set the audio category of the application to `AVAudioSessionCategoryAmbient` in order to allow the application to play audio files over other applications' audio playback.

10.6 Playing Video Files

Problem

You would like to be able to play video files in your iOS application.

Solution

Use an instance of the `MPMoviePlayerController` class.

 If you simply want to display a full-screen movie player, you can use the `MPMoviePlayerViewController` class and push your movie player view controller into the stack of view controllers of a navigation controller (for instance), or simply present your movie player view controller as a modal controller on another view controller using the `presentMovie PlayerViewControllerAnimated:` instance method of `UIViewController`. In this recipe, we will use `MPMoviePlayerController` instead of `MPMovie PlayerViewController` in order to get full access to various settings that a movie player view controller does not offer, such as windowed-mode video playback (not full-screen).

Discussion

The Media Player framework in the iOS SDK allows programmers to play audio and video files, among other interesting things. To be able to play a video file, we will instantiate an object of type `MPMoviePlayerController` like so:

```
self.moviePlayer = [[MPMoviePlayerController alloc] initWithContentURL:url];
```

In this code, `moviePlayer` is a property of type `MPMoviePlayerController` defined for the current view controller. In older iOS SDKs, programmers had very little control over how movies were played using the Media Player framework. With the introduction of the iPad, the whole framework changed drastically to give more control to programmers and allow them to present their contents with more flexibility than before.

An instance of `MPMoviePlayerController` has a property called `view`. This view is of type `UIView` and is the view in which the media, such as video, will be played. As a programmer, you are responsible for inserting this view into your application's view hierarchy to present your users with the content being played. Since you get a reference to an object of type `UIView`, you can shape this view however you want. For instance, you can simply change the background color of this view to a custom color.

Many multimedia operations depend on the notification system. For instance, `MPMoviePlayerController` does not work with delegates; instead, it relies on notifications. This allows for a very flexible decoupling between the system libraries and the applications that iOS programmers write. For classes such as `MPMoviePlayerController`, we start listening for notifications that get sent by instances of that class. We use the default notification center and add themselves as an observer for a notification.

To be able to test the recipe, we need a sample *.mov* file to play with the movie player. You can download an Apple-provided sample file from *http://bit.ly/TtfcP7*. Make sure you download the H.264 file format. If this file is zipped, unzip it and rename it to *Sample.m4v*. Now drag and drop this file into your application bundle in Xcode.

After doing this, we can go ahead and write a simple program that attempts to play the video file for us. Here is the *.h* file:

```
#import <UIKit/UIKit.h>
#import <MediaPlayer/MediaPlayer.h>

@interface Playing_Video_FilesViewController : UIViewController

@property (nonatomic, strong) MPMoviePlayerController *moviePlayer;
@property (nonatomic, strong) UIButton *playButton;

@end
```

Here is the implementation of the `startPlayingVideo:` method that we defined in the *.h* file:

```
- (void) startPlayingVideo:(id)paramSender{

    /* First let's construct the URL of the file in the application bundle
```

```
   that needs to get played by the movie player */
NSBundle *mainBundle = [NSBundle mainBundle];

NSString *urlAsString = [mainBundle pathForResource:@"Sample"
                                             ofType:@"m4v"];

NSURL    *url = [NSURL fileURLWithPath:urlAsString];

/* If we have already created a movie player before,
 let's try to stop it */
if (self.moviePlayer != nil){
  [self stopPlayingVideo:nil];
}

/* Now create a new movie player using the URL */
self.moviePlayer = [[MPMoviePlayerController alloc] initWithContentURL:url];

if (self.moviePlayer != nil){

  /* Listen for the notification that the movie player sends us
   whenever it finishes playing an audio file */
  [[NSNotificationCenter defaultCenter]
   addObserver:self
   selector:@selector(videoHasFinishedPlaying:)
   name:MPMoviePlayerPlaybackDidFinishNotification
   object:self.moviePlayer];

  NSLog(@"Successfully instantiated the movie player.");

  /* Scale the movie player to fit the aspect ratio */
  self.moviePlayer.scalingMode = MPMovieScalingModeAspectFit;

  /* Let's start playing the video in full screen mode */
  [self.moviePlayer play];

  [self.view addSubview:self.moviePlayer.view];

  [self.moviePlayer setFullscreen:YES
                         animated:YES];
} else {
  NSLog(@"Failed to instantiate the movie player.");
}

}
```

As you can see, we manage the movie player's view ourselves. If we add the view of the movie player to the view controller's view, we have to remove the view manually. This view will not get removed from the view controller's view even if we release the movie player. The following method stops the video and then removes the associated view:

```
- (void) stopPlayingVideo:(id)paramSender {

  if (self.moviePlayer != nil){
```

```
  [[NSNotificationCenter defaultCenter]
   removeObserver:self
   name:MPMoviePlayerPlaybackDidFinishNotification
   object:self.moviePlayer];

  [self.moviePlayer stop];

  if ([self.moviePlayer.view.superview isEqual:self.view]){
    [self.moviePlayer.view removeFromSuperview];
  }
}

}
```

In the startPlayingVideo: instance method of the view controller we are listening for
the MPMoviePlayerPlaybackDidFinishNotification notification that MKMoviePlayerView
Controller will send to the default notification center. We listen to this notification on
the videoHasFinishedPlaying: instance method of the view controller. Here, we can get
notified when the movie playback has finished and perhaps dispose of the movie player
object:

```
- (void) videoHasFinishedPlaying:(NSNotification *)paramNotification{

  /* Find out what the reason was for the player to stop */
  NSNumber *reason =
  [paramNotification.userInfo
   valueForKey:MPMoviePlayerPlaybackDidFinishReasonUserInfoKey];

  if (reason != nil){
    NSInteger reasonAsInteger = [reason integerValue];

    switch (reasonAsInteger){
      case MPMovieFinishReasonPlaybackEnded:{
        /* The movie ended normally */
        break;
      }
      case MPMovieFinishReasonPlaybackError:{
        /* An error happened and the movie ended */
        break;
      }
      case MPMovieFinishReasonUserExited:{
        /* The user exited the player */
        break;
      }
    }

    NSLog(@"Finish Reason = %ld", (long)reasonAsInteger);
    [self stopPlayingVideo:nil];
  } /* if (reason != nil){ */

}
```

You might have already noticed that we are invoking the stopPlayingVideo: instance
method that we implemented in the videoHasFinishedPlaying: notification handler.

We do this because the `stopPlayingVideo:` instance method takes care of unregistering the object from the notifications received by the media player, and removes the media player from the superview. In other words, when the video stops playing, it does not necessarily mean the resources we allocated for that player have been deallocated. We need to take care of that manually. Bear in mind that the `MPMoviePlayerController` class does not work in iPhone Simulator. You need to run this code on a real device and check the results for yourself.

See Also

Recipe 10.7

10.7 Capturing Thumbnails from a Video File

Problem

You are playing a video file using an instance of the `MPMoviePlayerController` class and would like to capture a screenshot from the movie at a certain time.

Solution

Use the `requestThumbnailImagesAtTimes:timeOption:` instance method of `MPMovie PlayerController` like so:

```
/* Capture the frame at the third second into the movie */
NSNumber *thirdSecondThumbnail = [NSNumber numberWithFloat:3.0f];

/* We can ask to capture as many frames as we
 want. But for now, we are just asking to capture one frame */
NSArray *requestedThumbnails =
[NSArray arrayWithObject:thirdSecondThumbnail];

/* Ask the movie player to capture this frame for us */
[self.moviePlayer
 requestThumbnailImagesAtTimes:requestedThumbnails
 timeOption:MPMovieTimeOptionExact];
```

Discussion

An instance of `MPMoviePlayerController` is able to capture thumbnails from the currently playing movie, synchronously and asynchronously. In this recipe, we are going to focus on asynchronous image capture for this class.

We can use the `requestThumbnailImagesAtTimes:timeOption:` instance method of `MPMoviePlayerController` to asynchronously access thumbnails. When I say "asynchronously," I mean that during the time the thumbnail is being captured and reported to your designated object (as we will soon see), the movie player will continue its work and will not block the playback. We must observe the `MPMoviePlayerThumbnail`

ImageRequestDidFinishNotification notification message the movie player sends to the default notification center in order to find out when the thumbnails are available:

```
- (void) startPlayingVideo:(id)paramSender{

    /* First let's construct the URL of the file in the application bundle
     that needs to get played by the movie player */
    NSBundle *mainBundle = [NSBundle mainBundle];

    NSString *urlAsString = [mainBundle pathForResource:@"Sample"
                                                 ofType:@"m4v"];

    NSURL    *url = [NSURL fileURLWithPath:urlAsString];

    /* If we have already created a movie player before,
     let's try to stop it */
    if (self.moviePlayer != nil){
      [self stopPlayingVideo:nil];
    }

    /* Now create a new movie player using the URL */
    self.moviePlayer = [[MPMoviePlayerController alloc] initWithContentURL:url];

    if (self.moviePlayer != nil){

      /* Listen for the notification that the movie player sends us
       whenever it finishes playing an audio file */
      [[NSNotificationCenter defaultCenter]
       addObserver:self
       selector:@selector(videoHasFinishedPlaying:)
       name:MPMoviePlayerPlaybackDidFinishNotification
       object:self.moviePlayer];

      [[NSNotificationCenter defaultCenter]
       addObserver:self
       selector:@selector(videoThumbnailIsAvailable:)
       name:MPMoviePlayerThumbnailImageRequestDidFinishNotification
       object:self.moviePlayer];

      NSLog(@"Successfully instantiated the movie player.");

      /* Scale the movie player to fit the aspect ratio */
      self.moviePlayer.scalingMode = MPMovieScalingModeAspectFit;

      /* Let's start playing the video in full screen mode */
      [self.moviePlayer play];

      [self.view addSubview:self.moviePlayer.view];

      [self.moviePlayer setFullscreen:YES
                             animated:YES];

      /* Capture the frame at the third second into the movie */
      NSNumber *thirdSecondThumbnail = [NSNumber numberWithFloat:3.0f];
```

```
      /* We can ask to capture as many frames as we
         want. But for now, we are just asking to capture one frame */
      NSArray *requestedThumbnails =
      [NSArray arrayWithObject:thirdSecondThumbnail];

      /* Ask the movie player to capture this frame for us */
      [self.moviePlayer
       requestThumbnailImagesAtTimes:requestedThumbnails
       timeOption:MPMovieTimeOptionExact];

    } else {
      NSLog(@"Failed to instantiate the movie player.");
    }

  }
```

You can see that we are asking the movie player to capture the frame at the third second into the movie. Once this task is completed, the videoThumbnailIsAvailable: instance method of the view controller will be called. Here is how we can access the captured image:

```
- (void) videoThumbnailIsAvailable:(NSNotification *)paramNotification{

  MPMoviePlayerController *controller = [paramNotification object];

  if (controller != nil &&
      [controller isEqual:self.moviePlayer]){
    NSLog(@"Thumbnail is available");

    /* Now get the thumbnail out of the user info dictionary */
    UIImage *thumbnail =
    [paramNotification.userInfo
     objectForKey:MPMoviePlayerThumbnailImageKey];

    if (thumbnail != nil){
      /* We got the thumbnail image. You can now use it here */
    }
  }

}
```

Since we started listening to the MPMoviePlayerThumbnailImageRequestDidFinishNotifi cation notifications when we instantiated the movie player object in the startPlaying Video: method, we must also stop listening for this notification whenever we stop the movie player (or whenever you believe is appropriate depending on your application architecture):

```
- (void) stopPlayingVideo:(id)paramSender {

  if (self.moviePlayer != nil){

    [[NSNotificationCenter defaultCenter]
     removeObserver:self
     name:MPMoviePlayerPlaybackDidFinishNotification
     object:self.moviePlayer];
```

```
[[NSNotificationCenter defaultCenter]
 removeObserver:self
 name:MPMoviePlayerThumbnailImageRequestDidFinishNotification
 object:self.moviePlayer];

[self.moviePlayer stop];

if ([self.moviePlayer.view.superview isEqual:self.view]){
  [self.moviePlayer.view removeFromSuperview];
}
}

}
```

When calling the requestThumbnailImagesAtTimes:timeOption: instance method of MPMoviePlayerController, we can specify one of two values for timeOption: MPMovieTimeOptionExact or MPMovieTimeOptionNearestKeyFrame. The former gives us the frame playing at the exact point we requested in the timeline of the video, whereas the latter is less exact, but uses fewer system resources and offers better performance when capturing thumbnails from a video. MPMovieTimeOptionNearestKeyFrame is usually adequate in terms of precision because it is just a couple of frames off.

10.8 Accessing the Music Library

Problem

You want to access an item that your user picks from her music library.

Solution

Use the MPMediaPickerController class:

```
MPMediaPickerController *mediaPicker = [[MPMediaPickerController alloc]
                                        initWithMediaTypes:MPMediaTypeAny];
```

Discussion

MPMediaPickerController is a view controller that the Music app displays to the user. By instantiating MPMediaPickerController, you can present a standard view controller to your users to allow them to select whatever item they want from their library and then transfer the control to your application. This is particularly useful in games, for instance, where the user plays the game and can have your application play his favorite tracks in the background.

You can get information from the media picker controller by becoming its delegate (conforming to MPMediaPickerControllerDelegate):

```
#import <UIKit/UIKit.h>
#import <MediaPlayer/MediaPlayer.h>
```

```
@interface Accessing_the_Music_LibraryViewController
          : UIViewController <MPMediaPickerControllerDelegate>

@end
```

Inside your `displayMediaPicker:` selector, implement the code required to display an instance of the media picker controller and present it to the user as a modal view controller:

```
- (void) displayMediaPicker{

  MPMediaPickerController *mediaPicker = [[MPMediaPickerController alloc]
                                    initWithMediaTypes:MPMediaTypeAny];

  if (mediaPicker != nil){

    NSLog(@"Successfully instantiated a media picker.");
    mediaPicker.delegate = self;
    mediaPicker.allowsPickingMultipleItems = NO;

    [self.navigationController presentModalViewController:mediaPicker
                                    animated:YES];

  } else {
    NSLog(@"Could not instantiate a media picker.");
  }

}
```

The `allowsPickingMultipleItems` property of the media picker controller lets you specify whether users can pick more than one item from their library before dismissing the media picker controller. This takes a `BOOL` value, so for now we just set it to `NO`; we will later see what this looks like. Now let's implement the various delegate messages defined in the `MPMediaPickerControllerDelegate` protocol:

```
- (void) mediaPicker:(MPMediaPickerController *)mediaPicker
  didPickMediaItems:(MPMediaItemCollection *)mediaItemCollection{

  NSLog(@"Media Picker returned");

  for (MPMediaItem *thisItem in mediaItemCollection.items){

    NSURL    *itemURL =
    [thisItem valueForProperty:MPMediaItemPropertyAssetURL];

    NSString *itemTitle =
    [thisItem valueForProperty:MPMediaItemPropertyTitle];

    NSString *itemArtist =
    [thisItem valueForProperty:MPMediaItemPropertyArtist];

    MPMediaItemArtwork *itemArtwork =
    [thisItem valueForProperty:MPMediaItemPropertyArtwork];
```

```
    NSLog(@"Item URL = %@", itemURL);
    NSLog(@"Item Title = %@", itemTitle);
    NSLog(@"Item Artist = %@", itemArtist);
    NSLog(@"Item Artwork = %@", itemArtwork);
  }

  [mediaPicker dismissModalViewControllerAnimated:YES];

}
```

You can access different properties of each selected item using the `valueForProperty:` instance method of `MPMediaItem`. Instances of this class will be returned to your application through the `mediaItemCollection` parameter of the `mediaPicker:didPickMediaItems:` delegate message.

Now let's write a program with a very simple GUI that allows us to ask the user to pick one music item from his Music library. After he picks the music file, we will attempt to play it using an `MPMusicPlayerController` instance. The GUI has two simple buttons: Pick and Play, and Stop Playing. The first button will ask the user to pick an item from his Music library to play, and the second button will stop the audio playback (if we are already playing the song). We will start with the design of the UI of the application. Let's create it in a simple way, as shown in Figure 10-1.

Figure 10-1. A very simple UI for the media picker and AV Audio Player

Now let's go ahead and define these two buttons in the *.h* of the view controller:

```
@interface Accessing_the_Music_LibraryViewController : UIViewController
        <MPMediaPickerControllerDelegate, AVAudioPlayerDelegate>

@property (nonatomic, strong) MPMusicPlayerController *myMusicPlayer;
@property (nonatomic, strong) UIButton *buttonPickAndPlay;
```

```
@property (nonatomic, strong) UIButton *buttonStopPlaying;

@end
```

When the view loads up, we will then instantiate these two buttons and place them on the view:

```
- (void)viewDidLoad {
  [super viewDidLoad];

  self.view.backgroundColor = [UIColor whiteColor];

  self.buttonPickAndPlay = [UIButton buttonWithType:UIButtonTypeRoundedRect];
  self.buttonPickAndPlay.frame = CGRectMake(0.0f,
                                            0.0f,
                                            200,
                                            37.0f);
  self.buttonPickAndPlay.center = CGPointMake(self.view.center.x,
                                              self.view.center.y - 50);
  [self.buttonPickAndPlay setTitle:@"Pick and Play"
                          forState:UIControlStateNormal];
  [self.buttonPickAndPlay addTarget:self
                             action:@selector(displayMediaPickerAndPlayItem)
                   forControlEvents:UIControlEventTouchUpInside];
  [self.view addSubview:self.buttonPickAndPlay];

  self.buttonStopPlaying = [UIButton buttonWithType:UIButtonTypeRoundedRect];
  self.buttonStopPlaying.frame = CGRectMake(0.0f,
                                            0.0f,
                                            200,
                                            37.0f);
  self.buttonStopPlaying.center = CGPointMake(self.view.center.x,
                                              self.view.center.y + 50);
  [self.buttonStopPlaying setTitle:@"Stop Playing"
                          forState:UIControlStateNormal];
  [self.buttonStopPlaying addTarget:self
                             action:@selector(stopPlayingAudio)
                   forControlEvents:UIControlEventTouchUpInside];
  [self.view addSubview:self.buttonStopPlaying];

  [self.navigationController setNavigationBarHidden:YES
                                           animated:NO];
}
```

The two most important methods in the view controller are the displayMediaPicker AndPlayItem and stopPlayingAudio:

```
- (void) stopPlayingAudio{

  if (self.myMusicPlayer != nil){

    [[NSNotificationCenter defaultCenter]
      removeObserver:self
      name:MPMusicPlayerControllerPlaybackStateDidChangeNotification
      object:self.myMusicPlayer];
```

```
    [[NSNotificationCenter defaultCenter]
     removeObserver:self
     name:MPMusicPlayerControllerNowPlayingItemDidChangeNotification
     object:self.myMusicPlayer];

    [[NSNotificationCenter defaultCenter]
     removeObserver:self
     name:MPMusicPlayerControllerVolumeDidChangeNotification
     object:self.myMusicPlayer];

    [self.myMusicPlayer stop];
  }

}

- (void) displayMediaPickerAndPlayItem{

  MPMediaPickerController *mediaPicker =
  [[MPMediaPickerController alloc]
   initWithMediaTypes:MPMediaTypeMusic];

  if (mediaPicker != nil){

    NSLog(@"Successfully instantiated a media picker.");
    mediaPicker.delegate = self;
    mediaPicker.allowsPickingMultipleItems = YES;

    [self.navigationController presentModalViewController:mediaPicker
                                                 animated:YES];

  } else {
    NSLog(@"Could not instantiate a media picker.");
  }

}
```

When the media picker controller succeeds, the mediaPicker:didPickMediaItems message will be called in the delegate object (in this case, the view controller). On the other
hand, if the user cancels the media player, we'll get the mediaPicker:mediaPickerDid
Cancel message. The following code implements the method that will be called in each
case:

```
- (void) mediaPicker:(MPMediaPickerController *)mediaPicker
  didPickMediaItems:(MPMediaItemCollection *)mediaItemCollection{

  NSLog(@"Media Picker returned");

  /* First, if we have already created a music player, let's
   deallocate it */
  self.myMusicPlayer = nil;

  self.myMusicPlayer = [[MPMusicPlayerController alloc] init];

  [self.myMusicPlayer beginGeneratingPlaybackNotifications];
```

```
/* Get notified when the state of the playback changes */
[[NSNotificationCenter defaultCenter]
 addObserver:self
 selector:@selector(musicPlayerStateChanged:)
 name:MPMusicPlayerControllerPlaybackStateDidChangeNotification
 object:self.myMusicPlayer];

/* Get notified when the playback moves from one item
 to the other. In this recipe, we are only going to allow
 the user to pick one music file */
[[NSNotificationCenter defaultCenter]
 addObserver:self
 selector:@selector(nowPlayingItemIsChanged:)
 name:MPMusicPlayerControllerNowPlayingItemDidChangeNotification
 object:self.myMusicPlayer];

/* And also get notified when the volume of the
 music player is changed */
[[NSNotificationCenter defaultCenter]
 addObserver:self
 selector:@selector(volumeIsChanged:)
 name:MPMusicPlayerControllerVolumeDidChangeNotification
 object:self.myMusicPlayer];

/* Start playing the items in the collection */
[self.myMusicPlayer setQueueWithItemCollection:mediaItemCollection];
[self.myMusicPlayer play];

/* Finally dismiss the media picker controller */
[mediaPicker dismissModalViewControllerAnimated:YES];

}

- (void) mediaPickerDidCancel:(MPMediaPickerController *)mediaPicker{

/* The media picker was cancelled */
NSLog(@"Media Picker was cancelled");
[mediaPicker dismissModalViewControllerAnimated:YES];

}
```

We are listening for the events the music player generates through the notifications that it sends. Here are the three methods that are going to be responsible for handling the notifications we are listening to for the music player:

```
- (void) musicPlayerStateChanged:(NSNotification *)paramNotification{

NSLog(@"Player State Changed");

/* Let's get the state of the player */
NSNumber *stateAsObject =
[paramNotification.userInfo
 objectForKey:@"MPMusicPlayerControllerPlaybackStateKey"];

NSInteger state = [stateAsObject integerValue];
```

```objc
/* Make your decision based on the state of the player */
switch (state){
  case MPMusicPlaybackStateStopped:{
    /* Here the media player has stopped playing the queue. */
    break;
  }
  case MPMusicPlaybackStatePlaying:{
    /* The media player is playing the queue. Perhaps you
       can reduce some processing that your application
       that is using to give more processing power
       to the media player */
    break;
  }
  case MPMusicPlaybackStatePaused:{
    /* The media playback is paused here. You might want
       to indicate this by showing graphics to the user */
    break;
  }
  case MPMusicPlaybackStateInterrupted:{
    /* An interruption stopped the playback of the media queue */
    break;
  }
  case MPMusicPlaybackStateSeekingForward:{
    /* The user is seeking forward in the queue */
    break;
  }
  case MPMusicPlaybackStateSeekingBackward:{
    /* The user is seeking backward in the queue */
    break;
  }
} /* switch (State){ */

}

- (void) nowPlayingItemIsChanged:(NSNotification *)paramNotification{

  NSLog(@"Playing Item Is Changed");   NSString *persistentID =
  [paramNotification.userInfo
   objectForKey:@"MPMusicPlayerControllerNowPlayingItemPersistentIDKey"];

  /* Do something with Persistent ID */
  NSLog(@"Persistent ID = %@", persistentID);

}

- (void) volumeIsChanged:(NSNotification *)paramNotification{
  NSLog(@"Volume Is Changed");
  /* The userInfo dictionary of this notification is normally empty */
}
```

By running the application and pressing the Pick and Play button on the view controller, we will be presented with the media picker controller. Once the picker view controller is displayed, the same Music UI will be presented to the user. After the user picks an item (or cancels the whole dialog), we will get appropriate delegate messages called in the view controller (since the view controller is the delegate of the media picker). After the items are picked (we only allow one item in this recipe, though), we will start the music player and start playing the whole collection.

If you want to allow your users to pick more than one item at a time, simply set the allowsPickingMultipleItems property of your media picker controller to YES:

```
mediaPicker.allowsPickingMultipleItems = YES;
```

 Sometimes when working with the media picker controller (MPMedia PickerController), the "MPMediaPicker: Lost connection to iPod li-brary" message will be printed to the console screen. This is because the media picker has been interrupted by an event, such as syncing with iTunes while the picker was being displayed to the user. Immediately, your mediaPickerDidCancel: delegate message will be called as well.

CHAPTER 11

Address Book

11.0 Introduction

On an iOS device, the Contacts application allows users to add contacts to, remove contacts from, and manipulate their address book. The address book can be a collection of people and groups. Each person can have properties such as first name, last name, phone number, and email address. Some properties can have a single value and some can have multiple values. For instance, the first name of a person is one value, but the phone number can be multiple values (e.g., if the user has two home phone numbers).

The AddressBook.framework framework in the iOS SDK allows you to interact with the address book database on the device. You can get the array of all entities in the user's address book, insert and change values, and much more.

To use the address-book-related functions in your application, follow these steps to first add AddressBook.framework to your application:

1. Click on your project's icon in Xcode.
2. Select the target to which you want to add the AddressBook framework.
3. On the top of the screen, select the Build Phases tab.
4. In the Build Phases tab, find and expand the Link Binary with Libraries box and press the + button, located at the bottom-left corner of that box.
5. In the list that gets displayed, select *AddressBook.framework* and press the Add button (see Figure 11-1).

After you've added the framework to your application, whenever you want to use address-book-related functions, you must include the main header file of the framework in your header (*.h*) or implementation (*.m*) file, like so:

```
#import <UIKit/UIKit.h>
#import <AddressBook/AddressBook.h>

@interface RootViewController : UIViewController
```

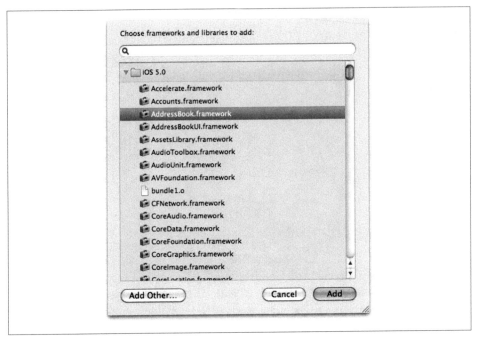

Choose frameworks and libraries to add:

▼ 🗀 iOS 5.0

🔲 Accelerate.framework
🔲 Accounts.framework
🔲 AddressBook.framework
🔲 AddressBookUI.framework
🔲 AssetsLibrary.framework
🔲 AudioToolbox.framework
🔲 AudioUnit.framework
🔲 AVFoundation.framework
🗋 bundle1.o
🔲 CFNetwork.framework
🔲 CoreAudio.framework
🔲 CoreData.framework
🔲 CoreFoundation.framework
🔲 CoreGraphics.framework
🔲 CoreImage.framework
🔲 CoreLocation.framework

Add Other...   Cancel   Add

Figure 11-1. Adding the AddressBook framework to your app

```
@end
```

You can use the Address Book framework on iOS Simulator, but the Contacts database on the simulator is empty by default. If you want to run the examples in this chapter on iOS Simulator, first populate your address book (on the simulator) using the Contacts application.

I have populated my iOS Simulator's contacts database with three entries, as shown in Figure 11-2.

I also suggest that you populate the address book of your iOS Simulator with as many values as possible: multiple phone numbers for work and home, different addresses, and so forth. Only through such diversity can you correctly test the Address Book framework's functions.

The examples in this chapter don't try to handle all the different types of errors that an Address Book API could throw. We simply check whether an API succeeds or fails. In your app, however, you might need to check these errors; for this reason, the code examples retrieve the references to errors that might happen during calls to each of the Address Book methods, just for your reference.

Figure 11-2. Contacts added to iOS Simulator

11.1 Requesting Access to the Address Book

Problem

You want to start accessing the user's address book, which requires the user to have granted your app access to the user's address book database. You want to check whether you have access so that you don't receive a runtime error when you attempt access.

Solution

In order to find the current authorization state of your app, call the function `ABAddress BookGetAuthorizationStatus` in the Address Book framework. This function can return any of the following values:

`kABAuthorizationStatusNotDetermined`
> The user has not yet decided whether she would like to grant access to your application.

`kABAuthorizationStatusDenied`
> The user has explicitly denied your application from having access to the address book.

`kABAuthorizationStatusAuthorized`
> The user has authorized your application to have access to the address book on her device.

`kABAuthorizationStatusRestricted`
> Parental controls or other permissions configured on the iOS device prevent your app from accessing and interacting with the address book database on the device.

If you find out that the status that you received from the `ABAddressBookGetAuthoriza tionStatus` function is `kABAuthorizationStatusNotDetermined`, you can use the `ABAd dressBookRequestAccessWithCompletion` function to ask for permission to access the user's address book database. You have to pass two parameters to this function:

An Address Book reference of type `ABAddressBookRef`
> The instance of the address book that you want to access.

A completion block of type `ABAddressBookRequestAccessCompletionHandler`
> After you call this function, iOS will ask the user if she wants to grant access to your application. Regardless of whether the user says Yes or No, this block object will be called and you will then, through a Boolean parameter, get to know whether the answer was Yes or No.

Discussion

Starting with iOS 6, Apple is quite rightly putting restrictions on how apps can access users' personal data, such as their contact information. This is done through a user interface designed by Apple that asks the users explicitly whether they allow these apps to access certain parts of their device and data, such as their address book database. Since we are all good iOS-land citizens, we will adhere to these rules and make sure that we access the user's address book only if we have been granted permission to do so.

Regardless of what you want to do with the address book, whether to read from it or write to it, you need to make sure that you have been granted sufficient privileges. If you are not sure about whether you can access the address book, simply call the `ABAd dressBookGetAuthorizationStatus` function as demonstrated in this recipe.

Here is a little example of what to do depending on what the `ABAddressBookGetAuthor izationStatus` function returns to your application. In this example, we will call the aforementioned function and just query the system about the authorization status of our app with regards to the address book database. If we are authorized to access it, fine. If we have been denied access, or there is a systemwide restriction on address book access, we will display an alert view on the screen. If we have not yet been given access, we will ask the user for her permission to access the address book:

```
#import "AppDelegate.h"
#import <AddressBook/AddressBook.h>

NSString *const kDenied = @"Access to address book is denied";
NSString *const kRestricted = @"Access to address book is restricted";

ABAddressBookRef addressBook;

@implementation AppDelegate
```

```objc
- (void) displayMessage:(NSString *)paramMessage{
    [[[UIAlertView alloc] initWithTitle:nil
                                message:paramMessage
                               delegate:nil
                      cancelButtonTitle:@"OK"
                      otherButtonTitles:nil] show];
}


- (BOOL)               application:(UIApplication *)application
    didFinishLaunchingWithOptions:(NSDictionary *)launchOptions{

    CFErrorRef error = NULL;

    switch (ABAddressBookGetAuthorizationStatus()){
        case kABAuthorizationStatusAuthorized:{
            addressBook = ABAddressBookCreateWithOptions(NULL, &error);
            /* Do your work and once you are finished ... */
            if (addressBook != NULL){
                CFRelease(addressBook);
            }
            break;
        }
        case kABAuthorizationStatusDenied:{
            [self displayMessage:kDenied];
            break;
        }
        case kABAuthorizationStatusNotDetermined:{
            addressBook = ABAddressBookCreateWithOptions(NULL, &error);
            ABAddressBookRequestAccessWithCompletion
            (addressBook, ^(bool granted, CFErrorRef error) {
                if (granted){
                    NSLog(@"Access was granted");
                } else {
                    NSLog(@"Access was not granted");
                }
                if (addressBook != NULL){
                    CFRelease(addressBook);
                }
            });
            break;
        }
        case kABAuthorizationStatusRestricted:{
            [self displayMessage:kRestricted];
            break;
        }
    }

    self.window = [[UIWindow alloc]
                  initWithFrame:[[UIScreen mainScreen] bounds]];
    self.window.backgroundColor = [UIColor whiteColor];
    [self.window makeKeyAndVisible];
    return YES;

}
```

11.2 Retrieving a Reference to an Address Book

Problem

You would like to work with a user's contacts. To do this, first you need to get a reference to the user's address book database. This reference is what you use to retrieve entries, as well as to make and save changes.

Solution

Use the `ABAddressBookCreateWithOptions` function in the Address Book framework. As the option, pass NULL and pass a reference to an error object to get any errors that may happen during the process:

```
addressBook = ABAddressBookCreateWithOptions(NULL, &error);
```

Discussion

To get a reference to the user's address book database you must first check whether you have permission, as discussed in Recipe 11.1. After permission is granted to your app, you can carry on to use the `ABAddressBookCreateWithOptions` function. This function returns a value of type `ABAddressBookRef` that will be `nil` if the address book cannot be accessed. You must check for `nil` values before accessing the address book reference returned by this function. Attempting to modify a `nil` address book will terminate your application with a runtime error.

After retrieving a reference to the user's address book, you can start making changes to the contacts, reading the entries, and so on. If you have made any changes to the address book, the `ABAddressBookHasUnsavedChanges` function will tell you by returning the value `YES`.

 An instance of the address book database returned by the `ABAddress BookCreate` function must be released when you are finished working with it, using the `CFRelease` Core Foundation method, as demonstrated in our example code.

After determining whether changes were made to the address book database, you can either save or discard these changes using the `ABAddressBookSave` or `ABAddressBook Revert` procedure, respectively.

Here is a little example that will demonstrate this. In the implementation file of your app delegate, define an instance variable of type `ABAddressBookRef` along with the error strings that you want to display to the user should your app *not* be granted permission to the address book:

```
#import "AppDelegate.h"
#import <AddressBook/AddressBook.h>
```

```
NSString *const kDenied = @"Access to address book is denied";
NSString *const kRestricted = @"Access to address book is restricted";

ABAddressBookRef addressBook;

@implementation AppDelegate

...
```

Now we go straight into the `application:didFinishLaunchingWithOptions:` instance method of our app delegate and start checking for the status of our app to see whether we can access the address book:

```
- (BOOL)                application:(UIApplication *)application
  didFinishLaunchingWithOptions:(NSDictionary *)launchOptions{

    CFErrorRef error = NULL;

    switch (ABAddressBookGetAuthorizationStatus()){
        case kABAuthorizationStatusAuthorized:{
            addressBook = ABAddressBookCreateWithOptions(NULL, &error);
            [self useAddressBook:addressBook];
            if (addressBook != NULL){
                CFRelease(addressBook);
            }
            break;
        }
        case kABAuthorizationStatusDenied:{
            [self displayMessage:kDenied];
            break;
        }
        case kABAuthorizationStatusNotDetermined:{
            addressBook = ABAddressBookCreateWithOptions(NULL, &error);
            ABAddressBookRequestAccessWithCompletion
            (addressBook, ^(bool granted, CFErrorRef error) {
                if (granted){
                    NSLog(@"Access was granted");
                    [self useAddressBook:addressBook];
                } else {
                    NSLog(@"Access was not granted");
                }
                if (addressBook != NULL){
                    CFRelease(addressBook);
                }
            });
            break;
        }
        case kABAuthorizationStatusRestricted:{
            [self displayMessage:kRestricted];
            break;
        }
    }

    self.window = [[UIWindow alloc]
```

```
                    initWithFrame:[[UIScreen mainScreen] bounds]];
        self.window.backgroundColor = [UIColor whiteColor];
        [self.window makeKeyAndVisible];
        return YES;

    }
```

You can see that if we are already or have just been granted permission to access the user's address book database, we are calling a method called useAddressBook:. In this method, if we have made any changes to the address book, we will save them:

```
- (void) useAddressBook:(ABAddressBookRef)paramAddressBook{
    /* Work with the address book here */

    /* Let's see whether we have made any changes to the
     address book or not, before attempting to save it */

    if (ABAddressBookHasUnsavedChanges(paramAddressBook)){
        /* Now decide if you want to save the changes to
         the address book */
        NSLog(@"Changes were found in the address book.");

        BOOL doYouWantToSaveChanges = YES;

        /* We can make a decision to save or revert the
         address book back to how it was before */
        if (doYouWantToSaveChanges){

            CFErrorRef saveError = NULL;

            if (ABAddressBookSave(paramAddressBook, &saveError)){
                /* We successfully saved our changes to the
                 address book */
            } else {
                /* We failed to save the changes. You can now
                 access the [saveError] variable to find out
                 what the error is */
            }

        } else {

            /* We did NOT want to save the changes to the address
             book so let's revert it to how it was before */
            ABAddressBookRevert(paramAddressBook);

        }

    } else {
        /* We have not made any changes to the address book */
        NSLog(@"No changes to the address book.");
    }
}
```

We created the doYouWantToSaveChanges local variable and set it to YES just to demonstrate that we can, if necessary, revert an address book whose contents have been changed (reversion is done through the ABAd dressBookRevert procedure). You can add code, for instance, asking the user if he wants the changes to be saved or not, and if not, you can revert the address book to its original state.

For more information about importing the Address Book framework into your application, please refer to this chapter's Introduction.

11.3 Retrieving All the People in the Address Book

Problem

You want to retrieve all the contacts in the user's address book.

Solution

Use the ABAddressBookCopyArrayOfAllPeople function to retrieve an array of all contacts:

```
- (void) readFromAddressBook:(ABAddressBookRef)paramAddressBook{

    NSArray *arrayOfAllPeople = (__bridge_transfer NSArray *)
    ABAddressBookCopyArrayOfAllPeople(paramAddressBook);

    NSUInteger peopleCounter = 0;
    for (peopleCounter = 0;
        peopleCounter < [arrayOfAllPeople count];
        peopleCounter++){

        ABRecordRef thisPerson =
        (__bridge ABRecordRef)
        [arrayOfAllPeople objectAtIndex:peopleCounter];

        NSLog(@"%@", thisPerson);

        /* Use the [thisPerson] address book record */
    }

}
```

Discussion

After accessing the user's address book database, we can call the ABAddressBook CopyArrayOfAllPeople function to retrieve an array of all the contacts in that address book. The return value of this function is an immutable array of type CFArrayRef. You can't work with this type of array as you would work with instances of NSArray, but you have two ways to traverse a CFArrayRef array. First, it natively supports two functions:

CFArrayGetCount

Gets the number of items in an instance of CFArrayRef. This is similar to the count instance method of an NSArray.

CFArrayGetValueAtIndex

Retrieves an item at a specific location of an instance of CFArrayRef. This is similar to the objectAtIndex: instance method of an NSArray.

Second, the CFArrayRef Core Foundation object is one of the objects that supports Toll-Free Bridging to its NS counterpart, NSArray. This means that we can simply bridge this Core Foundation array and type-cast it to an instance of NSArray. This works perfectly under ARC, using the __bridge_transfer keyword. That keyword decreases the reference count on the Core Foundation object, since our local array is a strong variable by default and will retain its contents without us having to do anything else. Just as a reminder, all local variables are strong variables, meaning that they will retain their contents. In this case, the ABAddressBookCopyArrayOfAllPeople function returns a Core Foundation array of all people in an address book. After we place the Core Foundation array into a local array (which will retain our Core Foundation array), we are going to have to dispose of the original Core Foundation object, before it was retained by the local variable (because of the strong local variable). Because of this, we are using __bridge_transfer to decrease the retain count on the Core Foundation array and let the strong local variable retain the toll-free array into an object of type NSArray.

The items that are put in an array of all people, retrieved by calling the ABAddressBookCopyArrayOfAllPeople function, are of type ABRecordRef. In Recipe 11.4, you will see how to access different properties of the entries, such as a person's entry, in the address book database.

See Also

Recipe 11.2

11.4 Retrieving Properties of Address Book Entries

Problem

You have retrieved a reference to an item in the address book, such as a person's entry, and you want to retrieve that person's properties, such as first and last names.

Solution

Use the ABRecordCopyValue function on the person's Address Book record.

Discussion

The records in the address book database are of type `ABRecordRef`. Each record could be either a group or a person. We have not discussed groups yet, so let's focus on people. Each person could have various types of information assigned to him, such as his first name, last name, email address, and so on. Bear in mind that many of these values are optional, and at the time of creating a new contact in the address book database, the user can simply leave out fields such as phone number, middle name, email address, URL, and so forth.

`ABRecordCopyValue` accepts an address book record and the property that has to be retrieved as its two parameters. The second parameter is the property of the record that we want to retrieve. Here are some of the common properties (all of these properties are defined as constant values in the *ABPerson.h* header file):

`kABPersonFirstNameProperty`
> This value will retrieve the first name of the given person. The return value is of type `CFStringRef`, which can be cast to `NSString` with a bridge cast, so you can do just about anything you want with the results.

`kABPersonLastNameProperty`
> This value will retrieve the last name of the given person. Like the first name property, the return value will be of type `CFStringRef`, which again can be cast to `NSString`.

`kABPersonMiddleNameProperty`
> This value will retrieve the middle name of the given person. Like the first name and the last name, the return value will be of type `CFStringRef`.

`kABPersonEmailProperty`
> This will retrieve the given person's email address. The return value in this case will be of type `ABMultiValueRef`. This is a data type that can contain multiple values inside it, like an array, but *not exactly* like an array. This type of data will be discussed next.

Some of the values that we retrieve from the `ABRecordCopyValue` function are straightforward, generic types, such as `CFStringRef`. But this function can also return more complicated values, such as the email of a contact. The email could be further broken down into home email address, work email address, and so on. Values that can be further broken down like this are called *multivalues* in the Address Book framework. Various functions allow us to work with multiple values (which are of type `ABMultiValueRef`):

`ABMultiValueGetCount`
> Returns the number of value/label pairs that are inside the multivalue.

`ABMultiValueCopyLabelAtIndex`

Returns the label associated with a multivalue item at a specific index (indexes are zero-based). For instance, if the user has three email addresses, such as work, home, and test addresses, the index of the first (work) email address in the email multivalue would be 0. This function will then retrieve the label associated with that address (in this example, *work*). Please bear in mind that multivalues do not necessarily have to have labels. Make sure you check for NULL values.

`ABMultiValueCopyValueAtIndex`

Returns the string value associated with a multivalue item at a specific index (indexes are zero-based). Suppose the user has work, home, and test email addresses. If we provide the index 0 to this function, it will retrieve the given contact's work email address.

 All Core Foundation array indexes are zero-based, just like their Cocoa counterpart array indexes.

Now let's go ahead and write a simple method that can retrieve all the people in the address book and print out their first name, last name, and email address objects, and place it in our app delegate:

```
- (void) readFromAddressBook:(ABAddressBookRef)paramAddressBook{

    NSArray *allPeople = (__bridge_transfer NSArray *)
    ABAddressBookCopyArrayOfAllPeople(paramAddressBook);

    NSUInteger peopleCounter = 0;
    for (peopleCounter = 0;
         peopleCounter < [allPeople count];
         peopleCounter++){

        ABRecordRef thisPerson = (__bridge ABRecordRef)
        [allPeople objectAtIndex:peopleCounter];

        NSString *firstName = (__bridge_transfer NSString *)
        ABRecordCopyValue(thisPerson, kABPersonFirstNameProperty);

        NSString *lastName = (__bridge_transfer NSString *)
        ABRecordCopyValue(thisPerson, kABPersonLastNameProperty);

        NSString *email = (__bridge_transfer NSString *)
        ABRecordCopyValue(thisPerson, kABPersonEmailProperty);

        NSLog(@"First Name = %@", firstName);
        NSLog(@"Last Name = %@", lastName);
        NSLog(@"Address = %@", email);

    }
}
```

We will obviously first ask for permission from the user whether or not we can access the device's address book database. Once permission is granted, we will call this method. I will not be repeating the code that requests for permission again, since we have already seen this code a few times in this chapter. Please refer to the Recipe 11.1 recipe for more information.

If you run this app in the iOS Simulator for iOS SDK 6, which has predefined contacts in the Contacts app, you will get the following printed to the console window:

```
First Name = Kate
Last Name = Bell
Address = ABMultiValueRef 0x73948f0 with 2 value(s)
    0: _$!<Work>!$_ (0x8d498c0) - kate-bell@mac.com (0x8d498e0)
    1: _$!<Work>!$_ (0x8d49130) - www.creative-consulting-inc.com (0x8d49920)
First Name = Daniel
Last Name = Higgins
Address = ABMultiValueRef 0x8d4a4a0 with 1 value(s)
    0: _$!<Home>!$_ (0x8d4a460) - d-higgins@mac.com (0x8d4a480)
 First Name = John
 Last Name = Appleseed
 Address = ABMultiValueRef 0x8856180 with 1 value(s)
    0: _$!<Work>!$_ (0x884a5b0) - John-Appleseed@mac.com (0x8856160)
First Name = Anna
Last Name = Haro
Address = ABMultiValueRef 0x8d4a0f0 with 1 value(s)
    0: _$!<Home>!$_ (0x8d4a0b0) - anna-haro@mac.com (0x8d4a0d0)
First Name = Hank
Last Name = Zakroff
Address = ABMultiValueRef 0x8d4a3c0 with 1 value(s)
    0: _$!<Work>!$_ (0x8d4a380) - hank-zakroff@mac.com (0x8d4a3a0)
First Name = David
Last Name = Taylor
Address = ABMultiValueRef 0x8d4a5b0 with 0 value(s)
```

It's immediately visible that the multivalue field (email) cannot be read as a plain string object. So, using the functions that we just learned, let's go ahead and implement a method to accept an object of type ABRecordRef, read that record's multivalue email field, and print the values out to the console:

```
- (void) logPersonEmails:(ABRecordRef)paramPerson{

  if (paramPerson == NULL){
    NSLog(@"The given person is NULL.");
    return;
  }

  ABMultiValueRef emails =
    ABRecordCopyValue(paramPerson, kABPersonEmailProperty);

  if (emails == NULL){
    NSLog(@"This contact does not have any emails.");
    return;
  }
```

```
    /* Go through all the emails */
    NSUInteger emailCounter = 0;

    for (emailCounter = 0;
         emailCounter < ABMultiValueGetCount(emails);
         emailCounter++){

      /* Get the label of the email (if any) */
      NSString *emailLabel = (__bridge_transfer NSString *)
                             ABMultiValueCopyLabelAtIndex(emails, emailCounter);

      NSString *localizedEmailLabel = (__bridge_transfer NSString *)
        ABAddressBookCopyLocalizedLabel((__bridge CFStringRef)emailLabel);

      /* And then get the email address itself */
      NSString *email = (__bridge_transfer NSString *)
                        ABMultiValueCopyValueAtIndex(emails, emailCounter);

      NSLog(@"Label = %@, Localized Label = %@, Email = %@",
            emailLabel,
            localizedEmailLabel,
            email);

    }

  CFRelease(emails);

}

- (void) readFromAddressBook:(ABAddressBookRef)paramAddressBook{

    NSArray *allPeople = (__bridge_transfer NSArray *)
    ABAddressBookCopyArrayOfAllPeople(paramAddressBook);

    NSUInteger peopleCounter = 0;
    for (peopleCounter = 0;
         peopleCounter < [allPeople count];
         peopleCounter++){

        ABRecordRef thisPerson = (__bridge ABRecordRef)
        [allPeople objectAtIndex:peopleCounter];

        NSString *firstName = (__bridge_transfer NSString *)
        ABRecordCopyValue(thisPerson, kABPersonFirstNameProperty);

        NSString *lastName = (__bridge_transfer NSString *)
        ABRecordCopyValue(thisPerson, kABPersonLastNameProperty);

        NSLog(@"First Name = %@", firstName);
        NSLog(@"Last Name = %@", lastName);

        [self logPersonEmails:thisPerson];

    }
}
```

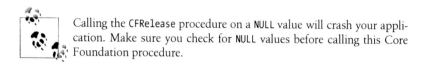

Calling the `CFRelease` procedure on a `NULL` value will crash your application. Make sure you check for `NULL` values before calling this Core Foundation procedure.

Label values returned by the `ABMultiValueCopyLabelAtIndex` function are rather cryptic and hard to read. Examples are `_$!<Other>!$_` and `_$!<Home>!$_`, which might be set for email addresses with labels of Other and Home. However, if you want to retrieve a plain and readable version of these labels, you can first copy the label using the `ABMultiValueCopyLabelAtIndex` function and pass the return value of this function to the `ABAddressBookCopyLocalizedLabel` function.

See Also

Recipe 11.2; Recipe 11.3

11.5 Inserting a Person Entry into the Address Book

Problem

You want to create a new person contact and insert it into the user's address book.

Solution

Use the `ABPersonCreate` function to create a new person. Set the person's properties using the `ABRecordSetValue` function and add the person to the address book using the `ABAddressBookAddRecord` function.

Discussion

After accessing the address book database using the `ABAddressBookCreate` function, you can start inserting new group and person records into the database. In this recipe, we will concentrate on inserting new person records. For information about inserting new groups into the address book, please refer to Recipe 11.6.

Use the `ABPersonCreate` function to create a new person record. Bear in mind that calling this function is not enough to add the person record to the address book. You must save the address book for your record to appear in the database.

By calling the `ABPersonCreate` function, you get a Core Foundation reference to a value of type `ABRecordRef`. Now you can call the `ABRecordSetValue` function to set the various properties of a new person entry. Once you are done, you must add the new person record to the database. You can do this using the `ABAddressBookAddRecord` function. After doing this, you must also save any unsaved changes to the address book database in order to truly preserve your new person record. Do this by using the `ABAddressBookSave` function.

So let's combine all this into a method that allows us to insert a new person entry into the address book:

```
- (ABRecordRef) newPersonWithFirstName:(NSString *)paramFirstName
                              lastName:(NSString *)paramLastName
                          inAddressBook:(ABAddressBookRef)paramAddressBook{

    ABRecordRef result = NULL;

    if (paramAddressBook == NULL){
        NSLog(@"The address book is NULL.");
        return NULL;
    }

    if ([paramFirstName length] == 0 &&
        [paramLastName length] == 0){
        NSLog(@"First name and last name are both empty.");
        return NULL;
    }

    result = ABPersonCreate();

    if (result == NULL){
        NSLog(@"Failed to create a new person.");
        return NULL;
    }

    BOOL couldSetFirstName = NO;
    BOOL couldSetLastName = NO;
    CFErrorRef setFirstNameError = NULL;
    CFErrorRef setLastNameError = NULL;

    couldSetFirstName = ABRecordSetValue(result,
                               kABPersonFirstNameProperty,
                               (__bridge CFTypeRef)paramFirstName,
                               &setFirstNameError);

    couldSetLastName = ABRecordSetValue(result,
                               kABPersonLastNameProperty,
                               (__bridge CFTypeRef)paramLastName,
                               &setLastNameError);

    CFErrorRef couldAddPersonError = NULL;
    BOOL couldAddPerson = ABAddressBookAddRecord(paramAddressBook,
                                        result,
                                        &couldAddPersonError);

    if (couldAddPerson){
        NSLog(@"Successfully added the person.");
    } else {
        NSLog(@"Failed to add the person.");
        CFRelease(result);
        result = NULL;
        return result;
    }
```

```
        if (ABAddressBookHasUnsavedChanges(paramAddressBook)){

            CFErrorRef couldSaveAddressBookError = NULL;
            BOOL couldSaveAddressBook = ABAddressBookSave(paramAddressBook,
                                                &couldSaveAddressBookError);

            if (couldSaveAddressBook){
                NSLog(@"Successfully saved the address book.");
            } else {
                NSLog(@"Failed to save the address book.");
            }

        }

        if (couldSetFirstName &&
            couldSetLastName){
            NSLog(@"Successfully set the first name and the last name of the person.");
        } else {
            NSLog(@"Failed to set the first name and/or last name of the person.");
        }

        return result;

    }

    - (void) createNewPersonInAddressBook:(ABAddressBookRef)paramAddressBook{

        ABRecordRef anthonyRobbins = [self newPersonWithFirstName:@"Anthony"
                                                lastName:@"Robbins"
                                            inAddressBook:paramAddressBook];

        if (anthonyRobbins != NULL){
            NSLog(@"Anthony Robbins' record is inserted into the Address Book.");
            CFRelease(anthonyRobbins);
        }

    }
```

In our app delegate, we will first check if we have permission to access the user's address book database. We have already seen this code in Recipe 11.1, so we won't be repeating it here. Once you have access, you can then call the createNewPersonInAddressBook: method that we have written and pass the instance of the address book object to this method.

The newPersonWithFirstName:lastName:inAddressBook: method that we implemented creates a new person entry in the address book database. After invoking this function, you will see the results (as shown in Figure 11-3) in the Contacts application on the iOS Simulator.

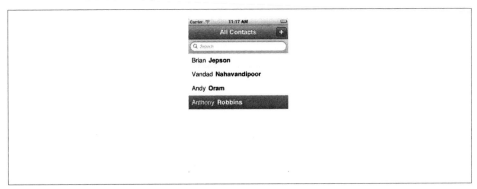

Figure 11-3. A new person record is added to the address book

 Memory management on Core Foundation is quite different from what you might be used to when writing applications for Cocoa Touch. As this topic is beyond the scope of this book, please make sure you read the "Memory Management Programming Guide for Core Foundation" documentation on Apple's website (*http://bit.ly/TtfcP7*).

11.6 Inserting a Group Entry into the Address Book

Problem

You want to categorize your contacts into groups.

Solution

Use the `ABGroupCreate` function.

Bear in mind that, as mentioned before, Core Foundation memory management is more complex than what Xcode's static analyzer could process. Therefore, attempting to use the LLVM compiler to compile Core Foundation code with static analysis turned on might give you a lot of warnings. You can ignore these and test the code with Instruments to make sure your code does not leak, but I encourage you to familiarize yourself with memory management in Core Foundation by reading Apple's "Memory Management Programming Guide for Core Foundation" document, as mentioned in the previous section.

Discussion

After retrieving the reference to the address book database, you can call the `ABGroup Create` function to create a new group entry. However, you must perform a few more operations before you can insert this group into the address book operation. The first thing you have to do is set the name of this group using the `ABRecordSetValue` function with the `kABGroupNameProperty` property, as shown in the example code.

After the name of the group is set, add it to the address book database just like you add a new person's entry—using the `ABAddressBookAddRecord` function. For more information about adding a new person's entry to the address book database, please read Recipe 11.5.

 Inserting a new group with a name that already exists in the address book database will create a new group with the same name but with no group members. In later recipes, we will learn how to avoid doing this by first finding the groups in the database and making sure a group with that name doesn't already exist.

After adding the group to the address book, you also need to save the address book's contents using the `ABAddressBookSave` function.

So, with all this in mind, let's go ahead and implement a method that allows us to create a new group with any desired name in the Address Book database:

```
- (ABRecordRef) newGroupWithName:(NSString *)paramGroupName
                    inAddressBook:(ABAddressBookRef)paramAddressBook{

    ABRecordRef result = NULL;

    if (paramAddressBook == NULL){
      NSLog(@"The address book is nil.");
      return NULL;
    }

    result = ABGroupCreate();

    if (result == NULL){
      NSLog(@"Failed to create a new group.");
      return NULL;
    }

    BOOL couldSetGroupName = NO;
    CFErrorRef error = NULL;

    couldSetGroupName = ABRecordSetValue(result,
                                         kABGroupNameProperty,
                                         (__bridge CFTypeRef)paramGroupName,
                                         &error);

    if (couldSetGroupName){

      BOOL couldAddRecord = NO;
      CFErrorRef couldAddRecordError = NULL;
```

```
      couldAddRecord = ABAddressBookAddRecord(paramAddressBook,
                                              result,
                                              &couldAddRecordError);

    if (couldAddRecord){

      NSLog(@"Successfully added the new group.");

      if (ABAddressBookHasUnsavedChanges(paramAddressBook)){
        BOOL couldSaveAddressBook = NO;
        CFErrorRef couldSaveAddressBookError = NULL;
        couldSaveAddressBook = ABAddressBookSave(paramAddressBook,
                                                 &couldSaveAddressBookError);
        if (couldSaveAddressBook){
          NSLog(@"Successfully saved the address book.");
        } else {
          CFRelease(result);
          result = NULL;
          NSLog(@"Failed to save the address book.");
        }
      } else {
        CFRelease(result);
        result = NULL;
        NSLog(@"No unsaved changes.");
      }
    } else {
      CFRelease(result);
      result = NULL;
      NSLog(@"Could not add a new group.");
    }
  } else {
    CFRelease(result);
    result = NULL;
    NSLog(@"Failed to set the name of the group.");
  }

  return result;

}

- (void) createNewGroupInAddressBook:(ABAddressBookRef)paramAddressBook{

    ABRecordRef personalCoachesGroup =
    [self newGroupWithName:@"Personal Coaches"
            inAddressBook:paramAddressBook];

    if (personalCoachesGroup != NULL){
        NSLog(@"Successfully created the group.");
        CFRelease(personalCoachesGroup);
    } else {
        NSLog(@"Could not create the group.");
    }

}
```

All we have to do now is to call the `createNewGroupInAddressBook:` method when our app delegate starts, to make sure that it works as expected. Before you attempt to call this method though, do make sure that your app has the required permission to access the user's address book database. To read more about this, please have a look at Recipe 11.1.

After running your code, you will see results like those shown in Figure 11-4 (you might have created other groups already, so your address book might not look exactly like that shown in the figure).

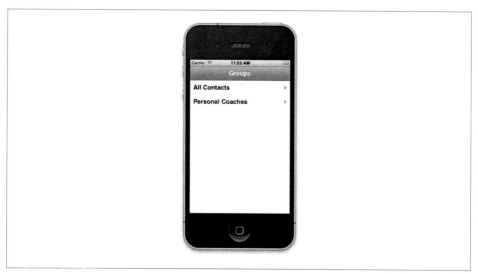

Figure 11-4. A new group created in the address book database

11.7 Adding Persons to Groups

Problem

You want to assign a person entry in the address book to a group.

Solution

Use the `ABGroupAddMember` function.

Discussion

We learned to insert both person entries (in Recipe 11.5) and group entries (in Recipe 11.6) into the address book database. In those recipes we implemented two custom methods named `newPersonWithFirstName:lastName:inAddressBook:` and `new GroupWithName:inAddressBook:`. Now we want to add the person entry to the group we created and save the information to the address book database. Combining these three recipes, we can use the following code to achieve our goal:

```
- (BOOL)    addPerson:(ABRecordRef)paramPerson
               toGroup:(ABRecordRef)paramGroup
    saveToAddressBook:(ABAddressBookRef)paramAddressBook{

    BOOL result = NO;

    if (paramPerson == NULL ||
        paramGroup == NULL ||
        paramAddressBook == NULL){
        NSLog(@"Invalid parameters are given.");
        return NO;
    }

    CFErrorRef error = NULL;

    /* Now attempt to add the person entry to the group */
    result = ABGroupAddMember(paramGroup,
                              paramPerson,
                              &error);

    if (result == NO){
        NSLog(@"Could not add the person to the group.");
        return result;
    }

    /* Make sure we save any unsaved changes */
    if (ABAddressBookHasUnsavedChanges(paramAddressBook)){
        BOOL couldSaveAddressBook = NO;
        CFErrorRef couldSaveAddressBookError = NULL;
        couldSaveAddressBook = ABAddressBookSave(paramAddressBook,
                                          &couldSaveAddressBookError);
        if (couldSaveAddressBook){
            NSLog(@"Successfully added the person to the group.");
            result = YES;
        } else {
            NSLog(@"Failed to save the address book.");
        }
    } else {
        NSLog(@"No changes were saved.");
    }

    return result;

}

- (void) addPersonsAndGroupsToAddressBook:(ABAddressBookRef)paramAddressBook{

    ABRecordRef richardBranson = [self
                                  newPersonWithFirstName:@"Richard"
                                  lastName:@"Branson"
                                  inAddressBook:paramAddressBook];
```

```
        if (richardBranson != NULL){

            ABRecordRef entrepreneursGroup = [self
                                    newGroupWithName:@"Entrepreneurs"
                                    inAddressBook:paramAddressBook];

            if (entrepreneursGroup != NULL){

                if ([self addPerson:richardBranson
                            toGroup:entrepreneursGroup
                    saveToAddressBook:paramAddressBook]){

                    NSLog(@"Successfully added Richard Branson \
                        to the Entrepreneurs Group");

                } else {
                    NSLog(@"Failed to add Richard Branson to the \
                        Entrepreneurs group.");
                }

                CFRelease(entrepreneursGroup);
            } else {
                NSLog(@"Failed to create the Entrepreneurs group.");
            }

            CFRelease(richardBranson);
        } else {
            NSLog(@"Failed to create an entity for Richard Branson.");
        }

    }
```

Once your app starts, you need to make sure your app has permission to access and update the user's address book. For more information about this, please see Recipe 11.1. Once you are sure that you have permission, you can call the addPerson sAndGroupsToAddressBook: method and pass the instance of address book that you retrieved from the system as a parameter to this method. Once that is done, We can see that the person entry we added to the "Entrepreneurs" group and to the database is, in fact, now inside this address book group, as shown in Figure 11-5.

See Also

Recipe 11.6

11.8 Searching the Address Book

Problem

You want to find a specific person or group in the address book database.

Figure 11-5. Adding a person to a group

Solution

Use the `ABAddressBookCopyArrayOfAllPeople` and `ABAddressBookCopyArrayOfAllGroups` functions to find all people and groups in the address book. Traverse the returned arrays to find the information you are looking for. Alternatively, you can use the `ABAddress BookCopyPeopleWithName` function to find an entry about a person with a specific name.

Discussion

Up to this point, we have been inserting group and person entries into the address book without checking whether such a group or person already exists. We can use the `AB AddressBookCopyArrayOfAllPeople` and `ABAddressBookCopyArrayOfAllGroups` functions to get the array of all people and groups in the address book and search in the array to see whether the person or group entries we are about to insert into the address book already exist. When we check whether strings match, we also have to check for null strings (which we assume mean that the contacts match). Here are two methods that will make use of these functions and that can also be used in other recipes:

```
- (BOOL) doesPersonExistWithFirstName:(NSString *)paramFirstName
                         lastName:(NSString *)paramLastName
                   inAddressBook:(ABRecordRef)paramAddressBook{

    BOOL result = NO;

    if (paramAddressBook == NULL){
        NSLog(@"The address book is null.");
        return NO;
    }

    NSArray *allPeople = (__bridge_transfer NSArray *)
```

```
    ABAddressBookCopyArrayOfAllPeople(paramAddressBook);

    NSUInteger peopleCounter = 0;
    for (peopleCounter = 0;
         peopleCounter < [allPeople count];
         peopleCounter++){

        ABRecordRef person = (__bridge ABRecordRef)
        [allPeople objectAtIndex:peopleCounter];

        NSString *firstName = (__bridge_transfer NSString *)
        ABRecordCopyValue(person, kABPersonFirstNameProperty);

        NSString *lastName = (__bridge_transfer NSString *)
        ABRecordCopyValue(person, kABPersonLastNameProperty);

        BOOL firstNameIsEqual = NO;
        BOOL lastNameIsEqual = NO;

        if ([firstName length] == 0 &&
            [paramFirstName length] == 0){
            firstNameIsEqual = YES;
        }
        else if ([firstName isEqualToString:paramFirstName]){
            firstNameIsEqual = YES;
        }

        if ([lastName length] == 0 &&
            [paramLastName length] == 0){
            lastNameIsEqual = YES;
        }
        else if ([lastName isEqualToString:paramLastName]){
            lastNameIsEqual = YES;
        }

        if (firstNameIsEqual &&
            lastNameIsEqual){
            return YES;
        }

    }

    return result;

}
```

Similarly, we can check the existence of a group by first retrieving the array of all the groups in the address book database, using the ABAddressBookCopyArrayOfAllGroups function:

```
- (BOOL) doesGroupExistWithGroupName:(NSString *)paramGroupName
                    inAddressBook:(ABAddressBookRef)paramAddressBook{

    BOOL result = NO;
```

```
    if (paramAddressBook == NULL){
        NSLog(@"The address book is null.");
        return NO;
    }

    NSArray *allGroups = (__bridge_transfer NSArray *)
    ABAddressBookCopyArrayOfAllGroups(paramAddressBook);

    NSUInteger groupCounter = 0;
    for (groupCounter = 0;
         groupCounter < [allGroups count];
         groupCounter++){

        ABRecordRef group = (__bridge ABRecordRef)
        [allGroups objectAtIndex:groupCounter];

        NSString *groupName = (__bridge_transfer NSString *)
        ABRecordCopyValue(group, kABGroupNameProperty);

        if ([groupName length] == 0 &&
            [paramGroupName length] == 0){
            return YES;
        }

        else if ([groupName isEqualToString:paramGroupName]){
            return YES;
        }

    }

    return result;

}
```

 Attempting to create a group with the name equal to @"" (an empty string), nil, or NULL will create a new group with the name "Contacts" in the address book database. Please try to avoid creating groups with empty names or names equal to nil or NULL.

We can use the doesGroupExistWithGroupName:inAddressBook: method in this way:

```
- (void) createGroupInAddressBook:(ABAddressBookRef)paramAddressBook{

    if ([self doesGroupExistWithGroupName:@"O'Reilly"
                           inAddressBook:addressBook]){
        NSLog(@"The O'Reilly group already exists in the address book.");
    } else {

        ABRecordRef oreillyGroup = [self newGroupWithName:@"O'Reilly"
                                            inAddressBook:addressBook];

        if (oreillyGroup != NULL){
            NSLog(@"Successfully created a group for O'Reilly.");
```

```
            CFRelease(oreillyGroup);
        } else {
            NSLog(@"Failed to create a group for O'Reilly.");
        }

    }

}
```

For the implementation of the `createNewGroupWithName:inAddressBook:` method, please refer to Recipe 11.6.

As we saw earlier, we have two ways of finding a person in the address book database:

- Retrieve the array of all people in the address book, using the `ABAddressBookCopy ArrayOfAllPeople` function. Next, get each record inside the array and compare the first and last name properties of each person with the strings you are looking for. You can search in any of the properties assigned to that person in the address book, including first name, last name, email, phone number, and so on.

- Ask the Address Book framework to perform the search based on a composite name. This is done using the `ABAddressBookCopyPeopleWithName` function.

Here is an example of using the `ABAddressBookCopyPeopleWithName` function to search for a contact with a specific name:

```
- (BOOL) doesPersonExistWithFullName:(NSString *)paramFullName
                    inAddressBook:(ABAddressBookRef)paramAddressBook{

    BOOL result = NO;

    if (paramAddressBook == NULL){
        NSLog(@"Address book is null.");
        return NO;
    }

    NSArray *allPeopleWithThisName = (__bridge_transfer NSArray *)
    ABAddressBookCopyPeopleWithName(paramAddressBook,
                            (__bridge CFStringRef)paramFullName);

    if ([allPeopleWithThisName count] > 0){
        result = YES;
    }

    return result;

}
```

Here is how we can use the method that we just implemented:

```
- (void) createPersonInAddressBook:(ABAddressBookRef)paramAddressBook{

    if ([self doesPersonExistWithFullName:@"Anthony Robbins"
                        inAddressBook:addressBook]){
        NSLog(@"Anthony Robbins exists in the address book.");
```

```
    } else {
        NSLog(@"Anthony Robbins does not exist in the address book.");

        ABRecordRef anthonyRobbins = [self newPersonWithFirstName:@"Anthony"
                                                        lastName:@"Robbins"
                                                   inAddressBook:addressBook];

        if (anthonyRobbins != NULL){
            NSLog(@"Successfully created a record for Anthony Robbins");
            CFRelease(anthonyRobbins);
        } else {
            NSLog(@"Failed to create a record for Anthony Robbins");
        }
    }

}
```

Using this function, you won't have to know the full name to be able to find a contact in the address book. You can just pass a part of the name—for instance, just the first name—in order to find all the contacts with that specific first name.

 The search performed by the `ABAddressBookCopyPeopleWithName` function is case-insensitive.

11.9 Retrieving and Setting a Person's Address Book Image

Problem

You want to be able to retrieve and set the images of address book people entries.

Solution

Use one of the following functions:

`ABPersonHasImageData`
> Use this function to find out if an address book entry has an image set.

`ABPersonCopyImageData`
> Use this function to retrieve the image data (if any).

`ABPersonSetImageData`
> Use this function to set the image data for an entry.

Discussion

As mentioned in this recipe's Solution, we can use the `ABPersonCopyImageData` function to retrieve the data associated with an image of a person entry in the address book. We can use this function in a method of our own to make it more convenient to use:

```
- (UIImage *) getPersonImage:(ABRecordRef)paramPerson{

    UIImage *result = nil;

    if (paramPerson == NULL){
        NSLog(@"The person is nil.");
        return NULL;
    }

    NSData *imageData = (__bridge_transfer NSData *)
    ABPersonCopyImageData(paramPerson);

    if (imageData != nil){
        UIImage *image = [UIImage imageWithData:imageData];
        result = image;
    }

    return result;

}
```

The ABPersonSetImageData function sets the image data for a person entry in the address book. Since this function uses data, not the image itself, we need to get NSData from UIImage. If we want the data pertaining to a PNG image, we can use the UIIma gePNGRepresentation function to retrieve the PNG NSData representation of the image of type UIImage. To retrieve JPEG image data from an instance of UIImage, use the UIImageJPEGRepresentation function. Here is the method that will allow you to set the image of a person entry in the address book database:

```
- (BOOL) setPersonImage:(ABRecordRef)paramPerson
        inAddressBook:(ABAddressBookRef)paramAddressBook
        withImageData:(NSData *)paramImageData{

    BOOL result = NO;

    if (paramAddressBook == NULL){
        NSLog(@"The address book is nil.");
        return NO;
    }

    if (paramPerson == NULL){
        NSLog(@"The person is nil.");
        return NO;
    }

    CFErrorRef couldSetPersonImageError = NULL;

    BOOL couldSetPersonImage =
    ABPersonSetImageData(paramPerson,
                         (__bridge CFDataRef)paramImageData,
                         &couldSetPersonImageError);

    if (couldSetPersonImage){
        NSLog(@"Successfully set the person's image. Saving...");
```

```
        if (ABAddressBookHasUnsavedChanges(paramAddressBook)){
            BOOL couldSaveAddressBook = NO;
            CFErrorRef couldSaveAddressBookError = NULL;

            couldSaveAddressBook =
            ABAddressBookSave(paramAddressBook,
                              &couldSaveAddressBookError);

            if (couldSaveAddressBook){
                NSLog(@"Successfully saved the address book.");
                result = YES;
            } else {
                NSLog(@"Failed to save the address book.");
            }
        } else {
            NSLog(@"There are no changes to be saved!");
        }
    } else {
        NSLog(@"Failed to set the person's image.");
    }

    return result;

}
```

Now let's write a simple application to demonstrate the use of these methods. In this example code, we want to achieve the following:

- Create a simple view controller with two labels and two image views.

- Attempt to retrieve a contact with the first name "Anthony" and the last name "Robbins" from our address book. If this contact doesn't exist, we will create it.

- Retrieve the previous image (if any) of the contact and display it in the first image view (the top image view).

- Set a new image for the contact, retrieved from our application bundle, and display the new image in the second image view (the bottom image view).

Let's get started. Here is the *.h* file of our view controller:

```
#import <UIKit/UIKit.h>
#import <AddressBook/AddressBook.h>

@interface ViewController : UIViewController

@property (nonatomic, strong) UILabel *labelOldImage;
@property (nonatomic, strong) UIImageView *imageViewOld;

@property (nonatomic, strong) UILabel *labelNewImage;
@property (nonatomic, strong) UIImageView *imageViewNew;

@end
```

The next stop is the viewDidLoad method of our view controller, where we will instantiate our labels and image views and place them on our view controller's view. We need to write our `viewDidLoad` method in a way that we can read a person's image from the address book and then set his image and display the new one, using the functions we've learned about in this and other recipes in this chapter:

```
- (void) changeYPositionOfView:(UIView *)paramView
                            to:(CGFloat)paramY{

    CGRect viewFrame = paramView.frame;
    viewFrame.origin.y = paramY;
    paramView.frame = viewFrame;

}

- (void) createLabelAndImageViewForOldImage{

    self.labelOldImage = [[UILabel alloc] initWithFrame:CGRectZero];
    self.labelOldImage.text = @"Old Image";
    self.labelOldImage.font = [UIFont systemFontOfSize:16.0f];
    [self.labelOldImage sizeToFit];
    self.labelOldImage.center = self.view.center;
    [self.view addSubview:self.labelOldImage];
    [self changeYPositionOfView:self.labelOldImage
                            to:80.0f];

    self.imageViewOld = [[UIImageView alloc] initWithFrame:CGRectMake(0.0f,
                                                                      0.0f,
                                                                      100.0f,
                                                                      100.0f)];
    self.imageViewOld.center = self.view.center;
    self.imageViewOld.contentMode = UIViewContentModeScaleAspectFit;
    [self.view addSubview:self.imageViewOld];
    [self changeYPositionOfView:self.imageViewOld
                            to:105.0f];

}

- (void) createLabelAndImageViewForNewImage{

    self.labelNewImage = [[UILabel alloc] initWithFrame:CGRectZero];
    self.labelNewImage.text = @"New Image";
    self.labelNewImage.font = [UIFont systemFontOfSize:16.0f];
    [self.labelNewImage sizeToFit];
    self.labelNewImage.center = self.view.center;
    [self.view addSubview:self.labelNewImage];
    [self changeYPositionOfView:self.labelNewImage
                            to:210.0f];

    self.imageViewNew = [[UIImageView alloc] initWithFrame:CGRectMake(0.0f,
                                                                      0.0f,
                                                                      100.0f,
                                                                      100.0f)];
    self.imageViewNew.center = self.view.center;
    self.imageViewNew.contentMode = UIViewContentModeScaleAspectFit;
    [self.view addSubview:self.imageViewNew];
    [self changeYPositionOfView:self.imageViewNew
```

```
                    to:235.0f];

   }

   - (void)viewDidLoad{
      [super viewDidLoad];

      self.view.backgroundColor = [UIColor whiteColor];
      [self createLabelAndImageViewForOldImage];
      [self createLabelAndImageViewForNewImage];

   }
```

The next stop would be to ask the user for permission to access the device's address
book database. The best place to do this is when we know our view has appeared on
the screen and that would be inside the `viewDidAppear:` instance method of our view
controller. In that method, we will simply query the system to see if our app has already
been authorized to access the user's address book:

```
   - (ABRecordRef) getPersonWithFirstName:(NSString *)paramFirstName
                             lastName:(NSString *)paramLastName
                        inAddressBook:(ABRecordRef)paramAddressBook{

      ABRecordRef result = NULL;

      if (paramAddressBook == NULL){
         NSLog(@"The address book is null.");
         return NULL;
      }

      NSArray *allPeople = (__bridge_transfer NSArray *)
      ABAddressBookCopyArrayOfAllPeople(paramAddressBook);

      NSUInteger peopleCounter = 0;
      for (peopleCounter = 0;
           peopleCounter < [allPeople count];
           peopleCounter++){

         ABRecordRef person = (__bridge ABRecordRef)
         [allPeople objectAtIndex:peopleCounter];

         NSString *firstName = (__bridge_transfer NSString *)
         ABRecordCopyValue(person, kABPersonFirstNameProperty);

         NSString *lastName = (__bridge_transfer NSString *)
         ABRecordCopyValue(person, kABPersonLastNameProperty);

         BOOL firstNameIsEqual = NO;
         BOOL lastNameIsEqual = NO;

         if ([firstName length] == 0 &&
             [paramFirstName length] == 0){
            firstNameIsEqual = YES;
         }
         else if ([firstName isEqualToString:paramFirstName]){
```

```
            firstNameIsEqual = YES;
        }

        if ([lastName length] == 0 &&
            [paramLastName length] == 0){
            lastNameIsEqual = YES;
        }
        else if ([lastName isEqualToString:paramLastName]){
            lastNameIsEqual = YES;
        }

        if (firstNameIsEqual &&
            lastNameIsEqual){
            return person;
        }

    }

    return result;

}

- (void) updateImagesInAddressBook:(ABAddressBookRef)paramAddressBook{

    ABRecordRef anthonyRobbins = [self getPersonWithFirstName:@"Anthony"
                                                    lastName:@"Robbins"
                                               inAddressBook:paramAddressBook];

    if (anthonyRobbins == NULL){
        NSLog(@"Couldn't find record. Creating one...");
        anthonyRobbins = [self newPersonWithFirstName:@"Anthony"
                                             lastName:@"Robbins"
                                        inAddressBook:paramAddressBook];
        if (anthonyRobbins == NULL){
            NSLog(@"Failed to create a new record for this person.");
            return;
        }
    }

    self.imageViewOld.image = [self getPersonImage:anthonyRobbins];

    NSString *newImageFilePath =
    [[NSBundle mainBundle] pathForResource:@"Anthony Robbins"
                                    ofType:@"jpg"];

    UIImage *newImage = [[UIImage alloc]
                        initWithContentsOfFile:newImageFilePath];

    NSData *newImageData = UIImagePNGRepresentation(newImage);

    if ([self setPersonImage:anthonyRobbins
               inAddressBook:paramAddressBook
              withImageData:newImageData]){
        NSLog(@"Successfully set this person's new image.");
        self.imageViewNew.image = [self getPersonImage:anthonyRobbins];
```

```objc
    } else {
        NSLog(@"Failed to set this person's new image.");
    }

    CFRelease(anthonyRobbins);

}

- (void) viewDidAppear:(BOOL)paramAnimated{
    [super viewDidAppear:paramAnimated];

    CFErrorRef error = NULL;

    switch (ABAddressBookGetAuthorizationStatus()){
        case kABAuthorizationStatusAuthorized:{
            addressBook = ABAddressBookCreateWithOptions(NULL, &error);
            [self updateImagesInAddressBook:addressBook];
            if (addressBook != NULL){
                CFRelease(addressBook);
            }
            break;
        }
        case kABAuthorizationStatusDenied:{
            [self displayMessage:kDenied];
            break;
        }
        case kABAuthorizationStatusNotDetermined:{
            addressBook = ABAddressBookCreateWithOptions(NULL, &error);
            ABAddressBookRequestAccessWithCompletion
            (addressBook, ^(bool granted, CFErrorRef error) {
                if (granted){
                    [self updateImagesInAddressBook:addressBook];
                } else {
                    NSLog(@"Access was not granted");
                }
                if (addressBook != NULL){
                    CFRelease(addressBook);
                }
            });
            break;
        }
        case kABAuthorizationStatusRestricted:{
            [self displayMessage:kRestricted];
            break;
        }
    }

}
```

The results are shown in Figure 11-6.

Figure 11-6. The old image for a contact is replaced by a new one

CHAPTER 12

Files and Folder Management

12.0 Introduction

iOS is based on Mac OS X, which itself is based on the UNIX operating system. In iOS, the operating system's full directory structure is not visible to an app because each app, written by an iOS app developer, lives in its own sandbox. A sandbox environment is exactly what it sounds like: a sanctioned area where only the app that owns the sandbox can access the contents of the folder. Every app has its own sandbox folder and the sandbox folders by default have subfolders that apps can access.

When an iOS app is installed on the device, the folder structure shown in Figure 12-1 will be created for that app by the system.

The root folder of every application contains various other folders, which I will explain here:

Name.app
> Despite the odd name with the *.app* extension, this is a folder. The contents of your main bundle will all go in here. For instance, all your app icons, your app binary, your different branding images, fonts, sounds, etc., will all be placed in this folder automatically when iOS installs your app on a device. The *name* is the product name that you have set for your app. So if your app is called MyApp, the .app folder will be called *MyApp.app*.

Documents/
> This folder is the destination for all user-created content. Content that your app has populated, downloaded, or created should not be stored in this folder.

Library/
> You use this directory to store cached files, user preferences, and so on. Usually, this folder on its own will not have any files sitting in it. It contains other folders that will contain files.

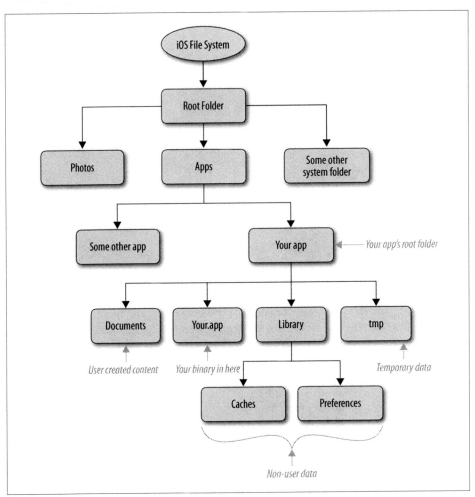

Figure 12-1. Depiction of the iOS file system

Library/Caches/

The folder where you store data that your app can later re-create, if need be. The contents of this folder are not backed up by iOS. Also, iOS may remove the contents of this folder if the device is running out of disk space while your app is not running! So do not allow your app to rely on the contents of this folder too much; be prepared to re-create this content. Once again: the contents of this folder will not be backed up by iOS and can be deleted while your app is suspended.

For instance, if your app is relying on files and folders that are to be created on disk, this folder would not be the best place to store this data. You are better off storing such files and folders in the */tmp* folder.

Library/Preferences/

As the name indicates, this folder contains the preferences that your app wants to remember between launches. We will talk about this in detail later. iOS does back up the contents of this folder.

Library/Application Support/

The data that your app creates, not including the data created by the user, must be stored in this folder. It is good to know that iOS backs up the contents of this folder. This folder may not be created for you automatically and you'll have to create it yourself if it doesn't exist. We will talk about folder creation later in this chapter.

tmp/

These are temporary files that your app may create, download, and so on. The contents of this folder are not backed up by iOS. For instance, you may download a few photos from the Internet and store them in this folder in order to increase the performance of your application, so that you won't have to download the files every time the user opens your app. This folder serves exactly this purpose. Make sure that you are not storing any user-created documents or files in this folder.

Now you know the folders that iOS creates for you when your app is installed on an iOS device. The next thing you want to do is find the path of the rest of the useful folders that we just talked about, using the APIs that Apple has exposed to you (these will be explained in this chapter).

12.1 Finding the Paths of the Most Useful Folders on Disk

Problem

You want to be able to find the path of some of the most useful folders that your app has access to (e.g., the folders that we talked about in Recipe 12.0), so that you can access their content or create new content in those folders.

 Programmers need to use APIs that are exposed in the iOS SDK to find the path of folders and/or files. In other words, you should never assume the path of a folder or a file. You should always make sure that you use the appropriate APIs to, for instance, find the paths that you are looking for, such as the *Documents* folder. Never, ever assume that this folder will be called *Documents* in your app's bundle. Simply use the appropriate APIs to find this path and, if you want to add or access files in the folder, attach your filenames to the end of this path.

Solution

Use the `URLsForDirectory:inDomains:` instance method of the `NSFileManager` class.

Discussion

The `NSFileManager` class offers a lot of file and folder related operations that you can do with iOS, right inside your apps, simply by making an instance of the class. I advise against using the shared file manager provided by this class through the `defaultMan ager` class method because it is not thread-safe. It is best to create and manage an instance of the `NSFileManager` class for yourself.

The `URLsForDirectory:inDomains:` instance method of the `NSFileManager` class allows you to search for specific directories on the iOS file system, mostly in your app's sandbox. There are two parameters to this method:

URLsForDirectory:
> This is the directory that you want to search for. Pass a value of type `NSSearchPath Directory` enumeration to this parameter. I will talk more about this soon.

inDomains
> This is *where* you look for the given directory. The value to this parameter must be of type `NSSearchPathDomainMask` enumeration.

Suppose you want to find the path to your app's *Documents* folder. This is how easily you can find it:

```
NSFileManager *fileManager = [[NSFileManager alloc] init];
NSArray *urls = [fileManager URLsForDirectory:NSDocumentDirectory
                                    inDomains:NSUserDomainMask];

if ([urls count] > 0){
    NSURL *documentsFolder = urls[0];
    NSLog(@"%@", documentsFolder);
} else {
    NSLog(@"Could not find the Documents folder.");
}
```

As you can see, after creating our own instance of `NSFileManager`, we passed the `NSDo cumentDirectory` value as the folder we are looking for and `NSUserDomainMask` as the domain. Let's go through some of the most important values that you can pass to each one of the parameters to the `URLsForDirectory:inDomains:` instance method of the `NSFileManager` class:

URLsForDirectory

NSLibraryDirectory
> The library folder for the app.

NSCachesDirectory
> The caches folder, as explained before.

NSDocumentDirectory
> The documents folder.

inDomains

> NSUserDomainMask
>> Specifies that the search be performed in the current user's folder. On OS X, this folder would be ~/.

Using this method, you can then find other folders such as the *caches* folder, as shown here:

```
NSFileManager *fileManager = [[NSFileManager alloc] init];
NSArray *urls = [fileManager URLsForDirectory:NSCachesDirectory
                                    inDomains:NSUserDomainMask];

if ([urls count] > 0){
    NSURL *cachesFolder = urls[0];
    NSLog(@"%@", cachesFolder);
} else {
    NSLog(@"Could not find the Caches folder.");
}
```

If you want to find the *tmp* folder, use the `NSTemporaryDirectory()` C function like so:

```
NSString *tempDirectory = NSTemporaryDirectory();
NSLog(@"Temp Directory = %@", tempDirectory);
```

When you execute this command on a device, the output will be similar to that shown here:

```
Temp Directory = /private/var/mobile/Applications/19E19C60-8A3A-41BF-
    AFCA-B1AB9746A4CB/tmp/
```

See Also

Recipe 12.0

12.2 Writing to and Reading from Files

Problem

You want to be able to save information to disk (e.g., text, data, images, etc.).

Solution

Cocoa classes that allow you to store information, such as `NSString`, `UIImage`, and `NSData`, all expose instance methods that allow you to store their data to disk under a given path.

Discussion

In order to store text to disk, assuming that your text is stored in an instance of `NSString` (or the immutable version of this class), you can use the `writeToFile:`

`atomically:encoding:error:` instance method of this class. This method works with strings that represent the destination path. Here are the different parameters:

writeToFile

> The path of the file to write to, as a string.

atomically

> A Boolean that, if set to YES, will first write the file to a temporary space and will then move the temporary file to the destination that you chose. This will ensure that the contents of the file will be saved to disk first and then saved to its destination, so that if iOS crashes before the file is saved to the final destination, your contents will still be saved later when the OS is back up again. It is recommended to set this value to YES when storing information that you don't want to lose under any circumstance while your app is running.

encoding

> Encoding of the text that you want to write to the path. Programmers usually use UTF8 for the encoding, using the `NSUTF8StringEncoding` constant value.

error

> Takes a pointer to an `NSError` object so that if the saving operation fails, you will be able to find the error that happened during the process. You can pass `nil` to this parameter if you are not interested in knowing about the errors that may occur during the saving process. Bear in mind that this function returns a Boolean value and you can simply use this value to find out whether an error has occurred.

For instance, if you have some text that you want to temporarily store in your app, and you don't want it to be backed up by iOS, you can do the following:

```
NSString *someText = @"Random string that won't be backed up.";
NSString *destinationPath = [NSTemporaryDirectory()
                      stringByAppendingPathComponent:@"MyFile.txt"];

NSError *error = nil;
BOOL succeeded = [someText writeToFile:destinationPath
                           atomically:YES
                             encoding:NSUTF8StringEncoding
                                error:&error];

if (succeeded) {
    NSLog(@"Successfully stored the file at: %@", destinationPath);
} else {
    NSLog(@"Failed to store the file. Error = %@", error);
}
```

Also, after you are done, to make sure things went fine, you can attempt to read the same string back into memory from the destination file, using the `stringWithContentsOfFile:encoding:error:` class method of the `NSString` class. This will return back the autorelease string that is the contents of the specified file. If you want to explicitly instantiate an object of type `NSString` with the contents of the file, simply use the `initWithContentsOfFile:encoding:error:` instance method of the `NSString` class like so:

```
- (BOOL) writeText:(NSString *)paramText toPath:(NSString *)paramPath{
    return [paramText writeToFile:paramPath
                       atomically:YES
                         encoding:NSUTF8StringEncoding
                            error:nil];
}

- (NSString *) readTextFromPath:(NSString *)paramPath{
    return [[NSString alloc] initWithContentsOfFile:paramPath
                                           encoding:NSUTF8StringEncoding
                                              error:nil];
}

- (BOOL)           application:(UIApplication *)application
  didFinishLaunchingWithOptions:(NSDictionary *)launchOptions{

    NSString *filePath = [NSTemporaryDirectory()
                    stringByAppendingPathComponent:@"MyFile.txt"];

    if ([self writeText:@"Hello, World!" toPath:filePath]){

        NSString *readText = [self readTextFromPath:filePath];
        if ([readText length] > 0){
            NSLog(@"Text read from disk = %@", readText);
        } else {
            NSLog(@"Failed to read the text from disk.");
        }

    } else {
        NSLog(@"Failed to write the file.");
    }

    self.window = [[UIWindow alloc]
                initWithFrame:[[UIScreen mainScreen] bounds]];
    self.window.backgroundColor = [UIColor whiteColor];
    [self.window makeKeyAndVisible];
    return YES;
}
```

What we have done is created two convenient methods that allow us to write text to and read text from a specified location. In our app delegate, then, we use these two methods to write some text to the *temp* folder and then read the same text back to memory in order to make sure our methods are working fine.

If you want to work with URLs encapsulated in instances of NSURL (or the mutable version of it), you can use the writeToURL:atomically:encoding:error: instance method instead.

 Instances of NSURL can point to resources (files, directories, etc.) locally or remotely. For instance, an instance of NSURL can represent a local file in the *Documents* folder of your app as easily as it can represent the website URL for www.apple.com. This class simply gives you functionality to access and work with URLs, regardless of which type of URL they are.

Other classes in foundation have methods similar to those of NSString. Let's take NSArray as an example. You can save the contents of an array using the writeTo File:atomically: instance method of NSArray. In order to read the contents of an array from disk, you can simply allocate an instance of the array and then initialize it using the initWithContentsOfFile: initializer of the array. Here is an example of both these:

```
NSString *filePath = [NSTemporaryDirectory()
                        stringByAppendingPathComponent:@"MyFile.txt"];

NSArray *arrayOfNames = @[@"Steve", @"John", @"Edward"];
if ([arrayOfNames writeToFile:filePath atomically:YES]){

    NSArray *readArray = [[NSArray alloc] initWithContentsOfFile:filePath];
    if ([readArray count] == [arrayOfNames count]){
        NSLog(@"Read the array back from disk just fine.");
    } else {
        NSLog(@"Failed to read the array back from disk.");
    }
} else {
    NSLog(@"Failed to save the array to disk.");
}
```

The writeToFile:atomically: instance method of NSArray class can save only an array that contains objects of the following type:

- NSString
- NSDictionary
- NSArray
- NSData
- NSNumber
- NSDate

If you attempt to insert any other objects in the array, your data will not be saved to disk, because this method first makes sure all the objects in the array are of one of the aforementioned types. This is simply because the Objective-C runtime will not, otherwise, have any idea how to store your data to disk. For instance, suppose you create a class called Per son and create a first name and last name property for the class, then instantiate an instance and add it to an array. How can an array then save your person to disk? It simply cannot do that, as it won't know what it has to save to disk. This is a problem known as *marshalling*, and is solved by iOS only for the data types just listed.

Dictionaries are also very similar to arrays and have the same way of saving their data to disk and reading data back into the dictionary. The method names are exactly the same, and the rules of saving an array also apply to dictionaries. Here is an example:

```
NSString *filePath = [NSTemporaryDirectory()
                        stringByAppendingPathComponent:@"MyFile.txt"];
```

```
NSDictionary *dict = @{
@"first name" : @"Steven",
@"middle name" : @"Paul",
@"last name" : @"Jobs",
};

if ([dict writeToFile:filePath atomically:YES]){
    NSDictionary *readDictionary = [[NSDictionary alloc]
                                    initWithContentsOfFile:filePath];

    /* Now compare the dictionaries and see if the one we read from disk
     is the same as the one we saved to disk */
    if ([readDictionary isEqualToDictionary:dict]){
       NSLog(@"The file we read is the same one as the one we saved.");
    } else {
       NSLog(@"Failed to read the dictionary from disk.");
    }

} else {
    NSLog(@"Failed to write the dictionary to disk.");
}
```

As you can see, this example writes the dictionary to disk and then reads it back from the same location. After reading, we compare the read dictionary to the one we saved to disk in order to make sure they both contain the same data.

Up to now, we have been using high-level classes such as NSString and NSArray to save our contents to disk. Now, what if we want to store raw array of bytes to disk? That's easy too. Suppose we have an array of four unsigned characters and we want to save that to disk:

```
unsigned char *bytes = {0x22, 0xA0, 0x41, 0x10};
```

The easiest way of saving this raw array of bytes to disk is to encapsulate it in another high-level data structure like NSData and then use the relevant methods of NSData to write to and read from the disk. The saving and loading methods for an NSData are virtually the same as those for NSArray and NSDictionary. Here is an example of saving raw data to disk and reading it back from the disk:

```
NSString *filePath = [NSTemporaryDirectory()
                      stringByAppendingPathComponent:@"MyFile.txt"];

char bytes[4] = {'a', 'b', 'c', 'd'};

NSData *dataFromBytes = [[NSData alloc] initWithBytes:bytes
                                              length:sizeof(bytes)];

if ([dataFromBytes writeToFile:filePath atomically:YES]){
    NSData *readData = [[NSData alloc] initWithContentsOfFile:filePath];
    if ([readData isEqualToData:dataFromBytes]){
        NSLog(@"The data read is the same data as was written to disk.");
    } else {
        NSLog(@"Failed to read the data from disk.");
```

```
        }
    } else {
        NSLog(@"Failed to save the data to disk.");
    }
```

See Also

Recipe 12.0

12.3 Creating Folders on Disk

Problem

You want to be able to create folders on disk to save some of your app's files in them.

Solution

Use the `createDirectoryAtPath:withIntermediateDirectories:attributes:error:` instance method of the `NSFileManager` class, as shown here:

```
NSFileManager *fileManager = [[NSFileManager alloc] init];

NSString *tempDir = NSTemporaryDirectory();
NSString *imagesDir = [tempDir stringByAppendingPathComponent:@"images"];

NSError *error = nil;
if ([fileManager createDirectoryAtPath:imagesDir
            withIntermediateDirectories:YES
                             attributes:nil
                                  error:&error]){

    NSLog(@"Successfully created the directory.");

} else {
    NSLog(@"Failed to create the directory. Error = %@", error);
}
```

Discussion

The APIs exposed by `NSFileManager` are very easy to use, and it's no surprise that you can use them to create folders on disk in a few lines. The `createDirectoryAtPath:with IntermediateDirectories:attributes:error:` method may look scary at first, but it's not that bad. I will explain the different parameters that you can pass to it:

createDirectoryAtPath
    The path to the folder that has to be created.

withIntermediateDirectories
    A Boolean parameter that, if set to YES, will create all the folders in the middle before it creates the final folder. For instance, if you want to create a folder named *images* in another folder named *data* inside the *tmp* folder of your app, but the

data folder doesn't exist yet, you could easily ask to create the *tmp/data/images/* folder and set the `withIntermediateDirectories` parameter to YES. This will make the system create the *data* for you as well as the *images* folder.

attributes

A dictionary of attributes that you can pass to the system in order to affect how your folder will be created. We won't be using these here, to keep things simple, but you can change things such as the modification date and time, the creation date and time, and other attributes of the created folder if you want to.

error

This parameter accepts a pointer to an error object of type `NSObject`, which will be populated with any errors that may happen while the folder is being created. It's generally a good idea to pass an error object to this parameter, so that if the method fails (returns NO), you can access the error and determine what went wrong.

See Also

Recipe 12.1

12.4 Enumerating Files and Folders

Problem

You either want to enumerate folders within a folder or you want to enumerate the list of files inside a folder. The act of enumerating means that you simply want to find all the folders and/or files within another folder.

Solution

Use the `contentsOfDirectoryAtPath:error:` instance method of the `NSFileManager` class as shown here. In this example, we are enumerating all the files, folders, and symlinks under our app's bundle folder:

```
NSFileManager *fileManager = [[NSFileManager alloc] init];
NSString *bundleDir = [[NSBundle mainBundle] bundlePath];

NSError *error = nil;
NSArray *bundleContents = [fileManager contentsOfDirectoryAtPath:bundleDir
                                                           error:&error];

if ([bundleContents count] > 0 &&
    error == nil){
    NSLog(@"Contents of the app bundle = %@", bundleContents);
}
else if ([bundleContents count] == 0 &&
         error == nil){
    NSLog(@"Call the police! The app bundle is empty.");
}
```

```
else {
    NSLog(@"An error happened = %@", error);
}
```

Discussion

In some of your iOS apps, you may need to enumerate the contents of a folder. Let me give you an example, in case this need is a bit vague right now. Imagine that the user asked you to download 10 images from the Internet and cache them in your app. You go ahead and save them, let's say, in the *tmp/images/* folder that you manually created. Now the user closes your app and reopens it, and in your UI, you want to display the list of already-downloaded-files in a table view. How can you achieve this? Well, it's easy. All you have to do is to enumerate the contents of the aforementioned folder using the NSFileManager class. As you saw in the Solution section of this recipe, the content sOfDirectoryAtPath:error: instance method of the NSFileManager class returns an array of NSString objects that will represent the files, folders, and symlinks within the given folder. However, it is not easy to say which one is a folder, which one is a file, and so on. To get more fine-grained detail from the file manager, invoke the contentsOfDirec toryAtURL:includingPropertiesForKeys:options:error:. Let's go through the different parameters that you need to pass to this method:

contentsOfDirectoryAtURL
> The path of the folder that you want to inspect. This path should be provided as an instance of NSURL. Don't worry about it if you don't know how to construct this instance. We will talk about it soon.

includingPropertiesForKeys
> This is an array of properties that you would like iOS to fetch for every file, folder, or item that it finds in the given directory. For instance, you can specify that you want the creation date of the items to be returned in the results, as part of the URL instance that is returned to you (in instances of NSURL that you get back from the framework). Here is the list of some of the most important values that you can place in this array:

NSURLIsDirectoryKey
> Allows you to determine later whether one of the URLs returned are directories.

NSURLIsReadableKey
> Allows you to determine later whether the returned URL is readable by your app's process.

NSURLCreationDateKey
> Returns the creation date of the item in the returned URL.

NSURLContentAccessDateKey
> Returns the last content access date in the returned results.

NSURLContentModificationDateKey

As its name indicates, this allows you to determine the last-modified-date for the returned URLs.

options

Only 0 or NSDirectoryEnumerationSkipsHiddenFiles may be entered for this parameter. If the latter value is entered, as the name of the value shows, all hidden items will be skipped during the enumeration.

error

A reference to an object that will be filled with an error should this method fail to execute its job. It's usually a good idea to provide error objects to these methods if you can. You get more control over why things fail, should they ever fail.

Now that we have more control over how the items are enumerated, let's enumerate all the items in the *.app* folder and print out the creation, last modified, and last accessed dates. We will also print out whether the items are hidden or not, and whether we have read access to the files or not. The last thing we'll print out will be whether the items are directories or not. Let's go:

```
- (NSArray *) contentsOfAppBundle{
    NSFileManager *manager = [[NSFileManager alloc] init];
    NSURL *bundleDir = [[NSBundle mainBundle] bundleURL];

    NSArray *propertiesToGet = @[
        NSURLIsDirectoryKey,
        NSURLIsReadableKey,
        NSURLCreationDateKey,
        NSURLContentAccessDateKey,
        NSURLContentModificationDateKey
    ];

    NSError *error = nil;
    NSArray *result = [manager contentsOfDirectoryAtURL:bundleDir
                              includingPropertiesForKeys:propertiesToGet
                                                 options:0
                                                   error:&error];

    if (error != nil){
        NSLog(@"An error happened = %@", error);
    }

    return result;
}

- (NSString *) stringValueOfBOOLProperty:(NSString *)paramProperty
                                   ofURL:(NSURL *)paramURL{

    NSNumber *boolValue = nil;
    NSError *error = nil;
    [paramURL getResourceValue:&boolValue
                        forKey:paramProperty
                         error:&error];
```

```objc
        if (error != nil){
            NSLog(@"Failed to get property of URL. Error = %@", error);
        }
        return [boolValue isEqualToNumber:@YES] ? @"Yes" : @"No";

}

- (NSString *) isURLDirectory:(NSURL *)paramURL{
    return [self stringValueOfBOOLProperty:NSURLIsDirectoryKey ofURL:paramURL];
}

- (NSString *) isURLReadable:(NSURL *)paramURL{
    return [self stringValueOfBOOLProperty:NSURLIsReadableKey ofURL:paramURL];
}

- (NSDate *) dateOfType:(NSString *)paramType inURL:(NSURL *)paramURL{
    NSDate *result = nil;
    NSError *error = nil;
    [paramURL getResourceValue:&result
                        forKey:paramType
                         error:&error];
    if (error != nil){
        NSLog(@"Failed to get property of URL. Error = %@", error);
    }
    return result;
}

- (void) printURLPropertiesToConsole:(NSURL *)paramURL{

    NSLog(@"Item name = %@", [paramURL lastPathComponent]);

    NSLog(@"Is a Directory? %@", [self isURLDirectory:paramURL]);

    NSLog(@"Is Readable? %@", [self isURLReadable:paramURL]);

    NSLog(@"Creation Date = %@",
          [self dateOfType:NSURLCreationDateKey inURL:paramURL]);

    NSLog(@"Access Date = %@",
          [self dateOfType:NSURLContentAccessDateKey inURL:paramURL]);

    NSLog(@"Modification Date = %@",
          [self dateOfType:NSURLContentModificationDateKey inURL:paramURL]);

    NSLog(@"--------------------------------");
}

- (BOOL)            application:(UIApplication *)application
  didFinishLaunchingWithOptions:(NSDictionary *)launchOptions{

    NSArray *itemsInAppBundle = [self contentsOfAppBundle];
    for (NSURL *item in itemsInAppBundle){
        [self printURLPropertiesToConsole:item];
    }
```

```
        self.window = [[UIWindow alloc]
                        initWithFrame:[[UIScreen mainScreen] bounds]];
        // Override point for customization after application launch.
        self.window.backgroundColor = [UIColor whiteColor];
        [self.window makeKeyAndVisible];
        return YES;
    }
```

The output of this program will be something similar to that shown here:

```
Item name = en.lproj
Is a Directory? Yes
Is Readable? Yes
Creation Date = 2012-08-11 20:07:49 +0000
Access Date = 2012-08-12 12:31:33 +0000
Modification Date = 2012-08-11 20:07:49 +0000
-----------------------------------
Item name = Enumerating Files and Folders
Is a Directory? No
Is Readable? Yes
Creation Date = 2012-08-12 12:31:30 +0000
Access Date = 2012-08-12 12:31:33 +0000
Modification Date = 2012-08-12 12:31:30 +0000
-----------------------------------
Item name = Info.plist
Is a Directory? No
Is Readable? Yes
Creation Date = 2012-08-11 20:07:48 +0000
Access Date = 2012-08-12 12:31:33 +0000
Modification Date = 2012-08-11 20:07:48 +0000
-----------------------------------
Item name = PkgInfo
Is a Directory? No
Is Readable? Yes
Creation Date = 2012-08-11 20:07:48 +0000
Access Date = 2012-08-11 20:07:48 +0000
Modification Date = 2012-08-11 20:07:48 +0000
-----------------------------------
```

 The important thing to note about this app is that we are using the getResourceValue:forKey:error: instance method of the NSURL class to get the value of each one of the keys that we are querying from the file manager, such as the creation and modification date. We pass these requirements to the file manager, asking it to fetch this information for us. And then, once we have our URLs, we use the aforementioned method to retrieve the different properties from the resulting URLs.

So let's have a look at the different parts of this app. I will simply explain what each one of these methods that we have written does:

contentsOfAppBundle
> This method searches the *.app* folder for all items (files, folders, symlinks, etc.) and returns the result as an array. All items in the array will be of type NSURL and contain their creation date, last modification date, and other attributes that we talked about before.

stringValueOfBOOLProperty:ofURL:
> This method will fetch the string equivalent (Yes or No) of a Boolean property of a URL. For instance, information about whether a URL is a directory or not is stored as a binary, Boolean value. However, if we want to print this Boolean value out to the console, we need to convert it to string. We have two query items for each URL that will return instances of NSNumber containing a Boolean value: NSURLIsDirectoryKey and NSURLIsReadableKey. So instead of writing this conversion code twice, methods are available to do the conversion of NSNumber to a string of Yes or No for us.

isURLDirectory:
> Takes in a URL and inspects it to see whether it is a directory. This method internally uses the stringValueOfBOOLProperty:ofURL: method and passes the NSURLIsDirectoryKey key to it.

isURLReadable:
> Determines whether your app has read access to a given URL. This method also internally uses the stringValueOfBOOLProperty:ofURL: method and passes the NSURLIsReadableKey key to it.

dateOfType:inURL:
> Since we are going to inspect three types of properties in each URL that will be of type NSDate, we have simply encapsulated the relevant code in this method, which will take the key and will return the date associated with that key in a given URL.

OK, that's about it, really. You now know how to enumerate folders and retrieve all items within the folder. You even know how to retrieve different attributes for different items.

See Also

Recipe 12.1; Recipe 12.2

12.5 Deleting Files and Folders

Problem

You have created some files and/or folders on disk and no longer need them, so you would like to delete them.

Solution

Use the `removeItemAtPath:error:` or the `removeItemAtURL:error:` instance method of the `NSFileManager` class. The former method takes the path as a string and the latter takes the path as a URL.

Discussion

Deleting files and folders is perhaps one of the easiest operations that you can perform using a file manager. In iOS, you need to be mindful of where you store your files and folders in the first place, and once you have done the storage, you need to get rid of files and folders when you no longer need them. For instance, let's create five text files in the *tmp/text* folder and then delete them once we are done. In the meantime, we can enumerate the contents of the folder before and after the deletion just to make sure things are working fine. Also, as you know, the *tmp/* folder exists when your app is installed, but the *tmp/text* doesn't. So we need to create it first. Once we are done with the files, we will delete the folder as well:

```
/* Creates a folder at a given path */
- (void) createFolder:(NSString *)paramPath{
    NSError *error = nil;
    if ([self.fileManager createDirectoryAtPath:paramPath
                    withIntermediateDirectories:YES
                                     attributes:nil
                                          error:&error] == NO){
        NSLog(@"Failed to create folder %@. Error = %@",
              paramPath,
              error);
    }
}

/* Creates 5 .txt files in the given folder, named 1.txt, 2.txt, etc */
- (void) createFilesInFolder:(NSString *)paramPath{
    /* Create 10 files */
    for (NSUInteger counter = 0; counter < 5; counter++){
        NSString *fileName = [NSString stringWithFormat:@"%lu.txt",
                             (unsigned long)counter+1];
        NSString *path = [paramPath stringByAppendingPathComponent:fileName];
        NSString *fileContents = [NSString stringWithFormat:@"Some text"];
        NSError *error = nil;
        if ([fileContents writeToFile:path
                           atomically:YES
                             encoding:NSUTF8StringEncoding
                                error:&error] == NO){
            NSLog(@"Failed to save file to %@. Error = %@", path, error);
        }
    }

}

/* Enumerates all files/folders at a given path */
- (void) enumerateFilesInFolder:(NSString *)paramPath{
```

```objectivec
    NSError *error = nil;
    NSArray *contents = [self.fileManager contentsOfDirectoryAtPath:paramPath
                                                              error:&error];

    if ([contents count] > 0 &&
        error == nil){
        NSLog(@"Contents of path %@ = \n%@", paramPath, contents);
    }
    else if ([contents count] == 0 &&
                error == nil){
        NSLog(@"Contents of path %@ is empty!", paramPath);
    }
    else {
        NSLog(@"Failed to enumerate path %@. Error = %@", paramPath, error);
    }

}

/* Deletes all files/folders in a given path */
- (void) deleteFilesInFolder:(NSString *)paramPath{

    NSError *error = nil;
    NSArray *contents = [self.fileManager contentsOfDirectoryAtPath:paramPath
                                                              error:&error];
    if (error == nil){
        error = nil;
        for (NSString *fileName in contents){
            /* We have the filename, to delete it,
             we have to have the full path */
            NSString *filePath = [paramPath
                                    stringByAppendingPathComponent:fileName];
            if ([self.fileManager removeItemAtPath:filePath
                                             error:&error] == NO){
                NSLog(@"Failed to remove item at path %@. Error = %@",
                    fileName,
                    error);
            }
        }
    } else {
        NSLog(@"Failed to enumerate path %@. Error = %@", paramPath, error);
    }

}

/* Deletes a folder with a given path */
- (void) deleteFolder:(NSString *)paramPath{
    NSError *error = nil;
    if ([self.fileManager removeItemAtPath:paramPath error:&error] == NO){
        NSLog(@"Failed to remove path %@. Error = %@", paramPath, error);
    }
}

- (BOOL)            application:(UIApplication *)application
  didFinishLaunchingWithOptions:(NSDictionary *)launchOptions{
```

```
        self.fileManager = [[NSFileManager alloc] init];

        NSString *txtFolder = [NSTemporaryDirectory()
                          stringByAppendingPathComponent:@"txt"];

        [self createFolder:txtFolder];
        [self createFilesInFolder:txtFolder];
        [self enumerateFilesInFolder:txtFolder];
        [self deleteFilesInFolder:txtFolder];
        [self enumerateFilesInFolder:txtFolder];
        [self deleteFolder:txtFolder];

        self.window = [[UIWindow alloc]
                    initWithFrame:[[UIScreen mainScreen] bounds]];
        self.window.backgroundColor = [UIColor whiteColor];
        [self.window makeKeyAndVisible];
        return YES;
    }
```

Bear in mind that the `fileManager` property, which we are using in various methods of our app delegate, is a property of the app delegate itself and is defined in this way in the app delegate's header file:

```
#import <UIKit/UIKit.h>

@interface AppDelegate : UIResponder <UIApplicationDelegate>

@property (nonatomic, strong) UIWindow *window;
@property (nonatomic, strong) NSFileManager *fileManager;

@end
```

This example code combines a lot of the things that you have learned in this chapter, from enumerating to creating to deleting files. It's all in this example. As you can see from the app's starting point, we are performing six main tasks, all of which have their associated methods to take care of them:

1. Creating the *tmp/txt* folder. We know the *tmp* folder will be created by iOS for every app, but the *txt* doesn't come already created by iOS when your app is installed on the device.

2. Creating five text files in the *tmp/txt* folder.

3. Enumerating all the files in the *tmp/txt* folder just to prove that we successfully created all five files in that folder.

4. Deleting the files that we created to prove the point of this recipe.

5. Enumerating the files again in the *tmp/txt* folder to demonstrate that the deletion mechanism worked just fine.

6. Deleting the *tmp/txt* folder, as we no longer need it. Again, as I mentioned before, be mindful of what folders and files you create on disk. Disk space doesn't grow on trees! So if you don't need your files and folders any longer, delete them.

Now you not only know how to create files and folders, but how to get rid of them when you longer need them.

See Also

Recipe 12.2

12.6 Securing Files on Disk

Problem

You want to make sure that the files that you are working with on disk are locked and encrypted when the iOS device is locked, and not accessible by an attacker.

Solution

Create your file using the `createFileAtPath:contents:attributes:` instance method or your folders using the `createDirectoryAtPath:withIntermediateDirectories:attributes:error:` instance method of the `NSFileManager` and use the `NSFileProtectionKey` key in the attributes dictionary with one of the following values:

`NSFileProtectionCompleteUnlessOpen`
> The file will be encrypted on disk and will be accessible by your app only after the user has unlocked the device. The user can then lock the device back, but while you have the handle to the file, you can continue to read from and write to the file.

`NSFileProtectionComplete`
> The file is encrypted on disk and is not accessible by your app unless the user unlocks the device. If you have a handle to the file when the device is unlocked, you will not be able to read from or write to the file if the user decides to lock the device again.

`NSFileProtectionCompleteUntilFirstUserAuthentication`
> The file is encrypted on disk and you can read from it or write to it only after the user has at least unlocked the device once. After that one-time unlocking, you can read from and write to the file. The user can lock the device, but that won't affect you and your file handle.

iOS uses the passcode that the user sets for her device as a seed to the encryption applied to sensitive data on the device. If you are storing sensitive files or folders on disk, you can use this mechanism, through `NSFileManager`, to ensure your data is securely stored on disk.

Discussion

If you noticed, I talked about a *file handle* in the `NSFileProtectionCompleteUntilFirst UserAuthentication` item of the list. What did I mean by that? Up to now, we have been saving complete data to disk and reading complete data back from disk. That's great, but sometimes you may want to open a file and keep writing to it and reading from it, appending data to it, and so on. For this purpose, the iOS SDK provides programmers with the NSFileHandle class. This is a high-level representation of a file and allows you to perform almost every operation possible to a file.

Let's have a look at a simple example. Say we want to write a simple text to a file under *tmp/file.txt*. This is how simple it is to do so:

```objc
- (BOOL)                    application:(UIApplication *)application
    didFinishLaunchingWithOptions:(NSDictionary *)launchOptions{

    NSFileManager *fileManager = [[NSFileManager alloc] init];

    NSString *filePath = [NSTemporaryDirectory()
                          stringByAppendingPathComponent:@"file.txt"];

    BOOL fileIsCreated = NO;
    if ([fileManager fileExistsAtPath:filePath] == NO){
        fileIsCreated = [fileManager createFileAtPath:filePath
                                              contents:nil
                                            attributes:nil];
    }

    if (fileIsCreated == YES){

        /* Open the file handle */
        NSFileHandle *fileHandle = [NSFileHandle
                                    fileHandleForUpdatingAtPath:filePath];

        if (fileHandle != nil){
            NSString *stringToWrite = @"Hello, World!";

            /* Write the data */
            [fileHandle writeData:
             [stringToWrite dataUsingEncoding:NSUTF8StringEncoding]];

            NSLog(@"Wrote to the file.");

        } else {
            NSLog(@"Failed to create the file handle.");
        }

        /* Close the file handle */
        [fileHandle closeFile];

        /* Delete the file now that we no longer need it */
        [fileManager removeItemAtPath:filePath error:nil];

    } else {
        NSLog(@"Failed to create the file on disk.");
    }

    self.window = [[UIWindow alloc]
```

```
                    initWithFrame:[[UIScreen mainScreen] bounds]];
        self.window.backgroundColor = [UIColor whiteColor];
        [self.window makeKeyAndVisible];
        return YES;
    }
```

As you can see, we are using the help of the NSFileManager to create the file if it doesn't exist and also to delete the file once we are done with it. Once the file is created, we can use the fileHandleForUpdatingAtPath: class method of the NSFileHandle class in order to open our file with read and write access. Here are the different important class methods on NSFileHandle that you can use to open files for various purposes:

fileHandleForUpdatingAtPath:
> Opens the file with read and write access. This will place the pointer of the file at the beginning of the file.

fileHandleForReadingAtPath:
> Opens the file with read access only.

fileHandleForWritingAtPath:
> Opens the file with write access only.

 None of these methods create the file at the given path if the file doesn't exist already.

Once the file is open, you can use one of the following instance methods of the NSFile Handle class to read from or write to the file, depending on what method you used to open the file:

readDataOfLength:
> Returns *n* number of bytes from the file as an instance of NSData.

writeData:
> Writes the given NSData to the file.

You can always find out how many bytes are already written to the file by getting the return value of the availableData instance method of the NSFileHandle.

Now that we know the basics of file handles, let's get on with the main purpose of this recipe, which is secure file storage.

Let's say you are capturing information about your user that you will use while your app is running. Next time your app runs, you will attempt to read from the file. If it doesn't exist, you will create it again. As we read in Recipe 12.0, the *Library/Caches/* folder is the best place to store this type of data, since it is data that our app is creating and the contents of this folder will not be backed up by iOS into backup storage device, such as iCloud or iTunes. So let's get started. In this example, we will use the NSFile ProtectionCompleteUnlessOpen protection for our file, which we will name *userdata.txt*.

There are two little things that we have to consider in this example code. We need to make sure:

- That we have set a passcode on the device where we are planning to run this app.
- That once the app is running on the device, we lock the device so the file becomes protected again.

In this example code, I am using techniques that are covered in Chapter 14, so don't feel bad if it seems a bit strange. The only thing strange that you may find in this example code is that we are waiting for the app to become inactive, which is what happens when the user locks her device while our app is running. This can also happen if the user sends the app to the background, but for the sake of simplicity, we won't consider that scenario. So make sure that when the app is executed on the device, you press the lock button to send the app to the inactive mode:

```
- (NSString *) cachesDirectory{

    NSArray *caches = [self.fileManager URLsForDirectory:NSCachesDirectory
                                            inDomains:NSUserDomainMask];
    if ([caches count] > 0){
        NSURL *result = caches[0];
        return [result path];
    } else {
        return nil;
    }

}

- (void) createFileIfDoesntExist:(NSString *)paramPath{

    NSDictionary *attributes = @{
    NSFileProtectionKey : NSFileProtectionComplete
    };

    if ([self.fileManager fileExistsAtPath:paramPath] == NO){
        [self.fileManager createFileAtPath:paramPath
                            contents:nil
                          attributes:attributes];
    }

}

- (BOOL)              application:(UIApplication *)application
  didFinishLaunchingWithOptions:(NSDictionary *)launchOptions{

    self.fileManager = [[NSFileManager alloc] init];

    NSString *filePath = [[self cachesDirectory]
                          stringByAppendingPathComponent:@"file.txt"];

    [self createFileIfDoesntExist:filePath];

    self.fileHandle = [NSFileHandle fileHandleForUpdatingAtPath:filePath];
```

```
            self.window = [[UIWindow alloc]
                          initWithFrame:[[UIScreen mainScreen] bounds]];
            self.window.backgroundColor = [UIColor whiteColor];
            [self.window makeKeyAndVisible];
            return YES;
        }

        - (void) writeToFile{

            @try {
                NSLog(@"Attempting to write to the file...");
                [self.fileHandle writeData:
                  [@"Hello World" dataUsingEncoding:NSUTF8StringEncoding]];
                NSLog(@"Successfully wrote to the file. Make sure you have a passcode\
                      set on your device. This method should have failed!");
            }
            @catch (NSException *exception) {
                NSLog(@"Failed to write to file. Is it locked?");
            }
            @finally {
                NSLog(@"Finishing our background task...");
                [[UIApplication sharedApplication]
                  endBackgroundTask:self.backgroundTask];
            }


        }

        - (void)applicationWillResignActive:(UIApplication *)application{

            if (self.fileHandle == nil){
                NSLog(@"The file wasn't opened. No point trying to write to it!");
                return;
            }

            NSLog(@"Scheduling writing to file in 10 seconds...");
            self.backgroundTask = [[UIApplication sharedApplication]
                                  beginBackgroundTaskWithExpirationHandler:^{
                                      self.backgroundTask = UIBackgroundTaskInvalid;
                                  }];

            [self performSelector:@selector(writeToFile)
                      withObject:nil
                      afterDelay:10.0f];

        }
```

There are a few methods in this example, all of which are explained here:

cachesDirectory

Returns the path of the *Library/Caches/* directory in your app's bundle.

createFileIfDoesntExist:

Takes the path of a file and creates it if it doesn't exist. The creation happens using the NSFileProtectionComplete value for the NSFileProtectionKey attribute so that the file will be locked, even if we have already opened it, when the device is locked.

application:didFinishLaunchingWithOptions:

Gets the handle to the file by utilizing the previously described methods.

applicationWillResignActive:

Schedules a write sequence to the file after 10 seconds. This method gets called in various situations, one of which being when the user presses the lock button on the device. So we are assuming this is the case.

writeToFile

Does the actual writing to the file.

 As you can see from the code, the writeData: instance method of the NSFileHandle class raises an exception if it cannot write to the file successfully. The readDataOfLength: instance method of this class does the same thing if it cannot read from the file.

If you run this app on a device that has a passcode, and then lock the device, you will see something similar to this showing up in the Console screen after 10 seconds:

```
Scheduling writing to file in 10 seconds...
Attempting to write to the file...
Failed to write to file. Is it locked?
Finishing our background task...
```

See Also

Recipe 12.5; Recipe 12.2

12.7 Saving Objects to Files

Problem

You have added a new class to your project and you would like to be able to save this object to disk as a file and then read it back from disk whenever required.

Solution

Make sure that your class conforms to the NSCoding protocol and implement all the required methods of this method. Don't worry; I will walk you through this in the Discussion section of this recipe.

Discussion

There are two really handy classes in iOS SDK for this specific purpose, which in the programming world is known as *marshalling*. They are called:

NSKeyedArchiver

    A class that can archive or save the contents of an object or object tree by keys. Each value in the class, let's say each property, can be saved to the archive, using a key that the programmer chooses. You will be given an archive file (we will talk more about this) and you will just save your values using keys that you choose. Just like a dictionary!

NSKeyedUnarchiver

    This class does the reverse of the archiver class. It simply gives you the unarchived dictionary and asks you to read the values into your object's properties.

In order for the archiver and the unarchiver to work, you need to make sure that the objects you are asking them to archive or unarchive conform to the NSCoding protocol. Let's start with a simple Person class. Here is the header file of our class:

```
@interface Person : NSObject <NSCoding>

@property (nonatomic, copy) NSString *firstName;
@property (nonatomic, copy) NSString *lastName;

@end
```

Now if you don't write any code for the implementation of this class and try to compile your code, you will see that the compiler will start to throw warnings at you saying you have not conformed to the NSCoding protocol and have not implemented its required methods. The methods that we have to implement are as follows:

- (void)encodeWithCoder:(NSCoder *)aCoder

    This method will give you a coder. You will use the coder just like you would use a dictionary. Simply store your values in it using keys that you choose.

- (id)initWithCoder:(NSCoder *)aDecoder;

    This method gets called on your class when you try to unarchive your class using NSKeyedUnarchiver. Simply read your values back from the NSCoder instance passed to this method.

Now, using this information, let's implement our class:

```
#import "Person.h"

NSString *const kFirstNameKey = @"FirstNameKey";
NSString *const kLastNameKey = @"LastNameKey";

@implementation Person

- (void)encodeWithCoder:(NSCoder *)aCoder{
    [aCoder encodeObject:self.firstName forKey:kFirstNameKey];
```

```
        [aCoder encodeObject:self.lastName forKey:kLastNameKey];
    }

    - (id)initWithCoder:(NSCoder *)aDecoder{
        self = [super init];
        if (self != nil){
            _firstName = [aDecoder decodeObjectForKey:kFirstNameKey];
            _lastName = [aDecoder decodeObjectForKey:kLastNameKey];
        }
        return self;
    }

    @end
```

You can see that the way we are using the instance of the NSCoder class is really similar to that of a dictionary except that, instead of setValue:forKey: in a dictionary, we are using encodeObject:forKey:, and instead of objectForKey: in a dictionary, we are using decodeObjectForKey:. All in all, very similar to the way we use dictionaries.

We are done with this class. So let's implement the archiving and unarchiving mechanism using the two aforementioned classes. Our plan is to first instantiate an object of type Person, archive it, get rid of it in memory, read it back from file, and see whether the unarchived value matches the value that we originally put in the class. We will be implementing this in our app delegate, because it's the easiest place to do this:

```
#import "AppDelegate.h"
#import "Person.h"

@implementation AppDelegate

- (BOOL)              application:(UIApplication *)application
  didFinishLaunchingWithOptions:(NSDictionary *)launchOptions{

    /* Define the name and the last name we are going to set in the object */
    NSString *const kFirstName = @"Steven";
    NSString *const kLastName = @"Jobs";

    /* Determine where we want to archive the object */
    NSString *filePath = [NSTemporaryDirectory()
                        stringByAppendingPathComponent:@"steveJobs.txt"];

    /* Instantiate the object */
    Person *steveJobs = [[Person alloc] init];
    steveJobs.firstName = kFirstName;
    steveJobs.lastName = kLastName;

    /* Archive the object to the file */
    [NSKeyedArchiver archiveRootObject:steveJobs toFile:filePath];

    /* Now unarchive the same class into another object */
    Person *cloneOfSteveJobs =
        [NSKeyedUnarchiver unarchiveObjectWithFile:filePath];
```

```
/* Check if the unarchived object has the same first name and last name
 as the previously archived object */
if ([cloneOfSteveJobs.firstName isEqualToString:kFirstName] &&
    [cloneOfSteveJobs.lastName isEqualToString:kLastName]){
    NSLog(@"Unarchiving worked");
} else {
    NSLog(@"Could not read the same values back. Oh no!");
}

/* We no longer need the temp file, delete it */
NSFileManager *fileManager = [[NSFileManager alloc] init];
[fileManager removeItemAtPath:filePath error:nil];

self.window = [[UIWindow alloc]
              initWithFrame:[[UIScreen mainScreen] bounds]];
self.window.backgroundColor = [UIColor whiteColor];
[self.window makeKeyAndVisible];
return YES;
}
```

So the archiving simply uses the `archiveRootObject:toFile` class method of the `NSKeyed Archiver` class, which takes an object and a file on which the content of the file has to be saved. Simple and easy. How about unarchiving? That is as easy as the archiving process. All you have to do is just pass the archived file path to the `unarchiveObject WithFile:` class method of the `NSKeyedUnarchiver` class and that class will do the rest for you.

See Also

Recipe 12.1

CHAPTER 13

Camera and the Photo Library

13.0 Introduction

Devices running iOS, such as the iPhone, are equipped with cameras—for instance, the iPhone 5 has two cameras and the iPhone 3G and 3GS each have one. Some iOS devices, such as the first generation of the iPad, do not have cameras. The `UIImagePickerController` class allows programmers to display the familiar Camera interface to their users and ask them to take a photo or shoot a video. The photos taken or the videos shot by the user with the `UIImagePickerController` class then become accessible to the programmer.

In this chapter, you will learn how to let users take photos and shoot videos from inside applications, access these photos and videos, and access the photos and videos that are placed inside the Photo Library on an iOS device, such as the iPod touch and iPad.

 iOS Simulator does not support the Camera interface. Please test and debug all your applications that require a Camera interface on a real iOS device with a camera.

In this chapter, we will first attempt to determine if a camera is available on the iOS device running the application. You can also determine whether the camera allows you (the programmer) to capture videos, images, or both. To do this, make sure you have added the *MobileCoreServices.framework* framework to your target by following these steps:

1. Click on your project's icon in Xcode.
2. Select the target to which you want to add the framework.
3. On the top of the screen, select the Build Phases tab.
4. In the Build Phases screen, expand the Link Binary with Libraries box and press the little + button on the bottom-left corner of that box.

5. Choose *MobileCoreServices.framework* from the list.

6. Click the Add button.

We will then move to other topics, such as accessing videos and photos from different albums on an iOS device. These are the same albums that are accessible through the Photos application built into iOS.

Accessing photos inside albums is more straightforward than accessing videos, however. For photos, we will be given the address of the photo and we can simply load the data of the image either in an instance of `NSData` or directly into an instance of `UIImage`. For videos, we won't be given a file address on the filesystem from which to load the data of the video. Instead, we will be given an address such as this:

```
assets-library://asset/asset.MOV?id=1000000004&ext=MOV
```

For addresses such as this, we need to use the Assets Library framework. The Assets Library framework allows us to access the contents accessible through the Photos application, such as videos and photos shot by the user. You can also use the Assets Library framework to save images and videos on the device. These photos and videos will then become accessible by the Photo Library as well as other applications that wish to access these contents.

To make sure the recipes in this chapter compile correctly, follow these steps to add the Assets Library framework to your target:

1. Click on your project's icon in Xcode.

2. Select the target to which you want to add the framework.

3. On the top of the screen, select the Build Phases tab.

4. In the Build Phases screen, expand the Link Binary with Libraries box and press the little + button on the bottom-left corner of that box.

5. Choose *AssetsLibrary.framework* from the list.

6. Click the Add button.

To access the data of an asset given the URL to the asset, follow these steps:

1. Allocate and initialize an object of type `ALAssetsLibrary`. The Assets Library object facilitates the bridge that you need in order to access the videos and photos accessible by the Photos application.

2. Use the `assetForURL:resultBlock:failureBlock` instance method of the Assets Library object (allocated and initialized in step 1) to access the asset. An asset could be an image, a video, or any other resource that Apple might later decide to add to the Photo Library. This method works with block objects. For more information about block objects and GCD, please refer to Chapter 6.

3. Release the Assets Library object allocated and initialized in step 1.

At this point, you might be wondering: how do I access the data for the asset? The resultBlock parameter of the assetForURL:resultBlock:failureBlock instance method of the Assets Library object will need to point to a block object that accepts a single parameter of type ALAsset. ALAsset is a class provided by the Assets Library that encapsulates an asset available to Photos and any other iOS application that wishes to use these assets. For more information about storing photos and videos in the Photo Library, please refer to Recipes 13.4 and 13.5. If you want to learn more about retrieving photos and videos from the Photo Library and the Assets Library, please refer to Recipes 13.6 and 13.7.

13.1 Detecting and Probing the Camera

Problem

You want to know whether the iOS device running your application has a camera that you can access. This is an important check to make before attempting to use the camera, unless you are sure your application will never run on a device that lacks one.

Solution

Use the isSourceTypeAvailable: class method of UIImagePickerController with the UIImagePickerControllerSourceTypeCamera value, like so:

```
- (BOOL) isCameraAvailable{

  return [UIImagePickerController isSourceTypeAvailable:
          UIImagePickerControllerSourceTypeCamera];

}

- (BOOL)          application:(UIApplication *)application
  didFinishLaunchingWithOptions:(NSDictionary *)launchOptions{

  if ([self isCameraAvailable]){
    NSLog(@"Camera is available.");
  } else {
    NSLog(@"Camera is not available.");
  }

  self.window = [[UIWindow alloc] initWithFrame:
                  [[UIScreen mainScreen] bounds]];

  self.window.backgroundColor = [UIColor whiteColor];
  [self.window makeKeyAndVisible];
  return YES;
}
```

Discussion

Before attempting to display an instance of UIImagePickerController to your user for taking photos or shooting videos, you must detect whether the device supports that interface. The isSourceTypeAvailable: class method allows you to determine three sources of data:

- The camera, by passing the UIImagePickerControllerSourceTypeCamera value to this method.
- The Photo Library, by passing the value UIImagePickerControllerSourceType PhotoLibrary to this method. This browses the root folder of the *Photos* directory on the device.
- The camera roll folder in the *Photos* directory, by passing the UIImagePickerCon trollerSourceTypeSavedPhotosAlbum value to this method.

If you want to check the availability of any of these facilities on an iOS device, you must pass these values to the isSourceTypeAvailable: class method of UIImagePicker Controller before attempting to present the interfaces to the user.

Now in the *.h* or the *.m* file of your object(s) (depending on your requirements), import the main header file of the framework we just added. Here I will import these framework into the *.h* file of my app delegate:

```
#import <UIKit/UIKit.h>
#import <AssetsLibrary/AssetsLibrary.h>
#import <MobileCoreServices/MobileCoreServices.h>

@interface Detecting_and_Probing_the_CameraAppDelegate
        : UIResponder <UIApplicationDelegate>

@property (strong, nonatomic) UIWindow *window;

@end
```

Now we can use the isSourceTypeAvailable: and availableMediaTypesForSource Type: class methods of UIImagePickerController to determine first if a media source is available (camera, Photo Library, etc.), and if so, whether media types such as image and video are available on that media source:

```
- (BOOL) cameraSupportsMedia:(NSString *)paramMediaType
              sourceType:(UIImagePickerControllerSourceType)paramSourceType{

  __block BOOL result = NO;

  if ([paramMediaType length] == 0){
    NSLog(@"Media type is empty.");
    return NO;
  }
```

```objective-c
    NSArray *availableMediaTypes =
    [UIImagePickerController availableMediaTypesForSourceType:paramSourceType];

    [availableMediaTypes enumerateObjectsUsingBlock:
     ^(id obj, NSUInteger idx, BOOL *stop) {

       NSString *mediaType = (NSString *)obj;
       if ([mediaType isEqualToString:paramMediaType]){
         result = YES;
         *stop= YES;
       }

     }];

    return result;

}

- (BOOL) doesCameraSupportShootingVideos{

  return [self cameraSupportsMedia:(__bridge NSString *)kUTTypeMovie
                       sourceType:UIImagePickerControllerSourceTypeCamera];

}

- (BOOL) doesCameraSupportTakingPhotos{

  return [self cameraSupportsMedia:(__bridge NSString *)kUTTypeImage
                       sourceType:UIImagePickerControllerSourceTypeCamera];

}

- (BOOL)             application:(UIApplication *)application
  didFinishLaunchingWithOptions:(NSDictionary *)launchOptions{

  if ([self doesCameraSupportTakingPhotos]){
    NSLog(@"The camera supports taking photos.");
  } else {
    NSLog(@"The camera does not support taking photos");
  }

  if ([self doesCameraSupportShootingVideos]){
    NSLog(@"The camera supports shooting videos.");
  } else {
    NSLog(@"The camera does not support shooting videos.");
  }

  self.window = [[UIWindow alloc] initWithFrame:
                   [[UIScreen mainScreen] bounds]];

  self.window.backgroundColor = [UIColor whiteColor];
  [self.window makeKeyAndVisible];
  return YES;
}
```

We are typecasting the kUTTypeMovie and the kUTTypeImage values to NSString using __bridge (as explained in Recipe 1.18). The reason behind this is that the two aforementioned values are of type CFString Ref and we need to retrieve their NSString representation. To help the static analyzer and the compiler and to avoid getting warnings from the compiler, it is best to do this typecasting.

Some iOS devices can have more than one camera. The two cameras might be called the front and the rear cameras. To determine whether these cameras are available, use the isCameraDeviceAvailable: class method of UIImagePickerController, like so:

```
- (BOOL) isFrontCameraAvailable{

  return [UIImagePickerController
          isCameraDeviceAvailable:UIImagePickerControllerCameraDeviceFront];

}

- (BOOL) isRearCameraAvailable{

  return [UIImagePickerController
          isCameraDeviceAvailable:UIImagePickerControllerCameraDeviceRear];

}
```

By calling these methods on an older iPhone with no rear camera, you will see that the isFrontCameraAvailable method returns NO and the isRearCameraAvailable method returns YES. Running the code on an iPhone with both front and rear cameras will prove that both methods will return YES, as iPhone 5 devices are equipped with both front- and rear-facing cameras.

If detecting which camera is present on a device isn't enough for your application, you can retrieve other settings using the UIImagePickerController class. One such setting is whether flash capability is available for a camera on the device. You can use the isFlashAvailableForCameraDevice: class method of UIImagePickerController to determine the availability of a flash capability on the rear or front camera. Please bear in mind that the isFlashAvailableForCameraDevice: class method of UIImagePickerCon troller checks the availability of the given camera device first, before checking the availability of a flash capability on that camera. Therefore, you can run the methods we will implement on devices that do not have front or rear cameras, without a need to first check if the camera is available.

```
- (BOOL) isFlashAvailableOnFrontCamera{

  return [UIImagePickerController isFlashAvailableForCameraDevice:
          UIImagePickerControllerCameraDeviceFront];

}- (BOOL) isFlashAvailableOnRearCamera{
```

```
    return [UIImagePickerController isFlashAvailableForCameraDevice:
            UIImagePickerControllerCameraDeviceRear];

}
```

Now if we take advantage of all the methods that we wrote in this recipe and test them in your app delegate (for example), we can see the results on different devices:

```
- (BOOL)                 application:(UIApplication *)application
    didFinishLaunchingWithOptions:(NSDictionary *)launchOptions{

  if ([self isFrontCameraAvailable]){
    NSLog(@"The front camera is available.");
    if ([self isFlashAvailableOnFrontCamera]){
      NSLog(@"The front camera is equipped with a flash");
    } else {
      NSLog(@"The front camera is not equipped with a flash");
    }
  } else {
    NSLog(@"The front camera is not available.");
  }

  if ([self isRearCameraAvailable]){
    NSLog(@"The rear camera is available.");
    if ([self isFlashAvailableOnRearCamera]){
      NSLog(@"The rear camera is equipped with a flash");
    } else {
      NSLog(@"The rear camera is not equipped with a flash");
    }
  } else {
    NSLog(@"The rear camera is not available.");
  }

  if ([self doesCameraSupportTakingPhotos]){
    NSLog(@"The camera supports taking photos.");
  } else {
    NSLog(@"The camera does not support taking photos");
  }

  if ([self doesCameraSupportShootingVideos]){
    NSLog(@"The camera supports shooting videos.");
  } else {
    NSLog(@"The camera does not support shooting videos.");
  }

  self.window = [[UIWindow alloc] initWithFrame:
                  [[UIScreen mainScreen] bounds]];

  self.window.backgroundColor = [UIColor whiteColor];
  [self.window makeKeyAndVisible];
  return YES;
}
```

Here are the results when we run the application on an iPhone 4:

```
The front camera is available.
The front camera is not equipped with a flash
The rear camera is available.
The rear camera is equipped with a flash
The camera supports taking photos.
The camera supports shooting videos.
```

Here is the output of the same code when run on an iPhone 3GS:

```
The front camera is not available.
The rear camera is available.
The rear camera is not equipped with a flash
The camera supports taking photos.
The camera supports shooting videos.
```

Running the same code on the first generation iPad will result in this output in the console window:

```
The front camera is not available.
The rear camera is not available.
The camera does not support taking photos
The camera does not support shooting videos
```

Running the same code on the iPad 2 will result in this output in the console window:

```
The front camera is available.
The front camera is not equipped with a flash
The rear camera is available.
The rear camera is not equipped with a flash
The camera supports taking photos.
The camera supports shooting videos.
```

13.2 Taking Photos with the Camera

Problem

You want to ask the user to take a photo with the camera on his iOS device, and you want to access that photo once the user is done.

Solution

Instantiate an object of type UIImagePickerController and present it as a modal view controller on your current view controller. Here is the *.h* file of the view controller:

```
#import <UIKit/UIKit.h>
#import <AssetsLibrary/AssetsLibrary.h>
#import <MobileCoreServices/MobileCoreServices.h>

@interface Taking_Photos_with_the_CameraViewController
            : UIViewController <UINavigationControllerDelegate,
                                UIImagePickerControllerDelegate>

@end
```

The delegate of an instance of UIImagePickerController must conform to the UINavigationControllerDelegate and UIImagePickerControllerDelegate protocols. If you forget to include them in the *.h* file of your delegate object, you'll get warnings from the compiler when assigning a value to the delegate property of your image picker controller. Please bear in mind that you can still assign an object to the delegate property of an instance of UIImagePickerController where that object does not explicitly conform to the UIImagePickerControllerDelegate and UINavigationControllerDelegate protocols, but implements the required methods in these protocols. I, however, suggest that you give a hint to the compiler that the delegate object does, in fact, conform to the aforementioned protocols in order to avoid getting compiler warnings.

In the implementation of the view controller (*.m* file), we will attempt to display an image picker controller as a modal view controller, like so:

```
- (void)viewDidLoad{
  [super viewDidLoad];

  if ([self isCameraAvailable] &&
      [self doesCameraSupportTakingPhotos]){

    UIImagePickerController *controller =
      [[UIImagePickerController alloc] init];

    controller.sourceType = UIImagePickerControllerSourceTypeCamera;

    NSString *requiredMediaType = (__bridge NSString *)kUTTypeImage;
    controller.mediaTypes = [[NSArray alloc]
                              initWithObjects:requiredMediaType, nil];

    controller.allowsEditing = YES;
    controller.delegate = self;

    [self.navigationController presentModalViewController:controller
                                                animated:YES];

  } else {
    NSLog(@"Camera is not available.");
  }

}
```

 We are using the isCameraAvailable and doesCameraSupportTakingPhotos methods in this example. These methods are implemented and explained in Recipe 13.1.

In this example, we are allowing the user to take photos using the image picker. You must have noticed that we are setting the delegate property of the image picker to self, which refers to the view controller. For this, we have to make sure we have implemented the methods defined in the UIImagePickerControllerDelegate protocol, like so:

```
- (void) imagePickerController:(UIImagePickerController *)picker
  didFinishPickingMediaWithInfo:(NSDictionary *)info{

  NSLog(@"Picker returned successfully.");

  NSString    *mediaType = [info objectForKey:
                              UIImagePickerControllerMediaType];

  if ([mediaType isEqualToString:(__bridge NSString *)kUTTypeMovie]){

    NSURL *urlOfVideo =
    [info objectForKey:UIImagePickerControllerMediaURL];

    NSLog(@"Video URL = %@", urlOfVideo);

  }

  else if ([mediaType isEqualToString:(__bridge NSString *)kUTTypeImage]){

    /* Let's get the metadata. This is only for
     images. Not videos */

    NSDictionary *metadata =
    [info objectForKey:
     UIImagePickerControllerMediaMetadata];

    UIImage *theImage =
    [info objectForKey:
     UIImagePickerControllerOriginalImage];

    NSLog(@"Image Metadata = %@", metadata);
    NSLog(@"Image = %@", theImage);

  }

  [picker dismissModalViewControllerAnimated:YES];

}

- (void)imagePickerControllerDidCancel:(UIImagePickerController *)picker{

  NSLog(@"Picker was cancelled");
  [picker dismissModalViewControllerAnimated:YES];

}
```

Discussion

There are a couple of important things that you must keep in mind about the image picker controller's delegate. First, two delegate messages are called on the delegate object of the image picker controller. The `imagePickerController:didFinishPick ingMediaWithInfo:` method gets called when the user finishes execution of the image picker (e.g., takes a photo and presses a button at the end), whereas the `imagePicker ControllerDidCancel:` method gets called when the image picker's operation is cancelled.

Also, the `imagePickerController:didFinishPickingMediaWithInfo:` delegate method contains information about the item that was captured by the user, be it an image or a video. The `didFinishPickingMediaWithInfo` parameter is a dictionary of values that tell you what the image picker has captured and the metadata of that item, along with other useful information. The first thing you have to do in this method is to read the value of the `UIImagePickerControllerMediaType` key in this dictionary. The object for this key is an instance of `NSString` that could be one of these values:

`kUTTypeImage`
> For a photo that was shot by the camera

`kUTTypeMovie`
> For a movie/video that was shot by the camera

The `kUTTypeImage` and `kUTTypeMovie` values are available in the Mobile Core Services framework and are of type `CFStringRef`. You can simply typecast these values to `NSString` if needed.

After determining the type of resource created by the camera (video or photo), you can access that resource's properties using the `didFinishPickingMediaWithInfo` dictionary parameter again.

For images (`kUTTypeImage`), you can access these keys:

`UIImagePickerControllerMediaMetadata`
> This key's value is an object of type `NSDictionary`. This dictionary contains a lot of useful information about the image that was shot by the user. A complete discussion of the values inside this dictionary is beyond the scope of this chapter.

`UIImagePickerControllerOriginalImage`
> This key's value is an object of type `UIImage` containing the image that was shot by the user.

`UIImagePickerControllerCropRect`
> If editing is enabled (using the `allowsEditing` property of `UIImagePicker Controller`), the object of this key will contain the rectangle of the cropped area.

`UIImagePickerControllerEditedImage`
> If editing is enabled (using the `allowsEditing` property of `UIImagePicker Controller`), this key's value will contain the edited (resized and scaled) image.

For videos (kUTTypeMovie) that are shot by the user, you can access the UIImagePicker ControllerMediaURL key in the didFinishPickingMediaWithInfo dictionary parameter of the imagePickerController:didFinishPickingMediaWithInfo: method. The value of this key is an object of type NSURL containing the URL of the video that was shot by the user.

After you get a reference to the UIImage instance that the user took with the camera, you can simply use that instance within your application.

 The images shot by the image picker controller within your application are not saved to the camera roll by default.

See Also

Recipe 13.1

13.3 Taking Videos with the Camera

Problem

You want to allow your users to shoot a video using their iOS device, and you would like to be able to use that video from inside your application.

Solution

Use UIImagePickerController with the UIImagePickerControllerSourceTypeCamera source type and the kUTTypeMovie media type:

```
- (void)viewDidLoad{
[super viewDidLoad];

if ([self isCameraAvailable] &&
    [self doesCameraSupportTakingPhotos]){

    UIImagePickerController *controller =
      [[UIImagePickerController alloc] init];

    controller.sourceType = UIImagePickerControllerSourceTypeCamera;

    NSString *requiredMediaType = (__bridge NSString *)kUTTypeMovie;
    controller.mediaTypes = [[NSArray alloc]
                             initWithObjects:requiredMediaType, nil];
    controller.allowsEditing = YES;
    controller.delegate = self;

    [self.navigationController presentModalViewController:controller
                                                animated:YES];
```

```
  } else {
    NSLog(@"Camera is not available.");
  }

}
```

 The isCameraAvailable and doesCameraSupportShootingVideos methods used in this sample code are implemented and discussed in Recipe 13.1.

We will implement the delegate methods of the image picker controller like so:

```
- (void)  imagePickerController:(UIImagePickerController *)picker
  didFinishPickingMediaWithInfo:(NSDictionary *)info{

  NSLog(@"Picker returned successfully.");

  NSLog(@"%@", info);

  NSString    *mediaType = [info objectForKey:
                               UIImagePickerControllerMediaType];

  if ([mediaType isEqualToString:(__bridge NSString *)kUTTypeMovie]){

    NSURL *urlOfVideo =
    [info objectForKey:UIImagePickerControllerMediaURL];

    NSLog(@"Video URL = %@", urlOfVideo);

    NSError *dataReadingError = nil;

    NSData *videoData =
    [NSData dataWithContentsOfURL:urlOfVideo
                         options:NSDataReadingMapped
                           error:&dataReadingError];

    if (videoData != nil){
      /* We were able to read the data */
      NSLog(@"Successfully loaded the data.");
    } else {
      /* We failed to read the data. Use the dataReadingError
       variable to determine what the error is */
      NSLog(@"Failed to load the data with error = %@",
          dataReadingError);
    }

  }

  [picker dismissModalViewControllerAnimated:YES];

}

- (void)imagePickerControllerDidCancel:(UIImagePickerController *)picker{
```

```
        NSLog(@"Picker was cancelled");
        [picker dismissModalViewControllerAnimated:YES];

}
```

Discussion

Once you detect that the iOS device your application is running on supports video recording, you can bring up the image picker controller with the UIImagePickerControl lerSourceTypeCamera source type and kUTTypeMovie media type to allow the users of your application to shoot videos. Once they are done, the imagePickerController:did FinishPickingMediaWithInfo: delegate method will get called and you can use the did FinishPickingMediaWithInfo dictionary parameter to find out more about the captured video (the values that can be placed inside this dictionary are thoroughly explained in Recipe 13.2).

When the user shoots a video using the image picker controller, the video will be saved in a temporary folder inside your application's bundle, not inside the camera roll. An example of such a URL is:

file://localhost/private/var/mobile/Applications/< APPID >/tmp/capture-T0x104e20. tmp.TQ9UTr/capturedvideo.MOV

 The value APPID in the URL represents your application's unique identifier, and will clearly be different depending on your application.

As the programmer, not only can you allow your users to shoot videos from inside your application, but also you can modify how the videos are captured. You can change two important properties of the UIImagePickerController class in order to modify the default behavior of video recording:

videoQuality
> This property specifies the quality of the video. You can choose a value such as UIImagePickerControllerQualityTypeHigh or UIImagePickerControllerQualityType Medium for the value of this property.

videoMaximumDuration
> This property specifies the maximum duration of the video. This value is measured in seconds.

For instance, if we were to allow the users to record high-quality videos for up to 30 seconds, we could simply modify the values of the aforementioned properties of the instance of UIImagePickerController like so:

```
- (void)viewDidLoad{
    [super viewDidLoad];
```

```
if ([self isCameraAvailable] &&
    [self doesCameraSupportTakingPhotos]){

  UIImagePickerController *controller =
    [[UIImagePickerController alloc] init];

  controller.sourceType = UIImagePickerControllerSourceTypeCamera;

  NSString *requiredMediaType = (__bridge NSString *)kUTTypeMovie;
  controller.mediaTypes = [[NSArray alloc]
                           initWithObjects:requiredMediaType, nil];

  controller.allowsEditing = YES;
  controller.delegate = self;

  /* Record in high quality */
  controller.videoQuality = UIImagePickerControllerQualityTypeHigh;

  /* Only allow 30 seconds of recording */
  controller.videoMaximumDuration = 30.0f;

  [self.navigationController presentModalViewController:controller
                                              animated:YES];

} else {
  NSLog(@"Camera is not available.");
}

}
```

See Also

Recipe 13.1

13.4 Storing Photos in the Photo Library

Problem

You want to be able to store a photo in the user's photo library.

Solution

Use the UIImageWriteToSavedPhotosAlbum procedure:

```
- (void) imageWasSavedSuccessfully:(UIImage *)paramImage
          didFinishSavingWithError:(NSError *)paramError
                       contextInfo:(void *)paramContextInfo{

  if (paramError == nil){
    NSLog(@"Image was saved successfully.");
  } else {
    NSLog(@"An error happened while saving the image.");
```

```
    NSLog(@"Error = %@", paramError);
  }

}

- (void)  imagePickerController:(UIImagePickerController *)picker
  didFinishPickingMediaWithInfo:(NSDictionary *)info{

  NSLog(@"Picker returned successfully.");

  NSLog(@"%@", info);

  NSString     *mediaType = [info objectForKey:
                               UIImagePickerControllerMediaType];

  if ([mediaType isEqualToString:(__bridge NSString *)kUTTypeImage]){

    UIImage *theImage = nil;

    if ([picker allowsEditing]){
      theImage = [info objectForKey:UIImagePickerControllerEditedImage];
    } else {
      theImage = [info objectForKey:UIImagePickerControllerOriginalImage];
    }

    SEL selectorToCall =
    @selector(imageWasSavedSuccessfully:didFinishSavingWithError:contextInfo:);

    UIImageWriteToSavedPhotosAlbum(theImage,
                                   self,
                                   selectorToCall,
                                   NULL);

  }

  [picker dismissModalViewControllerAnimated:YES];

}

- (void)imagePickerControllerDidCancel:(UIImagePickerController *)picker{

  NSLog(@"Picker was cancelled");
  [picker dismissModalViewControllerAnimated:YES];

}- (void)viewDidLoad{
  [super viewDidLoad];

  if ([self isCameraAvailable] &&
      [self doesCameraSupportTakingPhotos]){

    UIImagePickerController *controller =
    [[UIImagePickerController alloc] init];

    controller.sourceType = UIImagePickerControllerSourceTypeCamera;
```

```
    NSString *requiredMediaType = (__bridge NSString *)kUTTypeImage;
    controller.mediaTypes = [[NSArray alloc]
                            initWithObjects:requiredMediaType, nil];

    controller.allowsEditing = YES;
    controller.delegate = self;

    [self.navigationController presentModalViewController:controller
                                                animated:YES];

  } else {
    NSLog(@"Camera is not available.");
  }

}
```

The isCameraAvailable and doesCameraSupportTakingPhotos methods
used in this example are thoroughly explained in Recipe 13.1.

Discussion

Usually after a user is done taking a photo with her iOS device, she expects the photo
to be saved into her photo library. However, applications that are not originally shipped
with iOS can ask the user to take a photo, using the UIImagePickerController class, and
then process that image. In this case, the user will understand that the application we
provided might not save the photo to her photo library—it might simply use it internally. For instance, if an instant messaging application allows users to transfer their
photos to each other's devices, the user will understand that a photo he takes inside
the application will not be saved to his photo library, but will instead be transferred
over the Internet to the other user.

However, if you decide you want to store an instance of UIImage to the photo library
on the user's device, you can use the UIImageWriteToSavedPhotosAlbum function. This
function accepts four parameters:

1. The image
2. The object that will be notified whenever the image is fully saved
3. A parameter that specifies the selector that has to be called on the target object
   (specified by the second parameter) when the save operation finishes
4. A context value that will get passed to the specified selector once the operation is
   done

Providing the second, third, and fourth parameters to this procedure is optional. If you
do provide the second and third parameters, the fourth parameter still remains optional. For instance, this is the selector we have chosen in the example:

```
- (void) imageWasSavedSuccessfully:(UIImage *)paramImage
        didFinishSavingWithError:(NSError *)paramError
                    contextInfo:(void *)paramContextInfo{

  if (paramError == nil){
    NSLog(@"Image was saved successfully.");
  } else {
    NSLog(@"An error happened while saving the image.");
    NSLog(@"Error = %@", paramError);
  }

}
```

 If the error parameter that you receive in this selector is equal to nil, that means the image was saved in the user's photo library successfully. Otherwise, you can retrieve the value of this parameter to determine what the issue was.

13.5 Storing Videos in the Photo Library

Problem

You want to store a video accessible through a URL, such as a video in your application bundle, to the Photo Library.

Solution

Use the writeVideoAtPathToSavedPhotosAlbum:completionBlock: instance method of ALAssetsLibrary:

```
- (BOOL)          application:(UIApplication *)application
    didFinishLaunchingWithOptions:(NSDictionary *)launchOptions{

  self.assetsLibrary = [[ALAssetsLibrary alloc] init];

  NSURL *videoURL = [[NSBundle mainBundle] URLForResource:@"MyVideo"
                                            withExtension:@"MOV"];

  if (videoURL != nil){
    [self.assetsLibrary
     writeVideoAtPathToSavedPhotosAlbum:videoURL
     completionBlock:^(NSURL *assetURL, NSError *error) {

       if (error == nil){
         NSLog(@"no errors happened");
       } else {
         NSLog(@"Error happened while saving the video.");
         NSLog(@"The error is = %@", error);
       }

     }];
```

```
  } else {
    NSLog(@"Could not find the video in the app bundle.");
  }

  self.window = [[UIWindow alloc] initWithFrame:
                  [[UIScreen mainScreen] bounds]];

  self.window.backgroundColor = [UIColor whiteColor];
  [self.window makeKeyAndVisible];
  return YES;
}
```

In the example, assetsLibrary is a property of type ALAssetsLibrary. Although this example allocates and initializes this property in the app delegate, you do not necessarily have to use Assets Library objects in your app delegate. You can allocate, initialize, and use them anywhere in your application that you find most appropriate.

Discussion

The Assets Library framework is a convenient bridge between developers and the Photo Library. As mentioned in Recipe 13.6, the iOS SDK provides you with built-in GUI components that you can use to access the contents of the Photo Library. However, you might sometimes require direct access to these contents. In such instances, you can use the Assets Library framework.

After allocating and initializing the Assets Library object of type ALAssetsLibrary, you can use the writeVideoAtPathToSavedPhotosAlbum:completionBlock: instance method of this object to write a video from a URL to the Photo Library. All you have to do is provide the URL of the video in NSURL form and a block object whose code will be called when the video is saved. The block object must accept two parameters of type NSURL and NSError, respectively.

If the error parameter is nil, the save process went well and you don't have to worry about anything. One of the common errors that iOS could return to you is similar to this:

```
Error Domain=ALAssetsLibraryErrorDomain Code=-3302 "Invalid data"
UserInfo=0x7923590 {NSLocalizedFailureReason=
There was a problem writing this asset because
the data is invalid and cannot be viewed or played.,
NSLocalizedRecoverySuggestion=Try with different data,
NSLocalizedDescription=Invalid data}
```

You will get this error message if you attempt to pass a URL that is not inside your application bundle. If you are testing your application on iPhone Simulator, you might occasionally also get this error message:

```
Error Domain=ALAssetsLibraryErrorDomain Code=-3310 "Data unavailable"
UserInfo=0x6456810 {NSLocalizedRecoverySuggestion=
Launch the Photos application, NSLocalizedDescription=Data unavailable}
```

If so, please open the Photos application in iOS Simulator once, and then launch your application again. This will force the simulator to rebuild the necessary database for the photos that are available on the simulator—this will solve this issue, should you encounter it while developing iOS apps.

The first parameter passed to the block object provided to the `writeVideoAt PathToSavedPhotosAlbum:completionBlock:` method will point to the Assets Library URL of the stored video. A sample URL of this kind will look like this:

```
assets-library://asset/asset.MOV?id=1000000002&ext=MOV
```

In Recipe 13.7, we will learn how to use such a URL to load the data for the video file into memory.

13.6 Retrieving Photos and Videos from the Photo Library

Problem

You want users to be able to pick a photo or a video from their photo library and use it in your application.

Solution

Use the `UIImagePickerControllerSourceTypePhotoLibrary` value for the source type of your `UIImagePickerController` and the `kUTTypeImage` or `kUTTypeMovie` value, or both, for the media type, like so:

```
- (BOOL) isPhotoLibraryAvailable{

    return [UIImagePickerController isSourceTypeAvailable:
            UIImagePickerControllerSourceTypePhotoLibrary];

}

- (BOOL) canUserPickVideosFromPhotoLibrary{

    return [self
            cameraSupportsMedia:(__bridge NSString *)kUTTypeMovie
            sourceType:UIImagePickerControllerSourceTypePhotoLibrary];

}

- (BOOL) canUserPickPhotosFromPhotoLibrary{

    return [self
            cameraSupportsMedia:(__bridge NSString *)kUTTypeImage
            sourceType:UIImagePickerControllerSourceTypePhotoLibrary];

}

- (void)viewDidLoad{
```

```
    [super viewDidLoad];

    if ([self isPhotoLibraryAvailable]){

      UIImagePickerController *controller =
        [[UIImagePickerController alloc] init];

      controller.sourceType = UIImagePickerControllerSourceTypePhotoLibrary;

      NSMutableArray *mediaTypes = [[NSMutableArray alloc] init];

      if ([self canUserPickPhotosFromPhotoLibrary]){
        [mediaTypes addObject:(__bridge NSString *)kUTTypeImage];
      }

      if ([self canUserPickVideosFromPhotoLibrary]){
        [mediaTypes addObject:(__bridge NSString *)kUTTypeMovie];
      }

      controller.mediaTypes = mediaTypes;

      controller.delegate = self;

      [self.navigationController presentModalViewController:controller
                                                  animated:YES];

    }

  }
```

For the implementation of the cameraSupportsMedia:sourceType: method we are using in this example, please refer to Recipe 13.1.

Discussion

To allow your users to pick photos or videos from their photo library, you must set the sourceType property of an instance of UIImagePickerController to UIImagePickerCon trollerSourceTypePhotoLibrary before presenting them with the image picker. In addition, if you want to filter the videos or photos out of the items presented to your users once the image picker is shown, exclude the kUTTypeMovie or kUTTypeImage value (respectively) from the array of media types of the image picker (in the mediaTypes property).

Bear in mind that setting the mediaTypes property of an image picker controller to nil or an empty array will result in a runtime error.

After the user is done picking the image, you will get the usual delegate messages through the UIImagePickerControllerDelegate protocol. For more information on how you can implement the methods defined in this protocol for processing images, please refer to Recipe 13.2.

See Also

Recipe 13.7

13.7 Retrieving Assets from the Assets Library

Problem

You want to directly retrieve photos or videos from the Photo Library without the help of any built-in GUI components.

Solution

Use the Assets Library framework. Follow these steps:

1. Allocate and initialize an object of type `ALAssetsLibrary`.

2. Provide two block objects to the `enumerateGroupsWithTypes:usingBlock:failure Block:` instance method of the Assets Library object. The first block will retrieve all the groups associated with the type that we passed to this method. The groups will be of type `ALAssetsGroup`. The second block returns an error in case of failure.

3. Use the `enumerateAssetsUsingBlock:` instance method of each group object to enumerate the assets available in each group. This method takes a single parameter, a block that retrieves information on a single asset. The block that you pass as a parameter must accept three parameters, of which the first must be of type `ALAsset`.

4. After retrieving the `ALAsset` objects available in each group, you can retrieve various properties of each asset, such as their type, available URLs, and so on. Retrieve these properties using the `valueForProperty:` instance method of each asset of type `ALAsset`. The return value of this method, depending on the property passed to it, could be `NSDictionary`, `NSString`, or any other object type. We will see a few common properties that we can retrieve from each asset soon.

5. Invoke the `defaultRepresentation` instance method of each object of type `ALAsset` set to retrieve its representation object of type `ALAssetRepresentation`. Each asset in the Assets Library can have more than one representation. For instance, a photo might have a PNG representation by default, but a JPEG representation as well. Using the `defaultRepresentation` method of each asset of type `ALAsset`, you can retrieve the `ALAssetRepresentation` object, and then use that to retrieve different representations (if available) of each asset.

6. Use the size and the `getBytes:fromOffset:length:error:` instance methods of each asset representation to load the asset's representation data. You can then write the read bytes into an `NSData` object or do whatever else you need to do in your application. Additionally, for photos, you can use the `fullResolutionImage`, `fullScreen Image`, and `CGImageWithOptions:` instance methods of each representation to re-

trieve images of type CGImageRef. You can then construct a UIImage from CGImage
Ref using the imageWithCGImage: class method of UIImage:

```objective-c
- (void)viewDidLoad{
  [super viewDidLoad];
  self.assetsLibrary = [[ALAssetsLibrary alloc] init];

  [self.assetsLibrary
   enumerateGroupsWithTypes:ALAssetsGroupAll
   usingBlock:^(ALAssetsGroup *group, BOOL *stop) {
     [group enumerateAssetsUsingBlock:^(ALAsset *result,
                                        NSUInteger index,
                                        BOOL *stop) {

       /* Get the asset type */
       NSString *assetType = [result valueForProperty:ALAssetPropertyType];

       if ([assetType isEqualToString:ALAssetTypePhoto]){
         NSLog(@"This is a photo asset");
       }

       else if ([assetType isEqualToString:ALAssetTypeVideo]){
         NSLog(@"This is a video asset");
       }

       else if ([assetType isEqualToString:ALAssetTypeUnknown]){
         NSLog(@"This is an unknown asset");
       }

       /* Get the URLs for the asset */
       NSDictionary *assetURLs = [result valueForProperty:ALAssetPropertyURLs];

       NSUInteger    assetCounter = 0;
       for (NSString *assetURLKey in assetURLs){
         assetCounter++;
         NSLog(@"Asset URL %lu = %@",
               (unsigned long)assetCounter,
               [assetURLs valueForKey:assetURLKey]);
       }

       /* Get the asset's representation object */
       ALAssetRepresentation *assetRepresentation =
        [result defaultRepresentation];

       NSLog(@"Representation Size = %lld", [assetRepresentation size]);

     }];   }
   failureBlock:^(NSError *error) {
     NSLog(@"Failed to enumerate the asset groups.");
   }];

}
```

Discussion

The Assets Library is broken down into groups. Each group contains assets, and each asset has properties, such as URLs and representation objects.

You can retrieve all assets of all types from the Assets Library using the `ALAssetsGrou pAll` constant passed to the `enumerateGroupsWithTypes` parameter of the `enumerate GroupsWithTypes:usingBlock:failureBlock:` instance method of the Assets Library object. Here is a list of values you can pass to this parameter to enumerate different groups of assets:

`ALAssetsGroupAlbum`
> Groups representing albums that have been stored on an iOS device through iTunes.

`ALAssetsGroupFaces`
> Groups representing albums that contain face assets that were stored on an iOS device through iTunes.

`ALAssetsGroupSavedPhotos`
> Groups representing the saved photos in the Photo Library. These are accessible to an iOS device through the Photos application as well.

`ALAssetsGroupAll`
> All available groups in the Assets Library.

Now let's write a simple application that retrieves the data for the first image found in the Assets Library, creates a `UIImageView` out of it, and adds the image view to the view of the current view controller. This way, we will learn how to read the contents of an asset using its representation.

Let's start with the declaration of the view controller and define an image view in there, which we will use to display the first image that we can find in the assets library:

```
#import <UIKit/UIKit.h>
#import <AssetsLibrary/AssetsLibrary.h>
#import <MobileCoreServices/MobileCoreServices.h>

@interface Retrieving_Assets_from_the_Assets_LibraryViewController
            : UIViewController <UIImagePickerControllerDelegate,
                                UINavigationControllerDelegate>

@property (nonatomic, strong) ALAssetsLibrary *assetsLibrary;
@property (nonatomic, strong) UIImageView *imageView;

@end
```

Now when the view controller loads its view, we will initialize the assets library object and then start enumerating the assets library until we find the first photo. At that time, we will use the representation of that asset (photo) to display the photo on the image view:

```objective-c
- (void)viewDidLoad{
  [super viewDidLoad];

  self.view.backgroundColor = [UIColor whiteColor];
  self.assetsLibrary = [[ALAssetsLibrary alloc] init];

  dispatch_queue_t dispatchQueue =
    dispatch_get_global_queue(DISPATCH_QUEUE_PRIORITY_DEFAULT, 0);

  dispatch_async(dispatchQueue, ^(void) {

    [self.assetsLibrary
     enumerateGroupsWithTypes:ALAssetsGroupAll
     usingBlock:^(ALAssetsGroup *group, BOOL *stop) {

       [group enumerateAssetsUsingBlock:^(ALAsset *result,
                                          NSUInteger index,
                                          BOOL *stop) {

         __block BOOL foundThePhoto = NO;

         if (foundThePhoto){
           *stop = YES;
         }

         /* Get the asset type */
         NSString *assetType = [result valueForProperty:ALAssetPropertyType];

         if ([assetType isEqualToString:ALAssetTypePhoto]){
           NSLog(@"This is a photo asset");

           foundThePhoto = YES;
           *stop = YES;

           /* Get the asset's representation object */
           ALAssetRepresentation *assetRepresentation =
            [result defaultRepresentation];

           /* We need the scale and orientation to be able to construct a
            properly oriented and scaled UIImage out of the
            representation object */
           CGFloat imageScale = [assetRepresentation scale];

           UIImageOrientation imageOrientation =
            (UIImageOrientation)[assetRepresentation orientation];

           dispatch_async(dispatch_get_main_queue(), ^(void) {

             CGImageRef imageReference =
              [assetRepresentation fullResolutionImage];

             /* Construct the image now */
             UIImage    *image =
             [[UIImage alloc] initWithCGImage:imageReference
                                        scale:imageScale
```

```
                    orientation:imageOrientation];

        if (image != nil){
          self.imageView = [[UIImageView alloc]
                                initWithFrame:self.view.bounds];
          self.imageView.contentMode = UIViewContentModeScaleAspectFit;
          self.imageView.image = image;
          [self.view addSubview:self.imageView];

        } else {
          NSLog(@"Failed to create the image.");
        }
      });

    }

  }];
  }
  failureBlock:^(NSError *error) {
    NSLog(@"Failed to enumerate the asset groups.");
  }];

});

}
```

We enumerate the groups and every asset in the groups. Then we find the first photo asset and retrieve its representation. Using the representation, we construct a UIImage, and from the UIImage, we construct a UIImageView to display that image on the view. Quite simple, isn't it?

For video files, we are dealing with a slightly different issue, as the ALAsset Representation class does not have any methods that could return an object that encapsulates the video files. For this reason, we have to read the contents of a video asset into a buffer and perhaps save it to the *Documents* folder where it is easier for us to access later. Of course, the requirements depend on your application, but in this example code, we will go ahead and find the first video in the Assets Library and store it in the application's *Documents* folder under the name *Temp.MOV*:

```
- (void)viewDidLoad{
  [super viewDidLoad];

  self.view.backgroundColor = [UIColor whiteColor];
  self.assetsLibrary = [[ALAssetsLibrary alloc] init];

  dispatch_queue_t dispatchQueue =
  dispatch_get_global_queue(DISPATCH_QUEUE_PRIORITY_DEFAULT, 0);

  dispatch_async(dispatchQueue, ^(void) {

    [self.assetsLibrary
     enumerateGroupsWithTypes:ALAssetsGroupAll
     usingBlock:^(ALAssetsGroup *group, BOOL *stop) {
```

```
__block BOOL foundTheVideo = NO;

[group enumerateAssetsUsingBlock:^(ALAsset *result,
                                   NSUInteger index,
                                   BOOL *stop) {

  /* Get the asset type */
  NSString *assetType = [result valueForProperty:ALAssetPropertyType];

  if ([assetType isEqualToString:ALAssetTypeVideo]){
    NSLog(@"This is a video asset");

    foundTheVideo = YES;
    *stop = YES;

    /* Get the asset's representation object */
    ALAssetRepresentation *assetRepresentation =
     [result defaultRepresentation];

    const NSUInteger BufferSize = 1024;
    uint8_t buffer[BufferSize];
    NSUInteger bytesRead = 0;
    long long currentOffset = 0;
    NSError *readingError = nil;

    /* Find the documents folder (an array) */
    NSArray *documents =
    NSSearchPathForDirectoriesInDomains(NSDocumentDirectory,
                                        NSUserDomainMask,
                                        YES);

    /* Retrieve the one documents folder that we need */
    NSString *documentsFolder = [documents objectAtIndex:0];

    /* Construct the path where the video has to be saved */
    NSString *videoPath = [documentsFolder
                          stringByAppendingPathComponent:@"Temp.MOV"];

    NSFileManager *fileManager = [[NSFileManager alloc] init];

    /* Create the file if it doesn't exist already */
    if ([fileManager fileExistsAtPath:videoPath] == NO){
      [fileManager createFileAtPath:videoPath
                           contents:nil
                         attributes:nil];
    }

    /* We will use this file handle to write the contents
     of the media assets to the disk */
    NSFileHandle *fileHandle = [NSFileHandle
                               fileHandleForWritingAtPath:videoPath];

    do{

      /* Read as many bytes as we can put in the buffer */
```

```
            bytesRead = [assetRepresentation getBytes:(uint8_t *)&buffer
                                          fromOffset:currentOffset
                                              length:BufferSize
                                               error:&readingError];

            /* If we couldn't read anything, we will exit this loop */
            if (bytesRead == 0){
              break;
            }

            /* Keep the offset up to date */
            currentOffset += bytesRead;

            /* Put the buffer into an NSData */
            NSData *readData = [[NSData alloc]
                               initWithBytes:(const void *)buffer
                               length:bytesRead];

            /* And write the data to file */
            [fileHandle writeData:readData];

          } while (bytesRead > 0);
          NSLog(@"Finished reading and storing the \
                      video in the documents folder");

        }

      }];

      if (foundTheVideo){
        *stop = YES;
      }

    }
    failureBlock:^(NSError *error) {
      NSLog(@"Failed to enumerate the asset groups.");
    }];

  });

}
```

This is what's happening in the sample code:

- We get the default representation of the first video asset that we find in the Assets Library.

- We create a file called *Temp.MOV* in the application's *Documents* folder to save the contents of the video asset.

- We create a loop that runs as long as there is still data in the asset representation waiting to be read. The getBytes:fromOffset:length:error: instance method of the asset representation object reads as many bytes as we can fit into the buffer for as many times as necessary until we get to the end of the representation data.

- After reading the data into the buffer, we encapsulate the data into an object of type NSData using the initWithBytes:length: initialization method of NSData. We then write this data to the file we created previously using the writeData: instance method of NSFileHandle.

13.8 Editing Videos on an iOS Device

Problem

You want the user of your application to be able to edit videos straight from your application.

Solution

Use the UIVideoEditorController class. In this example, we will use this class in conjunction with an image picker controller. First we will ask the user to pick a video from her photo library. After she does, we will display an instance of the video editor controller and allow the user to edit the video she picked.

Discussion

The UIVideoEditorController in the iOS SDK allows programmers to display a video editor interface to the users of their applications. All you have to do is to provide the URL of the video that needs to be edited and then present the video editor controller as a modal view. You should not overlay the view of this controller with any other views, and you should not modify this view.

 Calling the presentModalViewController:animated: method immediately after calling the dismissModalViewControllerAnimated: method of a view controller will terminate your application with a runtime error. You must wait for the first view controller to be dismissed and then present the second view controller. You can take advantage of the view DidAppear: instance method of your view controllers to detect when your view is displayed. You know at this point that any modal view controllers must have disappeared.

So let's go ahead and declare the view controller and any necessary properties:

```
#import <UIKit/UIKit.h>
#import <AssetsLibrary/AssetsLibrary.h>
#import <MobileCoreServices/MobileCoreServices.h>

@interface Editing_Videos_on_an_iOS_DeviceViewController
        : UIViewController <UINavigationControllerDelegate,
                            UIVideoEditorControllerDelegate,
                            UIImagePickerControllerDelegate>
```

```
@property (nonatomic, strong) NSURL *videoURLToEdit;

@end
```

 The UIVideoEditorController is not designed to work in landscape mode. Even if the view controller that displays an instance of the video editor supports all orientations, the video editor will be shown in portrait mode only.

The next thing to do is to handle different video editor delegate messages in the view controller:

```
- (void)videoEditorController:(UIVideoEditorController *)editor
    didSaveEditedVideoToPath:(NSString *)editedVideoPath{
  NSLog(@"The video editor finished saving video");
  NSLog(@"The edited video path is at = %@", editedVideoPath);
  [editor dismissModalViewControllerAnimated:YES];
}

- (void)videoEditorController:(UIVideoEditorController *)editor
           didFailWithError:(NSError *)error{
  NSLog(@"Video editor error occurred = %@", error);
  [editor dismissModalViewControllerAnimated:YES];
}

- (void)videoEditorControllerDidCancel:(UIVideoEditorController *)editor{
  NSLog(@"The video editor was cancelled");
  [editor dismissModalViewControllerAnimated:YES];
}
```

When the view loads, we need to display a video picker to the user. She will then be able to pick a video from her library, and we will then proceed to allow her to edit that video:

```
- (BOOL) cameraSupportsMedia:(NSString *)paramMediaType
                  sourceType:(UIImagePickerControllerSourceType)paramSourceType{

  __block BOOL result = NO;

  if ([paramMediaType length] == 0){
    NSLog(@"Media type is empty.");
    return NO;
  }

  NSArray *availableMediaTypes =
  [UIImagePickerController availableMediaTypesForSourceType:paramSourceType];

  [availableMediaTypes enumerateObjectsUsingBlock:
   ^(id obj, NSUInteger idx, BOOL *stop) {

    NSString *mediaType = (NSString *)obj;
    if ([mediaType isEqualToString:paramMediaType]){
      result = YES;
```

```
        *stop= YES;
      }

   }];

   return result;

}

- (BOOL) canUserPickVideosFromPhotoLibrary{

   return [self cameraSupportsMedia:(__bridge NSString *)kUTTypeMovie
              sourceType:UIImagePickerControllerSourceTypePhotoLibrary];

}

- (BOOL) isPhotoLibraryAvailable{

   return [UIImagePickerController
           isSourceTypeAvailable:
           UIImagePickerControllerSourceTypePhotoLibrary];

}

- (void)viewDidLoad {
  [super viewDidLoad];

  if ([self isPhotoLibraryAvailable] &&
      [self canUserPickVideosFromPhotoLibrary]){

    UIImagePickerController *imagePicker =
      [[UIImagePickerController alloc] init];

    /* Set the source type to photo library */
    imagePicker.sourceType = UIImagePickerControllerSourceTypePhotoLibrary;

    /* And we want the user to be able to pick movies from the library */
    NSArray  *mediaTypes = [[NSArray alloc] initWithObjects:
                           (__bridge NSString *)kUTTypeMovie, nil];

    imagePicker.mediaTypes = mediaTypes;

    /* Set the delegate to the current view controller */
    imagePicker.delegate = self;

    /* Present the image picker */
    [self.navigationController presentModalViewController:imagePicker
                                          animated:YES];

  }

}
```

We now need to know when the user is done picking a video, so let's handle various delegate methods of the image picker control:

```
- (void)    imagePickerController:(UIImagePickerController *)picker
    didFinishPickingMediaWithInfo:(NSDictionary *)info{

  NSLog(@"Picker returned successfully.");

  NSString    *mediaType = [info objectForKey:
                                   UIImagePickerControllerMediaType];

  if ([mediaType isEqualToString:(NSString *)kUTTypeMovie]){
    self.videoURLToEdit = [info objectForKey:UIImagePickerControllerMediaURL];
  }

  [picker dismissModalViewControllerAnimated:YES];

}

- (void) imagePickerControllerDidCancel:(UIImagePickerController *)picker{

  NSLog(@"Picker was cancelled");
  self.videoURLToEdit = nil;
  [picker dismissModalViewControllerAnimated:YES];

}
```

When the view appears to the user after she has selected a video from the assets library on her device, we can proceed to display the video editor:

```
- (void) viewDidAppear:(BOOL)animated{
  [super viewDidAppear:animated];

  if (self.videoURLToEdit != nil){

    NSString *videoPath = [self.videoURLToEdit path];

    /* First let's make sure the video editor is able to edit the
     video at the path in the documents folder */
    if ([UIVideoEditorController canEditVideoAtPath:videoPath]){

      /* Instantiate the video editor */
      UIVideoEditorController *videoEditor =
      [[UIVideoEditorController alloc] init];

      /* We become the delegate of the video editor */
      videoEditor.delegate = self;

      /* Make sure to set the path of the video */
      videoEditor.videoPath = videoPath;

      /* And present the video editor */
      [self.navigationController presentModalViewController:videoEditor
                                                   animated:YES];

      self.videoURLToEdit = nil;
```

```
      } else {
        NSLog(@"Cannot edit the video at this path");
      }

   }

}
```

In the example, the user is allowed to pick any video from the photo library. Once she does, we will display the video editor controller by providing the path of the video that the video picker passes to us in a delegate method.

The video editor controller's delegate gets important messages about the state of the video editor. This delegate object must conform to the `UIVideoEditorControllerDele` `gate` and `UINavigationControllerDelegate` protocols. In the example, we chose the view controller to become the delegate of the video editor. Once the editing is done, the delegate object receives the `videoEditorController:didSaveEditedVideoToPath:` delegate method from the video editor controller. The path of the edited video will be passed through the `didSaveEditedVideoToPath` parameter.

Before attempting to display the interface of the video editor to your users, you must call the `canEditVideoAtPath:` class method of `UIVideoEditorController` to make sure the path you are trying to edit is editable by the controller. If the return value of this class method is `YES`, proceed to configuring and displaying the video editor's interface. If not, take a separate path, perhaps displaying an alert to your user.

See Also

Recipe 13.6; Recipe 13.7

CHAPTER 14

Multitasking

14.0 Introduction

Multitasking enables *background execution*, which means the application can keep working as usual—running tasks, spawning new threads, listening for notifications, and reacting to events—but simply does not display anything on the screen or have any way to interact with the user. When the user presses the Home button on his device, which in previous versions of the iPhone and iPad would terminate the application, the application is now sent into the background.

An application running on an iOS version that supports multitasking is, by default, opted into background execution. If you link your application against iOS SDK 4.0 and later, you can opt out of background execution, as you will see in Recipe 14.10. If you do, your application will be terminated when the user presses the Home button, as before.

When our application moves to the background (such as when the user presses the Home button) and then back to the foreground (when the user selects the application again), various messages are sent by the system and are expected to be received by an object we designate as our application delegate. For instance, when our application is sent to the background, our application delegate will receive the applicationDidEnter Background: method, and as the application comes back to the foreground for the user, the application delegate will receive the applicationWillEnterForeground: delegate message.

In addition to these delegate messages, iOS also sends notifications to the running application when it transitions the application to the background and from the background to the foreground. The notification that gets sent when the application is moved to the background is UIApplicationDidEnterBackgroundNotification, and the notification that gets sent when an application transitions from the background to the foreground is UIApplicationWillEnterForegroundNotification. You can use the default notification center to register for these notifications.

14.1 Detecting the Availability of Multitasking

Problem

You want to find out whether the iOS device running your application supports multitasking.

Solution

Call the isMultitaskingSupported instance method of UIDevice, like so:

```
- (BOOL) isMultitaskingSupported{

    BOOL result = NO;
    if ([[UIDevice currentDevice]
          respondsToSelector:@selector(isMultitaskingSupported)]){
      result = [[UIDevice currentDevice] isMultitaskingSupported];
    }
    return result;

}

- (BOOL)             application:(UIApplication *)application
    didFinishLaunchingWithOptions:(NSDictionary *)launchOptions{

    if ([self isMultitaskingSupported]){
      NSLog(@"Multitasking is supported.");
    } else {
      NSLog(@"Multitasking is not supported.");
    }

    self.window = [[UIWindow alloc] initWithFrame:
                       [[UIScreen mainScreen] bounds]];

    self.window.backgroundColor = [UIColor whiteColor];
    [self.window makeKeyAndVisible];
    return YES;
}
```

Discussion

Your application, depending on the iOS devices it targets, can be run and executed on a variety of devices on different versions of iOS. For instance, if you compile your application with iOS SDK 6 and your deployment target OS is 5.0, your application can be run on the iPhone 3G, iPhone 3GS, iPhone 4, iPhone 4S and iPod touch (second and third generations), provided that the iOS on these devices has been updated to iOS 4.0 or better. Furthermore, a device could have iOS 6.0 or later installed on it, but the underlying hardware might not be strong enough for multitasking to be supported. Because of this, your application must be aware of whether multitasking is enabled on that specific hardware (and on that specific iOS) before attempting to act like a multitasking application.

14.2 Completing a Long-Running Task in the Background

Problem

You want to borrow some time from iOS to complete a long-running task when your application is being sent to the background.

Solution

Use the `beginBackgroundTaskWithExpirationHandler:` instance method of `UIApplication`. After you have finished the task, call the `endBackgroundTask:` instance method of `UIApplication`.

Discussion

When an iOS application is sent to the background, its main thread is paused. The threads you create within your application using the `detachNewThreadSelector:toTarget:withObject:` class method of `NSThread` are also suspended. If you are attempting to finish a long-running task when your application is being sent to the background, you must call the `beginBackgroundTaskWithExpirationHandler:` instance method of `UIApplication` to borrow some time from iOS. The `backgroundTimeRemaining` property of `UIApplication` contains the number of seconds the application has to finish its job. If the application doesn't finish the long-running task before this time expires, iOS will terminate the application. Every call to the `beginBackgroundTaskWithExpirationHandler:` method must have a corresponding call to `endBackgroundTask:` (another instance method of `UIApplication`). In other words, if you ask for more time from iOS to complete a task, you must tell iOS when you are done with that task. Once this is done and no more tasks are requested to be running in the background, your application will be fully put into the background with all threads paused.

When your application is in the foreground, the `backgroundTimeRemaining` property of `UIApplication` is equal to the `DBL_MAX` constant, which is the largest value a value of type `double` can contain (the integer equivalent of this value is normally equal to −1 in this case). After iOS is asked for more time before the application is fully suspended, this property will indicate the number of seconds the application has before it finishes running its task(s).

You can call the `beginBackgroundTaskWithExpirationHandler:` method as many times as you wish inside your application. The important thing to keep in mind is that whenever iOS returns a token or a task identifier to your application with this method, you must call the `endBackgroundTask:` method to mark the end of that task once you are finished running the task. Failing to do so might cause iOS to terminate your application.

While in the background, applications are not supposed to be fully functioning and processing heavy data. They are indeed only supposed to *finish* a long-running task.

An example could be an application that is calling a web service API and has not yet received the response of that API from the server. During this time, if the application is sent to the background, the application can request more time until it receives a response from the server. Once the response is received, the application must save its state and mark that task as finished by calling the endBackgroundTask: instance method of UIApplication.

Let's have a look at an example. I will start by defining a property of type UIBackground TaskIdentifier in the app delegate. Also, let's define a timer of type NSTimer, which we will use to print a message to the console window every second when our app is sent to the background:

```
#import <UIKit/UIKit.h>

@interface Completing_a_Long_Running_Task_in_the_BackgroundAppDelegate
        : UIResponder <UIApplicationDelegate>

@property (nonatomic, strong) UIWindow *window;

@property (nonatomic, unsafe_unretained)
  UIBackgroundTaskIdentifier backgroundTaskIdentifier;

@property (nonatomic, strong) NSTimer *myTimer;

@end
```

Now let's move on to creating and scheduling our timer when the app gets sent to the background:

```
- (BOOL) isMultitaskingSupported{

  BOOL result = NO;
  if ([[UIDevice currentDevice]
      respondsToSelector:@selector(isMultitaskingSupported)]){
    result = [[UIDevice currentDevice] isMultitaskingSupported];
  }
  return result;

}

- (void) timerMethod:(NSTimer *)paramSender{

  NSTimeInterval backgroundTimeRemaining =
    [[UIApplication sharedApplication] backgroundTimeRemaining];

  if (backgroundTimeRemaining == DBL_MAX){
    NSLog(@"Background Time Remaining = Undetermined");
  } else {
    NSLog(@"Background Time Remaining = %.02f Seconds",
          backgroundTimeRemaining);
  }

}
```

```
- (void)applicationDidEnterBackground:(UIApplication *)application{

  if ([self isMultitaskingSupported] == NO){
    return;
  }

  self.myTimer =
  [NSTimer scheduledTimerWithTimeInterval:1.0f
                                   target:self
                                 selector:@selector(timerMethod:)
                                 userInfo:nil
                                  repeats:YES];

  self.backgroundTaskIdentifier =
  [application beginBackgroundTaskWithExpirationHandler:^(void) {
    [self endBackgroundTask];
  }];

}
```

You can see that in the completion handler for our background task, we are calling the endBackgroundTask method of our app delegate. This is a method which we have written and it looks like this:

```
- (void) endBackgroundTask{

  dispatch_queue_t mainQueue = dispatch_get_main_queue();

  __weak Completing_a_Long_Running_Task_in_the_BackgroundAppDelegate
    *weakSelf = self;

  dispatch_async(mainQueue, ^(void) {

    Completing_a_Long_Running_Task_in_the_BackgroundAppDelegate
      *strongSelf = weakSelf;

    if (strongSelf != nil){
      [strongSelf.myTimer invalidate];
      [[UIApplication sharedApplication]
       endBackgroundTask:self.backgroundTaskIdentifier];
      strongSelf.backgroundTaskIdentifier = UIBackgroundTaskInvalid;
    }

  });

}
```

There are a couple of things we need to do to clean up after a long-running task:

1. End any threads or timers, whether they are foundation timers or they are created with GCD.

2. End the background task by calling the endBackgroundTask: method of UIApplication.

3. Mark our task as ended by assigning the value of UIBackgroundTaskInvalid to our task identifiers.

Last but not least, when our app is brought to the foreground, if we still have our background task running, we need to ensure that we get rid of it:

```
- (void)applicationWillEnterForeground:(UIApplication *)application{

    if (self.backgroundTaskIdentifier != UIBackgroundTaskInvalid){
      [self endBackgroundTask];
    }

}
```

In our example, whenever the application is put into the background, we ask for more time to finish a long-running task (in this case, for instance, our timer's code). In our time, we constantly read the value of the backgroundTimeRemaining property of UIApplication 's instance and print that value out to the console. In the beginBackgroundTask WithExpirationHandler: instance method of UIApplication, we provided the code that will be executed just before our application's extra time to execute a long-running task finishes (usually about 5 to 10 seconds before the expiration of the task). In here, we can simply end the task by calling the endBackgroundTask: instance method of UIApplication.

> When an application is sent to the background and the application has requested more execution time from iOS, before the execution time is finished, the application could be revived and brought to the foreground by the user again. If you had previously asked for a long-running task to be executed in the background when the application was being sent to the background, you must end the long-running task using the end BackgroundTask: instance method of UIApplication.

See Also

Recipe 14.1

14.3 Receiving Local Notifications in the Background

Problem

You want to present an alert to your user even when your application is not running. You want to create this alert locally inside your application without using push notifications.

Solution

Instantiate an object of type UILocalNotification and schedule it using the schedule LocalNotification: instance method of UIApplication:

```
- (BOOL) localNotificationWithMessage:(NSString *)paramMessage
                   actionButtonTitle:(NSString *)paramActionButtonTitle
                         launchImage:(NSString *)paramLaunchImage
                     applicationBadge:(NSInteger)paramApplicationBadge
                      secondsFromNow:(NSTimeInterval)paramSecondsFromNow
                            userInfo:(NSDictionary *)paramUserInfo{

  if ([paramMessage length] == 0){
    return NO;
  }

  UILocalNotification *notification = [[UILocalNotification alloc] init];
  notification.alertBody = paramMessage;
  notification.alertAction = paramActionButtonTitle;

  if ([paramActionButtonTitle length]> 0){
    /* Make sure we have the action button for the user to press
     to open our application */
    notification.hasAction = YES;
  } else {
    notification.hasAction = NO;
  }

  /* Here you have a chance to change the launch image of your application
   when the notification's action is viewed by the user */
  notification.alertLaunchImage = paramLaunchImage;

  /* Change the badge number of the application once the notification is
   presented to the user. Even if the user dismisses the notification,
   the badge number of the application will change */
  notification.applicationIconBadgeNumber = paramApplicationBadge;

  /* This dictionary will get passed to your application
   later if and when the user decides to view this notification */
  notification.userInfo = paramUserInfo;

  /* We need to get the system time zone so that the alert view
   will adjust its fire date if the user's time zone changes */
  NSTimeZone *timeZone = [NSTimeZone systemTimeZone];
  notification.timeZone = timeZone;

  /* Schedule the delivery of this notification x seconds from now */
  NSDate *today = [NSDate date];

  NSDate *fireDate = [today dateByAddingTimeInterval:paramSecondsFromNow];

  NSCalendar *calendar = [NSCalendar autoupdatingCurrentCalendar];

  NSUInteger dateComponents =
  NSYearCalendarUnit |
```

```
NSMonthCalendarUnit |
NSDayCalendarUnit |
NSHourCalendarUnit |
NSMinuteCalendarUnit |
NSSecondCalendarUnit;

NSDateComponents *components = [calendar components:dateComponents
                                              fromDate:fireDate];

/* Here you have a chance to change these components. That's why we
 retrieved the components of the date in the first place. */
fireDate = [calendar dateFromComponents:components];

/* Finally set the schedule date for this notification */
notification.fireDate = fireDate;

[[UIApplication sharedApplication] cancelAllLocalNotifications];

[[UIApplication sharedApplication] scheduleLocalNotification:notification];

return YES;

}
```

Discussion

A *local notification* is an alert view (an object of type UIAlertView) that gets presented to the user if your application is running in the background or not running at all. You can schedule the delivery of a local notification using the scheduleLocalNotifica tion: instance method of UIApplication. The cancelAllLocalNotifications instance method cancels the delivery of all pending local notifications.

You can ask iOS to deliver a local notification to the user in the future when your application is not even running. These notifications could also be recurring—for instance, every week at a certain time. However, extra care must be taken when you are specifying the *fire date* for your notifications.

For instance, let's say the time is now 13:00 in London, the time zone is GMT+0, and your application is currently running on a user's device. You want to be able to deliver a notification at 14:00 to your user, even if your application is not running at that time. Now your user is on a plane at London's Gatwick Airport and plans to fly to Stockholm where the time zone is GMT+1. If the flight takes 30 minutes, the user will be in Stockholm at 13:30 GMT+0. However, when he lands, the iOS device will detect the change in the time zone and will change the user's device time to 14:30. Your notification was supposed to occur at 14:00 (GMT+0), so as soon as the time zone is changed, iOS detects that the notification is due to be displayed (30 minutes late, in fact, with the new time zone) and will display your notification.

The issue is that your notification was supposed to be displayed at 14:00 GMT+0 or 15:00 GMT+1, and not 14:30 GMT+1. To deal with occasions such as this (which may be more common than you think, with modern travel habits), when specifying a date and time for your local notifications to be fired, you should also specify the time zone of the date and time you are specifying.

The previous code did not include the alert view that you'd need to write in order to have something to display to the user. Let's go ahead and add that code in our application and see what happens on iPhone Simulator in different scenarios. Here is the *.h* file of our application delegate:

```
#import <UIKit/UIKit.h>

@interface Receiving_Local_Notifications_in_the_BackgroundAppDelegate
        : UIResponder <UIApplicationDelegate>

@property (nonatomic, strong) UIWindow *window;

@end
```

Perfect! Now we will go to the `application:didReceiveLocalNotification:` method and see if a local notification has woken our app up. If not, we will schedule one:

```
- (BOOL)              application:(UIApplication *)application
  didFinishLaunchingWithOptions:(NSDictionary *)launchOptions{

  self.window = [[UIWindow alloc] initWithFrame:
                    [[UIScreen mainScreen] bounds]];

  self.window.backgroundColor = [UIColor whiteColor];
  [self.window makeKeyAndVisible];

  id scheduledLocalNotification =
  [launchOptions valueForKey:
   UIApplicationLaunchOptionsLocalNotificationKey];

  if (scheduledLocalNotification != nil){

    /* We received a local notification while
     our application wasn't running. You can now typecase the
     ScheduledLocalNotification variable to UILocalNotification and
     use it in your application */

    NSString *message = @"Local Notification Woke Us Up";
    [[[UIAlertView alloc] initWithTitle:@"Notification"
                            message:message
                            delegate:nil
                    cancelButtonTitle:@"OK"
                    otherButtonTitles:nil, nil] show];

  } else {

    NSString *message =@"A new instant message is available. \
    Would you like to read this message?";

    /* If a local notification didn't start our application,
     then we start a new local notification */
```

```
[self localNotificationWithMessage:message
               actionButtonTitle:@"Yes"
                     launchImage:nil
                 applicationBadge:1
                  secondsFromNow:10.0f
                        userInfo:nil];

message = @"A new Local Notification is set up \
to be displayed 10 seconds from now";

[[[UIAlertView alloc] initWithTitle:@"Set Up"
                            message:message
                           delegate:nil
                  cancelButtonTitle:@"OK"
                  otherButtonTitles:nil, nil] show];

}

return YES;
}
```

Last but not least, we will handle the `application:didReceiveLocalNotification:` method of our `UIApplicationDelegate` in our app delegate to make sure we display a message to the user if she opens our app because of a local notification:

```
- (void)              application:(UIApplication *)application
    didReceiveLocalNotification:(UILocalNotification *)notification{

  NSString *message = @"The Local Notification is delivered.";

  [[[UIAlertView alloc] initWithTitle:@"Local Notification"
                              message:message
                             delegate:nil
                    cancelButtonTitle:@"OK"
                    otherButtonTitles:nil, nil] show];

}
```

Now let's test the code. Here is Scenario 1: the user has just installed our application and will launch it for the first time. Figure 14-1 shows what he will see.

The user taps the OK button and stays in the application. Figure 14-2 depicts the message that will be shown to the user after the notification is delivered to our application.

When the application is running or even in the background (that is, it hasn't been terminated yet), iOS will call the `application:didReceiveLocalNotification:` method of our application delegate to let our application know a local notification has been delivered to us. If the user is inside the application, iOS will not do anything special and will not display a message. However, iOS does display a notification message automatically when our application is running in the background.

In Scenario 2, the user opens our application for the first time (as shown earlier in Figure 14-1) and immediately after pressing the OK button, presses the Home button

Figure 14-1. An indication of local notifications being set up

Figure 14-2. A local notification delivered while our app is running (Scenario 1)

on his iOS device, sending our application to the background. Now when the notification is delivered, our user will see a message similar to Figure 14-3.

Because we set the application badge number property of our local notification to 1 when we created the notification, our application's badge number is immediately set to 1 when the notification is delivered. The user doesn't have to close or accept the notification for the badge number to be changed. Now if the user presses the Yes button, iOS will launch the application associated with this local notification and the user will

Figure 14-3. A local notification delivered to an app in the background (Scenario 2)

see a screen similar to Figure 14-2. Please note that in this scenario, our application has not been terminated but sent to the background.

Scenario 3 is when our application runs for the first time (as shown earlier in Figure 14-1) and the user sends our application to the background. Then the user terminates our application manually by double-tapping the Home button and closing the application with the Close button that appears on the application icon when the user presses and holds her finger on the icon for a few seconds, as shown in Figure 14-4.

Once our application is terminated, the local notification will be displayed to the user after a few seconds (10 seconds from the time we scheduled the notification). Once the notification is delivered, the user will see a screen similar to Figure 14-3. After the user presses the Yes button, iOS will relaunch our application and the user will see a screen similar to Figure 14-5.

So, you can visually see how local notifications work. When our application is running in the foreground or the background, iOS will deliver the local notification through the `application:didReceiveLocalNotification:` delegate method. However, if our application has been terminated either by the user or by iOS, we will receive the local notification (that is, if the user decides to view it) through the application's `didFinishLaunchingWithOptions:` method. We can retrieve the notification using the `UIApplicationLaunchOptionsLocalNotificationKey` key of the `didFinishLaunchingWithOptions` parameter.

A local notification does not necessarily have to be an action notification. Action notifications have two buttons. You can change the title of one button through the `alertAction` property of `UILocalNotification`. The other button is an OK button that simply

Figure 14-4. The user attempting to terminate our application before the local notification is delivered (Scenario 3)

Figure 14-5. A local notification waking up the terminated app

dismisses the alert; you cannot change the title or action. If a notification is not an action notification (when the `hasAction` property of `UILocalNotification` is set to `NO`), the notification will simply have an OK button, and pressing this button will *not* re-launch your application.

14.4 Playing Audio in the Background

Problem

You are writing an application that plays audio files (such as a music player) and you would like the audio files to be played even if your application is running in the background.

Solution

Create a new array key in your application's main *.plist* file. Set the name of the key to `UIBackgroundModes`. Add the value `audio` to this new key. Here is an example of the contents of a *.plist* file with the aforementioned key and value added:

```
<dict>
  ...
  ...
  ...
  <key>UIBackgroundModes</key>
  <array>
    <string>audio</string>
  </array>
  ...
  ...
  ...
</dict>
```

Now you can use the AV Foundation to play audio files, and your audio files will be played even if your application is in the background.

Discussion

In iOS, applications can request that their audio files continue playing even if the application is sent to the background. AV Foundation's `AVAudioPlayer` is an easy-to-use audio player that we will use in this recipe. Our mission is to start an audio player and play a simple song, and while the song is playing, send the application to the background by pressing the Home button. If we have included the `UIBackgroundModes` key in our application's *.plist* file, iOS will continue playing the music from our app's audio player, even in the background. While in the background, we should only play music and provide our music player with the data that is necessary for it to run. We should not be performing any other tasks, such as displaying new screens.

Here is the *.h* file of a simple app delegate that starts an `AVAudioPlayer`:

```
#import <UIKit/UIKit.h>
#import <AVFoundation/AVFoundation.h>

@interface Playing_Audio_in_the_BackgroundAppDelegate
            : UIResponder <UIApplicationDelegate, AVAudioPlayerDelegate>

@property (nonatomic, strong) UIWindow *window;
```

```
@property (nonatomic, strong) AVAudioPlayer *audioPlayer;

@end
```

When our app opens, we will allocate and initialize our audio player, read the contents
of a file named *MySong.mp4* into an instance of NSData and use that data in the initialization process of our audio player:

```
- (BOOL)               application:(UIApplication *)application
  didFinishLaunchingWithOptions:(NSDictionary *)launchOptions{

  dispatch_queue_t dispatchQueue =
    dispatch_get_global_queue(DISPATCH_QUEUE_PRIORITY_DEFAULT, 0);

  dispatch_async(dispatchQueue, ^(void) {
    NSError *audioSessionError = nil;
    AVAudioSession *audioSession = [AVAudioSession sharedInstance];
    if ([audioSession setCategory:AVAudioSessionCategoryPlayback
                            error:&audioSessionError]){
      NSLog(@"Successfully set the audio session.");
    } else {
      NSLog(@"Could not set the audio session");
    }

    NSBundle *mainBundle = [NSBundle mainBundle];

    NSString *filePath = [mainBundle pathForResource:@"MySong"
                                              ofType:@"mp3"];

    NSData   *fileData = [NSData dataWithContentsOfFile:filePath];

    NSError  *error = nil;

    /* Start the audio player */
    self.audioPlayer = [[AVAudioPlayer alloc] initWithData:fileData
                                                     error:&error];

    /* Did we get an instance of AVAudioPlayer? */
    if (self.audioPlayer != nil){
      /* Set the delegate and start playing */

      self.audioPlayer.delegate = self;

      if ([self.audioPlayer prepareToPlay] &&
          [self.audioPlayer play]){
        NSLog(@"Successfully started playing...");       } else {
        NSLog(@"Failed to play.");
      }

    } else {
      /* Failed to instantiate AVAudioPlayer */
    }
  });

  self.window = [[UIWindow alloc] initWithFrame:
```

```
                    [[UIScreen mainScreen] bounds]];

        self.window.backgroundColor = [UIColor whiteColor];
        [self.window makeKeyAndVisible];

        return YES;
    }
```

 Please bear in mind that playing audio in the background might not work in iPhone Simulator. You need to test this recipe on a real device. On the simulator, chances are that the audio will stop playing once your application is sent to the background.

In this example code, we are using AV audio sessions to silence music playback from other applications (such as the iPod application) before starting to play the audio. For more information about audio sessions, please refer to Recipe 10.5. When in the background, you are not limited to playing only the current audio file. If the currently playing audio file (in the background) finishes playing, you can start another instance of AVAudioPlayer and play a completely new audio file. iOS will adjust the processing required for this, but there is no guarantee that while in the background, your application will be given permission to allocate enough memory to accommodate the data of the new sound file.

Another important thing to keep in mind is that while your application is running an audio file in the background, the value returned by the backgroundTimeRemaining property of UIApplication will not be changed. In other words, an application that requests to play audio files in the background is not implicitly or explicitly asking iOS for extra execution time.

14.5 Handling Location Changes in the Background

Problem

You are writing an application whose main functionality is processing location changes, using Core Location. You want the application to retrieve the iOS device location changes even if the application is sent to the background.

Solution

Add the location value to the UIBackgroundModes key of your main application .*plist* file, like so:

```
<dict>
  ...
  ...
  ...
  <key>UIBackgroundModes</key>
```

```
<array>
  <string>location</string>
</array>
...
...
...
</dict>
```

Discussion

When your application is running in the foreground, you can receive delegate messages from an instance of `CLLocationManager` telling you when iOS detects that the device is at a new location. However, if your application is sent to the background and is no longer active, the location delegate messages will not be delivered normally to your application. They will instead be delivered in a batch when your application again becomes the foreground application.

If you still want to be able to receive changes in the location of the user's device while running in the background, you must add the `location` value to the `UIBack groundModes` key of your application's main *.plist* file, as shown in this recipe's Solution. Once in the background, your application will continue to receive the changes in the device's location. Let's test this in a simple app with just the app delegate.

What I intend to do in this app is to keep a boolean value in the app delegate, called *executingInBackground*. When the app goes to the background, I will set this value to YES; when the app comes back to the foreground, I will set this value to NO. When we get location updates from CoreLocation, we will check this flag. If this flag is set to YES, then we won't do any heavy calculations or any UI update because, well, our app is in the background, and as a responsible programmer we should not do heavy processing while our app is in the background. If our app is in the foreground, however, we have all the device's processing power for the normal processing that we wish to do. We also will attempt to get the best location change accuracy when our app is in the foreground; when the app is sent to the background, we will be sure to ask for less accuracy in location updates to ease the strain on the location sensors. So let's go ahead and define our app delegate:

```
#import <UIKit/UIKit.h>
#import <CoreLocation/CoreLocation.h>
@interface Handling_Location_Changes_in_the_BackgroundAppDelegate
           : UIResponder <UIApplicationDelegate, CLLocationManagerDelegate>

@property (nonatomic, strong) UIWindow *window;
@property (nonatomic, strong) CLLocationManager *myLocationManager;
@property (nonatomic, unsafe_unretained, getter=isExecutingInBackground)
  BOOL executingInBackground;

@end
```

Now let's go ahead and create and start our location manager when our app starts:

```
- (BOOL)            application:(UIApplication *)application
    didFinishLaunchingWithOptions:(NSDictionary *)launchOptions{

    self.myLocationManager = [[CLLocationManager alloc] init];
    self.myLocationManager.desiredAccuracy = kCLLocationAccuracyBest;
    self.myLocationManager.delegate = self;
    [self.myLocationManager startUpdatingLocation];

    self.window = [[UIWindow alloc] initWithFrame:
                    [[UIScreen mainScreen] bounds]];
    self.window.backgroundColor = [UIColor whiteColor];
    [self.window makeKeyAndVisible];
    return YES;
}
```

You can see that we have set the desired accuracy of our location manager to a high
level. However, when we go to the background, we want to lower this accuracy to give
iOS a bit of a rest:

```
- (void)applicationDidEnterBackground:(UIApplication *)application{
    self.executingInBackground = YES;

    /* Reduce the accuracy to ease the strain on
       iOS while we are in the background */
    self.myLocationManager.desiredAccuracy = kCLLocationAccuracyHundredMeters;
}
```

When our app is awakened from the background, we can change this accuracy back
to a high level:

```
- (void)applicationWillEnterForeground:(UIApplication *)application{
    self.executingInBackground = NO;

    /* Now that our app is in the foreground again, let's increase the location
       detection accuracy */
    self.myLocationManager.desiredAccuracy = kCLLocationAccuracyBest;
}
```

Additionally, we would like to avoid doing any intense processing when we get a new
location from the location manager while our app is in the background, so we need to
handle the locationManager:didUpdateToLocation:fromLocation: delegate method of
our location manager in this way:

```
- (void)locationManager:(CLLocationManager *)manager
    didUpdateToLocation:(CLLocation *)newLocation
           fromLocation:(CLLocation *)oldLocation{

    if ([self isExecutingInBackground]){
        /* We are in the background. Do not do any heavy processing */
    } else {
        /* We are in the foreground. Do any processing that you wish */
    }

}
```

The simple rule here is that if we are in the background, we should be using the smallest amount of memory and processing power to satisfy our application's needs. So, by decreasing the accuracy of the location manager while in the background, we are decreasing the amount of processing iOS has to do to deliver new locations to our application.

 Depending on the version of iOS Simulator you are testing your applications with, as well as the settings of your network connection and many other factors that affect this process, background location processing might not work for you. Please test your applications, including the source code in this recipe, on a real device.

14.6 Saving and Loading the State of Multitasking iOS Apps

Problem

You want the state of your iOS app to be saved when it is sent to the background, and for the same state to resume when the application is brought to the foreground.

Solution

Use a combination of the UIApplicationDelegate protocol's messages sent to your application delegate and the notifications sent by iOS to preserve the state of your multitasking apps.

Discussion

When an empty iOS application (an application with just one window and no code written for it) is run on an iOS device with support for multitasking for the first time (not from the background), the following UIApplicationDelegate messages will be sent to your app delegate, in this order:

1. application:didFinishLaunchingWithOptions:
2. applicationDidBecomeActive:

If the user presses the Home button on her iOS device, your app delegate will receive these messages, in this order:

1. applicationWillResignActive:
2. applicationDidEnterBackground:

Once the application is in the background, the user can press the Home button twice and select our application from the list of background applications. (The way our app is brought to the foreground doesn't really matter. For all we know, another app might launch our app through URI schemes that we can expose in our app.) Once our application is brought to the foreground again, we will receive these messages in the application delegate, in this order:

1. `applicationWillEnterForeground:`
2. `applicationDidBecomeActive:`

In addition to these messages, we will also receive various notification messages from iOS when our application is sent to the background or brought to the foreground again.

To save and load back the state of your apps, you need to think carefully about the tasks you need to pause when going into the background, and then resume when the application is brought to the foreground. Let me give you an example. As will be mentioned in Recipe 14.7, network connections can be easily resumed by the system itself, so we might not need to do anything special if we're downloading a file from the network. However, if you are writing a game, for instance, it is best to listen for the notifications iOS sends when your application is being sent to the background, and to act accordingly. In such a scenario, you can simply put the game engine into a paused state. You can also put the state of the sound engine into a paused state if necessary.

After an application is sent to the background, it has about 10 seconds to save any unsaved data and prepare itself to be brought to the foreground at any moment by the user. You can optionally ask for extra execution time if required (further information about this is available in Recipe 14.2).

Let's demonstrate saving your state with an example. Suppose we are writing a game for iOS. When our game is sent to the background, we want to:

1. Put the game engine into a paused state.
2. Save the user's score to disk.
3. Save the current level's data to disk. This includes where the user is in the level, the physical aspects of the level, the camera position, and so on.

When the user opens the application again, bringing the application to the foreground, we want to:

1. Load the user's score from disk.
2. Load the level the user was playing the last time from disk.
3. Resume the game engine.

Now let's say our app delegate is our game engine. Let's define a few methods in the app delegate's header file:

```
#import <UIKit/UIKit.h>

@interface Saving_and_Loading_the_State_of_Multitasking_iOS_AppsAppDelegate
        : UIResponder <UIApplicationDelegate>

@property (strong, nonatomic) UIWindow *window;
```

```
/* Saving the state of our app */
- (void) saveUserScore;
- (void) saveLevelToDisk;
- (void) pauseGameEngine;

/* Loading the state of our app */
- (void) loadUserScore;
- (void) loadLevelFromDisk;
- (void) resumeGameEngine;

@end
```

We will proceed to place stub implementations of these methods in the implementation file of our app delegate:

```
#import "Saving_and_Loading_the_State_of_Multitasking_iOS_AppsAppDelegate.h"

@implementation
  Saving_and_Loading_the_State_of_Multitasking_iOS_AppsAppDelegate

- (void) saveUserScore{
  /* Save the user score here */
}

- (void) saveLevelToDisk{
  /* Save the current level and the user's location on map to disk */
}

- (void) pauseGameEngine{
  /* Pause the game engine here */
}

- (void) loadUserScore{
  /* Load the user's location back to memory */
}

- (void) loadLevelFromDisk{
  /* Load the user's previous location on the map */
}

- (void) resumeGameEngine{
  /* Resume the game engine here */
}

...
```

Now we need to make sure that our app is able to handle interruptions, such as incoming calls on an iPhone. On such occasions, our app won't be sent to the background, but will become inactive. When the user finishes a phone call, for instance, iOS will bring our app to the active state. So when our app becomes inactive, we need to make sure we are pausing our game engine; when the app becomes active again, we can resume our game engine. We don't need to save anything to the disk when our app becomes inactive really (at least in this example), because iOS will bring our app to its previous state once it becomes active again:

```
- (void)applicationWillResignActive:(UIApplication *)application{
    [self pauseGameEngine];
}

- (void)applicationDidBecomeActive:(UIApplication *)application{
    [self resumeGameEngine];
}
```

And now, simply, when our app is sent to the background, we will save the state of our game and when our app is back in the foreground, we will load the state back:

```
- (void)applicationDidEnterBackground:(UIApplication *)application{
    [self saveUserScore];
    [self saveLevelToDisk];
    [self pauseGameEngine];
}

- (void)applicationWillEnterForeground:(UIApplication *)application{
    [self loadUserScore];
    [self loadLevelFromDisk];
    [self resumeGameEngine];
}
```

Not every application is a game. However, you can use this technique to load and save the state of your application in the multitasking environment of iOS.

See Also

Recipe 14.2

14.7 Handling Network Connections in the Background

Problem

You are using instances of NSURLConnection to send and receive data to and from a web server and are wondering how you can allow your application to work in the multitasking environment of iOS without connection failures.

Solution

Make sure you support connection failures in the block objects that you submit to your connection objects.

Discussion

For applications that use NSURLConnection but do not borrow extra time from iOS when they are sent to the background, connection handling is truly simple. Let's go through an example to see how an asynchronous connection will act if the application is sent to the background and brought to the foreground again. For this, let's send an asynchronous connection request to retrieve the contents of a URL (say, Apple's home page):

```
- (BOOL)                 application:(UIApplication *)application
  didFinishLaunchingWithOptions:(NSDictionary *)launchOptions{

    NSString *urlAsString = @"http://www.apple.com";
    NSURL *url = [NSURL URLWithString:urlAsString];
    NSURLRequest *urlRequest = [NSURLRequest requestWithURL:url];
    NSOperationQueue *queue = [[NSOperationQueue alloc] init];

    [NSURLConnection
     sendAsynchronousRequest:urlRequest
     queue:queue
     completionHandler:^(NSURLResponse *response, NSData *data, NSError *error) {

        if ([data length] > 0 &&
            error != nil){
          /* Date did come back */
        }
        else if ([data length] == 0 &&
                 error != nil){
          /* No data came back */
        }
        else if (error != nil){
          /* Error happened. Make sure you handle this properly */
        }

    }];

    self.window = [[UIWindow alloc] initWithFrame:
                   [[UIScreen mainScreen] bounds]];

    self.window.backgroundColor = [UIColor whiteColor];
    [self.window makeKeyAndVisible];
    return YES;
}
```

 I advise you to replace the Apple home page URL in this example with the URL to a rather large file on the Internet. The reason is that if your app is downloading a large file, you will have more time to play with the app and send it to the background and bring it to the foreground. Whereas, if you are on a rather fast Internet connection and you are just downloading Apple's home page, chances are that the connection is going to retrieve the data for you in a second or two.

In the foreground, our application will continue downloading the file. While downloading, the user can press the Home button and send the application to the background. What you will observe is true magic! iOS will automatically put the download process into a paused state for you. When the user brings your application to the foreground again, the downloading will resume without you writing a single line of code to handle multitasking.

Now let's see what happens with synchronous connections. We are going to download a very big file on the main thread (a very bad practice—do not do this in a production application!) as soon as our application launches:

```
- (BOOL)              application:(UIApplication *)application
    didFinishLaunchingWithOptions:(NSDictionary *)launchOptions{

    /* Replace this URL with the URL of a file that is rather big in size */
    NSString *urlAsString = @"http://www.apple.com";
    NSURL *url = [NSURL URLWithString:urlAsString];
    NSURLRequest *urlRequest = [NSURLRequest requestWithURL:url];
    NSError *error = nil;

    NSData *connectionData = [NSURLConnection  sendSynchronousRequest:urlRequest
                                                   returningResponse:nil
                                                               error:&error];

    if ([connectionData length] > 0 &&
        error == nil){    }
    else if ([connectionData length] == 0 &&
              error == nil){

    }
    else if (error != nil){

    }

    self.window = [[UIWindow alloc] initWithFrame:
                    [[UIScreen mainScreen] bounds]];

    self.window.backgroundColor = [UIColor whiteColor];
    [self.window makeKeyAndVisible];
    return YES;
}
```

If you run this application and send it to the background, you will notice that the application's GUI is sent to the background, but the application's core is never sent to the background and the appropriate delegate messages— applicationWillRe signActive: and applicationDidEnterBackground: —will never be received. I have conducted this test on an iPhone.

The problem with this approach is that we are consuming the main thread's time slice by downloading files synchronously. We can fix this by either downloading the files asynchronously on the main thread, as mentioned before, or downloading them synchronously on separate threads.

Take the previous sample code, for example. If we download the same big file synchronously on a global concurrent queue, the connection will be paused when the application is sent to the background, and will resume once it is brought to the foreground again:

```
- (BOOL)               application:(UIApplication *)application
  didFinishLaunchingWithOptions:(NSDictionary *)launchOptions{

  dispatch_queue_t dispatchQueue =
    dispatch_get_global_queue(DISPATCH_QUEUE_PRIORITY_DEFAULT, 0);

  dispatch_async(dispatchQueue, ^(void) {

    /* Replace this URL with the URL of a file that is rather big in size */
    NSString *urlAsString = @"http://www.apple.com";
    NSURL *url = [NSURL URLWithString:urlAsString];
    NSURLRequest *urlRequest = [NSURLRequest requestWithURL:url];
    NSError *error = nil;

    NSData *connectionData = [NSURLConnection  sendSynchronousRequest:urlRequest
                                                   returningResponse:nil
                                                               error:&error];

    if ([connectionData length] > 0 &&
        error == nil){

    }
    else if ([connectionData length] == 0 &&
             error == nil){

    }
    else if (error != nil){

    }
  });

  self.window = [[UIWindow alloc] initWithFrame:
                  [[UIScreen mainScreen] bounds]];

  self.window.backgroundColor = [UIColor whiteColor];
  [self.window makeKeyAndVisible];
  return YES;
}
```

See Also

Recipe 14.2

14.8 Handling Notifications Delivered to a Waking App

Problem

When your application is brought to the foreground, you want to be able to get notifications about important system changes, such as the user's locale changes.

Solution

Simply listen to one of the many system notifications that iOS sends to waking applications. Some of these notifications are listed here:

NSCurrentLocaleDidChangeNotification
> This notification is delivered to applications when the user changes her locale: for instance, if the user switches his iOS device's language from English to Spanish in the Settings page of the device.

NSUserDefaultsDidChangeNotification
> This notification is fired when the user changes the application's settings in the Settings page of the iOS device (if any settings are provided to the user).

UIDeviceBatteryStateDidChangeNotification
> This notification gets sent whenever the state of the battery of the iOS device is changed. For instance, if the device is plugged into a computer when the application is in the foreground and then unplugged when in the background, the application will receive this notification (if the application has registered for this notification). The state can then be read using the batteryState property of an instance of UIDevice.

UIDeviceProximityStateDidChangeNotification
> This notification gets sent whenever the state of the proximity sensor changes. The last state is available through the proximityState property of an instance of UIDevice.

Discussion

When your application is in the background, a lot of things could happen! For instance, the user might suddenly change the locale of her iOS device through the Settings page from English to Spanish. Applications can register themselves for such notifications. These notifications will be coalesced and then delivered to a waking application. Let me explain what I mean by the term *coalesced*. Suppose your application is in the foreground and you have registered for UIDeviceOrientationDidChangeNotification notifications. Now the user presses the Home button and your application gets sent to the background. The user then rotates the device from portrait, to landscape right, to portrait, and then to landscape left. When the user brings your application to the foreground, you will receive only one notification of type UIDeviceOrientationDidChangeNotification. This is coalescing. All the other orientations that happened along the way before your application opens are not important (since your application isn't on the screen) and the system will not deliver them to your application. However, the system will deliver you at least one notification for each aspect of the system, such as orientation, and you can then detect the most up-to-date orientation of the device.

Here is the implementation of a simple view controller that takes advantage of this technique to determine changes in orientation:

```
#import "Handling_Notifications_Delivered_to_a_Waking_AppViewController.h"

@implementation Handling_Notifications_Delivered_to_a_Waking_AppViewController

- (void) orientationChanged:(NSNotification *)paramNotification{
  NSLog(@"Orientation Changed");
}

- (void)viewDidLoad{
  [super viewDidLoad];

  [[NSNotificationCenter defaultCenter]
   addObserver:self
   selector:@selector(orientationChanged:)
   name:UIDeviceOrientationDidChangeNotification
   object:nil];

}

- (void)viewDidUnload{
  [super viewDidUnload];

  [[NSNotificationCenter defaultCenter] removeObserver:self];

}

- (BOOL)shouldAutorotateToInterfaceOrientation
        :(UIInterfaceOrientation)interfaceOrientation{
  return YES;
}

@end
```

Run the application on the device now. After the view controller is displayed on the screen, press the Home button to send the application to the background. Now try changing the orientation of the device a couple of times, and then relaunch the application. Observe the results, and you will see that initially when your application opens, at most one notification will be sent to the **orientationChanged:** method. You might get a second call, though, if your view hierarchy supports orientation changes.

14.9 Responding to Changes in App Settings

Problem

Your application exposes a settings bundle to the user. You want to get notified of the changes the user has made to your application's settings (while the application was in the background) as soon as your application is brought to the foreground.

Solution

Register for the NSUserDefaultsDidChangeNotification notification.

Discussion

Applications written for iOS can expose a bundle file for their settings. These settings will be available to users through the Settings application on their device. To get a better understanding of how this works, let's create a settings bundle:

1. In Xcode, choose File → New File.
2. Make sure the iOS category is selected on the left.
3. Choose the Resources subcategory.
4. Choose Settings Bundle as the file type and click Next.
5. Set the filename as *Settings.bundle*.
6. Click Save.

Now you have a file in Xcode named *Settings.bundle*. Leave this file as it is, without modifying it. Put the code in this recipe's Solution into your root view controller and run the application. Press the Home button on the device and go to the device's Settings application. If you have named your application "foo" you will see "Foo" in the Settings application, as shown in Figure 14-6 (the name of the sample application I created is "Responding to Changes in App Settings").

Figure 14-6. Our Settings.bundle displayed in the Settings app on iOS Simulator

Tap on your application's name to see the settings your application exposes to the user, as shown in Figure 14-7.

Let's go ahead and start listening for NSUserDefaultsDidChangeNotification notifications in our app delegate. When our app terminates, obviously, we will remove our app delegate from the notification chain:

```
#import "Responding_to_Changes_in_App_SettingsAppDelegate.h"
```

Figure 14-7. The contents of the default Settings.bundle

```
@implementation Responding_to_Changes_in_App_SettingsAppDelegate

- (void) settingsChanged:(NSNotification *)paramNotification{
  NSLog(@"Settings changed");
  NSLog(@"Notification Object = %@", [paramNotification object]);

}

- (BOOL)             application:(UIApplication *)application
  didFinishLaunchingWithOptions:(NSDictionary *)launchOptions{

  [[NSNotificationCenter defaultCenter]
   addObserver:self
   selector:@selector(settingsChanged:)
   name:NSUserDefaultsDidChangeNotification
   object:nil];

  self.window = [[UIWindow alloc] initWithFrame:
                 [[UIScreen mainScreen] bounds]];

  self.window.backgroundColor = [UIColor whiteColor];
  [self.window makeKeyAndVisible];
  return YES;
}

- (void)applicationWillTerminate:(UIApplication *)application{
  [[NSNotificationCenter defaultCenter] removeObserver:self];
}

@end
```

Now try to change some of these settings while your application is running in the background. After you are done, bring the application to the foreground and you will see that only one NSUserDefaultsDidChangeNotification notification will be delivered

to your application. The object attached to this notification will be of type `NSUser`
`Defaults` and will contain your application's settings `user defaults`.

14.10 Opting Out of Multitasking

Problem

You do not want your application to participate in multitasking.

Solution

Add the `UIApplicationExitsOnSuspend` key to your application's main *.plist* file and set
the value to `true`:

```
<dict>
   ...
   ...
   ...
   <key>UIApplicationExitsOnSuspend</key>
   <true/>
   ...
   ...
   ...
</dict>
```

Discussion

In some circumstances, you might require your iOS applications not to be multitasking
(although I strongly encourage you to develop your applications to be multitasking-
aware). In such cases, you can add the `UIApplicationExitsOnSuspend` key to your application's main *.plist* file. Devices on the latest iOS versions that support multitasking
understand this value and the OS will terminate an application with this key set to
true in the application's *.plist* file. On earlier iOS versions without support for multitasking, this value will have no meaning to the operating system and will be ignored.

When such an application runs on the latest iOS, the following application delegate
messages will be posted to your application:

1. `application:didFinishLaunchingWithOptions:`
2. `applicationDidBecomeActive:`

If the user presses the Home button on the device, the following messages will be sent
to your application delegate:

1. `applicationDidEnterBackground:`
2. `applicationWillTerminate:`

CHAPTER 15

Core Data

15.0 Introduction

Core Data is a powerful framework on the iOS SDK that allows programmers to store and manage data in an object-oriented way. Traditionally, programmers had to store their data on disk using the archiving capabilities of Objective-C, or write their data to files and manage them manually. With the introduction of Core Data, programmers can simply interact with its object-oriented interface to manage their data efficiently. In this chapter, you will learn how to use Core Data to create the model of your application (in the Model-View-Controller software architecture).

Core Data interacts with a persistent store at a lower level that is not visible to the programmer. iOS decides how the low-level data management is implemented. All the programmer must know is the high-level API she is provided with. But understanding the structure of Core Data and how it works internally is very important. Let's create a Core Data application to understand this a bit better.

Core Data in an iOS application needs a bit of setting up. Fortunately, with Xcode, this process is very easy. You can simply create a Core Data application and leave the rest up to Xcode.

Follow these instructions to create a project in Xcode that uses Core Data:

1. Open Xcode, if it's not open already.
2. From the File menu, select New → New Project...
3. In the New Project dialog, make sure iOS is the main category on the left and Application is the subcategory under it. Then on the righthand side of the dialog, choose Empty Application and press Next, as shown in Figure 15-1.
4. Now, for your product name, choose Introduction to Core Data and make sure the User Core Data checkbox is checked, as shown in Figure 15-2. Once done, press the Next button.

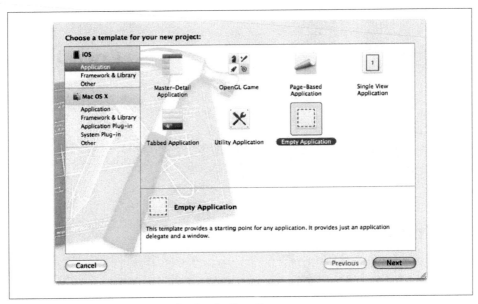

Figure 15-1. Creating an empty application for Core Data

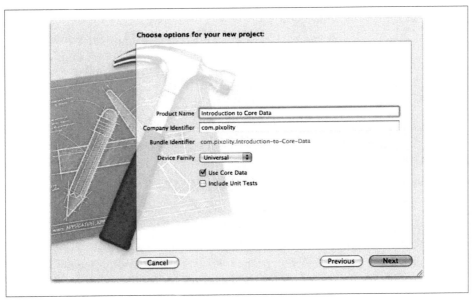

Figure 15-2. Setting up a project to use Core Data

5. Now you must choose where to save your project. Once you are done selecting the destination folder, press the Create button, as shown in Figure 15-3.

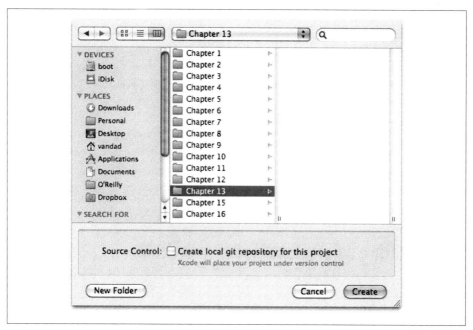

Figure 15-3. Selecting where to save our Core Data project

Now in Xcode, find the file named *Introduction_to_Core_DataAppDelegate.h*. This is the shared delegate of our application, since our application is universal. Both the iPad and iPhone application delegates will use this delegate as their superclass. If you have a look at the contents of this file, you will find that three properties were added to the declaration of the application delegate for you. These properties are:

- managedObjectContext (of type NSManagedObjectContext)
- managedObjectModel (of type NSManagedObjectModel)
- persistentStoreCoordinator (of type NSPersistentStoreCoordinator)

I know this is new and probably confusing to you, but by comparing these new concepts to existing database concepts, it will become easier for you to digest:

Persistent store coordinator
This is the bridge or the connection between the physical file that stores our data and our application. This bridge will be responsible for managing different object contexts.

Managed object model
This is the same concept as a schema in a database. This could represent the tables in a database or the different types of managed objects we can create in our database.

Managed object context

> This is the bridge between the programmer and the managed object model. Using the managed object context, you can insert a new row into a new table, read rows from a certain table, and so on. (Actually, Core Data doesn't use the concept of a "table," but I'm using the term here because it's familiar and will help you understand how Core Data works.)

Managed object

> This is similar to a row in a table. We insert managed objects into the managed object context and save the context. This way, we create a new row in a table in our database.

In Recipe 15.1, you will learn how to create a Core Data model using Xcode. This is the first step toward creating a database *schema*.

15.1 Creating a Core Data Model with Xcode

Problem

You want to visually design the data model of your iOS application using Xcode.

Solution

Follow the instructions in this chapter's Introduction to create a Core Data project. Then find the file with the extension of *xcdatamodel* in your application bundle in Xcode and click on it to open the visual data editor, as shown in Figure 15-4.

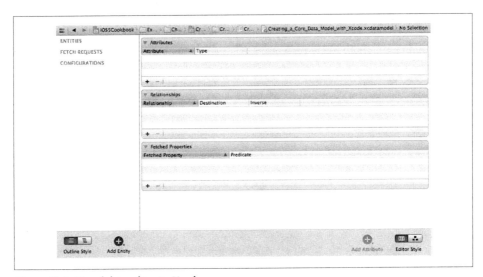

Figure 15-4. Visual data editor in Xcode

Discussion

Xcode's visual data editor is a fantastic tool that allows programmers to design the data model of their applications with ease. There are two important definitions you need to learn before you can work with this tool:

Entity
> Corresponds to a table in a database.

Attribute
> Corresponds to a column in a table.

Entities will later become objects (managed objects) when we generate the code based on our object model. This is explained in Recipe 15.2. For now, in this recipe, we will concentrate on creating the data model in this tool.

In the editor, find the + button at the bottom. Press and hold your mouse button on this button and then select Add Entity from the menu that will appear, as shown in Figure 15-5.

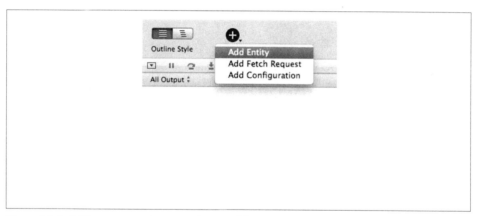

Figure 15-5. Adding a new entity to our data model

Your new entity will be created and will be in a state where you can immediately rename it after creation. Change the name of this entity to Person, as shown in Figure 15-6.

Select the `Person` entity, then select the + button in the Attributes pane (see Figure 15-7) and create the following three attributes for it (the results are shown in Figure 15-8:

* `firstName` (of type `String`).
* `lastName` (of type `String`).
* `age` (of type `Integer 32`).

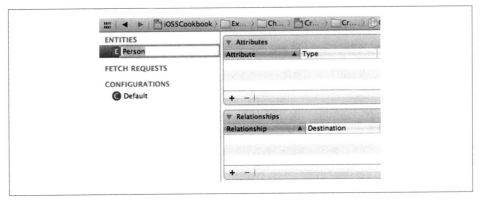

Figure 15-6. Changing the name of the new entity to Person

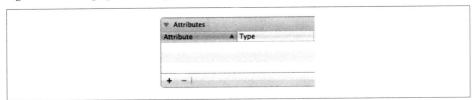

Figure 15-7. The Attributes box

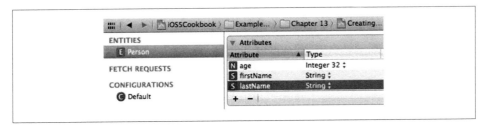

Figure 15-8. We have added three attributes to the Person entity

While you are in the data model editor, from the View menu in Xcode, choose Utilities→ Show Utilities. The utilities pane will open on the righthand side of Xcode. On top, choose the Data Model Inspector button and make sure that you have clicked on the Person entity that we just created. At this point, the Data Model inspector will be populated with items relevant to the Person entity, as shown in Figure 15-9.

Now click on the firstName, lastName, and the age attributes of the Person entity. Make sure the firstName and the lastName attributes are *not optional* by unticking the Optional checkbox and make sure the age field is optional by ticking the Optional checkbox.

Now your data model in the editor should look similar to that depicted in Figure 15-10.

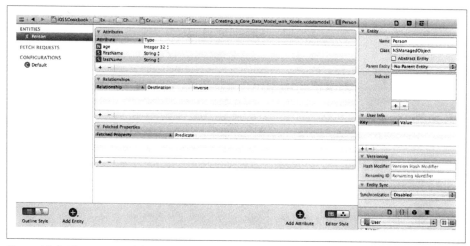

Figure 15-9. The Data Model Inspector shown on the right side of the Xcode window

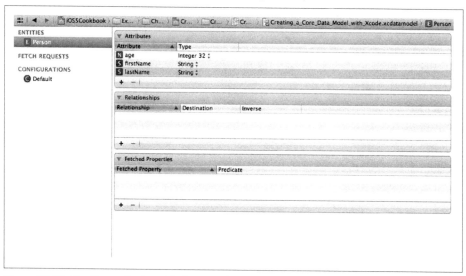

Figure 15-10. The Person Entity with three attributes

OK, we are done creating the model. Choose File → Save to make sure your changes are saved. To learn how to generate code based on the managed object you just created, refer to Recipe 15.2.

15.2 Generating Class Files for Core Data Entities

Problem

You followed the instructions inRecipe 15.1 and you want to know how to create code based on your object model.

Solution

Follow these steps:

1. In Xcode, find the file with the *xcdatamodel* extension that was created for your application when you created the application itself in Xcode. Click on the file, and you should see the editor on the righthand side of the Xcode window.

2. Select the Person entity that we created earlier (see Recipe 15.1).

3. Select File → New File in Xcode.

4. In the New File dialog, make sure you have selected iOS as the main category and Core Data as the subcategory. Then choose the NSManagedObject subclass item from the righthand side of the dialog and press Next, as shown in Figure 15-11.

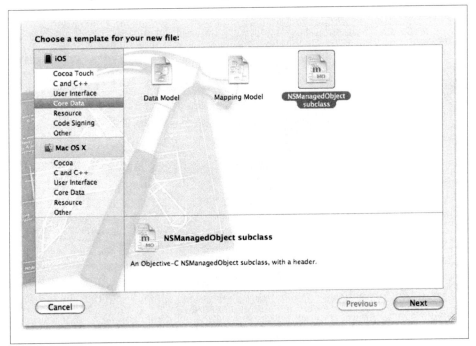

Figure 15-11. Creating a managed object subclass in Xcode

5. Now choose where to save your files in your project and press Create, as shown in Figure 15-12.

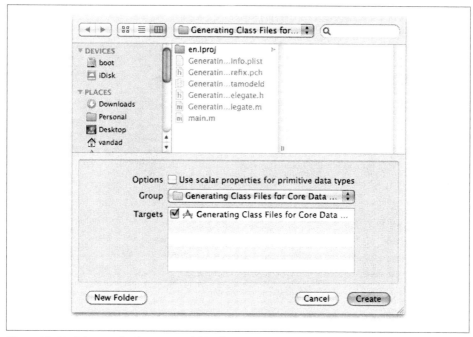

Figure 15-12. Selecting the destination folder for the managed object

Now you will see two new files in your project, called *Person.h* and *Person.m*. Open the contents of the *Person.h* file. It will look like the following:

```
#import <Foundation/Foundation.h>
#import <CoreData/CoreData.h>


@interface Person : NSManagedObject {
@private
}
@property (nonatomic, retain) NSString * firstName;
@property (nonatomic, retain) NSString * lastName;
@property (nonatomic, retain) NSNumber * age;

@end
```

The *Person.m* file is implemented for you in this way:

```
#import "Person.h"


@implementation Person
@dynamic firstName;
@dynamic lastName;
@dynamic age;

@end
```

There you go! We turned our managed object into a real definition and implementation. In Recipe 15.3, you will learn how to instantiate and save a managed object of type `Person` into the managed object context of your application.

Discussion

When you create your data model using the editor in Xcode, you are creating the data relationships, entities, attributes, and so forth. However, to be able to use your model in your app, you must generate the code for your model. If you view the *.h* and *.m* files for your entities, you will realize that all the attributes are assigned dynamically. You can even see the `@dynamic` directive in the *.m* file of your entities to tell the compiler that you will fulfill the request of each attribute at runtime using dynamic method resolution.

None of the code that Core Data runs on your entities is visible to you, and there is no need for it to be visible to the programmer in the first place. All you have to know is that a `Person` entity has three attributes named `firstName`, `lastName`, and `age`. You can assign values to these attributes (if they are read/write properties) and you can save to and load them from the context, as we'll see in Recipe 15.3.

15.3 Creating and Saving Data Using Core Data

Problem

You have already created a managed object and you want to instantiate it and insert that instance into your app's Core Data context.

Solution

Follow the instructions in Recipe 15.1 and Recipe 15.2. Now you can use the `insertNewObjectForEntityForName:inManagedObjectContext:` class method of `NSEntityDescription` to create a new object of a type specified by the first parameter of this method. Once the new entity (the managed object) is created, you can modify it by changing its properties. After you are done, save your managed object context using the `save:` instance method of the managed object context.

I'll assume that you have created a universal application in Xcode with the name Creating and Saving Data Using Core Data; now, follow these steps to insert a new managed object into the context:

1. Find the file named *Creating_and_Saving_Data_Using_Core_DataAppDelegate.m.*
2. Import the *Person.h* file into the app delegate's implementation file:

Person is the entity we created in Recipe 15.1.

```objc
#import "Creating_and_Saving_Data_Using_Core_DataAppDelegate.h"
#import "Person.h"

@implementation Creating_and_Saving_Data_Using_Core_DataAppDelegate

@synthesize managedObjectContext = _managedObjectContext;
@synthesize managedObjectModel = _managedObjectModel;
@synthesize persistentStoreCoordinator = _persistentStoreCoordinator;

...
```

3. In the `application:didFinishLaunchingWithOptions:` method of your shared application delegate, write this code:

```objc
- (BOOL)             application:(UIApplication *)application
didFinishLaunchingWithOptions:(NSDictionary *)launchOptions{
  self.window = [[UIWindow alloc] initWithFrame:
               [[UIScreen mainScreen] bounds]];

  Person *newPerson = [NSEntityDescription
                     insertNewObjectForEntityForName:@"Person"
                     inManagedObjectContext:self.managedObjectContext];

  if (newPerson != nil){

    newPerson.firstName = @"Anthony";
    newPerson.lastName = @"Robbins";
    newPerson.age = [NSNumber numberWithUnsignedInteger:51];

    NSError *savingError = nil;

    if ([self.managedObjectContext save:&savingError]){
      NSLog(@"Successfully saved the context.");
    } else {
      NSLog(@"Failed to save the context. Error = %@", savingError);
    }

  } else {
    NSLog(@"Failed to create the new person.");
  }

  self.window.backgroundColor = [UIColor whiteColor];
  [self.window makeKeyAndVisible];
  return YES;
}
```

Discussion

Previous recipes showed how to create entities and generate code based on them using the editor in Xcode. The next thing we need to do is start using those entities and instantiate them. For this, we use `NSEntityDescription` and call its `insertNewObjectFor EntityForName:inManagedObjectContext:` class method. This will look up the given entity (specified by its name as `NSString`) in the given managed object context. If the entity is found, the method will return a new instance of that entity. This is similar to creating a new row (managed object) in a table (entity) in a database (managed object context).

 Attempting to insert an unknown entity into a managed object context will raise an exception of type `NSInternalInconsistencyException`.

After inserting a new entity into the context, we must save the context. This will flush all the unsaved data of the context to the persistent store. We can do this using the `save:` instance method of our managed object context. If the `BOOL` return value of this method is `YES`, we can be sure that our context is saved. In Recipe 15.4, you will learn how to read the data back to memory.

15.4 Reading Data from Core Data

Problem

You want to be able to read the contents of your entities (tables) using Core Data.

Solution

Use an instance of `NSFetchRequest`:

```
- (BOOL) createNewPersonWithFirstName:(NSString *)paramFirstName
                            lastName:(NSString *)paramLastName
                                 age:(NSUInteger)paramAge{

    BOOL result = NO;

    if ([paramFirstName length] == 0 ||
        [paramLastName length] == 0){
      NSLog(@"First and Last names are mandatory.");
      return NO;
    }

    Person *newPerson = [NSEntityDescription
                         insertNewObjectForEntityForName:@"Person"
                         inManagedObjectContext:self.managedObjectContext];

    if (newPerson == nil){
```

```
      NSLog(@"Failed to create the new person.");
      return NO;
  }

  newPerson.firstName = paramFirstName;
  newPerson.lastName = paramLastName;
  newPerson.age = [NSNumber numberWithUnsignedInteger:paramAge];

  NSError *savingError = nil;

  if ([self.managedObjectContext save:&savingError]){
    return YES;
  } else {
    NSLog(@"Failed to save the new person. Error = %@", savingError);
  }

  return result;

}

- (BOOL)              application:(UIApplication *)application
  didFinishLaunchingWithOptions:(NSDictionary *)launchOptions{

  [self createNewPersonWithFirstName:@"Anthony"
                           lastName:@"Robbins"
                                age:51];

  [self createNewPersonWithFirstName:@"Richard"
                           lastName:@"Branson"
                                age:61];


  /* Create the fetch request first */
  NSFetchRequest *fetchRequest = [[NSFetchRequest alloc] init];

  /* Here is the entity whose contents we want to read */
  NSEntityDescription *entity =
  [NSEntityDescription
   entityForName:@"Person"
   inManagedObjectContext:self.managedObjectContext];

  /* Tell the request that we want to read the
   contents of the Person entity */
  [fetchRequest setEntity:entity];

  NSError *requestError = nil;
  /* And execute the fetch request on the context */
  NSArray *persons =
  [self.managedObjectContext executeFetchRequest:fetchRequest
                                         error:&requestError];

  /* Make sure we get the array */
  if ([persons count] > 0){

    /* Go through the persons array one by one */
```

```
        NSUInteger counter = 1;
        for (Person *thisPerson in persons){

            NSLog(@"Person %lu First Name = %@",
                  (unsigned long)counter,
                  thisPerson.firstName);

            NSLog(@"Person %lu Last Name = %@",
                  (unsigned long)counter,
                  thisPerson.lastName);

            NSLog(@"Person %lu Age = %ld",
                  (unsigned long)counter,
                  (unsigned long)[thisPerson.age unsignedIntegerValue]);

            counter++;
        }

    } else {
        NSLog(@"Could not find any Person entities in the context.");
    }

    self.window = [[UIWindow alloc] initWithFrame:
                   [[UIScreen mainScreen] bounds]];

    self.window.backgroundColor = [UIColor whiteColor];
    [self.window makeKeyAndVisible];
    return YES;
}
```

 In this code, we are using a counter variable inside a fast-enumeration block. The reason we need the counter in this fast-enumeration is for use in NSLog debugging messages that we are printing in order to see the index of the current enumerated person object in the array. An alternative to this solution would have been to use a classic for-loop with a counter variable.

For more information about fetch requests, please refer to this recipe's Discussion.

Discussion

For those of you who are familiar with database terminology, a *fetch request* is similar to a SELECT statement. In the SELECT statement, you specify which rows, with which conditions, have to be returned from which table. With a fetch request, we do the same thing. We specify the entity (table) and the managed object context (the database layer). We can also specify sort descriptors for sorting the data we read. But first we'll focus on reading the data to make it simpler.

To be able to read the contents of the Person entity (we created this entity in Recipe 15.1 and turned it into code in Recipe 15.2), we must first ask the NSEntity

Description class to search in our managed object context for an entity named Person. Once it is found, we will tell our fetch request what entity we want to read from. After this, all that's left to do is to execute the fetch request as we saw in this recipe's Solution.

The return value of the executeFetchRequest:error: instance method of NSManagedObjectContext is either nil (in case of an error) or an array of Person managed objects. If no results are found for the given entity, the returned array will be empty.

See Also

Recipe 15.1; Recipe 15.2

15.5 Deleting Data from Core Data

Problem

You want to delete a managed object (a row in a table) from a managed object context (your database).

Solution

Use the deleteObject: instance method of NSManagedObjectContext:

```
- (BOOL)              application:(UIApplication *)application
   didFinishLaunchingWithOptions:(NSDictionary *)launchOptions{

  [self createNewPersonWithFirstName:@"Anthony"
                           lastName:@"Robbins"
                                age:51];

  [self createNewPersonWithFirstName:@"Richard"
                           lastName:@"Branson"
                                age:61];

  /* Create the fetch request first */
  NSFetchRequest *fetchRequest = [[NSFetchRequest alloc] init];

  /* Here is the entity whose contents we want to read */
  NSEntityDescription *entity =
  [NSEntityDescription entityForName:@"Person"
            inManagedObjectContext:self.managedObjectContext];
  NSSortDescriptor *ageSort =
  [[NSSortDescriptor alloc] initWithKey:@"age"
            ascending:YES];
  /* Tell the request that we want to read the
     contents of the Person entity */
  [fetchRequest setEntity:entity];

  NSError *requestError = nil;
```

```
        /* And execute the fetch request on the context */
        NSArray *persons =
        [self.managedObjectContext executeFetchRequest:fetchRequest
                                            error:&requestError];

        /* Make sure we get the array */
        if ([persons count] > 0){

          /* Delete the last person in the array */
          Person *lastPerson = [persons lastObject];

          [self.managedObjectContext deleteObject:lastPerson];

          NSError *savingError = nil;
          if ([self.managedObjectContext save:&savingError]){
            NSLog(@"Successfully deleted the last person in the array.");
          } else {
            NSLog(@"Failed to delete the last person in the array.");
          }

        } else {
          NSLog(@"Could not find any Person entities in the context.");
        }

        self.window = [[UIWindow alloc] initWithFrame:
                        [[UIScreen mainScreen] bounds]];

        self.window.backgroundColor = [UIColor whiteColor];
        [self.window makeKeyAndVisible];
        return YES;
    }
```

 In this example code, we are using the `createNewPersonWithFirst Name:lastName:age:` method that we coded in Recipe 15.4.

Discussion

You can delete managed objects (records of a table in a database) using the `deleteOb ject:` instance method of `NSManagedObjectContext`.

This method doesn't return an error to you in any of its parameters, nor does it return a `BOOL` value, so you really have no good way of knowing whether an object was successfully deleted using the managed object context. The best way to determine this to use that managed object's `isDeleted` method.

With this information, let's change the code that we wrote previously in this recipe:

```
- (BOOL)            application:(UIApplication *)application
  didFinishLaunchingWithOptions:(NSDictionary *)launchOptions{

  [self createNewPersonWithFirstName:@"Anthony"
```

```
                            lastName:@"Robbins"
                                age:51];

[self createNewPersonWithFirstName:@"Richard"
                          lastName:@"Branson"
                               age:61];

/* Create the fetch request first */
NSFetchRequest *fetchRequest = [[NSFetchRequest alloc] init];

/* Here is the entity whose contents we want to read */
NSEntityDescription *entity =
[NSEntityDescription entityForName:@"Person"
            inManagedObjectContext:self.managedObjectContext];

/* Tell the request that we want to read the
 contents of the Person entity */
[fetchRequest setEntity:entity];

NSError *requestError = nil;

/* And execute the fetch request on the context */
NSArray *persons =
[self.managedObjectContext executeFetchRequest:fetchRequest
                                         error:&requestError];

/* Make sure we get the array */
if ([persons count] > 0){

  /* Delete the last person in the array */
  Person *lastPerson = [persons lastObject];

  [self.managedObjectContext deleteObject:lastPerson];

  if ([lastPerson isDeleted]){
    NSLog(@"Successfully deleted the last person...");

    NSError *savingError = nil;
    if ([self.managedObjectContext save:&savingError]){
      NSLog(@"Successfully saved the context.");
    } else {
      NSLog(@"Failed to save the context.");
    }

  } else {
    NSLog(@"Failed to delete the last person.");
  }

} else {
  NSLog(@"Could not find any Person entities in the context.");
}

self.window = [[UIWindow alloc] initWithFrame:
                [[UIScreen mainScreen] bounds]];
```

```
    self.window.backgroundColor = [UIColor whiteColor];
    [self.window makeKeyAndVisible];
    return YES;
}
```

Once you run the app, you will get results similar to this, printed to the console window:

```
Successfully deleted the last person...
Successfully saved the context.
```

15.6 Sorting Data in Core Data

Problem

You want to sort the managed objects (records) that you fetch from a managed object context (database).

Solution

Create instances of NSSortDescriptor for each attribute (column, in the database world) of an entity that has to be sorted. Add the sort descriptors to an array and assign the array to an instance of NSFetchRequest using the setSortDescriptors: instance method. In this example code, Sorting_Data_in_Core_DataAppDelegate is the class that represents the app delegate in a universal app. To understand how the Person entity is created, please refer to Recipes 15.1 and 15.2:

```
- (BOOL)              application:(UIApplication *)application
    didFinishLaunchingWithOptions:(NSDictionary *)launchOptions{

    [self createNewPersonWithFirstName:@"Richard"
                              lastName:@"Branson"
                                   age:61];

    [self createNewPersonWithFirstName:@"Anthony"
                              lastName:@"Robbins"
                                   age:51];

    /* Create the fetch request first */
    NSFetchRequest *fetchRequest = [[NSFetchRequest alloc] init];

    /* Here is the entity whose contents we want to read */
    NSEntityDescription *entity =
    [NSEntityDescription entityForName:@"Person"
                inManagedObjectContext:self.managedObjectContext];
    NSSortDescriptor *ageSort =
    [[NSSortDescriptor alloc] initWithKey:@"age"
                                ascending:YES];

    NSSortDescriptor *firstNameSort =
    [[NSSortDescriptor alloc] initWithKey:@"firstName"
                                ascending:YES];
```

```
    NSArray *sortDescriptors = [[NSArray alloc] initWithObjects:
                                ageSort,
                                firstNameSort, nil];

    fetchRequest.sortDescriptors = sortDescriptors;

    /* Tell the request that we want to read the
     contents of the Person entity */
    [fetchRequest setEntity:entity];

    NSError *requestError = nil;

    /* And execute the fetch request on the context */
    NSArray *persons =
    [self.managedObjectContext executeFetchRequest:fetchRequest
                                             error:&requestError];

    for (Person *person in persons){

      NSLog(@"First Name = %@", person.firstName);
      NSLog(@"Last Name = %@", person.lastName);
      NSLog(@"Age = %lu", (unsigned long)[person.age unsignedIntegerValue]);

    }

    self.window = [[UIWindow alloc] initWithFrame:
                   [[UIScreen mainScreen] bounds]];

    self.window.backgroundColor = [UIColor whiteColor];
    [self.window makeKeyAndVisible];
    return YES;
}
```

Discussion

An instance of NSFetchRequest can carry with itself an array of NSSortDescriptor instances. Each sort descriptor defines the attribute (column) on the current entity that
has to be sorted and whether the sorting has to be ascending or descending. For instance, the Person entity we created in Recipe 15.1 has firstName, lastName, and age
attributes. If we want to read all the persons in a managed object context and sort them
from youngest to oldest, we would create an instance of NSSortDescriptor with the
age key and set it to be ascending:

```
    NSSortDescriptor *ageSortDescriptor =
    [[NSSortDescriptor alloc] initWithKey:@"age"
                                ascending:YES];
```

 You can assign more than one sort descriptor to one fetch request. The
order in the array determines the order in which descriptors are provided. In other words, The output is sorted according to the first descriptor of the array, and within that order, entries are sorted according
to the second descriptor of the array, etc.

Recipe 15.4

15.7 Boosting Data Access in Table Views

Problem

In an application that uses table views to present managed objects to the user, you want to be able to fetch and present the data in a more fluid and natural way than managing your data manually.

Solution

Use fetched results controllers, which are instances of `NSFetchedResultsController`.

Discussion

Fetched results controllers work in the same way as table views. Both have sections and rows. A fetched results controller can read managed objects from a managed object context and separate them into sections and rows. Each section is a group (if you specify it) and each row in a section is a managed object. You can then easily map this data to a table view and display it to the user. There are a few very important reasons why you might want to modify your application to use fetched results controllers:

- After a fetched results controller is created on a managed object context, any change (insertion, deletion, modification, etc.) will immediately be reflected on the fetched results controller as well. For instance, you could create your fetched results controller to read the managed objects of the `Person` entity. Then in some other place in your application, you might insert a new `Person` managed object into the context (the same context the fetched results controller was created on). Immediately, the new managed object will become available in the fetched results controller. This is just magical!

- With a fetched results controller, you can manage cache more efficiently. For instance, you can ask your fetched results controller to keep only *N* number of managed objects in memory per controller instance.

- Fetched results controllers are exactly like table views in the sense that they have sections and rows, as explained before. You can use a fetched results controller to present managed objects in the GUI of your application with table views with ease.

Here are some of the important properties and instance methods of fetched results controllers (all are objects of type `NSFetchedResultsController`):

---

sections *(property, of type* NSArray*)*

A fetched results controller can group data together using a key path. The designated initializer of the NSFetchedResultsController class accepts this grouping filter through the sectionNameKeyPath parameter. The sections array will then contain each grouped section. Each object in this array conforms to the NSFetche dResultsSectionInfo protocol.

objectAtIndexPath: *(instance method, returns a managed object)*

Objects fetched with a fetched results controller can be retrieved using their section and row index. Each section's rows are numbered 0 through *N*-1, where *N* is the total number of items in that section. An index path object comprises a section and row index, and perfectly matches the information needed to retrieve objects from a fetched results controller. The objectAtIndexPath: instance method accepts index paths. Each index path is of type NSIndexPath. If you need to construct a table view cell using a managed object in a fetched results controller, simply pass the index path object in the cellForRowAtIndexPath parameter of the tableView:cell ForRowAtIndexPath: delegate method of a table view. If you want to construct an index path yourself anywhere else in your application, use the indexPathFor Row:inSection: class method of NSIndexPath.

fetchRequest *(property, of type* NSFetchRequest*)*

If at any point in your application, you believe you have to change the fetch request object for your fetched results controllers, you can do so using the fetchRequest property of an instance of NSFetchedResultsController. This is useful, for example, if you want to change the sort descriptors (refer to Recipe 15.6 for information about this) of the fetch request object after you have allocated and initialized your fetched results controllers.

To demonstrate the usefulness of fetch results controllers, we need to create an app that lets us add new managed objects to and delete managed objects from our managed objects context with a user interface. For this, we will need two view controllers:

Persons List View Controller

This will be our root view controller. In it we will display a table view; inside the table view we will list all the Person managed objects that we have in our managed objects context. Please refer to Recipe 15.1 to see how we created the Person managed object. The table view on this view controller must allow the user to delete Person objects by swiping or pressing the Edit button on the navigation bar. We will display a + button on the navigation bar as well, to allow the user to add new Person objects to the managed object context.

Add New Person View Controller

We will use this view controller to allow the user to add new Person objects to the managed object context.

To do this, simply follow these instructions:

1. Let's start with an empty application. Go to Xcode, select File → New → New Project..., and choose an Empty Application universal iOS project. (You should also enable Core Data; see Recipe 15.1 for more information.) Name the project *Boosting Data Access in Table Views*. Next, select the *Boosting_Data_Access_in_Table_Views.xcdatamodeld* in Xcode and create the same exact Person entity that we created in Recipe 15.1 and save it as Person.

2. In your project, create two view controllers, both subclassing `UIViewController`. Name one *PersonListViewController* and the other *AddPersonViewController*. Create both these view controllers without an xib file (we won't need Interface Builder as our UI is very simple indeed).

3. Now open the declaration of your app delegate and define a new property of type `PersonListViewController` and call it `personListViewController`. This will be the root view controller that we will display to our users. Remember that you also need a navigation controller, so define that as a property too:

```
#import <UIKit/UIKit.h>

@class PersonListViewController;

@interface Boosting_Data_Access_in_Table_ViewsAppDelegate
          : UIResponder <UIApplicationDelegate>

@property (strong, nonatomic) UIWindow *window;

@property (nonatomic, strong)
  PersonListViewController *personListViewController;

@property (nonatomic, strong) UINavigationController *navigationController;

@property (readonly, strong, nonatomic)
  NSManagedObjectContext *managedObjectContext;

@property (readonly, strong, nonatomic)
  NSManagedObjectModel *managedObjectModel;

@property (readonly, strong, nonatomic)
  NSPersistentStoreCoordinator *persistentStoreCoordinator;

- (void)saveContext;
- (NSURL *)applicationDocumentsDirectory;

@end
```

4. When your app loads up, you want to display the Person List View Controller to the user, so do that now in the `application:didFinishLaunchingWithOptions:` method of your app delegate:

```
- (BOOL)            application:(UIApplication *)application
  didFinishLaunchingWithOptions:(NSDictionary *)launchOptions{

  self.personListViewController =
```

```
[[PersonListViewController alloc]
 initWithNibName:nil
 bundle:nil];

self.navigationController =
[[UINavigationController alloc]
 initWithRootViewController:self.personListViewController];

self.window = [[UIWindow alloc] initWithFrame:
                [[UIScreen mainScreen] bounds]];

self.window.backgroundColor = [UIColor whiteColor];
[self.window makeKeyAndVisible];

self.window.rootViewController = self.navigationController;

return YES;
}
```

5. When the Person List view controller is displayed, place a table view on it to list all the person entities in your managed object context. Let's create the table now and set up our view controller as that table view's delegate and data source. You also need an Add button on the navigation bar with a + sign on it, so when the user taps on that button, it will take him to the Add Person view controller. In addition to these two properties, you also need to have your fetched results controller in the root view controller. So let's define all these in our view controller's definition:

```
#import <UIKit/UIKit.h>
#import <CoreData/CoreData.h>

@interface PersonListViewController : UIViewController
            <UITableViewDelegate,
             UITableViewDataSource,
             NSFetchedResultsControllerDelegate>

@property (nonatomic, strong) UITableView *tableViewPersons;
@property (nonatomic, strong) UIBarButtonItem *barButtonAddPerson;
@property (nonatomic, strong) NSFetchedResultsController *personsFRC;

@end
```

6. Next, you need to start implementing our view controller. In the `viewDidLoad` method, instantiate your Add navigation bar button. Also, instantiate your table view and set up the edit button on the navigation bar:

```
- (void)viewDidLoad{
[super viewDidLoad];

self.title = @"Persons";

self.tableViewPersons =
[[UITableView alloc] initWithFrame:self.view.bounds
                             style:UITableViewStylePlain];
self.tableViewPersons.delegate = self;
```

```
self.tableViewPersons.dataSource = self;

[self.view addSubview:self.tableViewPersons];

self.barButtonAddPerson = [[UIBarButtonItem alloc]
                           initWithBarButtonSystemItem:UIBarButtonSystemItemAdd
                           target:self
                           action:@selector(addNewPerson:)];

[self.navigationItem setLeftBarButtonItem:[self editButtonItem]
                          animated:NO];
[self.navigationItem setRightBarButtonItem:self.barButtonAddPerson
                          animated:NO];

}
```

7. Obviously, now that you've elected the root view controller to become the delegate and the data source of the table view, you need to implement the required methods for the delegate and the data source. For now, we will return 0 cells to the table view. Later, when we properly read Person entities from the managed object context using the fetched results controller, we can return the appropriate count of Person objects:

```
- (NSInteger)tableView:(UITableView *)tableView
numberOfRowsInSection:(NSInteger)section{
  return 0;
}

- (UITableViewCell *)tableView:(UITableView *)tableView
        cellForRowAtIndexPath:(NSIndexPath *)indexPath{
  return nil;
}
```

8. Now it's time to hook the + button to the Add Person view controller, so make sure you have imported the *AddPersonViewController.h* header file into the implementation file of the Person List view controller:

```
- (void) addNewPerson:(id)paramSender{

  AddPersonViewController *controller = [[AddPersonViewController alloc]
                                         initWithNibName:nil
                                         bundle:nil];
  [self.navigationController pushViewController:controller
                                animated:YES];

}
```

9. In the Add Person view controller, you need four properties. Three are text fields: first name, last name, and age. The fourth property is for an Add navigation button, which you will place on the navigation bar. The user will press this button once she is done, to add the new person to the list:

```
#import <UIKit/UIKit.h>
#import <CoreData/CoreData.h>
```

```
@interface AddPersonViewController : UIViewController

@property (nonatomic, strong) UITextField *textFieldFirstName;
@property (nonatomic, strong) UITextField *textFieldLastName;
@property (nonatomic, strong) UITextField *textFieldAge;
@property (nonatomic, strong) UIBarButtonItem *barButtonAdd;

@end
```

10. Now in the `viewDidLoad` method of your Add Person view controller, instantiate these properties and place them on the view and put the bar button on the navigation bar:

```
- (void)viewDidLoad{
  [super viewDidLoad];

  self.title = @"New Person";

  CGRect textFieldRect = CGRectMake(20.0f,
                                    20.0f,
                                    self.view.bounds.size.width - 40.0f,
                                    31.0f);

  self.textFieldFirstName = [[UITextField alloc] initWithFrame:textFieldRect];
  self.textFieldFirstName.placeholder = @"First Name";
  self.textFieldFirstName.borderStyle = UITextBorderStyleRoundedRect;
  self.textFieldFirstName.autoresizingMask = UIViewAutoresizingFlexibleWidth;
  self.textFieldFirstName.contentVerticalAlignment =
    UIControlContentVerticalAlignmentCenter;
  [self.view addSubview:self.textFieldFirstName];

  textFieldRect.origin.y += 37.0f;
  self.textFieldLastName = [[UITextField alloc] initWithFrame:textFieldRect];
  self.textFieldLastName.placeholder = @"Last Name";
  self.textFieldLastName.borderStyle = UITextBorderStyleRoundedRect;
  self.textFieldLastName.autoresizingMask = UIViewAutoresizingFlexibleWidth;
  self.textFieldLastName.contentVerticalAlignment =
    UIControlContentVerticalAlignmentCenter;
  [self.view addSubview:self.textFieldLastName];

  textFieldRect.origin.y += 37.0f;
  self.textFieldAge = [[UITextField alloc] initWithFrame:textFieldRect];
  self.textFieldAge.placeholder = @"Age";
  self.textFieldAge.borderStyle = UITextBorderStyleRoundedRect;
  self.textFieldAge.autoresizingMask = UIViewAutoresizingFlexibleWidth;
  self.textFieldAge.keyboardType = UIKeyboardTypeNumberPad;
  self.textFieldAge.contentVerticalAlignment =
    UIControlContentVerticalAlignmentCenter;
  [self.view addSubview:self.textFieldAge];  self.barButtonAdd =
  [[UIBarButtonItem alloc] initWithTitle:@"Add"
                                   style:UIBarButtonItemStylePlain
                                  target:self
                                  action:@selector(createNewPerson:)];
```

```
[self.navigationItem setRightBarButtonItem:self.barButtonAdd
                                  animated:NO];
```

}

11. As you can see, the Add button is now linked to the createNewPerson: method of your Add Person view controller, so all you have to do is to implement this method, get the values in your text fields, and place them in a new Person object. Then you will need to save this object into the managed object context and pop the view controller to go back to the Person List view controller (at which time the Person view controller will need to display the new person in the list). To do all this, you first need to make sure we have imported the *Person.h* and the *Boosting_Data_Access_in_Table_ViewsAppDelegate.h* header files into the Add Person view controller's implementation file so that you can create a new person and use the managed object context in the app delegate to insert that person into the database:

12. Now let's implement the createNewPerson: method in the Add Person view controller:

```
- (void) createNewPerson:(id)paramSender{

    Boosting_Data_Access_in_Table_ViewsAppDelegate *appDelegate =
      (Boosting_Data_Access_in_Table_ViewsAppDelegate *)
        [[UIApplication sharedApplication] delegate];

    NSManagedObjectContext *managedObjectContext =
      appDelegate.managedObjectContext;

    Person *newPerson =
    [NSEntityDescription insertNewObjectForEntityForName:@"Person"
                             inManagedObjectContext:managedObjectContext];

    if (newPerson != nil){

      newPerson.firstName = self.textFieldFirstName.text;
      newPerson.lastName = self.textFieldLastName.text;
      newPerson.age = [NSNumber numberWithInteger:
                        [self.textFieldAge.text integerValue]];

      NSError *savingError = nil;

      if ([managedObjectContext save:&savingError]){
        [self.navigationController popViewControllerAnimated:YES];
      } else {
        NSLog(@"Failed to save the managed object context.");
      }

    } else {
      NSLog(@"Failed to create the new person object.");
    }

}
```

13. To offer a better user experience, when your view appears on the screen, you can automatically display the keyboard on the first name text field:

```
- (void) viewDidAppear:(BOOL)paramAnimated{
  [super viewDidAppear:paramAnimated];
  [self.textFieldFirstName becomeFirstResponder];
}
```

14. You are done with the Add Person view controller. You can actually now go ahead and try it out for yourself. Let's now go to the Person List view controller and during its initialization, instantiate our fetched results controller:

```
#import "PersonListViewController.h"
#import "AddPersonViewController.h"
#import "Boosting_Data_Access_in_Table_ViewsAppDelegate.h"
#import "Person.h"

@implementation PersonListViewController

- (NSManagedObjectContext *) managedObjectContext{

  Boosting_Data_Access_in_Table_ViewsAppDelegate *appDelegate =
    (Boosting_Data_Access_in_Table_ViewsAppDelegate *)
      [[UIApplication sharedApplication] delegate];

  NSManagedObjectContext *managedObjectContext =
    appDelegate.managedObjectContext;

  return managedObjectContext;

}

- (id) initWithNibName:(NSString *)nibNameOrNil
              bundle:(NSBundle *)nibBundleOrNil{

  self = [super initWithNibName:nibNameOrNil
                         bundle:nibBundleOrNil];

  if (self != nil){

    /* Create the fetch request first */
    NSFetchRequest *fetchRequest = [[NSFetchRequest alloc] init];

    /* Here is the entity whose contents we want to read */
    NSEntityDescription *entity =
    [NSEntityDescription entityForName:@"Person"
              inManagedObjectContext:[self managedObjectContext]];

    NSSortDescriptor *ageSort =
    [[NSSortDescriptor alloc] initWithKey:@"age"
                               ascending:YES];

    NSSortDescriptor *firstNameSort =
    [[NSSortDescriptor alloc] initWithKey:@"firstName"
                               ascending:YES];
```

```
          NSArray *sortDescriptors = [[NSArray alloc] initWithObjects:
                                       ageSort,
                                       firstNameSort, nil];

          fetchRequest.sortDescriptors = sortDescriptors;

          /* Tell the request that we want to read the
           contents of the Person entity */
          [fetchRequest setEntity:entity];

          self.personsFRC =
          [[NSFetchedResultsController alloc]
           initWithFetchRequest:fetchRequest
           managedObjectContext:[self managedObjectContext]
           sectionNameKeyPath:nil
           cacheName:nil];

          self.personsFRC.delegate = self;
          NSError *fetchingError = nil;
          if ([self.personsFRC performFetch:&fetchingError]){
            NSLog(@"Successfully fetched.");
          } else {
            NSLog(@"Failed to fetch.");
          }

      }

      return self;

  }
```

15. Now go ahead and implement various methods of your table view delegate (we left
    them to their minimum required implementation before). You can read the fetched
    managed objects from the fetched results controller and display the Person man-
    aged objects in the table view:

```
- (NSInteger)tableView:(UITableView *)tableView
 numberOfRowsInSection:(NSInteger)section{

  id <NSFetchedResultsSectionInfo> sectionInfo = [self.personsFRC.sections
                                                  objectAtIndex:section];
  return [sectionInfo numberOfObjects];

}

- (UITableViewCell *)tableView:(UITableView *)tableView
        cellForRowAtIndexPath:(NSIndexPath *)indexPath{

  UITableViewCell *result = nil;

  static NSString *PersonTableViewCell = @"PersonTableViewCell";

  result = [tableView dequeueReusableCellWithIdentifier:PersonTableViewCell];
```

```
if (result == nil){
  result =
  [[UITableViewCell alloc] initWithStyle:UITableViewCellStyleSubtitle
                      reuseIdentifier:PersonTableViewCell];

  result.selectionStyle = UITableViewCellSelectionStyleNone;

}

Person *person = [self.personsFRC objectAtIndexPath:indexPath];

result.textLabel.text =
  [person.firstName stringByAppendingFormat:@" %@", person.lastName];

result.detailTextLabel.text =
[NSString stringWithFormat:@"Age: %lu",
 (unsigned long)[person.age unsignedIntegerValue]];

return result;
}
```

16. You can now run the app and test it for yourself. One of the issues in our app at the moment is that if the user goes to the Add Person view controller and adds a new person to the managed object context, when she is sent back to the Person List view controller, the new person she just inserted into the context will not appear in the list. That is because our view controller doesn't know about the new object in the managed object context. The way to solve this is to implement the controllerDidChangeContent: delegate method of our fetched results controller object in the Person List view controller. When we created our fetched results controller, we nominated this view controller to become the delegate of the fetched results controller, so let's implement this method. This method gets called when the fetched results controller detects a change in the objects in the managed object context, so once this method gets called, we can go ahead and reload our table view:

```
- (void)controllerDidChangeContent:(NSFetchedResultsController *)controller{
[self.tableViewPersons reloadData];
}
```

17. The next thing we have to do in our Person List view controller is to handle editing:

```
- (void)    tableView:(UITableView *)tableView
  commitEditingStyle:(UITableViewCellEditingStyle)editingStyle
    forRowAtIndexPath:(NSIndexPath *)indexPath{

Person *personToDelete = [self.personsFRC objectAtIndexPath:indexPath];

/* Very important: we need to make sure we are not reloading the table view
 while deleting the managed object */
self.personsFRC.delegate = nil;

[[self managedObjectContext] deleteObject:personToDelete];

if ([personToDelete isDeleted]){
```

```
    NSError *savingError = nil;
    if ([[self managedObjectContext] save:&savingError]){

      NSError *fetchingError = nil;
      if ([self.personsFRC performFetch:&fetchingError]){
        NSLog(@"Successfully fetched.");

        NSArray *rowsToDelete = [[NSArray alloc]
                                  initWithObjects:indexPath, nil];

        [tableViewPersons
         deleteRowsAtIndexPaths:rowsToDelete
         withRowAnimation:UITableViewRowAnimationAutomatic];

      } else {
        NSLog(@"Failed to fetch with error = %@", fetchingError);
      }

    } else {
      NSLog(@"Failed to save the context with error = %@", savingError);
    }
  }

  self.personsFRC.delegate = self;

}

- (UITableViewCellEditingStyle)tableView:(UITableView *)tableView
         editingStyleForRowAtIndexPath:(NSIndexPath *)indexPath{
  return UITableViewCellEditingStyleDelete;
}

- (void) setEditing:(BOOL)paramEditing
           animated:(BOOL)paramAnimated{

  [super setEditing:paramEditing
           animated:paramAnimated];

  if (paramEditing){
    [self.navigationItem setRightBarButtonItem:nil
                                      animated:YES];
  } else {
    [self.navigationItem setRightBarButtonItem:self.barButtonAddPerson
                                      animated:YES];
  }

  [self.tableViewPersons setEditing:paramEditing
                           animated:YES];

}
```

We are all done. Go ahead and try it out for yourself.

15.8 Implementing Relationships in Core Data

Problem

You want to be able to link your managed objects to each other: for instance, linking a Person to the Home he lives in.

Solution

Use inverse relationships in the model editor.

Discussion

Relationships in Core Data can be one-to-one, inverse one-to-many, or inverse many-to-many. Here is an example of each type of relationship:

One-to-one relationship
> An example is the relationship between a person and her nose. Each person can have only one nose, and each nose can belong to only one person.

Inverse one-to-many relationship
> An example is the relationship between an employee and his manager. The employee can have only one direct manager, but his manager can have multiple employees working for her. Here, the relationship of the employee with the manager is one-to-one, but from the manager's perspective, the relationship is one (manager) to many (employees); hence the word *inverse*.

Inverse many-to-many relationship
> An example is the relationship between a person and a car. One car can be used by more than one person, and one person can have more than one car.

In Core Data, you can create one-to-one relationships, but I highly recommend that you avoid doing so because, going back to the example in the preceding list, the person will know what nose she has but the nose will not know who it belongs to. Please note that this is a different one-to-one model than what you might have seen in other database management systems where Object A and B will be linked together when they have a one-to-one relationship. In a Core Data one-to-one relationship, Object A will know about Object B, but not the other way around. In an object-oriented programming language such as Objective-C, it is always best to create inverse relationships so that child elements can refer to parent elements of that relationship. In a one-to-many relationship, the object that can have association with many other objects will retain a set of those objects. The set will be of type NSSet. However, in a one-to-one relationship, objects on both sides of the fence keep a reference to one another using the proper class names of one another since, well, the relationship is one-to-one and an instance of one object in another object can easily be represented with the class name of that object.

Let's go ahead and create a data model that takes advantage of an inverse one-to-many relationship:

1. In Xcode, find the *xcdatamodel* file that was created for you when you started your Core Data project, as shown earlier in Figure 15-1 (refer to Recipe 15.1 to create such a project).

2. Open the data model file in the editor by clicking on it.

3. Remove any entities that were created for you previously by selecting them and pressing the Delete key on your keyboard.

4. Create a new entity and name it Employee. Create three attributes for this entity, named firstName (of type String), lastName (of type String), and age (of type Integer 32), as shown in Figure 15-13.

5. Create another entity named Manager with the same attributes you created for the Employee entity (firstName of type String, lastName of type String, and age of type Integer 32). See Figure 15-14.

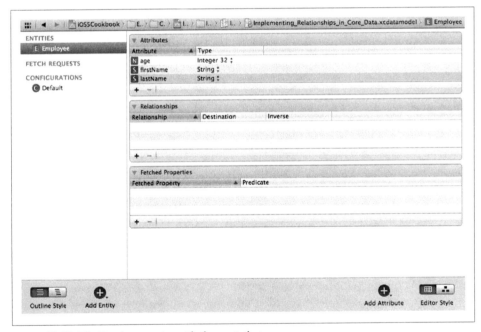

Figure 15-13. The Employee entity with three attributes

6. Create a new relationship for the Manager entity by first selecting the Manager entity in the list and then pressing the + button in the bottom of the Relationships box (see Figure 15-15).

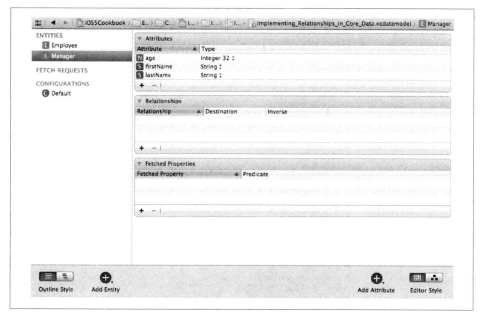

Figure 15-14. The Manager entity with three attributes

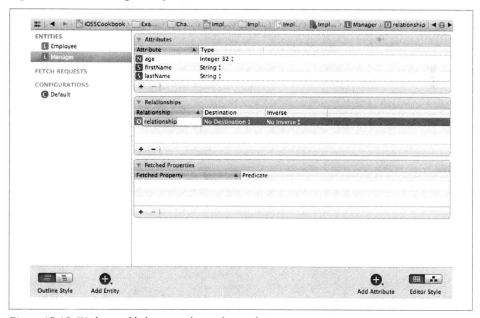

Figure 15-15. We have added a new relationship to the Manager entity

7. Set the name of the new relationship to `FKManagerToEmployees` (see Figure 15-16).

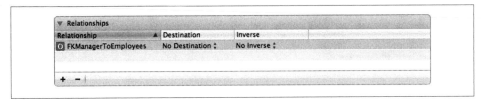

Figure 15-16. Changing the name of the new Manager-to-Employees relationship

8. Select the `Employee` entity and create a new relationship for it. Name the relationship `FKEmployeeToManager` (see Figure 15-17).

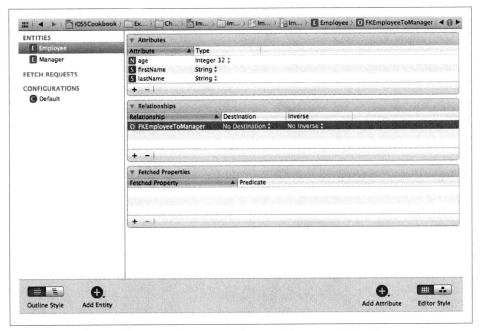

Figure 15-17. Changing the name of the new Employee-to-Manager relationship

9. Choose the `Manager` entity, and then select the `FKManagerToEmployees` relationship for the `Manager`. In the Relationships box, choose Employee in the Destination drop-down menu (because we want to connect a `Manager` to an `Employee` entity through this relationship), set the Inverse box's value to `FKEmployeeToManager` (because the `FKEmployeeToManager` relationship of the `Employee` will link an employee to her `Manager`), and tick the To-Many Relationship box in Data Model inspector (see Recipe 15.1). The results are shown in Figure 15-18.

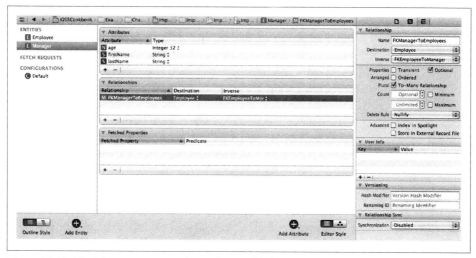

Figure 15-18. The Manager inverse relationship established with employees

10. Select both your `Employee` and `Manager` entities, select File → New File, and create
    the managed object classes for your model, as described in Recipe 15.2.

After creating the inverse one-to-many relationship, open the *.h* file of your `Employee`
entity:

```
#import <Foundation/Foundation.h>
#import <CoreData/CoreData.h>

@class Manager;

@interface Employee : NSManagedObject {
@private
}
@property (nonatomic, retain) NSString * firstName;
@property (nonatomic, retain) NSString * lastName;
@property (nonatomic, retain) NSNumber * age;
@property (nonatomic, retain) Manager *FKEmployeeToManager;

@end
```

You can see that a new property has been added to this file. The property is named
`FKEmployeeToManager` and its type is `Manager`, meaning that from now on, if we have a
reference to any object of type `Employee`, we can access its `FKEmployeeToManager` property
to access that specific employee's `Manager` object (if any). Let's have a look at the *.h* file
of the `Manager` entity:

```
#import <Foundation/Foundation.h>
#import <CoreData/CoreData.h>

@class Employee;
```

```
@interface Manager : NSManagedObject {
@private
}
@property (nonatomic, retain) NSNumber * age;
@property (nonatomic, retain) NSString * firstName;
@property (nonatomic, retain) NSString * lastName;
@property (nonatomic, retain) NSSet *FKManagerToEmployees;
@end

@interface Manager (CoreDataGeneratedAccessors)

- (void)addFKManagerToEmployeesObject:(Employee *)value;
- (void)removeFKManagerToEmployeesObject:(Employee *)value;
- (void)addFKManagerToEmployees:(NSSet *)values;
- (void)removeFKManagerToEmployees:(NSSet *)values;
@end
```

The FKManagerToEmployees property is also created for the Manager entity. The data type of this object is NSSet. This simply means the FKManagerToEmployees property of any instance of the Manager entity can contain 1 to *N* number of Employee entities (a one-to-many relationship: one manager, many employees).

Another type of relationship that you might want to create is a many-to-many relationship. Going back to the Manager to Employee relationship, with a many-to-many relationship, any manager could have *N* number of employees and one employee could have *N* number of managers. To do this, follow the same instructions for creating a one-to-many relationship, but select the Employee entity and then the FKEmployeeToManager relationship. Change this name to FKEmployeeToManagers and tick the To-Many Relationship box, as shown in Figure 15-19. Now the arrow has double arrowheads on both sides.

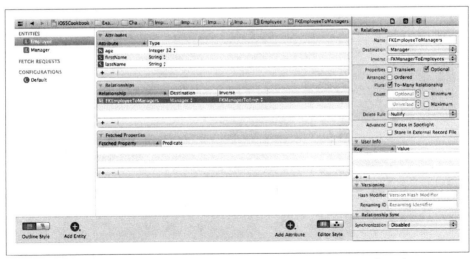

Figure 15-19. Creating a Many-to-Many relationship between the Manager and Employee entities

In your code, for a one-to-many relationship, you can simply create a new `Manager` managed object (read how you can insert objects to a managed object context in Recipe 15.3), save it to the managed object context, and then create a couple of `Employee` managed objects and save them to the context as well. Now, to associate the manager with an employee, set the value of the `FKEmployeeToManager` property of an instance of `Employee` to an instance of the `Manager` managed object. Core Data will then create the relationship for you.

If you would like to retrieve all employees (of type `Employee`) that are associated to a manager object (of type `Manager`), all you have to do is to use the `allObjects` instance method of the `FKManagerToEmployees` property of our manager object. This object is of type `NSSet`, so you can use its `allObjects` instance method to retrieve the array of all employee objects associated with a particular manager object.

CHAPTER 16

Dates, Calendars, and Events

16.0 Introduction

The Event Kit and Event Kit UI frameworks allow iOS developers to access the Calendar database on an iOS device. You can insert, read, and modify events using the Event Kit framework. The Event Kit UI framework allows you to present built-in SDK GUI elements that allow the user to manipulate the Calendar database manually. In this chapter, we will focus on the Event Kit framework first, and then learn about the Event Kit UI framework.

With the Event Kit framework, a programmer can modify the user's Calendar database without him knowing. However, this is not a very good practice. In fact, Apple prohibits programmers from doing so and asks us to always notify users about any changes that the program might make to the Calendar database. Here is a quote from Apple:

> If your application modifies a user's Calendar database programmatically, it must get confirmation from the user before doing so. An application should never modify the Calendar database without specific instruction from the user.

iOS comes with a built-in Calendar app. The Calendar app can work with different types of calendars, such as local, CalDAV, and so forth. In this chapter, we will be working with different types of calendars as well. To make sure you are prepared to run the code in some of the recipes in this chapter, please create a Google account and associate it with Google Calendar. To get started, head over to *http://www.google.com/ calendar/*.

Once there, create a Google account. After you are done, add Google Calendar to your iOS device by following these steps:

1. Go to the home screen of your iOS device.
2. Go to Settings.
3. Select Mail, Contacts, Calendars.
4. Select Add Account...
5. Select Other.

6. Under the Calendars group, select the Add CalDAV Account button.

7. On the CalDAV screen, enter the following (see Figure 16-1):

   a. **www.google.com** for the Server

   b. Your Google username for User Name

   c. Your Google password for Password

   d. A description of your choice for Description

8. Tap Next.

Figure 16-1. Adding a Google calendar to an iOS device

Once you add the new Google account with Calendar access to your iOS device, you can see this calendar appear in the Calendars list in the Calendar application, as shown in Figure 16-2.

CalDAV is a protocol that allows access to the standard Calendar format used by Google Calendar and is supported by iOS. For more information about CalDAV, please refer to RFC 4791 at *http://tools.ietf.org/html/rfc4791*.

Almost all the recipes in this chapter demonstrate the use of the Event Kit and Event Kit UI frameworks using a CalDAV calendar. Before reading the recipes, please take a few minutes and follow the instructions provided here to create a new CalDAV calendar and link it to your iOS device. Here are some of the benefits of using a CalDAV calendar:

Figure 16-2. The new Google Calendar added to the list of calendars on an iOS device

- It's easy to set up.
- It can be shared among different platforms, so changes to a local instance of a CalDAV calendar object will be reflected—automatically by iOS—to the CalDAV server. This will give you a better understanding of how calendars work in iOS, and you can simply check your Google Calendar online and make sure the local changes are reflected there.
- You can add participants to an event using a CalDAV calendar. This is explained in Recipe 16.6.
- You can add a CalDAV calendar to iCal on your Mac, as well as your iOS devices, syncing events across all machines.

To run the example code in this chapter, you must add the Event Kit framework, and in some cases the Event Kit UI framework, to your application by following these steps:

1. Click on your project's icon in Xcode
2. Select the target to which you want to add the frameworks.
3. Select the Build Phases tab from the top of the screen.
4. Expand the Link Binary with Libraries box under the Build Phases tab and press the little + button located on the bottom-left corner of this box.
5. Choose the Event Kit and Event Kit UI frameworks and click Add.

The iOS Simulator on Mac OS X does not simulate the Calendar app on an iOS device. To test the recipes in this chapter, you must run and debug your program on a real iOS device. All examples in this chapter have been tested on the iPhone 4 and iPad 2.

In most of the example code in this chapter, we will focus on manually reading and manipulating events in a calendar. If you want to use the built-in iOS capabilities to allow your users to quickly access their calendar events, please refer to Recipes 16.9 and 16.10.

16.1 Retrieving the List of Calendars

Problem

You want to retrieve the list of calendars available on the user's device before you attempt to insert new events into them.

Solution

Access the calendars array property of an instance of EKEventStore. Each calendar is of type EKCalendar:

```
- (BOOL)            application:(UIApplication *)application
    didFinishLaunchingWithOptions:(NSDictionary *)launchOptions{

    EKEventStore *eventStore = [[EKEventStore alloc] init];

    /* These are the calendar types an iOS Device can have. Please note
       that the "type" property of an object of type EKCalendar
       is of type EKCalendarType. The values in the "CalendarTypes"
       array reflect the exact same values in the EKCalendarType
       enumeration, but as NSString values */
    NSArray *calendarTypes = @[
    @"Local",
    @"CalDAV",
    @"Exchange",
    @"Subscription",
    @"Birthday"
    ];

    /* Go through the calendars one by one */
    NSUInteger counter = 1;
    for (EKCalendar *thisCalendar in eventStore.calendars){

        /* The title of the calendar */
        NSLog(@"Calendar %lu Title = %@",
              (unsigned long)counter, thisCalendar.title);

        /* The type of the calendar */
        NSLog(@"Calendar %lu Type = %@",
```

```
            (unsigned long)counter,
            [calendarTypes objectAtIndex:thisCalendar.type]);

    /* The color that is associated with the calendar */
    NSLog(@"Calendar %lu Color = %@",
          (unsigned long)counter,
          [UIColor colorWithCGColor:thisCalendar.CGColor]);

    /* And whether the calendar can be modified or not */
    if ([thisCalendar allowsContentModifications]){
      NSLog(@"Calendar %lu can be modified.",
            (unsigned long)counter);
    } else {
      NSLog(@"Calendar %lu cannot be modified.",
            (unsigned long)counter);
    }

    counter++;
  }

  self.window = [[UIWindow alloc] initWithFrame:
                 [[UIScreen mainScreen] bounds]];

  self.window.backgroundColor = [UIColor whiteColor];
  [self.window makeKeyAndVisible];
  return YES;
}
```

Running this code on an iOS device with six calendars (see Figure 16-2) will print results similar to this in the console window:

```
Calendar 1 Title = Birthdays
Calendar 1 Type = Birthday
Calendar 1 Color = UIDeviceRGBColorSpace 0.509804 0.584314 0.686275 1
Calendar 1 cannot be modified.
Calendar 2 Title = Calendar
Calendar 2 Type = Local
Calendar 2 Color = UIDeviceRGBColorSpace 0.054902 0.380392 0.72549 1
Calendar 2 can be modified.
Calendar 3 Title = Calendar
Calendar 3 Type = CalDAV
Calendar 3 Color = UIDeviceRGBColorSpace 0.054902 0.380392 0.72549 1
Calendar 3 can be modified.
Calendar 4 Title = Home
Calendar 4 Type = CalDAV
Calendar 4 Color = UIDeviceRGBColorSpace 0.443137 0.101961 0.462745 1
Calendar 4 can be modified.Calendar 5 Title = Work
Calendar 5 Type = CalDAV
Calendar 5 Color = UIDeviceRGBColorSpace 0.964706 0.309804 0 1
Calendar 5 can be modified.
Calendar 6 Title = vandad.np@gmail.com
Calendar 6 Type = CalDAV
Calendar 6 Color = UIDeviceRGBColorSpace 0.160784 0.321569 0.639216 1
Calendar 6 can be modified.
```

Discussion

By allocating and initializing an object of type EKEventStore, you can access different types of calendars that are available on an iOS device. iOS supports common calendar formats such as CalDAV and Exchange. The calendars property of an instance of EKEventStore is of type NSArray and contains the array of calendars that are on an iOS device. Each object in this array is of type EKCalendar and each calendar has properties that allow us to determine whether, for instance, we can insert new events into that calendar.

As we'll see in Recipe 16.2, a calendar object allows modifications only if its allowsContentModifications property has a YES value.

 You can use the colorWithCGColor: instance method of UIColor to retrieve an object of type UIColor from CGColorRef.

See Also

Recipe 16.2

16.2 Adding Events to Calendars

Problem

You would like to be able to create new events in users' calendars.

Solution

Find the calendar you want to insert your event into (please refer to Recipe 16.1). Create an object of type EKEvent using the eventWithEventStore: class method of EKEvent and save the event into the user's calendar using the saveEvent:span:error: instance method of EKEventStore:

```
- (BOOL)   createEventWithTitle:(NSString *)paramTitle
                      startDate:(NSDate *)paramStartDate
                        endDate:(NSDate *)paramEndDate
             inCalendarWithTitle:(NSString *)paramCalendarTitle
              inCalendarWithType:(EKCalendarType)paramCalendarType
                          notes:(NSString *)paramNotes{

    BOOL result = NO;

    EKEventStore *eventStore = [[EKEventStore alloc] init];

    /* Are there any calendars available to the event store? */
    if ([eventStore.calendars count] == 0){
```

```
    NSLog(@"No calendars are found.");
    return NO;
  }

  EKCalendar *targetCalendar = nil;

  /* Try to find the calendar that the user asked for */
  for (EKCalendar *thisCalendar in eventStore.calendars){
    if ([thisCalendar.title isEqualToString:paramCalendarTitle] &&
        thisCalendar.type == paramCalendarType){
      targetCalendar = thisCalendar;
      break;
    }
  }

  /* Make sure we found the calendar that we were asked to find */
  if (targetCalendar == nil){
    NSLog(@"Could not find the requested calendar.");
    return NO;
  }

  /* If a calendar does not allow modification of its contents
   then we cannot insert an event into it */
  if (targetCalendar.allowsContentModifications == NO){
    NSLog(@"The selected calendar does not allow modifications.");
    return NO;
  }

  /* Create an event */
  EKEvent *event = [EKEvent eventWithEventStore:eventStore];
  event.calendar = targetCalendar;

  /* Set the properties of the event such as its title,
   start date/time, end date/time, etc. */
  event.title = paramTitle;
  event.notes = paramNotes;
  event.startDate = paramStartDate;
  event.endDate = paramEndDate;

  /* Finally, save the event into the calendar */
  NSError *saveError = nil;

  result = [eventStore saveEvent:event
                            span:EKSpanThisEvent
                           error:&saveError];

  if (result == NO){
    NSLog(@"An error occurred = %@", saveError);
  }

  return result;

}
```

You can use the method we just implemented to insert new events into a user's calendar:

```
- (BOOL)              application:(UIApplication *)application
  didFinishLaunchingWithOptions:(NSDictionary *)launchOptions{

    /* The event starts from today, right now */
    NSDate *startDate = [NSDate date];

    /* And the event ends this time tomorrow.
     24 hours, 60 minutes per hour and 60 seconds per minute
     hence 24 * 60 * 60 */
    NSDate *endDate = [startDate
                   dateByAddingTimeInterval:24 * 60 * 60];

    /* Create the new event */
    BOOL createdSuccessfully = [self createEventWithTitle:@"My event"
                                     startDate:startDate
                                       endDate:endDate
                          inCalendarWithTitle:@"Calendar"
                           inCalendarWithType:EKCalendarTypeLocal
                                        notes:nil];

    if (createdSuccessfully){
      NSLog(@"Successfully created the event.");
    } else {
      NSLog(@"Failed to create the event.");
    }

    self.window = [[UIWindow alloc] initWithFrame:
                   [[UIScreen mainScreen] bounds]];

    self.window.backgroundColor = [UIColor whiteColor];
    [self.window makeKeyAndVisible];
    return YES;
}
```

Discussion

To programmatically create a new event in a calendar on an iOS device, we must:

1. Allocate and initialize an instance of EKEventStore.

2. Find the calendar we want to save the event to (please refer to Recipe 16.1). We must make sure the target calendar supports modifications by checking that the calendar object's allowsContentModifications property is YES. If it is not, you must choose a different calendar or forego saving the event.

3. Once you find your target calendar, create an event of type EKEvent using the eventWithEventStore: class method of EKEvent.

4. Set the properties of the new event such as its title, startDate, and endDate.

5. Associate your event with the calendar that you found in step 2 using the calendars property of an instance of EKEvent.

6. Once you are done setting the properties of your event, add that event to the calendar using the saveEvent:span:error: instance method of EKEventStore. The

---

return value of this method (a `BOOL` value) indicates whether the event was successfully inserted into the Calendar database. If the operation fails, the `NSError` object passed to the `error` parameter of this method will contain the error that has occurred in the system while inserting this event.

If you attempt to insert an event without specifying a target calendar, or if you insert an event into a calendar that cannot be modified, the `saveEvent:span:error:` instance method of `EKEventStore` will fail with an error similar to this:

```
Error Domain=EKErrorDomain Code=1 "No calendar has been set."
UserInfo=0x15d860 {NSLocalizedDescription=No calendar has been set.}
```

Running our code on an iOS device, we will see an event created in the Calendar database, as shown in Figure 16-3.

Figure 16-3. Programmatically adding an event to a calendar

iOS syncs online calendars with the iOS calendar. These calendars could be Exchange, CalDAV, and other common formats. Creating an event on a CalDAV calendar on an iOS device will create the same event on the server. The server changes are also reflected in the iOS Calendar database when the Calendar database is synced with the server.

See Also

Recipe 16.1

16.3 Accessing the Contents of Calendars

Problem

You want to retrieve events of type `EKEvent` from a calendar of type `EKCalendar` on an iOS device.

Solution

Follow these steps:

1. Instantiate an object of type `EKEventStore`.
2. Using the `calendars` property of the event store (instantiated in step 1), find the calendar you want to read from.
3. Determine the time and date where you want to start the search in the calendar and the time and date where the search must stop.
4. Pass the calendar object (found in step 2), along with the two dates you found in step 3, to the `predicateForEventsWithStartDate:endDate:calendars:` instance method of `EKEventStore`.
5. Pass the predicate created in step 4 to the `eventsMatchingPredicate:` instance method of `EKEventStore`. The result of this method is an array of `EKEvent` objects (if any) that fell between the given dates (step 3) in the specified calendar (step 2).

This code illustrates the above steps:

```
- (EKCalendar *) calDAVCalendarWithTitleContaining
                 :(NSString *)paramDescription{

  EKCalendar *result = nil;

  EKEventStore *eventStore = [[EKEventStore alloc] init];

  for (EKCalendar *thisCalendar in eventStore.calendars){
    if (thisCalendar.type == EKCalendarTypeCalDAV){
      if ([thisCalendar.title
           rangeOfString:paramDescription].location != NSNotFound){
        return thisCalendar;
      }
    }
  }

  return result;

}

- (void) readEvents{

  /* Find a calendar to base our search on */
  EKCalendar *targetCalendar =
    [self calDAVCalendarWithTitleContaining:@"gmail.com"];
```

```
/* If we could not find a CalDAV calendar that we were looking for,
 then we will abort the operation */
if (targetCalendar == nil){
  NSLog(@"No CalDAV calendars were found.");
  return;
}

/* We have to pass an array of calendars to the event store to search */
NSArray *targetCalendars = [[NSArray alloc] initWithObjects:
                              targetCalendar, nil];

/* Instantiate the event store */
EKEventStore *eventStore = [[EKEventStore alloc] init];

/* The start date will be today */
NSDate *startDate = [NSDate date];

/* The end date will be one day from today */
NSDate *endDate = [startDate dateByAddingTimeInterval:24 * 60 * 60];

/* Create the predicate that we can later pass to the
 event store in order to fetch the events */
NSPredicate *searchPredicate =
[eventStore predicateForEventsWithStartDate:startDate
                                    endDate:endDate
                                  calendars:targetCalendars];

/* Make sure we succeeded in creating the predicate */
if (searchPredicate == nil){
  NSLog(@"Could not create the search predicate.");
  return;
}

/* Fetch all the events that fall between
 the starting and the ending dates */
NSArray *events = [eventStore eventsMatchingPredicate:searchPredicate];

/* Go through all the events and print their information
 out to the console */
if (events != nil){

  NSUInteger counter = 1;
  for (EKEvent *event in events){

    NSLog(@"Event %lu Start Date = %@",
          (unsigned long)counter,
          event.startDate);

    NSLog(@"Event %lu End Date = %@",
          (unsigned long)counter,
          event.endDate);

    NSLog(@"Event %lu Title = %@",
          (unsigned long)counter,
```

```
                event.title);

        counter++;
    }

} else {
    NSLog(@"The array of events for this start/end time is nil.");
}

}

- (BOOL)            application:(UIApplication *)application
    didFinishLaunchingWithOptions:(NSDictionary *)launchOptions{

    [self readEvents];

    self.window = [[UIWindow alloc] initWithFrame:
                    [[UIScreen mainScreen] bounds]];

    self.window.backgroundColor = [UIColor whiteColor];
    [self.window makeKeyAndVisible];
    return YES;
}
```

When we run this code on an iOS device with six calendars set up (one of which is a Google CalDAV calendar), as shown in Figure 16-2, we will see the events that are available between the day that we run the app and the next day.

The Calendar app in iOS displays the same events in the format shown in Figure 16-4. Please bear in mind that you will not see results similar to this unless you create the events in your Google Calendar just as I have created them, at the exact same date and time. However, if you do decide to create events in other calendars, such as the local calendar, on different dates, make sure you change the starting and ending dates of the event predicate and the calendar in which you are performing the search. For more information, please refer to this recipe's Discussion.

Discussion

As mentioned in this chapter's Introduction, an iOS device can be configured with different types of calendars using CalDAV, Exchange, and so on. Each calendar that is accessible by the Event Kit framework is encompassed within an EKCalendar object that can be accessed using the calendars array property of an instance of EKEventStore. You can fetch events inside a calendar in different ways, but the easiest way is to create and execute a specially formatted specification of dates and times, called a *predicate*, inside an event store.

A predicate of type NSPredicate that we can use in the Event Kit framework can be created using the predicateForEventsWithStartDate:endDate:calendars: instance method of an EKEventStore. The parameters to this method are:

Figure 16-4. The Calendar app on an iOS device

predicateForEventsWithStartDate
    The starting date and time from when the events have to be fetched.

endDate
    The ending date up until which the events will be fetched.

calendars
    The array of calendars to search for events between the starting and ending dates.

See Also

Recipe 16.1

16.4 Removing Events from Calendars

Problem

You want to be able to delete a specific event or series of events from users' calendars.

Solution

Use the removeEvent:span:commit:error: instance method of EKEventStore.

Discussion

The `removeEvent:span:commit:error:` instance method of `EKEventStore` can remove an instance of an event or all instances of a recurring event. For more information about recurring events, please refer to Recipe 16.5. In this recipe, we will only remove an instance of the event and not the other instances of the same event in the calendar.

The parameters that we can pass to this method are:

removeEvent
> This is the `EKEvent` instance to be removed from the calendar.

span
> This is the parameter that tells the event store whether we want to remove only this event or all the occurrences of this event in the calendar. To remove only the current event, specify the `EKSpanThisEvent` value for the `removeEvent` parameter. To remove all occurrences of the same event from the calendar, pass the `EKSpanFutureEvents` value for the parameter.

commit
> A boolean value that tells the event store if the changes have to be saved on the remote/local calendar immediately or not.

error
> This parameter can be given a reference to an `NSError` object that will be filled with the error (if any), when the return value of this method is `NO`.

To demonstrate this, let's use the event creation method that we implemented in Recipe 16.2. What we can do then is to create an event in our Google CalDAV calendar and after it has been created, attempt to delete it from the event store:

```
- (BOOL)    createEventWithTitle:(NSString *)paramTitle
                       startDate:(NSDate *)paramStartDate
                         endDate:(NSDate *)paramEndDate
               inCalendarWithTitle:(NSString *)paramCalendarTitle
               inCalendarWithType:(EKCalendarType)paramCalendarType
                           notes:(NSString *)paramNotes{

  BOOL result = NO;

  EKEventStore *eventStore = [[EKEventStore alloc] init];

  /* Are there any calendars available to the event store? */
  if ([eventStore.calendars count] == 0){
    NSLog(@"No calendars are found.");
    return NO;
  }

  EKCalendar *targetCalendar = nil;

  /* Try to find the calendar that the user asked for */
  for (EKCalendar *thisCalendar in eventStore.calendars){
    if ([thisCalendar.title isEqualToString:paramCalendarTitle] &&
```

```
      thisCalendar.type == paramCalendarType){
      targetCalendar = thisCalendar;
      break;
    }
  }

  /* Make sure we found the calendar that we were asked to find */
  if (targetCalendar == nil){
    NSLog(@"Could not find the requested calendar.");
    return NO;
  }

  /* If a calendar does not allow modification of its contents
   then we cannot insert an event into it */
  if (targetCalendar.allowsContentModifications == NO){
    NSLog(@"The selected calendar does not allow modifications.");
    return NO;
  }

  /* Create an event */
  EKEvent *event = [EKEvent eventWithEventStore:eventStore];
  event.calendar = targetCalendar;

  /* Set the properties of the event such as its title,
   start date/time, end date/time, etc. */
  event.title = paramTitle;
  event.notes = paramNotes;
  event.startDate = paramStartDate;
  event.endDate = paramEndDate;

  /* Finally, save the event into the calendar */
  NSError *saveError = nil;

  result = [eventStore saveEvent:event
                            span:EKSpanThisEvent
                           error:&saveError];

  if (result == NO){
    NSLog(@"An error occurred = %@", saveError);
  }

  return result;

}

- (BOOL)    removeEventWithTitle:(NSString *)paramTitle
                      startDate:(NSDate *)paramStartDate
                        endDate:(NSDate *)paramEndDate
            inCalendarWithTitle:(NSString *)paramCalendarTitle
             inCalendarWithType:(EKCalendarType)paramCalendarType
                          notes:(NSString *)paramNotes{

  BOOL result = NO;

  EKEventStore *eventStore = [[EKEventStore alloc] init];
```

```objectivec
/* Are there any calendars available to the event store? */
if ([eventStore.calendars count] == 0){
  NSLog(@"No calendars are found.");
  return NO;
}

EKCalendar *targetCalendar = nil;

/* Try to find the calendar that the user asked for */
for (EKCalendar *thisCalendar in eventStore.calendars){
  if ([thisCalendar.title isEqualToString:paramCalendarTitle] &&
      thisCalendar.type == paramCalendarType){
    targetCalendar = thisCalendar;
    break;
  }
}

/* Make sure we found the calendar that we were asked to find */
if (targetCalendar == nil){
  NSLog(@"Could not find the requested calendar.");
  return NO;
}

/* If a calendar does not allow modification of its contents
 then we cannot insert an event into it */
if (targetCalendar.allowsContentModifications == NO){
  NSLog(@"The selected calendar does not allow modifications.");
  return NO;
}

NSArray *calendars = [[NSArray alloc] initWithObjects:targetCalendar, nil];

NSPredicate *predicate =
[eventStore predicateForEventsWithStartDate:paramStartDate
                                    endDate:paramEndDate
                                  calendars:calendars];

/* Get all the events that match the parameters */
NSArray *events = [eventStore eventsMatchingPredicate:predicate];

if ([events count] > 0){

  /* Delete them all */
  for (EKEvent *event in events){
    NSError *removeError = nil;
    /* Do not commit here, we will commit in batch after we have
     removed all the events that matched our criteria */
    if ([eventStore removeEvent:event
                           span:EKSpanThisEvent
                         commit:NO
                          error:&removeError] == NO){
      NSLog(@"Failed to remove event %@ with error = %@",
            event,
            removeError);
```

```
      }
    }

    NSError *commitError = nil;
    if ([eventStore commit:&commitError]){
      result = YES;
    } else {
      NSLog(@"Failed to commit the event store.");
    }

  } else {
    NSLog(@"No events matched your input.");
  }

  return result;

}

- (BOOL)              application:(UIApplication *)application
  didFinishLaunchingWithOptions:(NSDictionary *)launchOptions{


  NSDate *startDate = [NSDate date]; /* Now */

  const NSTimeInterval NSOneHour = 60 * 60; /* 60 minutes, each 60 seconds */
  NSDate *endDate = [startDate dateByAddingTimeInterval:NSOneHour];

  BOOL createdSuccessfully = [self createEventWithTitle:@"Shopping"
                                              startDate:startDate
                                                endDate:endDate
                                  inCalendarWithTitle:@"vandad.np@gmail.com"
                                   inCalendarWithType:EKCalendarTypeCalDAV
                                                  notes:@"Get bread"];

  if (createdSuccessfully){

    NSLog(@"Successfully created the event.");

    BOOL removedSuccessfully =
    [self removeEventWithTitle:@"Shopping"
                     startDate:startDate
                       endDate:endDate
           inCalendarWithTitle:@"vandad.np@gmail.com"
            inCalendarWithType:EKCalendarTypeCalDAV
                         notes:@"Get bread"];

    if (removedSuccessfully){
      NSLog(@"Successfully removed the event.");
    } else {
      NSLog(@"Failed to remove the event.");
    }

  } else {
    NSLog(@"Failed to create the event.");
  }
```

```
    }
    self.window = [[UIWindow alloc] initWithFrame:
                    [[UIScreen mainScreen] bounds]];

    self.window.backgroundColor = [UIColor whiteColor];
    [self.window makeKeyAndVisible];
    return YES;
}
```

In this example, we are not committing the deletion of every event one by one. We are simply setting the `commit` parameter of the `removeEvent:span:commit:error:` method to `NO`. After we are done, we are invoking the `commit:` method of the event store explicitly. The reason for this is that we don't really want to commit every single deletion. That would create a lot of overhead. We can delete as many events as we need to, and then commit them all in one batch.

See Also

Recipe 16.1; Recipe 16.3

16.5 Adding Recurring Events to Calendars

Problem

You want to add a recurring event to a calendar.

Solution

In this example, we are creating an event that occurs on the same day, every month, for an entire year. The steps are as follows:

1. Create an instance of `EKEventStore`.
2. Find a modifiable calendar inside the `calendars` array of the event store (for more information, refer to Recipe 16.1).
3. Create an object of type `EKEvent` (for more information, refer to Recipe 16.2).
4. Set the appropriate values for the event, such as its `startDate` and `endDate` (for more information, refer to Recipe 16.2).
5. Instantiate an object of type `NSDate` that contains the exact date when the recurrence of this event ends. In this example, this date is one year from today's date.
6. Use the `recurrenceEndWithEndDate:` class method of `EKRecurrenceEnd` and pass the `NSDate` you created in step 5 to create an object of type `EKRecurrenceEnd`.
7. Allocate and then instantiate an object of type `EKRecurrenceRule` using the `initRecurrenceWithFrequency:interval:end:` method of `EKRecurrenceRule`. Pass the

---

recurrence end date that you created in step 6 to the end parameter of this method. For more information about this method, please refer to this recipe's Discussion.

8. Assign the recurring event that you created in step 7 to the `recurringRule` property of the `EKEvent` object that was created in step 3.

9. Invoke the `saveEvent:span:error:` instance method with the event (created in step 3) as the `saveEvent` parameter and the value `EKSpanFutureEvents` for the `span` parameter. This will create our recurring event for us.

The following code illustrates these steps:

```
- (void) createRecurringEventInLocalCalendar{

  /* Step 1: And now the event store */
  EKEventStore *eventStore = [[EKEventStore alloc] init];

  /* Step 2: Find the first local calendar that is modifiable */
  EKCalendar *targetCalendar = nil;

  for (EKCalendar *thisCalendar in eventStore.calendars){
    if (thisCalendar.type == EKCalendarTypeLocal &&
        [thisCalendar allowsContentModifications]){
      targetCalendar = thisCalendar;
    }
  }

  /* The target calendar wasn't found? */
  if (targetCalendar == nil){
    NSLog(@"The target calendar is nil.");
    return;
  }

  /* Step 3: Create an event */
  EKEvent *event = [EKEvent eventWithEventStore:eventStore];

  /* Step 4: Create an event that happens today and happens
   every month for a year from now */

  NSDate *eventStartDate = [NSDate date];

  /* Step 5: The event's end date is one hour from the moment it is created */
  NSTimeInterval NSOneHour = 1 * 60 * 60;
  NSDate *eventEndDate = [eventStartDate dateByAddingTimeInterval:NSOneHour];

  /* Assign the required properties, especially
   the target calendar */
  event.calendar = targetCalendar;
  event.title = @"My Event";
  event.startDate = eventStartDate;
  event.endDate = eventEndDate;

  /* The end date of the recurring rule
   is one year from now */
  NSTimeInterval NSOneYear = 365 * 24 * 60 * 60;
```

```
    NSDate *oneYearFromNow = [eventStartDate dateByAddingTimeInterval:NSOneYear];

    /* Step 6: Create an Event Kit date from this date */
    EKRecurrenceEnd *recurringEnd =
    [EKRecurrenceEnd recurrenceEndWithEndDate:oneYearFromNow];

    /* Step 7: And the recurring rule. This event happens every
     month (EKRecurrenceFrequencyMonthly), once a month (interval:1)
     and the recurring rule ends a year from now (end:RecurringEnd) */

    EKRecurrenceRule *recurringRule =
    [[EKRecurrenceRule alloc]
     initRecurrenceWithFrequency:EKRecurrenceFrequencyMonthly
     interval:1
     end:recurringEnd];

    /* Step 8: Set the recurring rule for the event */
    event.recurrenceRules = [[NSArray alloc] initWithObjects:recurringRule, nil];

    NSError *saveError = nil;

    /* Step 9: Save the event */
    if ([eventStore saveEvent:event
                     span:EKSpanFutureEvents
                     error:&saveError]){
      NSLog(@"Successfully created the recurring event.");
    } else {
      NSLog(@"Failed to create the recurring event %@", saveError);
    }

}
```

Discussion

A recurring event is an event that happens more than once. We can create a recurring event just like a normal event. Please refer to Recipe 16.2 for more information about inserting normal events into the Calendar database. The only difference between a recurring event and a normal event is that you apply a recurring rule to a recurring event. A recurring rule tells the Event Kit framework how the event has to occur in the future.

We create a recurring rule by instantiating an object of type EKRecurrenceRule using the initRecurrenceWithFrequency:interval:end: initialization method. The parameters for this method are:

initRecurrenceWithFrequency
> Specifies whether you want the event to be repeated daily (EKRecurrenceFre quencyDaily), weekly (EKRecurrenceFrequencyWeekly), monthly (EKRecurrenceFre quencyMonthly), or yearly (EKRecurrenceFrequencyYearly).

interval

> A value greater than zero that specifies the interval between each occurrence's start and end period. For instance, if you want to create an event that happens every week, specify the `EKRecurrenceFrequencyWeekly` value with an `interval` of 1. If you want this event to happen every other week, specify `EKRecurrenceFrequency Weekly` with an `interval` of 2.

end

> A date of type `EKRecurrenceEnd` that specifies the date when the recurring event ends in the specified calendar. This parameter is not the same as the event's end date (the `endDate` property of `EKEvent`). The end date of an event specifies when that specific event ends in the calendar, whereas the `end` parameter of the `initRe currenceWithFrequency:interval:end:` method specifies the final occurrence of the event in the database.

Figure 16-5 depicts how our recurring event appears in the Calendar app on the device.

Figure 16-5. Calendar app showing the recurring event we created (My Event)

By editing this event (see Figure 16-6) in the Calendar application on an iOS device, you can see that the event is truly a recurring event that happens every month, on the same day the event was created, for a whole year.

Figure 16-6. Editing a recurring event in the Calendar app on an iOS device

See Also

Recipe 16.2

16.6 Retrieving the Attendees of an Event

Problem

You want to retrieve the list of attendees for a specific event.

Solution

Use the `attendees` property of an instance of `EKEvent`. This property is of type `NSArray` and includes objects of type `EKParticipant`.

The example code that follows will retrieve all the events that happen today (whatever the day may be) and print out useful event information, including the attendees of that event, to the console window:

```
- (EKCalendar *) calDAVCalendarWithTitleContaining
                :(NSString *)paramDescription{

    EKCalendar *result = nil;
```

```
  EKEventStore *eventStore = [[EKEventStore alloc] init];

  for (EKCalendar *thisCalendar in eventStore.calendars){
    if (thisCalendar.type == EKCalendarTypeCalDAV){
      if ([thisCalendar.title
           rangeOfString:paramDescription].location != NSNotFound){
        return thisCalendar;
      }
    }
  }

  return result;

}

- (void) enumerateTodayEvents{

  /* Find a calendar to base our search on */
  EKCalendar *targetCalendar =
    [self calDAVCalendarWithTitleContaining:@"vandad.np@gmail.com"];

  /* If we could not find a CalDAV calendar that
   we were looking for, then we will abort the operation */
  if (targetCalendar == nil){
    NSLog(@"No CalDAV calendars were found.");
    return;
  }

  /* We have to pass an array of calendars
   to the event store to search */
  NSArray *targetCalendars = [[NSArray alloc]
                              initWithObjects:targetCalendar, nil];

  /* Instantiate the event store */
  EKEventStore *eventStore = [[EKEventStore alloc] init];

  /* Construct the starting date for today */
  NSDate *startDate = [NSDate date];

  /* The end date will be 1a day from now */
  NSTimeInterval NSOneDay = 1 * 24 * 60 * 60;
  NSDate *endDate = [startDate dateByAddingTimeInterval:NSOneDay];

  /* Create the predicate that we can later pass to
   the event store in order to fetch the events */
  NSPredicate *searchPredicate =
  [eventStore predicateForEventsWithStartDate:startDate
                                      endDate:endDate
                                    calendars:targetCalendars];

  /* Make sure we succeeded in creating the predicate */
  if (searchPredicate == nil){
    NSLog(@"Could not create the search predicate.");
    return;
  }
```

```
/* Fetch all the events that fall between the
 starting and the ending dates */
NSArray *events = [eventStore eventsMatchingPredicate:searchPredicate];

/* Array of NSString equivalents of the values
 in the EKParticipantRole enumeration */
NSArray *attendeeRole = [NSArray arrayWithObjects:
                         @"Unknown",
                         @"Required",
                         @"Optional",
                         @"Chair",
                         @"Non Participant",
                         nil];

/* Array of NSString equivalents of the values
 in the EKParticipantStatus enumeration */
NSArray *attendeeStatus = [NSArray arrayWithObjects:
                           @"Unknown",
                           @"Pending",
                           @"Accepted",
                           @"Declined",
                           @"Tentative",
                           @"Delegated",
                           @"Completed",
                           @"In Process",
                           nil];

/* Array of NSString equivalents of the values
 in the EKParticipantType enumeration */
NSArray *attendeeType = [NSArray arrayWithObjects:
                         @"Unknown",
                         @"Person",
                         @"Room",
                         @"Resource",
                         @"Group",
                         nil];

/* Go through all the events and print their information
 out to the console */
if (events != nil){

  NSUInteger eventCounter = 0;
  for (EKEvent *thisEvent in events){

    eventCounter++;

    NSLog(@"Event %lu Start Date = %@",
          (unsigned long)eventCounter,
          thisEvent.startDate);

    NSLog(@"Event %lu End Date = %@",
          (unsigned long)eventCounter,
          thisEvent.endDate);
```

```objc
            NSLog(@"Event %lu Title = %@",
                  (unsigned long)eventCounter,
                  thisEvent.title);

            if (thisEvent.attendees == nil ||
                [thisEvent.attendees count] == 0){
              NSLog(@"Event %lu has no attendees",
                    (unsigned long)eventCounter);
              continue;
            }

            NSUInteger attendeeCounter = 1;
            for (EKParticipant *participant in thisEvent.attendees){

              NSLog(@"Event %lu Attendee %lu Name = %@",
                    (unsigned long)eventCounter,
                    (unsigned long)attendeeCounter,
                    participant.name);

              NSLog(@"Event %lu Attendee %lu Role = %@",
                    (unsigned long)eventCounter,
                    (unsigned long)attendeeCounter,
                    [attendeeRole objectAtIndex:
                     participant.participantRole]);

              NSLog(@"Event %lu Attendee %lu Status = %@",
                    (unsigned long)eventCounter,
                    (unsigned long)attendeeCounter,
                    [attendeeStatus objectAtIndex:
                     participant.participantStatus]);

              NSLog(@"Event %lu Attendee %lu Type = %@",
                    (unsigned long)eventCounter,
                    (unsigned long)attendeeCounter,
                    [attendeeType objectAtIndex:
                     participant.participantType]);

              NSLog(@"Event %lu Attendee %lu URL = %@",
                    (unsigned long)eventCounter,
                    (unsigned long)attendeeCounter,
                    participant.URL);

              attendeeCounter++;

            }

        } /* for (EKEvent *Event in Events){ */

      } else {
        NSLog(@"The array of events is nil.");
      }

    }

    - (BOOL)             application:(UIApplication *)application
```

```
didFinishLaunchingWithOptions:(NSDictionary *)launchOptions{

    [self enumerateTodayEvents];

    self.window = [[UIWindow alloc] initWithFrame:
                   [[UIScreen mainScreen] bounds]];

    self.window.backgroundColor = [UIColor whiteColor];
    [self.window makeKeyAndVisible];
    return YES;
}
```

When we run this code on an iOS device with a couple of events set up on a CalDAV calendar named *vandad.np@gmail.com* (refer to this chapter's Introduction for more information about CalDAV calendars and how you can set one up on your iOS device), we get results similar to these in the console window.

Discussion

Different types of calendars, such as CalDAV, can include participants in an event. iOS allows users to add participants to a calendar on the server, although not to the calendar on the iOS device. You can do this using Google Calendar, for instance.

Once the user adds participants to an event, you can use the `attendees` property of an instance of `EKEvent` to access the participant objects of type `EKParticipant`. Each participant has properties such as:

name
:   This is the name of the participant. If you just specified the email address of a person to add him to an event, this field will be that email address.

URL
:   This is usually the "mailto" URL for the attendee.

participantRole
:   This is the role the attendee plays in the event. Different values that can be applied to this property are listed in the `EKParticipantRole` enumeration.

participantStatus
:   This tells us whether this participant has accepted or declined the event request. This property could have other values, all specified in the `EKParticipantStatus` enumeration.

participantType
:   This is of type `EKParticipantType`, which is an enumeration and, as its name implies, specifies the type of participant, such as group (`EKParticipantTypeGroup`) or individual person (`EKParticipantTypePerson`).

See Also

Recipe 16.2; Recipe 16.3

16.7 Adding Alarms to Calendars

Problem

You want to add alarms to the events in a calendar.

Solution

Use the `alarmWithRelativeOffset:` class method of `EKAlarm` to create an instance of `EKAlarm`. Add the alarm to an event using the `addAlarm:` instance method of `EKEvent`, like so:

```
- (EKCalendar *) getFirstModifiableLocalCalendar{

  EKCalendar *result = nil;

  EKEventStore *eventStore = [[EKEventStore alloc] init];

  for (EKCalendar *thisCalendar in eventStore.calendars){
    if (thisCalendar.type == EKCalendarTypeLocal &&
        [thisCalendar allowsContentModifications]){
      return thisCalendar;
    }
  }

  return result;

}

- (void) addAlarmToCalendar{

  EKCalendar *targetCalendar = [self getFirstModifiableLocalCalendar];

  if (targetCalendar == nil){
    NSLog(@"Could not find the target calendar.");
    return;
  }

  EKEventStore *eventStore = [[EKEventStore alloc] init];

  /* The event starts 60 seconds from now */
  NSDate *startDate = [NSDate dateWithTimeIntervalSinceNow:60.0f];

  /* And end the event 20 seconds after its start date */
  NSDate *endDate = [startDate dateByAddingTimeInterval:20.0f];

  EKEvent *eventWithAlarm = [EKEvent eventWithEventStore:eventStore];

  eventWithAlarm.calendar = targetCalendar;
  eventWithAlarm.startDate = startDate;
  eventWithAlarm.endDate = endDate;

  /* The alarm goes off two seconds before the event happens */
```

```
        EKAlarm *alarm = [EKAlarm alarmWithRelativeOffset:-2.0f];

        eventWithAlarm.title = @"Event with Alarm";
        [eventWithAlarm addAlarm:alarm];

        NSError *saveError = nil;

        if ([eventStore saveEvent:eventWithAlarm
                              span:EKSpanThisEvent
                             error:&saveError]){
          NSLog(@"Saved an event that fires 60 seconds from now.");
        } else {
          NSLog(@"Failed to save the event. Error = %@", saveError);
        }


}

- (BOOL)            application:(UIApplication *)application
    didFinishLaunchingWithOptions:(NSDictionary *)launchOptions{

    [self addAlarmToCalendar];

    self.window = [[UIWindow alloc] initWithFrame:
                     [[UIScreen mainScreen] bounds]];

    self.window.backgroundColor = [UIColor whiteColor];
    [self.window makeKeyAndVisible];
    return YES;
}
```

Discussion

An event of type EKEvent can have multiple alarms. Simply create the alarm using either the alarmWithAbsoluteDate: or alarmWithRelativeOffset: class method of EKAlarm. The former method requires an absolute date and time (you can use the CFAbsoluteTimeGet Current function to get the current absolute time), whereas the latter method requires a number of seconds relative to the start date of the event when the alarm must be fired. For instance, if the event is scheduled for today at 6:00 a.m., and we go ahead and create an alarm with the relative offset of -60 (which is counted in units of seconds), our alarm will be fired at 5:59 a.m. the same day. Only zero and negative numbers are allowed for this offset. Positive numbers will automatically be changed to zero by iOS. Once an alarm is fired, iOS will display the alarm to the user, as shown in Figure 16-7.

You can use the removeAlarm: instance method of EKEvent to remove an alarm associated with that event instance.

See Also

Recipe 16.1

Figure 16-7. iOS displaying an alert on the screen when an alarm is fired

16.8 Handling Event Changed Notifications

Problem

You want to get notified in your application when the user changes the contents of the Calendar database.

Solution

Register for the EKEventStoreChangedNotification notification:

```
- (EKCalendar *)
    calDAVCalendarWithTitleContaining:(NSString *)paramDescription
                        inEventStore:(EKEventStore *)paramEventStore{

    EKCalendar *result = nil;

    for (EKCalendar *thisCalendar in paramEventStore.calendars){
        if (thisCalendar.type == EKCalendarTypeCalDAV){
            if ([thisCalendar.title
                    rangeOfString:paramDescription].location != NSNotFound){
                return thisCalendar;
            }
        }
    }
```

```
    return result;
}

- (void) eventsChanged:(NSNotification *)paramNotification{

  NSMutableArray *invalidatedEvents = [[NSMutableArray alloc] init];

  NSLog(@"Refreshing array of events...");

  for (EKEvent *event in self.eventsForOneYear){
    if ([event refresh] == NO){
      [invalidatedEvents addObject:event];
    }
  }

  if ([invalidatedEvents count] > 0){
    [self.eventsForOneYear removeObjectsInArray:invalidatedEvents];
  }

}

- (BOOL)             application:(UIApplication *)application
    didFinishLaunchingWithOptions:(NSDictionary *)launchOptions{

  self.eventStore = [[EKEventStore alloc] init];

  EKCalendar *calendar =
  [self calDAVCalendarWithTitleContaining:@"vandad.np@gmail.com"
                            inEventStore:self.eventStore];

  NSTimeInterval NSOneYear = 1 * 365 * 24 * 60 * 60;

  NSDate *startDate = [NSDate date];
  NSDate *endDate = [startDate dateByAddingTimeInterval:NSOneYear];

  NSArray *calendars = [[NSArray alloc] initWithObjects:calendar, nil];

  NSPredicate *predicate =
  [self.eventStore predicateForEventsWithStartDate:startDate
                                           endDate:endDate
                                         calendars:calendars];

  NSArray *events = [self.eventStore eventsMatchingPredicate:predicate];

  self.eventsForOneYear = [[NSMutableArray alloc] initWithArray:events];

  [[NSNotificationCenter defaultCenter]
    addObserver:self
    selector:@selector(eventsChanged:)
    name:EKEventStoreChangedNotification
    object:nil];

  self.window = [[UIWindow alloc] initWithFrame:
                  [[UIScreen mainScreen] bounds]];
```

```
        self.window.backgroundColor = [UIColor whiteColor];
        [self.window makeKeyAndVisible];
        return YES;
    }
```

Discussion

Multitasking is possible on iOS. Imagine you have fetched a series of events from
EKEventStore into an array and you allow your user to work with them (edit them, add
to them, and remove from them). The user could simply switch from your application to the Calendar application and delete the same event she is trying to delete in your
application. Such a sequence of activities will generate an EKEventStoreChangedNotifi
cation notification that you can choose to receive.

The EKEventStoreChangedNotification notification will be sent to your application (at
least, if you subscribe to this notification) even if your application is in the foreground.
Because of this, you must make sure you treat this notification differently depending
on whether your application is in the background or the foreground. Here are a couple
of things to consider:

- If you receive the EKEventStoreChangedNotification notification while your application is in the foreground, it is best to implement a mechanism to find out whether
  the changes to the event store originated inside your own application or came from
  someone else outside the application. If they came from outside the application,
  you must make sure you are retaining the latest version of the events in the store,
  and not the old events. If for any reason you copied one of the events in the event
  store and kept the copy somewhere, you must call the refresh instance method of
  that event of type EKEvent. If the return value of this method is YES, you can keep
  the object in memory. If the return value is NO, you must dispose of the object,
  because someone outside your application has deleted or somehow invalidated the
  event.

- If you receive the EKEventStoreChangedNotification notification while your application is in the background, according to documentation from Apple, your application should not attempt to do any GUI-related processing and should, in fact,
  use as little processing power as possible. You must therefore refrain from adding
  new screens to, or modifying in any way, the GUI of your application.

- If you receive the EKEventStoreChangedNotification notification while your application is in the background, you must make note of it inside the application
  (perhaps store this in a property of type BOOL) and react to this change when the
  application is brought to the foreground again. Normally, if you receive any notification about a change to an event while you are in the background, you should
  retrieve all events stored in the application when you return to the foreground.

Coalescing is not enabled on the EKEventStoreChangedNotification event store notification. In other words, you can receive multiple notifications of the same type if a single event changes in the Calendar database. It is up to you to determine how and when you need to refetch your retained events.

16.9 Presenting Event View Controllers

Problem

You want to use the built-in iOS SDK view controllers to display the properties of an event in the Calendar database.

Solution

Create an instance of EKEventViewController and push it into a navigation controller or present it as a modal view controller on another view controller.

Discussion

Users of iOS devices are already familiar with the interface they see on the Calendar application. When they select an event, they can see that event's properties and they might be allowed to modify the event. To present a view to a user using built-in iOS SDK event view controllers, we can instantiate an object of type EKEventView Controller and assign an event of type EKEvent to its event property. Once that's done, we can push the event view controller into our navigation controller and let iOS take care of the rest.

We want to find an event (any event) in any of the calendars available on an iOS device, from one year ago to now. We will use EKEventViewController to present that event to the user. Here is the *.h* file of our view controller:

```
#import <UIKit/UIKit.h>
#import <EventKit/EventKit.h>
#import <EventKitUI/EventKitUI.h>

@interface Presenting_Event_View_ControllersViewController
        : UIViewController <EKEventViewDelegate>
@property (nonatomic, strong) EKEventStore *eventStore;

@end
```

Now in the viewDidLoad method of our view controller, let's go ahead and display the instance of EKEventViewController on the first event we find in any of the calendars on the device, from a year ago:

```
- (void)viewDidLoad{
  [super viewDidLoad];
```

```
self.eventStore = [[EKEventStore alloc] init];

NSTimeInterval NSOneYear = 1 * 365 * 24.0f * 60.0f * 60.0f;
NSDate *startDate = [[NSDate date] dateByAddingTimeInterval:-NSOneYear];
NSDate *endDate = [NSDate date];

NSPredicate *predicate =
[self.eventStore predicateForEventsWithStartDate:startDate
                                         endDate:endDate
                                       calendars:self.eventStore.calendars];

NSArray *events = [self.eventStore eventsMatchingPredicate:predicate];

if ([events count] > 0){
  EKEvent *event = [events objectAtIndex:0];
  EKEventViewController *controller = [[EKEventViewController alloc] init];
  controller.event = event;
  controller.allowsEditing = NO;
  controller.allowsCalendarPreview = YES;
  controller.delegate = self;

  [self.navigationController pushViewController:controller
                                      animated:YES];
}

}
```

Last but not least, as you can see in the code, we have become the delegate object of the event view controller, so let's make sure we are handling the delegate methods if required:

```
- (void)eventViewController:(EKEventViewController *)controller
    didCompleteWithAction:(EKEventViewAction)action{

  switch (action){

    case EKEventViewActionDeleted:{
      NSLog(@"User deleted the event.");
      break;
    }
    case EKEventViewActionDone:{
      NSLog(@"User finished viewing the event.");
      break;
    }
    case EKEventViewActionResponded:{
      NSLog(@"User responsed to the invitation in the event.");
      break;
    }

  }

}
```

Once we run this application on an iOS device, we can see the built-in event view controller displaying the contents of the event that we have found (see Figure 16-8).

Figure 16-8. The built-in iOS event view controller

Different properties of an instance of `EKEventViewController` that we can use to change the behavior of this object are as follows:

`allowsEditing`

If this property's value is set to `YES`, the Edit button will appear on the navigation bar of the event view controller, allowing the user to edit the event. This happens only on modifiable calendars and only for events that have been created by the user on this device. For instance, if you create an event on the Web using Google Calendar and the event appears in your iOS device, you are not allowed to edit that event.

`allowsCalendarPreview`

If this property's value is set to `YES` and the event the user is viewing is an invitation, the user will be given the option to view this current event in a calendar with other events that have been scheduled on the same date.

`event`

This property must be set before presenting the event view controller. This will be the event that the event view controller will display to the user.

When you push the event view controller, the Back button will appear with the title "Back" by default, so you do not have to change it manually. However, if you decide to change the Back button, you can do so by assigning a new object of type `UIBarButtonItem` to the `backBarButtonItem` property of your navigation item. In our example code, we can modify the pushController: method to give our root view controller a custom Back button before pushing the event view controller.

```
- (void)viewDidLoad{
    [super viewDidLoad];

    self.eventStore = [[EKEventStore alloc] init];

    NSTimeInterval NSOneYear = 1 * 365 * 24.0f * 60.0f * 60.0f;
    NSDate *startDate = [[NSDate date] dateByAddingTimeInterval:-NSOneYear];
    NSDate *endDate = [NSDate date];

    NSPredicate *predicate =
    [self.eventStore predicateForEventsWithStartDate:startDate
                                             endDate:endDate
                                           calendars:self.eventStore.calendars];

    NSArray *events = [self.eventStore eventsMatchingPredicate:predicate];

    if ([events count] > 0){
        EKEvent *event = [events objectAtIndex:0];
        EKEventViewController *controller = [[EKEventViewController alloc] init];
        controller.event = event;
        controller.allowsEditing = YES;
        controller.allowsCalendarPreview = YES;
        controller.delegate = self;    self.navigationItem.backBarButtonItem =
        [[UIBarButtonItem alloc] initWithTitle:@"Go Back"
                                         style:UIBarButtonItemStylePlain
                                        target:nil
                                        action:nil];

        [self.navigationController pushViewController:controller
                                            animated:YES];
    }

}
```

The results of this modification are depicted in Figure 16-9 (please note that in this example, editing is enabled for the event view controller).

See Also

Recipe 16.10

16.10 Presenting Event Edit View Controllers

Problem

You want to allow your users to edit (insert, delete, and modify) events in the Calendar database from inside your application, using built-in SDK view controllers.

Figure 16-9. An edit view controller with editing enabled and a custom back button

Solution

Instantiate an object of type `EKEventEditViewController` and present it on a navigation controller using the `presentModalViewController:animated:` instance method of `UINavigationController`.

Discussion

An instance of the `EKEventEditViewController` class allows us to present an event edit view controller to the user. This view controller, depending on how we set it up, can allow the user to either edit an existing event or create a new event. If you want this view controller to edit an event, set the event property of this instance to an event object. If you want the user to be able to insert a new event into the system, set the event property of this instance to `nil`.

The `editViewDelegate` property of an instance of `EKEventEditViewController` is the object that will receive delegate messages from this view controller telling the programmer about the action the user has taken. One of the most important delegate messages your delegate object must handle (a required delegate selector) is the `eventEditViewController:didCompleteWithAction:` method. This delegate method will be called whenever the user dismisses the event edit view controller in one of the possible ways indicated by the `didCompleteWithAction` parameter. This parameter can have values such as the following:

`EKEventEditViewActionCanceled`
> The user pressed the Cancel button on the view controller.

`EKEventEditViewActionSaved`

> The user saved (added/modified) an event in the Calendar database.

`EKEventEditViewActionDeleted`

> The user deleted an event from the Calendar database.

Please make sure to dismiss the event edit view controller after receiving this delegate message, if you are displaying the edit view controller as a modal view controller.

So let's go ahead and define our view controller:

```
#import <UIKit/UIKit.h>
#import <EventKit/EventKit.h>
#import <EventKitUI/EventKitUI.h>

@interface Presenting_Event_Edit_View_ControllersViewController
        : UIViewController <EKEventEditViewDelegate>

@property (nonatomic, strong) EKEventStore *eventStore;

@end
```

Now let's try to find the first event from a year ago (whatever event that might be) and allow the user to edit that event by displaying an edit event view controller:

```
- (void)eventEditViewController:(EKEventEditViewController *)controller
        didCompleteWithAction:(EKEventEditViewAction)action{

  switch (action){

    case EKEventEditViewActionCanceled:{
      NSLog(@"Cancelled");
      break;
    }
    case EKEventEditViewActionSaved:{
      NSLog(@"Saved");
      break;
    }
    case EKEventEditViewActionDeleted:{
      NSLog(@"Deleted");
      break;
    }

  }

}

- (void)viewDidLoad{
  [super viewDidLoad];

  self.eventStore = [[EKEventStore alloc] init];

  NSTimeInterval NSOneYear = 1 * 365 * 24.0f * 60.0f * 60.0f;
  NSDate *startDate = [[NSDate date] dateByAddingTimeInterval:-NSOneYear];
  NSDate *endDate = [NSDate date];
```

```
NSPredicate *predicate =
  [self.eventStore predicateForEventsWithStartDate:startDate
                                           endDate:endDate
                                         calendars:self.eventStore.calendars];

NSArray *events = [self.eventStore eventsMatchingPredicate:predicate];

if ([events count] > 0){
  EKEvent *event = [events objectAtIndex:0];
  EKEventEditViewController *controller =
    [[EKEventEditViewController alloc] init];

  controller.event = event;
  controller.editViewDelegate = self;

  [self.navigationController presentModalViewController:controller
                                              animated:YES];
}

}
```

Depending on the event that is found on the device, the user will see something similar to Figure 16-10.

Figure 16-10. An edit event view controller displaying an event

See Also

Recipe 16.9

CHAPTER 17

Graphics and Animations

17.0 Introduction

You've certainly seen applications with beautiful graphics effects on iPhones or iPads. And you've probably also encountered impressive animations in games and other apps. Working together, the iOS runtime and Cocoa programming frameworks make possible an amazing variety of graphics and animation effects with relatively simple coding. The quality of these graphics and animations depends partly, of course, on the aesthetic sensitivities of the programmer and artistic collaborators. But in this chapter, you'll see how much you can accomplish with modest programming skills.

I'll dispense with conceptual background, preferring to introduce ideas such as color spaces, transformation, and the graphics context as we go along. I'll just mention a few basics before leaping into code.

In Cocoa Touch, an app is made up of *windows* and *views*. An app with a UI has at least one window that contains, in turn, one or more views. In Cocoa Touch, a window is an instance of `UIWindow`. Usually, an app will open to the main window and the programmer will then add views to the window to represent different parts of the UI: parts such as buttons, labels, images, and custom controls. All these UI-related components are handled and drawn by UIKit.

Some of these things might sound relatively difficult to understand, but I promise you that as we proceed through this chapter, you will understand them step-by-step with the many examples I will give.

Apple has provided developers with powerful frameworks that handle graphics and animations in iOS and OS X. Some of these frameworks and technologies are:

UIKit
> The high-level framework that allows developers to create views, windows, buttons, and other UI related components. It also incorporates some of the low-level APIs into an easier-to-use high-level API.

Quartz 2D

The main engine running under the hood to facilitate drawing in iOS; UIKit uses Quartz.

Core Graphics

A framework that supports the graphics context (more on this later), loading images, drawing images, and so on.

Core Animation

A framework that, as its name implies, facilitates animations in iOS.

When drawing on a screen, one of the most important concepts to grasp is the relation between points and pixels. I'm sure you're familiar with pixels, but what are *points*? They're the device-independent counterpart of pixels. For instance, compare the iPhone 3GS to the iPhone 4. Both devices have 3.5-inch displays. However, the number of pixels that iPhone 3GS can draw in portrait mode is 320×480. The same screen size on the iPhone 4 is capable of drawing twice as many, or 640×960, pixels in portrait mode.

Now imagine you are writing an iPhone app that has only one screen, and that you are simply filling the whole screen with the color green. Imagine that you naïvely specify a rectangular area of 320×480 pixels. When iPhone 3GS users run your app, they will be quite happy because "it does what it says it does": fill the entire screen with the color green. iPhone 4 users, on the other hand, will be quite unhappy: what they will see is quite different, as shown in Figure 17-1.

Figure 17-1. Device-dependent pixel rendering yields different results on different devices

To remedy this problem, Apple introduced device-independent drawing methods to help developers focus on how their shapes and graphics have to appear on a device instead of worrying about the screen sizes and resolutions of different devices that run the same code. To fix the issue we saw in Figure 17-1, the developer of the app can simply use the relevant APIs to specify the green rectangle in points instead of pixels. That will allow the same code to run on the iPhone 3GS and the iPhone 4, ensuring that the screen on the iPhone 4 will be filled with the rectangle. For this reason, many of the methods that you will see in this chapter will rely on points (or as Apple calls them, *logical points*) instead of pixels.

The origin point of the screen on an iOS device is the top-left corner. Screens whose drawing origin is on the top-left corner are also referred to as Upper Left Origin, or ULO, screens. This means that point (0, 0) is the topmost and the leftmost point on the screen, and that positive values of the *x* axis extend towards the right, while positive values of the *y* axis extend towards the bottom. In other words, an *x* position of 20 is further right on the screen than a position of 10 is. On the *y* axis, point 20 is further down than point 10.

In this chapter, we will be using view objects of type UIView to draw shapes, strings, and everything else that's visible on the screen.

I assume you have the latest Xcode from Apple. If not, please head to Xcode's website (*http://developer.apple.com/xcode/*) and download it.

In order to be able to incorporate some of these code snippets in an application, I will first show you the required steps to create a new project in Xcode and subclass UIView, where we can place the code:

1. Open Xcode.
2. From the File menu, select New → Project.
3. On the left side of the screen, make sure the iOS category is selected. Select Application under that category (see Figure 17-2).
4. On the right side of the screen, select Single View Application, and press Next (see Figure 17-2).

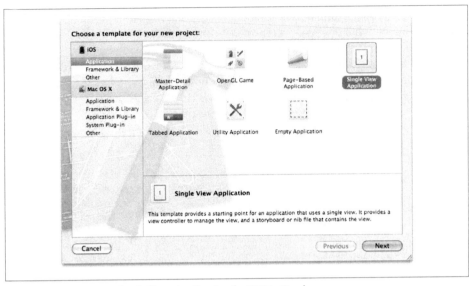

Figure 17-2. Creating a Single View Application for iOS in Xcode

5. In the Product Name box (Figure 17-3), select a name for your project. I've entered *Graphics*, and I suggest you choose the same name to avoid confusion later on.

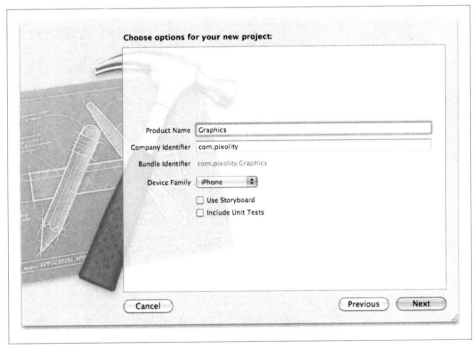

Figure 17-3. Setting the options for a new project in Xcode

6. In the Company Identifier box, enter a bundle identifier prefix, which will be prepended to the Product Name you chose. This is usually com.company. I have chosen *com.pixolity*. Xcode usually will pick this up automatically for you.

7. In the Device Family, select iPhone, and then press Next.

8. On the next screen (Figure 17-4), select where you want to save your project and press Create.

Figure 17-4. Saving the Xcode project on disk

Now your Xcode project is open. On the left side of Xcode, expand the Graphics group to reveal all the files that Xcode created when you created the project. Now we shall create a view object for the view controller. Please follow these steps to do so:

1. Select the Graphics group from the lefthand side in Xcode.

2. Right-click on the Graphics group and select New File....

3. In the New File dialog box, make sure iOS is selected as the category on the left side, and select Cocoa Touch as the subcategory (see Figure 17-5).

4. On the right side, select Objective-C class, and then press Next (see Figure 17-5).

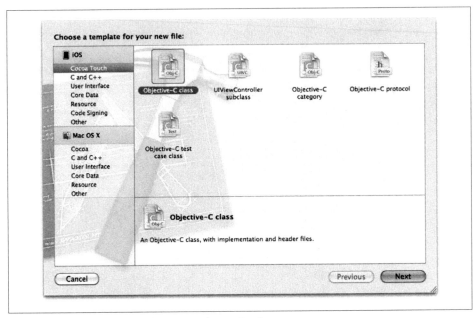

Figure 17-5. Creating a new Objective-C class in Xcode

5. In the next screen (Figure 17-6), make sure that the Subclass box has *UIView* written inside it, and then press Next.

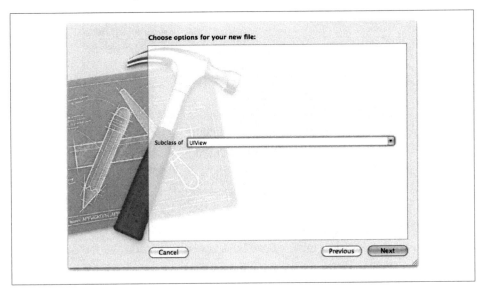

Figure 17-6. Creating a subclass of UIView

6. In the Save As dialog, set the file name to *GraphicsViewControllerView.m*.

7. Select Graphics in the Group drop-down box (see Figure 17-7).

8. Make sure the "Add to targets" checkbox is selected for the project that we created earlier, and then press Save (see Figure 17-7).

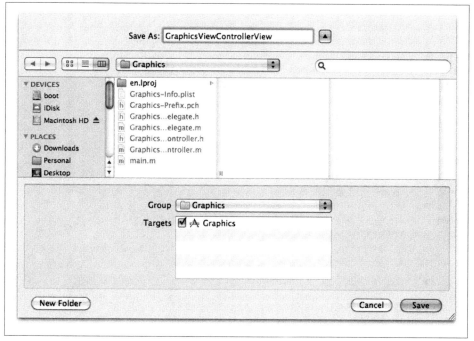

Figure 17-7. Saving a subclass of UIView to disk

9. On the left side of Xcode's main window, click on the *GraphicsViewController.xib* file. Interface Builder will be displayed on the right side of Xcode's screen, as shown in Figure 17-8. We will not be using the *.xib* file at this point.

10. From the Xcode menu, select View → Utilities → File Inspector. The file inspector will be displayed, by default, on the right side of Xcode's window.

11. Click somewhere inside the gray view that is created for you in Interface Builder. The contents displayed in File Inspector (on the right) will change to reflect your selection (see Figure 17-9).

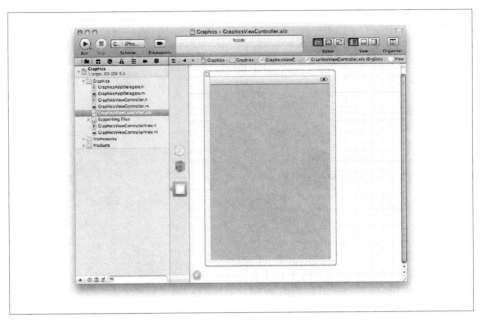

Figure 17-8. Selecting the xib file of the view controller

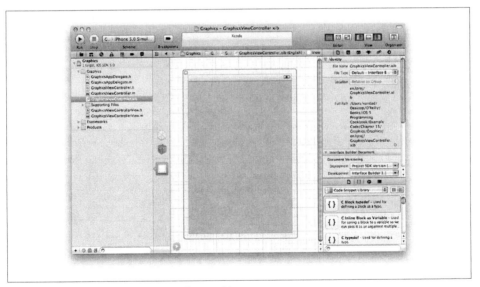

Figure 17-9. The file inspector in Interface Builder

12. In File Inspector, choose the Identity Inspector tab on top (see Figure 17-10).

Figure 17-10. The Identity Inspector shows information for the view object

13. In the Class box, under the Custom Class section, enter GraphicsViewController
    View (the view object we created before), and press Return on your keyboard.

Now we are ready to start coding. What we did was simply create a view class of type
UIView so that later in this chapter, we can change the code in that class. Then we used
Interface Builder to set the view controller's view class to the same view object that we
created. This means that the view controller's view will now be an instance of the
GraphicsViewControllerView class that we created.

You have probably already looked at the contents of the view object that Xcode generated. One of the most important methods inside this object is drawRect:. Cocoa
Touch automatically calls this method whenever it is time to draw the view, and uses
it to ask the view object to draw its contents on the graphical context that Cocoa Touch
automatically prepares for the view. A graphical context can be thought of as a canvas,
offering an enormous number of properties such as pen color, pen thickness, etc. Given
the context, you can start *painting* straight away inside the drawRect: method, and
Cocoa Touch will make sure that the attributes and properties of the context are applied
to your drawings. We will talk about this more later, but for now, let's move on to more
interesting subjects.

17.1 Enumerating and Loading Fonts

Problem

You want to use fonts which come pre-installed on an iOS device, in order to render
some text on the screen.

Solution

Use the UIFont class.

Discussion

Fonts are fundamental to displaying text on a graphical user interface. The UIKit framework provides programmers with high-level APIs that facilitate the enumerating, loading, and use of fonts. Fonts are encapsulated in the UIFont class in Cocoa Touch. Each iOS device comes with built-in system fonts. Fonts are organized into *families*, and each family contains *faces*. For instance, Helvetica is a font family, and Helvetica *Bold* is one of the faces of the Helvetica family. To be able to load a font, you must know the font's face (that is, its name)—and to know the face, you have to know the family. So first, let's enumerate all the font families that are installed on the device, using the familyNames class method of the UIFont class:

```
- (void) enumerateFonts{

  for (NSString *familyName in [UIFont familyNames]){
    NSLog(@"Font Family = %@", familyName);
  }

}
```

Running this program in iOS Simulator, I get results similar to this:

```
Font Family = Heiti TC
Font Family = Sinhala Sangam MN
Font Family = Kannada Sangam MN
Font Family = Georgia
Font Family = Heiti J
Font Family = Times New Roman
Font Family = Snell Roundhand
Font Family = Geeza Pro
Font Family = Helvetica Neue
...
```

After getting the font families, we can enumerate the font names inside each family. We'll use the fontNamesForFamilyName: class method of the UIFont class, and get back an array of font names for the family name that we pass as a parameter:

```
- (void) enumerateFonts{

  for (NSString *familyName in [UIFont familyNames]){
    NSLog(@"Font Family = %@", familyName);
    for (NSString *fontName in
        [UIFont fontNamesForFamilyName:familyName]){
      NSLog(@"\t%@", fontName);

    }
  }

}
```

Running this code in iOS Simulator gives me the following results:

```
...
Font Family = Geeza Pro
```

```
    GeezaPro
    GeezaPro-Bold
Font Family = Helvetica Neue
  HelveticaNeue-Italic
  HelveticaNeue-Bold
  HelveticaNeue-BoldItalic
  HelveticaNeue
...
```

So as you can see, *Helvetica Neue* is the font family and *HelveticaNeue-Bold* is one of the font names in this family. Now that we know the font name, we can load the fonts into objects of type UIFont using the fontWithName:size: class method of the UIFont class:

```
UIFont *helveticaBold = [UIFont fontWithName:@"HelveticaNeue-Bold"
                                        size:12.0f];
```

 If the result of the fontWithName:size: class method of the UIFont class is nil, the given font name could not be found. Make sure that the font name you have provided is available in the system by first enumerating all the font families and then all font names available in each family.

You can also use the systemFontOfSize: instance method of the UIFont class (or its bold alternative, boldSystemFontOfSize:) to load local system fonts, whatever they might be, from the device that is running your code. The default system font for iOS devices is Helvetica.

After you have loaded fonts, you can proceed to Recipe 17.2, where we will use the fonts that we loaded here in order to draw text on a graphical context.

See Also

Recipe 17.2

17.2 Drawing Text

Problem

You want to be able to draw text on the screen of an iOS device.

Solution

Use the drawAtPoint:withFont: method of NSString.

Discussion

To draw text, we can use some really handy methods built into the NSString class, such as drawAtPoint:withFont:. Before we proceed further, make sure that you have followed the instructions in Recipe 17.0. You should now have a view object, subclassed from UIView, named GraphicsViewControllerView. Open that file. If the drawRect: instance method of the view object is commented out, remove the comments until you have that method in your view object:

```
#import "GraphicsViewControllerView.h"

@implementation GraphicsViewControllerView

- (id)initWithFrame:(CGRect)frame{
  self = [super initWithFrame:frame];
  if (self) {
    // Initialization code
  }
  return self;
}

- (void)drawRect:(CGRect)rect{

}

@end
```

The drawRect: method is where we'll do the drawing, as mentioned before. Here, we can start loading the font, and then draw a simple string on the screen at point 40 on the x axis and 180 on the y axis (Figure 17-11):

```
- (void)drawRect:(CGRect)rect{

  UIFont *helveticaBold = [UIFont fontWithName:@"HelveticaNeue-Bold"
                                          size:40.0f];

  NSString *myString = @"Some String";

  [myString drawAtPoint:CGPointMake(40, 180)
               withFont:helveticaBold];

}
```

In this code, we are simply loading a bold Helvetica font at size 40, and using it to draw the text Some String at point (40, 180).

17.3 Constructing, Setting, and Using Colors

Problem

You want to be able to obtain references to color objects in order to use them while you are drawing various forms on a view, such as text, rectangles, triangles, and line segments.

Figure 17-11. A random string drawn on the graphical context of a view

Solution

Use the UIColor class.

Discussion

UIKit provides programmers with a high-level abstraction of colors, encapsulated in the UIColor object. This class has a few really handy class methods such as redColor, blueColor, brownColor, and yellowColor. However, if the color you are looking for isn't one of the explicitly named UIColor methods, you can always use the color WithRed:green:blue:alpha: class method of UIColor class to load the color that you are looking for. The return value of this class method is a value of type UIColor. The parameters of this method are:

red

> The amount of red to use in the color. This value can be anything between 0.0f to 1.0f, where 0.0f omits all red and 1.0f makes the red component as dark as possible.

green

> The amount of green to mix with the red in the color. This value also ranges from 0.0f to 1.0f.

blue

> The amount of blue to mix with the red and green in the color. This value also ranges from 0.0f to 1.0f.

alpha

The opaqueness of the color. This value can range from 0.0f to 1.0f, with 1.0f making the color completely opaque and 0.0f making the color completely transparent (in other words, invisible).

After you have an object of type UIColor, you can use its set instance method to make the current graphics context use that color for subsequent drawing.

 You can use the colorWithRed:green:blue:alpha: class method of the UIColor class to load primary colors like red by simply passing 1.0f as the red parameter, and 0.0f for the green and blue parameters. The alpha is up to you.

If you look at Figure 17-11, you will notice that the background color of the view object we have created by default is an ugly gray color. Let's change that, shall we? Simply find the viewDidLoad instance method of your view controller, GraphicsViewController, and set the background color of your view to white, as shown here:

```
- (void)viewDidLoad{
  [super viewDidLoad];
  self.view.backgroundColor = [UIColor whiteColor];
}
```

 We will be using instance methods of the NSString class to draw text on the current graphics context, as we shall soon discuss.

Now let's load a magenta color into an object of type UIColor and then draw the text I Learn Really Fast on the view's graphical context using a bold Helvetica font of size 30 (see Recipe 17.1 for loading fonts):

```
- (void)drawRect:(CGRect)rect{
  // Drawing code

  /* Load the color */
  UIColor *magentaColor =[UIColor colorWithRed:0.5f
                                         green:0.0f
                                          blue:0.5f
                                         alpha:1.0f];

  /* Set the color in the graphical context */
  [magentaColor set];

  /* Load the font */
  UIFont *helveticaBold = [UIFont fontWithName:@"HelveticaNeue-Bold"
                                          size:30.0f];

  /* the string to be drawn */
```

```
NSString *myString = @"I Learn Really Fast";

/* Draw the string using the font. The color has
   already been set */
[myString drawAtPoint:CGPointMake(25, 190)
            withFont:helveticaBold];

}
```

The results are shown in Figure 17-12.

Figure 17-12. String drawn with a color on a graphical context

We can also use the `drawInRect:withFont:` instance method of the `NSString` class to draw text inside a rectangular space. The text will get stretched to fit into that rectangle. UIKit will even wrap the text if it doesn't fit horizontally within the given rectangle. Rectangular bounds are encapsulated in `CGRect` structures. You can use the `CGRect` `Make` function to create the bounds of a rectangle:

```
- (void)drawRect:(CGRect)rect{
    // Drawing code

    /* Load the color */
    UIColor *magentaColor = [UIColor colorWithRed:0.5f
                                            green:0.0f
                                             blue:0.5f
                                            alpha:1.0f];

    /* Set the color in the graphical context */
    [magentaColor set];

    /* Load the font */
    UIFont *helveticaBold = [UIFont boldSystemFontOfSize:30];
```

```
/* the string to be drawn */
NSString *myString = @"I Learn Really Fast";

/* Draw the string using the font. The color has
  already been set */
[myString drawInRect:CGRectMake(100,  /* x */
                                120,  /* y */
                                100,  /* width */
                                200)  /* height */
             withFont:helveticaBold];

}
```

This function takes four parameters:

x

> The x position of the origin point of the rectangle in relation to the graphics context. In iOS, this is the number of points heading right, starting from the left side of the rectangle.

y

> The y position of the origin point of the rectangle in relation to the graphics context. In iOS, this is the number of points heading down, starting from the top of the rectangle.

width
> The width of the rectangle in points.

height
> The height of the rectangle in points.

The output is shown in Figure 17-13.

UIColor is really a UIKit wrapper around the Core Graphics class CGColor. When we get as low-level as Core Graphics, we suddenly gain more control over how we use the color objects, and we can even determine the components from which the color is made. Let's say some other code passed you an object of type UIColor, and you want to detect its red, green, blue, and alpha components. To get the components that make up a UIColor object, follow these steps:

1. Use the CGColor instance method of the instance of the UIColor class. This will give us a color object of type CGColorRef, which is a Core Graphics Color Reference object.

2. Use the CGColorGetComponents function to get the components that construct the color object.

3. Use the CGColorGetNumberOfComponents function to determine the number of components that were used to construct the color (red + green + etc.) if need be.

Here is an example:

Figure 17-13. Drawing a string in a rectangular space

```
/* Load the color */
UIColor *steelBlueColor = [UIColor colorWithRed:0.3f
                                          green:0.4f
                                           blue:0.6f
                                          alpha:1.0f];

CGColorRef colorRef = [steelBlueColor CGColor];

const CGFloat *components = CGColorGetComponents(colorRef);

NSUInteger componentsCount = CGColorGetNumberOfComponents(colorRef);

NSUInteger counter = 0;
for (counter = 0;
     counter < componentsCount;
     counter++){
  NSLog(@"Component %lu = %.02f",
        (unsigned long)counter + 1,
        components[counter]);
}
```

The output that we get in the console window after running this code is:

```
Component 1 = 0.30
Component 2 = 0.40
Component 3 = 0.60
Component 4 = 1.00
```

See Also

Recipe 17.1

17.4 Drawing Images

Problem

You want to be able to draw images on the screen of an iOS device.

Solution

Use the `UIImage` class to load an image and then use the `drawInRect:` method of the image to draw it on a graphics context.

Discussion

UIKit helps you draw images with ease. All you have to do is to load your images in instances of type `UIImage`. The `UIImage` class provides various class and instance methods to load your images. Here are some of the important ones in iOS:

`imageNamed:` *class method*
> Loads the image (and caches the image if it can load it properly). The parameter to this method is the name of the image in the bundle, such as *Tree Texture.png*.

`imageWithData:` *class method*
> Loads an image from the data encapsulated in an instance of an `NSData` object that was passed as the parameter to this method.

`initWithContentsOfFile:` *instance method (for initialization)*
> Uses the given parameter as the path to an image that has to be loaded and used to initialize the image object.

 This path should be the full path to the image in the app bundle.

`initWithData:` *instance method (for initialization)*
> Uses the given parameter of type `NSData` to initialize the image. This data should belong to a valid image.

Please follow these steps to add an image to your Xcode project:

1. Find where the image is located in your computer.

2. Drag and drop the image into Xcode (onto the lefthand side, where the rest of your project files are stored).

3. A new dialog box will appear on the screen. Check the "Copy items into destination group's folder (if needed)" checkbox only if you want the image file to be copied into your project's structure. Uncheck this box if you don't intend to copy the

image into your project file, instead allowing Xcode to read it from the original file that you dragged and dropped.

4. In the Folders section, make sure that the "Create groups for any added folders" radio button is selected.

5. In the "Add to targets" section, make sure that you check the targets to which you want to add your image.

You can retrieve Xcode's icon by following these steps:

1. Find the Xcode app in the finder.

2. Press Command+I on Xcode in Finder to get information on it.

3. Click on the icon in the upper left of the Xcode Info window.

4. Press Command+C to copy it.

5. Open the Preview app.

6. Hit Command+V to paste the Xcode icon into a new image.

7. You will now have an ICNS file with five separate pages. Save it as a PDF, then delete all but the highest-resolution icon (page 1).

We will be drawing this image on a graphics context to demonstrate how to draw images in this section of the book. I've already found the file, and dragged and dropped that image into my iOS app. Now I have an image called *xcode.png* in my app bundle. The image is shown in Figure 17-14.

Figure 17-14. Xcode's icon, found in your Xcode app

Here is the code for drawing an image:

```objc
- (void)drawRect:(CGRect)rect{

  UIImage *image = [UIImage imageNamed:@"Xcode.png"];

  if (image != nil){
    NSLog(@"Successfully loaded the image.");
  } else {
    NSLog(@"Failed to load the image.");
  }

}
```

If you have the *Xcode.png* image in your app bundle, running this code will print Successfully loaded the image. in the console. If you don't have the image, Failed to load the image. will get printed. For the remainder of this section, I assume you have this image in your app bundle. Feel free to place other images in your app bundle and refer to those images instead of *Xcode.png*, which I will be using in example code.

The two easiest ways to draw an image of type UIImage on a graphics context are:

drawAtPoint: *instance method of* UIImage *class*
  Draws the image at its original size at the given point. Construct the point using the CGPointMake function.

drawInRect: *instance method of* UIImage *class*
  Draws the image in the given rectangular space. To construct this rectangular space, use the CGRectMake function:

```objc
- (void)drawRect:(CGRect)rect{

  /* Assuming the image is in your app bundle and we can load it */
  UIImage *xcodeIcon = [UIImage imageNamed:@"Xcode.png"];

  [xcodeIcon drawAtPoint:CGPointMake(0.0f,
                                     20.0f)];

  [xcodeIcon drawInRect:CGRectMake(50.0f,
                                   10.0f,
                                   40.0f,
                                   35.0f)];
}
```

The drawAtPoint: call shown above will draw the image at its full size at point (0, 20), and the drawInRect: call will draw the image at point (50, 10) at 40×35 points, as shown in Figure 17-15.

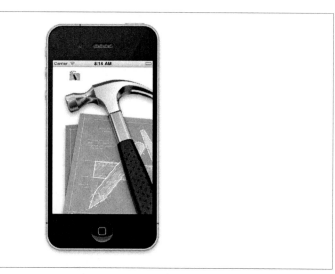

Figure 17-15. Drawing an image on a graphics context can be accomplished with two different methods

Aspect ratio is the ratio between the width and the height of an image (or a computer screen). Let's assume you have an image that is 100×100 pixels. If you draw this image at point (0, 0) with a size of (100, 200), you can immediately see on the screen that the image is stretched in height (200 pixels instead of 100). The drawInRect: instance method of UIImage leaves it up to you how you want to draw your images. In other words, it is *you* who has to specify the *x*, *y*, width, and height of your image as it appears on the screen.

See Also

Recipe 13.6

17.5 Constructing Resizable Images

Problem

You want to be   able to save some memory and disk space by creating resizable images for your UI components. You may also want to be able to create different sizes of the same UI component, such as a button, using only a single background image.

Resizable images refer to simple PNG or JPG images that can be loaded into an instance of UIImage.

Solution

Create a resizable image using the resizableImageWithCapInsets: instance method of the UIImage class.

Discussion

Resizable images may sound a bit strange at first, but they make sense when you understand the different display needs of your app. For instance, you may be working on an iOS app where you want to provide a background image for your buttons. The bigger the text in the button, the wider the button. So you now have two options on how you want to provide the background images of your buttons:

- Create one image per size of button. This will add to the size of your bundle, consumes more memory, and requires much more work from you. In addition, any change to the text requires a new image to make the button fit.

- Create one resizable image and use that throughout the app for all the buttons.

Without a doubt, the second option is much more appealing. So what are resizable images? They are simply images that are divided into two virtual areas:

- An area that will not be stretched.
- An area that will be stretched to fit any size.

As you can see in Figure 17-16, we have created an image for a button. After a better look at the image, you can clearly see that it is made out of a gradient. The area that I have drawn a rectangle around is the area that can be cut out of the image. You might be wondering why. Have a closer look! If I cut that area and made it only 1 pixel wide and as tall as it is now, I could, in my app, put as many of those vertical slices that I cut together to form the same area that is highlighted in this photo. See Figure 17-17.

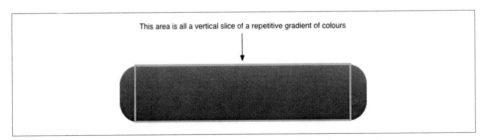

Figure 17-16. An image with a redundant area is a great candidate for a resizable image

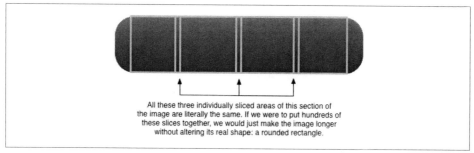

Figure 17-17. Individual slices of the center section of the image are all the same

So how can one make this image smaller and still be able to construct a button out of it? The answer is simple. In this case, where the image is consistently the same across the length of the image, we will simply cut the center of it into a slice that is 1 point wide while keeping it as tall as it is right now. Figure 17-18 shows what our image will look like after this operation.

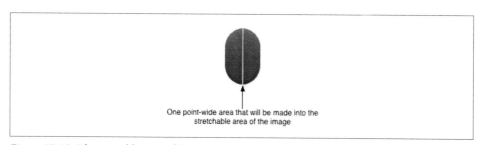

Figure 17-18. The resizable area of the image is made into a one-point wide area

Now comes the interesting part! How can we tell the iOS SDK which part of the image to keep intact and which part to stretch? It turns out that iOS SDK has already taken care of this. First, load your image into memory using the UIImage APIs that you learned in this chapter. After constructing an instance of UIImage with an image that you know you can stretch, transform the image instance into a resizable image using the `resiza bleImageWithCapInsets:` instance method of the same instance. The parameter that this method takes is of type UIEdgeInsets, which is itself defined in this way:

```
typedef struct UIEdgeInsets {
    CGFloat top, left, bottom, right;
} UIEdgeInsets;
```

Edge insets are there to allow us to create what Apple calls *nine-part images*. A nine-part image is an image that has the following nine components:

- Upper left corner
- Top edge
- Upper right corner

- Right edge
- Lower right corner
- Bottom edge
- Lower left corner
- Left edge
- Center

Figure 17-19 illustrates this concept much better than words can.

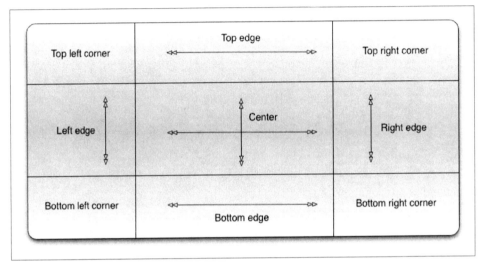

Figure 17-19. Illustration of a nine-part image

The purpose of storing an image as a nine-part image is that programmers can resize it vertically and horizontally to pretty much any size they want. When the programmer requires the image to be resized, some of these components will stay unchanged and some will be resized. The parts that stay unchanged are the corners, which aren't resized at all. The other parts of the image will be resized as follows:

Top edge
    This part of the image will be resized in its width but not in its height.

Right edge
    This part of the image will be resized in its height but not in its width.

Bottom edge
    This part of the image, just like the top edge, will be resized in its width, but not in its height.

Left edge

Just like the right edge, this part of the image will be resized in its height, but not in its width.

Center

Will be resized in both its width and its height.

The top, left, bottom, and right values of the inset mark the area that you don't want to stretch. For instance, if you specified the value of 10 for the left, 11 for the top, 14 for the right, and 5 for the bottom, you are telling iOS to put a vertical *line* on the image at 10 points from the left, a horizontal line at 11 points from the top, another vertical line at 14 points from the right, and a final horizontal line at 5 points from the bottom. The rectangular area *trapped* between these virtual lines is the resizable area of the image and the area outside this rectangle is not stretched. This may sound a bit confusing, but imagine a rectangle (your image) and then you draw another rectangle inside it. The inner rectangle is resizable but the outer rectangle stays intact. I think looking at a picture demonstrating these values will clarify this (Figure 17-20).

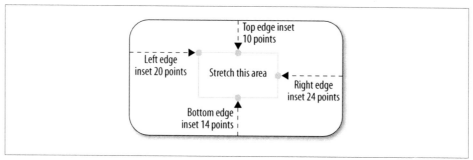

Figure 17-20. The stretchable portion of the image is defined by the edge insets

 The left and right distances are really the same in Figure 17-20. So are the top and the bottom distances. I have just set them to different values to make the edge inset construction a bit more straightforward and easier to understand. If all the values were the same, when we construct the edge insets later you may ask: which one is which?!

For an image like this (Figure 17-20), we should construct the edge inset like so:

```
UIEdgeInsets edgeInsets;
edgeInsets.left = 20.0f;
edgeInsets.top = 10.0f;
edgeInsets.right = 24.0f;
edgeInsets.bottom = 14.0f;
```

OK, now let's go back to our example code. What we are trying to do here is use the stretchable image that we created in Figure 17-18 for a real application. We will create a button and place it at the center of our only view controller's view. The button's text will read "Stretched Image on Button" and its size will be 200 points wide and 44 points tall. Here is our code:

```
#import "ViewController.h"

@interface ViewController ()
@property (nonatomic, strong) UIButton *button;
@end

@implementation ViewController

- (void)viewDidLoad{
    [super viewDidLoad];

    /* Instantiate the button */
    self.button = [UIButton buttonWithType:UIButtonTypeCustom];
    [self.button setFrame:CGRectMake(0.0f, 0.0f, 200.0f, 44.0f)];

    /* Set the title of the button */
    [self.button setTitle:@"Stretched Image on Button"
                forState:UIControlStateNormal];

    /* Adjust the font for our text */
    self.button.titleLabel.font = [UIFont systemFontOfSize:15.0f];

    /* Construct the stretchable image */
    UIImage *image = [UIImage imageNamed:@"Button"];
    UIEdgeInsets edgeInsets;
    edgeInsets.left = 14.0f;
    edgeInsets.top = 0.0f;
    edgeInsets.right = 14.0f;
    edgeInsets.bottom = 0.0f;
    image = [image resizableImageWithCapInsets:edgeInsets];

    /* Set the background image of the button */
    [self.button setBackgroundImage:image forState:UIControlStateNormal];

    [self.view addSubview:self.button];
    self.button.center = self.view.center;

}

- (void)didReceiveMemoryWarning{
    [super didReceiveMemoryWarning];
}


@end
```

Now if you run the app, you will see something similar to Figure 17-21.

Figure 17-21. A button is displayed on the screen with a stretchable background image

See Also

Recipe 17.4

17.6 Drawing Lines

Problem

You simply want to be able to draw lines on a graphics context.

Solution

Retrieve the handle to your graphics context and then use the `CGContextMoveToPoint` and the `CGContextAddLineToPoint` functions to draw your line.

Discussion

When we talk about drawing shapes in iOS or OS X, we are implicitly talking about *paths*. What are paths, you may ask? A path is constructed from one or more series of points drawn on a screen. There is a big difference between paths and lines. A path can contain many lines, but a line cannot contain many paths. Think of paths as series of points—it's as simple as that.

Lines have to be drawn using paths. Specify the start and end points, and then ask Core Graphics to fill that path for you. Core Graphics realizes that you have created a line on that path, and will paint that path for you using the color that you specified (see Recipe 17.3).

We will be talking about paths in more depth later (see Recipe 17.7), but for now let's focus on using paths to create straight lines. To do this, follow these steps:

1. Choose a color on your graphics context (see Recipe 17.3).

2. Retrieve the handle to the graphics context, using the `UIGraphicsGetCurrentContext` function.

3. Set the starting point for your line using the `CGContextMoveToPoint` procedure.

4. Move your pen on the graphics context using the `CGContextAddLineToPoint` procedure to specify the ending point of your line.

5. Create the path that you have laid out using the `CGContextStrokePath` procedure. This procedure will draw the path using the current color that has been set on the graphics context.

Optionally, you can use the `CGContextSetLineWidth` procedure to set the width of the lines that you are drawing on a given graphics context. The first parameter to this procedure is the graphics context that you are drawing on, and the second parameter is the width of the line, expressed as a floating-point number (`CGFloat`).

 In iOS, the line width is measured in logical points.

Here is an example:

```
- (void)drawRect:(CGRect)rect{

    /* Set the color that we want to use to draw the line */
    [[UIColor brownColor] set];

    /* Get the current graphics context */
    CGContextRef currentContext = UIGraphicsGetCurrentContext();

    /* Set the width for the line */
    CGContextSetLineWidth(currentContext,
                          5.0f);

    /* Start the line at this point */
    CGContextMoveToPoint(currentContext,
                         50.0f,
                         10.0f);

    /* And end it at this point */
```

```
CGContextAddLineToPoint(currentContext,
                        100.0f,
                        200.0f);

/* Use the context's current color to draw the line */
CGContextStrokePath(currentContext);

}
```

Running this code in iOS Simulator will show you results similar to Figure 17-22.

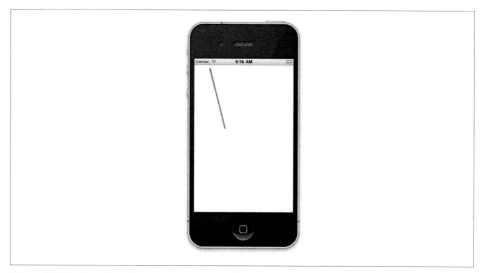

Figure 17-22. Drawing a line on a current graphics context

Let me show you another example. As mentioned earlier, the CGContextAddLineTo Point procedure specifies the end point of the current line. Now what if we have already drawn a line from point (20, 20) to point (100, 100), and want to draw a line from (100, 100) to (300, 100)? You might think that after drawing the first line, we have to move the pen to point (100, 100) using the CGContextMoveToPoint procedure, and then draw the line to point (300, 100) using the CGContextAddLineToPoint procedure. While that will work, there is a more efficient way to do this. After you call the CGContextAddLine ToPoint procedure to specify the ending point of your current line, your pen's position will change to what you pass to this method. In other words, after you issue a method using the pen, it leaves the pen's position at the ending point of whatever it drew. So to draw another line from the current ending point to another point, all you have to do is to call the CGContextAddLineToPoint procedure again with another ending point. Here is an example:

```
- (void)drawRect:(CGRect)rect{
  // Drawing code

  /* Set the color that we want to use to draw the line */
```

```
[[UIColor brownColor] set];

/* Get the current graphics context */
CGContextRef currentContext = UIGraphicsGetCurrentContext();

/* Set the width for the lines */
CGContextSetLineWidth(currentContext,
                      5.0f);

/* Start the line at this point */
CGContextMoveToPoint(currentContext,
                     20.0f,
                     20.0f);

/* And end it at this point */
CGContextAddLineToPoint(currentContext,
                        100.0f,
                        100.0f);

/* Extend the line to another point */
CGContextAddLineToPoint(currentContext,
                        300.0f,
                        100.0f);

/* Use the context's current color to draw the lines */
CGContextStrokePath(currentContext);

}
```

The results are shown in Figure 17-23. You can see that both lines are successfully drawn without us having to move the pen for the second line.

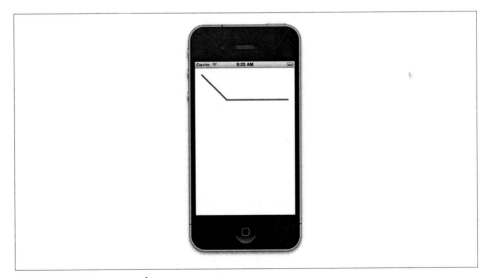

Figure 17-23. Drawing two lines at once

The point where two lines meet is, not surprisingly, called a join. With Core Graphics, you can specify what type of join you want to have between lines that are connected to each other. To make your choice, you must use the `CGContextSetLineJoin` procedure. It takes two parameters: a graphics context on which you are setting the join type, and the join type itself, which must be of type `CGLineJoin`. `CGLineJoin` is an enumeration of the following values:

`kCGLineJoinMiter`

Joins will be made out of sharp corners. This is the default join type.

`kCGLineJoinBevel`

Joins will be squared off on the corner.

`kCGLineJoinRound`

As the name implies, this makes round joins.

Let's have a look at an example. Let's say we want to write a program that can draw "rooftops" on a graphics context (three of them, one for each join type), and also draws text below each rooftop describing the type of join it is using. Something similar to Figure 17-24 will be the result.

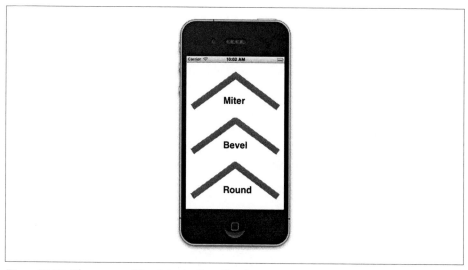

Figure 17-24. Three types of line joins in Core Graphics

To accomplish this, I've written a method named `drawRooftopAtTopPointof:textToDis play:lineJoin:`, which takes three parameters:

1. A point at which the top of the rooftop should be placed.
2. The text to display inside the rooftop.
3. The join type to be used.

The code is as follows:

```
- (void) drawRooftopAtTopPointof:(CGPoint)paramTopPoint
              textToDisplay:(NSString *)paramText
                  lineJoin:(CGLineJoin)paramLineJoin{

  /* Set the color that we want to use to draw the line */
  [[UIColor brownColor] set];

  /* Get the current graphics context */
  CGContextRef currentContext = UIGraphicsGetCurrentContext();

  /* Set the line join */
  CGContextSetLineJoin(currentContext,
                       paramLineJoin);

  /* Set the width for the lines */
  CGContextSetLineWidth(currentContext,
                        20.0f);

  /* Start the line at this point */
  CGContextMoveToPoint(currentContext,
                       paramTopPoint.x - 140,
                       paramTopPoint.y + 100);

  /* And end it at this point */
  CGContextAddLineToPoint(currentContext,
                          paramTopPoint.x,
                          paramTopPoint.y);

  /* Extend the line to another point to
   make the rooftop */
  CGContextAddLineToPoint(currentContext,
                          paramTopPoint.x + 140,
                          paramTopPoint.y + 100);

  /* Use the context's current color to draw the lines */
  CGContextStrokePath(currentContext);

  /* Draw the text in the rooftop using a black color */
  [[UIColor blackColor] set];

  /* Now draw the text */
  CGPoint drawingPoint = CGPointMake(paramTopPoint.x - 40.0f,
                                     paramTopPoint.y + 60.0f);
  [paramText drawAtPoint:drawingPoint
              withFont:[UIFont boldSystemFontOfSize:30.0f]];

}
```

Now let's call this   method in the drawRect: instance method of the view object where
we have a graphics context:

```
- (void)drawRect:(CGRect)rect{

  [self drawRooftopAtTopPointof:CGPointMake(160.0f, 40.0f)
              textToDisplay:@"Miter"
                  lineJoin:kCGLineJoinMiter];
```

```
[self drawRooftopAtTopPointof:CGPointMake(160.0f, 180.0f)
               textToDisplay:@"Bevel"
                    lineJoin:kCGLineJoinBevel];

[self drawRooftopAtTopPointof:CGPointMake(160.0f, 320.0f)
               textToDisplay:@"Round"
                    lineJoin:kCGLineJoinRound];

}
```

See Also

Recipe 17.3; Recipe 17.7

17.7 Constructing Paths

Problem

You want to be able to draw any shape that you wish on a graphics context.

Solution

Construct and draw paths.

Discussion

A series of points placed together can form a shape. A series of shapes put together builds a path. Paths can easily be managed by Core Graphics. In Recipe 17.6, we worked indirectly with paths using CGContext functions. But Core Graphics also has functions that work directly with paths, as we shall soon see.

Paths belong to whichever graphics context they are drawn on. Paths do not have boundaries or specific shapes, unlike the shapes we draw on them. But paths do have bounding boxes. Please bear in mind that boundaries are not the same as bounding boxes. Boundaries are limits above which you cannot draw on a canvas, while the bounding box of a path is the smallest rectangle that contains all the shapes, points, and other objects that have been drawn on that specific path. Think of paths as stamps and think of your graphics context as the envelope. Your envelope could be the same every time you mail something to your friend, but what you put on that context (the stamp or the path) can be different.

After you finish drawing on a path, you can then draw that path on the graphics context. Developers familiar with game programming know the concept of *buffers*, which draw their scenes and, at appropriate times, *flush* the images onto the screen. Paths are those buffers. They are like blank canvases that can be drawn on graphics contexts when the time is right.

The first step in directly working with paths is to create them. The method creating the path returns a handle that you use whenever you want to draw something on that path, passing the handle to Core Graphics for reference. After you create the path, you can add different points, lines, and shapes to it and then draw the path. You can either fill the path or paint it with a stroke on a graphics context. Here are the methods you have to work with:

CGPathCreateMutable *function*
> Creates a new mutable path of type CGMutablePathRef and returns its handle. We should dispose of this path once we are done with it, as you will soon see.

CGPathMoveToPoint *procedure*
> Moves the current pen position on the path to the point specified by a parameter of type CGPoint.

CGPathAddLineToPoint *procedure*
> Draws a line segment from the current pen position to the specified position (again, specified by a value of type CGPoint).

CGContextAddPath *procedure*
> Adds a given path (specified by a path handle) to a graphics context, ready for drawing.

CGContextDrawPath *procedure*
> Draws a given path on the graphics context.

CGPathRelease *procedure*
> Releases the memory allocated for a path handle.

CGPathAddRect *procedure*
> Adds a rectangle to a path. The rectangle's boundaries are specified by a CGRect structure.

There are three important drawing methods that you can ask the CGContextDrawPath procedure to perform:

kCGPathStroke
> Draws a line (stroke) to mark the boundary or edge of the path, using the currently selected stroke color.

kCGPathFill
> Fills the area surrounded by the path with the currently selected fill color.

kCGPathFillStroke
> Combines stroke and fill. Uses the currently selected fill color to fill the path, and the currently selected stroke color to draw the edge of the path. We'll see an example of this method in the following section.

Let's have a look at an example. We will draw a blue line from the top-left to the bottom-right corner, and another from the top-right to the bottom-left corner, to create a gigantic X across the screen.

For this example, I have removed the status bar from the application in iOS Simulator. If you don't want to bother doing this, please continue to the example code. With a status bar, the output of this code will only be slightly different from the screenshot I'll show. To hide the status bar, find the *Info.plist* file in your Xcode project and add a key to it named `UIStatusBarHidden` with the value of `YES`, as shown in Figure 17-25. This will force your app's status bar to be hidden when it opens.

Key	Type	Value
Localization native development region	String	en
Bundle display name	String	${PRODUCT_NAME}
Executable file	String	${EXECUTABLE_NAME}
Icon file	String	
Bundle identifier	String	com.pixolity.${PRODUCT_NAME:rfc1034identifier}
InfoDictionary version	String	6.0
Bundle name	String	${PRODUCT_NAME}
Bundle OS Type code	String	APPL
Bundle versions string, short	String	1.0
Bundle creator OS Type code	String	????
Bundle version	String	1.0
Application requires iPhone environmer	Boolean	YES
Main nib file base name	String	MainWindow
Status bar is initially hidden	Boolean	YES
▶ Supported interface orientations	Array	(3 items)

Figure 17-25. Hiding the status bar in an iOS app using the Info.plist file

```
- (void)drawRect:(CGRect)rect{

    /* Create the path */
    CGMutablePathRef path = CGPathCreateMutable();

    /* How big is the screen? We want the X to cover
     the whole screen */
    CGRect screenBounds = [[UIScreen mainScreen] bounds];

    /* Start from top-left */
    CGPathMoveToPoint(path,
                      NULL,
                      screenBounds.origin.x,
                      screenBounds.origin.y);

    /* Draw a line from top-left to bottom-right of the screen */
    CGPathAddLineToPoint(path,
                         NULL,
                         screenBounds.size.width,
                         screenBounds.size.height);

    /* Start another line from top-right */
    CGPathMoveToPoint(path,
                      NULL,
                      screenBounds.size.width,
```

```
                        screenBounds.origin.y);

    /* Draw a line from top-right to bottom-left */
    CGPathAddLineToPoint(path,
                         NULL,
                         screenBounds.origin.x,
                         screenBounds.size.height);

    /* Get the context that the path has to be drawn on */
    CGContextRef currentContext = UIGraphicsGetCurrentContext();

    /* Add the path to the context so we can
     draw it later */
    CGContextAddPath(currentContext,
                     path);

    /* Set the blue color as the stroke color */
    [[UIColor blueColor] setStroke];

    /* Draw the path with stroke color */
    CGContextDrawPath(currentContext,
                      kCGPathStroke);

    /* Finally release the path object */
    CGPathRelease(path);

}
```

 The NULL parameters getting passed to procedures such as CGPathMove
ToPoint represent possible transformations that can be used when drawing the shapes and lines on a given path. For information about transformations, refer to Recipes 17.11, 17.12, and 17.13.

You can see how easy it is to draw a path on a context. All you really have to remember
is how to create a new mutable path (CGPathCreateMutable), add that path to your
graphics context (CGContextAddPath), and draw it on a graphics context (CGContextDraw
Path). If you run this code, you will get an output similar to that shown in Figure 17-26.

See Also

Recipe 17.6; Recipe 17.11; Recipe 17.12; Recipe 17.13

17.8 Drawing Rectangles

Problem

You want to be able to draw rectangles on a graphics context.

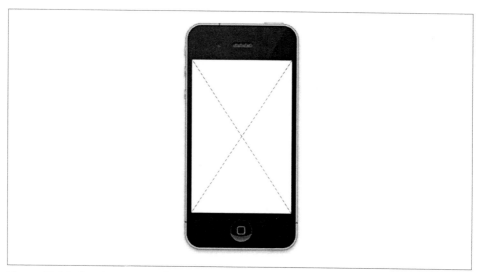

Figure 17-26. Drawing on a graphics context using paths

Solution

Use the `CGPathAddRect` to add a rectangle to a path and then draw that path on a graphics context.

Discussion

As we learned in Recipe 17.7, you can construct and use paths quite easily. One of the procedures that you can use on paths in Core Graphics is `CGPathAddRect`, which lets you draw rectangles as part of paths. Here is an example:

```
- (void)drawRect:(CGRect)rect{

    /* Create the path first. Just the path handle. */
    CGMutablePathRef path = CGPathCreateMutable();

    /* Here are the rectangle boundaries */
    CGRect rectangle = CGRectMake(10.0f,
                                  10.0f,
                                  200.0f,
                                  300.0f);

    /* Add the rectangle to the path */
    CGPathAddRect(path,
                  NULL,
                  rectangle);

    /* Get the handle to the current context */
    CGContextRef currentContext = UIGraphicsGetCurrentContext();
```

```
/* Add the path to the context */
CGContextAddPath(currentContext,
                 path);

/* Set the fill color to cornflower blue */
[[UIColor colorWithRed:0.20f
               green:0.60f
                blue:0.80f
               alpha:1.0f] setFill];

/* Set the stroke color to brown */
[[UIColor brownColor] setStroke];

/* Set the line width (for the stroke) to 5 */
CGContextSetLineWidth(currentContext,
                      5.0f);

/* Stroke and fill the path on the context */
CGContextDrawPath(currentContext,
                  kCGPathFillStroke);

/* Dispose of the path */
CGPathRelease(path);

}
```

Here, we are drawing a rectangle on the path, filling it with cornflower blue, and stroking the edges of the rectangle with brown. Figure 17-27 shows how the output will look when we run the program.

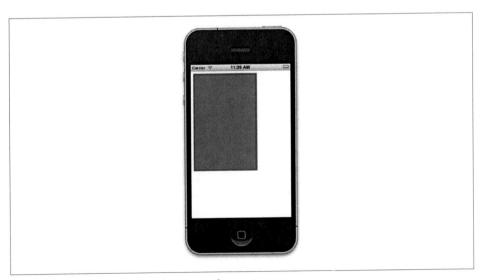

Figure 17-27. Drawing a rectangle using paths

If you have multiple rectangles to draw, you can pass an array of CGRect objects to the CGPathAddRects procedure. Here is an example:

```
- (void)drawRect:(CGRect)rect{

    /* Create the path first. Just the path handle. */
    CGMutablePathRef path = CGPathCreateMutable();

    /* Here are the first rectangle boundaries */
    CGRect rectangle1 = CGRectMake(10.0f,
                                   10.0f,
                                   200.0f,
                                   300.0f);

    /* And the second rectangle */
    CGRect rectangle2 = CGRectMake(40.0f,
                                   100.0f,
                                   90.0f,
                                   300.0f);

    /* Put both rectangles into an array */
    CGRect rectangles[2] = {
      rectangle1, rectangle2
    };

    /* Add the rectangles to the path */
    CGPathAddRects(path,
                   NULL,
                   (const CGRect *)&rectangles,
                   2);

    /* Get the handle to the current context */
    CGContextRef currentContext = UIGraphicsGetCurrentContext();

    /* Add the path to the context */
    CGContextAddPath(currentContext,
                     path);

    /* Set the fill color to cornflower blue */
    [[UIColor colorWithRed:0.20f
                    green:0.60f
                     blue:0.80f
                    alpha:1.0f] setFill];

    /* Set the stroke color to black */
    [[UIColor blackColor] setStroke];

    /* Set the line width (for the stroke) to 5 */
    CGContextSetLineWidth(currentContext,
                          5.0f);

    /* Stroke and fill the path on the context */
    CGContextDrawPath(currentContext,
                      kCGPathFillStroke);
```

```
    /* Dispose of the path */
    CGPathRelease(path);

}
```

Figure 17-28 shows how the output of this code will look when run in iOS Simulator. The parameters that we pass to the `CGPathAddRects` procedure are (in this order):

1. The handle to the path where we will add the rectangles.
2. The transformation, if any, to use on to the rectangles. (For information about transformations, refer to Recipes 17.11, 17.12, and 17.13.)
3. A reference to the array holding the `CGRect` rectangles.
4. The number of rectangles in the array that we passed in the previous parameter. It is very important that you pass exactly as many rectangles as you have in your array, to avoid unknown behavior by this procedure.

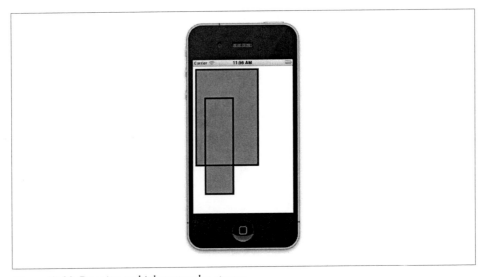

Figure 17-28. Drawing multiple rectangles at once

See Also

Recipe 17.7; Recipe 17.11; Recipe 17.12; Recipe 17.13

17.9 Adding Shadows to Shapes

Problem

You want to be able to apply shadows to shapes that you draw on graphic contexts.

Solution

Use the CGContextSetShadow procedure.

Discussion

It is easy to draw shadows using Core Graphics. The graphics context is the element that bears the shadow. What that means is that you need to apply the shadow to the context, draw the shapes that need the shadow, and then remove the shadow from the context (or set a new context). We will see an example of this soon.

In Core Graphics, we can use two procedures to apply a shadow to a graphics context:

CGContextSetShadow *procedure*

This procedure, which creates black or gray shadows, accepts three parameters:

- The graphics context on which the shadow has to be applied.
- The offset, specified by a value of type CGSize, from the right and the bottom part of each shape where the shadow has to be applied. The greater the *x* value of this offset is, the farther to the right of each shape the shadow will extend. The greater the *y* value of this offset is, the lower the shadow will extend.
- The blur value that has to be applied to the shadow, specified as a floating-point value (CGFloat). Specifying 0.0f will cause the shadow to be a solid shape. The higher this value goes, the more blurred the shadow will get. We will see an example of this soon.

CGContextSetShadowWithColor *procedure*

This procedure accepts the exact same parameters as CGContextSetShadow, with one addition. This fourth parameter, of type CGColorRef, sets the color of the shadow.

At the beginning of this section, I mentioned that the graphics context retains its shadow properties until we explicitly remove the shadow. Let me make that point clearer by showing you an example. Let us go ahead and write code that allows us to draw two rectangles, the first one with a shadow and the second one without a shadow. We will draw the first one in this way:

```
- (void) drawRectAtTopOfScreen{

    /* Get the handle to the current context */
    CGContextRef currentContext = UIGraphicsGetCurrentContext();

    CGContextSetShadowWithColor(currentContext,
                            CGSizeMake(10.0f, 10.0f),
                            20.0f,
                            [[UIColor grayColor] CGColor]);

    /* Create the path first. Just the path handle. */
    CGMutablePathRef path = CGPathCreateMutable();

    /* Here are the rectangle boundaries */
    CGRect firstRect = CGRectMake(55.0f,
```

```
                                    60.0f,
                                    150.0f,
                                    150.0f);

/* Add the rectangle to the path */
CGPathAddRect(path,
              NULL,
              firstRect);

/* Add the path to the context */
CGContextAddPath(currentContext,
                 path);

/* Set the fill color to cornflower blue */
[[UIColor colorWithRed:0.20f
                 green:0.60f
                  blue:0.80f
                 alpha:1.0f] setFill];

/* Fill the path on the context */
CGContextDrawPath(currentContext,
                  kCGPathFill);

/* Dispose of the path */
CGPathRelease(path);

}
```

If we call this method in the `drawRect:` instance method of the view object, we will see the rectangle drawn on the screen with a nice shadow just like we wanted it, as shown in Figure 17-29.

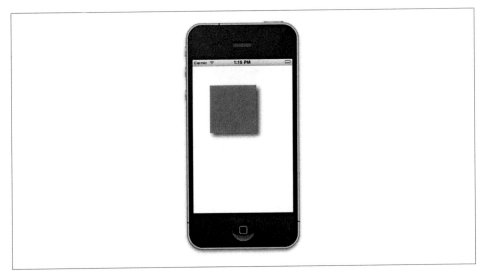

Figure 17-29. Shadow applied to a rectangle

Now let's go ahead and draw a second rectangle after the first one. We won't ask for a shadow, but we'll leave the shadow property of the graphics context as it was for the first rectangle:

```
- (void) drawRectAtBottomOfScreen{

    /* Get the handle to the current context */
    CGContextRef currentContext = UIGraphicsGetCurrentContext();

    CGMutablePathRef secondPath = CGPathCreateMutable();

    CGRect secondRect = CGRectMake(150.0f,
                                   250.0f,
                                   100.0f,
                                   100.0f);
    CGPathAddRect(secondPath,
                  NULL,
                  secondRect);

    CGContextAddPath(currentContext,
                     secondPath);

    [[UIColor purpleColor] setFill];

    CGContextDrawPath(currentContext,
                      kCGPathFill);

    CGPathRelease(secondPath);

}

- (void)drawRect:(CGRect)rect{
    [self drawRectAtTopOfScreen];
    [self drawRectAtBottomOfScreen];
}
```

The drawRect: method first calls the drawRectAtTopOfScreen method, and right after that, calls the drawRectAtBottomOfScreen method. We haven't asked for a shadow for the drawRectAtBottomOfScreen rectangle, yet if you run the app, you will see something similar to Figure 17-30.

It's immediately obvious that the shadow is applied to the second rectangle at the bottom of the screen. To avoid this, we will save the state of the graphics context *before* applying the shadow effect, and then restore the state when we want to remove the shadow effect.

Broadly speaking, saving and restoring the state of a graphics context is not limited to shadows only. Restoring the state of a graphics context restores everything (fill color, font, line thickness, etc.) to the values they had before you set them. So for instance, if you applied fill and stroke colors in the meantime, those colors will be reset.

You can save the state of a graphics context through the CGContextSaveGState procedure and restore the previous state through the CGContextRestoreGState procedure. So if we

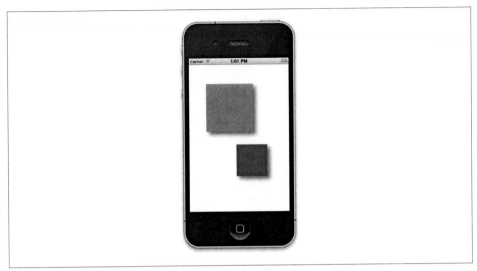

Figure 17-30. A shadow is unintentionally applied to the second rectangle

modify the drawRectAtTopOfScreen procedure by saving the state of the graphics context before applying the shadow, and restore that state after drawing the path, we will have different results, shown in Figure 17-31:

```
- (void) drawRectAtTopOfScreen{

    /* Get the handle to the current context */
    CGContextRef currentContext = UIGraphicsGetCurrentContext();

    CGContextSaveGState(currentContext);

    CGContextSetShadowWithColor(currentContext,
                                CGSizeMake(10.0f, 10.0f),
                                20.0f,
                                [[UIColor grayColor] CGColor]);

    /* Create the path first. Just the path handle. */
    CGMutablePathRef path = CGPathCreateMutable();

    /* Here are the rectangle boundaries */
    CGRect firstRect = CGRectMake(55.0f,
                                  60.0f,
                                  150.0f,
                                  150.0f);

    /* Add the rectangle to the path */
    CGPathAddRect(path,
                  NULL,
                  firstRect);

    /* Add the path to the context */
    CGContextAddPath(currentContext,
                     path);
```

```
/* Set the fill color to cornflower blue */
[[UIColor colorWithRed:0.20f
               green:0.60f
                blue:0.80f
               alpha:1.0f] setFill];

/* Fill the path on the context */
CGContextDrawPath(currentContext,
                  kCGPathFill);

/* Dispose of the path */
CGPathRelease(path);

/* Restore the context to how it was
 when we started */
CGContextRestoreGState(currentContext);

}
```

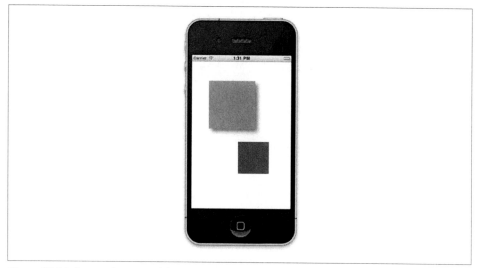

Figure 17-31. Saving the state of the graphics context for accurate shadows

17.10 Drawing Gradients

Problem

You want to draw gradients on graphics contexts, using different colors.

Solution

Use the CGGradientCreateWithColor function.

Discussion

After learning about colors in Recipe 17.3, we're ready to put these skills to better use than drawing simple rectangles and colorful text!

Core Graphics allows programmers to create two types of gradients: axial and radial. (We will only discuss axial gradients in this book.) Axial gradients are gradients that start from one point with one color and end at another point with another color (although they can start and stop with the same color, which does not make them much of a gradient). "Axial" means relating to an axis. The two points (start and end point) create a line segment, which will be the axis on which the gradient will be drawn. An example of an axial gradient is shown in Figure 17-32.

Figure 17-32. An axial gradient starting from the color blue and ending in the color green

In order to create an axial gradient, you must call the `CGGradientCreateWithColorCom`
`ponents` function. The return value of this function will be the new gradient of type `CGGradientRef`. This is the handle to the gradient. Once you are done with the gradient, you *must* call the `CGGradientRelease` procedure, passing the handle to the gradient that you had previously retrieved from `CGGradientCreateWithColorComponents`.

The `CGGradientCreateWithColorComponents` function takes four parameters:

A color space
> This is a container for a range of colors, and must be of type `CGColorSpaceRef`. For this parameter, we can just pass the return value of the `CGColorSpaceCreateDevi`
> `ceRGB` function, which will give us an RGB color space.

An array of color components (for details, see Recipe 17.3)
> This array has to contain red, green, blue, and alpha values, all represented as `CGFloat` values. The number of elements in the array is tightly linked to the next

two parameters. Essentially, you have to include enough values in this array to specify the number of locations in the fourth parameter. So if you ask for two locations (the start and end point), you have to provide two colors in the array here. And since each color is made out of red, green, blue, and alpha, this array has to have 2×4 items: four for the first color and four for the second. Don't worry if you didn't get all this; you will eventually understand it through the examples that follow in this section.

Locations of colors in the array of colors

This parameter controls how quickly the gradient shifts from one color to another. The number of elements must be the same as the value of the fourth parameter. If we ask for four colors, for example, and we want the first color to be the starting color and the last color to be the ending color in the gradient, we have to provide an array of two items of type CGFloats, with the first item set to 0.0f (as in the *first* item in the array of colors) and the second item set to 3.0f (as in the *fourth* item in the array of colors). The values of the two intermediate colors determine how the gradient actually inserts colors to get from the start to the end. Again, don't worry if this is too difficult to grasp. I will give you many examples to help you fully understand the concept.

Number of locations

This specifies how many colors and locations we want.

Let's have a look at an example. Suppose we want to draw the same gradient we saw in Figure 17-32? Here's how:

1. Pick the start and end points of the gradient—the axis along which it will shift. In this case, I've chosen to move from left to right. Think of this as changing color as you move along a hypothetical horizontal line. Along that line, we will spread the colors so that every perpendicular line to this horizontal line contains only one color. In this case, the perpendicular lines would be every vertical line in Figure 17-32. Look at those vertical lines closely. Every single one contains only one color, which runs all the way from top to the bottom. That's how axial gradients work. OK, that's enough theory—let's go to the second step.

2. Now we have to create a color space to pass to the first parameter of the CGGra dientCreateWithColorComponents function, as mentioned before:

```
CGColorSpaceRef colorSpace =
  CGColorSpaceCreateDeviceRGB();
```

 We will release this color space once we are done with it.

3. Select blue as the starting point (left) and green as the ending point (right), according to the colors chosen in Figure 17-32. The names I've selected (startColor

Components and endColorComponents) are arbitrarily chosen to help us remember what we're doing with each color. We'll actually use array positions to specify which one is the start and which one is the end:

```
UIColor *startColor = [UIColor blueColor];
  CGFloat *startColorComponents =
  (CGFloat *)CGColorGetComponents([startColor CGColor]);

  UIColor *endColor = [UIColor greenColor];
  CGFloat *endColorComponents =
  (CGFloat *)CGColorGetComponents([endColor CGColor]);
```

 If you don't remember the concept behind color components, I suggest that you look at Recipe 17.3 before you continue reading these instructions.

4. After retrieving the components of each color, we place them all in one flat array to pass to the CGGradientCreateWithColorComponents function:

```
CGFloat colorComponents[8] = {

    /* Four components of the blue color (RGBA) */
    startColorComponents[0],
    startColorComponents[1],
    startColorComponents[2],
    startColorComponents[3], /* First color = blue */


    /* Four components of the green color (RGBA) */
    endColorComponents[0],
    endColorComponents[1],
    endColorComponents[2],
    endColorComponents[3], /* Second color = green */

};
```

5. Because we have only two colors in this array, we need to specify that the first is positioned at the very beginning of the gradient (position 0.0) and the second at the very end (position 1.0). So let's place these indices in an array to pass to the CGGradientCreateWithColorComponents function:

```
CGFloat colorIndices[2] = {
    0.0f, /* Color 0 in the colorComponents array */
    1.0f, /* Color 1 in the colorComponents array */
};
```

6. Now all we have to do is to actually call the CGGradientCreateWithColorCompo nents function with all these values that we generated:

```
CGGradientRef gradient =
CGGradientCreateWithColorComponents
(colorSpace,
```

```
(const CGFloat *)&colorComponents,
(const CGFloat *)&colorIndices,
2);
```

7. Fantastic! Now we have the gradient object in the `gradient` variable. Before we forget, we have to release the color space that we created using the `CGColorSpace CreateDeviceRGB` function:

```
CGColorSpaceRelease(colorSpace);
```

Now we'll use the `CGContextDrawLinearGradient` procedure to draw the axial gradient on a graphics context. This procedure takes five parameters:

Graphics context
Specifies the graphics context on which the axial gradient will be drawn.

Axial gradient
The handle to the axial gradient object. We created this gradient object using the `CGGradientCreateWithColorComponents` function.

Start point
A point on the graphics context, specified by a `CGPoint`, that indicates the start point of the gradient.

End point
A point on the graphics context, specified by a `CGPoint`, that indicates the end point of the gradient.

Gradient drawing options
Specifies what happens if your start or end point isn't at the edge of the graphical context. You can use your start or end color to fill the space that lies outside the gradient. Specify one of the following values for this parameter:

`kCGGradientDrawsAfterEndLocation`
Extends the gradient to all points after the ending point of the gradient.

`kCGGradientDrawsBeforeStartLocation`
Extends the gradient to all points before the starting point of the gradient.

`0`
Does not extend the gradient in any way.

To extend colors on both sides, specify both the "after" and "before" parameters as a logical OR (using the | operator). We'll see an example later:

```
CGRect screenBounds = [[UIScreen mainScreen] bounds];

CGPoint startPoint, endPoint;

startPoint = CGPointMake(0.0f,
                         screenBounds.size.height / 2.0f);

endPoint = CGPointMake(screenBounds.size.width,
                       startPoint.y);
```

```
CGContextDrawLinearGradient
(currentContext,
 gradient,
 startPoint,
 endPoint,
 0);

CGGradientRelease(gradient);
```

 The gradient handle we are releasing at the end of this code was created in another code block in an earlier example.

The output of this code will obviously look similar to Figure 17-32. Because we started the gradient from the leftmost point of the view and stretched it all the way to the rightmost point, we couldn't take advantage of all the values that could be passed to the final *Gradient drawing options* parameter of the `CGContextDrawLinearGradient` procedure. Let's remedy that, shall we? How about we draw a gradient that looks similar to that shown in Figure 17-33?

Figure 17-33. An axial gradient with start and end point color extensions

We will use the same procedure explained earlier in this section to code the result:

```
- (void)drawRect:(CGRect)rect{

    CGContextRef currentContext = UIGraphicsGetCurrentContext();

    CGContextSaveGState(currentContext); CGColorSpaceRef colorSpace =
    CGColorSpaceCreateDeviceRGB();
```

```
UIColor *startColor = [UIColor orangeColor];
CGFloat *startColorComponents =
(CGFloat *)CGColorGetComponents([startColor CGColor]);

UIColor *endColor = [UIColor blueColor];
CGFloat *endColorComponents =
(CGFloat *)CGColorGetComponents([endColor CGColor]);

CGFloat colorComponents[8] = {

  /* Four components of the orange color (RGBA) */
  startColorComponents[0],
  startColorComponents[1],
  startColorComponents[2],
  startColorComponents[3], /* First color = orange */


  /* Four components of the blue color (RGBA) */
  endColorComponents[0],
  endColorComponents[1],
  endColorComponents[2],
  endColorComponents[3], /* Second color = blue */

};

CGFloat colorIndices[2] = {
  0.0f, /* Color 0 in the colorComponents array */
  1.0f, /* Color 1 in the colorComponents array */
};

CGGradientRef gradient = CGGradientCreateWithColorComponents
(colorSpace,
 (const CGFloat *)&colorComponents,
 (const CGFloat *)&colorIndices,
 2);

CGColorSpaceRelease(colorSpace);

CGPoint startPoint, endPoint;

startPoint = CGPointMake(120,
                         260);

endPoint = CGPointMake(200.0f,
                       220);

CGContextDrawLinearGradient (currentContext,
                             gradient,
                             startPoint,
                             endPoint,
                             kCGGradientDrawsBeforeStartLocation |
                             kCGGradientDrawsAfterEndLocation);

CGGradientRelease(gradient);
```

```
    CGContextRestoreGState(currentContext);

}
```

It might be difficult to understand how mixing kCGGradientDrawsBeforeStartLoca
tionand kCGGradientDrawsAfterEndLocation values passed to the CGContextDrawLin
earGradient procedure is creating a diagonal effect like that shown in Figure 17-33. So
let's remove those values and set the parameter of the CGContextDrawLinearGradient
procedure to 0, as we had it before. Figure 17-34 shows what the results will be.

Figure 17-34. Axial gradient without stretched colors

It's easy to conclude that the gradient in Figure 17-34 is the same gradient shown in
Figure 17-33. However, the gradient in Figure 17-33 extends the start and end points'
colors all the way across the graphics context, which is why you can see the whole
screen covered with color.

See Also

Recipe 17.3

17.11 Displacing Shapes Drawn on Graphic Contexts

Problem

You want to move everything that is drawn on a graphics context to a new location,
without changing your drawing code—or you would simply like to displace your con‐
text's contents with ease.

Solution

Use the CGAffineTransformMakeTranslation function to create an affine translation transformation.

Discussion

Recipe 17.8 mentioned transformations. These are exactly what the name suggests: changes to the way a graphic is displayed. Transformations in Core Graphics are objects that you apply to shapes before they get drawn. For instance, you can create a translation transformation. Translating what, you might be asking? A translation transformation is a mechanism by which you can *displace* a shape or a graphics context.

Other types of transformations include rotation (see Recipe 17.13) and scaling (see Recipe 17.12). These are all examples of *affine* transformations, which map each point in the origin to another point in the final version. All the transformations we discuss in this book will be affine transformations.

A translation transformation *translates* the current position of a shape on a path or graphics context to another relative place. For instance, if you draw a point at location (10, 20), apply a translation transformation of (30, 40) to it, and then draw it, the point will be drawn at (40, 60), because 40 is the sum of 10+30 and 60 is the sum of 20+40.

In order to create a new translation transformation, we must use the CGAffineTrans formMakeTranslation function, which will return an affine transformation of type CGAffineTransform. The two parameters to this function specify the x and the y translation in points.

In Recipe 17.8, we saw that the CGPathAddRect procedure accepts, as its second parameter, a transformation object of type CGAffineTransform. To displace a rectangle from its original place to another, you can simply create an affine transformation specifying the changes you want to make in the x and y coordinates, and pass the transformation to the second parameter of the CGPathAddRect procedure as shown here:

```
- (void)drawRect:(CGRect)rect{

    /* Create the path first. Just the path handle. */
    CGMutablePathRef path = CGPathCreateMutable();

    /* Here are the rectangle boundaries */
    CGRect rectangle = CGRectMake(10.0f,
                                  10.0f,
                                  200.0f,
                                  300.0f);

    /* We want to displace the rectangle to the right by
      100 points but want to keep the y position
      untouched */
    CGAffineTransform transform = CGAffineTransformMakeTranslation(100.0f,
                                                                   0.0f);
```

```
/* Add the rectangle to the path */
CGPathAddRect(path,
              &transform,
              rectangle);

/* Get the handle to the current context */
CGContextRef currentContext =
UIGraphicsGetCurrentContext();

/* Add the path to the context */
CGContextAddPath(currentContext,
                 path);

/* Set the fill color to cornflower blue */
[[UIColor colorWithRed:0.20f
                 green:0.60f
                  blue:0.80f
                 alpha:1.0f] setFill];

/* Set the stroke color to brown */
[[UIColor brownColor] setStroke];

/* Set the line width (for the stroke) to 5 */
CGContextSetLineWidth(currentContext,
                      5.0f);

/* Stroke and fill the path on the context */
CGContextDrawPath(currentContext,
                  kCGPathFillStroke);

/* Dispose of the path */
CGPathRelease(path);

}
```

Figure 17-35 shows the output of this block of code when placed inside a view object.

Compare Figure 17-35 with Figure 17-27. Can you see the difference? Check the source code for both figures and you'll see that the *x* and *y* points specified for both rectangles in both code blocks are the same. It is just that in Figure 17-35, we have applied an affine translation transformation to the rectangle when we added it to the path.

In addition to applying transformations to shapes that get drawn to a path, we can apply transformations to graphics contexts using the CGContextTranslateCTM procedure. This applies a translation transformation on the current transformation matrix (CTM). The current transformation matrix, although its name might be complex, is quite simple to understand. Think of CTM as how your graphics context's center is set up, and how each point that you draw gets projected onto the screen. For instance, when you ask Core Graphics to draw a point at (0, 0), Core Graphics finds the center of the screen by looking at the CTM. The CTM will then do some calculations and tell Core Graphics that point (0, 0) is indeed at the top-left corner of the screen. Using procedures such as CGContextTranslateCTM, you can change how CTM is configured

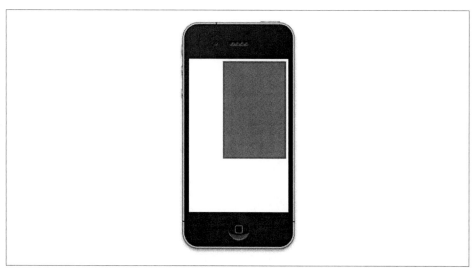

Figure 17-35. A rectangle with an affine translation transformation

and subsequently force every shape drawn on the graphics context to be shifted to another place on the canvas. Here is an example where we achieve the exact same effect we saw in Figure 17-35 by applying a translation transformation to the CTM instead of directly to the rectangle:

```
- (void)drawRect:(CGRect)rect{

  /* Create the path first. Just the path handle. */
  CGMutablePathRef path = CGPathCreateMutable();

  /* Here are the rectangle boundaries */
  CGRect rectangle = CGRectMake(10.0f,
                                10.0f,
                                200.0f,
                                300.0f);

  /* Add the rectangle to the path */
  CGPathAddRect(path,
                NULL,
                rectangle);

  /* Get the handle to the current context */
  CGContextRef currentContext = UIGraphicsGetCurrentContext();

  /* Save the state of the context to revert
   back to how it was at this state, later */
  CGContextSaveGState(currentContext);

  /* Translate the current transformation matrix
   to the right by 100 points */
  CGContextTranslateCTM(currentContext,
                        100.0f,
```

```
                        0.0f);

    /* Add the path to the context */
    CGContextAddPath(currentContext,
                    path);

    /* Set the fill color to cornflower blue */
    [[UIColor colorWithRed:0.20f
                    green:0.60f
                     blue:0.80f
                    alpha:1.0f] setFill];

    /* Set the stroke color to brown */
    [[UIColor brownColor] setStroke];  /* Set the line width (for the stroke) to 5 */
    CGContextSetLineWidth(currentContext,
                    5.0f);

    /* Stroke and fill the path on the context */
    CGContextDrawPath(currentContext,
                    kCGPathFillStroke);

    /* Dispose of the path */
    CGPathRelease(path);

    /* Restore the state of the context */
    CGContextRestoreGState(currentContext);

}
```

After running this program, you will notice that the results are exactly like those shown in Figure 17-35.

See Also

Recipe 17.8; Recipe 17.12; Recipe 17.13

17.12 Scaling Shapes Drawn on Graphic Contexts

Problem

You want to scale   shapes on your graphics context up and down dynamically.

Solution

Create an affine scale transformation using the CGAffineTransformMakeScale function.

Discussion

Recipe 17.11 explained what a transformation is, and how to apply it to shapes and graphics contexts. One of the transformations that you can apply is scaling. You can easily ask Core Graphics to scale a shape, such as a circle, to 100 times its original size.

To create an affine scale transformation, use the `CGAffineTransformMakeScale` function, which returns a transformation object of type `CGAffineTransform`. If you want to apply a scale transformation directly to a graphics context, use the `CGContextScaleCTM` procedure to scale the Current Transformation Matrix (CTM). For more information about CTM, see Recipe 17.11.

Scale transformation functions take two parameters: one to scale the *x* axis and the other to scale the *y* axis. Take another look at the rectangle in Figure 17-27. If we want to scale this rectangle to half its normal length and width, shown in Figure 17-27, we can simply scale the *x* and the *y* axis by 0.5 (half their original value), as shown here:

```
/* Scale the rectangle to half its size */
CGAffineTransform transform =
  CGAffineTransformMakeScale(0.5f, 0.5f);

/* Add the rectangle to the path */
CGPathAddRect(path,
              &transform,
              rectangle);
```

Figure 17-36 shows what we will see after applying the scale transformation to the code we wrote in Recipe 17.8.

Figure 17-36. Scaling a rectangle

In addition to the `CGAffineTransformMakeScale` function, you can use the `CGContextScaleCTM` procedure to apply a scale transformation to a graphics context. The following code will achieve the exact same effect as the previous example, as you can see in Figure 17-36:

```
- (void)drawRect:(CGRect)rect{

    /* Create the path first. Just the path handle. */
    CGMutablePathRef path = CGPathCreateMutable();

    /* Here are the rectangle boundaries */
    CGRect rectangle = CGRectMake(10.0f,
                                  10.0f,
                                  200.0f,
                                  300.0f);

    /* Add the rectangle to the path */
    CGPathAddRect(path,
                  NULL,
                  rectangle);

    /* Get the handle to the current context */
    CGContextRef currentContext = UIGraphicsGetCurrentContext();

    /* Scale everything drawn on the current
     graphics context to half its size */
    CGContextScaleCTM(currentContext,
                      0.5f,
                      0.5f);

    /* Add the path to the context */
    CGContextAddPath(currentContext,
                     path);

    /* Set the fill color to cornflower blue */
    [[UIColor colorWithRed:0.20f
                     green:0.60f
                      blue:0.80f
                     alpha:1.0f] setFill];

    /* Set the stroke color to brown */
    [[UIColor brownColor] setStroke];

    /* Set the line width (for the stroke) to 5 */
    CGContextSetLineWidth(currentContext,
                          5.0f);

    /* Stroke and fill the path on the context */
    CGContextDrawPath(currentContext,
                      kCGPathFillStroke);

    /* Dispose of the path */
    CGPathRelease(path);

}
```

See Also

Recipe 17.11

17.13 Rotating Shapes Drawn on Graphic Contexts

Problem

You want to be able to rotate the contents that you have drawn on a graphics context without changing your drawing code.

Solution

Use the `CGAffineTransformMakeRotation` function to create an affine rotation transformation.

Discussion

 I strongly suggest that you read the material in Recipes 17.11and in 17.12before proceeding with this section. To avoid redundancy, I have tried to keep material that has been taught in earlier sections out of later sections.

Just like scaling and translation, you can apply rotation translation to shapes drawn on paths, and graphics contexts. You can use the `CGAffineTransformMakeRotation` function and pass the rotation value in radians to get back a rotation transformation, of type `CGAffineTransform`. You can then apply this transformation to paths and shapes. If you want to rotate the whole context by a specific angle, you must use the `CGContextRota teCTM` procedure.

Let's rotate the same rectangle we had in Figure 17-27 45 degrees clockwise (see Figure 17-37). The values you supply for rotation must be in radians. Positive values cause clockwise rotation, while negative values cause counterclockwise rotation:

```
/* Rotate the rectangle 45 degrees clockwise */
CGAffineTransform transform =
CGAffineTransformMakeRotation((45.0f * M_PI) / 180.0f);

/* Add the rectangle to the path */
CGPathAddRect(path,
            &transform,
            rectangle);
```

As we saw in Recipe 17.12, we can also apply a transformation directly to a graphics context using the `CGContextRotateCTM` procedure.

See Also

Recipe 17.11; Recipe 17.12

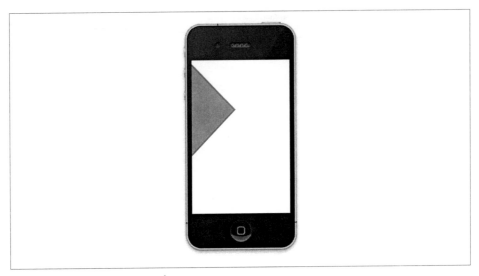

Figure 17-37. Rotating a rectangle

17.14 Animating and Moving Views

Problem

You want to   animate the displacement of views.

Solution

Use the animation methods of UIView while displacing your views.

Discussion

There are various ways of performing animations in iOS: capabilities are provided at a relatively low level, but also at a higher level. The highest level we can get is through UIKit, which is what we will be discussing in this section. UIKit includes some low-level Core Animation functionalities and presents us with a really clean API to work with.

The starting point for   performing animations in UIKit is to call the beginAnima tions:context: class method of the UIView class. Its first parameter is an optional name that you choose for your animation, and the second is an optional context that you can retrieve later to pass to delegate methods of the animations. We will talk about these shortly.

After you start an animation with the `beginAnimations:context:` method, it won't actually take place until you call the `commitAnimations` class method of `UIView` class. The calculation you perform on a view object (such as moving it) between calling `beginAnimations:context:` and `commitAnimations` will be animated after the `commitAnimations` call. Let's have a look at an example.

As we saw in Recipe 17.4, I included in my bundle an image called *Xcode.png*. This is Xcode's icon, which I found by searching in Google Images (see Figure 17-14). Now, in my view controller (see Recipe 17.0), I want to place this image in an image view of type `UIImageView` and then move that image view from the top-left corner of the screen to the bottom-right corner.

Here are the steps that complete this task:

1. Open the *.h* file of your view controller.

2. Define an instance of `UIImageView` as a property of the view controller, and call it `xcodeImageView`, like so:

   ```
   #import <UIKit/UIKit.h>

   @interface Animating_and_Moving_ViewsViewController : UIViewController

   @property (nonatomic, strong) UIImageView *xcodeImageView;

   @end
   ```

3. Load the *Xcode.png* image into an instance of `UIImage` when your view is loaded:

   ```
   - (void) viewDidLoad{
     [super viewDidLoad];

     UIImage *xcodeImage = [UIImage imageNamed:@"Xcode.png"];

     self.xcodeImageView = [[UIImageView alloc]
                           initWithImage:xcodeImage];

     /* Just set the size to make the image smaller */
     [self.xcodeImageView setFrame:CGRectMake(0.0f,
                                              0.0f,
                                              100.0f,
                                              100.0f)];

     self.view.backgroundColor = [UIColor whiteColor];
     [self.view addSubview:self.xcodeImageView];

   }
   ```

4. Figure 17-38 shows how the view will look when we run the program in iOS Simulator.

Figure 17-38. Adding an image view to a view object

5. Now when the view appears on the screen, in the `viewDidAppear:` instance method of the view controller, we will start the animation block for the image view and start an animation that moves the image from its initial location at the top-left corner of the screen to the bottom-right corner. We will make sure this animation happens over a five-second time period:

```
- (void) viewDidAppear:(BOOL)paramAnimated{

  [super viewDidAppear:paramAnimated];

  /* Start from top-left corner */
  [self.xcodeImageView setFrame:CGRectMake(0.0f,
                                           0.0f,
                                           100.0f,
                                           100.0f)];

  [UIView beginAnimations:@"xcodeImageViewAnimation"
                  context:(__bridge void *)self.xcodeImageView];

  /* Five seconds animation */
  [UIView setAnimationDuration:5.0f];

  /* Receive animation delegates */
  [UIView setAnimationDelegate:self];

  [UIView setAnimationDidStopSelector:
   @selector(imageViewDidStop:finished:context:)];

  /* End at the bottom-right corner */
  [self.xcodeImageView setFrame:CGRectMake(200.0f,
                                           350.0f,
```

```
                                          100.0f,
                                          100.0f)];

    [UIView commitAnimations];

}
```

6. Provide the implementation for a `imageViewDidStop:finished:context:` delegate method for your view controller, so that it gets called by UIKit when the animation finishes. This is optional, and for this example I will just log some messages to prove that the method was called. Later examples will show how you can use the method to kick off other activity the moment the animation is finished:

```
- (void)imageViewDidStop:(NSString *)paramAnimationID
                finished:(NSNumber *)paramFinished
                 context:(void *)paramContext{

    NSLog(@"Animation finished.");

    NSLog(@"Animation ID = %@", paramAnimationID);

    UIImageView *contextImageView = (__bridge UIImageView *)paramContext;
    NSLog(@"Image View = %@", contextImageView);

}
```

Now if you run the app, you will notice that as soon as your view gets displayed, the image shown in Figure 17-38 will start moving towards the bottom-right corner, as shown in Figure 17-39, over a period of five seconds.

Figure 17-39. The image is animated to the bottom-right corner of the screen

Also, if you look at the output printed to the console, you will see something similar to this if you wait for the animation to finish:

```
Animation finished.
Animation ID = xcodeImageViewAnimation
Image View = <UIImageView: 0x68221a0;
              frame = (200 350; 100 100);
              opaque = NO;
              userInteractionEnabled = NO;
              layer = <CALayer: 0x68221d0>>
```

Now let's go through some of the concepts and how we actually animated this image view. Here are the important class methods of UIView that you should know about when performing animations using UIKit:

beginAnimations:context:
: Starts an animation block. Any animatable property change that you apply to views after calling this class method will be animated after the animation is committed.

setAnimationDuration:
: Sets the duration of the animation in seconds.

setAnimationDelegate:
: Sets the object that will receive delegate objects for various events that could happen before, during, or after the animation. Setting a delegate object will *not* immediately start firing animation delegates. You must also use different setter class methods on the view object to tell UIKit which selectors in your delegate object have to receive which delegate messages.

setAnimationDidStopSelector:
: Sets the method in the delegate object that has to be called when the animation finishes. This method has to accept three parameters in this order:

1. An animation identifier of type NSString: this will contain the animation identifier passed to the beginAnimations:context: class method of UIView when the animation was started.

2. A "finished" indicator, of type NSNumber: this parameter contains a boolean value inside the NSNumber, which the runtime sets to YES if it could fully finish the animation before it was stopped by the code. If this is value is set to NO, it means the animation was interrupted before it was completed.

3. A context of type void *: this is the context that was passed to the beginAnimations:context: class method of UIView when the animation was started.

setAnimationWillStartSelector:
: Sets the selector   that has to be called in the delegate object when the animation is about to start. The selector passed to this class method has to have two parameters, in this order:

1. An animation identifier of type `NSString`: the runtime sets this to the animation identifier passed to the `beginAnimations:context:` class method of `UIView` when the animation was started.

2. A context of type `void *`: this is the context that was passed to the `beginAnimations:context:` class method of `UIView` when the animation was started.

`setAnimationDelay:`

Sets a delay (in seconds) for the animation before it starts. If this value is set to `3.0f`, for instance, the animation will start 3 seconds after it has been committed.

`setAnimationRepeatCount:`

Sets the number of times an animation block has to repeat its animation.

Now that we know some of the most useful `UIView` class methods that help us animate views, let's look at another animation. In this example code, I want to have two image views (both displaying the same image) appear on the screen at the same time: one at the top-left corner and the other at the bottom-right corner, as shown in Figure 17-40.

Figure 17-40. The starting position of the animation

 In this section, I will call the top-left image *image 1* and the bottom-right image *image 2*.

What we are going to do in this code is create two images, as mentioned, in the top-left and bottom-right corners. Next, we want *image 1* to start moving towards *image 2* over a three-second period, and then fade away. While *image 1* is approaching *image 2*, we want *image 2* to start its animation and move towards the top-left corner of the screen, where *image 1* used to be. We also want *image 2* to complete its animation over a three-second time period, and fade away at the end. This will look *really* cool when you run it on a device or the iOS Simulator. Let me show you how to code it:

1. In the *.h* file of your view controller, define two image views:

```
#import <UIKit/UIKit.h>

@interface Animating_and_Moving_ViewsViewController : UIViewController

@property (nonatomic, strong) UIImageView *xcodeImageView1;
@property (nonatomic, strong) UIImageView *xcodeImageView2;

@end
```

2. In the `viewDidLoad` instance method of your view controller, initialize both of the image views and place them on your view:

```
- (void) viewDidLoad{
  [super viewDidLoad];

  UIImage *xcodeImage = [UIImage imageNamed:@"Xcode.png"];
  self.xcodeImageView1 = [[UIImageView alloc]
                            initWithImage:xcodeImage];

  self.xcodeImageView2 = [[UIImageView alloc]
                            initWithImage:xcodeImage];

  /* Just set the size to make the images smaller */
  [xcodeImageView1 setFrame:CGRectMake(0.0f,
                                       0.0f,
                                       100.0f,
                                       100.0f)];

  [xcodeImageView2 setFrame:CGRectMake(220.0f,
                                       350.0f,
                                       100.0f,
                                       100.0f)];


  self.view.backgroundColor = [UIColor whiteColor];
  [self.view addSubview:self.xcodeImageView1];
  [self.view addSubview:self.xcodeImageView2];

}
```

3. Implement an instance method called `startTopLeftImageViewAnimation` for your view controller. This method, as its name suggests, will carry out the animation for *image 1*, moving it from the top-left corner of the screen to the bottom-right corner while fading it out. Fading is accomplished simply by setting the alpha value to 0:

```
- (void) startTopLeftImageViewAnimation{

  /* Start from top-left corner */
```

```
[self.xcodeImageView1 setFrame:CGRectMake(0.0f,
                                          0.0f,
                                          100.0f,
                                          100.0f)];

[self.xcodeImageView1 setAlpha:1.0f];

[UIView beginAnimations:@"xcodeImageView1Animation"
                context:(__bridge void *)self.xcodeImageView1];

/* 3 seconds animation */
[UIView setAnimationDuration:3.0f];

/* Receive animation delegates */
[UIView setAnimationDelegate:self];

[UIView setAnimationDidStopSelector:
 @selector(imageViewDidStop:finished:context:)];

/* End at the bottom-right corner */
[self.xcodeImageView1 setFrame:CGRectMake(220.0f,
                                          350.0f,
                                          100.0f,
                                          100.0f)];

[self.xcodeImageView1 setAlpha:0.0f];

[UIView commitAnimations];

}
```

4. When the animation for any of these image views stops, we intend to remove those image views from their parent views, as they are not useful anymore. As we saw in the startTopLeftImageViewAnimation method, we passed a delegate selector to the setAnimationDidStopSelector: class method of UIView, and this selector will get called when the animations for *image 1* (as we saw before) and for *image 2* (as we will soon see) stop. Here is the implementation for this delegate selector:

```
- (void)imageViewDidStop:(NSString *)paramAnimationID
                finished:(NSNumber *)paramFinished
                 context:(void *)paramContext{

UIImageView *contextImageView = (__bridge UIImageView *)paramContext;
[contextImageView removeFromSuperview];

}
```

5. We also need a method that will animate *image 2*. There is a little difference between how I've written the animation method for *image 2* as compared to that for *image 1*. I want to be able to start *image 2*'s animation *almost* as *image 1* is finishing its animation. So if *image 1* performs its animation in three seconds, I want *image 2* to start its animation at second 2.0 in *image 1*'s animation, so that I can see *image 2* starting to animate before *image 1* gets to the bottom-right corner of the screen

and fades away. To accomplish this, I am starting both animations at the same time, but the animation for *image 2* will include a two-second delay at the beginning. So if I start both animations at 1 p.m., *image 1* will start its animation at 13:00:00 and finish it at 13:00:03, while *image 2* starts at 13:00:02 and finishes at 13:00:05. Here is how we will animate *image 2*:

```objc
- (void) startBottomRightViewAnimationAfterDelay:(CGFloat)paramDelay{

    /* Start from bottom-right corner */
    [self.xcodeImageView2 setFrame:CGRectMake(220.0f,
                                              350.0f,
                                              100.0f,
                                              100.0f)];

    [self.xcodeImageView2 setAlpha:1.0f];

    [UIView beginAnimations:@"xcodeImageView2Animation"
                    context:(__bridge void *)self.xcodeImageView2];

    /* 3 seconds animation */
    [UIView setAnimationDuration:3.0f];

    [UIView setAnimationDelay:paramDelay];

    /* Receive animation delegates */
    [UIView setAnimationDelegate:self];

    [UIView setAnimationDidStopSelector:
     @selector(imageViewDidStop:finished:context:)];

    /* End at the top-left corner */
    [self.xcodeImageView2 setFrame:CGRectMake(0.0f,
                                              0.0f,
                                              100.0f,
                                              100.0f)];

    [self.xcodeImageView2 setAlpha:0.0f];

    [UIView commitAnimations];

}
```

6. Last but not least, we have to fire both the startTopLeftImageViewAnimation and the startBottomRightViewAnimationAfterDelay: methods at the same time when the view becomes visible:

```objc
- (void) viewDidAppear:(BOOL)paramAnimated{

    [super viewDidAppear:paramAnimated];
    [self startTopLeftImageViewAnimation];
    [self startBottomRightViewAnimationAfterDelay:2.0f];

}
```

17.15 Animating and Scaling Views

Problem

You want to be able to animate the scaling up or down of your views.

Solution

Create a scale affine transformation for your view and use the UIView animation methods to animate the scale transformation.

Discussion

 I highly recommend that you read Recipe 17.14 before proceeding with this section of the book.

In order to scale a view while animating it, you can either apply a scale transformation to it within an animation block (see Recipe 17.12), or just increase the view's width and/or height.

Let's have a look at scaling an image view by applying a scale transformation to it:

```
- (void) viewDidAppear:(BOOL)paramAnimated{
  [super viewDidAppear:paramAnimated];

  /* Place the image view at the center of the view of this view controller */
  self.xcodeImageView.center = self.view.center;

  /* Make sure no translation is applied to this image view */
  self.xcodeImageView.transform = CGAffineTransformIdentity;

  /* Begin the animation */
  [UIView beginAnimations:nil
                  context:NULL];

  /* Make the animation five seconds long */
  [UIView setAnimationDuration:5.0f];

  /* Make the image view twice as large in
   width and height */
  self.xcodeImageView.transform = CGAffineTransformMakeScale(2.0f,
                                                             2.0f);

  /* Commit the animation */
  [UIView commitAnimations];

}
```

This code uses an affine scale transformation to scale the image view to become twice as big as it originally was. The best thing about applying scale transformations to a view is that the width and height are scaled using the center of the view as the center of the scaling. Suppose that the center of your view is at point (100, 100) on the screen, and you scale your view to be twice as big in width and height. The resulting view will have its center remain at point (100, 100) on the screen, while being twice as big in each direction. If you were to scale a view by increasing its frame's width and height explicitly, you would end up with the final view being located somewhere else on the screen. That's because when changing the frame of the image view to scale the width and height, you are also changing the value of the *x* and the *y* of the frame, whether you want to or not. Because of that, your image view will not be scaled up from its center. Fixing this issue is outside the scope of this book, but feel free to play with it for a while and maybe you will find the solution. One hint that I *will* give you is that you can run two animations at the same time in parallel: one for changing the width and height, and the other for changing the center of the image view!

See Also

Recipe 17.12; Recipe 17.14

17.16 Animating and Rotating Views

Problem

You want to animate the rotation of your views.

Solution

Create a rotation affine transform and use the animation methods of UIView to animate the rotation.

Discussion

 I highly recommend that you read Recipe 17.14 before proceeding with this section of the book.

In order to rotate a view while animating it, you must apply a rotation transformation to it while in an animation block (see Recipe 17.12). Let's have a look at some sample code that will make this clearer. Let's say we have an image named *Xcode.png* (see Figure 17-14), and we want to display it in the center of the screen. After the image is displayed, we want to rotate it 90 degrees over a five-second time period and then rotate it back to its original orientation. So when the view appears on the screen, let's rotate the image view 90 degrees clockwise:

```
- (void) viewDidAppear:(BOOL)paramAnimated{
  [super viewDidAppear:paramAnimated];

  self.xcodeImageView.center = self.view.center;

  /* Begin the animation */
  [UIView beginAnimations:@"clockwiseAnimation"
                  context:NULL];

  /* Make the animation five seconds long */
  [UIView setAnimationDuration:5.0f];

  [UIView setAnimationDelegate:self];

  [UIView setAnimationDidStopSelector:
   @selector(clockwiseRotationStopped:finished:context:)];

  /* Rotate the image view 90 degrees */
  self.xcodeImageView.transform =
  CGAffineTransformMakeRotation((90.0f * M_PI) / 180.0f);

  /* Commit the animation */
  [UIView commitAnimations];

}
```

We've chosen the clockwiseRotationStopped:finished:context: selector to get called when the clockwise rotation animation finishes. In that method, we will be rotating the image view counterclockwise back to 0 degrees (where it originally was) over a five-second time period:

```
- (void)clockwiseRotationStopped:(NSString *)paramAnimationID
                        finished:(NSNumber *)paramFinished
                         context:(void *)paramContext{

  [UIView beginAnimations:@"counterclockwiseAnimation"
                  context:NULL];

  /* Five seconds long */
  [UIView setAnimationDuration:5.0f];

  /* Back to original rotation */
  self.xcodeImageView.transform = CGAffineTransformIdentity;

  [UIView commitAnimations];

}
```

As you saw in Recipe 17.14, Recipe 17.15, and in this section, there are many ways to animate views (direct or indirect subclasses of UIView) and many properties that you can modify while carrying out your animations. Be creative and inspect other properties in UIView which you might have not previously known about. You may also want to take a look at the documentation for UIView in Xcode Organizer.

See Also

Recipe 17.13; Recipe 17.14; Recipe 17.15

CHAPTER 18

Core Motion

18.0 Introduction

iOS devices such as the iPhone and iPad are usually equipped with accelerometer hardware. Some iOS devices might also include a gyroscope, such as the iPhone 5 and the new iPad. Before attempting to use either the accelerometer or the gyroscope in your iOS applications, you must check the availability of these sensors on the iOS device on which your app runs. Recipes 18.1 and 18.2 include techniques you can use to detect the availability of the accelerometer and gyroscope. With a gyroscope, iOS devices such as the iPhone 4 and iPad 2 are able to detect motion in six axes.

Let's go through a situation that will show you the value of the gyroscope. The accelerometer cannot detect the rotation of the device around its vertical axis if you are holding the device perfectly still in your hands, sitting in a computer chair, and rotating your chair in a clockwise or counterclockwise fashion. From the standpoint of the floor or the Earth, the device is rotating around the vertical axis, but it's not rotating around its own y-axis, which is the vertical center of the device. So, the accelerometer does not detect any motion.

However, the gyroscope included in some iOS devices allows us to detect such movements. This allows more fluid and flawless movement detection routines. This is typically useful in games, where the developers need to know not only whether the device is moving on the x-, y-, and z-axes (information they can get from the accelerometer), but also whether it is changing in relation to the Earth along these directions, which requires a gyroscope.

Programmers can use the Core Motion framework to access both the accelerometer and the gyroscope data (if available). All recipes in this chapter make use of the Core Motion framework. Please follow these steps to add this framework to your project:

1. Click on your project icon in Xcode.
2. Select the target to which you want to add the Core Motion framework.
3. On the top of the screen, select the Build Phases tab.

4. Under Build Phases, find and expand the Link Binary with Libraries box and press the little + button on its bottom-left corner.

5. In the list of frameworks, select the CoreMotion.framework and press the Add button (see Figure 18-1).

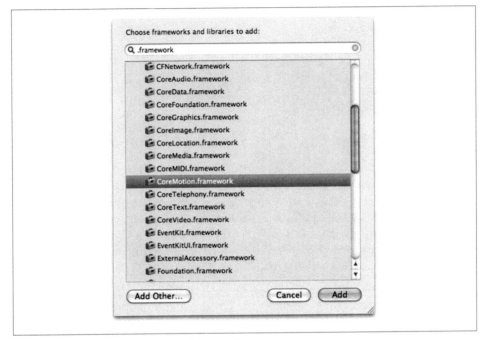

Figure 18-1. Adding the Core Motion framework to a target

iOS Simulator does not simulate the accelerometer or the gyroscope hardware. However, you can generate a *shake* with iOS Simulator using Hardware → Shake Gesture (see Figure 18-2).

18.1 Detecting the Availability of an Accelerometer

Problem

In your program, you want to detect whether the accelerometer hardware is available.

Solution

Use the `isAccelerometerAvailable` method of `CMMotionManager` to detect the accelerometer hardware. The `isAccelerometerActive` method can also be used to detect whether the accelerometer hardware is currently sending updates to the program.

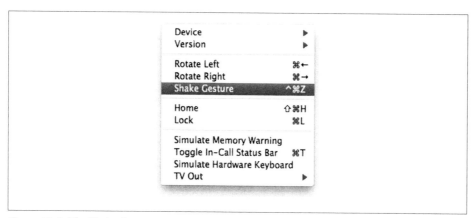

Figure 18-2. The Shake Gesture option in iOS Simulator

Let's first make sure we have imported the required header files:

```
#import <UIKit/UIKit.h>
#import <CoreMotion/CoreMotion.h>

@interface Detecting_the_Availability_of_an_AccelerometerAppDelegate
        : UIResponder <UIApplicationDelegate>

@property (strong, nonatomic) UIWindow *window;

@end
```

Next, go on to detect the availability of accelerometer in the implementation file of our app delegate:

```
- (BOOL)                application:(UIApplication *)application
  didFinishLaunchingWithOptions:(NSDictionary *)launchOptions{

  CMMotionManager *motionManager = [[CMMotionManager alloc] init];

  if ([motionManager isAccelerometerAvailable]){
    NSLog(@"Accelerometer is available.");
  } else{
    NSLog(@"Accelerometer is not available.");
  }

  if ([motionManager isAccelerometerActive]){
    NSLog(@"Accelerometer is active.");
  } else {
    NSLog(@"Accelerometer is not active.");
  }

  self.window = [[UIWindow alloc] initWithFrame:
                 [[UIScreen mainScreen] bounds]];

  self.window.backgroundColor = [UIColor whiteColor];
  [self.window makeKeyAndVisible];
```

```
    return YES;
}
```

Accelerometer hardware might be available on the iOS device running your program. This, however, does not mean the accelerometer hardware is sending updates to your program. If the accelerometer or gyroscope *is* sending updates to your program, we say it is *active* (which requires you to define a delegate object, as we will soon see).

If you run this code on iOS Simulator, you will get values similar to these in the console window:

```
Accelerometer is not available.
Accelerometer is not active.
```

Running the same code on an iPhone 4 device, you will get values similar to these:

```
Accelerometer is available.
Accelerometer is not active.
```

Discussion

An iOS device could have a built-in accelerometer. As we don't yet know which iOS devices might have accelerometer hardware built in and which ones won't, it is best to test the availability of the accelerometer before using it.

You can detect the availability of this hardware by instantiating an object of type CMMotionManager and accessing its isAccelerometerAvailable method. This method is of type BOOL and returns YES if the accelerometer hardware is available and NO if not.

In addition, you can detect whether the accelerometer hardware is currently sending updates to your application (whether it is active) by issuing the isAccelerometerActive method of CMMotionManager. You will learn about retrieving accelerometer data in Recipe 18.3.

See Also

Recipe 18.3

18.2 Detecting the Availability of a Gyroscope

Problem

You want to find out whether the current iOS device that is running your program has gyroscope hardware available.

Solution

Use the isGyroAvailable method of an instance of CMMotionManager to detect the gyroscope hardware. The isGyroActive method is also available if you want to detect whether the gyroscope hardware is currently sending updates to your program (in other words, whether it is active):

```
- (BOOL)              application:(UIApplication *)application
didFinishLaunchingWithOptions:(NSDictionary *)launchOptions{

    CMMotionManager *motionManager = [[CMMotionManager alloc] init];

    if ([motionManager isGyroAvailable]){
      NSLog(@"Gryo is available.");
    } else {
      NSLog(@"Gyro is not available.");
    }

    if ([motionManager isGyroActive]){
      NSLog(@"Gryo is active.");
    } else {
      NSLog(@"Gryo is not active.");
    }

    self.window = [[UIWindow alloc] initWithFrame:
                    [[UIScreen mainScreen] bounds]];

    self.window.backgroundColor = [UIColor whiteColor];
    [self.window makeKeyAndVisible];
    return YES;
}
```

iOS Simulator does not have gyroscope simulation in place. If you run this code on the simulator, you will receive results similar to these in the console window:

```
Gyro is not available.
Gyro is not active.
```

If you run the same code on the original iPad, you will get the same results as you get from iOS Simulator. However, if you run this code on an iOS device with a gyroscope, such as the iPhone 4 or iPad 2, the results could be different:

```
Gyro is available.
Gyro is not active.
```

Discussion

If you plan to release an application that makes use of the gyroscope, you must make sure other iOS devices without this hardware can run your application. If you are using the gyroscope as part of a game, for instance, you must make sure other iOS devices that are capable of running your application can play the game, although they might not have a gyroscope installed. Not all iOS devices have a gyroscope. This recipe shows you how to determine whether a device has a gyroscope.

To achieve this, you must first instantiate an object of type CMMotionManager. After this, you must access the isGyroAvailable method (of type BOOL) and see whether the gyroscope is available on the device running your code. You can also use the isGyro

Active method of the `CMMotionManager` instance to find out whether the gyroscope is currently sending your application any updates. For more information about this, please refer to Recipe 18.5.

See Also

Recipe 18.5

18.3 Retrieving Accelerometer Data

Problem

You want to ask iOS to send accelerometer data to your application.

Solution

Use the `startAccelerometerUpdatesToQueue:withHandler:` instance method of `CMMotion Manager`. Here is the header file of a view controller that utilizes `CMMotionManager` to get accelerometer updates:

```
#import <UIKit/UIKit.h>
#import <CoreMotion/CoreMotion.h>

@interface Retrieving_Accelerometer_DataViewController : UIViewController

@property (nonatomic, strong) CMMotionManager *motionManager;

@end
```

We will now implement our view controller and take advantage of the `startAccelero meterUpdatesToQueue:withHandler:` method of the `CMMotionManager` class:

```
#import "Retrieving_Accelerometer_DataViewController.h"

@implementation Retrieving_Accelerometer_DataViewController

- (void)viewDidLoad{
  [super viewDidLoad];

  self.motionManager = [[CMMotionManager alloc] init];

  if ([self.motionManager isAccelerometerAvailable]){
    NSOperationQueue *queue = [[NSOperationQueue alloc] init];
    [self.motionManager
     startAccelerometerUpdatesToQueue:queue
     withHandler:^(CMAccelerometerData *accelerometerData, NSError *error) {
       NSLog(@"X = %.04f, Y = %.04f, Z = %.04f",
             accelerometerData.acceleration.x,
             accelerometerData.acceleration.y,
             accelerometerData.acceleration.z);
     }];
  } else {
```

```
        NSLog(@"Accelerometer is not available.");
    }
}

- (BOOL)shouldAutorotateToInterfaceOrientation
        :(UIInterfaceOrientation)interfaceOrientation{
    return YES;
}

@end
```

Discussion

The accelerometer reports three-dimensional data (three axes) that iOS reports to your program as *x*, *y*, and *z* values. These values are encapsulated in a `CMAcceleration`structure:

```
typedef struct {
    double x;
    double y;
    double z;
} CMAcceleration;
```

If you hold your iOS device in front of your face with the screen facing you in portrait mode:

- The x-axis runs from left to right at the horizontal center of the device, with values ranging from −1 to +1 from left to right.
- The y-axis runs from bottom to top at the vertical center of the device, with values ranging from −1 to +1 from bottom to top.
- The z-axis runs from the back of the device, through the device toward you, with values ranging from −1 to +1 from back to front.

The best way to understand the values reported from the accelerometer hardware is by taking a look at a few examples. Here is one: let's assume you have your iOS device facing you with the bottom of the device pointing to the ground and the top pointing up. If you hold it perfectly still without tilting it in any specific direction, the values you have for the x-, y-, and z-axes at this moment will be (x: 0.0, y: -1.0, z: 0.0). Now try the following while the screen is facing you and the bottom of the device is pointing to the ground:

1. Turn the device 90 degrees clockwise. The values you have at this moment are (x: +1.0, y: 0.0, z: 0.0).
2. Turn the device a further 90 degrees clockwise. Now the top of the device must be pointing to the ground. The values you have at this moment are (x: 0.0, y: +1.0, z: 0.0).

3. Turn the device a further 90 degrees clockwise. Now the top of the device must be pointing to the left. The values you have right now are (x: -1.0, y: 0.0, z: 0.0).

4. Finally, if you rotate the device a further 90 degrees clockwise, where the top of the device once again points to the sky and the bottom of the device points to the ground, the values will be as they were originally (x: 0.0, y: -1.0, z: 0.0).

So, from these values, we can conclude that rotating the device around the z-axis changes the *x* and *y* values reported by the accelerometer, but not the *z* value.

Let's conduct another experiment. Hold the device again so it's facing you with its bottom pointing to the ground and its top pointing to the sky. The values that a program will get from the accelerometer, as you already know, are (x: 0.0, y: -1.0, z: 0.0). Now try these movements:

1. Tilt the device backward 90 degrees around the x-axis so that its top will be pointing backward. In other words, hold it as though it is sitting face up on a table. The values you get at this moment will be (x: 0.0, y: 0.0, z: -1.0).

2. Now tilt the device backward 90 degrees again so that its back is facing you, its top is facing the ground, and its bottom is facing the sky. The values you get at this moment will be (x: 0.0, y: 1.0, z: 0.0).

3. Tilt the device backward 90 degrees so that it's facing the ground with its back facing the sky and its top pointing toward you. The reported values at this moment will be (x: 0.0, y: 0.0, z: 1.0).

4. And finally, if you tilt the device one more time in the same direction, so the device is facing you and its top is facing the sky, the values you get will be the same values you started with.

Therefore, we can observe that rotating the device around the x-axis changes the values of the y- and z-axes, but not x. I encourage you to try the third type of rotation—around the y-axis (pointing from top to bottom)—and observe the changes in the values reported for the x- and the z-axes.

To be able to receive accelerometer updates, you have two options:

- The `startAccelerometerUpdatesToQueue:withHandler:` instance method of `CMMotionManager`.

  This method will deliver accelerometer updates on an operation queue (of type `NSOperationQueue`) and will require a basic knowledge of blocks that are used extensively in Grand Central Dispatch (GCD). For more information about blocks, please refer to Chapter 6.

- The `startAccelerometerUpdates` instance method of `CMMotionManager`.

  Once you call this method, the accelerometer (if available) will start updating accelerometer data in the motion manager object. You need to set up your own thread to continuously read the value of the `accelerometerData` property (of type `CMAccelerometerData`) of `CMMotionManager`.

In this recipe, we are using the first method (with blocks). I highly recommend that you first readChapter 6 before proceeding with this recipe. The block we provide to the `startAccelerometerUpdatesToQueue:withHandler:` instance method of `CMMotionMan ager` must be of type `CMAccelerometerHandler`:

```
typedef void (^CMAccelerometerHandler)
            (CMAccelerometerData *accelerometerData, NSError *error);
```

In other words, we must accept two parameters on the block. The first one must be of type `CMAccelerometerData` and the second must be of type `NSError`, as implemented in our example code.

See Also

Recipe 18.1

18.4 Detecting Shakes on an iOS Device

Problem

You want to know when the user shakes an iOS device.

Solution

Use the `motionEnded:withEvent:` method of your app's window object.

Discussion

The `motionEnded:withEvent:` method of your app's window will get called whenever a motion has been captured by iOS. The simplest implementation of this method is this:

```
- (void) motionEnded:(UIEventSubtype)motion
          withEvent:(UIEvent *)event{

  /* Do something with the motion */

}
```

The `motion` parameter, as you can see, is of type `UIEventSubtype`. One of the values of type `UIEventSubtype` is `UIEventSubtypeMotionShake`, which is what we are interested in. As soon as we detect this event, we know that the user has shaken her iOS device. In order to get to our app's window, though, we need to subclass `UIWindow`. To do so, follow these steps:

1. In Xcode, while you have your project opened, go to File → New File.
2. From the lefthand side, make sure iOS is the main category and Cocoa Touch is the subcategory.

3. In the list on the righthand side, select Objective-C class and then press Next, as shown in Figure 18-3.

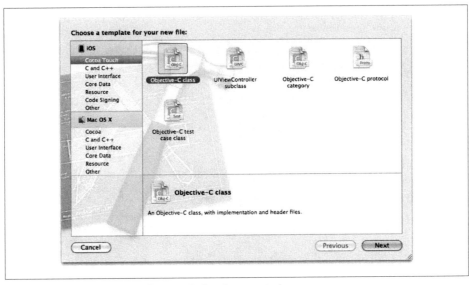

Figure 18-3. Creating a new Objective-C class for our window

4. Now make sure that you are subclassing `UIWindow` and then press Next, as shown in Figure 18-4.

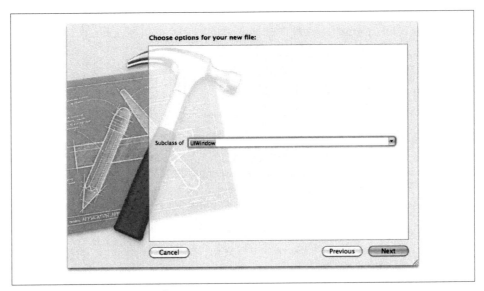

Figure 18-4. Subclassing UIWindow

5. In this screen, set the file name to *MyWindow* and press the Save button, as shown in Figure 18-5.

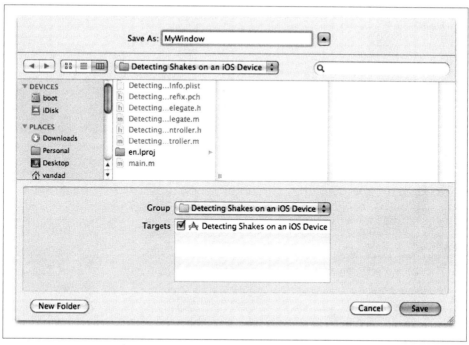

Figure 18-5. Saving the class file

Now that you have your window class, go to our app delegate and make sure that the app delegate's window object is an instance of the class, `MyWindow`:

```
#import "Detecting_Shakes_on_an_iOS_DeviceAppDelegate.h"
#import "Detecting_Shakes_on_an_iOS_DeviceViewController.h"
#import "MyWindow.h"

@implementation Detecting_Shakes_on_an_iOS_DeviceAppDelegate

- (BOOL)              application:(UIApplication *)application
  didFinishLaunchingWithOptions:(NSDictionary *)launchOptions{

  self.window = [[MyWindow alloc] initWithFrame:
                  [[UIScreen mainScreen] bounds]];

  UIUserInterfaceIdiom device = [[UIDevice currentDevice] userInterfaceIdiom];

  if (device == UIUserInterfaceIdiomPhone) {

    self.viewController =
    [[Detecting_Shakes_on_an_iOS_DeviceViewController alloc]
     initWithNibName:@"Detecting_Shakes_on_an_iOS_DeviceViewController_iPhone"
     bundle:nil];
```

```
  } else {
    self.viewController =
    [[Detecting_Shakes_on_an_iOS_DeviceViewController alloc]
      initWithNibName:@"Detecting_Shakes_on_an_iOS_DeviceViewController_iPad"
      bundle:nil];
  }

  self.window.rootViewController = self.viewController;
  [self.window makeKeyAndVisible];
  return YES;
}
```

Now go to the implementation of the `MyWindow` class and handle the `motionEnded:with Event:` method:

```
#import "MyWindow.h"

@implementation MyWindow

- (void) motionEnded:(UIEventSubtype)motion
          withEvent:(UIEvent *)event{

  if (motion == UIEventSubtypeMotionShake){
    NSLog(@"Detected a shake");
  }

}

@end
```

If you now simulate a shake event even if you are on iOS Simulator (see Recipe 18.0), you will see that our window prints the text *Detected a shake* to the console window.

18.5 Retrieving Gyroscope Data

Problem

You want to be able to retrieve information about the device's motion from the gyroscope hardware on an iOS device.

Solution

Follow these steps:

1. Find out whether the gyroscope hardware is available on the iOS device. Please refer to Recipe 18.2 for directions on how to do this.
2. If the gyroscope hardware is available, make sure it is not already sending you updates. Please refer to Recipe 18.2 for directions.

---

3. Use the `setGyroUpdateInterval:` instance method of `CMMotionManager` to set the number of updates you want to receive per second. For instance, for 20 updates per second (one second), set this value to 1.0/20.0.

4. Invoke the `startGyroUpdatesToQueue:withHandler:` instance method of `CMMotion Manager`. The queue object could simply be the main operation queue (as we will see later) and the handler block must follow the `CMGyroHandler` format.

The following code implements these steps:

```
- (BOOL)              application:(UIApplication *)application
  didFinishLaunchingWithOptions:(NSDictionary *)launchOptions{

  CMMotionManager *manager = [[CMMotionManager alloc] init];

  if ([manager isGyroAvailable]){

    if ([manager isGyroActive] == NO){

      [manager setGyroUpdateInterval:1.0f / 40.0f];

      NSOperationQueue *queue = [[NSOperationQueue alloc] init];

      [manager
        startGyroUpdatesToQueue:queue
        withHandler:^(CMGyroData *gyroData, NSError *error) {

          NSLog(@"Gyro Rotation x = %.04f", gyroData.rotationRate.x);
          NSLog(@"Gyro Rotation y = %.04f", gyroData.rotationRate.y);
          NSLog(@"Gyro Rotation z = %.04f", gyroData.rotationRate.z);

        }];
    } else {
      NSLog(@"Gyro is already active.");
    }

  } else {
    NSLog(@"Gyro isn't available.");
  }

  self.window = [[UIWindow alloc] initWithFrame:
                  [[UIScreen mainScreen] bounds]];

  self.window.backgroundColor = [UIColor whiteColor];
  [self.window makeKeyAndVisible];
  return YES;
}
```

Discussion

With `CMMotionManager`, application programmers can attempt to retrieve gyroscope updates from iOS. You must first make sure the gyroscope hardware is available on the iOS device on which your application is running (please refer to Recipe 18.2). After doing so, you can call the `setGyroUpdateInterval:` instance method of `CMMotion`

Manager to set the number of updates you would like to receive per second on updates from the gyroscope hardware. For instance, if you want to be updated *N* times per second, set this value to 1.0/*N*.

After you set the update interval, you can call the startGyroUpdatesToQueue:withHandler: instance method of CMMotionManager to set up a handler block for the updates. For more information about blocks, please refer to Chapter 6. Your block object must be of type CMGyroHandler, which accepts two parameters:

gyroData
> The data that comes from the gyroscope hardware, encompassed in an object of type CMGyroData. You can use the rotationRate property of CMGyroData (a structure) to get access to the *x*, *y*, and *z* values of the data, which represent all three Euler angles known as roll, pitch, and yaw, respectively. You can learn more about these by reading about flight dynamics.

error
> An error of type NSError that might occur when the gyroscope is sending us updates.

If you do not wish to use block objects, you must call the startGyroUpdates instance method of CMMotionManager instead of the startGyroUpdatesToQueue:withHandler: instance method, and set up your own thread to read the gyroscope hardware updates posted to the gyroData property of the instance of CMMotionManager you are using.

See Also

Recipe 18.2

iCloud

19.0 Introduction

iCloud is Apple's cloud infrastructure. A cloud is a name given to a service that stores information on a centralized location, where the user cannot physically access the disk/memory that stores the information. For instance, an iCloud storage space could be allocated by Apple in California, and all iPhone devices in New York could have all their iCloud traffic go to the California iCloud data center.

The purpose of using iCloud, from a programmer's perspective, is to give their users the ability to seamlessly have their apps' data transferred from one machine to the other. Let's have a look at a real life example of when iCloud would come in very handy: imagine that you have developed an app called Game XYZ. Sarah is a hypothetical user of your game and she has purchased it through the App Store. Your game is a universal app, and hence can be run on both the iPhone and the iPad. It just so happens that Sarah has an iPad and an iPhone, and has installed your game on both her devices. She is playing your game at the office, and is at level 12. She goes back home and picks up her iPad to play some more, only to discover that the game starts from level 1 on her iPad because she was playing on her iPhone all along. This is definitely not a pretty situation. What is better is for your game to be intelligent enough to save its state and resume that state when your users start the game, regardless of which device they have been running the game. To handle this situation, you could use iCloud to store Sarah's game state on her iPhone and let iCloud synchronize this data to the data centers that are maintained by Apple. When she picks her iPad up, you could use your app to contact iCloud and find out if there is a recent game state saved for Sarah. If yes, then you can load that state for her to give her the feeling that she really didn't even leave your game. She just switched devices. This is a bit more work for you, but in the end you will get really happy customers.

Before being able to use iCloud services, you first need to enable your app for iCloud. This requires creating the correct provisioning profiles in iOS Provisioning Portal and then enabling the correct entitlements in your project. You can read more about this in Recipe 19.1.

I use the terms "folder" and "directory" interchangeably throughout this chapter.

19.1 Setting Up Your App for iCloud

Problem

You want to start using iCloud in your apps and you would like to know how you should set up your Xcode project.

Solution

Follow these steps to enable iCloud storage in your app:

1. Create an app in Xcode and set its bundle identifier using a reverse-domain style. For instance, *com.pixolity.Setting-Up Your-App-For-iCloud*.

2. Using the iOS Provisioning Portal, create a new App ID for your app. Enable iCloud for that App ID by selecting it in the portal, enabling the checkbox for iCloud, and saving your changes.

3. In iOS Provisioning Portal, create new Ad Hoc App Store and Development provisioning profiles, and make sure they are linked to your new App ID.

4. Select your target in Xcode and set the appropriate provisioning profiles for different schemes, such as Debug, Release, etc.

5. In Xcode, select your target and in the Summary tab, scroll down to the Entitlements section and enable entitlements for your target. This will prepopulate the relevant iCloud storage entitlements for you.

Discussion

To enable iCloud for an app, you need to do a bit of setting up. The high level requirement was described in the Solution section, but let's now go into details about what we really need to do:

1. Open Xcode and from the File menu select New → New Project...

2. On the lefthand side of the New Project dialog, make sure iOS is the main category and Application is the subcategory. From the list that now appears on the righthand side of the New Project dialog, choose Empty Application and press the Next button (see Figure 19-1).

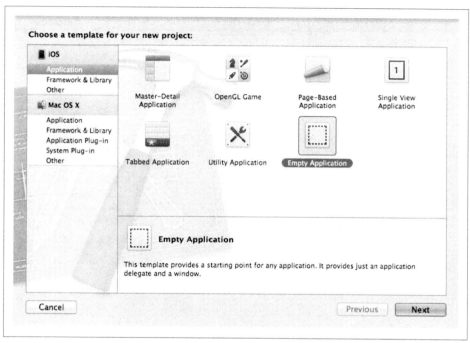

Choose a template for your new project:

iOS
- Application
- Framework & Library
- Other

Mac OS X
- Application
- Framework & Library
- Application Plug-in
- System Plug-in
- Other

Master-Detail Application

OpenGL Game

Page-Based Application

Single View Application

Tabbed Application

Utility Application

Empty Application

Empty Application

This template provides a starting point for any application. It provides just an application delegate and a window.

Cancel   Previous   **Next**

Figure 19-1. Creating an Empty Application to use with iCloud storage

3. In this screen (see Figure 19-2), set the Product Name to `Setting Up Your App For iCloud` and set the Company Identifier to the reverse domain name of your company name. For instance, I have set this value to `com.pixolity`. If your company name is XYZ, then you set this value to `com.XYZ`. Once you are done and your settings look like those shown in Figure 19-2, press the Next button.

4. Now you are asked to save your project. Simply save the project on disk or wherever you wish. Once done, press the Create button.

5. We now need to create the App ID in iOS Provisioning Portal. Log in to the iOS Dev Center (*http://bit.ly/PUtjlY*) and from the menus, select the iOS Provisioning Portal.

6. In the provisioning portal, select the App IDs option and then press the New App ID button.

7. In the Description field (see Figure 19-3), enter `Setting Up Your App For iCloud`. In the Bundle Seed ID (App ID Prefix), select the Use Team ID option. In the Bundle Identifier (App ID Suffix) box, choose `com. TEAM ID.Setting-Up-Your-App-For-iCloud`, where `TEAM ID` is your company name. For my example, this would be `com.pixolity.Setting-Up-Your-App-For-iCloud`. Once you are done, press the Submit button.

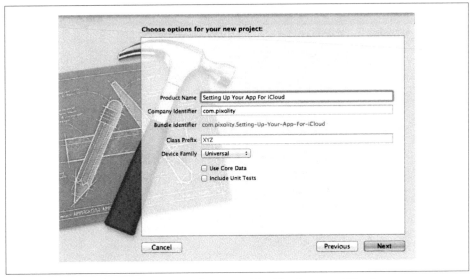

Figure 19-2. Setting the product name and company identifier for a new iCloud app

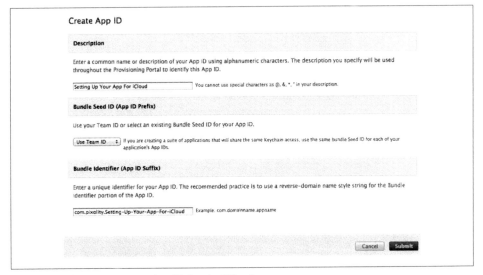

Figure 19-3. Setting up a new App ID for the iCloud app

8. You are now back in the provisioning portal. Select the Provisioning item from the menu and then under the Development tab, select the New Profile button.

9. In the Profile Name field, enter `Setting Up Your App For iCloud Development`. In the Certificates field, check the box for the your Development Certificate. In the App ID drop-down, select the *Setting Up Your App For iCloud* ID that we created earlier. In the Devices section, select the devices you would like to allow the

development version of your app to run. After you are done, select the Submit button (see Figure 19-4).

Figure 19-4. Creating a new Development provision profile for iCloud

10. Once the app goes through the development and testing process, we are going to want to submit it to the App Store, so let's go ahead and create the App Store provisioning profile as well. In the Provisioning section of the iOS Provisioning Portal, select the Distribution tab and then press the New Profile button.

11. Set the Distribution Method to App Store. Set the Profile Name to *Setting Up Your App For iCloud App Store*. In the App ID drop-down, select the *Setting Up Your App For iCloud* ID that we created earlier. Once you are done, press the Submit button (see Figure 19-5).

12. Navigate to the Development and then the Distribution tabs of the Provisioning section of the iOS Provisioning Portal screen and press the Download button on the Development and the App Store provisioning profiles that you just created.

13. Once you have downloaded the two provision profiles, drag and drop them into iTunes. iTunes will then automatically install these provision profiles for you.

14. In Xcode, select your project file (with the blue icon), select your target, and then choose the Build Settings tab. From the bar menu, make sure the All and the Combined options are selected, as shown in Figure 19-6.

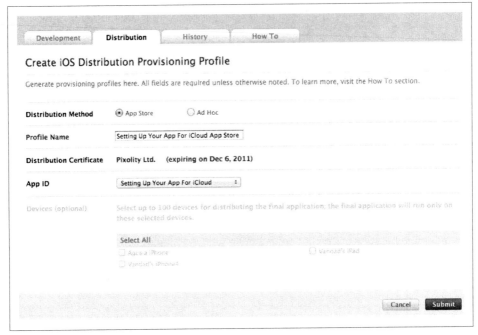

Figure 19-5. Creating a new Distribution provision profile for iCloud

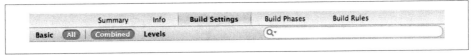

Figure 19-6. The Combined and All bar items should be selected in the Build Settings tab

15. Scroll down the Build Settings list until you get to the Code Signing section. In that section, for Debug, select the Development provision profile and for Release, select the App Store provision profile we created earlier (see Figure 19-7).

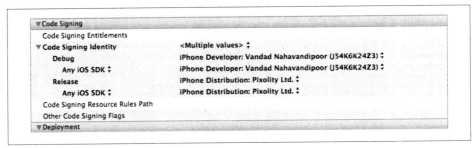

Figure 19-7. Setting the appropriate provisioning profiles for the Debug and Release schemes

If you cannot see these profiles in your list, it could be because you have not yet installed them. Downloading the profiles is not sufficient. You need to drag and drop the downloaded provision profiles into iTunes. iTunes will then install those profiles for you.

16. While you have your target selected, move from the Build Settings tab to the Summary tab (see Figure 19-8).

Figure 19-8. The Summary tab of the target

17. Scroll down in the Summary tab until you get to the Entitlements section. In that section, tick the Enable Entitlements checkbox and Xcode will automatically set the required entitlements values for iCloud for you.

Fantastic. We are now done. The app is now set up for iCloud because of the entitlements and the provision profiles that we created earlier and used in the Build Settings of the target. Now it's time to start using iCloud in the apps.

19.2 Storing and Synchronizing Dictionaries in iCloud

Problem

You want to store key-value data in dictionary form in iCloud, and seamlessly read and write to this centralized and synchronized dictionary from various devices and from various iCloud accounts.

Solution

Use the NSUbiquitousKeyValueStore class.

The data that you store in iCloud using the NSUbiquitousKeyValueStore is uniquely created in iCloud using the provision profile with which you sign the app and the end-user's iCloud account. In other word, you simply store values in iCloud using the NSUbiquitousKeyValueStore class, not worrying if one user's data is going to clash with another user's data. iCloud does that separation for you.

Discussion

The NSUbiquitousKeyValueStore class works very similar to the NSUserDefaults class. It can store strings, boolean, integer, float and other values. Each one of the values has to have a key associated with it. You will then be able to read the values by passing the keys to this class. The difference between the NSUbiquitousKeyValueStore and the

`NSUserDefaults` class is that the former synchronizes its dictionary data with iCloud, whereas the latter only stores the dictionary locally to a *.plist* file—this data will be deleted once the app gets deleted from the user's device.

Before you can use the `NSUbiquitousKeyValueStore` class to store key-value data in iCloud, you must set up the appropriate entitlements for your project. Please refer to Recipe 19.1 to learn how to do this.

An instance of your application uses a unique identifier to store data in the iCloud. This unique identifier is made up of three key pieces:

Team ID
> This is the unique identifier for your iOS Developer Program. When you sign up for iOS Developer Program, Apple will automatically generate a unique identifier for your account. To retrieve this identifier, simply log into Developer Center (*http://bit.ly/Qdj3FC*) and then select Your Account from the top menu items. Then choose Organization Profile from the menus on the left. On the screen to the right, your Team ID is displayed under the *Company/Organization ID* section. No two iOS Developer accounts can have the same Team ID.

Reverse domain-style of company identifier
> This string is usually in the form of *com.COMPANYNAME*, where *COMPANYNAME* is the name of your company and *APPNAME* is the name of your app. For instance, my company name is `Pixolity`, so my reverse domain style of company identifier will be *com.pixolity*.

App identifier and optional suffix
> This is the string that gets attached as the suffix to the Reverse domain-style of company identifier. For instance *Storing and Synchronizing Dictionaries in iCloud* is the name of the product that I have created for this recipe. Once I fed this value to Xcode's project dialog when creating the project itself, the resulting string became *Storing-and-Synchronizing-Dictionaries-in-iCloud*, since spaces are not allowed in the app identifier.

The Team ID is always bound to the provision profile with which you will sign your app. You do *not* have to enter this value into your project settings. For instance, if my company name is *Pixolity* and I set the reverse domain style name for my app to *com.pixolity* and my app ID to *Storing-and-Synchronizing-Dictionaries-in-iCloud*, the name that iCloud will use in the entitlements will be *$(TeamIdentifierPrefix) com.pixolity.Storing-and-Synchronizing-Dictionaries-in-iCloud*.

The `$(TeamIdentifierPrefix)` value is the Team ID, which will be resolved to my actual Team ID when Xcode compiles my application and signs it with a provision profile.

Now that we are sure we have set up the project properly and entitlements are set up as well, then we can move on to using the NSUbiquitousKeyValueStore class to store keys and values in iCloud. There are various methods that NSUbiquitousKey ValueStore class exposes to us in order for us to save the values in iCloud. Some of these methods are listed and explained here:

setString:forKey:
Sets a string value for the given key. The string must be of type NSString. Obviously, classes that subclass NSString, such as NSMutableString can also be stored in iCloud using this method.

setArray:forKey:
Sets an array value for the given key. The array can be either a mutable or an immutable array.

setDictionary:forKey:
Sets a mutable or an immutable dictionary for the given key.

setBool:forKey:
Sets a boolean value of type BOOL for the given key.

setData:forKey:
Sets a mutable or an immutable data for the given key.

None of these methods will actually do the saving for you. If you are done setting the values, then you must call the synchronize method of NSUbiquitousKeyValueStore for your settings to be flushed first to iOS and then synchronized with iCloud.

All the work that we do with the NSUbiquitousKeyValueStore is done through the defaultStore class method of this class. This class method will return an instance of the NSUbiquitousKeyValueStore class, which is ready for us to use.

Obviously, after setting the values for keys, we are going to want to retrieve those values at some point during the runtime of the app. We can do this using some of the methods that the NSUbiquitousKeyValueStore provides us with. Some of these methods are listed here:

stringForKey:
Returns the string associated with the given key, or nil if that key cannot be found. This will be an immutable string even if you used this key to store a mutable string in iCloud.

arrayForKey:
Returns the array associated with the given key, or nil if that key cannot be found. This will be an immutable array even if the original array you stored in iCloud for this key was mutable.

dictionaryForKey:

Returns the dictionary associated with the given key, or `nil` if that key cannot be found. The dictionary returned by this method will be immutable even if the original dictionary you stored into iCloud for this key was mutable.

boolForKey:

Returns the boolean value of type `BOOL` associated with the given key, or `nil` if that key cannot be found.

dataForKey:

Returns the data of type `NSData` associated with the given key, or `nil` if that key cannot be found. The data returned by this method will be immutable even if the original data stored in iCloud for this key was mutable.

So let's have a look at how we can perhaps use this class in the apps. As you already know, iCloud's power really proves handy when you are sharing data between two or more devices for the same user. For instance, if the user picks up his iPhone and reads a book up to page 40, and then picks up his iPad, the app that presents the book can see the last page the user was at, and opens the book right there. In effect, we have two devices pretending to be one, for the sake of usability for the end-user. For this example, we will store a string and a boolean value into iCloud using the `NSUbiquitousKeyValue` `Store` class. We will place a check to see if those values had already been stored in iCloud; if yes, we will read their value. I can then build this app, run it on my iPhone and then on my iPad, and see what happens:

```
- (BOOL)              application:(UIApplication *)application
 didFinishLaunchingWithOptions:(NSDictionary *)launchOptions{

 NSUbiquitousKeyValueStore *kvoStore =
   [NSUbiquitousKeyValueStore defaultStore];

 NSString *stringValue = @"My String";
 NSString *stringValueKey = @"MyStringKey";

 BOOL boolValue = YES;
 NSString *boolValueKey = @"MyBoolKey";

 BOOL mustSynchronize = NO;

 if ([[kvoStore stringForKey:stringValueKey] length] == 0){
   NSLog(@"Could not find the string value in iCloud. Setting...");
   [kvoStore setString:stringValue
              forKey:stringValueKey];
   mustSynchronize = YES;
 } else {
   NSLog(@"Found the string in iCloud, getting...");
   stringValue = [kvoStore stringForKey:stringValueKey];
 }
```

```
if ([kvoStore boolForKey:boolValueKey] == NO){
  NSLog(@"Could not find the boolean value in iCloud. Setting...");
  [kvoStore setBool:boolValue
             forKey:boolValueKey];
  mustSynchronize = YES;
} else {
  NSLog(@"Found the boolean in iCloud, getting...");
  boolValue = [kvoStore boolForKey:boolValueKey];
}

if (mustSynchronize){
  if ([kvoStore synchronize]){
    NSLog(@"Successfully synchronized with iCloud.");
  } else {
    NSLog(@"Failed to synchronize with iCloud.");
  }
}

self.window = [[UIWindow alloc] initWithFrame:
               [[UIScreen mainScreen] bounds]];

self.window.backgroundColor = [UIColor whiteColor];
[self.window makeKeyAndVisible];
return YES;
}
```

After setting up the correct provision profiles, enabling entitlements for this project, and running this app on an iPhone that has already been set up with an iCloud account, we can observe these results printed to the console screen:

```
Could not find the string value in iCloud. Setting...
Could not find the boolean value in iCloud. Setting...
Successfully synchronized with iCloud.
```

Now, I will leave my iPhone sitting here for a minute or two just to make sure that iCloud has enough time to synchronize my data with the cloud. I will then run the same code on an iPad to see what happens:

```
Found the string in iCloud, getting...
Found the boolean in iCloud, getting...
```

Fantastic. This demonstrates that iCloud is indeed synchronizing the data for multiple iOS devices that are hooked to the same iCloud account.

19.3 Creating and Managing Folders for Apps in iCloud

Problem

You want to store specific files into specific folders within the user's iCloud storage for your app.

Solution

Follow these steps:

1. Make sure your app is set up to use iCloud (see Recipe 19.1)

2. Select your project file (with the blue icon) in Xcode and select the Summary tab.

3. In the Summary tab, scroll down until you get to the Entitlements section. Find the iCloud Containers list and copy the first value in that list. The value for the project that I have set up for this recipe is *com.pixolity.Creating-and-Managing-Folders-for-Apps-in-iCloud*. This value will be different for your app.

4. In your app delegate, place the string that you copied from iCloud Containers list, into a string. Prefix this string with your Team ID (see Recipe 19.2 on how to find your Team ID).

5. Now instantiate an object of type `NSFileManager` and pass the path that you created in the previous two steps, to the `URLForUbiquityContainerIdentifier:` method of this class. The value of this method will be the *local* address for iCloud storage on the device that is running your app. Let's call this path *Root iCloud Path*.

6. Append the folder name that you want to create to the Root iCloud Path (see previous step). Keep the resulting path in a string or an instance of `NSURL`.

7. Invoke the `fileExistsAtPath:isDirectory:` method of your file manager. If this method returns `NO`, then go on to create the folder using the `createDirectoryAtPath:withIntermediateDirectories:attributes:error:`method of the file manager. If the return value of the `fileExistsAtPath:isDirectory:` method is `YES`, check whether the boolean value that comes out of the `isDirectory` parameter is `NO`. If it is `NO`, then you must create your folder again as instructed, because the path that was found by the `fileExistsAtPath:isDirectory:` method was not a directory, but rather a file.

Discussion

One of the things that can make iCloud *sound* complicated to developers is that they assume, since it is a cloud storage, that they have to deal with URLs outside their apps or URLs on the Internet. Well, this is not true. With iCloud, the URLs that you deal with are actually iOS-related. By that, I mean that the URLs are local to the device connected to iCloud. iCloud will then synchronize these local URLs and their data with the iCloud storage hosted by Apple in the cloud. The developer doesn't really have to worry about this part, unless there are conflicts that need to be resolved because two devices running your app and using the same iCloud account simultaneously modified a resource that cannot automatically be merged. We will talk about this later; let's just focus on creating folders in iCloud for now.

So let's now implement what we learned in the Solution section of this chapter:

```
- (BOOL)          application:(UIApplication *)application
    didFinishLaunchingWithOptions:(NSDictionary *)launchOptions{
```

```objc
NSFileManager *fileManager = [[NSFileManager alloc] init];

/* Place your team ID here */
NSString *teamID = @"TEAM ID";

NSString *rootFolderIdentifier = [NSString stringWithFormat:
  @"%@.com.pixolity.Creating-and-Managing-Folders-for-Apps-in-iCloud",
                                  teamID];

NSURL *containerURL =
  [fileManager URLForUbiquityContainerIdentifier:rootFolderIdentifier];

NSString *documentsDirectory = [[containerURL path]
                                stringByAppendingPathComponent:@"Documents"];
BOOL isDirectory = NO;
BOOL mustCreateDocumentsDirectory = NO;

if ([fileManager fileExistsAtPath:documentsDirectory
                      isDirectory:&isDirectory]){
  if (isDirectory == NO){
    mustCreateDocumentsDirectory = YES;
  }
} else {
  mustCreateDocumentsDirectory = YES;
}

if (mustCreateDocumentsDirectory){
  NSLog(@"Must create the directory.");

  NSError *directoryCreationError = nil;

  if ([fileManager createDirectoryAtPath:documentsDirectory
            withIntermediateDirectories:YES
                             attributes:nil
                                  error:&directoryCreationError]){
    NSLog(@"Successfully created the folder.");
  } else {
    NSLog(@"Failed to create the folder with error = %@",
          directoryCreationError);
  }

} else {
  NSLog(@"This folder already exists.");
}

self.window = [[UIWindow alloc] initWithFrame:
              [[UIScreen mainScreen] bounds]];

self.window.backgroundColor = [UIColor whiteColor];
[self.window makeKeyAndVisible];
return YES;
}
```

The Container Identifier that Xcode sets up by default for your application is made out of a Team ID and a Bundle Identifier. If you want, you can simply change this. One of the great features of iCloud for developers is that the container identifiers that you specify for your app's iCloud storage don't have to necessarily be linked in any way to your app or your app's bundle identifier. If you believe the default identifier is confusing, just change it to something that makes more sense to you and your team.

What we can do now is to wrap the code into a method for re-use:

```objc
- (BOOL) createiCloudDirectory:(NSString *)paramDirectory
           recursiveCreation:(BOOL)paramRecursiveCreation
                      teamID:(NSString *)paramTeamID
              iCloudContainer:(NSString *)paramContainer
                   finalPath:(NSString **)paramFinalPath{

    BOOL result = NO;

    NSFileManager *fileManager = [[NSFileManager alloc] init];

    NSString *rootFolderIdentifier = [NSString stringWithFormat:
                                      @"%@.%@", paramTeamID, paramContainer];

    NSURL *containerURL =
      [fileManager URLForUbiquityContainerIdentifier:rootFolderIdentifier];

    NSString *documentsDirectory = [[containerURL path]
                              stringByAppendingPathComponent:@"Documents"];

    if (paramFinalPath != nil){
      *paramFinalPath = documentsDirectory;
    }  BOOL isDirectory = NO;
    BOOL mustCreateDocumentsDirectory = NO;

    if ([fileManager fileExistsAtPath:documentsDirectory
                          isDirectory:&isDirectory]){
      if (isDirectory == NO){
        mustCreateDocumentsDirectory = YES;
      }
    } else {
      mustCreateDocumentsDirectory = YES;
    }

    if (mustCreateDocumentsDirectory){
      NSLog(@"Must create the directory.");

      NSError *directoryCreationError = nil;

      if ([fileManager createDirectoryAtPath:documentsDirectory
                withIntermediateDirectories:paramRecursiveCreation
                                 attributes:nil
                                      error:&directoryCreationError]){
```

```
      result = YES;
      NSLog(@"Successfully created the folder.");
    } else {
      NSLog(@"Failed to create the folder with error = %@",
          directoryCreationError);
    }

  } else {
    NSLog(@"This folder already exists.");
    result = YES;
  }

  return result;

}

- (BOOL)              application:(UIApplication *)application
didFinishLaunchingWithOptions:(NSDictionary *)launchOptions{


  /* Place your Team ID here */
  NSString *teamID = @"TEAM ID";

  NSString *containerID =
  @"com.pixolity.Creating-and-Managing-Folders-for-Apps-in-iCloud";

  NSString *documentsDirectory = nil;

  if ([self createiCloudDirectory:@"Documents"
              recursiveCreation:YES
                      teamID:teamID
                iCloudContainer:containerID
                    finalPath:&documentsDirectory]){
    NSLog(@"Successfully created the directory in %@", documentsDirectory);
  } else {
    NSLog(@"Failed to create the directory.");
  }

  self.window = [[UIWindow alloc] initWithFrame:
              [[UIScreen mainScreen] bounds]];

  self.window.backgroundColor = [UIColor whiteColor];
  [self.window makeKeyAndVisible];
  return YES;
}
```

 The finalPath parameter in the new method is an out parameter, meaning that it can store the final path of the directory that you created into an output string, should you need it for any other method (or anywhere in your app).

OK, now that we have this method, we can go ahead and save a resource into the Documents folder for the current user's iCloud storage for the app:

```objc
- (BOOL)              application:(UIApplication *)application
    didFinishLaunchingWithOptions:(NSDictionary *)launchOptions{

    /* Place your Team ID here */
    NSString *teamID = @"TEAM ID";

    NSString *containerID =
      @"com.pixolity.Creating-and-Managing-Folders-for-Apps-in-iCloud";

    NSString *documentsDirectory = nil;

    if ([self createiCloudDirectory:@"Documents"
                   recursiveCreation:YES
                             teamID:teamID
                    iCloudContainer:containerID
                          finalPath:&documentsDirectory]){
      NSLog(@"Successfully created the directory in %@", documentsDirectory);

      NSString *stringToSave = @"My String";

      NSString *pathToSave = [documentsDirectory
                              stringByAppendingPathComponent:@"MyString.txt"];

      NSError *savingError = nil;

      if ([stringToSave writeToFile:pathToSave
                         atomically:YES
                           encoding:NSUTF8StringEncoding
                              error:&savingError]){
        NSLog(@"Successfully saved the string in iCloud.");
      } else {
        NSLog(@"Failed to save the string with error = %@", savingError);
      }


    } else {
      NSLog(@"Failed to create the directory.");
    }

    self.window = [[UIWindow alloc] initWithFrame:
                   [[UIScreen mainScreen] bounds]];

    self.window.backgroundColor = [UIColor whiteColor];
    [self.window makeKeyAndVisible];
    return YES;
}
```

 Saving a file in a cloud URL does not explicitly tell iOS that the file has to be placed in cloud storage. We will learn about saving files in cloud storage in Recipe 19.5.

If I run this app on an iPad that has been set up to backup data and files to an iCloud account, I can go to the Settings app and then select the iCloud option in the list. In the iCloud screen, I would then select Storage & Backup. Once in the Storage & Backup screen, select Manage Storage, and you will be presented with a screen similar to that shown in Figure 19-9.

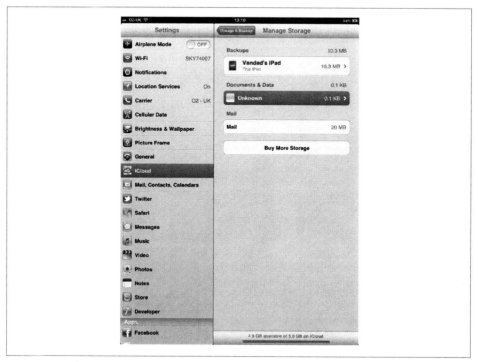

Figure 19-9. The Documents and Data of the app are listed in the Settings app on the iPad

Now if you select your app from the list (our app is listed as Unknown, for reasons we will go through later in this chapter), you can see a screen similar to Figure 19-10).

See Also

Recipe 19.1; Recipe 19.2; Recipe 19.5

19.4 Searching for Files and Folders in iCloud

Problem

You want to search for files and/or folders inside the current iCloud user's cloud space allocated for your app.

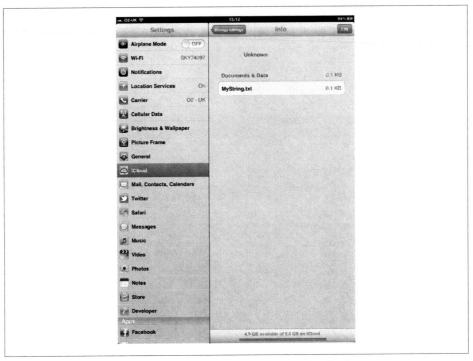

Figure 19-10. Our string saved into the disk is indeed syncing with iCloud

Solution

Use the `NSMetadataQuery` class.

Discussion

OS X Developers are probably familiar with the `NSMetadataQuery` class. This class allows developers to query Spotlight items, whether they are files or folders. In iOS, we will use this class to search for files and folders in the iCloud space assigned to the app for the current user, if she has set up iCloud for the iOS device on which the app is running.

To set up a metadata query, there are three very important things that we need to do:

1. We need to set the predicate of the metadata query. The predicate is the *search criteria* of the query. This predicate will tell the query what items we are searching for.

2. We also need to set the query's search scope. In order to search in the user's iCloud Documents folder, we set this scope to `NSMetadataQueryUbiquitousDocuments Scope`. Otherwise, you can use the `NSMetadataQueryUbiquitousDataScope`, which represents the Data folder in iCloud, a folder your app can use to store data related to the user-created documents. Remember that the files you store in the user's iCloud should not be your app's temporary files or any other files that your app

can retrieve in some other way if those files weren't present in the user's iCloud storage. Things that you store in the user's iCloud storage should be his or her creations.

3. After we start the query, we shall start listening for the `NSMetadataQueryDidFinish GatheringNotification` notification. This notification gets called when the query has finished its search. In the method that handles this notification, we can then look through the results the query gathered for us and determine if any of those files/folders are the ones we're looking for.

The `setPredicate:` instance method of `NSMetadataQuery` class allows us to set the predicate of the query. The predicate must be of type `NSPredicate`. We will use the `predicateWithFormat:` class method of `NSPredicate` class to initialize the predicate. Remember, the predicate will tell the query what to search for. The `predicateWithFormat:` accepts a format string in the following format:

```
QUERY_ITEM COMPARISON_CRITERIA PATTERN
```

The *QUERY_ITEM* part of the format of the predicate can be any of the `NSMetadataItem` constant values. For instance, we can use the `NSMetadataItemFSNameKey` constant value to tell the predicate that the search pattern targets the file-system name of the items in the cloud. Since the format provided to the `predicateWithFormat:` method can be a variable number of arguments, with the first argument dictating the format of the rest of the arguments, you can pass `%K` as the *QUERY_ITEM*. For instance, the following two predicates are basically the same in terms of how they will supply an input to the meta data query:

```
NSPredicate *predicate = [NSPredicate predicateWithFormat:@"%K like %@",
                          NSMetadataItemFSNameKey,
                          @"*"];

NSPredicate *samePredicate = [NSPredicate predicateWithFormat:
                              @"NSMetadataItemFSNameKey like %@",
                              @"*"];
```

The *COMPARISON_CRITERIA* part of the format of the predicate can be any of the following values:

>

To indicate that you are searching for query items that are, in value, bigger than your criteria patterns. For instance, you can search in the documents folder in the iCloud container of an app for all files whose size is bigger than X kilobytes, where X is defined by you.

<

This comparison criteria is similar to the previous criteria. This criteria looks for items in the iCloud container of an app whose size (as an example) is smaller than the file size that you have specified in the pattern.

like

This comparison criteria is used for searching for file names and display names of files. You can even use wildcards with this criteria; for instance, looking for all files whose names start with a specific character.

We can go on and on about this, but I suggest we dive into the development piece to get a better understanding of how metadata queries work. For this example, here is what we will do:

1. When the app loads (in the app delegate), we will simply search for *all* files in the app's iCloud container.

2. We will then log the names of all the files that we found to the console, using NSLog.

3. At the end of every search, we will create a new file whose name is generated randomly using a random integer. We will then make sure that file doesn't already exist in the iCloud container for the app. If it doesn't, we will save it to the iCloud container. Simple, isn't it? This way, whenever the app opens up, we are creating a new file to the user's iCloud storage.

 Storing unnecessary files in users' iCloud storage is a really bad practice. Make sure, as stated before, that you only use iCloud to store files that have been directly created by your user, such as documents or creative images. For this example, since we need to find files/folders in the user's iCloud container to prove that the solution works, we need to at least have something stored in the iCloud container for the app.

Although we are going to learn about storing files in the iCloud in Recipe 19.5, for the sake of this recipe, we will use another, easier method to store files into iCloud. We will accomplish this using the setUbiquitous:itemAtURL:destinationURL:error: instance method of NSFileManager. The parameters that we will pass to this method are:

setUbiquitous
 This is a boolean value that you set to YES if you want to move a file to the iCloud.

itemAtURL
 The parameter passed to this method is the NSURL pointing to the file in your app's bundle that needs to be moved to iCloud.

destinationURL
 This is the URL of where the source file has to be copied in the user's iCloud storage. This URL must be an iCloud URL.

error
 A pointer to an NSError object that will get set to an error, if one occurs during process.

So let's go ahead and create a Single View Application, and then define the view controller with a metadata query property that we will use for searching in the app's iCloud container:

```
#import <UIKit/UIKit.h>

@interface ViewController : UIViewController

@property (nonatomic, strong) NSMetadataQuery *metadataQuery;

@end
```

When the view controller is loaded, in the `viewDidLoad` method, we shall start the query and search for all files in the Documents directory of the app's iCloud container:

```
- (void)viewDidLoad{

  [super viewDidLoad];

  /* Listen for a notification that gets fired when the metadata query
   has finished finding the items we were looking for */
  [[NSNotificationCenter defaultCenter]
   addObserver:self
   selector:@selector(handleMetadataQueryFinished:)
   name:NSMetadataQueryDidFinishGatheringNotification
   object:nil];

  // Do any additional setup after loading the view, typically from a nib.
  self.metadataQuery = [[NSMetadataQuery alloc] init];
  NSArray *searchScopes = [[NSArray alloc] initWithObjects:
                           NSMetadataQueryUbiquitousDocumentsScope, nil];
  [self.metadataQuery setSearchScopes:searchScopes];
  NSPredicate *predicate = [NSPredicate predicateWithFormat:
                            @"%K like %@",
                            NSMetadataItemFSNameKey,
                            @"*"];
  [self.metadataQuery setPredicate:predicate];
  if ([self.metadataQuery startQuery]){
    NSLog(@"Successfully started the query.");
  } else {
    NSLog(@"Failed to start the query.");
  }
}
```

In this code, we have elected the `handleMetadataQueryFinished:` instance method of the view controller (yet to be implemented) as the method that the query will call whenever it has finished searching inside the Documents folder of the app's iCloud container. Let's go and implement this method. What we want to do in this method is to look for all the files that the metadata query found (if any), and then list them by printing them out to the console. After this, we will create a new random file and place it in the app's iCloud container. Here are the steps that we have to take in order to achieve this:

1. Generate a URL for a new random file in the app's iCloud container. For this, we first need to find the app's iCloud container URL.

2. If the URL for this new random file already exists in the results returned by the metadata query, we will ignore the whole operation.

3. If a file with the exact same name as the new random file has *not* been created in the Documents directory of the app's iCloud container, we will save a file with the same name to the app's Documents directory in the app's sandbox on the device.

4. After the file has been created in the app's sandbox, we will set it to ubiquitous, where the file will be moved to iCloud and will automatically be deleted from the app's sandbox.

As described before, we are going to have to store a file into the app's Documents folder, on the app's sandbox, and in iCloud. Therefore, we need to have some methods that give us these URLs. First we will start with a method that will return the URL for the app's Documents folder in iCloud:

```
- (NSURL *) urlForDocumentsFolderIniCloud{

  NSURL *result = nil;

  #error Put your TEAM ID here
  const NSString *TeamID = @"YOUR TEAM ID";

  NSString *containerID = [[NSBundle mainBundle] bundleIdentifier];

  NSString *teamIDAndContainerID = [[NSString alloc] initWithFormat:@"%@.%@",
                                    TeamID,
                                    containerID];

  NSFileManager *fileManager = [[NSFileManager alloc] init];

  NSURL *appiCloudContainerURL =
  [fileManager URLForUbiquityContainerIdentifier:teamIDAndContainerID];

  result = [appiCloudContainerURL URLByAppendingPathComponent:@"Documents"
                                  isDirectory:YES];

  if ([fileManager fileExistsAtPath:[result path]] == NO){

    /* The Documents directory does NOT exist in the app's iCloud container;
     attempt to create it now */

    NSError *creationError = nil;
    BOOL created = [fileManager createDirectoryAtURL:result
                    withIntermediateDirectories:YES
                                    attributes:nil
                                        error:&creationError];

    if (created){
      NSLog(@"Successfully created the Documents folder in iCloud.");
    } else {
```

```
        NSLog(@"Failed to create the Documents folder in iCloud. Error = %@",
            creationError);
        result = nil;
    }

} else {
    /* the Documents directory already exists in the app's iCloud container;
    we don't have to do anything */
}

return result;

}
```

Now we will use this method to determine the URL of the random file in the Documents folder in the iCloud container for the app:

```
- (NSURL *) urlForRandomFileInDocumentsFolderIniCloud{

    NSURL *result = nil;

    NSUInteger randomNumber = arc4random() % NSUIntegerMax;

    NSString *randomFileName = [[NSString alloc] initWithFormat:@"%llu.txt",
                                (unsigned long)randomNumber];

    /* Check in the metadata query if this file already exists */
    __block BOOL fileExistsAlready = NO;
    [self.metadataQuery.results enumerateObjectsUsingBlock:
     ^(NSMetadataItem *item, NSUInteger idx, BOOL *stop) {
        NSString *itemFileName = [item valueForAttribute:NSMetadataItemFSNameKey];
        if ([itemFileName isEqualToString:randomFileName]){
            NSLog(@"This file already exists. Aborting...");
            fileExistsAlready = YES;
            *stop = YES;
        }
     }];

    if (fileExistsAlready){
        return nil;
    }

    result = [[self urlForDocumentsFolderIniCloud]
            URLByAppendingPathComponent:randomFileName];

    return result;

}
```

Now that we have the URL for the random file (yet to be created) in iCloud, we also need to write a method that we can use to get the URL for the same file in the app bundle. Since we created this random file name in the urlForRandomFileInDocuments FolderIniCloud method, the new method won't know about this name and thus we need to pass the file name to the method as a parameter:

```
- (NSURL *) urlForRandomFileInDocumentsFolderInAppSandbox
            :(NSString *)paramFileName{

  NSURL *result = nil;

  NSString *documentsFolderInAppSandbox =
  [NSSearchPathForDirectoriesInDomains(NSDocumentDirectory,
                                       NSUserDomainMask,
                                       YES) objectAtIndex:0];

  NSString *filePath = [documentsFolderInAppSandbox
                        stringByAppendingPathComponent:paramFileName];

  result = [NSURL fileURLWithPath:filePath];

  return result;

}
```

Next, we have to implement a method that we will soon use to enumerate through the metadata items returned by the metadata query:

```
- (void) enumerateMetadataResults:(NSArray *)paramResults{

  [paramResults enumerateObjectsUsingBlock:
   ^(NSMetadataItem *item, NSUInteger index, BOOL *stop) {

     NSString *itemName = [item valueForAttribute:NSMetadataItemFSNameKey];
     NSURL *itemURL = [item valueForAttribute:NSMetadataItemURLKey];
     NSNumber *itemSize = [item valueForAttribute:NSMetadataItemFSSizeKey];

     NSLog(@"Item name = %@", itemName);
     NSLog(@"Item URL = %@", itemURL);
     NSLog(@"Item Size = %llu",
           (unsigned long long)[itemSize unsignedLongLongValue]);

   }];

}
```

Last but not least, we will implement the handleMetadataQueryFinished: method, which will get called by the notification center when the metadata query finishes searching for the query:

```
- (void) handleMetadataQueryFinished:(id)paramSender{

  NSLog(@"Search finished");

  if ([[paramSender object] isEqual:self.metadataQuery] == NO){
    NSLog(@"An unknown object called this method. Not safe to proceed.");
    return;
  }

  /* Stop listening for notifications as we are not expecting anything more */
  [[NSNotificationCenter defaultCenter] removeObserver:self];
```

```objective-c
/* We are done with the query, let's stop the process now */
[self.metadataQuery disableUpdates];
[self.metadataQuery stopQuery];

[self enumerateMetadataResults:self.metadataQuery.results];

if ([self.metadataQuery.results count] == 0){
  NSLog(@"No files were found.");
}

NSURL *urlForFileIniCloud = [self urlForRandomFileInDocumentsFolderIniCloud];

if (urlForFileIniCloud == nil){
  NSLog(@"Cannot create a file with this URL. URL is empty.");
  return;
}

NSString *fileName = [[[urlForFileIniCloud path]
                       componentsSeparatedByString:@"/"] lastObject];

NSURL *urlForFileInAppSandbox =
[self urlForRandomFileInDocumentsFolderInAppSandbox:fileName];

NSString *fileContent =
[[NSString alloc] initWithFormat:@"Content of %@",
 [[self urlForRandomFileInDocumentsFolderIniCloud] path]];

/* Save the file temporarily in the app bundle and then move
 it to the cloud */
NSError *writingError = nil;
BOOL couldWriteToAppSandbox =
[fileContent writeToFile:[urlForFileInAppSandbox path]
             atomically:YES
               encoding:NSUTF8StringEncoding
                  error:&writingError];

/* If we cannot save the file, just return from method because it won't make
 any sense to continue as we, ideally, should have stored the file in iCloud
 from the app sandbox but here, if an error has occurred,
 we cannot continue */
if (couldWriteToAppSandbox == NO){
  NSLog(@"Failed to save the file to app sandbox. Error = %@", writingError);
  return;
}

NSFileManager *fileManager = [[NSFileManager alloc] init];

/* Now move the file to the cloud */
NSError *ubiquitousError = nil;
BOOL setUbiquitousSucceeded =
[fileManager setUbiquitous:YES
                itemAtURL:urlForFileInAppSandbox
            destinationURL:urlForFileIniCloud
                    error:&ubiquitousError];
```

```
   if (setUbiquitousSucceeded){
     NSLog(@"Successfully moved the file to iCloud.");
     /* The file has been moved from App Sandbox to iCloud */
   } else {
     NSLog(@"Failed to move the file to iCloud with error = %@",
           ubiquitousError);
   }

 }
```

You can now go ahead and run the app and see for yourself. Once you open and close the app a few times, you will be able to see something similar to Figure 19-11 in the Settings app on your iOS device.

Our app only creates a new file when the metadata query finishes. The metadata query gets fired in the `viewDidLoad` method of the view controller, which itself gets fired when the only view gets loaded. Therefore, if you simply open the app and press the Home button on your iOS device, and then open the app again, the app might not create a new file—the app was simply sent to the background instead of being terminated and reopened. To make sure the app creates a new file every time you open it, before opening the app, close it manually from the apps bar in iOS by double-pressing the Home button and closing the app from the list of running apps.

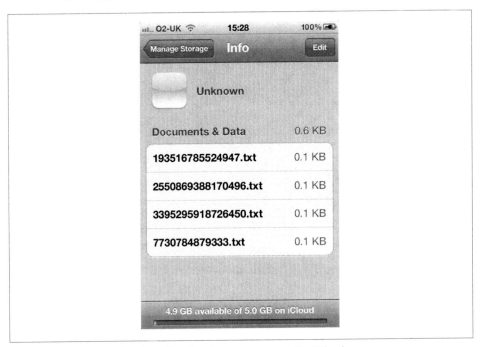

Figure 19-11. The list of random files that the app has created in iCloud

See Also

Recipe 19.5

19.5 Storing User Documents in iCloud

Problem

You want to allow the users of your app to create documents in your app and you want to have those documents present on all devices that the user owns.

Solution

Use UIDocument.

Discussion

Although a user can have many files of different types stored on her device by different apps, each app has to be considerate of the amount of data that it puts in the user's iCloud storage. Therefore, only the data that the user generates while using your app might need to be saved to the user's iCloud storage space. For instance, if you are creating a web-browser app, the data that your browser app caches on disk on the device should not be stored in the cloud. Why? Because that data was not generated by the user. Your app simply was trying to give a better user experience by caching the data so that the next time it accessed the same series of web pages, the pages would load faster. If you look at it from the user's perspective, she didn't really ask you to cache the data. What's even worse is that your app is now using the user's iCloud storage (for which she might have probably paid) to store cached data. That is simply wrong. You must tell the user what data your app is storing in the cloud, and if she doesn't allow you to use her cloud storage space, you should avoid using that space and just store the data locally in your app's sandbox.

One of the most confusing facts about iCloud is how you, as the programmer, will need to manage the data stored in the cloud. Before iCloud, as programmers, we were only concerned about the data we stored in the app's sandbox. Now we need to learn about a secondary storage space called iCloud storage. A lot of programmers tend to get confused when it comes to iCloud storage, and I personally think that Apple might have made it a bit complicated in their documentation. Perhaps this is something that will be solved at a later stage of iOS development, but for now, here are a few key points you will need to learn about in order to integrate iCloud storage into your apps and allow the loading and saving of users' documents from and to iCloud:

1. A file that is present on the user's cloud storage is ubiquitous. Ubiquitous files are files that are stored outside an app's sandbox. We will talk about these more, but for now, remember that a ubiquitous file is a file that is no longer present in the app's sandbox, but rather in the cloud.

2. We have to subclass the UIDocument class in order to manage users' documents. Each document will be given a ubiquitous URL to load its contents from. In the subclass, all we really have to do is to implement two very important methods that will allow iOS to pass data to us (when iOS reads the data from iCloud) and for us to be able to pass data to iOS to store on iCloud.

3. Your ubiquitous files do *not* necessarily have to be in your app sandbox. If you want to store a file in iCloud, you will simply retrieve a direct URL to the iCloud folder (more on this later) and place your files there.

4. Before you go and create files in the user's iCloud storage, you must first query the iCloud storage to see if that file already exists or not.

5. Each app has an identifier; iCloud uses that identifier to separate the iCloud files for that app from files from other apps present on users' iOS devices. If you use the same app identifier across multiple apps, all those apps will be able to share each other's iCloud storage space. This can be good if you are developing a "lite" version of your app and you want the full version to be able to access the iCloud storage of the "lite" version of your app, and vice versa.

6. You can search for files in your app's iCloud storage for the current user, using the NSMetadataQuery class (refer to Recipe 19.4 for more information).

In this recipe, we would like to write an app that simply creates a document for the user (text file) and allows him to edit that document. In the background, we will save that document to iCloud so that if he has another iOS device set up with the same iCloud credentials (username and password), he can see the most up-to-date version of the file, regardless of which iOS device he is editing it on. Here is the checklist for this app:

1. We need to set up the appropriate provision profiles for the app, as well as entitlements (see Recipe 19.1 for more information).

2. Now we have to give the document a name (for now, let's call the document file *UserDocument.txt*).

3. When the app opens (whether it is for the first time or not), we will fire up a metadata query and try to find the file in the user's iCloud storage. If that file already exists, we will retrieve its URL. If that file doesn't exist, we will create an empty/dummy file in that URL.

4. Now that we have the URL for the document file in the user's iCloud storage, we will open that document into the instance of the subclass of UIDocument. We will learn about this in a minute.

Something that can confuse any programmer is using the UIDocument class—but to be perfectly honest, if you want to start with the basics, there are only four things you need to learn about this class:

1. You must always subclass this class. This class itself doesn't know how to load its contents or how to pass its contents as data to iOS to store in the cloud.

2. You must initialize this class with the URL of a file. In this recipe, we will pass the URL of a file in the user's cloud storage to the designated initializer of this class.

3. In your subclass, you must override the contentsForType:error: instance method of UIDocument. The return value of this method can be an NSData snapshot of the document you are managing. For instance, if it is a text file whose URL you passed to the initializer of your document class, then you must simply convert that text (presumably in the form of NSString) to NSData and return that data as the return value of this method. iOS calls this method in your document whenever it needs to store that data to the cloud or needs to read that content to present it to the user.

4. You must override the loadFromContents:ofType:error: instance method of your UIDocument subclass. In this method, iOS passes you the data (that perhaps was read from the cloud storage), and you must read that data into text (if text is what your document manages).

So, assuming that we have already set up the app with iCloud (see Recipe 19.1), we will go ahead and start subclassing UIDocument. In this recipe, we want to create a Documents folder in the user's iCloud storage for the app (if this folder doesn't exist yet). We will then read from/store a file named *UserDocument.txt* in this folder. Follow these steps to subclass the UIDocument class:

1. In Xcode, select File → New → New File... from the menus.

2. In the New File dialog, make sure the Cocoa Touch subcategory of the iOS category is selected on the lefthand side. Then select the Objective-C class item on the righthand side of the dialog and press the Next button (see Figure 19-12).

3. In the next screen, name your new class CloudDocument and make sure you are subclassing UIDocument, as shown in Figure 19-13. Once you are done, press the Next button.

4. In the next dialog, select where you wish to save the new class and press the Create button (see Figure 19-14).

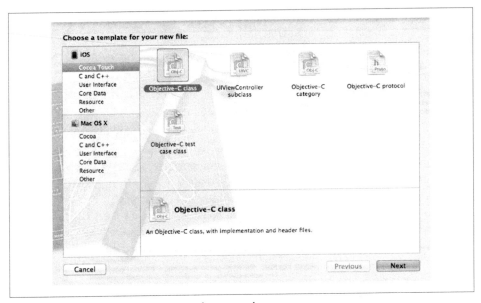

Figure 19-12. Beginning to create a new document class

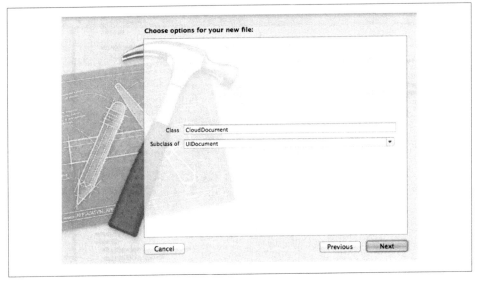

Figure 19-13. Subclassing UIDocument

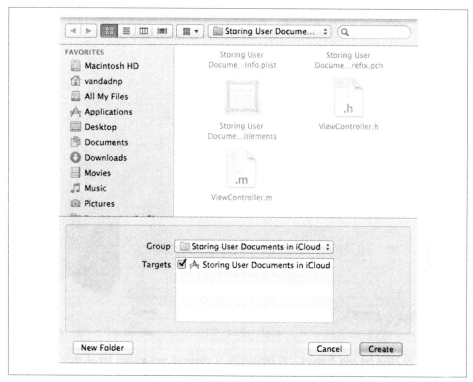

Figure 19-14. Saving the subclass to disk

Now that we have the UIDocument subclass, we need to see how we can initialize it. The designated initializer of UIDocument class is the initWithFileURL: method. However, we need to change this a bit, as we are going to need a delegate object as well. Why do we need a delegate object, you might be asking? We want to let the delegate object know whenever iOS downloads a newer version of the document from iCloud. Imagine this scenario: the user has two iOS devices running your app and she has already set up those devices with her iCloud credentials. Now she opens your app on her iPhone and starts writing some text into the text view. She leaves the app and goes to run some errands. She comes back and picks up her *iPad* (as opposed to her iPhone, which she originally used to write content in the app), and sees that the app picked up the latest version of the document and shows that content. Remember that the app is still present in the background on her iPhone. She adds some text to the document on the iPad and goes back to the iPhone. At this point, iCloud has probably already picked up the version that her iPad synced to the cloud and has downloaded that document into her iPhone. At this point, the document object has to be intelligent enough to present the new content to a delegate object. In this case, we can nominate the view controller (the owner of the text view) as the delegate object of the document. The whole point is that we need to create a delegate object that will be notified whenever iCloud gives a new version of data, which we need to initialize the document. Let's define this protocol in the header file of the document and define a new designated initializer for the class:

```
#import <UIKit/UIKit.h>

@class CloudDocument;

@protocol CloudDocumentProtocol<NSObject>
- (void) cloudDocumentChanged:(CloudDocument *)paramSender;
@end

@interface CloudDocument : UIDocument

@property (nonatomic, strong) NSString *documentText;
@property (nonatomic, weak) id<CloudDocumentProtocol> delegate;

/* Designated Initializer */
- (id) initWithFileURL:(NSURL *)paramURL
            delegate:(id<CloudDocumentProtocol>)paramDelegate;

@end
```

Here is a brief description of what is going on in this header file:

The CloudDocumentProtocol *protocol*
:   This is the protocol that this document's delegate object has to adapt in order to stay up-to-date about the changes to the current document that are brought into the user's current device via iCloud.

The documentText *string*
:   This is a simple string that we will use to house the content of the document. The user will pass the URL of the file that we need to initialize the document to the class's designated initializer. The UIDocument class will then read the contents of that URL for us (we don't have to do it manually) and will pass the data of that file to the class. All we have to do is convert that data to the format we are managing in the document (in this case, NSString).

The initWithFileURL:delegate: *designated initializer*
:   This is the class's designated initializer, and very similar to the designated initializer of the superclass. The difference is that we are asking for a second parameter that will be the delegate of an instance of the class. We will keep the delegate object updated whenever new content is downloaded by iOS from iCloud for the document we are managing.

We will follow that with the implementation of the class's designated initializer:

```
- (id) initWithFileURL:(NSURL *)paramURL
            delegate:(id<CloudDocumentProtocol>)paramDelegate{

  self = [super initWithFileURL:paramURL];

  if (self != nil){
```

```
    if (paramDelegate == nil){
      NSLog(@"Warning: no delegate is given.");
    }

    _delegate = paramDelegate;
  }

  return self;

}

- (id) initWithFileURL:(NSURL *)paramURL{
  return [self initWithFileURL:paramURL
                      delegate:nil];
}
```

As described before, we shall now implement the contentsForType:error: instance method of the class. This method gets called whenever iOS decides to read the contents of the document that the instance of the class is managing. For instance, iOS might ask the instance to say what contents it is managing so that iOS can store that content on iCloud. In this method, we will simply convert the string to an instance of NSData and return it:

```
- (id) contentsForType:(NSString *)typeName
                 error:(NSError *__autoreleasing *)outError{

  if ([self.documentText length] == 0){
    self.documentText = @"New Document";
  }

  return [self.documentText dataUsingEncoding:NSUTF8StringEncoding];
}
```

 We are setting a default text for the document if the text that we are managing at the moment is empty, so that when the user first creates a new document (our app creates the document for the user), the text won't be empty and the user at least sees something on the screen.

Moving on to the implementation of the loadFromContents:ofType:error: instance method of the document class now, we shall simply read the content that is passed to us as the first parameter of this method and turn it into the text that the document instance is managing. This method gets called when iOS reads the contents of the URL with which the instance of the class gets initialized. So we will take the data and turn it into a string in this example. In addition to that, we also let the delegate object know (if one is set) that the text the instance is managing has changed:

```
- (BOOL) loadFromContents:(id)contents
                   ofType:(NSString *)typeName
                    error:(NSError *__autoreleasing *)outError{

  NSData *data = (NSData *)contents;
```

```
if ([data length] == 0){
  self.documentText = @"New Document";
} else {
  self.documentText = [[NSString alloc] initWithData:data
                                       encoding:NSUTF8StringEncoding];
}

if ([_delegate respondsToSelector:@selector(cloudDocumentChanged:)]){
  [_delegate cloudDocumentChanged:self];
}

return YES;

}
```

 In this method, we will notify the delegate object that the contents of the document have changed, to give the delegate object a chance to update things, such as the UI.

That was really all we had to implement in the document class. The rest of the heavy lifting has to happen in the view controller. The first thing that we need to do in the view controller is to find the iCloud path of the *UserDocument.txt* file we are creating for the user. For this, as we learned in Recipe 19.3, we will use the `URLForUbiq uityContainerIdentifier:` instance method of `NSFileManager`. Also, as we learned in Recipe 19.3, we will create a Documents directory in the app's root iCloud directory if one doesn't exist. Let's begin with a method that returns the URL for the Documents directory in iCloud for the app and creates the directory if it doesn't exist already:

```
- (NSURL *) urlForDocumentsDirectoryIniCloud{

  NSURL *result = nil;

  #error Replace this with your own Team ID
  NSString *teamID = @"TEAM ID";

  NSString *containerID = @"com.pixolity.Storing-User-Documents-in-iCloud";

  NSString *teamIDAndContainerID = [NSString stringWithFormat:@"%@.%@",
                                    teamID,
                                    containerID];

  NSFileManager *fileManager = [[NSFileManager alloc] init];

  NSURL *iCloudURL = [fileManager
                      URLForUbiquityContainerIdentifier:teamIDAndContainerID];

  NSURL *documentsFolderURLIniCloud =
  [iCloudURL URLByAppendingPathComponent:@"Documents"
                          isDirectory:YES];
```

```
    /* If it doesn't exist, create it */
    if ([fileManager fileExistsAtPath:[documentsFolderURLIniCloud path]] == NO){
      NSLog(@"The documents folder does NOT exist in iCloud. Creating...");
      NSError *folderCreationError = nil;
      BOOL created = [fileManager createDirectoryAtURL:documentsFolderURLIniCloud
                         withIntermediateDirectories:YES
                                          attributes:nil
                                               error:&folderCreationError];

      if (created){
        NSLog(@"Successfully created the Documents folder in iCloud.");
        result = documentsFolderURLIniCloud;
      } else {
        NSLog(@"Failed to create the Documents folder in iCloud. Error = %@",
            folderCreationError);
      }
    } else {
      NSLog(@"The Documents folder already exists in iCloud.");
      result = documentsFolderURLIniCloud;
    }

    return result;

}
```

We will use the URL returned by the `urlForDocumentsDirectoryIniCloud` method to create the URL for the *UserDocument.txt* that the app wants to create/edit/manage:

```
- (NSURL *) urlForFileInDocumentsDirectoryIniCloud{

  return [[self urlForDocumentsDirectoryIniCloud]
          URLByAppendingPathComponent:@"UserDocument.txt"];

}
```

Now let's go to the header file of the view controller and define the appropriate instance variables. We need:

1. An instance of the `CloudDocument` class that will manage the document in the cloud.

2. An instance of the `UITextView` class that we will use to allow the user to enter his text, which we will sync to iCloud as he types.

3. An instance of the `NSMetadataQuery` class that we will use to find the existing document in the cloud, if one exists.

```
#import <UIKit/UIKit.h>
#import "CloudDocument.h"

@interface ViewController : UIViewController
                           <CloudDocumentProtocol, UITextViewDelegate>

@property (nonatomic, strong) CloudDocument *cloudDocument;
@property (nonatomic, strong) UITextView *textViewCloudDocumentText;
```

```
@property (nonatomic, strong) NSMetadataQuery *metadataQuery;

@end
```

Now that we have the text view declared in the header file of the view controller, let's go instantiate it in the implementation of the view controller:

```
- (void) setupTextView{
  /* Create the text view */

  CGRect textViewRect = CGRectMake(20.0f,
                                   20.0f,
                                   self.view.bounds.size.width - 40.0f,
                                   self.view.bounds.size.height - 40.0f);

  self.textViewCloudDocumentText = [[UITextView alloc] initWithFrame:
                                    textViewRect];
  self.textViewCloudDocumentText.delegate = self;
  self.textViewCloudDocumentText.font = [UIFont systemFontOfSize:20.0f];
  [self.view addSubview:self.textViewCloudDocumentText];
}
```

We will be using this method in the `viewDidLoad` method of the view controller, which will be discussed soon. Now let's start implementing a method that will allow the view controller to react to keyboard notifications. As it was discussed in Recipe 2.29, when the user starts to change the text in the text view, the keyboard will pop up (if a Bluetooth keyboard isn't set up) and the keyboard will cover almost half of the iPhone screen. So in this case, we need to change the content inset of the text view. We start by listening to keyboard notifications:

```
- (void) listenForKeyboardNotifications{
  /* As we have a text view, when the keyboard shows on screen, we want to
  make sure the textview's content is fully visible, so start
  listening for keyboard notifications */
  [[NSNotificationCenter defaultCenter]
   addObserver:self
   selector:@selector(handleKeyboardWillShow:)
   name:UIKeyboardWillShowNotification
   object:nil];

  [[NSNotificationCenter defaultCenter]
   addObserver:self
   selector:@selector(handleKeyboardWillHide:)
   name:UIKeyboardWillHideNotification
   object:nil];
}
```

The next thing that we shall take care of is to search for existing user documents when the view controller's view is loaded (in the `viewDidLoad` method). If a document exists in the cloud, then we will load that; if not, we will create a new document:

```
- (void) startSearchingForDocumentIniCloud{
  /* Start searching for existing text documents */
  self.metadataQuery = [[NSMetadataQuery alloc] init];
```

```
    NSPredicate *predicate = [NSPredicate predicateWithFormat:@"%K like %@",
                              NSMetadataItemFSNameKey,
                              @"*"];
    [self.metadataQuery setPredicate:predicate];
    NSArray *searchScopes = [[NSArray alloc] initWithObjects:
                              NSMetadataQueryUbiquitousDocumentsScope,
                              nil];
    [self.metadataQuery setSearchScopes:searchScopes];

    NSString *metadataNotification =
      NSMetadataQueryDidFinishGatheringNotification;

    [[NSNotificationCenter defaultCenter]
      addObserver:self
      selector:@selector(handleMetadataQueryFinished:)
      name:metadataNotification
      object:nil];

    [self.metadataQuery startQuery];
  }
```

Let's utilize all these methods in the view controller:

```
- (void)viewDidLoad{
  [super viewDidLoad];
  [self listenForKeyboardNotifications];
  self.view.backgroundColor = [UIColor brownColor];
  [self setupTextView];
  [self startSearchingForDocumentIniCloud];
}
```

In the `startSearchingForDocumentIniCloud` method, we started listening for `NSMeta
dataQueryDidFinishGatheringNotification` notifications on the `handleMetadataQuery
Finished:` method. We need to have a look at the implementation of this method. The
way we have to implement this method is to first find out if the metadata query could
find any existing iCloud documents. If yes, then we will look for the specific document
that the app creates for the user, which is called *UserDocument.txt*. If this file is found
in the user's cloud space, then we will open that document. If not, we will create it:

```
- (void) handleMetadataQueryFinished:(NSNotification *)paramNotification{

  /* Make sure this is the metadata query that we were expecting... */
  NSMetadataQuery *senderQuery = (NSMetadataQuery *)[paramNotification object];

  if ([senderQuery isEqual:self.metadataQuery] == NO){
    NSLog(@"Unknown metadata query sent us a message.");
    return;
  }

  [self.metadataQuery disableUpdates];

  /* Now we stop listening for these notifications because we don't really
    have to, anymore */
  NSString *metadataNotification =
    NSMetadataQueryDidFinishGatheringNotification;
```

```objectivec
[[NSNotificationCenter defaultCenter] removeObserver:self
                                      name:metadataNotification
                                      object:nil];

[self.metadataQuery stopQuery];

NSLog(@"Metadata query finished.");


/* Let's find out if we had previously created this document in the user's
 cloud space because if yes, then we have to avoid overwriting that
 document and just use the existing one */
__block BOOL documentExistsIniCloud = NO;
NSString *FileNameToLookFor = @"UserDocument.txt";

NSArray *results = self.metadataQuery.results;

[results enumerateObjectsUsingBlock:^(id obj, NSUInteger idx, BOOL *stop) {
  NSMetadataItem *item = (NSMetadataItem *)obj;
  NSURL *itemURL = (NSURL *)[item valueForAttribute:NSMetadataItemURLKey];
  NSString *lastComponent = (NSString *)[[itemURL pathComponents] lastObject];
  if ([lastComponent isEqualToString:FileNameToLookFor]){
    if ([itemURL isEqual:[self urlForFileInDocumentsDirectoryIniCloud]]){
      documentExistsIniCloud = YES;
      *stop = YES;
    }
  }
}];

NSURL *urlOfDocument = [self urlForFileInDocumentsDirectoryIniCloud];
self.cloudDocument = [[CloudDocument alloc] initWithFileURL:urlOfDocument
                                            delegate:self];


__weak ViewController *weakSelf = self;

/* If the document exists, open it */
if (documentExistsIniCloud){
  NSLog(@"Document already exists in iCloud. Loading it from there...");
  [self.cloudDocument openWithCompletionHandler:^(BOOL success) {
    if (success){
      ViewController *strongSelf = weakSelf;
      NSLog(@"Successfully loaded the document from iCloud.");
      strongSelf.textViewCloudDocumentText.text =
        strongSelf.cloudDocument.documentText;
    } else {
      NSLog(@"Failed to load the document from iCloud.");
    }
  }];

} else {
  NSLog(@"Document does not exist in iCloud. Creating it...");

  /* If the document doesn't exist, ask the CloudDocument class to
   save a new file on that address for us */
  [self.cloudDocument saveToURL:[self urlForFileInDocumentsDirectoryIniCloud]
```

```
                forSaveOperation:UIDocumentSaveForCreating
            completionHandler:^(BOOL success) {
              if (success){
                NSLog(@"Successfully created the new file in iCloud.");
                ViewController *strongSelf = weakSelf;
      strongSelf.textViewCloudDocumentText.text =
                  strongSelf.cloudDocument.documentText;

              } else {
                NSLog(@"Failed to create the file.");
              }
            }];

    }

  }
```

What is left now is to listen for changes in the text view—once the changes have been applied by the user, we will try to save them into the document. We do this by implementing the `textViewDidChange:` delegate method of the `UITextViewDelegate` protocol:

```
- (void) textViewDidChange:(UITextView *)textView{
  self.cloudDocument.documentText = textView.text;
  [self.cloudDocument updateChangeCount:UIDocumentChangeDone];
}
```

With this method, we let the document know that the user has updated the contents of the text in the text view. We call the `updateChangeCount:` instance method of `UIDocu ment` to get the document to reflect those changes to the cloud. We also have to implement the `cloudDocumentChanged:` delegate method of the `CloudDocumentProtocol` protocol, and change the text inside the text view when the text in the document changes. This method will get called, for instance, when the user opens the app in two devices with the same iCloud credentials, changes the document in one device, and leaves the document open in the other device. The second device's iCloud daemon will then retrieve the latest version of the document from the cloud, and the document class will call the `cloudDocumentChanged:` delegate message to give us a chance to update the UI:

```
- (void) cloudDocumentChanged:(CloudDocument *)paramSender{
  self.textViewCloudDocumentText.text = paramSender.documentText;
}
```

Before we forget, we also have to implement the keyboard notification handlers:

```
- (void) handleKeyboardWillShow:(NSNotification *)paramNotification{

  NSDictionary *userInfo = [paramNotification userInfo];

  NSValue *animationCurveObject =
  [userInfo valueForKey:UIKeyboardAnimationCurveUserInfoKey];

  NSValue *animationDurationObject =
  [userInfo valueForKey:UIKeyboardAnimationDurationUserInfoKey];

  NSValue *keyboardEndRectObject =
```

```
        [userInfo valueForKey:UIKeyboardFrameEndUserInfoKey];

    NSUInteger animationCurve = 0;
    double animationDuration = 0.0f;
    CGRect keyboardEndRect = CGRectMake(0, 0, 0, 0);

    [animationCurveObject getValue:&animationCurve];
    [animationDurationObject getValue:&animationDuration];
    [keyboardEndRectObject getValue:&keyboardEndRect];

    UIWindow *window = [[[UIApplication sharedApplication] delegate] window];

    /* Convert the frame from window's coordinate system to
       the view's coordinate system */
    keyboardEndRect = [self.view convertRect:keyboardEndRect
                                    fromView:window];

    [UIView beginAnimations:@"changeTextViewContentInset"
                    context:NULL];
    [UIView setAnimationDuration:animationDuration];
    [UIView setAnimationCurve:(UIViewAnimationCurve)animationCurve];

    CGRect intersectionOfKeyboardRectAndWindowRect =
    CGRectIntersection(window.frame, keyboardEndRect);

    CGFloat bottomInset = intersectionOfKeyboardRectAndWindowRect.size.height;

    self.textViewCloudDocumentText.contentInset = UIEdgeInsetsMake(0.0f,
                                                                   0.0f,
                                                                   bottomInset,
                                                                   0.0f);

    [UIView commitAnimations];

}

- (void) handleKeyboardWillHide:(NSNotification *)paramNotification{

    if (UIEdgeInsetsEqualToEdgeInsets(self.textViewCloudDocumentText.contentInset,
                                      UIEdgeInsetsZero)){
      /* the text view's content inset is intact, so no need to reset it */
      return;
    }

    NSDictionary *userInfo = [paramNotification userInfo];

    NSValue *animationCurveObject =
    [userInfo valueForKey:UIKeyboardAnimationCurveUserInfoKey];

    NSValue *animationDurationObject =
    [userInfo valueForKey:UIKeyboardAnimationDurationUserInfoKey];

    NSUInteger animationCurve = 0;
    double animationDuration = 0.0f;
```

```
[animationCurveObject getValue:&animationCurve];
[animationDurationObject getValue:&animationDuration];

[UIView beginAnimations:@"changeTextViewContentInset"
            context:NULL];
[UIView setAnimationDuration:animationDuration];
[UIView setAnimationCurve:(UIViewAnimationCurve)animationCurve];

self.textViewCloudDocumentText.contentInset = UIEdgeInsetsZero;

[UIView commitAnimations];

}
```

Go ahead and run this app on a device. It is actually better if you can run the same app on two iOS devices with the same iCloud credentials, and then update the document on one device and wait for the second device to automatically update its contents from the cloud.

See Also

Recipe 2.29; Recipe 19.1; Recipe 19.3

19.6 Managing the State of Documents in iCloud

Problem

You want to be able to detect conflicts and other issues that could occur as a result of syncing documents to iCloud.

Solution

Stat listening to the UIDocumentStateChangedNotification notification.

 I highly recommend reading Recipe 19.5 before proceeding with this recipe, as the material described here highly relies on what was taught in that section.

Discussion

The UIDocumentStateChangedNotification notification gets sent when the state of an iCloud document (of type UIDocument) is changed. The object carried by this notification is the instance of the UIDocument whose state was changed. You can listen to this notification and then analyze the documentState property of your iCloud document; this property is of type UIDocumentState and can be a mixture of these values:

UIDocumentStateNormal

Things are normal and no conflicts have occurred in the document.

UIDocumentStateClosed

This means that the document has not yet been opened, or was open and has just been closed. You might want to disallow the user from editing the document while the document is in this state. Apple recommends that you do not display alert views to your users, but instead, perhaps, display graphical components on the screen to indicate to the user that editing has been disabled.

UIDocumentStateInConflict

This state indicates that a conflict has happened in the document. For instance, the same document could had been edited by two or more people at the same time causing a conflict. In such cases, you will have two options. Either fix the conflict programmatically for the user, or prompt the user to choose which version of that document she wants to keep.

UIDocumentStateSavingError

This document state indicates that an error has occurred in saving the document to iCloud. You *might* want to allow the user to continue editing the document while the document is in this state, but there is no guarantee as to whether the user changes will be saved to iCloud or not. Obviously, you might want to implement some smart mechanisms in your apps that will temporarily store the contents of the document in the app bundle while the document is in this state, and reflect those changes to iCloud at a later time. The solution is up to you. Alternatively, you might want to let your users know that an error has happened to their document, and that there is a possibility of data loss.

UIDocumentStateEditingDisabled

This state indicates that editing has been disabled on the document because of an error. It is best in this case to disallow the user from editing the document.

 As explained before, the documentState property of UIDocument can be a mixture of the aforementioned values.

To demonstrate how we can take advantage of the UIDocumentStateChangedNotifica tion notification, let's build on top of the example code in Recipe 19.5 and change the viewDidLoad method of the view controller to subscribe to this notification:

```
- (void) listenForDocumentStateChangesNotification{

  /* Start listening for the Document State Changes notification */
  [[NSNotificationCenter defaultCenter]
   addObserver:self
   selector:@selector(handleDocumentStateChanged:)
   name:UIDocumentStateChangedNotification
```

```
    object:nil];

  }

  - (void)viewDidLoad{
    [super viewDidLoad];

    [self listenForDocumentStateChangesNotification];
    [self listenForKeyboardNotifications];
    self.view.backgroundColor = [UIColor brownColor];
    [self setupTextView];
    [self startSearchingForDocumentIniCloud];
  }
```

We have elected the handleDocumentStateChanged: method of the view controller to listen for the UIDocumentStateChangedNotification notification. Now let's go ahead and implement this method:

```
  - (void) handleDocumentStateChanged:(NSNotification *)paramNotification{
    NSLog(@"Document state has changed");
    NSLog(@"Notification Object = %@", [paramNotification object]);

    NSLog(@"Notification Object Class = %@",
          NSStringFromClass([[paramNotification object] class]));

    CloudDocument *senderDocument = (CloudDocument *)paramNotification.object;
    NSLog(@"Document State = %d", senderDocument.documentState);


    /* Since we don't yet know how to solve conflicts, we'll disallow the user
      from editing the document if an error of any sort happens. Later, when
      we learn about handling conflicts, we'll handle these issues more gracefully*/

    if (senderDocument.documentState & UIDocumentStateInConflict){
      NSLog(@"Conflict found in the document.");
      self.textViewCloudDocumentText.editable = NO;
    }
    if (senderDocument.documentState & UIDocumentStateClosed){
      NSLog(@"Document is closed.");
      self.textViewCloudDocumentText.editable = NO;
    }
    if (senderDocument.documentState & UIDocumentStateEditingDisabled){
      NSLog(@"Editing is disabled on this document.");
      self.textViewCloudDocumentText.editable = NO;
    }
    if (senderDocument.documentState & UIDocumentStateNormal){
      NSLog(@"Things are normal. We are good to go.");
      self.textViewCloudDocumentText.editable = YES;
    }
    if (senderDocument.documentState & UIDocumentStateSavingError){
      NSLog(@"A saving error has happened.");
      self.textViewCloudDocumentText.editable = NO;
    }

  }
```

As you can see, we are using if statements instead of else-if statements in this example, simply because the state of a cloud document can be more than one of the aforementioned values at the same time. Therefore, we have to be able to handle them in conjunction. You will also notice that we are disallowing the user from entering text into the text view while an error has been detected in the state of the document, be it a saving error or a conflict. This is not a very good user experience, and I highly recommend that you have a look at Recipe 19.7 to learn how to solve conflicts in iCloud documents and provide a better user experience in your apps.

See Also

Recipe 19.5

19.7 Handling Conflicts in iCloud Documents

Problem

You want to be able to solve conflicts between two or more versions of a document (managed through UIDocument) in iCloud.

Solution

Use the otherVersionsOfItemAtURL: class method of the NSFileVersion class to detect different versions of the current revision of the document you are managing using an instance of UIDocument. Each version of a document is of type NSFileVersion. The procedure to take is as follows:

1. Instantiate and open a document.
2. Listen for UIDocumentStateChangedNotification notifications (see Recipe 19.6).
3. Check if the documentState property of the document that caused the aforementioned notification to be fired has the UIDocumentStateInConflict state. If yes, then we will proceed to the next step. If not, we will handle the issue in a different way.

 When a conflict occurs in a document, iCloud will automatically attempt to resolve that conflict by either merging two or more revisions of that document together, or simply taking the latest version. Whatever iCloud does, it will give you *a* revision of the document to work with. This revision is called the *current version* of that document.

4. We will use the currentVersionOfItemAtURL: class method of the NSFileVersion class to get the current version of the document by passing the URL of the document to this method.

---

5. Next, we will use the `otherVersionsOfItemAtURL:` class method of the `NSFileVer`
sion class to get all other versions of the document, by passing the URL of the
document to this method. The return value of this method is an array of type
`NSFileVersion`. Now that we have all the other versions, as well as the current
version of the document, we will put them in an array for processing. Remember,
all these version objects are of type `NSFileVersion`.

6. Now that we have all the versions, we can display a table view to the user asking
him which version he would like to use, now that a conflict has occurred.

7. If he chose the current version, we will simply get rid of the table view and display
the main UI of the app, since the current version is the one that the document is
currently managing—iCloud has managed to solve the conflict on that version, so
there really is nothing we need to do on that document. Since the user chose the
current version, we will *not* proceed to the next steps.

8. If the user does *not* choose the current version, we will proceed to the steps that
follow.

9. We will first close the document that we are currently managing, using the `close`
`WithCompletionHandler:` instance method of `UIDocument`.

10. Then we will use the `removeOtherVersionsOfItemAtURL:error:` class method of
`NSFileVersion` class, and pass the URL of the version that the user picked as the
first parameter to this method. This method will then automatically dispose of the
other versions that are available for the current document (in conflict, or not in
conflict), except for the version to which we pass the URL in the second argument
of this method. That version will be kept safe. We do this in order to let iCloud
know we are handling the conflict manually. If we don't take this step, the next
time the app opens, the document will go into a conflict state because iCloud will
detect all the in-conflict versions of the document we were managing.

11. The next step is to re-instantiate the document object using the URL to the version
that the user just picked. This will get rid of the previous document object, as there
is no good way of switching between two or more document files using the same
instance of `UIDocument`.

12. Last but not least, we will attempt to open the new version of the document, using
the `openWithCompletionHandler:` instance method of the document object (of type
`UIDocument`).

 This recipe builds on top of Recipes 19.6 and 19.5. I highly recommend
that you thoroughly cover those recipes before proceeding with this one.

Discussion

In this recipe, we will assume that we have two iOS devices running the same app, that both have one document open, and that the user is sharing her iCloud account on both devices (in other words, both devices belong to the same user). We have a text view that allows the user to enter text, and we will attempt to save the text in the current document. We also start listening for `UIDocumentStateChangedNotification` notifications (see Recipe 19.6) and once we detect a conflict, we will display a modal table view on the screen and list all available versions of the document. The user can then pick a version, which we will keep as the current version and allow her to continue editing the document.

One of the first things we need to accomplish is creating a view controller with a table view in it. We will use this table view to display the available versions of the document that the user is editing, should there be a conflict between versions. So let's go ahead and create the view controller by following these steps:

1. In Xcode, select File → New → New File...

2. Make sure you have selected the Cocoa Touch subcategory under the iOS category on the lefthand side of the New File dialog. Once that is done, select the UIView-Controller subclass item on the righthand side and press the Next button, as shown in Figure 19-15.

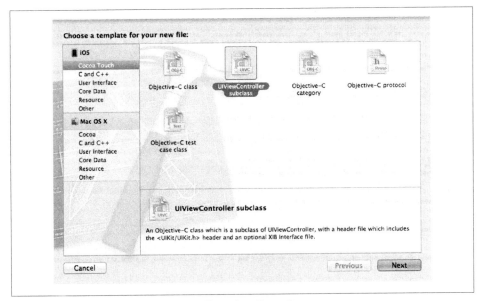

Figure 19-15. Creating a new view controller to handle conflicts

3. In the next screen, set your view controller's class to *ConflictViewController* and make sure Xcode creates a XIB file alongside the view controller's header and

implementation file, as shown in Figure 19-16. Once you are done, press the Next button.

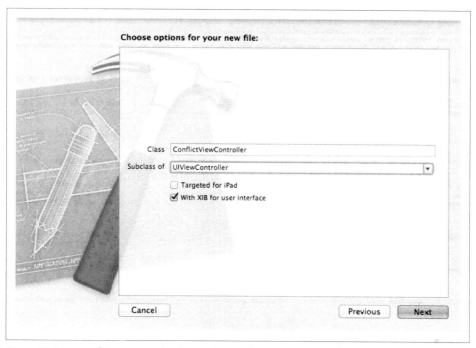

Figure 19-16. Specifying a name for the conflict resolution view controller

4. In the next screen, specify where you would like to save the view controller and its .xib file and then press the Create button.

Perfect! Now we have the view controller. We want the app's main view controller to be in charge of populating data into the table view inside the conflict view controller so let's define the interface of the conflict view controller with a new designated initializer:

```
#import <UIKit/UIKit.h>

@interface ConflictViewController : UIViewController

@property (nonatomic, strong) UITableView *tableViewVersions;

/* Designated Initializer */
- (id) initWithNibName:(NSString *)nibNameOrNil
              bundle:(NSBundle *)nibBundleOrNil
    tableViewDelegate:(id<UITableViewDelegate>)paramTableViewDelegate
  tableViewDataSource:(id<UITableViewDataSource>)paramTableViewDataSource;

@end
```

The next step is to implement this view controller. There's not much code to write here, except for implementing the designated initializer and setting up the table view:

```objc
#import "ConflictViewController.h"

@implementation ConflictViewController

- (id) initWithNibName:(NSString *)nibNameOrNil
                bundle:(NSBundle *)nibBundleOrNil
     tableViewDelegate:(id<UITableViewDelegate>)paramTableViewDelegate
   tableViewDataSource:(id<UITableViewDataSource>)paramTableViewDataSource{

  self = [super initWithNibName:nibNameOrNil
                         bundle:nibBundleOrNil];

  if (self != nil){
    /* No view exists at this point so let's set the table view's frame
       to a zero-rectangle and then we will adjust it when the view loads */
    tableViewVersions = [[UITableView alloc]
                          initWithFrame:CGRectZero
                          style:UITableViewStylePlain];
    tableViewVersions.delegate = paramTableViewDelegate;
    tableViewVersions.dataSource = paramTableViewDataSource;
  }

  return self;

}

- (id) initWithNibName:(NSString *)nibNameOrNil
                bundle:(NSBundle *)nibBundleOrNil{

  return [self initWithNibName:nibNameOrNil
                        bundle:nibBundleOrNil
             tableViewDelegate:nil
           tableViewDataSource:nil];

}

- (void)viewDidLoad{
  [super viewDidLoad];

  self.view.autoresizingMask = UIViewAutoresizingFlexibleWidth |
                               UIViewAutoresizingFlexibleHeight;
  self.tableViewVersions.autoresizingMask = self.view.autoresizingMask;
  self.tableViewVersions.frame = self.view.bounds;
  [self.view addSubview:self.tableViewVersions];

}

- (BOOL)shouldAutorotateToInterfaceOrientation
        :(UIInterfaceOrientation)interfaceOrientation{
```

```
    return (interfaceOrientation == UIInterfaceOrientationPortrait);
}

@end
```

OK, now let's go to the app's main view controller's header file and make sure that we have:

1. An array of type NSArray in which we can store different versions of the document, should there be a conflict.

2. An instance of the ConflictViewController class that we will use to display to the user when we detect a conflict on the document.

```
#import <UIKit/UIKit.h>
#import "CloudDocument.h"

@class ConflictViewController;

@interface ViewController : UIViewController <UITextFieldDelegate,
        CloudDocumentProtocol, UITextViewDelegate,
        UITableViewDelegate, UITableViewDataSource>

@property (nonatomic, strong) UITextView *textViewCloudDocumentText;
@property (nonatomic, strong) CloudDocument *cloudDocument;
@property (nonatomic, strong) NSMetadataQuery *metadataQuery;
@property (nonatomic, copy) NSArray *arrayOfCloudDocumentVersions;
@property (nonatomic, strong) ConflictViewController *conflictViewController;

@end
```

Obviously, we will now move to the implementation of the file and define our private method there:

```
#import "ViewController.h"
#import "ConflictViewController.h"

@interface ViewController(Private)
- (NSURL *) urlForDocumentsDirectoryIniCloud;
@end

@implementation ViewController

...
```

What we have to do now is to listen to and handle incoming UIDocumentStateChanged Notification notifications. Once a notification arrives, we will:

1. Find out if the document's state now contains the UIDocumentStateInConflict flag or not. If yes, we will proceed to the next step.

2. Once we find a conflict, we will use the currentVersionOfItemAtURL: and the otherVersionsOfItemAtURL: class methods of NSFileVersion, and place all the available versions in the arrayOfCloudDocumentVersions array.

3. Now that we have all the available versions of the document in the `arrayOfCloud DocumentVersions` array, we will place the conflict view controller inside a navigation controller and present it as a modal view controller on top of the current view controller. This will then give the user the ability to view all available versions and pick one.

So let's dig in and handle the incoming `UIDocumentStateChangedNotification`s:

```
- (void) listenForDocumentStateChangesNotification{

    /* Start listening for the Document State Changes notification */
    [[NSNotificationCenter defaultCenter]
     addObserver:self
     selector:@selector(handleDocumentStateChanged:)
     name:UIDocumentStateChangedNotification
     object:nil];

}

- (void) prepareFileVersionsTableView{

    self.conflictViewController = [[ConflictViewController alloc]
                                    initWithNibName:@"ConflictViewController"
                                    bundle:nil
                                    tableViewDelegate:self
                                    tableViewDataSource:self];

}

- (void)viewDidLoad{
    [super viewDidLoad];
    [self prepareFileVersionsTableView];
    [self listenForDocumentStateChangesNotification];
    [self listenForKeyboardNotifications];
    self.view.backgroundColor = [UIColor brownColor];
    [self setupTextView];
    [self startSearchingForDocumentIniCloud];
}
```

Here is the implementation of the `handleDocumentStateChanged:` method that will do the heavy lifting of finding all the file versions and so on:

```
- (void) handleDocumentStateChanged:(NSNotification *)paramNotification{
    NSLog(@"Document state has changed");
    NSLog(@"Notification Object = %@", [paramNotification object]);

    NSLog(@"Notification Object Class = %@",
        NSStringFromClass([[paramNotification object] class]));

    CloudDocument *senderDocument = (CloudDocument *)paramNotification.object;
    NSLog(@"Document State = %d", senderDocument.documentState);


    /* Since we don't yet know how to solve conflicts, we will disallow the user
       from editing the document if an error of any sort has happened. Later, when
```

```
we will learn about handling conflicts, we will handle these issues
more gracefully*/

if (senderDocument.documentState & UIDocumentStateInConflict){
  NSLog(@"Conflict found in the document.");

  NSMutableArray *versions = [[NSMutableArray alloc] init];

  /* The first item in the list will be the current version */
  [versions addObject:[NSFileVersion currentVersionOfItemAtURL:
                       self.cloudDocument.fileURL]];

  /* Then add the other available versions of this document to the list */
  [versions addObjectsFromArray:
   [NSFileVersion otherVersionsOfItemAtURL:senderDocument.fileURL]];

  self.arrayOfCloudDocumentVersions = [NSArray arrayWithArray:versions];

  NSLog(@"There are %lu versions of this document available.",
        (unsigned long)[self.arrayOfCloudDocumentVersions count]);

  UINavigationController *tempNavController =
  [[UINavigationController alloc] initWithRootViewController:
   self.conflictViewController];

  [self presentModalViewController:tempNavController
                          animated:YES];

  [self.conflictViewController.tableViewVersions reloadData];

}

if (senderDocument.documentState & UIDocumentStateClosed){
  NSLog(@"Document is closed.");
  self.textViewCloudDocumentText.editable = NO;
}
if (senderDocument.documentState & UIDocumentStateEditingDisabled){
  NSLog(@"Editing is disabled on this document.");
  self.textViewCloudDocumentText.editable = NO;
}
if (senderDocument.documentState & UIDocumentStateNormal){
  NSLog(@"Things are normal. We are good to go.");
}
if (senderDocument.documentState & UIDocumentStateSavingError){
  NSLog(@"A saving error has happened.");
  self.textViewCloudDocumentText.editable = NO;
}

}
```

We shall now feed the table view inside the conflict view controller, with data relevant
to the various file versions of each conflict that we can find on the document we are
currently managing. Let's go ahead and do that right now:

```
- (NSInteger) numberOfSectionsInTableView:(UITableView *)tableView{
  return 1;
}

- (NSInteger) tableView:(UITableView *)tableView
  numberOfRowsInSection:(NSInteger)section{

  return [self.arrayOfCloudDocumentVersions count];

}

- (UITableViewCell *) tableView:(UITableView *)tableView
           cellForRowAtIndexPath:(NSIndexPath *)indexPath{

  UITableViewCell *result = nil;

  static NSString *FileVersionTableViewCell = @"FileVersionTableViewCell";

  result = [tableView dequeueReusableCellWithIdentifier:
            FileVersionTableViewCell];

  if (result == nil){
    result = [[UITableViewCell alloc] initWithStyle:UITableViewCellStyleSubtitle
                                    reuseIdentifier:FileVersionTableViewCell];
    result.detailTextLabel.numberOfLines = 2;
  }

  NSFileVersion *version = [self.arrayOfCloudDocumentVersions objectAtIndex:
                            indexPath.row];

  if (indexPath.row == 0){
    result.textLabel.text = [NSString stringWithFormat:
                             @"(Current) Version at: %@",
                             version.modificationDate];
  } else {
    result.textLabel.text = [NSString stringWithFormat:@"Version at: %@",
                             version.modificationDate];
  }


  result.detailTextLabel.text = [NSString stringWithFormat:@"Modified by: %@",
                                 version.localizedNameOfSavingComputer];

  return result;

}
```

 The first instance of NSFileVersion we place in the array of file versions (that gets fed to the table view) is always the current version. Because of this, in the table view, we will label the first cell *Current* to let the user know that if he picks that version, it will be the version he is currently working on after conflicts were handled by iCloud automatically.

When the user selects one of the versions we have presented in the table view on the conflict view controller, we would like to retrieve that version and present it to the user. As mentioned in the Solution of this recipe, there are a few steps that we have to take in order to achieve this. I strongly suggest that you refer to those steps before having a look at this code:

```objc
- (void)             tableView:(UITableView *)tableView
       didSelectRowAtIndexPath:(NSIndexPath *)indexPath{

  if (indexPath.row == 0){
    [self dismissModalViewControllerAnimated:YES];
    return;
  }

  self.textViewCloudDocumentText.text = [NSString string];

  NSFileVersion *selectedFileVersion = [self.arrayOfCloudDocumentVersions
                                 objectAtIndex:indexPath.row];

  NSLog(@"Closing the document...");

  /* Step 1: First close the document */
  [self.cloudDocument closeWithCompletionHandler:^(BOOL success) {
    if (success){
      NSLog(@"Successfully closed the current document.");

      /* Step 2: Remove all other versions of the selected revision */
      NSLog(@"Removing all other versions of the selected revision...");
      NSError *removeError = nil;
      BOOL removed = [NSFileVersion
                      removeOtherVersionsOfItemAtURL:selectedFileVersion.URL
                      error:&removeError];
      if (removed &&
          removeError == nil){
        NSLog(@"Successfully removed all other versions of selected revision.");

        /* Step 3: Open the selected revision */
        NSLog(@"Opening the selected revision...");
        self.cloudDocument = [[CloudDocument alloc]
                               initWithFileURL:selectedFileVersion.URL
                               delegate:self];

        [self.cloudDocument openWithCompletionHandler:^(BOOL success) {
          if (success){
            NSLog(@"Successfully opened the new file.");
            self.textViewCloudDocumentText.text =
            self.cloudDocument.documentText;
          } else {
            NSLog(@"Failed to open the new file.");
          }
        }];

      } else {
        NSLog(@"Failed to remove other versions of this revision. Error = %@",
```

```
                removeError);
        }
    } else {
        NSLog(@"Failed to close the current document.");
        }
    }];

    [self dismissModalViewControllerAnimated:YES];

}
```

Now if you run this app on two devices simultaneously using the same iCloud account, you will see an interface similar to Figure 19-17 pop up to ask you which version of the document you would prefer to keep.

Figure 19-17. Selecting a version to handle conflicts

See Also

Recipe 19.5; Recipe 19.6

CHAPTER 20

Pass Kit

20.0 Introduction

We're all familiar with coupons and tickets. For instance, you may go to a coffee shop that gives you a loyalty card that offers you a free cup of coffee after you have accumulated some number of stamps for previous coffee purchases. We also use coupons when we shop. You can buy X amount of food and the shop may give you a coupon to spend when you next shop there.

Figure 20-1 depicts what a simple railway ticket (presented as a pass) looks like in Passbook on a real iOS device.

Figure 20-1. A railway ticket presented as a pass in Passbook on an iOS device

iOS apps can use the Passbook framework to interact with passes as well. Going back to the coffee shop example, the app for this coffee shop may allow the user to top up their loyalty card with cash to allow them to take advantage of other cool things that the shop has to offer, such as WiFi access across the country. So, when the user opens the app, it will detect a pass in the user's Passbook database related to the coffee shop, allow the user to top the pass up right there on her phone, and then contact a barista to say that the pass installed on the user's device has been topped up with cash.

Pass Kit is how Apple represents this type of transaction digitally. Apple also introduced Passbook in iOS 6. So let's get our terminology right before we dig any deeper:

Pass Kit
> The framework Apple provides to developers to allow digitally signed passes to be delivered to compatible iOS devices running iOS 6 or later.

Passbook
> The client application on iOS 6 devices able to store, handle, and manage passes created by developers.

Therefore, we as developers will be using Pass Kit to create digitally signed passes and deliver them to our users. Our users will use Passbook on their devices to interact with the passes we create for them. Of course, this allows us developers to deliver coupons, rail passes, public transportation tickets, loyalty cards, and so on to our users in the form of digitally signed passes instead of the traditional, paper-based approach where people have to carry multiple cards in their wallets. Passbook on iOS devices is the place where all this content can be stored in a single place, without users having to carry all these passes in their pockets.

Before attempting to use new technology, you should get a grasp of the big picture: the high-level design of the technology and how it enables us to achieve our goals. For Pass Kit, I have broken this big picture down into small steps so that you can hopefully learn how you can use it to deliver digitally signed passes to your users:

1. The developer creates a certificate and its corresponding private key using Apple's Provisioning Portal.
2. The developer then creates a series of files that will represent the pass that the user will be given later.
3. The developer signs the created pass with the certificate that she created at the first step.
4. The developer delivers the pass to the user through various means of delivery.
5. The user will see the pass and will have the opportunity to add that pass to her device.
6. Once the pass is added to the user's device, Passbook will retain it for future use until the user decides to delete the pass.

I know that it can be difficult to understand the big picture simply by reading a few paragraphs of text. Figure 20-2 shows the sequence in more detail.

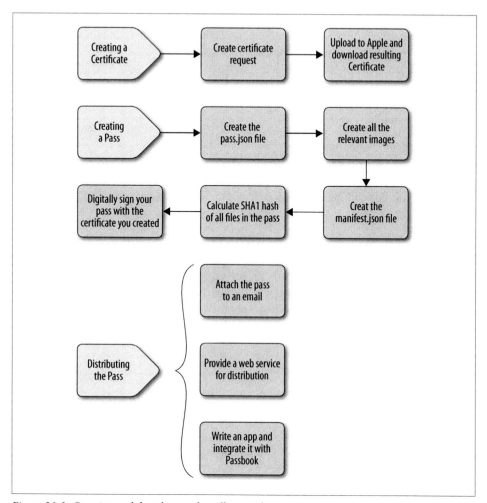

Figure 20-2. Creating and distributing digitally signed passes to users, iOS 6 and above

The recipes in this chapter will thoroughly explain the details of this process. A few bits and pieces related to Pass Kit as a technology—keeping your pass up-to-date and learning how to push updates from a server—require you to know a bit about server-side development. For the sake of simplicity, we won't be covering those parts in this chapter and instead will be focusing on creating passes. Once you know how to create a pass, you can distribute it in a variety of ways, two of which are explained in this chapter. However, parts that are not relevant to iOS, such as those that require server-side development knowledge, are skipped in this chapter for this reason.

20.1 Creating Pass Kit Certificates

Problem

You have decided to distribute digitally signed passes to your users and would like to begin with the first step, creating certificates to sign your passes with.

Solution

Create your certificates in the iOS Provisioning Portal.

Discussion

As explained in Recipe 20.0, in order to distribute passes to your users, you need to digitally sign them, and before doing that, you need to request a certificate from Apple that will uniquely bind all your passes to your developer account. That way, Apple knows which passes are legitimate and which ones are not.

Follow these steps to create your certificate:

1. Navigate your browser to the iOS Dev Center. I have avoided putting the URL to the iOS Dev Center here, as this URL is subject to change and I don't want to give you the wrong URL. If you don't know where this is, simply type it in a search engine and I bet you will find it in a matter of seconds.

2. If you are not logged in already, log in now.

3. Once logged in, go to the iOS Provisioning Portal page.

4. In the iOS Provisioning Portal, navigate to the Pass Type IDs page on the lefthand side of the screen.

5. When you first land there, the page will look empty, as shown in Figure 20-3. Find and select the New Pass Type ID button on the screen.

6. Now, in the Description box, enter text that will describe your pass type ID.

7. In the Identifier box, enter a reverse-domain-style identifier of your pass. For instance, if your app ID is *com.pixolity.testingpasskit*, then for passes that integrate with that app you can use *pass.pixolity.testingpasskit*. The pass identifier is really something that should make sense to you and your application. However, the practice is that the whole identifier name should start with *pass.* and then you use whatever you wish for the rest of the identifier. Figure 20-4 demonstrates how you can fill in the details in this page.

Once you are done populating the details in this page, press the Submit button. Now you have a pass type ID. However, this pass type ID is not linked to any certificate as such. Now we have to associated our pass type ID to a certificate. That's also easy. Follow these steps to create the certificate and associate it with your pass type ID:

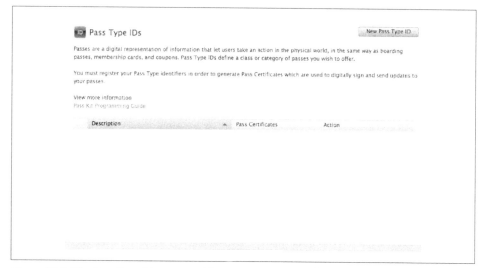

Figure 20-3. The Pass Type IDs screen with no pass types created yet

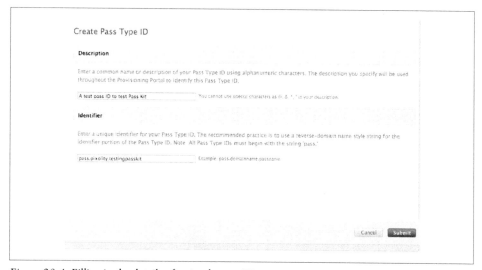

Figure 20-4. Filling in the details of a simple pass ID

1. In the Pass Type IDs section of the iOS Provisioning Portal, find the pass type ID that you created (Figure 20-5). Under the Pass Certificates column of the list, you can see that for your pass type ID, it will say *None*. Under the Action column, select the Configure link.

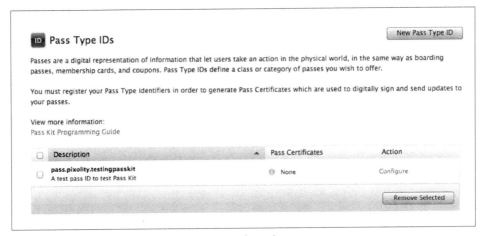

Figure 20-5. A pass type ID that has not been configured yet

2. In the new screen, you can see that the status of your pass certificate is *Configurable* and the light next to it is amber (see Figure 20-6). This means the certificate has *not* been configured for your pass type ID yet. Now select the Configure button again in the new screen.

Figure 20-6. A certificate has not yet been associated with our pass type ID

3. Once you press the Configure button, you will be presented with a modal dialog on your browser instructing you to create a certificate signing request using the Keychain on your Mac. Simply follow the steps, create the certificate signing request (Figure 20-7), and once you are done, press the Continue button (Figure 20-8).

It is possible to create the Certificate signing request on a non-Mac machine. In order to do so, you need to make sure that Open SSL is installed on that machine. The instructions on how to generate these certificates on non-Mac machines are outside the scope of this book, but if you are interested, a simple web search will help you understand the process on those machines.

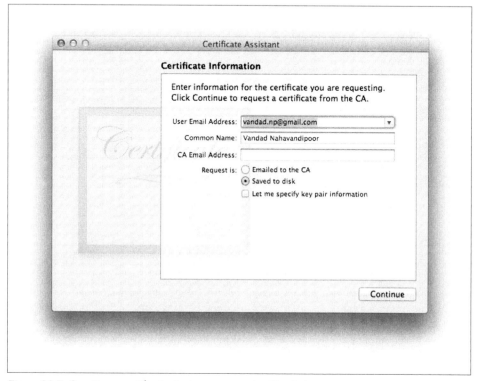

Figure 20-7. Creating a certificate signing request using Keychain

 The certificate requests that you create on your computer using Keychain Access will also create a private key that is associated with that certificate. Apple recommends that you back up your Keychain database every now and then so that you won't lose your private keys, as Apple will not be saving your private keys on the iOS Provisioning Portal. If you are moving to a new computer, you need to move your private keys with you manually. That's why they are called private keys. Exporting private keys is simple: right-click on your private key and press the Export menu item.

Figure 20-8. Follow the on-screen instructions to create a certificate signing request

4. Now you will be asked on your browser to upload the certificate signing request to Apple in order to retrieve your certificate. The private key was created on your computer the moment you created the certificate signing request. The certificate that Apple will issue you at the end of this process will match your private key. So now select the Choose File button in this screen in order to select the certificate signing request that Keychain created for you (see Figure 20-9) and once done, press the Generate button.

5. Once the certificate has been generated, you will be presented with a screen similar to Figure 20-10. Press the Continue button on this screen.

Submit Certificate Signing Request

The creation of a CSR will prompt Keychain Access to simultaneously generate a public and private key pair. Your private key is stored on your Mac in the login Keychain by default and can be viewed in the Keychain Access application under the "Keys" category.

Select the Certificate Signing request (CSR) file that you saved to your disk.

Choose File   Certificate...ningRequest

Figure 20-9. Uploading the certificate signing request to Apple to get a certificate back

6. Now you are presented with a screen where you can download your certificate (see Figure 20-11). Simply press the Download button and once the certificate file is downloaded to your computer, press the Done button.

7. Now you should have the downloaded certificate on your disk. Locate that file and double-click on it in order to import it into your Keychain. To make sure everything worked successfully, open Keychain Access on your computer and navigate to the Login section and then the My Certificate subsection. Now on the righthand side of the screen, confirm that your certificate is present and that it is associated with a private key, as shown in Figure 20-12.

Figure 20-10. Apple letting you know that your certificate was created successfully

Figure 20-11. You can now download your generated certificate

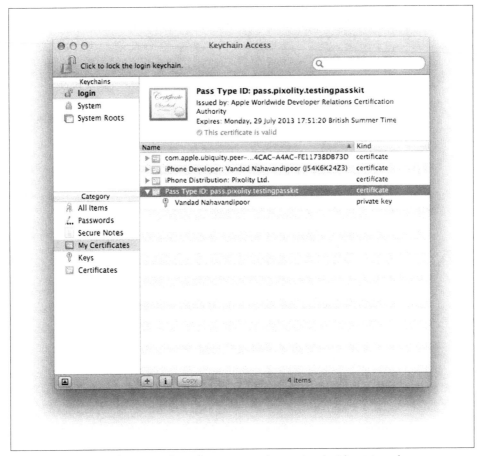

Figure 20-12. The Apple generated certificate is correctly associated with a private key

You are now done creating your certificate, and ready to sign your passes, ready to be sent to iOS devices.

See Also

Recipe 20.0

20.2 Creating Pass Files

Problem

You want to create a pass file that represents the data that you want your users to hold in their iOS devices.

Solution

Create a *pass.json* file and populate it with appropriate keys and values.

Discussion

Apple has chosen JSON files to represent passes for Pass Kit. JSON stands for *JavaScript Object Notation* and is extensively used in web applications and services. However, as an iOS developer, you don't necessarily have to know about JSON files.

JSON files are simple key-value files, just like a dictionary. A key can have a value and the value can range from a simple string to a dictionary that contains keys and values itself. Here is a simple JSON that will pretty much demonstrate all there is to know about JSON files:

```
{
  "key 1" : "value 1",
  "key 2 - dictionary" : {
     "key 2.1" : "value 2.1",
     "key 2.2" : "value 2.2"
  },
  "key 3 - array" : [
     {
        "array item 1, key1" : "value",
        "array item 1, key2" : "value"
     },
     {

        "array item 2, key1" : "value",
        "array item 2, key2" : "value"
     }
  ]
}
```

You can see that dictionaries are represented with square brackets and arrays with curly brackets. Other values are just simple key value pairs. If we were to represent this same JSON object with a normal `NSDictionary`, this is what the resulting code would be:

```
NSDictionary *json = @{
@"key1" : @"value1",
@"key 2 - dictionary" : @{
    @"key 2.1" : @"value 2.1",
    @"key 2.2" : @"value 2.2",
},
@"key 3 - array" : @[
    @{
        @"array item 1, key1" : @"value",
        @"array item 1, key2" : @"value"
    },
    @{
        @"array item 2, key1" : @"value",
        @"array item 2, key2" : @"value"
    }
]
};
```

For more information about JSON, you can refer to JSON.org (*http://www.json.org*). Let's move on to creating our pass files. A pass file, as mentioned before, is a simple JSON file. Don't confuse pass files with passes. A pass is a collection of files, including the *pass.json* file, that will, as a whole, represent the digitally signed pass that users can install on their devices. A pass file is a file that explains how the pass should appear on the device.

The *pass.json* file can be constructed using high- and low-level keys. High-level keys are the keys that will be immediately visible in the top hierarchy of the *pass.json* file. The low-level keys will appear as children of the high-level keys. Don't worry if this sounds confusing for now. I know I was confused when I first heard about this, but if you read on, I promise it will all click eventually.

Let's start by creating a *pass.json* in Xcode. I should warn you that Xcode is unfortunately not the best editor for JSON files; However, it is our primary IDE, so we will stick with it. Follow these steps to create a *pass.json* file:

1. Create an empty iOS project in Xcode by choosing File → New → Project...
2. On the lefthand side of the New Project dialog, make sure you are under the iOS category. Then choose Other and on the righthand side, choose Empty, as shown in Figure 20-13. Once done, press the Next button.

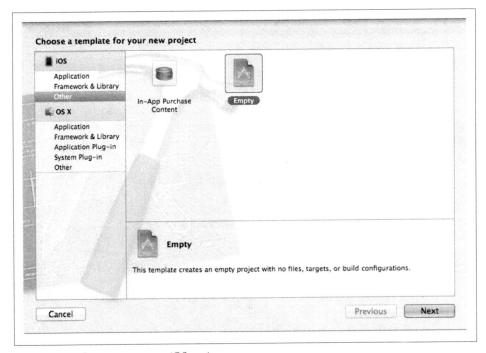

Figure 20-13. Creating an empty iOS project

3. Now, give your project a name under the Product Name box and once done, press the Next button. Now you get the chance to save your file on disk. Once you have successfully chosen the path to save the project, you are ready to create the *pass.json* file.

4. In your new empty project, in Xcode, choose File → New → File...

5. In the New File dialog, make sure you are under the iOS category, then choose Other. On the righthand side, choose Empty, as shown in Figure 20-14. Once you are done, press the Next button.

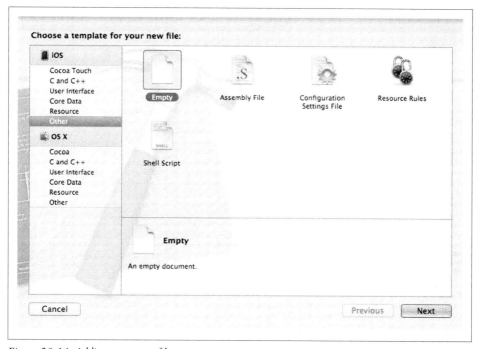

Figure 20-14. Adding an empty file to our project

6. After pressing the Next button, you are now asked to save this file on disk. Make sure that you save this file as *pass.json*. Once you are done, press the Create button and your file is now added on disk and added to your project.

OK, fantastic, now we have our *pass.json* created on disk. We need to populate it with some keys and values. Before we go into the details of the keys and the values, let me show you a simple pass file populated with keys and values so that you can get a better idea of what a pass file actually contains:

```
{
  "formatVersion" : 1,
  "passTypeIdentifier" : "",
  "serialNumber" : "p69f2J",
```

```
    "teamIdentifier" : "",
    "description" : "Train Ticket Example",
    "locations" : [
      {
        "longitude" : -0.170867,
        "latitude" : 50.834948
      }
    ],
    "barcode" : {
      "message" : "1234567890",
      "format" : "PKBarcodeFormatPDF417",
      "messageEncoding" : "iso-8859-1"
    },
    "organizationName" : "O'Reilly Railways",
    "logoText" : "O'Reilly Railways",
    "foregroundColor" : "rgb(255, 255, 255)",
    "backgroundColor" : "rgb(100, 100, 100)",
    "boardingPass" : {
      "transitType" : "PKTransitTypeTrain",
      "primaryFields" : [
        {
          "key" : "departure",
          "label" : "Departs From",
          "value" : "Hove, 07:37",
        },
        {
          "key" : "departurePlatform",
          "label" : "Departs from Platform",
          "value" : "2",
        }
      ],
      "auxiliaryFields" : [
        {
          "key" : "arrival",
          "label" : "Arrives At",
          "value" : "London Bridge, 08:41"
        },
        {
          "key" : "arrivalPlatform",
          "label" : "Arrives at Platform",
          "value" : "13"
        }
      ],
      "backFields" : [
        {
          "key" : "oreillyRailways",
          "label" : "O'Reilly Railways",
          "value" : "For more information about our services, visit www.oreilly.com"
        },
        {
          "key" : "termsAndConditions",
          "label" : "Terms and Conditions",
          "value" : "To be filled later"
        }
      ]
```

```
        }
    }
```

 I have intentionally left the `teamIdentifier` and `passTypeIdentifier` keys' values empty. You need to make sure that you populate the values of these keys to something that you have set up in your provisioning portal as a pass type ID. It is imperative that you fill the values of these keys with accurate information.

Fantastic, now we have our *pass.json* ready to be included in our digitally signed pass. Remember, a pass is more than just the *pass.json* file. We need to include a handful of images and a manifest file that will list all the files included in our pass.

Here are some of the most important keys that you can place in the *pass.json* file:

formatVersion
> This key specifies the version of the pass format. Please set this value to the constant value of *1*.

passTypeIdentifier
> This is the identifier of the pass that you created in the iOS Provisioning Portal before, minus your team ID. For instance, if my full pass ID is *TEAMID.pass.pixolity.testingpasskit*, I will set the value of the pass identifier to *pass.pixolity.testingpasskit*.

teamIdentifier
> This is your team identifier. To find this value, simply navigate to the main page of iOS Dev Center, and then navigate to Member Center. Choose Your Account and then Organization Profile. You should now be able to see a field that reads *Company/Organization ID*. That is your Team ID. Simply copy and paste that value in this key in your *pass.json* file.

description
> A short description of what this pass is for. Accessibility in iOS will use this description.

organizationName
> This is the name of your company.

serialNumber
> A unique serial number for your pass. You can make this up as you go. It should make sense to you and your organization. Note that if two or more passes are using the same pass type identifier, their serial numbers *cannot* be the same.

barcode
> A barcode for your pass. It is highly recommended that you include barcode information with your digital passes. The keys that you can enter in this dictionary are explained here:

message
> The message to be encoded within your barcode.

format
> The format of your barcode. The value of this key must be `PKBarcodeFormat Text`, `PKBarcodeFormatQR`, `PKBarcodeFormatPDF417`, or `PKBarcodeFormatAztec`. A discussion of barcode formats is outside the scope of this book so we won't go into details about barcodes and what each format means.

messageEncoding
> The encoding that you want to use for your barcode. Leave the value of this key at `iso-8859-1`.

logoText
> This text will appear next to the logo of your pass in the Passbook app on the device.

foregroundColor
> The foreground color of your pass. This value is specified in red, green, and blue values, each ranging from 0 to 255 inclusive. Wrap the value inside an `rgb()` function. For instance, for pure red color, specify `rgb(255, 0, 0)`, or for white, specify `rgb(255, 255, 255)`.

backgroundColor
> This is the background color of your pass, specified in the same format as the `foregroundColor`.

Once you are done setting the values for these keys, you can now specify what type of pass you are creating. You can do this by putting one of the following keys in your pass's top level keys, just like all the previously mentioned keys:

 The following keys in your *pass.json* will contain a dictionary of values (keys and values) that will specifically dictate what the pass is for and what values it contains.

eventTicket
> This tells Passbook that your pass is for an event, such as a concert.

coupon
> This tells Passbook that your pass is a coupon. For instance, the user can use a pass like this to get some items more cheaply in the store that issued the pass.

storeCard
> This tells Passbook that your pass is a store card (e.g., a loyalty card that you can use in a store to collect points).

boardingPass
> This tells Passbook that your pass is a boarding pass (e.g., for plane, train, or bus travel).

generic

> A pass that doesn't fit into any of the aforementioned categories.

Once you have included one of these pass types as a key into your *pass.json*, it is now time to specify the keys and values for the pass type dictionary (which we just talked about). Each pass type dictionary can contain the following keys:

transitType

> This key is required only inside the boardingPass dictionary; otherwise, you can just ignore this key. The possible values for this key are PKTransitTypeAir, PKTran sitTypeBus, PKTransitTypeTrain, PKTransitTypeBoat, and PKTransitTypeGeneric. All these are self-explanatory.

headerFields

> The visible part of the top of the pass in Passbook on the device. Make sure you don't put too much information here, as these values are always visible to the user even when all passes are stacked on top of each other in the Passbook app on the device.

primaryFields

> The most important information about your pass, which will be displayed on the front side of the pass. For instance, for a boarding pass at an airport, the gate, seat number, and airline name may be the most important pieces of information to display. For another type of pass, these values may be different.

secondaryFields

> Less important information about the pass, also displayed on the front side of the pass. Again, for a boarding pass at an airport, the secondary fields might be the boarding time, boarding date, and aircraft type.

auxiliaryFields

> The least important information to be displayed on the front side of the pass. Again, going back to our example of a boarding pass at an airport, this might be the expected arrival time.

backFields

> The values to display on the back of the pass.

All the aforementioned keys have dictionaries as their values, and those dictionaries can contain any of the following keys:

label

> The value of the field that has to be displayed on the pass (back or front of the pass, depending on the key that it has been added to).

key

> The key that your app can use to read the value of this field.

value

> The value of this field.

`textAlignment`

An optional key that can describe the alignment of the label visually on the pass. You can specify any of the following values for this field (these values are really self-explanatory):

- PKTextAlignmentRight
- PKTextAlignmentCenter
- PKTextAlignmentLeft
- PKTextAlignmentNatural
- PKTextAlignmentJustified

Phew! Those are a lot of keys and values to remember. Don't worry, though, you'll get used to them after some time! So let's create a simple *pass.json* now. I believe if we put our requirements down first and then tackle the creation of the pass file itself, it will be much easier to map what we learned so far to how we create the *pass.json* file. So here is what we'll do for an example:

- The type of pass is a train boarding pass.
- The train departs from a city called Hove in the United Kingdom at 07:37. The platform from which the train departs at Hove is Platform 2.
- The train will arrive into London Bridge station in London at 08:41 on Platform 13.
- The ticket is valid for all trains operated by a made-up company named O'Reilly Railways.

Before we move on, though, we need to go through the `locations` array in our *pass.json* file. This key is an array in which every element has two keys I will describe in a moment. But the cool thing about this key is that it can describe the geolocations where the pass that you are creating belongs. When the pass is imported in the Passbook app on the user's device, iOS will display a message on the user's screen with the details of your pass, telling the user that your pass is relevant at the current location where the user is. Think of it this way: in our example, the user has to display the train ticket at the ticket barriers every time she reaches the train station at Hove (the departure city). So you can put the location of the departure train station in the pass (under the `loca tions` key) so that iOS will automatically display the pass on the screen when the user reaches the train station. You can do the same thing for the destination train station because when the user is coming back home to the Hove train station via London Bridge, London Bridge will be the departing station. It's just the other way around. If you go from point A to B, A is the source and B is the destination. Once you come back, B is the source and A is the destination. So you can put the location of both point A and B, or even some other points where your pass is relevant, inside the `locations` array. Here are the keys that every location can contain:

longitude
> The longitude of the location. This value is of type `double`. Do not put quotation marks around this value.

latitude
> The latitude of the location. This value is of type `double`. Do not put quotation marks around this value.

See Also

Recipe 20.2; Recipe 20.0

20.3 Providing Icons and Images for Passes

Problem

You want to make sure that your pass will be branded according to your company's style, or give your pass a distinct flavor or image.

Solution

Create backgrounds, icons, and logos and embed them inside your digitally signed pass.

Discussion

A pass can contain different images:

Background (background.png and background@2x.png)
> The background image of the pass. Not all passes can have background images.

Logo (logo.png and logo@2x.png)
> The logo that will appear on the upper left corner of the pass, depending on which type of pass it is.

Icon (icon.png and icon@2x.png)
> The icon for the pass. Not all passes can have icons. We will have a look at creating icons for passes in this chapter.

Thumbnail (thumbnail.png and thumbnail@2x.png)
> The thumbnail image that will be visible when the passes are stacked on top of each other.

All images, as you can see from the filenames, have to come in the non-retina and the retina flavors. Apple doesn't strictly say that this is a must, but don't we all as developers value our customers? Retina displays are so popular now that they are becoming industry standard, so please do provide the retina images for your passes.

Now that we know the image filenames, let's move on to the image dimensions. I will list only the retina images, so please divide the image width and height that I provide below in half to get the dimensions of the non-retina images:

background@2x.png
> 640 pixels wide and 960 pixels tall

logo@2x.png
> 60 pixels wide and 60 pixels tall

icon@2x.png
> 58 pixels wide and 29 pixels tall

thumbnail@2x.png
> 200 pixels wide and 200 pixels tall

For the purposes of this recipe, I have created all these images in a very simple way. Figure 20-15 shows them together on one canvas.

 The figure is for demonstration purposes and just to show you how many images you have to prepare for one pass. You do *not* have to create such an image where all your images appear on one canvas.

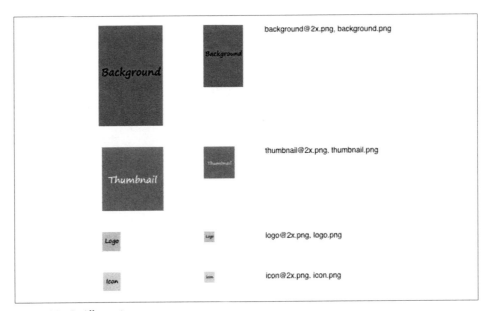

Figure 20-15. All pass images on one canvas

Now that your images are ready, place them in the same folder that you have placed your *pass.json* file. We will move on to the next stage now, which is preparing our manifest file.

See Also

Recipe 20.2

20.4 Preparing Your Passes for Digital Signature

Problem

You want to prepare your passes for digital signature. This is the step that you have to take before you are able to digitally sign your passes.

Solution

Create a file named *manifest.json* in the same folder where you placed your *pass.json* and your pass images. The manifest file will be a JSON file. Its root object is a dictionary. The keys to the dictionary are the names of the files (all your images, plus the *pass.json* file). The value of each key is the SHA1 hash of the file.

Discussion

Simply create the *manifest.json* file with the keys for all your images and leave the values empty for now. Your *manifest.json* file's contents should look similar to that shown here:

```
{
    "background.png"     :    "",
    "background@2x.png"  :    "",
    "icon.png"           :    "",
    "icon@2x.png"        :    "",
    "logo.png"           :    "",
    "logo@2x.png"        :    "",
    "pass.json"          :    "",
    "thumbnail.png"      :    "",
    "thumbnail@2x.png"   :    ""
}
```

Now off to do the interesting part. We have to calculate the SHA1 hashes of all these files. Remember that every time you change the files from now on (for instance, if you find an issue with the *pass.json* file), you will have to recalculate the SHA1 hash and place the new SHA1 value in the *manifest.json* file. In order to calculate the SHA1 hash of any file in OS X, simply follow these steps:

1. Open up Terminal and navigate to the folder where the target file sits, using the cd command.

2. Issue an *openssl* command in Terminal. Pass sha1 as the first argument and the filename as the second argument to this command.

For instance, in my project folder, I have a folder called *pass* and I have placed my *pass.json* and my almost-empty *manifest.json* files in there along the images (background, logo, etc.). Now in Terminal, I shall calculate the SHA1 hashes of all these files and place them in the manifest file. So the following listing shows my *openssl* command on the first line, and the output with all the hashes on the rest of the lines.

```
openssl sha1 *.*
SHA1(background.png)= 0744d456ce7ada02ac581d0fa5c99a5f5eb97539
SHA1(background@2x.png)= 75b5cc40951bcc18750b4230d6334f48f66e8215
SHA1(icon.png)= ed698ab24c5bd7f0e7496b2897ec054bbd426747
SHA1(icon@2x.png)= 90381c84cfea22136c951ddb3b368ade71f49eef
SHA1(logo.png)= c3bd8c5533b6c9f500bbadbdd957b9eac8a6bfe9
SHA1(logo@2x.png)= 1a56a5564dec5e8742ad65dc47aa9bd64c39222f
SHA1(manifest.json)= a7319cf48c0e34cac75001aada9d0767208bf73c
SHA1(pass.json)= af56398ccc5a0faf73667eacabf76d04c961566f
SHA1(thumbnail.png)= 58883d22196eb73f33ea556a4b7ea735f90a6213
SHA1(thumbnail@2x.png)= 0903df90165ef1a8909a15b4f652132c27368560
```

 We calculated the SHA1 of all files, including the SHA1 of the *manifest.json*. However, we are not going to need the SHA1 of *manifest.json* because it holds the hashes for all the other files, and doesn't have to hold its own. So just ignore the SHA1 of this file.

What we have to do now is to populate the *manifest.json* with the SHA1 values of the rest of the files that we just calculated:

```
{
    "background.png"      :   "0744d456ce7ada02ac581d0fa5c99a5f5eb97539",
    "background@2x.png"   :   "75b5cc40951bcc18750b4230d6334f48f66e8215",
    "icon.png"            :   "ed698ab24c5bd7f0e7496b2897ec054bbd426747",
    "icon@2x.png"         :   "90381c84cfea22136c951ddb3b368ade71f49eef",
    "logo.png"            :   "c3bd8c5533b6c9f500bbadbdd957b9eac8a6bfe9",
    "logo@2x.png"         :   "1a56a5564d0fec5e8742ad65dc47aa9bd64c39222f",
    "pass.json"           :   "af56398ccc5a0faf73667eacabf76d04c961566f",
    "thumbnail.png"       :   "58883d22196eb73f33ea556a4b7ea735f90a6213",
    "thumbnail@2x.png"    :   "0903df90165ef1a8909a15b4f652132c27368560"
}
```

All is good now. We can now move on to the next step, which is the signature of our pass.

See Also

Recipe 20.1

20.5 Signing Passes Digitally

Problem

You have prepared your *pass* folder with the manifest and the *pass.json* and all the images, and now you want to be able to digitally sign the pass folder and its content to create your pass file, ready to be distributed.

Solution

Use `openssl` to sign your passes.

Discussion

Every pass has to be signed using the certificate that we created in Recipe 20.1. We will use `openssl` again in Terminal in order to sign our passes. Before you continue reading, make sure that you have created a folder named *pass* and place your *pass.json*, *manifest.json* and all your images in this folder. The folder name doesn't necessarily have to be called *pass*. However, to make sure you can follow through the steps in this recipe and the rest of this chapter, it's best to do what I've done and put the files in a folder named *pass* so you can follow along more easily.

 Some of you may be a bit confused as to what keys are which and what certificates do what. I hope I can make it a bit more clear here. When you request a new certificate in the iOS Provisioning Portal, Keychain creates a private key on your computer along with a Certificate Request file (CSR). The certificate will be generated by Apple. When you download the certificate, its file extension will be *.cer*. This is just the certificate! When you import this certificate into your Keychain, Keychain will automatically associate the certificate with the private key that it created before. Now if you export the certificate from Keychain, the resulting file will be of type *.p12*, which contains both the certificate and the private key for the certificate.

Before we can dive into the signing process, we will need to export our certificate from Keychain Access. Keep in mind that the certificate that you downloaded from iOS Provisioning Profile is not the same certificate as you will now export from Keychain Access, so make sure that you follow these steps to export your pass ID certificate from your Keychain:

1. Open up Keychain Access on your Mac.
2. On the upper-left side of the window under Keychains, make sure that you have selected the Login keychain.
3. Under the Category section on the left side, choose My Certificates.

4. Locate your Pass Type ID certificate on the righthand side of the screen and then right-click on it.

5. Now choose the Export option, as shown in Figure 20-16, and proceed to export your certificate to disk as a *.p12* file (as shown in Figure 20-17). Do not save the certificate in the *pass* folder. Keep the certificate outside that folder.

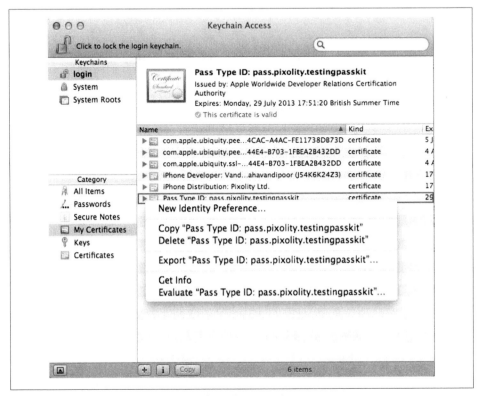

Figure 20-16. Exporting our pass ID certificate from Keychain Access

6. After you attempt to export your certificate, you will be asked for two pieces of information: a password that you need to set on your certificate and the password of your OS X user, who owns the Keychain Access. The first password is on the certificate, which will make sure the certificate cannot be imported into any random machine if the user doesn't have the password. The second password makes sure the person who is exporting your certificate from your Keychain really has permission to do so. For instance, if you leave your computer on and unlocked and your friend attempts to export a certificate from your Keychain, he or she will have to enter your user account's password in order to do so. It's always good practice to make sure different accounts on the system have different passwords. For instance, if you and your brother both use the same Mac, you need to make sure that

Figure 20-17. Saving the certificate to disk as part of exporting from Keychain Access

your account's password is something unique to your account. If you and your brother have the same password on both your accounts on the same Mac, that defies the whole purpose of security on your Mac.

 Make sure that you *do not* save the certificate inside the *pass* folder. You should not ship your certificate inside your pass.

Now that you have exported your certificate, you have ended up with a file that is probably named *Certificates.p12*. Now it is time to split this file into the certificate part and the private key. As you may know, when you export a certificate from Keychain Access, the resulting *.p12* file contains both the certificate and the private key. However, when you use openssl to sign your pass, you will need to pass the private key and the certificate separately. So to retrieve the private key and the certificate from your *Certificates.p12* file that we just exported from Keychain Access, follow these steps:

1. Open up Terminal if it's not open already.
2. Navigate to the folder where you saved the exported certificate `.p12` file.
3. In order to get the certificate out, issue the following command:

```
openssl pkcs12 -in "NAME OF YOUR .P12 CERTIFICATE FILE" -clcerts \
-nokeys -out "NAME OF THE OUTPUT CERTIFICATE"
```

For instance, the certificate and private key file exported from my Keychain is named *Certificates.p12* and I want to export the certificate out of it, under the name *exported-certificate*. To do this, I have to issue the following command in Terminal:

```
openssl pkcs12 -in Certificates.p12 -clcerts -nokeys -out exported-certificate
```

 Once you issue this command, you will be asked to assign your exported certificate a password. For this example, I am setting the password as *1234*, but please give yours a better password.

4. In order to export the private key out of the Keychain-exported certificate, you will need to issue the following command in Terminal:

```
openssl pkcs12 -in "NAME OF YOUR .P12 CERTIFICATE FILE" \
-nocerts -out "NAME OF THE OUTPUT KEY"
```

I will name the exported private key *exported-key*, but feel free to choose another name if you want to:

```
openssl pkcs12 -in Certificates.p12 -nocerts -out exported-key
```

Again, you will be asked to enter passwords for your key. I have set mine up with the password of *1234* so that I can easily remember it, and it's the same password I have set up for my certificate. In an organization where you need to make sure things are done in a secure way, of course, you wouldn't want to choose this type of password. Choose something that makes sense for you and make sure the passwords that you choose for different certificates/keys that you export are distinct for maximum protection.

Fantastic, now we have our exported certificate and private key files. We can now move on to signing our pass with these files. Follow these steps in order to do so:

1. If you haven't already, place all the files related to the pass (*pass.json*, *manifest.json*, and all the relevant images) inside a folder called *pass*. You can name this folder anything you want, but for the purpose of clarity in this recipe, it's best that the folder name that you create be the same folder that I have here. That way, it will be easier for all of us to know which folder we are in and what we are doing in Terminal.

2. Use the `cd` command to change the current working directory to the *pass* directory where all your pass files exist.

3. Execute the *rm -f .DS_Store* command to make sure no unnecessary OS X hidden system files are present in your *pass* folder. You need to make sure all the files in this folder are listed in the *manifest.json* along with their SHA1 hashes. If any other files, hidden or not hidden, creep into this folder without being listed in the manifest file, the resulting pass will be invalid and not readable by Passbook on iOS devices or the simulator.

4. Issue the following command in Terminal in order to generate a *signature* file inside your *pass* folder:

```
openssl smime -binary -sign -signer "PATH TO YOUR EXPORTED CERTIFICATE" \
-inkey "PATH TO YOUR EXPORTED PRIVATE KEY" -in manifest.json \
-out signature -outform DER
```

 This command has to be issued inside the *pass* folder where all your pass assets exist. The exported certificate and private key are the certificate and the private key that you extracted from the Keychain-exported certificate. Avoid providing the actual Keychain-exported certificate to this command. Before this, we learned how to extract the real certificate and the private key out of the Keychain-exported *.p12* file, so you may want to have a look at that again to make sure things are going as planned.

As part of the last step, you will be asked to provide the password for your private key. Do you remember it? That is the password that you set when you were extracting the private key from the Keychain-exported certificate. This command has now created a file named *signature* in the *pass* folder. We are almost done; all we have to do now is to compress the *pass* directory into a ZIP file with the extension of *.pkpass*. In order to do that, follow these steps:

1. Open up Terminal and using the `cd` command, navigate to your *pass* folder.

2. Issue the following command in order to zip your *pass* folder into a file called *pass.pkpass* in the current folder:

```
zip -r pass.pkpass . -x '.DS_Store'
```

This will zip up all the pass files into the *pass.pkpass* and again, makes sure that a file named *.DS_Store* will not be included in the output archive.

See Also

Recipe 20.4; Recipe 20.1

20.6 Distributing Passes Using Email

Problem

You want to be able to send your digitally signed passes to people using their email address.

Solution

Simply send the passes as attachments in your email.

Discussion

The pass that you signed and packaged up in Recipe 20.5 is now ready to be distributed. One of the easiest way of distributing passes is through email. Follow these steps to distribute your pass through email using the Mail.app on your installation of OS X:

1. Open up Mail.app on your installation of OS X.
2. From the File menu, choose New Message.
3. Enter the email address of the person to whom you want to send the pass.
4. Enter a title for your email.
5. Enter the message for your email and simply drag and drop the *pass.pkpass* file, which you prepared in Recipe 20.5, into the message of your email at the end, as shown in Figure 20-18.

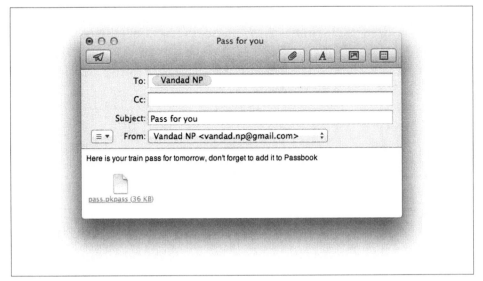

Figure 20-18. Distributing digitally signed passes using Mail.app on OS X

6. Now send the email. The user will receive it in her inbox. The email will appear as shown in Figure 20-19 on the user's device.

Figure 20-19. A pass sent through email

Note that the icon that we specified for our pass in Recipe 20.3 is appearing in Mail.app on iOS devices when a pass is attached to an email.

Now the user has the ability to tap on the pass that is attached to the email. This will cause Passbook to pop up and display the pass in its interface, allowing the user to add the pass to Passbook, right on the device Figure 20-20.

If the user presses the Add button on the pass, it will get added to Passbook right on the device. Now the user has the ability to see the front (Figure 20-21) or the back (Figure 20-22) of the pass.

Figure 20-21 differs from Figure 20-20 in that when the pass is added to the Passbook on the device (Figure 20-21), there is no Add button on the top of the screen. This simply shows that the pass is already installed on the device.

Figure 20-20. Opening a pass attached to an email will display the Passbook interface on an iOS device

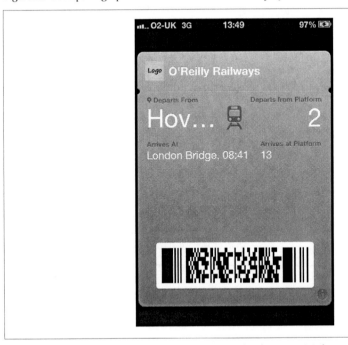

Figure 20-21. Displaying the front of a pass in Passbook on an iOS device

Figure 20-22. Displaying the back of a pass in Passbook on an iOS device

See Also

Recipe 20.7

20.7 Distributing Passes Using Web Services

Problem

You want users to be able to download your digitally signed passes right from your website.

Solution

In your web pages, create hyperlinks to your *.pkpass* passes. When users view the web pages on their devices, they can simply tap on those links. Once they tap on the link, Safari will detect that the link leads to a *.pkpass* file and will hand the link to Passbook which will display the pass on the website and allow the users to add your passes to their Passbook.

Discussion

Safari on iOS does not handle direct downloading of *.pkpass* pass files. In order to let your users download the *.pkpass* passes, you need to create web pages with hyperlinks in them that point to the *.pkpass* files. A simple HTML code file that serves a *pass.pkpass* to the user is displayed here:

```
<html>
    <header>
        <title>Passbook Site</title>
    </header>
    <body>
        <a href="http://localhost:8888/pass.pkpass">Download your pass here</a>
    </body>
</html>
```

 I have put the link as *localhost* because I'm running an instance of Apache web server on my installation of OS X. You need to make sure the link in this HTML file makes sense in your web development environment.

Now when the user opens this link in Safari on her device, she will see something similar to Figure 20-23.

Figure 20-23. Viewing our website in Safari on iOS Simulator

When the user taps on the link, Passbook will pop up and will display its familiar UI to the user, allowing her to add your pass to her device's Passbook, similar to that shown in Figure 20-20.

See Also

Recipe 20.6

20.8 Enabling Your iOS Apps to Access Passes on iOS Devices

Problem

You want to deploy your Passbook-enabled app to iOS devices and you want to make sure that your app can read the digitally signed passes that you have pushed into those devices.

Solution

Create an appropriate provision profile for your app, linked to an App ID that has Passes access enabled for it.

Discussion

You need to sign your apps with an appropriate provisioning profile that has been created in the same portal that your pass IDs were created in, in order to be able to read our own passes from the Passbook app on users' devices. The whole process is depicted in Figure 20-24.

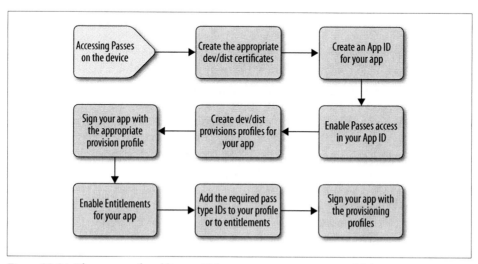

Figure 20-24. The process of enabling an iOS app to access passes on an iOS device

So let's begin! Here I assume that you already have a Dev/Dist certificate. We'll create an app ID for the pass ID that we created in Recipe 20.1 and then move on to create the appropriate provisioning profile for that app ID. Here we go:

1. Navigate to iOS Dev Center in your browser, and log in if you are not logged in already.

2. Navigate to iOS Provisioning Portal now.

3. Navigate to the App IDs section and press the New App ID button.

4. In the Description box, describe your app ID; something that is meaningful to you and your team or organization.

5. Leave the Bundle Seed ID as Use Team ID.

6. In the Bundle Identifier (App ID Suffix), enter the reverse domain style name of your bundle ID. For me, for the pass with an ID of *pass.pixolity.testingpasskit*, I have set the bundle identifier of my app ID to *com.pixolity.testingpasskit*.

7. Once you are done, press the Submit button. Great, now you have an App ID.

8. Back in the App IDs section of the portal, locate your newly created app ID. You should see something similar to that shown in Figure 20-25.

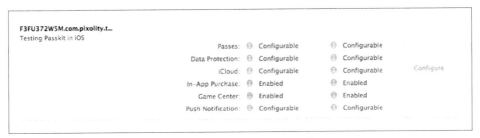

Figure 20-25. Locating our app ID in the iOS provisioning portal

9. As you can see, passes are not configured for this app ID. Press the Configure link on the righthand side of the screen for the app ID that you just generated.

10. In the new screen, you will see a few configuration options, such as those for iCloud and push notifications. Ignore all those and move over to the Enable for Passes section and tick the box next to it, as shown in Figure 20-26.

11. Once you tick that check box, you will be prompted with a screen asking whether you want to enable passes for this app ID. Press the OK button on that dialog and then press the Done button at the bottom of the screen to finish your work with the app ID (Figure 20-27).

Figure 20-26. Enabling Pass access on our app ID

Figure 20-27. Pressing OK on this dialog will finally enable Passes access on our app ID

12. Now that we have enabled Passes for our app ID, it is time to create our provisioning profile. Head to the Provisioning section of the iOS Provisioning Profile now.

13. We are going to create a developer provisioning profile as opposed to an Ad Hoc build, so in the Provisioning section, under the Development tab, press the New Profile button.

14. Under the Profile name, give your profile a meaningful name. I have set the profile name as *Testing Passkit.*

15. Under the Certificates section, choose your developer certificate and tick it.

16. Under the App ID section, choose the App ID that you just created.

17. Under the Devices, choose the list of devices on which you are intending to test your app. Once you are done, press the Submit button (as shown in Figure 20-28).

Figure 20-28. Creating a developer provisioning profile for our passkit app

18. Once you are done, you should be able to download your provisioning profile from the iOS Provisioning Portal. After you have downloaded the profile, simply drag and drop it into iTunes in order to install it.

There are various ways of installing a provisioning profile on your OS X installation. The best and fastest way is to drag and drop the profile into iTunes. You can also use Xcode to install the profile. Whatever method you choose, make sure that you avoid double-clicking on the profile in order to install it. Double-clicking will install your profile with a really cryptic name on your disk, and later it will be very difficult to distinguish which profile is which. To keep your disk clean, use iTunes or Xcode to install your provisioning profiles. You can view all installed provisioning profiles on your disk in the file *~/Library/MobileDevice/ Provisioning Profiles/*.

19. Now open your project in Xcode. In the Build Settings of your target app, choose the provisioning profile that you just created for Debug-only builds. You can do the same thing for Ad Hoc builds, but under the Release scheme in Build Settings.

20. Now go to the Summary tab of your target, and under the Entitlements section, tick the Enable Entitlements box to enable entitlements for your target.

21. Under Entitlements, under the Passes section, choose the "Use selected pass type identifiers" option and then press the Refresh button. This will contact the iOS

Provisioning Portal and will retrieve all the pass type IDs that your provisioning profile is linked to. Remember, a provisioning profile is linked to an app ID and you configured your app ID to enable access to passes. So you will end up with something like that shown in Figure 20-29.

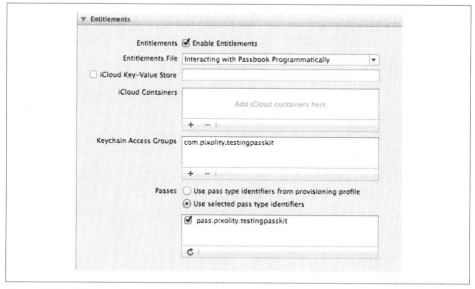

Figure 20-29. Choosing the pass IDs that we want to access

 If you want to be able to access all pass type IDs that your provision profile can read, simply leave the Passes option as "Use pass type identifiers from provisioning profile."

And with this task, we are all done setting up Pass Kit! All we need is to write an app that can access the passes that we created and imported into passbook, as mentioned in Recipe 20.6 and Recipe 20.7. The app will be described in Recipe 20.9.

See Also

Recipe 20.6; Recipe 20.7

20.9 Interacting with Passbook Programmatically

Problem

You want to be able to interact with the installed passes on a user's device programmatically.

Solution

Include the PassKit.framework into your project and use the `PKPassLibrary` to find the passes that you are interested in. Passes will be of type `PKPass`, so using this class you can retrieve information about your passes.

Discussion

 As a prerequisite to this recipe, please make sure that you have read Recipe 20.8 and now have an Xcode iOS project that has the appropriate provisioning profile to access your passes in the user's Passbook library.

Apple has provided the PassKit.framework for iOS developers. Using this framework, you can interact with passes that the user has installed on her devices. To be able to use this framework, you have to first add it to our project. Follow these steps:

1. On the lefthand side in the Navigator pane, select your project (with the blue icon).
2. Choose the target that you are building next to the Navigator pane.
3. On the top of the screen, choose the Build Phases tab.
4. Move over to and expand the Link Binary With Libraries section and press the + button for it.
5. In the list of frameworks and libraries that appear on your list, find and choose PassKit.framework and add it to your project, as shown in Figure 20-30.

Now that you have this framework, you can get started with your project. Go to your app delegate's header file and import the *PassKit/PassKit.h* header file from the PassKit framework:

```
#import <UIKit/UIKit.h>
#import <PassKit/PassKit.h>

@interface AppDelegate : UIResponder <UIApplicationDelegate>

@property (strong, nonatomic) UIWindow *window;

@end
```

The next thing that we are going to do is declare a private property of type `PKPassLibrary` in the implementation file of our app delegate. The aforementioned class in PassKit.framework will allow you to interact with the passes that have been added to the device. While you are at it, you will also need to know the keys in the *pass.json* file that you created in Recipe 20.2 in order to be able to read values such as the departure platform and departure city. So declare these keys as well, all in the implementation file of your app delegate:

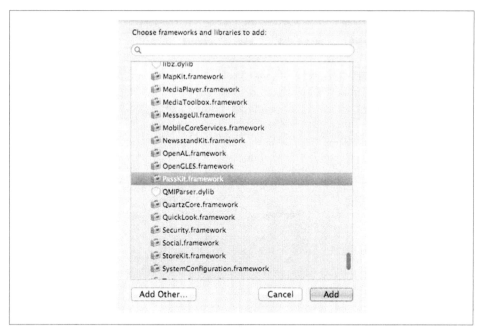

Figure 20-30. Adding the PassKit.framework to our target in Xcode

```objc
#import "AppDelegate.h"

@interface AppDelegate ()
@property (nonatomic, strong) PKPassLibrary *passLibrary;
@end

NSString *PassIdentifier       = @"pass.pixolity.testingpasskit";
NSString *PassSerialNumber     = @"p69f2J";

NSString *DepartureKey         = @"departure";
NSString *DeparturePlatformKey = @"departurePlatform";
NSString *Arrival              = @"arrival";
NSString *ArrivalPlatform      = @"arrivalPlatform";

@implementation AppDelegate

...
```

Fantastic! After you are done with that, you need to start accessing the Passbook library on the device. But wait a minute: what if the device doesn't have Passbook installed on it? You have to first check whether Passbook is available on the device. Do that using the `isPassLibraryAvailable` class method of the `PKPassLibrary` class.

The next thing you need to do is instantiate your `passLibrary` property of type `PK PassLibrary` and then use the `passWithPassTypeIdentifier:serialNumber:` instance method of the pass library to find the pass that you are looking for. So now you know why we have also defined our pass identifier and its serial number among the keys to different fields within the pass. The aforementioned method will return an object of type PKPass that will represent your pass object. Once you have this pass object, you can read the values from its different keys.

Default keys, such as organization name and serial number, are mapped to properties for you by Apple in the PKPass class itself. However, if you want to access the values within primaryFields or other similar places, you will need to use the localizedValue ForFieldKey: instance method of the PKPass class and pass your keys to this method to get the values associated with those keys. So here is a little code snippet that can read the departure and arrival city and platforms from the pass that we created in Recipe 20.2:

 This is inside the implementation file of our app delegate.

```objectivec
#import "AppDelegate.h"

@interface AppDelegate ()
@property (nonatomic, strong) PKPassLibrary *passLibrary;
@end

NSString *PassIdentifier      = @"pass.pixolity.testingpasskit";
NSString *PassSerialNumber    = @"p69f2J";

NSString *DepartureKey         = @"departure";
NSString *DeparturePlatformKey = @"departurePlatform";
NSString *Arrival              = @"arrival";
NSString *ArrivalPlatform      = @"arrivalPlatform";

@implementation AppDelegate

- (void) displayPassInformation:(PKPass *)paramPass{

    if (paramPass == nil){
        NSLog(@"The given pass is nil.");
        return;
    }

    NSLog(@"Departs From = %@",
        [paramPass localizedValueForFieldKey:DepartureKey]);
    NSLog(@"Departure Platform = %@",
      [paramPass localizedValueForFieldKey:DeparturePlatformKey]);

    NSLog(@"Arrives at = %@",
      [paramPass localizedValueForFieldKey:Arrival]);
    NSLog(@"Arrival Platform = %@",
      [paramPass localizedValueForFieldKey:ArrivalPlatform]);

}
```

```
- (BOOL)                  application:(UIApplication *)application
    didFinishLaunchingWithOptions:(NSDictionary *)launchOptions{

    if ([PKPassLibrary isPassLibraryAvailable]){
        self.passLibrary = [[PKPassLibrary alloc] init];

        PKPass *pass =
        [self.passLibrary passWithPassTypeIdentifier:PassIdentifier
                                        serialNumber:PassSerialNumber];
        [self displayPassInformation:pass];

    } else {
        /* Take another action here perhaps */
        NSLog(@"The pass library is not available.");
    }

    self.window = [[UIWindow alloc]
                   initWithFrame:[[UIScreen mainScreen] bounds]];

    // Override point for customization after application launch.
    self.window.backgroundColor = [UIColor whiteColor];
    [self.window makeKeyAndVisible];
    return YES;
}
```

The pass identifier and serial number provided are for the pass that I created using my certificate. However, your pass identifier will be different. The serial number may be the same, but the pass identifier will certainly be different, and will be something that makes more sense for you and your provisioning portal/organization.

See Also

Recipe 20.2

Index

Symbols

" " (double quotes), in strings, 23
%s vs. %@ format specifier, 24
- (id)initWithCoder:(NSCoder *)aDecoder; method, 596
- (void)encodeWithCoder:(NSCoder *)aCoder method, 596
.h files, 60
.ipa files, 19
.mobileprovision files, 19
.plist file
    adding key and setting to true, 662
    adding location Key to, 648
    setting array key in .plist file, 646–648
.png files
    finding path in images folder to all, 90
    loading as image, 87
.xib files, 147
= (equal sign), setting properties using, 49
== (double equal sign), inside conditional statement, 28
@ (at-sign)
    as prefix to double quotes, 23
    in expression boxing, 71
@ [ ] collection format, 73
@" " (an empty string), creating group with name equal to, 560
@property keyword, 48
@synthesize keyword, 49
^ (caret) character, marking block object with, 77
_bridge_retained typecast, 58
__block storage type
    prefix integerValue variable with, 370–371

prefix outsideVariable, 366–367
__bridge typecast, 58
__bridge_transfer keyword, 544
__bridge_transfer typecast, 58
{ } (curly braces), in if-else statement, 29
| (pipe) character, using in constructing swipe gesture, 457

A

ABAddressBookAddRecord function, 549–551
ABAddressBookCopyArrayOfAllGroups function, 558–562
ABAddressBookCopyArrayOfAllPeople function, 543, 558–562
ABAddressBookCopyLocalizedLabel function, 549
ABAddressBookCopyPeopleWithName function, 562
ABAddressBookCreate function, 540
ABAddressBookCreateWithOptions function, 540–543
ABAddressBookGetAuthorizationStatus function, 537–540, 538
ABAddressBookHasUnsavedChanges function, 540
ABAddressBookRevert procedure, 543
ABAddressBookSave function, 553
ABGroupAddMember function, 555–557
ABGroupCreate function, 552–555
ABMultiValueCopyLabelAtIndex function, 549
ABMultiValueCopyLabelAtIndex function, label values, 549
ABMultiValueRef values, 545

We'd like to hear your suggestions for improving our indexes. Send email to *index@oreilly.com*.

About the Author

Vandad Nahavandipoor has developed software using Cocoa, Cocoa Touch, Assembly, Delphi, and .NET for many years. As a staff member of a company that is a global leader in mobile money solutions in London, he has worked with some of the world's biggest brands—such as Visa and US Bank—to deliver mobile applications to their customers. Vandad brings an interest in management, leadership, and entrepreneurship to his work, believing in the synergy that is achieved as a result of cooperation and working together in a team.

Colophon

The cover image for *iOS6 Programming Cookbook* is the Cowan's shrew tenrec (*Microgale cowani*). One of 20 known species of *Microgales* native to Madagascar, Cowan's shrew tenrec is 4 to 6 inches in length and weighs less than an ounce, with a tail smaller than its body. Because it has poor eyesight, the shrew tenrec instead uses its stiff, sensitive whiskers and a keen sense of smell to navigate the dense tropical rainforests of eastern Madagascar. The tenrecs are one of the few mammals that retain a cloaca, a single urogenital opening that was characteristic of the earliest known mammals and the modern day platypus and marsupials.

An insectivore like many tenrecs, Cowan's shrew tenrec is also known to eat small mammals and earthworms. Its natural predators include larger tenrecs and Madagascan red owls, although it can evade most predators by fleeing and hiding in the leafy underbrush of the forest floor, where it also forages for insects.

Some speculate that the tenrecs migrated to Madagascar from Africa through oceanic dispersal, or rafting over, after the island had broken off from the continent 165 million years ago. The earliest known tenrecs appeared on the island some 60 million years ago and have evolved into widely diversified species, having arrived at a time when there were no other mammals, which allowed them to adapt to their ecological niches with little to no competition. Most African tenrecs have disappeared and are known only through fossils. The larger tenrecs of Madagascar evolved into quill-bearing mammals similar to hedgehogs, while the smaller tenrecs look like shrews or moles; however, tenrecs are not related to any of those other animals.

The cover image is from a loose page, origin unknown. The text font is Linotype Birka; the heading font is Adobe Myriad Condensed; and the code font is LucasFont's The-SansMonoCondensed.

Get even more for your money.

Join the O'Reilly Community, and register the O'Reilly books you own. It's free, and you'll get:

- $4.99 ebook upgrade offer
- 40% upgrade offer on O'Reilly print books
- Membership discounts on books and events
- Free lifetime updates to ebooks and videos
- Multiple ebook formats, DRM FREE
- Participation in the O'Reilly community
- Newsletters
- Account management
- 100% Satisfaction Guarantee

Signing up is easy:

1. **Go to: oreilly.com/go/register**
2. **Create an O'Reilly login.**
3. **Provide your address.**
4. **Register your books.**

Note: English-language books only

To order books online:
oreilly.com/store

For questions about products or an order:
orders@oreilly.com

To sign up to get topic-specific email announcements and/or news about upcoming books, conferences, special offers, and new technologies:
elists@oreilly.com

For technical questions about book content:
booktech@oreilly.com

To submit new book proposals to our editors:
proposals@oreilly.com

O'Reilly books are available in multiple DRM-free ebook formats. For more information:
oreilly.com/ebooks

O'REILLY®

Spreading the knowledge of innovators   oreilly.com

CPSIA information can be obtained at www.ICGtesting.com
Printed in the USA
BVOW062333071212

307084BV00003B/1/P